Research Methods and Statistics in
PSYCHOLOGY

Research Methods and Statistics in
PSYCHOLOGY

Hugh Coolican
SECOND EDITION

Hodder & Stoughton

A MEMBER OF THE HODDER HEADLINE GROUP

ACKNOWLEDGEMENTS

Peter Richardson and Kevin Buchanan at Nene College for reviewing several pieces of material; Martin Tolley, also at Nene, for many invaluable snippets and examples; Kate Arnold, at Nene, for information on ethics; Nicky Hayes (Huddersfield University), Karen Henwood (Brunel University), Derek Edwards and Jonathan Potter (Loughborough University), Paula Nicolson (University of Sheffield) for extremely useful qualitative methods information; Shelley Gooding (ATP) for the Statpak information; David Howell (University of Vermont) for statistical information; and finally, Bob Potter, Bert Brummell and John Hunt for queries leading to modifications.

Very special thanks to Richard Gross for continuing and much valued support and advice, and to Tim Gregson-Williams and Louise Tooms for their invaluable editorial support. Finally, my thanks to, and absolute admiration for, all the students I've met who have suffered my tricks (and 'jokes') and have let me know what's needed in the book.

The authors and publishers would also like to thank the following for permission to reproduce material in this book:

The British Psychological Society and Dr S. Halliday for Table 7.2 on p. 96; J. Wiley & Sons for Figure 10.1 (adapted) p. 161; Blackwell and the *Journal of Personality and Social Psychology* for Figures 13.5 and 13.6 on p. 215; the British Psychological Society and Professor Chapman for Figure 13.8 on p. 217; the *Journal of Personality and Social Psychology* and Harcourt Brace Javonovich for Figure 21.2 (adapted) on p. 348.

We are grateful to the Longman Group UK Ltd, on behalf of the Literary Executor of the late Sir Ronald A. Fisher, FRS and Dr Frank Yates, FRS, for permission to reproduce the tables 'Random numbers', 'Critical values of Chi squared' and 'Critical values of *t*' from *Statistical Tables for Biological, Agricultural and Medical Research* (6th ed.) (1974).

British Library Cataloguing in Publication Data

A catalogue for this title is available from the British Libr

ISBN 0 340 60082 9

First published 1994
Impression number 10 9 8 7 6 5 4 3
Year   1999 1998 1997 1996 1995
Copyright © 1994 Hugh Coolican

Typeset by Wearset, Boldon, Tyne & Wear
Printed in Great Britain for Hodder & Stoughton Educational, a division of Hodder Headline Plc, 338 Euston Road, London NW1 3BH by The Bath Press

DEDICATION

To everyone who has helped get this book to its second edition, but in particular, to Rama (with love) for unending support, and, most of all, to Kiran, who has given us so many surprises.

CONTENTS

Preface to the first edition   xi

Preface to the second edition   xii

PART I   **Introduction**   1

Chapter 1   Psychology and research   3
Scientific research; empirical method; hypothetico-deductive method;
falsifiability; descriptive research; hypothesis testing; the null-hypothesis;
one- and two-tailed hypotheses; planning research.

Chapter 2   Variables and definitions   22
Psychological variables and constructs; operational definitions;
independent and dependent variables; extraneous variables; random and
constant error; confounding.

Chapter 3   Samples and groups   34
Populations and samples; sampling bias; representative samples; random
samples; stratified, quota, cluster, snowball, self-selecting and
opportunity samples; sample size. Experimental, control and placebo
groups.

PART II   **Methods**   47

Chapter 4   Some general themes   49
Reliability. Validity; internal and external validity; threats to validity;
ecological validity; construct validity. Standardised procedure; participant
variance; confounding; replication; meta-analysis. The quantitative–
qualitative dimension.

Chapter 5   The experimental method I: nature of the method   66
Experiments; non-experimental work; the laboratory; field experiments;
quasi-experiments; natural experiments; *ex post facto* research; criticisms
of the experiment.

Chapter 6   The experimental method II: experimental designs   81
Repeated measures; related designs; order effects. Independent samples
design; participant (subject) variables. Matched pairs. Single participant.

Chapter 7   Observational methods   93
Observation as technique and design; participant and non-participant
observation; structured observation; controlled observation; naturalistic
observation; objections to structured observation; qualitative non-
participant observation; role-play and simulation; the diary method;
participant observation; indirect observation; content analysis; verbal
protocols.

Chapter 8   Asking questions I: interviews and surveys   114
Structure and disguise; types of interview method; the clinical method;
the individual case-study; interview techniques; surveys.

Chapter 9   Asking questions II: questionnaires, scales and tests   135
Questionnaires; attitude scales; questionnaire and scale items; projective
tests; sociometry; psychometric tests. Reliability, validity and
standardisation of tests.

Chapter 10   Comparison studies   159
Cross-sectional studies; longitudinal studies; short-term longitudinal
studies. Cross-cultural studies; research examples; indigenous
psychologies; ethnicity and culture within one society.

Chapter 11   New paradigms   169
Positivism; doubts about positivism; the establishment paradigm;
objections to the traditional paradigm; new paradigm proposals;
qualitative approaches; feminist perspective; discourse analysis;
reflexivity.

PART III   Dealing with data   185

Chapter 12   Measurement   187
Nominal level; ordinal level; interval level; plastic interval scales; ratio
level; reducing from interval to ordinal and nominal level; categorical and
measured variables; continuous and discrete scales of measurement.

Chapter 13   Descriptive statistics   200
Central tendency; mean; median; mode. Dispersion; range; semi-
interquartile range; mean deviation; standard deviation and variance.
Population parameters and sample statistics. Distributions; percentiles;
deciles and quartiles. Graphical representation; histogram; bar chart;
frequency polygon; ogive. Exploratory data analysis; stem-and-leaf
display; box plots. The normal distribution; standard (z-) scores; skewed
distributions; standardisation of psychological measurements.

PART IV   Using data to test predictions   231

Section 1   An introduction to significance testing   233

Chapter 14   Probability and significance   233
Logical, empirical and subjective probability; probability distributions.
Significance; levels of significance; the 5% level; critical values; tails of
distributions; the normal probability distribution; significance of z-scores;
importance of 1% and 10% levels; type I and type II errors.

Section 2   Simple tests of difference – non-parametric   254
Using tests of significance – general procedure

Chapter 15   Tests at nominal level   256
Binomial sign test. Chi-square test of association; goodness of fit; one
variable test; limitations of chi-square.

Chapter 16   Tests at ordinal level   269
Wilcoxon signed ranks. Mann–Whitney *U*. Wilcoxon rank sum. Testing
when *N* is large.

Section 3   Simple tests of difference – parametric   278

Chapter 17   Tests at interval/ratio level   278
Power; assumptions underlying parametric tests; robustness. *t* test for
related data; *t* test for unrelated data.

Section 4   Correlation   293

Chapter 18   Correlation and its significance   293
The nature of correlation; measurement of correlation; scattergrams.
Calculating correlation; Pearson's product-moment coefficient;
Spearman's Rho. Significance and correlation coefficients; strength and
significance; guessing error; variance estimate; coefficient of
determination. What you can't assume with a correlation; cause and
effect assumptions; missing middle; range restriction; correlation when
one variable is nominal; general restriction; dichotomous variables and
the point biserial correlation; the Phi coefficient. Common uses of
correlation in psychology.

Section 5   Tests for more than two conditions
Introduction to more complex tests

Chapter 19   Non-parametric tests – more than two conditions   320
Kruskal-Wallis (unrelated differences). Jonckheere (unrelated trend).
Friedman (related differences). Page (related trend).

Chapter 20   One way ANOVA   327
Comparing variances; the *F* test; variance components; sums of squares;
calculations for one-way; the significance and interpretation of *F*. A priori
and post hoc comparisons; error rates; Bonferroni *t* tests; linear contrasts
and coefficients; Newman–Keuls; Tukey's HSD; unequal sample
numbers.

Chapter 21   Multi-factor ANOVA   343
Factors and levels; unrelated and related designs; interaction effects;
main effects; simple effects; partitioning the sums of squares; calculation
for two-way unrelated ANOVA; three-way ANOVA components.

Chapter 22   Repeated measures ANOVA   355
Rationale; between subjects variation; division of variation for one-way
repeated measures design; calculation for one-way design; two-way
related design; mixed model – one repeat and one unrelated factor;
division of variation in mixed model.

Chapter 23   Other useful complex multi-variate tests – a brief summary 367
MANOVA, ANCOVA; multiple regression and multiple predictions.

Section 6   What analysis to use?   374

Chapter 24   Choosing an appropriate test   374
Tests for two samples; steps in making a choice; decision chart; examples
of choosing a test; hints. Tests for more than two samples. Some
information on computer programmes.

Chapter 25   Analysing qualitative data   382
Qualitative data and hypothesis testing; qualitative analysis of qualitative
content; methods of analysis; transcribing speech; grounded theory; the
final report. Validity. On doing a qualitative project. Analysing discourse.
Specialist texts.

PART V   Ethics and practice   391

Chapter 26   Ethical issues and humanism in psychological research   393
Publication and access to data; confidentiality and privacy; the Milgram
experiment; deception; debriefing; stress and discomfort; right to non-
participation; special power of the investigator; involuntary participation;
intervention; research with animals.

Chapter 27   Planning practicals   408

Chapter 28   Writing your practical report   413

Appendix 1   Structured questions   434
Appendix 2   Statistical tables   447
Appendix 3   Answers to exercises and structured questions   469

References   484

Index   491

PREFACE TO THE FIRST EDITION

After the domination of behaviourism in Anglo-American psychology during the middle of the century, the impression has been left, reflected in the many texts on research design, that the experimental method is the central tool of psychological research. In fact, a glance through journals will illuminate a wide array of data-gathering instruments in use outside the experimental laboratory and beyond the field experiment. This book takes the reader through details of the experimental method, but also examines the many criticisms of it, in particular the argument that its use, as a paradigm, has led to some fairly arid and unrealistic psychological models, as has the empirical insistence on quantification. The reader is also introduced to non-experimental method in some depth, where current A-level texts tend to be rather superficial. But, further, it takes the reader somewhat beyond current A-level minimum requirements and into the world of qualitative approaches.

Having said that, it is written at a level which should feel 'friendly' and comfortable to the person just starting their study of psychology. The beginner will find it useful to read part one first, since this section introduces fundamental issues of scientific method and techniques of measuring or gathering data about people. Thereafter, any reader can and should use it as a manual to be dipped into at the appropriate place for the current research project or problem, though the early chapters of the statistics section will need to be consulted in order to understand the rationale and procedure of the tests of significance.

I have tried to write the statistical sections as I teach them, with the mathematically nervous student very much in mind. Very often, though, people who think they are poor at mathematical thinking find statistics far less difficult than they had feared, and the tests in this book which match current A-level requirements involve the use of very few mathematical operations. Except for a few illuminative examples, the statistical concepts are all introduced via realistic psychological data, some emanating from actual studies performed by students.

This book will provide the A-level, A/S-level or International Baccalaureate student with all that is necessary, not only for selecting methods and statistical treatments for practical work and for structured questions on research examples, but also for dealing with general issues of scientific and research methods. Higher education students, too, wary of statistics as vast numbers of psychology beginners often are, should also find this book an accessible route into the area. Questions throughout are intended to engage the reader in active thinking about the current topic, often by stimulating the prediction of problems before they are presented. The final structured questions imitate those found in the papers of several Examination Boards.

I hope, through using this book, the reader will be encouraged to *enjoy* research; not to see it as an intimidating add-on, but, in fact, as the engine of theory without which we would be left with a broad array of truly fascinating ideas about human experience and behaviour with no means of telling which are sheer fantasy and which might lead us to models of the human condition grounded in reality.

If there are points in this book which you wish to question, please get in touch via the publisher.

Hugh Coolican

PREFACE TO THE SECOND EDITION

When I wrote the first edition of this book I was writing as an A-level teacher knowing that we all needed a comprehensive book of methods and statistics which didn't then exist at the appropriate level. I was pleasantly surprised, therefore, to find an increasing number of Higher Education institutions using the book as an introductory text. In response to the interests of higher education students, I have included chapters on significance tests for three or more conditions, both non-parametric and using ANOVA. The latter takes the student into the world of the interactions which are possible with the use of more than one independent variable. The point about the 'maths' involved in psychological statistics still holds true, however. The calculations involve no more than those on the most basic calculator – addition, subtraction, multiplication and division, squares, square roots and decimals. The chapter on other useful complex tests is meant only as a signpost to readers venturing further into more complex designs and statistical investigation.

Although this introduction of more complex test procedures tends to weight the book further towards statistics, a central theme remains the importance of the whole spectrum of possible research methods in psychology. Hence, I have included a brief introduction to the currently influential, if controversial, qualitative approaches of discourse analysis and reflexivity, along with several other minor additions to the variety of methods. The reader will find a general updating of research used to exemplify methods.

In the interest of student learning through engagement with the text, I have included a glossary at the end of each chapter which doubles as a self-test exercise, though A-level tutors, and those at similar levels, will need to point out that students are not expected to be familiar with every single key term. The glossary definition for each term is easily found by consulting the main index and turning to the page referred to in heavy type. To stem the tide of requests for sample student reports, which the first edition encouraged, I have written a bogus report, set at an 'average' level (I believe), and included possible marker's comments, both serious and hair-splitting.

Finally, I anticipate, as with the first edition, many enquiries and arguments critical of some of my points, and these I welcome. Such enquiries have caused me to alter, or somewhat complicate, several points made in the first edition. For instance, we lose Yates' correction, find limitations on the classic Spearman's rho formula, learn that correlation with dichotomous (and therefore nominal) variables *is* possible, and so on. These points do not affect anything the student needs to know for their A-level exam but may affect procedures used in practical reports. Nevertheless, I have withstood the temptation to enter into many other subtle debates or niceties simply because the main aim of the book is still, of course, to clarify and not to confuse through density. I do hope that this aim has been aided by the inclusion of yet more teaching 'tricks' developed since the last edition, and, at last, a few of my favourite illustrations. If only some of these could move!

Hugh Coolican

Introduction

1

PSYCHOLOGY AND RESEARCH

This introduction sets the scene for research in psychology. The key ideas are that:

* Psychological researchers generally follow a scientific approach.
* This involves the logic of testing hypotheses produced from falsifiable theories.
* Hypotheses need to be precisely stated before testing.
* Scientific research is a continuous and social activity, involving promotion and checking of ideas amongst colleagues.
* Researchers use probability statistics to decide whether effects are 'significant' or not.
* Research has to be carefully planned with attention to design, variables, samples and subsequent data analysis. If *all* these areas are not fully planned, results may be ambiguous or useless.
* Some researchers have strong objections to the use of traditional scientific methods in the study of persons. They support qualitative and 'new paradigm' methods which may *not* involve rigid pre-planned testing of hypotheses.

Student: I'd like to enrol for psychology please.
Lecturer: You do realise that it includes quite a bit of statistics, and you'll have to do some experimental work and write up practical reports?
Student: Oh . . .

When enrolling for a course in psychology, the prospective student is very often taken aback by the discovery that the syllabus includes a fair-sized dollop of statistics and that practical research, experiments and report-writing are all involved. My experience as a tutor has commonly been that many 'A' level psychology students are either 'escaping' from school into further education or tentatively returning after years away from academic study. Both sorts of student are frequently dismayed to find that this new and exciting subject is going to thrust them back into two of the areas they most disliked in school. One is maths – but rest assured! Statistics, in fact, will involve you in little of the maths on a traditional syllabus and will be performed on real data most of which you have gathered yourself. Calculators and computers do the 'number crunching' these days. The other area is science.

It is strange that of all the sciences – natural and social – the one which directly concerns ourselves as individuals in society is the least likely to be found in schools, where teachers are preparing young people for social life, amongst other things! It is also strange that a student can study all the 'hard' natural sciences – physics, chemistry, biology – yet never be asked to consider what a science *is* until they study psychology or sociology.

These are generalisations of course. Some schools teach psychology. Others nowadays teach the underlying principles of scientific research. Some of us actually enjoyed science and maths at school. If you did, you'll find some parts of this book fairly easy going. But can I state one of my most cherished beliefs right now, for the sake of those who hate numbers and think this is all going to be a struggle, or, worse still, boring? Many of the ideas and concepts introduced in this book will already be in your head in an informal way, even 'hard' topics like probability. My job is partly to give names to some concepts you will easily think of for yourself. At other times it will be to formalise and tighten up ideas that you have gathered through experience. For instance, you already have a fairly good idea of how many cats out of ten ought to choose 'Poshpaws' cat food in preference to another brand, in order for us to be convinced that this is a real difference and not a fluke. You can probably start discussing quite competently what would count as a representative sample of people for a particular survey.

Returning to the prospective student then, he or she usually has little clue about what sort of research psychologists do. The notion of 'experiments' sometimes produces anxiety. 'Will we be conditioned or brainwashed?'

If we ignore images from the black-and-white film industry, and think carefully about what psychological researchers might do, we might conjure up an image of the street survey. Think again, and we might suggest that psychologists watch people's behaviour. I agree with Gross (1992) who says that, at a party, if one admits to teaching, or even studying, psychology, a common reaction is 'Oh, I'd better be careful what I say from now on'. Another strong contender is 'I suppose you'll be analysing my behaviour' (said as the speaker takes one hesitant step backwards) in the mistaken assumption that psychologists go around making deep, mysterious inter-pretations of human actions as they occur. (If you meet someone who does do this, ask them something about the evidence they use, after you've finished with this book!) The notion of such analysis is loosely connected to Freud who, though popularly portrayed as a psychiatric Sherlock Holmes, used very few of the sorts of research outlined in this book – though he did use unstructured clinical interviews and the case-study method (Chapter 8).

SO WHAT IS THE NATURE OF PSYCHOLOGICAL RESEARCH?

Although there are endless and furious debates about what a science is and what sort of science, if any, psychology should be, a majority of psychologists would agree that research should be scientific, and at the very least that it should be objective, controlled and checkable. There is no final agreement, however, about precisely *how* scientific method should operate within the very broad range of psychological research topics. There are many definitions of science but, for present purposes, Allport's (1947) is useful. Science, he claims, has the aims of:

> '. . . understanding, prediction and control above the levels achieved by unaided common sense.'

What does Allport, or anyone, mean by 'common sense'? Aren't some things blindly obvious? Isn't it indisputable that babies are born with different personalities, for instance? Let's have a look at some other popular 'common-sense' claims.

Before reading my comments on the right-hand side of Box 1.1, have a think about any challenge you might wish to make to the claims made. In particular, what evidence would you want to get hold of?

I have used these statements, including the controversial ones, because they are just the sort of things people claim confidently, yet with no hard evidence. They are 'hunches' masquerading as fact. I call them 'armchair certainties (or theories)' because this is where they are often claimed from.

Box 1.1   *'Common-sense' claims*

1 Women obviously have a maternal instinct – look how strongly they want to stay with their child and protect it

Have we checked how men would feel after several months alone with a baby? Does the term 'instinct' *add* to our understanding, or does it simply describe what mothers do and, perhaps, feel? Do *all* mothers feel this way?

2 Michelle is so good at predicting people's star sign – there must be something in astrology

Have we checked that Michelle gets a lot more signs correct than anyone would by just guessing? Have we counted the times when she's wrong?

3 So many batsmen get out on 98 or 99 – it must be the psychological pressure

Have we compared with the numbers of batsmen who get out on other high totals?

4 Women are less logical, more suggestible and make worse drivers than men

Women score the same as men on logical tests in general. They are equally 'suggestible', though boys are more likely to agree with views they don't hold but which are held by their peer group. Statistically, women are more likely to obey traffic rules and have less expensive accidents. Why else would 'one lady owner' be a selling point?

5 I wouldn't obey someone who told me to seriously hurt another person if I could possibly avoid it

About 62% of people who could have walked free from an experiment, continued to obey an experimenter who asked them to give electric shocks to a 'learner' who had fallen silent after screaming horribly

6 'The trouble with having so many black immigrants is that the country is too small' (Quote from *Call Nick Ross* phone-in, BBC Radio 4, 3.11.92)

In 1991, the total black population of the UK (African Caribbean and Indian sub-continental Asian) was a little under 5%. Almost every year since the second world war, more people have left than have entered Britain to live. Anyway, *whose* country?

I hope you see why we need evidence from research. One role for a scientific study is to challenge 'common-sense' notions by checking the facts. Another is to produce 'counter-intuitive' results like those in item five. Let me say a little more about what scientific research is by dispelling a few myths about it.

MYTH NO. 1: 'SCIENTIFIC RESEARCH IS THE COLLECTION OF FACTS'

All research is about the collection of data but this is not the sole aim. First of all, facts are not data. Facts do not speak for themselves. When people say they do they are omitting to mention essential background theory or assumptions they are making.

> A sudden crash brings us running to the kitchen. The accused is crouched in front of us, eyes wide and fearful. Her hands are red and sticky. A knife lies on the floor. So does a jam jar and its spilled contents. The accused was about to lick her tiny fingers.

I hope you made some false assumptions before the jam was mentioned. But, as it is, do the facts alone tell us that Jenny was stealing jam? Perhaps the cat knocked the jam over and Jenny was trying to pick it up. We constantly assume a lot beyond the present data in order to explain it (see Box 1.2). Facts are DATA interpreted through THEORY. Data are what we get through EMPIRICAL observation, where 'empirical' refers to information obtained through our senses. It is difficult to get raw data. We almost always interpret it immediately. The time you took to run 100 metres (or, at least, the position of the watch hands) is raw data. My saying you're 'quick' is interpretation. If we lie on the beach looking at the night sky and see a 'star' moving steadily we 'know' it's a satellite, but only because we have a lot of received astronomical knowledge, from our culture, in our heads.

Box 1.2 *Fearing or clearing the bomb?*

> In psychology we constantly challenge the simplistic acceptance of facts 'in front of our eyes'. A famous bomb disposal officer, talking to Sue Lawley on *Desert Island Discs*, told of the time he was trying urgently to clear the public from the area of a live bomb. A newspaper published his picture, advancing with outstretched arms, with the caption, 'terrified member of public flees bomb', whereas another paper correctly identified him as the calm, but concerned expert he really was.

Data are interpreted through what psychologists often call a 'schema' – our learned prejudices, stereotypes and general ideas about the world and even according to our current purposes and motivations. It is difficult to see, as developed adults, how we could ever avoid this process. However, rather than despair of ever getting at any psychological truth, most researchers share common ground in following some basic principles of contemporary science which date back to the revolutionary use of EMPIRICAL METHOD to start questioning the workings of the world in a consistent manner.

The empirical method

The original empirical method had two stages:

1 Gathering of data, directly, through our external senses, with no preconceptions as to how it is ordered or what explains it.

2 INDUCTION of patterns and relationships within the data.

'Induction' means to move from individual observations to statements of general patterns (sometimes called 'laws').

If a 30-metre-tall Martian made empirical observations on Earth, it (Martians have one sex) might focus its attention on the various metal tubes which hurtle around, some in the air, some on the ground, some under it, and stop every so often to take on little bugs and to shed others.

The Martian might then conclude that the tubes were important life-forms and that the little bugs taken on were food . . . and the ones discharged . . . ?

Now we have gone beyond the original empirical method. The Martian is constructing *theory*. This is an attempt to explain *why* the patterns are produced, what forces or processes underly them.

It is inevitable that human thinking will go beyond the patterns and combinations discovered in data analysis to ask, 'But why?'. It is also naïve to assume we could ever gather data without some background theory in our heads, as I tried to demonstrate above. Medawar (1963) has argued this point forcefully, as has Bruner who points out that, when we perceive the world, we always and inevitably 'go beyond the information given'.

Testing theories – the hypothetico-deductive method

This Martian's theory, that the bugs are food for the tubes, can be tested. If the tubes get no bugs for a long time, they should die. This prediction is a HYPOTHESIS. A hypothesis is a statement of exactly what should be the case *if* a certain theory is true. Testing the hypothesis shows that the tubes can last indefinitely without bugs. Hence the hypothesis is not supported and the theory requires alteration or dismissal. This manner of thinking is common in our everyday lives. Here's another example:

> Suppose you and a friend find that every Monday morning the wing mirror of your car gets knocked out of position. You suspect the dustcart which empties the bin that day. Your friend says, 'Well, OK. If you're so sure let's check next Tuesday. They're coming a day later next week because there's a Bank Holiday.'

The logic here is essential to critical thinking in psychological research.

- The *theory* investigated is that the dustcart knocks the mirror.
- The *hypothesis* to be tested is that the mirror will be knocked next Tuesday.
- Our *test* of the hypothesis is to check whether the mirror *is* knocked next Tuesday.
- If the mirror *is* knocked the theory is *supported*.
- If the mirror is *not* knocked the theory appears wrong.

Notice, we say only 'supported' here, not 'proven true' or anything definite like that. This is because there could be an alternative reason why it got knocked. Perhaps the boy who follows the cart each week on his bike does the knocking. This is an example of 'confounding' which we'll meet formally in the next chapter. If you and your friend were seriously scientific you could rule this out (you could get up early). This demonstrates the need for complete control over the testing situation where possible.

We say 'supported' then, rather than 'proved', because D (the dustcart) might not have caused M (mirror getting knocked) – our theory. Some *other* event may have been the cause, for instance B (boy cycling with dustcart). Very often we think we have evidence that X causes Y when, in fact, it may well be that Y causes X. You might think that a blown fuse caused damage to your washing machine, which now won't run, when actually the machine broke, overflowed and caused the fuse to blow. In psychological research, the theory that mothers talk more to young daughters (than to young sons) because girls are naturally more talkative, and the opposite theory, that girls are more talkative because their mothers talk more to them are both supported by the evidence that mothers do talk more to their daughters. Evidence is more useful when it supports one theory and *not* its rival.

Ben Elton (1989) is onto this when he says:

> Lots of Aboriginals end up as piss-heads, causing people to say 'no wonder they're so poor, half of them are piss-heads'. It would, of course, make much more sense to say 'no wonder half of them are piss-heads, they're so poor'.

Deductive logic

Theory-testing relies on the logical arguments we were using above. These are examples of DEDUCTION. Stripped to their bare skeleton they are:

	Applied to theory-testing	*Applied to the dustcart and mirror problem*
1 If X is true then Y must be true	1 If theory A is true, then hypothesis H will be confirmed	1 If the dustcart knocks the mirror then the mirror will get knocked next Tuesday
2 Y isn't true	2 H is disconfirmed	2 The mirror didn't get knocked
3 Therefore X is true	3 Theory A is wrong*	3 Therefore it isn't the dustcart
or	or	
2 Y is true	2 H is confirmed	2 The mirror *did* get knocked
3 X could still be true	3 Theory A could be true	3 Perhaps it *is* the dustcart

* At this point, according to the 'official line', scientists should drop the theory with the false prediction. In fact, many famous scientists, including Newton and Einstein, and most not-so-famous-ones, have clung to theories *despite* contradictory results because of a 'hunch' that the data were wrong. This hunch was sometime shown to be correct. The beauty of a theory *can* outweigh pure logic in real science practice.

It is often not a lot of use getting more and more of the same sort of support for your theory. If I claim that all swans are white because the sun bleaches their feathers, it gets a bit tedious if I keep pointing to each new white one saying 'I told you so'. All we need is one sun-loving black swan to blow my theory wide apart.

If your hypothesis is disconfirmed, it is not always necessary to abandon the theory which predicted it, in the way that my simple swan theory must go. Very often you would have to adjust your theory to take account of new data. For instance, your friend might have a smug look on her face. 'Did you know it was the Council's "be-ever-so-nice-to-our-customers" promotion week and the collectors get bonuses if there are no complaints?' 'Pah!' you say 'That's no good as a test then!' Here, again, we see the need to have complete control over the testing situation in order to keep external events as constant as possible. 'Never mind,' your friend soothes, 'we can always write this up in our psychology essay on scientific method'.

Theories in science don't just get 'proven true' and they rarely rest on totally unambiguous evidence. There is often a balance in favour with several anomalies yet to explain. Theories tend to 'survive' or not against others depending on the quality, not just the quantity, of their supporting evidence. But for every *single* supportive piece of evidence in social science there is very often an alternative explanation. It might be claimed that similarity between parent and child in intelligence is evidence for the view that intelligence is genetically transmitted. However, this evidence supports *equally* the view that children *learn* their skills from their parents, and similarity between adoptive parent and child is a *challenge* to the theory.

Falsifiability

Popper (1959) has argued that for any theory to count as a theory we must at least be able to see how it *could* be falsified – we don't have to be able to falsify it; after all, it might be true! As an example, consider the once popular notion that Paul McCartney died some years ago (I don't know whether there is *still* a group who believe this). Suppose we produce Paul in the flesh. This won't do – he is, of course, a cunning replacement. Suppose we show that no death certificate was issued anywhere around the time of his purported demise. Well, of course, there was a cover up; it was made out in a different name. Suppose we supply DNA evidence from the current Paul and it exactly matches the original Paul's DNA. Another plot; the current sample was switched behind the scenes . . . and so on. This theory is useless because there is only (rather stretched) supporting evidence and *no* accepted means of falsification. Freudian theory often comes under attack for this weakness. Reaction formation can excuse many otherwise damaging pieces of contradictory evidence. A writer once explained the sexual symbolism of chess and claimed that the very hostility of chess players to these explanations was evidence of their validity! They were defending against the powerful threat of the truth. Women who claim publicly that they do *not* desire their babies to be male, contrary to 'penis-envy' theory, are reacting internally against the very real threat that the desire they harbour, originally for their father, might be exposed, so the argument goes. With this sort of explanation *any* evidence, desiring males or not desiring them, is taken as support for the theory. Hence, it is unfalsifiable and therefore untestable in Popper's view.

Conventional scientific method

Putting together the empirical method of induction, and the hypothetico-deductive method, we get what is traditionally taken to be the 'scientific method', accepted by many psychological researchers as the way to follow in the footsteps of the successful natural sciences. The steps in the method are shown in Box 1.3.

Box 1.3 *Traditional scientific method*

1 Observation, gathering and ordering of data
2 Induction of generalisations, laws
3 Development of explanatory theories
4 Deduction of hypotheses to test theories
5 Testing of the hypotheses
6 Support or adjustment of theory

Scientific research projects, then, may be concentrating on the early or later stages of this process. They may be exploratory studies, looking for data from which to create theories, or they may be hypothesis-testing studies, aiming to support or challenge a theory.

There are many doubts about, and criticisms of, this model of scientific research, too detailed to go into here though several aspects of the arguments will be returned to throughout the book, particularly in Chapter 11. The reader might like to consult Gross (1992) or Valentine (1992).

MYTH NO. 2: 'SCIENTIFIC RESEARCH INVOLVES DRAMATIC DISCOVERIES AND BREAKTHROUGHS'

If theory testing was as simple as the dustcart test was, life would produce dramatic breakthroughs every day. Unfortunately, the classic discoveries are all the lay person hears about. In fact, research plods along all the time, largely according to Figure 1.1. Although, from reading about research, it is easy to think about a single project beginning and ending at specific points of time, there is, in the research world, a constant cycle occurring.

A project is developed from a combination of the current trends in research thinking (theory) and methods, other challenging past theories and, within psychology at least, from important events in the everyday social world. The investigator might wish to replicate (repeat) a study by someone else in order to verify it. Or they

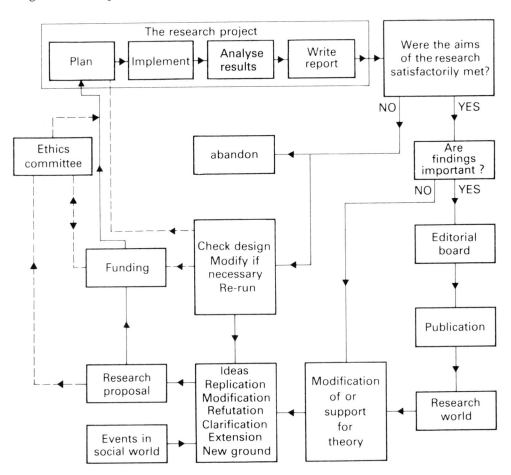

Figure 1.1 *The research cycle*

might wish to extend it to other areas, or to modify it because it has weaknesses. Every now and again an investigation breaks completely new ground but the vast majority develop out of the current state of play.

Politics and economics enter at the stage of funding. Research staff, in universities, colleges or hospitals, have to justify their salaries and the expense of the project. Funds will come from one of the following: university, college or hospital research funds; central or local government; private companies; charitable institutions; and the odd private benefactor. These, and the investigator's direct employers, will need to be satisfied that the research is worthwhile to them, to society or to the general pool of scientific knowledge, and that it is ethically sound.

The actual testing or 'running' of the project may take very little time compared with all the planning and preparation along with the analysis of results and report-writing. Some procedures, such as an experiment or questionnaire, may be tried out on a small sample of people in order to highlight snags or ambiguities for which adjustments can be made before the actual data gathering process is begun. This is known as PILOTING. The researcher would run PILOT TRIALS of an experiment or would PILOT a questionnaire, for instance.

The report will be published in a research journal if successful. This term 'successful' is difficult to define here. It doesn't always mean that original aims have been entirely met. Surprises occurring during the research may well make it important, though usually such surprises would lead the investigator to rethink, replan and run again on the basis of the new insights. As we saw above, failure to confirm one's hypothesis can be an important source of information. What matters overall, is that the research results are an important or useful contribution to current knowledge and theory development. This importance will be decided by the editorial board of an academic journal (such as the *British Journal of Psychology*) who will have the report reviewed, usually by experts 'blind' as to the identity of the investigator.

Theory will then be adjusted in the light of this research result. Some academics may argue that the design was so different from previous research that its challenge to their theory can be ignored. Others will wish to query the results and may ask the investigator to provide 'raw data' – the whole of the originally recorded data, unprocessed. Some will want to replicate the study, some to modify . . . and here we are, back where we started on the research cycle.

MYTH NO. 3: 'SCIENTIFIC RESEARCH IS ALL ABOUT EXPERIMENTS'

An experiment involves the researcher's control and manipulation of conditions or 'variables, as we shall see in Chapter 5.

Astronomy, one of the oldest sciences, could not use very many experiments until relatively recently when technological advances have permitted direct tests of conditions in space. It has mainly relied upon *observation* to test its theories of planetery motion and stellar organisation.

It is perfectly possible to test hypotheses without an experiment. Much psychological testing is conducted by observing what children do, asking what people think and so on. The evidence about male and female drivers, for instance, was obtained by observation of actual behaviour and insurance company statistics.

MYTH NO. 4: 'SCIENTISTS HAVE TO BE UNBIASED'

It is true that investigators try to remove bias from the way a project is run and from the way data is gathered and analysed. But they are biased about theory. They interpret ambiguous data to fit their particular theory as best they can. This happens whenever we're in a heated argument and say things like 'Ah, but that could be because . . .'. Investigators *believe* in their theory and attempt to produce evidence to support it. Mitroff (1974) interviewed a group of scientists and all agreed that the notion of the purely objective, uncommited scientist was naïve. They argued that:

> . . . in order to be a good scientist, one had to have biases. The best scientist, they said, not only has points of view but also defends them with gusto. Their concept of a scientist did not imply that he would cheat by making up experimental data or falsifying it; rather he does everything in his power to defend his pet hypotheses against early and perhaps unwarranted death caused by the introduction of fluke data.

DO WE GET ON TO PSYCHOLOGICAL RESEARCH NOW?

Yes. We've looked at some common ideas in the language and logic of scientific research, since most, but not all, psychological investigators would claim to follow a scientific model. Now let's answer some 'wh' questions about the practicalities of psychological research.

WHAT IS THE SUBJECT MATTER FOR PSYCHOLOGICAL RESEARCH?

The easy answer is 'humans'. The more controversial answer is 'human behaviour' since psychology is literally (in Greek) the study of mind. This isn't a book which will take you into the great debate on the relationship between mind and body or whether the study of mind is at all possible. This is available in other general textbooks (e.g. Gross 1992, Valentine 1992).

Whatever type of psychology you are studying you should be introduced to the various major 'schools' of psychology (Psycho-analytic, Behaviourist, Cognitive Humanist, . . .) It is important to point out here, however, that each school would see the focus for its subject matter differently – behaviour, the conscious mind, even the unconscious mind. Consequently, different investigatory methods have been developed by different schools.

Nevertheless, the initial raw data which psychologists gather directly from humans can *only* be observed behaviour (including physiological responses) or language (verbal report).

WHY DO PSYCHOLOGISTS DO RESEARCH?

All research has the overall aim of collecting data to expand knowledge. To be specific, research will usually have one of two major aims: To gather purely descriptive data or to test hypotheses.

Descriptive research

A piece of research may establish the ages at which a large sample of children reach certain language development milestones or it may be a survey (Chapter 8) of current adult attitudes to the use of nuclear weapons. If the results from this are in numerical form then the data are known as QUANTITATIVE and we would make use of DESCRIPTIVE STATISTICS (Chapter 13) to present a summary of findings. If the research presents a report of the contents of interviews or case-studies (Chapter 8), or of detailed observations (Chapter 7), then the data may be largely QUALITATIVE (Chapters 4, 11, 25), though parts may well become quantified.

Moving to level 3 of Box 1.3, the descriptive data may well be analysed in order to generate hypotheses, models, theories or further research directions and ideas.

Hypothesis testing

A large amount of research sets out to examine one RESEARCH HYPOTHESIS or more by showing that differences in relationships between people already exist, or that they can be created through experimental manipulation. In an experiment, the research hypothesis would be called the EXPERIMENTAL HYPOTHESIS. Tests of differences or relationships between sets of data are performed using INFERENTIAL STATISTICS (Chapters 15–24). Let me describe two examples of HYPOTHESIS TESTING, one laboratory based, the other from 'the field'.

1 IN THE LABORATORY: A TEST OF SHORT-TERM MEMORY THEORY – A theory popular in the 1960s was the model of short-term (ST) and long-term (LT) memory. This claimed that the small amount of information, say seven or eight digits or a few unconnected words, which we can hold in the conscious mind at any one time (our short-term store) is transferred to a LT store by means of rehearsal – repetition of each item in the ST store. The more rehearsal an item received, the better it was stored and therefore the more easily it was recalled.

A challenge to this model is that simply rehearsing items is not efficient and rarely what people actually do, even when so instructed. Humans tend to make incoming information meaningful. Repetition of words does not, in itself, make them more meaningful. One way an unconnected list of words *could* be made more meaningful is to form a vivid mental image of each one and to link it to the next in a bizarre fashion. If 'wheel' is followed by 'plane', for instance, imagine a candy striped little aeroplane flying through the centre hole of the previously imaged wheel.

From this a prediction can be made. Our hypothesis for testing is:

'People will recall significantly more correct items after learning by image-linking than after learning by rehearsal.'

Every time this experiment is conducted the hypothesis is clearly supported. Most people are much better using imagery. This is not the obvious result it may seem. Many people feel far more comfortable simply repeating things. They predict that the 'silly' method will confuse them. However, even if it does, the information still sticks better. So, a useful method for exam revision? Well, making sense of your notes, playing with them, is a lot better than simply reading and repeating them. Lists of examples can also be stored this way.

2 IN THE FIELD: A TEST OF MATERNAL DEPRIVATION – Bowlby (1951) proposed a controversial theory that young infants have a natural (that is, biological or innate) tendency to form a special attachment with just one person, usually the mother, different in kind and quality from any other.

What does this theory predict? Well, coupled with other arguments, Bowlby was able to predict that children unable to form such an attachment, or those for whom this attachment was severed within the first few years of life, especially before three years old, would later be more likely than other children to become maladjusted.

Bowlby produced several examples of seriously deprived children exhibiting greater maladjustment. Hence, he could *support* his theory. In this case, he didn't do something to people and demonstrate the result (which is what an experiment like our memory example above does). He predicted something to be the case, showed it was, and then related these results back to what had happened to the children in the past.

But remember that continual support does not *prove* a theory to be correct. Rutter (1971) challenged the theory with evidence that boys on the Isle of Wight who suffered early deprivation, even death of their mother, were *not* more likely to be rated as maladjusted than other boys so long as the separation had not also involved continuing social difficulties within the family. Here, Bowlby's theory has to be adjusted in the light of contradictory evidence.

Hypotheses are **not** *aims or theories!*

Researchers state their hypothesis extremely precisely and clearly. I have given the memory hypothesis in the example above. There are certain features of hypotheses that may help you write them in your own practical reports:

1 No theory is included: we *don't* say, 'People will recall more scores *because* . . . (imagery makes words more meaningful, etc.). . .'. We just simply state what we expect to happen.

2 Effects are precisely defined. We *don't* say, 'Memory will be better. . .', we define *exactly* how improvement will be measured, '. . . people will recall significantly more items. . .'. Definition and precision are dealt with in Chapter 2.

The term 'significant' has been introduced here. It is tackled fully in Chapter 14. For now let's take it to mean that we're predicting a difference large enough to be considered *not a fluke*. That is to say, a difference so large that we can dismiss the idea it's just a chance occurrence. Researchers would refer, here, to the 'rejection of the NULL HYPOTHESIS'.

The null hypothesis

Students always find it odd that psychological researchers emphasise so strongly the logic of the null hypothesis and its acceptance or rejection. The whole notion is not simple and has engendered huge, even hostile debate over the years. One reason for its prominence is that psychological evidence is so firmly founded on the theory of probability i.e. decisions about the genuine nature of effects are based on mathematical *likelihood*. Hence, this concept, too, will be more thoroughly tackled in Chapter 14. For the time being, consider this debate. You, and a friend, have each just bought a box of matches ('average contents 40'). Being particularly bored or masochistic you both decide to count them. It turns out that your friend has 45 whereas you have a meagre 36. 'I've been done!' you exclaim, 'just because the newsagent didn't want to change a £50 note'. Your friend tries to explain that there will always be variation around the average of 40 and that your number is actually closer to the mean than his is. 'But you've got 9 more than me', you wail, 'Well I'm sure the shopkeeper couldn't both have it in for you *and* favour me – there isn't time to check all the boxes the way you're suggesting.'

What's happening is that you're making a non-obvious claim about reality, challenging the status quo, with no other evidence than the matches. Hence, it's down to you to provide some good 'facts' with which to argue your case. What you have is a difference from the pure average. But is it a difference *large* enough to convince anyone that it isn't just random variation? It's obviously not convincing your friend. He is staying with the 'null hypothesis' that the average content really is 40 (and that your difference could reasonably be expected by chance).

Let's look at another field research example. Penny and Robinson (1986) proposed the theory that young people smoke *partly* to reduce stress. The hypothesis they tested was that smokers would differ from non-smokers on a measure of anxiety (the Spielberger Trait Anxiety Inventory). Note the precision. The *theory* is not in the hypothesis and the measure of stress is precisely defined. We shall discuss psychological measures, such as this one, in Chapter 9. The null hypothesis here, then, is that smokers and non-smokers have a real difference of zero on this scale. Now, *any* test of two groups will *always* produce *some* difference, just as any test of two bottles of washing up liquid will inevitably produce a slightly different number of plates washed successfully. The question is, again, do the groups differ enough to reject the status quo view that they are similar? The notion is a bit like that of being innocent until proved guilty. There's usually *some* sort of evidence against an accused but if it isn't strong enough we stick, however uncomfortably, to the innocent view. This doesn't mean that researchers give up nobly. They often talk of 'retaining' or just 'not rejecting' the null hypothesis. The null hypothesis will not automatically be treated as therefore *true*. In the smoking and anxiety case the null hypothesis was rejected – smokers were significantly higher than non-smokers on *this* measure of anxiety.

In the maternal deprivation example, above, we can see that after testing, Rutter claimed the null hypothesis (no difference between deprived and non-deprived boys) could *not* be rejected, whereas Bowlby's results had been used to *support* rejection. A further cross-cultural example is given by Joe (1991) in Chapter 10. Have a look at the way we might use the logic of null hypothesis thinking in everyday life, as described in Box 1.4.

Box 1.4 *The null hypothesis – the truth standing on its head*

Everyday thinking	**Formal research thinking**
Women just don't have a chance of management promotion in this place. In the last four interviews they picked a male each time out of a shortlist of two females and two males	Hypothesis of interest: more males get selected for management
Really? Let's see, how many males *should* they have selected if you're wrong?	Construct null hypothesis – what would happen if our theory is *not* true?
How do you mean?	
Well, there were the same number of female as male candidates each time, so there should have been just as many females as males selected in all. That's two!	Express the null hypothesis statistically. Very often this is that the difference between the two sets of scores is really zero. Here, it is that the difference between females and males selected will be zero
Oh yeah! That's what I meant to start with. There should have been at *least* two new women managers from that round of selection	Note: if there had been three female candidates and only one male each time, the null hypothesis would predict three females selected in all
Well *just* two unless we're compensating for past male advantage! Now is none out of four different *enough* from two out of four to give us hard evidence of selection bias?	Conduct a statistical test to assess the probability that the actual figures would differ as much as they do from what the null hypothesis predicts

One- and two-tailed hypotheses *(or 'one- and two-sided', or 'directional' and 'non-directional')*

If smokers use cigarettes to reduce stress you might argue that, rather than finding them *higher* on anxiety, they'd be *lower* – so long as they had a good supply! Hence, Penny and Robinson could predict that smokers might be higher *or* lower than non-smokers on anxiety. The hypothesis would be known as 'two-tailed' (some say 'two-sided' or 'non-directional') – where the direction of effect is *not* predicted. A one-tailed hypothesis *does* predict the direction e.g., that people using imagery will recall *more* words. Again, the underlying notion here is statistical and will be dealt with more fully in Chapter 14.

When is a hypothesis test 'successful'?

The decision is based entirely on a TEST OF SIGNIFICANCE, which estimates the unlikelihood of the null hypothesis being true. We will discuss these in Chapter 14. However, note that, as with Rutter's case, a demonstration of no real difference can be very important. Although young women consistently *rate* their IQ lower than do young men, it's important to demonstrate that there is, in fact, no real difference in IQ.

Students doing practical work often get quite despondent when what they predicted does not occur. It feels very much as though the project hasn't worked. Some students I was teaching recently failed to show, contrary to their expectations, that the 'older generation' were more negative about homosexuality than their own generation. I explained that it was surely important information that the 'older generation' were just as liberal as they were (or, perhaps, that their generation were just as hostile).

If hypothesis tests 'fail' we either accept the null hypothesis as important information or we critically assess the design of the project and look for weaknesses in it. Perhaps we asked the wrong questions or the wrong people? Were instructions clear enough? Did we test everybody fairly and in the same manner? The process of evaluating our design and procedure is educational in itself and forms an important part of our research report – the 'Discussion'. The whole process of writing a report is outlined in Chapter 28.

HOW DO PSYCHOLOGISTS CONDUCT RESEARCH?

A huge question and basically an introduction to the rest of the book! A very large number of psychologists use the experimental method or some form of well controlled careful investigation, involving careful measurement in the data gathering process.

In Chapter 11, however, we shall consider why a growing number of psychologists reject the use of the experiment and may also tend to favour methods which gather qualitative data – information from people which is in descriptive, non-numerical, form. Some of these psychologists also reject the scientific method as I have outlined it. They accept that this has been a successful way to study inert matter, but seek an alternative approach to understanding ourselves. Others reinterpret 'science' as it applies to psychology.

One thing we can say, though, is, whatever the outlook of the researcher, there are three major ways to get information about people. You either ask them, observe them or meddle. These are covered in 'Asking questions', 'Observational methods' and 'The experimental method (part 1 and part 2)'.

PLANNING RESEARCH

To get us started, and to allow me to introduce the rest of this book, let's look at the key decision areas facing anyone about to conduct some research. I have identified these in Figure 1.2. Basically, the four boxes are answers to the questions:

Variables: WHAT shall we study? (what human characteristics under what conditions?)
Design: HOW shall we study these?
Samples: WHO shall we study?
Analysis: WHAT sort of evidence will we get, in what form?

> Before looking at these a little more closely, try planning a piece of research which tests the (loosely-worded) hypothesis that 'people are more irritable in hot weather'.

VARIABLES

Variables are tricky things. They are the things which alter so that we can make comparisons, such as 'Are you tidier than I am?' Heat is a variable in our study. How shall we define it? How shall we make sure that it isn't humidity, rather than temperature, that is responsible for any irritability?

But the real problem is how to measure 'irritability'. We could, of course, devise some sort of questionnaire. The construction of these is dealt with in Chapter 9. We could observe people's behaviour at work on hot and cool days. Are there more arguments? Is there more swearing or shouting? We could observe these events in the street or in some families. Chapter 7 will deal with methods of observation.

We could even bring people into the 'laboratory' and see whether they tend to answer our questionnaire differently under a well-controlled change in temperature. We could observe their behaviour whilst carrying out a frustrating task (for instance, balancing pencils on a slightly moving surface) and we could ask them to assess this task under the two temperature conditions.

The difficulty of defining variables, stating exactly what it is we mean by a term and how, if at all, we intend to measure it, seemed to me to be so primary that I gave it the first chapter in the main body of the book (Chapter 2).

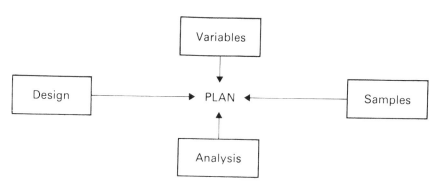

Figure 1.2 *Key decision areas in research*

DESIGN

The decisions about variable measurement have taken us into decisions about the DESIGN. The design is the overall structure and strategy of the research. Decisions on measuring irritability may determine whether we conduct a laboratory study or 'field' research. If we want realistic irritability we might wish to measure it as it occurs naturally, 'in the field'. If we take the laboratory option described above, we would be running an experiment. However, experiments can be run using various designs. Shall we, for instance, have the same group of people perform the frustrating task under the two temperature conditions? If so, mightn't they be getting practice at the task which will make changes in their performance harder to interpret? The variety of experimental designs is covered in Chapter 6.

There are several constraints on choice of design:

1 RESOURCES – The researcher may not have the funding, staff or time to carry out a long-term study. The most appropriate technical equipment may be just too expensive. Resources may not stretch to testing in different cultures. A study in the natural setting – say in a hospital – may be too time consuming or ruled out by lack of permission. The laboratory may just have to do.

2 NATURE OF RESEARCH AIM – If the researcher wishes to study the effects of maternal deprivation on the three-year-old, certain designs are ruled out. We can't experiment by artificially depriving children of their mothers (I hope you agree!) and we can't question a three-year-old in any great depth. We may be left with the best option of observing the child's behaviour, although some researchers have turned to experiments on animals in lieu of humans. The ethics of such decisions are discussed more fully in Chapter 26.

3 PREVIOUS RESEARCH – If we intend to *repeat* an earlier study we must use the same design and method. An *extension* of the study may require the same design, because an extra group is to be added, or it may require use of a different design which complements the first. We may wish to demonstrate that a laboratory discovered effect can be reproduced in a natural setting, for instance.

4 THE RESEARCHER'S ATTITUDE TO SCIENTIFIC INVESTIGATION – There can be hostile debates between psychologists from different research backgrounds. Some swear by the strictly controlled laboratory setting, seeking to emulate the 'hard' physical sciences in their isolation and precise measurement of variables. Others prefer the more realistic 'field' setting, while there is a growing body of researchers with a humanistic, 'action research' or 'new paradigm' approach who favour qualitative methods. We shall look more closely at this debate in the methods section.

SAMPLES

These are the people we are going to study or work with. If we carry out our field observations on office workers (on hot and cool days) we might be showing only that these sort of people get more irritable in the heat. What about builders or nurses? If we select a sample for our laboratory experiment, what factors shall we take into account in trying to make the group representative of most people in general? Is this possible? These are issues of 'sampling' and are dealt with in Chapter 3.

One word on terminology here. It is common to refer to the people studied in psychological research, especially in experiments, as 'subjects'. There are objections to this, particularly by psychologists who argue that a false model of the human being is generated by referring to (and possibly treating) people studied in this distant, coolly scientific manner. The British Psychological Society's 'Revised Ethical Principles for Conducting Research with Human Participants' were in provisional operation from February 1992. These include the principle that, on the grounds of courtesy and gratitude to participants, the terminology used about them should carry obvious respect (although traditional psychologists did not intend 'subjects' to be derogatory). The principles were formally adopted in October 1992. However, through 1992 and up to mid-1993, in the *British Journal of Psychology*, there was only one use of 'participants' in over 30 research reports, so we are in a transition phase on this term.

Some important terminology uses 'subject', especially 'subject variables' (Chapter 3), and 'between' or 'within subjects' (Chapters 20–22). In the interest of clarity I have included both terms in Chapter 3 but stuck to the older one in Chapters 20–22 in order not to confuse readers checking my text with others on a difficult statistical topic. Elsewhere, in this second edition, you should find that 'subjects' has been purged except for appearances in quotes.

ANALYSIS

The design chosen, and method of measuring variables, will have a direct effect on the statistical or other analysis which is possible at the end of data collection. In a straightforward hypothesis-testing study, it is pointless to steam ahead with a design and procedure, only to find that the results can barely be analysed in order to support the hypothesis.

There is a principle relating to computer programming which goes: *'garbage in – garbage out'*. It applies here too. If the questionnaire contains items like 'How do you feel?', what is to be done with the largely unquantifiable results?

Thoughts of the analysis should not stifle creativity but it is important to keep it central to the planning.

ONE LAST WORD ON THE NATURE OF SCIENTIFIC RESEARCH (FOR NOW)

Throughout the book, and in any practical work, can I suggest that the reader keep the following words from Rogers (1961) in mind? If taken seriously to heart and practised, whatever the arguments about various methods, I don't think the follower of this idea will be far away from 'doing science'.

> Scientific research needs to be seen for what it truly is; a way of preventing me from deceiving myself in regard to my creatively formed subjective hunches which have developed out of the relationship between me and my material.

Note: at the end of each chapter in this book there is a set of definitions for terms introduced. If you want to use this as a self test, cover up the right-hand column. You can then write in your guess as to the term being defined or simply check after you read each one. Heavy white lines enclose a set of similar terms, as with the various types of hypotheses, overleaf.

GLOSSARY

Relatively uninterpreted information received through human senses	____	data
Logical argument where conclusions follow automatically from premises	_____	deduction
Methods for numerical summary of set of sample data	_____ _____	descriptive statistics
Overall structure and strategy of a piece of research	_____	design
Observation, recording and organisation of (sense) data, creating form which will reveal any patterns	_____ _____	empirical method
Precise prediction of relationship between data to be measured; usually made to support more general theoretical explanation	_____	hypothesis
		types of hypothesis
Hypothesis tested in a particular experiment	_____	experimental
Prediction that data do not vary significantly in the way which will support the theory under investigation; very often the prediction that differences or correlations will be zero	____	null
Hypothesis in which direction of difference or relationship is predicted before testing	___ _____	one tailed (one-sided, directional)
Hypothesis tested in a particular piece of research	_____	research
Hypothesis in which direction of differences or relationship is not predicted before testing	___ _____	two tailed (two-sided, non-directional)
Method of recording observations and regularities, developing theories to explain regularities and testing predictions from those theories	_____ - _____ _____	hypothetico-deductive method
Methods for assessing the probability of chance occurrence of certain data differences or relationships	_____ _____	inferential statistics
Estimating form of a relationship between variables using a limited set of sample measures	_____	induction

Trying out prototype of a study or questionnaire on a small sample in order to discover snags or errors in design or to develop workable measuring instrument	_____; _____ _____	piloting; pilot trials
Data gathered which is not susceptible to, or dealt with by, numerical measurement or summary	_____ ____	qualitative data
Data gathered which is susceptible to numerical measurement or summary	_____ ____	quantitative data
People or things taken as a small subset that exemplify the larger population	_____	sample
Method used to verify truth or falsity of theoretical explanations of why events occur	_____ _____	scientific method
Proposed explanation of observable events	_____	theory
Phenomenon (thing in the world) which goes through observable changes	_____	variable

Variables and Definitions

This chapter is an introduction to the language and concepts of measurement in social science.

- **Variables** are identified events which change in value.
- Many explanatory concepts in psychology are unobservable directly but are treated as **hypothetical constructs**, as in other sciences.
- Variables to be measured need precise 'operational' definition (the steps taken to measure the phenomenon) so that researchers can communicate effectively about their findings.
- **Independent variables** are assumed to affect **dependent variables** especially if they are controlled in experiments.
- Other variables affecting the events under observation must be accounted for and, if possible, controlled, especially in experimental work. **Random errors** have unpredictable effects on the dependent variable, whereas **constant errors** affect it in a consistent manner.
- **Confounding** occurs when a variable related to the independent variable obscures a real effect or produces the false impression that the independent variable is producing observed changes.

A variable is anything which varies. Rather a circular definition I know, but it gets us started. Let's list some things which vary:

1 Height – varies as you grow older
          – varies between individuals

2 Time – to respond with 'yes' or 'no' to questions
          – to solve a set of anagrams

3 The political party people vote for

4 Your feelings towards your partner or parent

5 Extroversion

6 Attitude towards vandals

7 Anxiety

Notice that all of these can vary – within yourself from one time to another
          – between different individuals in society

A variable can take several or many values across a range. The value given is often numerical but not necessarily so. In example **3** above, for instance, the different values are names.

The essence of studying anything (birds, geology, emotion) is the observation of changes in variables. If nothing changed there would be nothing to observe. The essence of science is to relate these changes in variables to changes in other variables.

MEASURING VARIABLES

Some of the variables above are easy to measure and we are familiar with the type of measuring instrument required. Height is one of these and time another, though the equipment required to measure 'reaction times' (as in example 2) is quite sophisticated, because of the very brief intervals involved.

Some variables are familiar in concept but measuring them numerically seems a very difficult, strange or impossible thing to do, as in the case of *attitude* or *anxiety*. However, we often make estimates of others' attitudes when we make such pronouncements as 'He is very strongly opposed to smoking' or 'She didn't seem particularly averse to the idea of living in Manchester'.

Variables like *extroversion* or *dissonance* are at first both strange and seemingly unmeasurable. This is because they have been invented by psychologists in need of a unifying concept to explain their observations of people.

If we are to work with variables such as *attitude* and *anxiety* we must be able to specify them precisely, partly because we want to be accurate in the measurement of their change, and partly because we wish to communicate with others about our findings. If we wish to be taken seriously in our work it must be possible for others to replicate our findings using the same measurement procedures. But what *are* 'attitude' and 'anxiety'?

DEFINING PSYCHOLOGICAL VARIABLES

First, try to write down your *own* definition of:
(a) intelligence
(b) anxiety
(c) superstition
Perhaps that was difficult. Now, give some examples of people displaying those characteristics.

You probably found the definitions quite hard, especially the first. Why is it we have such difficulty defining terms we use every day with good understanding? You must have used these terms very many times in your communications with others, saying, for instance:

I think Jenny has a lot of intelligence
Bob gets anxious whenever a dog comes near him
Are people today less superstitious than they were?

PSYCHOLOGICAL CONSTRUCTS

I hope you found it relatively easier, though, to give examples of people being intelligent, anxious or superstitious. Remember, I said in Chapter 1 that information about people must come, somehow, from what they say or do. When we are young we are little psychologists. We build up a concept of 'intelligence' or 'anxiety' from learning what are signs or manifestations of it; biting lips, shaking hand, tremulous voice in the latter case, for instance.

Notice that we learn that certain things are done 'intelligently'; getting sums right, doing them quickly, finishing a jigsaw. People who do these things consistently get called 'intelligent' (the adverb has become an adjective). It is one step now to statements like the one made about Jenny above where we have a noun instead of an adjective. It is easy to think of intelligence as having some thing-like quality, of existing independently, because we can use it as a noun. We can say 'What is X?'. The Greek philosopher Plato ran into this sort of trouble asking questions like 'What is justice?'. The tendency to treat an abstract concept as if it had independent existence is known as REIFICATION.

Some psychologists (especially the behaviourist Skinner, who took an extreme empiricist position) would argue that observable events (like biting lips), and, for anxiety, directly measurable internal ones (like increased heart rate or adrenalin secretion), are all we need to bother about. Anxiety just *is* all these events, no more. They would say that we don't need to assume *extra* concepts over and above these things which we can observe and measure. To assume the existence of internal structures or processes, such as 'attitude' or 'drive' is 'mentalistic', unobjective and unscientific.

Other psychologists argue that there is more. That a person's attitude, for instance, is more than the sum of statements about, and action towards, the attitude object. They would argue that the concept is useful in theory development, even if they are unable to trap and measure it in accurate detail. They behave, in fact, like the 'hard' scientists in physics.

No physicist has ever directly seen an atom or a quark. This isn't physically possible. (It may be *logically* impossible ever to 'see' intelligence, but that's another matter.) What physicists do is to *assume* that atoms and quarks exist and then work out how much of known physical evidence is explained by them. Quarks are HYPOTHETICAL CONSTRUCTS. They will survive as part of an overall theory so long as the amount they explain is a good deal more than the amount they contradict.

Taking a careful path, psychologists treat concepts like intelligence, anxiety or attitude as hypothetical constructs too. They are *assumed* to exist as factors which explain observable phenomena. If, after research which attempts both to support and refute the existence of the constructs, the explanations remain feasible, then the constructs can remain as theoretical entities. A state of anxiety is assumed from observation of a person's sweating, stuttering and shaking. But we don't *see* 'anxiety' as such. Anxiety is, then, a hypothetical construct.

ORGANISATION OF CONSTRUCTS

A construct can be linked to others in an explanatory framework from which further predictions are possible and testable. We might, for instance, infer low self-esteem in people who are very hostile to members of minority ethnic groups. The low self-esteem might, in turn, be related to authoritarian upbringing which could be checked up on. We might then look for a relationship between authoritarian rearing and prejudiced behaviour as shown in Figure 2.1.

If psychologists are to use such constructs in their research work and theorising, they must obviously be very careful indeed in explaining how these are to be treated as variables. Their definitions must be precise. Even for the more easily measurable variables, such as short-term memory capacity, definitions must be clear.

One particular difficulty for psychologists is that a large number of terms for variables they might wish to research already exist in everyday English with wide variation in possible meaning.

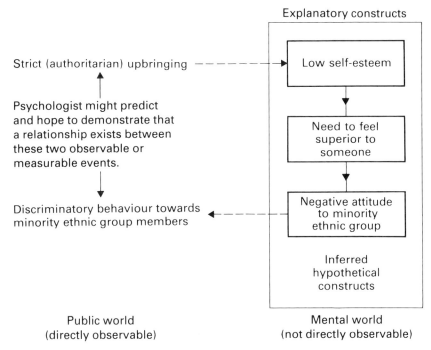

Figure 2.1 *Explanatory framework of hostility to minority ethnic groups*

Discuss with a colleague, or think about, the terms shown below:

Identity	Instinct	Reinforcement	Egocentric	Attitude
Neurotic	Attention	Conformity	Unconscious	Conscience

How could any of these be measured or assessed?

OPERATIONAL DEFINITIONS

In search of objectivity, scientists conducting research attempt to OPERATIONALISE their variables. An OPERATIONAL DEFINITION of variable X gives us *the set of activities required to measure X*. It is like a set of instructions. For instance, in physics, pressure is precisely defined as weight or mass per unit area. To measure pressure we have to find out the weight impinging on an area and divide by that area.

Even in measuring a person's height, if we want to agree with others' measurements, we will need to specify conditions such as what to take as the top of the head and how the person should stand. In general though, height and time present us with no deep problem since the units of measurement are already clearly and universally defined.

In a particular piece of memory research we might define short-term memory capacity as 'the longest list of digits on which the participant has perfect recall in more than 80% of trials'. Here, on each trial, the participant has to try to recall the digit string presented in the order it was given. Several trials would occur with strings from three to, say, 12 digits in length. At the end of this it is relatively simple to calculate our measure of short-term memory capacity according to our operational definition.

If a researcher had measured the 'controlling' behaviour of mothers with their children, he or she would have to provide the coding scheme given to assistants for making recordings during observation. This might include categories of 'physical restraint', 'verbal warning', 'verbal demand' and so on, with detailed examples given to observers during training.

The notorious example, within psychological research, is the definition of intelligence as 'that which is measured by the (particular) intelligence test used'. Since intelligence tests differ, we obviously do not have in psychology the universal agreement enjoyed by physicists. It might be argued that physicists have many ways to measure pressure but they know what pressure *is*. Likewise, can't psychologists have several ways to test intelligence? But psychologists aren't in the same position. Physicists get almost exactly the same results with their various alternative measures. Psychologists, on the other hand, are still using the tests to try to establish agreement on the nature of intelligence itself. (See 'factor analysis' in Chapter 9.)

An operational definition gives us a more or less valid method for measuring some *part* of a hypothetical construct. It rarely covers the whole of what is usually understood by that construct. It is hard to imagine an operational definition which could express the rich and diverse meaning of human intelligence. But for any particular piece of research we must state exactly what we are counting as a measure of the construct we are interested in. As an example, consider a project carried out by some students who placed a ladder against a wall and observed men and women walking round or under it. For this research, 'superstitious behaviour' was (narrowly) operationalised as the avoidance of walking under the ladder.

Imagine you were about to start testing the hypotheses stated below. In each case, try to provide operationalised definitions for the variables involved. If it helps, ask yourself 'What will *count* as (aggression) in this study? How exactly will it be measured?' Think carefully, and then state the exact procedure you would use to carry out the measurement of the variables.

1 Physically punished children are more aggressive

2 Memory deterioration can be the result of stress at work

3 Language development is advanced in infants by parents who provide a lot of visual and auditory stimulation

4 People will be more likely to comply with a request from a person they trust

5 People told an infant is male will be more likely to describe the infant according to the popular male stereotype than will those told it is female

Here are some ideas:

1 *Physical punishment*: number of times parent reports striking per week; questionnaire to parents on attitudes to physical punishment. *Aggression*: number of times child initiates rough-and-tumble behaviour observed in playground at school; number of requests for violent toys in Santa Claus letters.

2 *Stress*: occupations defined as more stressful the more sickness, heart attacks etc. reported within them. *Memory* could be defined as on page 25, or participants could keep a diary of forgetful incidents.

3 *Language development*: length of child's utterances; size of vocabulary, etc. *Stimulation*: number of times parent initiates sensory play, among other things, during home observation.

4 *Compliance*: if target person agrees to researcher's request for change in street.

Trust: defined in terms of dress and role. In one case, the researcher dressed smart with doctor's bag. In the other, with scruffy clothes. We could also use post-encounter assessment rating by the target person.

5 *Stereotype response*: number of times participant, in describing the infant, uses terms coming from a list developed by asking a panel of the general public what infant features were typically masculine and typically feminine.

INDEPENDENT AND DEPENDENT VARIABLES

In the experiment on memory described in Chapter 1 there were two variables. One was manipulated by the experimenter and had just two values – learning by rehearsal or learning by imagery. Notice this variable does not have numerical values as such, but it is operationally defined. The other variable, operationally defined, was the number of items recalled correctly, in any order, during two minutes.

Considering these two variables, which of the following statements makes more sense to you?

1 'The mode of learning depends upon the number of items recalled'

2 'The number of items recalled depends upon the mode of learning'

Not too difficult I hope? Now, one of these variables is known as the DEPENDENT VARIABLE (commonly DV for short) and the other is known as the INDEPENDENT VARIABLE (IV). I hope it is obvious that, since the number of items recalled *depends* upon which learning mode is used, the number of items recalled gets called the 'dependent variable'. The variable it depends on gets known as the 'independent variable'. It isn't affected by the DV, it is independent of it. The DV *is*, we hope, affected by the IV.

Suppose we give participants a list of words to learn under two conditions. In one they have 30 seconds to learn and in the other they have one minute. These different values of the IV are often referred to as LEVELS. The time given for learning (IV) will, we expect, be related to the number of words correctly recalled (DV). This is the hypothesis under test.

Figure 2.2 *Relationship of IV and DV*

Figure 2.3 *Specific examples of IV–DV relationship*

Try to identify the IV and DV in the other examples given on page 26.

A fundamental process in scientific research has been to relate IV to DV through experimental manipulation, holding all other relevant variables constant while only the IV changes. Some psychology textbooks assume that IV and DV apply only to experiments. However, the terms originate from mathematics, are common through-out scientific research and relate to any linked variation. *In an experiment the IV is completely in the control of the experimenter.* It is what the experimenter manipulates. In other research, the IV, for instance the amount of physical punishment or sex-role socialisation, is assumed to have varied way beyond any control of the researcher. These points are explored more thoroughly in Chapter 5.

In our imagery-or-rehearsal experiment we found that the group using imagery did, indeed, recall far more words than the rehearsal group. Try to find some answers to the following questions:

1 What would interfere with your ability to perform at your best in either of these memory tasks?

2 Could something *other* than the imagery be responsible for the differences?

EXTRANEOUS VARIABLES

This is a general term referring to any variable other than the IV which might have an effect on the measured DV. It tends to be used in reference mainly to experiments where we would normally be interested in controlling the unwanted effects of all variables except the IV, so that we can compare conditions fairly.

If all variables are controlled – kept from altering – then any change in the DV can more confidently be attributed to changes in the IV.

The unwanted effects of extraneous variables are often known as 'errors'. Have a look at Figure 2.4. Imagine each picture shows the deliveries of a bowler. In Figure 2.4b there are few errors. In Figure 2.4c there seems to be one systematic error. If the bowler could correct this, all the deliveries would be accurate. In Figure 2.4a there seems to be no systematic error but deliveries vary quite widely about the wicket in a seemingly random pattern. In Figure 2.4d we can only sympathise! Deliveries vary randomly *and* are systematically off the wicket. We will now look at the way these two sorts of CONSTANT (systematic) ERROR and RANDOM ERROR are dealt with in research.

Random error (or random variable)

Maybe your answers to question **1** included some of the following:

• the way you were feeling on the day

Figure 2.4 *Random and constant errors*

- the stuffy atmosphere in the room
- the noise of the heater
- the fact that you'd just come from a Sociology exam

The heater may go on and off by thermostat. Experimental apparatus may behave slightly differently from trial to trial. A technician may cough when you're trying to concentrate. Some of the variables above affect only you as participant. Others vary across everyone. Some people will pay more attention than others. The words presented have different meanings to each person. These last two 'people' differences are known as PARTICIPANT (or SUBJECT) VARIABLES (see Chapter 3).

All these variables are unpredictable (well, something could have been done about the heater!). They are sometimes called 'nuisance variables'. They are random in their effect. They do not affect one condition more than the other, we hope. In fact, we assume that they will just about balance out across the two groups, partly because we *randomly allocated* participants to conditions (see Chapter 3).

Where possible, everything is done to remove obviously threatening variables. In general though, random errors cannot be entirely eliminated. We have to hope they balance out.

Random errors, then, are unsystematic extraneous variables.

Constant error

For question 2, did you suggest that:

- participants might be better in the imagery condition because it came second and they had practice?
- the list of words used in the imagery condition might have been easier?
- in the imagery condition the instructions are more interesting and therefore more motivating?

In these examples an extraneous variable is operating *systematically*. It is affecting the performances in one condition more than in the other. This is known as a CONSTANT ERROR.

If the effect of an extraneous variable is systematic it is serious because we may assume the IV has affected the DV when it hasn't.

Suppose babies lying in a cot look far more at complex visual patterns. Suppose though, the complex patterns were always presented on the right-hand side, with a simple pattern on the left. Maybe the cot makes it more comfortable to look to the right. Perhaps babies have a natural tendency to prefer looking to the right. This is a constant error which is quite simple to control for. We don't have to know that left or right *does* make a difference. To be safe we might as well present half the complex designs to the left, and half to the right, unpredictably, in order to rule out the possibility. This is an example of RANDOMISATION of stimulus position (see Chapter 6 for this and other ways of dealing with constant error).

Confounding (or confounding variables)

The fundamentally important point made in the last section was that, *whenever differences or relationships are observed in results, it is always possible that a variable, other than the independent variable has produced the effect*. In the example above, left or right side is acting as an uncontrolled IV. By making the side on which complex and simple designs will appear *unpredictable* the problem would have been eliminated. This *wasn't* done, however, and our experiment is said to be CONFOUNDED.

Notice, from Figure 2.5, that at least three explanations of our results are now

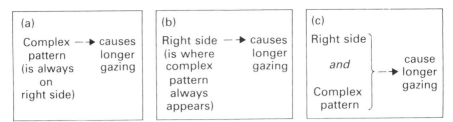

Figure 2.5 *Alternative explanations of gazing effect*

possible. Figure 2.5c refers to two possibilities. First, perhaps *some* babies prefer looking to the right whilst others prefer more complex patterns. Second, perhaps the *combination* of right side and complex pattern tips the balance towards preference in most babies.

Consideration of Figure 2.5 presents another possibility. Suppose our results had been inconclusive – no significant difference in preference for pattern was found. However, suppose also that, all things being equal, babies *do* prefer more complex patterns (they do). The constant presentation of complex patterns to the right might have produced inconclusive results because, with the particular cot used, babies are far more comfortable looking to the left. Now we have an example of confounding which *obscures* a valid effect, rather than one that produces an artificial effect.

Confounding is a regular feature of our attempts to understand and explain the world around us. Some time ago, starting a Christmas vacation, a friend told me that switching to decaffeinated coffee might reduce some physical effects of tension which I'd been experiencing. To my surprise, after a couple of weeks, the feelings had subsided. The alert reader will have guessed that the possible confounding variable here is the vacation period, when *some* relaxation might occur anyway.

There is a second possible explanation of this effect. I might have been expecting a result from my switch to the far less preferred decaffeinated coffee. This alone might have caused me to reappraise my inner feelings – a possibility one always has to keep in mind in psychological research when participants know in advance what behaviour changes are expected. This is known as a PLACEBO EFFECT and is dealt with in Chapter 3.

Confounding is said to occur, then, whenever the true nature of an effect is obscured by the operation of unwanted variables. Very often these variables are not recognised by the researcher but emerge through critical inspection of the study by others.

In the imagery experiment, it may not be the *images* that cause the improvement. It may be the meaningful links, amounting to a story, that people create for the words. How could we check this hypothesis? Some students I was teaching once suggested we ask people without sight from birth to create the links. I'm absolutely sure this would work. It certainly does work on people who report very poor visual imagery. They improve as much as others using image-linking. So we must always be careful not to jump to the conclusion that it is the variable we *thought* we were examining that has, in fact, created any demonstrated effects.

Look back at the exercise on page 26. Assume that in each example research is carried out which supports the link between IV and DV (groups under greater stress *do* have poorer memory performance, for example). Can you think of a confounding variable in each example which might explain the link?

CONFOUNDING IN NON-EXPERIMENTAL RESEARCH

In non-experimental work the researcher does not control the IV. The researcher measures variables which already exist in people and in society, such as social class of child and child's academic achievement.

One of the reasons for doing psychological research is to challenge the 'common-sense' assumptions people often make between an observed IV and DV. It is easy to assume, for instance, that poor home resources are responsible for low academic achievement when a relationship is discovered between these two variables. But those with low resources are more likely to live in areas with poorer schools which attract less well-trained staff. The relationship is confounded by these latter variables.

Confounding occurred when Bowlby (1953) observed that children without mothers and reared in institutions often developed serious psychological problems. He attributed the cause of these problems almost entirely to lack of a single maternal bond. Later checks revealed that along with no mother went regimented care, a serious lack of social and sensory stimulation, reduced educational opportunity and a few other variables possibly contributing to later difficulties in adjustment.

In the world of occupational psychology a resounding success has recently been reported (Jack, 1992) for British Home Stores in improvement of staff performance through a thorough programme of training (using National Vocational Qualifications) and incentives. One indicator of this improvement is taken to be the highly significant drop in full-time staff turnover from 1989–1990 (50%) to 1990–1991 (24%). Unfortunately, this period happened to coincide with a massive upturn in general unemployment, which cannot therefore be ruled out as a serious confounding variable.

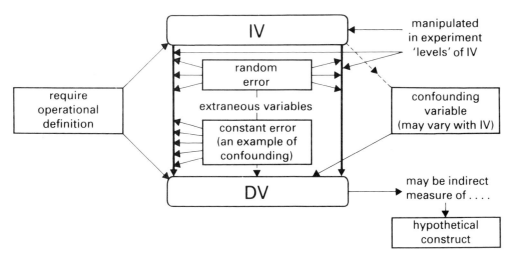

Figure 2.6 *Summary of variables and errors*

GLOSSARY

Systematic error in measurement; i.e. affects measurement always in one direction only	_____ _____	constant error
Phenomenon which is assumed to exist but is (as yet) unconfirmed; it is assumed to be responsible for effects or variations already observed; stays as a possible explanation of effects while evidence continues to support it	_____ _____	hypothetical construct
Definition of variable in exact terms and these terms are the steps taken in measurement of the variable	_____ _____	operational definition
Any error possible in measuring a variable, excluding error which is systematic	_____ _____	random error
Tendency to treat abstract concepts as real entities	_____	reification

		variables
Variable which is uncontrolled and obscures any effect sought, usually in a systematic manner	_____	confounding
Variable which is assumed to be directly affected by changes in the IV	_____	dependent
Anything other than the IV which *could* affect the dependent variable; it may or may not have been allowed for and/or controlled	_____	extraneous
Variable which experimenter *manipulates* in an experiment and which is assumed to have a direct affect on the DV	_____	independent
A variable which creates unpredictable error in measurement	_____	random

EXERCISES

I Identify the assumed independent and dependent variables in the following statements:
  a) Attitudes can be influenced by propaganda messages
  b) Noise affects efficiency of work
  c) Time of day affects span of attention
  d) Performance is improved with practice
  e) Smiles given tend to produce smiles in return
  f) Aggression can be the result of frustration
  g) Birth order in the family influences the individual's personality and intellectual achievement

h) People's behaviour in crowds is different from behaviour when alone

2 In exercise **1**, what could be an operational definition of: 'noise', 'span of attention', 'smile'?

3 Two groups of six-year-old children are assessed for their cognitive skills and sociability. One group has attended some form of preschool education for at least a year before starting school. The other group has not received any preschool experience. The preschool educated group are superior on both variables.
   a) Identify the independent and dependent variables
   b) Identify possible confounding variables
   c) Outline ways in which the confounding variables could be eliminated as possible explanations of the differences

SAMPLES AND GROUPS

This chapter looks at how people are selected for study in psychological research and on what basis they are divided into various groups required for ideal scientific experimentation. Issues arising are:

- Samples should be **representative** of those to whom results may be generalised.
- **Random** selection provides representative samples only with large numbers.
- Various non-random selection techniques (**stratified**, **quota**, **cluster**, **snowball sampling**, **critical cases**) aim to provide representative, or at least useful *small* samples. **Opportunity** and **self-selecting samples** may well be biased.
- *Size* of samples for experiments is a subject of much debate; large is not always best.
- In strict experimental work, variance in participant performance should be kept to a minimum.
- **Control groups** and **placebo groups** serve as comparisons, showing what might occur in experimental conditions excluding only the independent variable.

SAMPLES

Suppose you had just come back from the airport with an Indian friend who is to stay with you for a few weeks and she switches on the television. To your horror, one of the worst imaginable game shows is on and you hasten to tell her that this is not typical of British TV fare. Suppose, again, that you are measuring attitudes to trade unions and you decide to use the college canteen to select people to answer your questionnaire. Unknown to you, the men and women you select are mainly people with union positions on a training course for negotiation skills. In both these cases an unrepresentative sample has been selected. In each case our view of reality can be distorted.

POPULATIONS AND SAMPLES

One of the main aims of scientific study is to be able to generalise from examples. A psychologist might be interested in establishing some quality of all human behaviour, or in the characteristics of a certain group, such as those with strong self-confidence or those who have experienced preschool education. In each case the POPULATION is all the existing members of that group. Since the population itself will normally be too large for each individual within it to be investigated, we would normally select a SAMPLE from it to work with. A population need not consist of people. A biologist might be interested in a population consisting of all the cabbages in one field. A psychologist might be measuring participants' reaction times, in which case the population is the times (not the people) and is infinite, being all the times which could ever be produced.

The particular population we are interested in (managers, for instance), and from which we draw our samples, is known as the TARGET POPULATION.

SAMPLING BIAS

We need our sample to be typical of the population about which we wish to generalise results. If we studied male and female driving behaviour by observing drivers in a town at 11.45 a.m. or 3.30 p.m. our sample of women drivers is likely to contain a larger than usual number driving cars with small children in the back.

This weighting of a sample with an over-representation of one particular category is known as SAMPLING BIAS. The sample tested in the college canteen was a biased sample, if we were expecting to acquire from it an estimation of the general public's current attitude to trade unions.

According to Ora (1965), many experimental studies may be biased simply because the sample used are volunteers. Ora found that volunteers were significantly different from the norm on the following characteristics: dependence on others, insecurity, aggressiveness, introversion, neuroticism and being influenced by others.

A further common source of sampling bias is the student. It is estimated that some 75% of American and British psychological research studies are conducted on students (Valentine, 1992). To be fair, the estimates are based on studies occurring around the late 1960s and early 1970s. Well over half of the UK participants were volunteers. To call many of the USA participants 'volunteers' is somewhat misleading. In many United States institutions the psychology student is required to participate in a certain number of research projects. The 'volunteering' only concerns which particular ones. This system also operates now in some UK establishments of higher education.

PARTICIPANT VARIABLES (OR 'SUBJECT VARIABLES')

In many laboratory experiments in psychology, the nature of the individuals being tested is not considered to be an important issue. The researcher is often specifically interested in an experimental effect, in a difference between conditions rather than between types of person. In this case the researcher needs, in a sense, 'an average bunch of people' in each condition.

> An experimental group searches a word list for words rhyming with 'tree' whilst counting backwards in sevens. A control group does the same thing but does not have to count. The control group performance is superior. Could this difference be caused by anything other than the distraction of counting?

I hope that one of your possible explanations was that the control group might just happen to be better with the sound of words. There may be quite a few good poets or songwriters among them. This would have occurred by chance when the people were allocated to their respective groups. If so, the study would be said to be confounded

Group A   Group B

Figure 3.1 *Participant variables might affect experiment on diet*

by PARTICIPANT (or SUBJECT) VARIABLES. These are variations between persons acting as participants, and which are relevant to the study at hand. Until the recent shift in terminology, explained earlier, these would have been known as 'subject variables'.

SAMPLING

REPRESENTATIVE SAMPLES

What we need then, are samples representative of the population from which they are drawn. The target population for each sample is often dictated by the hypothesis under test. We might need one sample of men and one of women. Or we may require samples of eight-year-old and 12-year-old children, or a group of children who watch more than 20 hours of television a week and one watching less than five hours.

Within each of these populations, however, how are we to ensure that the individuals we select will be representative of their category? The simple truth is that a truly representative sample is an abstract ideal unachievable in practice. The practical goal we can set ourselves is to remove as much sampling bias as possible. We need to ensure that no members of the target population are more likely than others to get into our sample. One way to achieve this goal is to take a truly RANDOM SAMPLE since this is strictly defined as *a sample in which every member of the target population has an equal chance of being included.*

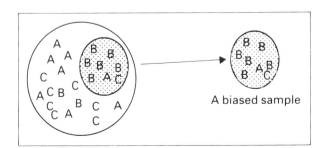

A biased sample

Figure 3.2 *A biased sample*

WHAT IS MEANT BY RANDOM?

Random is not just haphazard. The strict meaning of random sequencing is that no event is ever predictable from *any* of the preceding sequence. Haphazard human choices *may* have some underlying pattern of which we are unaware. This is not true for the butterfly. Evolution has led it to make an endlessly random sequence of turns in flight (unless injured) which makes prediction impossible for any of its much more powerful predators.

RANDOM SAMPLES

Which of the following procedures do you think would produce a group of people who would form a random sample?
a) Picking anybody off the street to answer a questionnaire
(Target population: the general public)
b) Selecting every fifth home in a street
(Target population: the street)
c) Selecting every 10th name on the school register
(Target population: the school)
d) Sticking a pin in a list of names
(Target population: the names on the list)
e) Selecting slips from a hat containing the names of all Wobbly College students and asking those selected to answer your questionnaire on sexual behaviour
(Target population: Wobbly College students)

The answer is that none of these methods will produce a tested random sample. In item (a) we may avoid people we don't like the look of, or they may avoid us. In items (b) and (c) the definition obviously isn't satisfied (though these methods are sometimes known as QUASI-RANDOM SAMPLING or SYSTEMATIC SAMPLING). In (d) we are less likely to drop our pin at the top or bottom of the paper. In (e) the initial selection is random but our sample will end up not containing those who refuse to take part.

If no specific type of person (teachers, drug addicts, four to five-year-olds . . .) is the subject of research then, technically, a large random sample is the only sure way to acquire a fully representative sample of the population. Most psychological research, however, does not use random samples. A common method is to advertise in the local press; commoner still is to acquire people by personal contact, and most common of all is to use students. A very common line in student practical reports is 'a random sample was selected'. This has never been true in my experience unless the population was the course year or college, perhaps.

What students can reasonably do is attempt to obtain as random a sample as possible, or to make the sample fairly representative, by selecting individuals from important subcategories (some working class, some middle class and so on) as is described under 'stratified sampling' below. Either way, it is important to discuss this issue when interpreting results and evaluating one's research.

The articles covered in the survey cited by Valentine did not exactly set a shining example. Probably 85% used inadequate sampling methods and, of these, only 5% discussed the consequent weaknesses and implications.

HOW TO SAMPLE RANDOMLY

Computer selection

The computer can generate an endless string of random numbers. These are numbers which have absolutely no relationship to each other as a sequence and which are selected with equal frequency. Given a set of names the computer would use these to select a random set.

Random number tables

Alternatively, we can use the computer to generate a set of random numbers which we record and use to do any selecting ourselves. Such a table appears as Table 1 in Appendix 2. Starting anywhere in the table and moving either vertically or horizontally a random sequence of numbers is produced. To select five people at random from a group of 50, give everyone a number from 1 to 50 and enter the table by moving through it vertically or horizontally. Select the people who hold the first five numbers which occur as you move through the table.

Manual selection

The numbered balls in a Bingo session or the numbers on a roulette wheel are selected almost randomly as are raffle tickets drawn from a barrel or hat so long as they are all well shuffled, the selector can't see the papers and these are all folded so as not to feel any different from one another. You *can* select a sample of 20 from the college population this way, but you'd need a large box rather than the 'hat' so popular in answers to questions on random selection.

These methods of random selection can be put to uses other than initial sample selection:

Random allocation to experimental groups

We may need to split 40 participants into two groups of 20. To ensure, as far as possible, that participant variables are spread evenly across the two groups, we need to give each participant an equal chance of being in either group. In fact, we are selecting a sample of 20 from a population of 40, and this can be done as described in the methods above.

Random ordering

We may wish to put 20 words in a memory list into random order. To do this give each word a random number as described before. Then put the random numbers into

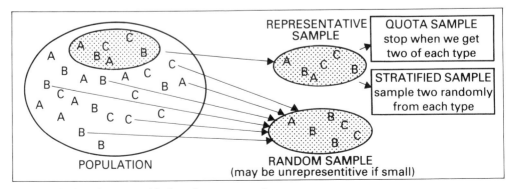

Figure 3.3 *Random, stratified and quota samples*

numerical order, keeping the word with its number. The words will now be randomly ordered.

Random sequencing of trials

In the experiment on infants' preference for simple and complex patterns, described in the last chapter, we saw a need to present the complex figure to right and left at random. Here, the ordering can be decided by calling the first 20 trials 'left' and the rest 'right'. Now give all 40 trials a random number. Put these in order and the left–right sequencing will become random.

ENSURING A REPRESENTATIVE SAMPLE

If a researcher, conducting a large survey (see Chapter 8), wanted to ensure that as many types of people from one town could be selected for the sample, which of the following methods of contacting people would provide the greatest access?
a) Using the telephone directory
b) Selecting from all houses
c) Using the electoral roll
d) Questioning people on the street

I hope you'll agree that the electoral roll will provide us with the widest, unbiased section of the population, though it won't include prisoners, the homeless, new residents and persons in psychiatric care. The telephone directory eliminates non-phone owners and the house selection eliminates those in residential institutions. The street will not contain people at work, those with a severe disability unless they have a helper, and so on.

If we use near-perfect random sampling methods on the electoral roll then a representative sample should, theoretically, be the result. We should get numbers of men, women, over 60s, diabetics, young professionals, members of all cultural groups and so on, in proportion to their frequency of occurrence in the town as a whole. This will only happen, though, if the sample is fairly large as I hope you'll agree, at least after reading the section on sample sizes further below.

STRATIFIED SAMPLING

We may not be able to use the electoral roll or we may be taking too small a sample to expect representativeness by chance. In such cases we may depart from complete random sampling. We may pre-define those groups of people we want represented.

If you want a representative sample of students within your college you might decide to take business studies students, art students, catering students and so on, in proportion to their numbers. If 10% of the college population comprises art students, then 10% of your sample will be art students. If the sample is going to be 50 students then five will be chosen randomly from the art department.

The strata of the population we identify as relevant will vary according to the particular research we are conducting. If, for instance, we are researching the subject of attitudes to unemployment, we would want to ensure proportional representation of employed and unemployed, whilst on abortion we might wish to represent various religions. If the research has a local focus, then the local, not national, proportions would be relevant. In practice, with small scale research and limited samples, only a few relevant strata can be accommodated.

QUOTA SAMPLING

This method has been popular amongst market research companies and opinion pollsters. It consists of obtaining people from strata in proportion to their occurrence in the general population but with the selection from each stratum being left entirely to the devices of the interviewer who would be unlikely to use pure random methods, but would just stop interviewing 18–21-year-old males, for instance, when the quota had been reached.

CLUSTER SAMPLES

It may be that, in a particular town, a certain geographical area can be fairly described as largely working class, another as largely middle class and another as largely Chinese. In this case 'clusters' (being housing blocks or whole streets) may be selected from each such area and as many people as possible from within that cluster will be included in the sample. This, it is said, produces large numbers of interviewees economically because researcher travel is reduced, but of course it is open to the criticism that each cluster may not be as representative as intended.

SNOWBALL SAMPLING

This refers to a technique employed in the more qualitative techniques (see Chapter 11) where a lot of information is required just to get an overall view of an organisational system or to find out what is happening around a certain issue such as alcoholism. A researcher might select several key people for interview and these contacts may lead on to further important contacts to be interviewed.

CRITICAL CASES

A special case may sometimes highlight things which can be related back to most non-special cases. Freud's studies of people with neuroses led him to important insights about the unconscious workings possible in anybody's mind. Researchers interested in perceptual learning have studied people who have regained sight dramatically.

THE SELF-SELECTING SAMPLE

You may recall some students who placed a ladder against a wall and observed how many men and women passed under or around it. In this investigation the sample

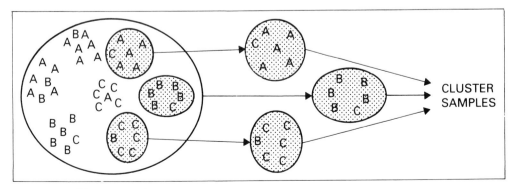

Figure 3.4 *Cluster samples*

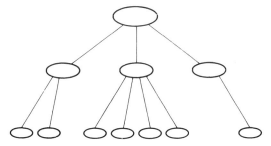

Figure 3.5 *A snowball sample*

could not be selected by the researchers. They had to rely on taking the persons who walked along the street at that time as their sample. Several studies involve this kind of sample. In one study, people using a phone booth were asked if they had picked up a coin left in the booth purposely by the researchers. The independent variable was whether the person was touched while being asked or not. The dependent variable was whether they admitted picking up the coin or not.

Volunteers for experimental studies are, of course, a self-selecting sample.

THE OPPORTUNITY OR CONVENIENCE SAMPLE

Student practical work is very often carried out on other students. For that matter, so is a lot of research carried out in universities. If you use the other students in your class as a sample you are using them as an opportunity sample. They just happen to be the people you can get hold of.

The samples available in a 'natural experiment' (see Chapter 5) are also opportunistic in nature. If there is a chance to study children about to undergo an educational innovation, the researcher who takes it has no control over the sample.

SAMPLE SIZE

One of the most popular items in many students' armoury of prepared responses to 'Suggest modifications to this research' is 'The researcher should have tested more participants'. If a significant difference has been demonstrated between two groups this is not necessary unless (i) we have good reason to suspect sampling bias or (ii) we are replicating the study (see Chapter 4).

If the research has failed to show a significant difference we may well suspect our samples of bias. But is it a good idea to simply add a lot more to our tested samples?

Figure 3.6 *An opportunity sample?*

The argument FOR large samples

It is easier to produce a biased sample with small samples. I hope this example will make this clear. If you were to select five people from a group containing five Catholics, five Muslims, five Hindus and five Buddhists, you'd be more likely to get a religious bias in your sample than if you selected 10 people. For instance, if you select only five they could all be Catholics, but with 10 this isn't possible.

In general, the larger the sample the less the likely sampling bias.

Does this mean then that we should always test as many people as possible? Another argument for large samples is demonstrated by the following example. Suppose there are somewhat more pro- than anti-abortionists in the country as a whole, the ratio being six to five. A small sampling strategy, producing 12 for and 10 against will not convince anyone that this difference represents reality, but a difference of 360 to 300 might. Although we haven't yet covered probability, I hope that your acquired sense of chance factors would agree with this.

The argument AGAINST large samples

One reason we can't always take such large samples is economic, concerning time and money. But another limitation is that larger samples may obscure a relevant participant variable or specific effect.

Suppose, for instance, there is a task which, when performed under condition B produces improvement over condition A but only for left-handed participants (left-handers are disadvantaged when writing left to right with ink which has to dry, for instance). These contributions to the total scores are illustrated by the two left-hand columns in Figure 3.7. Here, the increased total score for all participants on condition B is due almost completely to the difference for left-handers (distance X shown by the middle two columns (b) in Figure 3.7). If only left-handed scores were considered, the difference would be seen as significant (not just chance) but the overall difference for the whole sample is not. The difference shown by the two right-hand columns (c) of Figure 3.7, where a lot more people have been tested is significant. However, the researcher might conclude that there is a slight but significant difference across *all* participants. A specific and interesting effect (sharp improvements for left-handers) is being obscured by simply taking a much larger sample, rather than stopping after the first 'failure' to examine possible participant variables (left- or right-handedness) which are hiding the effect.

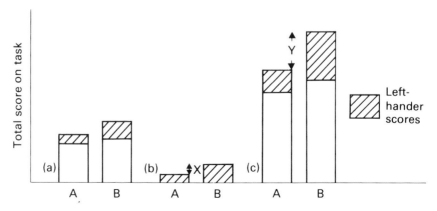

Figure 3.7 *Task scores for right- and left-handed participants*

A large sample, then, may disguise an important participant variable which needs teasing out.

Large samples may also disguise weaknesses in the *design* of an experiment. If there are a large number of uncontrolled variables present then differences between two small groups may seem insignificant (just chance variation). It may take large samples to show that the difference *is* consistent. In field studies (outside the laboratory – see Chapter 5) we may have to put up with this lack of control, but in laboratory experiments such random variables can be controlled so that small samples will demonstrate the real difference.

It has been argued that the optimum sample size, when investigating an experimental IV assumed to have a similar effect on most people, is about 25 to 30. If significance is not shown then the researcher investigates participant variables and the design of the study.

GROUPS

CONTROL GROUPS AND EXPERIMENTAL GROUPS

Suppose we were interested in attempting to reduce racial prejudice in children by use of a specific training programme. After one year the children's attitudes are indeed more positive than they were at the start. Can we say that the procedure obviously works? Is there an alternative explanation of the prejudice reduction? Where's the confounding variable?

Well, perhaps the children would have reached this greater maturity in thought without the treatment, through the increasing complexity of their encounters with the environment. We need to compare these children's development with that of a group who do not experience the programme. This latter group would be known as a CONTROL GROUP and the group receiving the programme as an EXPERIMENTAL GROUP or TREATMENT GROUP.

In selecting these two groups we must be careful to avoid confounding by participant variables and ensure that they are equivalent in composition. We can select each entirely at random or on a stratified basis. In studies like this, the children might be chosen as matched pairs (see Chapter 6) so that for each child in one group there was a child to compare with in the other, matched on relevant characteristics such as age, sex, social class and so on.

PLACEBO GROUP

The experimental group in the example above may have lowered their output of prejudice responses because they knew they were in an experimental programme, especially if they knew what outcomes the researchers were expecting. In trials of new drugs some people are given a salt pill or solution in order to see whether the expectation of improvement and knowledge of having been given a cure alone will produce improvement. Similarly, psychologists create PLACEBO GROUPS in order to eliminate the possibility that results are confounded by expectancy variables.

A common experimental design within physiological psychology has been to inject participants with a substance which stimulates the physiological reactions which occur when individuals are emotionally aroused. A control group then experiences everything the injected (experimental) group experience, except the injection. The placebo group receives an injection of a harmless substance with no physiological effects. Performances are then observed and if both the control and placebo groups differ in the same way from the experimental group we can rule out expectancy as the cause of the difference. Some of the children in the prejudice study above could be given a programme unrelated to prejudice reduction, and also informed of expected results, in order to serve as a placebo group.

GLOSSARY

Special case (usually a person) who/ which highlights specific phenomenon for study	_____ _____	critical case
		groups
Group used as baseline measure against which, performance of experimental, treatment or criterion group is assessed	_____	control
Group who receive values of the IV in an experiment or quasi-experiment	_____ or _____	experiment or treatment
Group who don't receive the critical 'treatment' but everything else the experimental group receive and who are (sometimes) led to believe that their treatment will have an effect; used to check expectancy effects	_____	placebo
Variables which differ between groups of people and which may need to be controlled in order to demonstrate an effect of the IV	_____ _____	participant (or subject) variables
Effect on participants simply through knowing they are expected to exhibit changed behaviour	_____ _____	placebo effect
All possible members of group from which a sample is taken	_____	population
Number which has absolutely no relationship with the other numbers in its set	_____ _____	random number
Group selected from population for study or experiment	_____	sample

		samples
Sample in which members of a subgroup of the target population are over- or under-represented	_____	biased
Sample selected from specific area as being representative of a population	_____	cluster
Sample selected because they are easily available for testing	_____	opportunity
Sample selected by taking every nth case	_____-_____ or _____	quasi-random or systematic
Sample selected so that specified groups will appear in numbers proportional to their size in the target population; selection ceases when enough of specific subgroup has been found	_____	quota
Sample selected in which every member of the target population has an equal chance of being selected	_____	random
Sample selected so that specified groups will appear in numbers proportional to their size in the target population	_____	representative
Systematic tendency towards over- or under-representation of some categories (of people) in a sample	_____ ____	sampling bias
Sample selected for study on the basis of their own action in arriving at the sampling point	____-_____	self-selecting
Sample selected for study by asking key figures for people they think will be important or useful to include	_____	snowball
Sample selected so that specified groups will appear in numbers proportional to their size in the target population; within each subgroup cases are selected on a random basis	_____	stratified
The (often theoretical) group of all possible cases from which, it is hoped, a sample has been taken	_____ _____	target population

EXERCISES

1 A researcher shows that participants in a conformity experiment quite often give an obviously wrong answer to simple questions when six other confederates of the experimenter have just given the same wrong answer by prearrangement. What else must the researcher do in order to demonstrate that the real participants actually are conforming to group pressure?

2 The aim of a particular investigation is to compare the attitudes of working-class and middle-class mothers to discipline in child rearing. What factors should be taken into account in selecting two comparable samples (apart from social class)?

3 A psychologist advertises in the university bulletin for students willing to participate in an experiment concerning the effects of alcohol consumption on appetite. For what reasons might the sample gathered not be a random selection of students?

4 A random sample of business studies students in the county of Suffex could be drawn by which one of these methods?
  a) Selecting one college at random and using all the business studies students within it.
  b) Group all business studies students within each college by surname initial (A, B, . . . Z). Select one person at random from each initial group in each college.
  c) Put the names of all business studies students at all colleges into a very large hat, shake and draw out names without looking.

5 A psychologist visits a group of 20 families with a four-year-old child and trains the mother to use a special programme for promoting reading ability. Results in reading ability at age six are compared with those of a control group who were not visited and trained. A research assistant suggests that a third group of families should have been included in the study. What sort of group do you think the assistant is suggesting?

6 A psychology lecturer requires two groups to participate in a memory experiment. She divides the students in half by splitting the left side from the right side of the class. The left side get special instructions and do better on the problem-solving task. The lecturer claims that the instructions are therefore effective. Her students argue that a confounding variable could be operating. What are they thinking of, perhaps?

Methods

SOME GENERAL THEMES

This chapter introduces the general themes of **reliability** and **validity**, **standardisation** and the **qualitative-quantitative** dimension in research.

- **Reliability** refers to a measure's *consistency* in producing similar results on different but comparable occasions.
- **Validity** has to do with whether a measure is really measuring what it was intended to measure.
- In particular, for experimental work, there has been a debate about **'threats to internal and external validity'**.
- **'Internal validity'** refers to the issue of whether an effect was genuine or rather the result of incorrectly applied statistics, sampling biases or extraneous variables unconnected with the IV.
- **'External validity'** concerns whether an effect generalises from the specific people, place and measures of variables tested to the population, other populations, other places and to other, perhaps fuller, measures of the variables tested.
- The main message of the chapter is not that students need (now) to get embroiled in hair-splitting debate about what exactly is internal or external, or a case of this or that type of validity. The point is to study the various 'threats' and try to avoid them in practical work, or at least discuss them in writing about practical studies.
- **Standardised procedures** reduce **variance** in people's performances, exclude bias from different treatment of groups and make **replication** possible. Replication is fundamental to the establishment of scientific credibility.
- **Meta-analysis** is the statistical review of many tests of the same hypothesis in order to establish the extent of valid replication and to produce objective reviews of results in topic areas.
- The **qualitative-quantitative** dimension is introduced as a fundamental division within the theory of methods in contemporary psychological research. The dimension will be referred to throughout as research varies in the extent to which it employs aspects of either approach. Some researchers see the two approaches as complementary rather than antagonistic.

So far, we have discussed the sorts of things we might want to measure or control in research studies, and the sort of groups required by investigations. Whenever psychologists discuss measurement – in the form of scales, tests, surveys, etc. – the issue arises of whether the measures are RELIABLE and VALID. Both these terms will be discussed in some detail in Chapter 9 where they are applied to psychological tests. However, the next few chapters are about overall methods in psychological research and, at times, we will need to refer to the general meaning of these terms, and a few others.

RELIABILITY

Any measure we use in life should be reliable, otherwise it's useless. You wouldn't want your car speedometer or a thermometer to give you different readings for the same values on different occasions. This applies to psychological measures as much as any other. Hence, questionnaires should produce the same results when retested on the same people at different times (so long as nothing significant has happened to them between tests) and different observers measuring aggression in children should come up with similar ratings.

VALIDITY

In addition to being consistent we should also be able to have confidence that our measuring device is measuring what it's supposed to measure. You wouldn't want your speedometer to be recording oil pressure or your thermometer to be actually measuring humidity. In psychology, this issue is of absolutely crucial importance since, as you saw in the 'variables' chapter, it is often difficult to agree on *what* a concept 'really is' and things in psychology are not as touchable or get-at-able as things in physics or chemistry. Hence, validity is the issue of whether psychological measures really *do* make some assessment of the phenomenon under study.

INTERNAL AND EXTERNAL VALIDITY

There are two rather special meanings of the term 'validity' now popular in psychological debate about the design of research studies, especially experiments. The terms were coined by Campbell and Stanley in the 1960s and produce deep, difficult and sometimes hostile argument about meanings and the importance of various types of validity. There is not room to go into this in great depth here, but my reason for including the general ideas is to help us to focus and categorise all the problems in designing research which will lead us as close as possible to what is and what is not the case in the world of psychological investigation. I say 'as close as possible' because there is an underlying theme, which I'm sure you've caught hold of by now, that scientific research, in psychology as elsewhere, does not get at any *exact* truth in the world of theory. Many people would argue that the best we can hope to do is to rule out what *isn't* true. We can be very confident that a null hypothesis *isn't* true but we can never be sure exactly *why* there was a difference in our results. Was it really the IV or was something else responsible? This is a good starting point for our discussion of internal and external validity. Before we go further though, would you like to try and generate some of the basic ideas by having a go at the exercise below?

Consider the following project carried out by a student at Rip-off College where staff have responsibility for 60 students per class, one hour a week and therefore have very little time to monitor what students set out to test. Tabatha feels she can train people to draw better. To do this she asks student friends to be participants in her study which involves training one group and having the other as a control. She tells friends that the training will take quite some time so those who are rather busy go into the control group, who only turn up for the test sessions. Both groups of participants are tested for artistic ability at the beginning and end of the training period and improvement is measured as the difference between these two scores. The test is to copy a drawing of Mickey Mouse. A slight problem occurs in that Tabatha lost the original pre-test cartoon, but she was fairly confident that her post-test one was much the same. She also found the training was too much for her to conduct on her own so she had to get an artist acquaintance to help, after giving him a rough idea of how her training method worked. The trained group have ten sessions of one hour and at the end of this period Tabatha feels she has got on very well with them, even though rather a lot have dropped out because of the time needed. One of the control group participants even remarks on how matey they all seem to be and that some members of the control group had noted that the training group seemed to have a good time in the bar each week after the sessions. Some of her trainees sign up for a night class in drawing because they want to do well on the final test. Quite a few others are on a BTEC Health Studies course and started a module on creative art during the training which they thought was quite fortunate. The final difference between groups was quite small but the trained group did better. Tabatha loathes statistics so she decides to present the data as they were recorded. She hasn't yet reached the recommended reading on significance tests in her Rip-off College self-study pack.

Now, please list all the things you think Tabatha might have got a bit wrong in this study. *In particular,* list all the reasons she might have got a difference but *not* because of the specific training plan she used.

'THREATS' TO VALIDITY

I hope that, even if you're new to the idea of scientific or experimental research, Tabatha's project offended your sense of balanced, fair, objective investigation. There are obviously many ways in which Tabatha might have got some differences but *not* because of her particular training programme. These things, *other than the IV,* which could have produced the results, Campbell and Stanley called 'threats to validity'. It is time to distinguish between internal and external threats:

Threats to internal *validity*

Did the design of the study really illuminate the effect of one variable on another? Was there a genuine effect?

Threats to external *validity*

To what extent is it legitimate to generalise these findings to other people, places, times and instance of the variables measured?

INTERNAL VALIDITY

Within this concept two questions are asked:
1 Is there a real effect here?
   Is the difference in the measures of the dependent variable one we can take seriously? (i.e., is there a 'real' statistical difference?)

Table 4.1   *Threats to internal and external validity of research studies*

Threats to internal validity	Description	Comments
Using a low power statistical test	Different tests have varying sensitivity to detect difference	Dealt with in the statistics Chapters 14–24
Violating assumptions of statistical test used	Tests should not be used if the data don't fit the assumptions	Dealt with in the statistics Chapters 14–24
'Fishing'/capitalising on chance	Multiple testing of the same data gives a higher chance of getting a fluke 'significant' result – see p. 318	For all these three statistical points note that Tabatha didn't bother with testing her data, and that differences were small
Reliability of measures	Reliability as described in this Chapter and Chapter 9	Dealt with on p. 50 and pp. 150
Reliability of procedures	Standardisation of procedures – described in this Chapter	Tabatha doesn't seem to have given *precise* instructions to her extra trainer
Random errors in the research setting	Described in Chapter 3	
Participant variance	Problem described in this Chapter	Also covered in Chapter 3
History	Events which happen to participants during the research which affect results but are not linked to the IV	Some of Tabatha's trainees started an art module
Maturation	Participants may mature during the study	A problem in child development studies, especially where there is not an adequate control group
Testing	Participants may get 'wise' to the tests if they're repeated	Tabatha's trainees might have practised on Mickey Mouse or at least recalled their original mistakes
Instrumentation	Measures may change in effect between first and second testing. A particular problem if participants approach a 'ceiling' (see p. 225) at the end of the study. They can't show their true ability	Tabatha changed her measure because she lost the first version

Threats to internal validity	Description	Comments
Selection bias	Occurs when more of one type of person gets into one group for the study — a big problem in field research where many unwanted factors may differ between, say, two groups of children under study	Those who were more busy selected themselves into the control group in Tabatha's study. Also, since the students knew what it was about, keener ones may have joined the training group
Drop-out	More of one type of person may drop out of one of the groups	More students dropped out of Tabatha's trainee group because of the time taken
Imitation of treatment	Control participants may get to know what treatment groups are doing	If mothers are being helped to stimulate their children, the techniques may pass to control group mothers simply by meeting in the community
Rivalry or demoralisation of control group	'Control' participants may try to do as well as the 'treatment' group *or* they may resent the 'treatment'	Some of Tabatha's control students seem to resent not being in the trainee group
Threats to external validity		
Construct validity	To what extent do the measures employed actually tap the concept under study?	Discussed in this Chapter. How accurately or fully is Tabatha measuring 'artistic ability'? Suppose synchro-swimming ability were judged simply by the time swimmers could remain underwater?
Inadequate variable definition	To what extent are the measures used adequately defined?	Tabatha's 'rough idea' of her training, given to her extra trainer, suggests it isn't well defined
Mono-method bias	Construct validity is improved by taking a *variety* of measures of the same concept	For instance, better to have people give their 'sentence' of a fictitious criminal in writing *and* in public, and perhaps to get them to rate for guilt or 'criminality' also
Hypothesis guessing	'Treatment' participants	Tabatha's trainees certainly

Threats to external validity	Description	Comments
	may well guess what is required of them in the study	knew what they were expected to do
Evaluation apprehension ('pleasing the experimenter' or 'looking good')	Hypothesis guessing *may* lead to trying to please the experimenter or looking good	See 'demand characteristics' p. 75. Note that Tabatha's trainees tried to do well
Experimenter expectancy	Dealt with in this Chapter	See also p. 74
Level of the independent variable (IV)	The levels of the IV used may not be far enough apart. Better to use *several* levels (in more advanced work)	One and three cups of coffee may make no difference but one and 10 might! Better to try one, four, seven and 10, perhaps
Generalisation to the population	Dealt with in this Chapter	See also Chapter 3
Generalisation to other populations	Dealt with in this Chapter	See also Chapter 3
Generalisation to other settings; 'ecological validity'	Dealt with in this Chapter	Will Tabatha's training work out of college?

2 Was the effect caused by the IV or something else?
   If the difference *is* treated as statistically valid, did it occur because the IV had a direct effect, or did manipulating the IV, or just running the study in general, produce some other, hidden effect?

1 This question mainly concerns statistical significance and will be dealt with in Chapters 14–23. It's about whether we say, 'Sure there was a difference but it could have been just chance, it's so small' – the sort of question we ask about those lines of plates in washing-up liquid commercials. For now, note, from Table 4.1 (see p. 52) that if we use the wrong statistical test, use a test without satisfying its assumptions, do too many tests on the same data, or introduce too many random errors into the experimental setting or into the procedure, we may be unable to state confidently that any differences found were true differences. Random errors can be dealt with to some extent by operating a STANDARDISED PROCEDURE and we'll look at exactly what this entails after this section on validity.

2 From Table 4.1 note that the other, non-statistical threats to internal validity concern reasons why the differences might have occurred even though the IV *didn't* cause them. Several of these are to do with getting an imbalance of people of certain types in one of the conditions. We'll deal with this problem in Chapter 6 – Experimental designs. Note that rivalry or resentment by the control group, and so on, is seen as a threat to *internal* validity because the *treatment* isn't causing any effect on the treatment group. The control group is creating the difference. Tabatha's control group might draw half-heartedly since at least some appear to feel a bit left out. This factor, then, has nothing to do with the programme as such, which therefore can't be said to be *causing* any differences found.

EXTERNAL VALIDITY

Suppose the IV *is* responsible for the change. For various reasons which I hope are, or will become, fairly obvious, the results of such a 'successful' study may not be generalised to all other situations without some serious considerations. There are four major ways in which generalisation may be limited. We can ask:

1 Would this happen with other sorts of people or with *all* the people of whom our sample was an example?

2 Would this happen in other *places*?

3 Would this happen at other *times*? (Consider Asch's famous conformity studies in the 1950s. Would people be as likely to conform now as then?)

4 Would this happen with other *measures*? (e.g. 'racial discrimination' might be assessed by having people give sentences to a black and a white fictitious 'criminal'. Would the effect found occur if a questionnaire had been used instead?)

Bracht and Glass (1968) categorised **1** as 'population validity' and **2** as 'ECOLOGICAL' VALIDITY. I have treated this second term as a 'key term' because, unlike the first, it is a very popular term, although its original use (Brunswik, 1947) was limited to perception. It is a term you are likely to come across quite often in other textbooks or in class discussion, especially on the issue of the laboratory study in psychology.

Population validity

Think how often you've been frustrated by a news or magazine article which, on the basis of some single study, goes on to make claims such as '. . . so we see that women (do such and such) whilst men (do so and so). . .'. Obviously a class experiment can't be generalised to *all* students nor can it be generalised to all other groups of people. The matter of how important this issue is varies with the type of study. External validity is of crucial importance to *applied* researchers who want to know that a programme (of training or therapy, for instance) 'works' and they may be less worried about the *exact* (conceptual) variable responsible for the effect.

Ecological validity

A big problem with psychological laboratory research is that it is often very difficult to see how results could be generalised to real-life circumstances, to naturally occurring behaviour in an everyday setting. A study's 'ecological validity', according to Bracht and Glass, has to do with the extent to which it generalises to other settings or places. A study has higher ecological validity if it generalises beyond the laboratory to field settings but a field study, in a naturalistic setting is *not* automatically 'ecologically valid'. This depends on whether it will generalise to *other* natural settings (some quite artificial and limited field settings are mentioned below). The term, unfortunately, is used today rather variably and some texts assume ecological validity simply where a study is 'naturalistic', where the data gathered are 'realistic' even though the result may obviously *not* be valid for another context. Nevertheless, if you claimed that many experiments in psychology are criticised because they lack ecological validity, this being because their results would not be replicated in real-life settings, you'd be correct. Carlsmith et al. (1976) used the term MUNDANE REALISM to refer to research set-ups which were close to real life, whereas EXPERIMENTAL REALISM occurs when an experimental set up, though 'artificial', is so engaging and attention grabbing that any artificiality is compensated for.

As an example of laboratory limitation, Asch's famous demonstrations of conformity were conducted among total strangers, who had to judge the length of lines with no discussion. Real-life conformity almost always concerns familiarity and social interaction with one's peers. Asch's study would demonstrate more ecological validity if we could reproduce the effect, say, among friends in a school classroom setting. Milgram (1961) increased conformity simply by having participants hear tape-recorded criticisms of their nonconforming judgements.

What counts as a 'naturalistic environment' is also sometimes hard to gauge. Much human behaviour occurs in what is not, to the individuals concerned, a natural environment, for example, the doctor's surgery, a visit to the police station, or the inside of an aeroplane. For some participants the laboratory can be no less natural than many other places. In Ainsworth's (1971) study of infant attachments, behaviour was observed when the mother was present, when she was absent, when a stranger was present and when the mother returned. From the infant's point of view it probably wasn't of great consequence where this study was carried out – the local nursery, a park or the laboratory (which looked something like a nursery anyway!). The infant is very often in situations just as strange, and what mattered over-whelmingly was whether the mother was there or not. We shall return to this line of discussion when we consider the advantages and disadvantages of the laboratory in the next chapter. If the infant behaves at home as she did in the laboratory, then the laboratory study has high ecological validity.

Construct validity

The other aspect of Table 4.1 I'd like to stress here is that concerning generalisation from the measures taken to the intended concept, item 4, above. The issue here is, to what extent do *our* measures of a concept under study really reflect the breadth of that concept? We are back to the issue of hypothetical constructs and operational definitions first encountered in the 'variables' chapter.

WHAT EXACTLY WAS YOUR MEASURE? – Although this can be a heady debate, at the very heart of what psychology tries to do, the practical point, which I cannot emphasise too strongly here, for new psychology students, is the threat from weak definition of variables and 'mono-method' bias. I have already stressed in Chapter 3, how important it is to define *exactly* what it is you are counting as the IV and DV in your project. The worst crimes usually concern the DV. Tutors often despair of writing 'how was this measured?' by the side of hypotheses or statements of aims in practical reports! Some examples are 'aggression will be greater . . .', '. . . will have better memory', '. . . are sexist in their attitudes'. What usually *has* been shown is that one group of children hits peers more, higher numbers of words are recalled, more 'feminine' than 'masculine' terms have been used to describe a baby or a particular occupation. These are only a (small) *part* of the whole concept mentioned in the definitions. It may sound as though we're being pretty finicky here, like Stephen Fry and Hugh Laurie telling the waitress off because she brought them a glass of water and they didn't ask for the glass! But in psychology it is of crucial importance not to claim you've discovered or demonstrated something which you haven't. Consider the common psychology class practical where we devise a questionnaire concerning say, homosexuality. This is discussed as the measurement of an 'attitude'. However, almost *all* definitions of 'attitude' include something about an *enduring* belief – yet we've only measured a person's view at *one* moment. Will they think this next week? What *have* we measured exactly? In any case, does our questionnaire tap *anything like* the full range and depth of an 'attitude to homosexuality'?

It is also unwise to try to generalise from *one* ('mono') method. Measures taken on paper cannot be generalised to people's behaviour in *all* of their life outside the classroom or laboratory. People may well 'look good' on paper ('social desirability' – to be discussed in Chapter 8) yet continue to discriminate in daily life, tell 'homophobic' jokes and so on.

WHY BOTHER WITH INTERNAL AND EXTERNAL VALIDITY?

There are two major aspects to the debate on validity. One is an often hair-splitting debate on just what threats should go into what categories. The other has to do with the practical issues of designing research. As I said earlier, the main reasons for going into a little depth on this issue are to focus your attention on how careful you need to be in defining variables and designing your study. This is so you don't end up with worthless data about which nothing much can be said because there are too many ways to interpret it and/or because you haven't got the necessary comparisons to make any confident statement about differences. As far as the debate on categories is concerned, even the crack writers on this issue don't agree. The reader who *is* interested in more on this debate might like to look at the readings below. The first is the original presentation of the terms. The second is a much later and more easily available text with a chapter on the issue.

Campbell, D. T. and Stanley, J. C. (1966) *Experimental and Quasi-Experimental Designs for Research* Chicago: Rand McNally

Cook, T. D. and Campbell, D. T. (1979) *Quasi-Experimentation: Design and Analysis Issues for Field Settings* Boston: Houghton Mifflin

STANDARDISED PROCEDURE

Here, the ideal is that, for each common aspect of an experimental procedure, every participant has *exactly* the same experience. There are at least three strong reasons for desiring a standardised procedure.

1 We want to keep unwanted VARIANCE in participants' performance to a minimum so that real differences aren't clouded.

2 We don't want different treatment of groups to *confound* the effect of the independent variable.

3 Good scientific experiments are recorded so that others can REPLICATE them.

1 Participant variance

Very often, in the teaching of psychology, the form is to introduce an interesting idea to test (e.g. are smokers more anxious?), explain what is to be done and then to send students off to test their friends, family and/or who they can get hold of (the typical opportunity sample). This is very often all that *can* be done, given school or college resources. However, does anyone in these circumstances really believe that the procedure will be at all standard? Different testers are operating for a start. Even for the same tester, with the best will in the world, it is difficult to run an identical procedure with your dad at tea time and with your boy/girl friend later that same evening. Paid researchers try to do better but, nevertheless, it would be naïve to assume that features of the tester (accent, dress, looks, etc.), their behaviour, or the surrounding physical environment do not produce unwanted random error. Random errors, in turn, will produce higher levels of what is known as variance among the participants' scores and this makes it more difficult to demonstrate real statistical differences, as we shall see later in the statistical section. This, then, is a threat to *internal* validity, since it's a reason why we may not demonstrate a real difference.

2 Confounding

There are all sorts of ways in which Tabatha's control group has been treated differently. Any one of these factors *could* be responsible for any differences found. The acid test *should* be that trainees perform better under *exactly* the same conditions as the untrained group.

Barber (1976) gives an example of what he calls 'the investigator loose procedure effect'. It also includes the problem of what we shall call 'experimenter bias' in the next chapter. The study (Raffetto, 1967) led one group of experimenters (people who conduct research for investigators) to believe that sensory deprivation produces many reports of hallucinations and another group to believe the opposite. The experimenters then interviewed people who had undergone sensory deprivation. The instructions for interviewing were purposely left vague. Experimenters reported results in accordance with what they had been led to believe – more hallucinatory reports from experimenters expecting them.

Even with standardised procedures, experimenters do not always follow them. Friedman (1967) argued that this is partly because experimenters may not recognise that social interaction and non-verbal communication play a crucial role in the procedure of an experiment. Male experimenters, when the participant is female, are more likely to use her name, smile and look directly at her. Procedures do not usually tell the experimenter exactly how to greet participants, engage in casual pleasantries, arrange seating and how much to smile.

Notice that 'loose procedure', as such, is a threat to *internal* validity, since it's likely to create more variance in people's performance, but the 'experimenter bias' (or expectancy) is treated as a threat to *external* validity. This is because we can't be sure that the same bias effect would occur in other research situations. The experimenter's bias varies *with* the IV but it *isn't* the IV. It is not wanted and has a *confounding* effect.

3 Replication

In traditional scientific method, replication plays a very important role. Not long ago, there was immense excitement in the world of physics when one group of researchers claimed to have successfully produced 'cold fusion' – a process which could potentially release enormous amounts of cheap energy – at normal room temperature. One replication, by different scientists, was announced. But one replication is not enough. Several more attempts failed and, just three months after the jubilant announcements, the effect was back in its place as part of the still imaginary future.

If you tell me you have shown that, with special training, anyone can be trained to telepathise, I should want to see your evidence and experience the phenomenon for myself. It's not that I don't trust you, but we need others to check our wilder claims or to look coolly at processes which, because we are so excited about them, we are failing to analyse closely enough. I may discover an alternative explanation of what is happening or point out a flaw in your procedure. In the interests of replication, then, it is essential that I can follow your procedure exactly. In other words, this would be a challenge to the internal validity of your apparent training effect.

This is why you'll find that tutors, along with being strict about your definition of variables, will be equally concerned that you record every essential detail of your procedure and the order in which you carried it out. They're not being pernickety. They're encouraging you to communicate effectively and arming you with skills which will help you to defend your project against critics.

REPLICATION AND EXTERNAL VALIDITY

Each time an effect is demonstrated on samples not specifically different from the original, we have a test of how well the effect generalises *to* the population from which the samples were drawn. Sometimes we may attempt to replicate *across* populations, to see whether the effect works on Ys as well as Xs, for instance, managers as well as students. The Milgram (1961) study, cited earlier, was a replication in Norway and France, and is an example of cross-cultural research (see Chapter 10). Both these cases of generalisation support the effect's external validity, in Campbell's terms.

META-ANALYSIS

Unfortunately for the scientific model of psychology which many psychologists adhere to, it is the exception, rather than the rule, to find a procedure which 'works' reliably every time it is tested. The world of psychological research is littered with conflicting results and areas of theoretical controversy, often bitterly disputed. Here are some areas in which literally hundreds of studies have been carried out and yet without bringing us much closer to a definitive conclusion about the relationships they explore:

- sex differences and origin of differences in sex role
- the origins of intelligence – nature or nurture
- socio-economic position and educational or occupational achievement
- conformity and its relation to other personality variables
- cognitive dissonance (and alternative explanations)
- language development and parental stimulation
- deprivation of parental attachment and emotional disturbance

Much of the conflict in results arises from the fact that the studies use a huge variety of methods, variable definitions, different samples and so on. Periodically, it has been the tradition to conduct a LITERATURE REVIEW of a certain research topic area such as those above. Examples of these will be found in the *Annual Review of Psychology* which is published each year. The problem here is that reviewers can be highly selective and subjectively weight certain of the studies. They can interpret results with their own theoretical focus and fail to take account of common characteristics of *some* of the studies which might explain consistencies or oddities. In other words, the traditional review of scientific studies in psychology has been pretty unscientific.

Meta-analysis is a relatively recent approach to this problem employing a set of statistical techniques in order to use the results of possibly hundreds of studies of the same hypothesis as a new 'data set'. The result of each study is treated rather like an individual participant's result in a single study. The statistical procedures are beyond the scope of this book but here are two examples of meta-analytic research.

In one of the most famous and early meta-analytic studies, Smith and Glass (1977) included about 400 studies of the efficacy of psychotherapy (does it work?). The main findings were that the average therapy patient showed improvement superior to 75%

of non-therapy patients and that behavioural and non-behavioural therapies were not significantly different in their effects.

Born (1987) meta-analysed 189 studies of sex differences in Thurstone-type intelligence measures across several cultures. In general, traditional sex differences were found but these were small and there were also some significant differences between clusters of cultures.

Meta-analysis takes account of sample size and various statistical features of the data from each study. There are many arguments about features which merge in the analysis, such as Presby's (1978) argument that some non-behavioural therapies covered by Smith and Glass were better than others. The general point, however, is that meta-analysis seems to be a way of gathering together and refining knowledge (a general goal of science) in a subject area where one cannot expect the commonly accepted and standardised techniques of the natural sciences.

STANDARDISED PROCEDURES AND QUALITATIVE RESEARCH

As we shall see in a little while, there are psychological research methods for which the requirement of a rigid standardised procedure would stifle the kind of relationship sought with the people the researcher studies, or works with. Such methods tend to sacrifice aspects of design validity in favour of richer and more realistic data, a debate we shall now go on to consider.

THE QUANTITATIVE–QUALITATIVE DIMENSION

In the chapter on variables, and in Chapter 1, I introduced a conventional approach to scientific study and measurement in psychological research. This would include an emphasis on the directly and physically observable, the assumption that cause and effect relationships must be logically analysed, and the use of quantitative methods wherever possible – loosely speaking, a form of POSITIVISM. Not everyone agrees that this is the appropriate method for the study of active human beings rather than inert matter. I mentioned this briefly at the end of Chapter 1. Some argue that a QUALITATIVE approach is possible in the investigation of psychological phenomena.

QUANTIFICATION AND QUALITATIVE EXPERIENCE

'Quantification' means to measure on some numerical basis, if only by frequency. Whenever we count or categorise, we quantify. Separating people according to astrological sign is quantification. So is giving a grade to an essay.

A qualitative research, by contrast, emphasises meanings, experiences (often verbally described), descriptions and so on. Raw data will be exactly what people have said (in interview or recorded conversations) or a description of what has been observed. Qualitative data can be later quantified to some extent but a 'qualitative approach' tends to value the data *as* qualitative.

It is rather like the difference between counting the shapes and colours of a pile of sweets as against feeling them, playing with them, eating them. Or counting sunsets rather than appreciating them. The difference between each one may be somehow quantifiable but such measurements will not convey the importance and the special impact of some over others.

By strict definition a variable can only be quantitative. As it changes it takes different values. There may only be two values, for instance male and female. A positivist would argue that psychologists can only study variables because contrast and comparison can only be achieved where there is change; what changes is a variable and variables must be quantifiable.

The case against is eloquently put by Reason and Rowan (1981) in a statement on what they call 'quantophrenia':

> There is too much measurement going on. Some things which are numerically precise are not true; and some things which are not numerical are true. Orthodox research produces results which are statistically significant but humanly insignificant; in human inquiry it is much better to be deeply interesting than accurately boring.

This is a sweeping statement, making it sound as though all research not using the methods which the authors prefer is 'humanly insignificant'. This is not so. Many possibly boring but accurate research exercises have told us a lot about perceptual processes, for instance. However, the statement would not have been made had there not been an excess of emphasis, within psychological research history, on the objective measurement and direct observation of every concept, such that, important topics, not susceptible to this treatment, were devalued.

On the topic of 'emotion', for instance, in mainstream textbooks you will find little that relates to our everyday understanding of that term. You will find strange studies in which people are injected with drugs and put with either a happy or angry actor, and studies in which people are given false information about events they are normally oblivious of – such as their heart or breathing rate. These things are quantifiable, as are the responses such subjects give to structured questionnaires.

VARYING RESEARCH CONTEXTS

The debate about qualitative research represents, to some extent, differences of interest in the way psychology should be practised or applied. If you're interested in the accuracy of human perception in detecting colour changes, or in our ability to process incoming sensory information at certain rates, then it seems reasonable to conduct highly controlled experimental investigations using a strong degree of accurate quantification. If your area is psychology applied to social work practice, awareness changes in ageing, or the experience of mourning, you are more likely to find qualitative methods and data of greater use.

But the debate also represents fundamental disagreement over what is the most appropriate model for understanding human behaviour and, therefore, the best way to further our understanding. We shall investigate this point further in Chapter 11.

A compromise position is often found by arguing that the gathering of basically qualitative data, and its inspection and analysis *during* the study, can lead to the stimulation of new insights which can then be investigated more thoroughly by quantitative methods at a later stage. This might still be considered a basically positivist approach, however.

An old example of this reasoning occurred in some research which studied the effects of long-term unemployment in Austria in the 1930s (Jahoda-Lazarsfeld and Zeisl, 1932). A small boy, in casual conversation with a research worker, expressed the wish to become an Indian tribal chief but added 'I'm afraid it will be hard to get the job'. The investigators developed and tested quantitatively the hypothesis that parental unemployment has a limiting effect on children's fantasies. Children of unemployed parents mentioned significantly less expensive items in their Christmas present wishes, compared with children of employed parents. (We assume, of course, that the parental groups were matched for social class!)

More recently there have been examples of quantitative analysis *preceding* a qualitative major design as when Reicher and Emler (1986) conducted qualitative interviews on groups originally identified through a quantitative survey.

RELATIVE VALUES OF QUANTITATIVE AND QUALITATIVE STUDIES

In general, methods which are tighter and more rigorous give rise to more reliable and internally valid data, replicable effects and a claim to greater objectivity. However, results are open to the criticism of giving narrow, unrealistic information using measures which trap only a tiny portion of the concept originally under study. More qualitative enquiries, with looser controls and conducted in more natural,

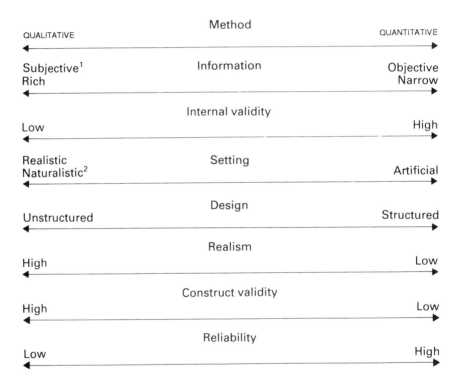

Figure 4.1 *Variations in construction and control – qualitative and quantitative studies*

Note:

1 Some qualitative proponents argue strongly that their methods do not necessarily invoke greater subjectivity at all. Numbers can be used subjectively, as when 'trained raters' use a rating scale to 'code' observed behaviour. A descriptive account of an abused person's experience can be written objectively and can be checked with them for accuracy and true reflection. A person's own, major reasons for objecting to abortion could be counted as more objective data than a number which places them at five on a zero to 30 abortion attitude scale.

2 Naturalistic studies (those carried out in natural surroundings) may use fully quantified data gathering procedures. Qualitative studies however, will almost always tend to be naturalistic.

everyday circumstances give richer results and more realistic information. Therefore, it is often claimed that they have greater ecological validity though they may lack validity in other respects (e.g. internal). Findings may also be less reliable and more subjective.

Loosely controlled methods will produce unpredictable amounts and types of information which the researcher has to sift, organise and select for importance. Such methods leave more room for the researcher to manoeuvre in questioning the participants and in deciding what observations are more worthwhile, thus fostering more natural, less stilted human interaction with more realistic results. The price is greater individual bias and less comparability across studies.

Studies can vary in their construction and control across all the dimensions shown in Figure 4.1. The qualitative-quantitative dimension tends to correlate with the other dimensions as shown, and it is worth bearing these in mind as we progress through the research methods commonly in use in psychological investigation today. Qualitative approaches are integrated into the chapters on observation and on asking questions. Others are covered in Chapter 11.

GLOSSARY

Effect of attention grabbing, interesting experiment in compensating for artificiality or 'demand characteristics' (see Chapter 5)	_____ _____	experimental realism
Statistical analysis of multiple studies of the same, or very similar, hypotheses; an allegedly more objective version of the traditional literature review of all studies in a topic area	____-_____	meta-analysis
Effect of research design which resembles everyday life but which is not necessarily engaging to participants	_____ _____	mundane realism
Methodological belief that description of the world's phenomena, including human experience and social behaviour, is reducible to observable facts (at the most extreme, 'sense-data') and the mathematical relationships between them	_____	positivism
Methodological stance which holds that information about human events and experience, if reduced to numerical form, loses most of its important meaning and value for research and understanding	_____ _____	qualitative approach
Information gathered which is not in, or reducible to, numerical form	_____ ____	qualitative data

Information gathered which is in, or reduced to, numerical form	_____ __	quantitative data
Extent to which findings or measures can be repeated with similar results	_____	reliability
Repetition of a study to check its validity	_____	replication
Way of testing or acquiring measures from participants which is repeated in exactly the same way each time for all common parts of the method	_____ _____	standardised procedure
Extent to which instruments measure what it is intended that they should measure; also, extent to which a research effect can be trusted, is not 'contaminated'	_____	**validity**
Extent to which investigation can be generalised to other places and conditions, in particular, from the artificial and/or controlled (e.g. laboratory) to the natural environment	_____	ecological
Extent to which results of research can be generalised across people, places, times and other measures of the variables	_____	external
Extent to which effect found in a study can be taken to be real and caused by the identified independent variable	_____	internal
Any aspect of the design or method of a study which weakens the likelihood that a real effect has been demonstrated	_____ to _____	threat to validity
Statistical measure of extent to which data vary	_____	variance

EXERCISES

1 Which of the measures below might produce the best construct validity of a person's attitude to the elderly?

   a) answers to a questionnaire
   b) what they say to a close friend in conversation
   c) what they say in an informal interview
   d) the number of elderly people they count as close friends?

   Which of these might be the most reliable measure?

2 Think of examples where we could obtain data which were:
   a) internally but not externally valid
   b) externally but not internally valid
   c) reliable but not valid

3 Two psychologists have recently completed research into the experiences of persons with disabilities in the able-bodied world. One conducted informal interviews and looked for illuminating points brought out by the interviewees. The other used a pre-structured questionnaire and published significant differences in attitude, measured by the questionnaire, between the interviewees and a control group of able-bodied people. Construct the list of criticisms which each might make of the other's procedure and findings. Chapters 8 and 9 contain detailed evaluations of these methods.

4 Give examples of human experiences which might be very difficult to quantify in any useful or meaningful way.

THE EXPERIMENTAL METHOD I

The nature of the method

This chapter introduces the general division of research into experimental and non-experimental designs.
- A **true experiment** occurs when an independent variable is manipulated and participants are randomly allocated to conditions.
- **Quasi-experiments** occur when participants are not allocated by the experimenter into conditions of the manipulated independent variable.
- Non-experiments investigate variables which exist among people irrespective of any researcher intervention.
- Any of these studies may be used to eliminate hypotheses and therefore support theories.
- The **laboratory experiment** has traditionally been considered more powerful in terms of control of variables but is criticised for artificiality and on several other grounds.
- In the use of experiments there are many threats to validity such as **demand characteristics**, **expectancy** and **loose procedures**.
- Humanists object to the **'dehumanisation'** of people in many mainstream psychological experiments.

Among the variety of research methods and designs popular with psychological researchers, there is a rather sharp divide. Designs are seen as either *experimental* or *non-experimental*, the latter often being called INVESTIGATIONS, although, of course, experiments are investigations too, in the general sense. This conceptual divide between methods is further sharpened by the fact that, in various learning institutions, it is possible to take a degree course in 'experimental psychology'.

Table 5.1 gives some terminology for these two groupings with some indication, I hope, of where some methods lie on the dimension of investigator control which weakens as studies move away (to the right) from the traditional laboratory experiment.

EXPERIMENTS

In experiments, the ideal is to control all relevant variables whilst altering only the IV. A strong and careful attempt is made to even out random variables and to eliminate constant errors. The reason for this is that, if all other variables are controlled, only the IV can be responsible for changes in the DV. The reasoning here is not confined to scientific experiment but is used as 'common-sense' thinking in many practical situations in everyday life. If you're trying to work out what causes interference on your TV set you would probably try turning off one piece of electrical equipment at a time, leaving all others just as they were, until the interference stops.

Complete control of the IV is the hallmark of an experiment. As an example, consider a researcher who very briefly exposes concrete or abstract words to participants who have the task of recognising them as soon as possible. The IV here (the variable which the experimenter alters) is the concrete or abstract word sets. The DV is the time taken to recognise each word. When looking for the IV in a straightforward experiment it is helpful to ask 'what were the various conditions which participants underwent?'

To make this a well-controlled experiment, all other variables, as far as is feasible, should be held constant. Hence the experimenter would ensure that each word was of exactly the same size, colour, print style and so on. Machine settings, ambient light and background noise should not be allowed to vary. Also, each list would have to contain words of fairly comparable frequency of occurrence in everyday reading, otherwise frequency might act as a confounding variable.

RANDOM ALLOCATION OF PARTICIPANTS

Most important of all, any possible differences between the people in the different conditions of an experiment which tests separate groups ('independent samples' – see next chapter) will be evened out by allocating participants at random to conditions. This is the major difference between 'true' experiments and what are known as 'quasi-experiments'. This difference is explained further below. In an experiment where the same people are in each condition ('repeated measures' – see next chapter) the variable of differences-between-groups is completely controlled by elimination.

INVESTIGATIONS WHICH ARE NOT EXPERIMENTS

In contrast with the experiment, consider the study of the effect of early visual stimulation on children's later cognitive development. We can't take a group of children and deprive them of visual experience under controlled conditions. (If you're not convinced, please read the chapter on ethics now!)

In non-experimental investigations, the researcher gathers data through a variety of methods *but does not intervene* in order to control an independent variable. Other forms of control may well occur in order to enhance the accuracy of measurement, as when children of specific ages take a highly structured test of intelligence in a quiet and uninterrupted environment.

The weakness of non-experimental investigations is that, since the researcher does not have control over all relevant variables, confounding is much more likely.

> Assume it is found that children deprived of good visual stimulation at home are slower in cognitive development. What confounding variables (*not* the lack of visual experience itself) could explain the children's slower development?

Two reasons I could think of were:

1 Parents who do not stimulate visually might also not stimulate in ways that have

an important effect on cognitive development. For instance, they may not talk very much to their children.

2 Lack of visual stimulation may occur where working parents are busy and also can't afford good child care facilities. The general lack of resources might in some way affect cognitive development.

The diagram below shows the essential difference between an experiment and a non-experimental investigation:

Experiment		Non-experimental investigation	
Manipulated	Measured	Measured	Measured
IV ⟶ DV		IV ⟶ DV	

The control of the IV, and our ability to eliminate as many extraneous variables as

Table 5.1 *Experimental terminology*

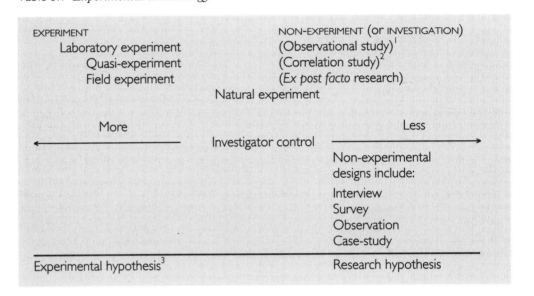

Notes:

1 This term is sometimes used for all methods other than experimental. The idea is that, if we aren't manipulating, we can only be observing what occurs or has occurred naturally. Unfortunately, it is easy to confuse this wide use with the sense of observation as a technique (or method) where it literally means to watch and record behaviour as it is produced. This is different from, say, interviewing. Observation, as a technique, may be employed in a straightforward experiment.

2 This term can *also* be used for non-experimental designs but it only makes sense to use it where changes in one recorded variable (say income) are related to changes in another variable (say, educational standards expected for children). Correlation is explained in Chapter 18. Many studies of variables existing in the social world do not, however, use statistical correlation but look for significant *differences* between groups.

3 These are the appropriate terms for the hypotheses. All hypotheses are research hypotheses first, but the experiment earns this special title.

possible, give us greater confidence that changes in the DV are produced by changes in the IV.

ELIMINATION OF HYPOTHESES IN NON-EXPERIMENTAL WORK

In an experiment we can eliminate alternative explanations of an effect by controlling variables. Where we do not have an experimental level of control we can still eliminate possible explanations. If we wish to investigate my explanation above that children lacking visual stimulation may also be lacking language stimulation, we can conduct a study of parents who are poor visual stimulators but competent in verbal stimulation. If their children are behind in cognitive development then my explanation has to be invalid.

Remember that, in Chapter 1, I pointed out that scientific research does not require that experiments be conducted. Astronomers did very well with careful observation and hypothesis testing. A vast amount of psychological research has been carried out using non-experimental methods.

FROM NON-EXPERIMENT TO EXPERIMENT

Very often a non-experimental study can lead to experiments being conducted to 'tighten up' knowledge of the variables under study. For instance, the observation has been made that children, during their preschool years, change their reasoning about 'wrong' and 'right' actions, concentrating their attention at first on the objective consequences of the act rather than taking the actor's intention into account too. This has led to direct (and successful) experimental attempts to alter the child's predominant style of reasoning by having them observe an adult model using the more advanced judgement style.

In many areas of psychological research, children can only be observed, not experimented with. However, some psychologists have performed experiments on animals as a substitute. Monkeys, for instance, have been deprived of their mothers and many animals have been subjected to various forms of physical punishment. These studies obviously raise ethical issues and we shall discuss these in some detail in Chapter 20.

THE LABORATORY

Most studies carried out in laboratories are experiments, but not all. It is possible to bring children into a laboratory simply to observe their behaviour in a play setting without subjecting them to any changes in an independent variable.

Control

If an aim of the experiment is to reduce relevant extraneous variables by strict control then this is best achieved in a laboratory setting, particularly where highly accurate recordings of human cognitive functions (such as memory, perception, selective attention) are required. The IV and DV can be very precisely defined and accurately measured.

Bandura's (1965) research used controlled observation to record amounts and types of aggression shown by children after they had watched an adult model being rewarded, unrewarded or punished for aggression. These three conditions represent the strictly controlled IV of an experimental design. Each child was observed in an identical play setting with an identical (now notorious) Bobo doll.

Consider the difference between this experimental setting and the 'field' setting of raters observing the aggressive behaviour of children in a school playground. In the playground, children may move off, be obscured by others or simply lack energy in cold weather. They may wish to play with the observer if he or she isn't hidden.

Bandura had strict control over timing, position and analysis of filmed records of behaviour. Ainsworth, mentioned earlier, had complete control over the departure of a mother and arrival of a stranger when testing infants' reactions to separation in a laboratory setting, as well as highly accurate recordings of the infants' behaviour.

Artificial conditions

In physical science it is often necessary to study phenomena under completely artificial and controlled conditions in order to eliminate confounding variables. Only in this way would we know that feathers obey gravity in exactly the same way as lead. Critics of the laboratory method in psychology however, argue that behaviour studied out of context in an artificial setting is meaningless, as we shall see below.

Later on we shall discuss various criticisms of the experiment as a research method. Here we shall list some related criticisms of the laboratory as a research focus.

CRITICISMS OF THE LABORATORY AS RESEARCH LOCATION

1 *Narrowness of the IV and DV* (low construct validity). The aggression measured in Bandura's experiments is a very narrow range of what children are capable of in the way of destructive or hostile behaviour. Bandura might argue that at least this fraction of aggressive behaviour, we are now aware, could be modelled. However, Heather (1976) has argued persuasively:

> Psychologists have attempted to squeeze the study of human life into a laboratory situation where it becomes unrecognisably different from its naturally occurring form.

2 *Inability to generalise* (ecological validity). A reliable effect in the laboratory may have little relationship to life outside it. The concept of an 'iconic memory' or very short-term 'visual information store', holding 'raw' sensory data from which we rapidly process information, has been considered by later psychologists to be an artifact of the particular experiments which produced evidence for it.

Certainly there is a lot less faith now in the idea that experiments on rats, pigeons or even chimpanzees can tell us a lot about complex human behaviour.

3 *Artificiality*. A laboratory is an intimidating, possibly even frightening place. People may well be unduly meek and overimpressed by their surroundings. If the experimenter compounds this feeling by sticking rigidly to a standardised procedure, reciting a formal set of instructions without normal interactive gestures such as smiles and helpful comments, a participant (until recently known as a 'subject') is hardly likely to feel 'at home' and behave in a manner representative of normal everyday behaviour.

SOME DEFENCE

In defence of the laboratory it can be said that:

1 In the study of brain processes, or of human performance, stimulus detection and so on, not only does the artificiality of the laboratory hardly matter, it is the only place where highly technical and accurate measurements can be made.

If we study human vigilance in detecting targets, for instance, does it matter whether this is done in the technical and artificial surroundings of a laboratory or the equally technical and artificial environment of a radar monitoring centre where research results will be usefully applied? If we wish to discover how fine new-born babies' perceptual discriminations are, this can be done with special equipment and the control of a laboratory. The infant, at two weeks, is hardly likely to know or care whether it is at home or not.

2 Physicists would not have been able to split atoms in the natural environment, nor observe behaviour in a vacuum. Psychologists have discovered effects in the laboratory which, as well as being interesting in themselves, have produced practical applications. Without the laboratory we would be unaware of differences in hemispheric function, the phenomena of perceptual defence or the extreme levels of obedience to authority which are possible. In each case, the appropriate interpretation of results has been much debated but the phenomena themselves have been valuable in terms of human insight and further research.

3 Research conducted under laboratory conditions is generally far easier to *replicate*, a feature valued very highly by advocates of the experimental method (see Chapter 4).

4 Some effects must surely be *stronger* outside the laboratory, not just artificially created within it. For instance, in Milgram's famous obedience study (see Chapter 26) participants were free to leave at any time yet, in real life, there are often immense social pressures and possibly painful sanctions to suffer if one disobeys on principle. So Milgram's obedience effects could be expected to operate even more strongly in real life than he dramatically illustrated in his laboratory.

FIELD EXPERIMENTS

The obvious alternative to the laboratory experiment is to conduct one's research 'in the field'. A field experiment is a study carried out in the natural environment of those studied, perhaps the school, hospital or street, whilst the IV is still manipulated by the experimenter. Other variables may well be tightly controlled but, in general, the experimenter cannot maintain the high level of control associated with the laboratory.

In addition to his notorious laboratory studies of obedience Milgram also asked people in subway trains to give up their seats (yes, *he* did it, not just his research students). Piliavin et al. (1969) had students collapse in the New York subway carrying either a cane or made to appear drunk (the IV). The DV was the number of times they were helped within 70 seconds. Notice that many extraneous variables are uncontrolled, especially the number of people present in the train compartment. The ethical issues are interesting too – suppose you were delayed for an important appointment through offering help? This issue of involuntary participation will be discussed in Chapter 26.

It used to be thought that the laboratory should be the starting point for investigating behaviour patterns and IV–DV links. The effects of such studies could then be tried out in 'the field'. The comparison was with the physicist harnessing electricity in the laboratory and putting it to work for human benefit in the community. In the last few decades many psychologists have become disaffected with the laboratory as solely appropriate for psychological research and have concentrated more on 'field' results in their own right.

Two examples of field experiments are:

1 An elegant design by Friedrich and Stein (1973) involved observation of nursery school children to obtain a baseline for cooperative, helpful and friendly behaviour for each child. Children were then randomly assigned to two groups. Over a month, at regular intervals, one group watched 'pro-social' television programmes whilst the other (control) group watched neutral films of circuses and farm activity. The children were observed again at the end of the period and there was a significant rise in cooperativeness and peer-directed affection for the experimental group.

2 Ganster et al. (1982) randomly allocated 79 public service employees to a treatment group and a control group. The 'treatment' involved stress management training sessions and, at the end, this group showed relatively lower levels of adrenaline secretion, depression and anxiety. The effects, though small, were still present some four months later. The control group later received the same training.

Notice the random allocation to 'treatment' or control groups in both these field experiments.

ADVANTAGES AND DISADVANTAGES OF THE FIELD EXPERIMENT

By studying effects in the natural environment, the field experiment avoids the criticism that results can't be generalised to real situations, though of course, one may not be able to generalise to real situations markedly unlike this particular field setting. The field experiment therefore is likely to have higher ecological validity, though control, and therefore internal validity, is generally lower.

In many cases, participants are unaware of being involved in an experiment until effects have been recorded. The extent to which they are aware of the aims of the experiment determines the extent to which it may be queried for bias from participants and the effects of 'demand characteristics' (see below). Still, even with some distortion through this awareness, it will not involve the apprehension and artificiality of the laboratory.

The field experiment may be more expensive and time consuming. The researcher may require skills of tact and persuasion, not needed in the laboratory, in dealing with those who need convincing that the research is necessary, and in arranging details of the design which will ensure valid results whilst retaining cooperation with personnel such as the teacher or hospital worker.

The major disadvantage, however, is in the lack of control which the investigator can exert over extraneous variables, over strict manipulation of the IV and over careful, accurate measurement of the DV. All these are vulnerable to far more fluctuation in the field setting, compared with a laboratory.

QUASI-EXPERIMENTS

Some studies don't qualify as true experiments. Remember that the experimenter has to have control over all possible confounding and 'nuisance' variables in order that changes in the DV can be attributed confidently to manipulation of the IV. This includes random allocation of participants to experimental and control groups since, if not, differences in the DV could be attributable to differences between the groups. We will discuss this issue further in Chapter 6, 'Experimental designs'.

The term 'QUASI-EXPERIMENT' is given to studies in which experimental procedures are applied but random allocation to conditions is not possible.

An example is the pre-test/treatment/post-test design. A group of people with dyslexia, attending one centre, might be tested prior to implementation of a new training programme, and tested again after it has been completed. To eliminate the possibility that the 'treatment group' might have improved anyway, without the programme, a more thorough design would include a control group. These could be other persons with dyslexia attending the centre on a different day or from a quite different centre. This design uses a 'non-equivalent control group', however. The control group might fail to improve, not because they did not receive the 'treatment' but because their centre lacks some other variable associated with the 'treatment' group's centre. Confounding cannot be ruled out.

Note that if the experimenter had been allowed to use people at one centre and allocate these at random to experimental or control groups then the study would qualify for full experimental status.

NATURAL EXPERIMENTS

There are occasions when a natural event is about to occur which a psychologist may exploit for research purposes. For instance, a headteacher may be about to introduce a 'discovery learning' approach in one infant class of the school. The regime in one ward of a psychiatric hospital may change to an emphasis on patient autonomy, nurses to guide and train rather than to care and guard. In both cases there will be a naturally occurring control group – a similar group not experiencing the change – with which behaviour changes can be compared. The IV, however, is not at all controlled by the experimenter. The experiment is 'quasi' since no control is possible over group differences.

The advantage here is that participants are not aware that they are part of an 'experiment', though there may still be distortion of normal behaviour as a response to the real-life changes and novelty they are experiencing. However, the investigator is not guilty of interfering, though his or her presence may have some unwanted effects.

EX POST FACTO RESEARCH

Very many studies reported in the psychological journals are those in which *existing* differences are sought between groups of people and no IV is manipulated by the researcher. As we saw in Chapter 1, it is legitimate to hold a theory, produce hypotheses from it and to check these out by measurement. The Rutter (1971) and Penny and Robinson (1986) studies mentioned there were examples. It is assumed here that the IV is a naturally occurring one which has already operated. In a sense, we look back 'after the fact' (*post facto*) to relate our measured dependent variable(s) to the independent variable.

A researcher might record differences in reaction to a finger-painting exercise between working-class and middle-class children. Males and females might be tested for differences in verbal ability. In cases like these, it is argued, the IV is class or gender and the researcher cannot claim to have controlled these since the people studied were socialised throughout their lives prior to the test.

Sex, class, years of education and so on are variables which the researcher can have no influence over. The problem is that, because the IV is confounded by so many other variables, we cannot state that it is the *cause* of changes in the DV. We can use techniques like matching, and random selection of subjects from the appropriate populations, in order to try to eliminate some confounding variables but there are far too many of these to ever be able to state that a difference is unambiguously the result of sex or class difference.

CRITICISMS OF THE EXPERIMENT

Many criticisms of the experimental method involve the implicit assumption that the experiment is being carried out in a laboratory. We have already considered the advantages and disadvantages of laboratory research. The following criticisms, then, apply to the experiment as a design, irrespective of where it is carried out, though some carry more weight when applied to the laboratory experiment.

FROM WITHIN THE EXPERIMENTAL RESEARCH TRADITION

Even those who strongly favour the use of the experimental method have realised that there are very many pitfalls involved in running experiments, some of which are not obvious and have been brought to our attention by sometimes dramatic demonstrations.

Barber (1976) has documented many of these pitfalls and he categorises these into the following groups:

1 Investigator paradigm effect
2 Investigator experimental design effect
3 Investigator loose procedure effect
4 Investigator data analysis effect
5 Investigator fudging effect
6 Experimenter personal attributes effect
7 Experimenter failure to follow the procedure effect
8 Experimenter misrecording effect
9 Experimenter fudging effect
10 Experimenter unintentional expectancy effect

Most of these speak for themselves and several could be applied to non-experimental studies. The 'investigator' is the person with overall control of the research whereas the 'experimenter' is a person carrying out the procedure on each participant, often as a research student or as a paid employee.

Experimenters may fudge results because they are hired for the job and wish to 'succeed' or because they will be compared with others in order to assess EXPERIMENTER RELIABILITY – the extent to which two experimenters' results agree. They may misrecord or fail to follow procedure because the investigator has designed a loose procedure. The personal attributes of experimenters (attractiveness, sex, etc.) may well affect participant behaviour. The design which an investigator uses, or their own psychological 'paradigms' (roughly speaking, their theoretical perspective) may well produce different results from other designs. The most notorious investigator fudging in psychological history was conducted by Sir Cyril Burt, as documented by Leon Kamin (1977).

EXPERIMENTER EXPECTANCY

Since psychology experiments are carried out by humans on humans, it has been argued that the necessary social interaction which must occur between experimenter and participant makes the psychological experiment different in kind from any other.

Is it possible that the experimenter could unintentionally 'give the game away' to the participant? This is Barber's point **10**.

Rosenthal (1966) showed that students given groups of 'bright' and 'dull' rats (who were actually randomly mixed for maze learning ability) produced results consistent with the label of their rats. This was originally used to show that experimenter expectancies can even affect the behaviour of laboratory rats. However, Barber argues that the results were almost certainly due to other effects from his list of 10 above, such as deviation from procedure.

Forty experiments between 1968 and 1976 failed to show evidence of experimenters passing on influence which the investigators tried to produce. However, some studies have shown that experimenters *can* affect participants' responses through facial or verbal cues and that certain participants are more likely to pick up experimenter influence than others, particularly those high in need for approval.

DEMAND CHARACTERISTICS

If participants who need approval are affected by experimenter influence, then it suggests that they perhaps want to 'please the experimenter' and get the 'right' result. To do this they would have to know what was required in the first place.

Orne (1962) argued that there are many cues in an experimental situation which give participants an idea of what the study is about, what behaviour is under study and perhaps even what changes are expected or required of them. These cues which may reveal the experimental hypothesis Orne named DEMAND CHARACTERISTICS. 'Experimental realism', mentioned in the last chapter, was thought by Aronson to *lower* the likely effects of demand characteristics, because participants' attention is entirely grabbed by the interest of the procedure.

Participant reactions

Participants could react to demand characteristics in several ways. They may engage in what is termed PLEASING THE EXPERIMENTER.

In fact, Weber and Cook (1972) found little evidence that participants do try to respond as they think the experimenter might wish. Masling (1966) has even suggested that, knowing the experimental aims, behaviour might be altered away from expectancy – the 'screw you' effect. Research suggests, however, that most participants try to appear normal and competent since they are concerned about how their behaviour will be judged. This may well influence them to behave as naturally as possible and show that they cannot be influenced.

EVALUATION APPREHENSION may occur when participants are worried what the researcher may find out about them and this anxiety may affect results. Some may try to 'look good'. This is known as SOCIAL DESIRABILITY. Others may just not concentrate as well on the task at hand. A further problem, sometimes known as 'enlightenment', is the increasing awareness of psychology students (who are most often participants) and the general public about psychological research findings, even if these are often poorly understood.

REACTIVE AND NON-REACTIVE STUDIES

It must be emphasised that *any* research study, experiment or not, in so far as participants are aware of the research aims, can be affected by some of the variables just described, perhaps 'social desirability' in particular. Such studies use what is called a REACTIVE design (or use a 'reactive measure') since the participant is

Table 5.2 *What* are *experiments?*

	Common element: independent variable is manipulated by the experimenter	
Laboratory	**Field**	**Quasi**
Conducted in laboratory Random allocation of participants to conditions	Conducted in field setting Random allocation of participants to conditions	Almost always conducted in field setting. Participants *not* randomly allocated to conditions and often selection is automatic because one IV is the difference between groups (e.g. smoker/non-smoker)
Natural	**Ex post facto research**	
Quasi experiment where researcher exploits occurrence of natural IV *about* to be applied	No manipulation of an independent variable	Independent variable is naturally occurring; differences sought between people who differ in a specific way, e.g. neurotic/ non-neurotic; high/low self- esteem; smoker/non-smoker

Experiments *and ex post facto* research both suffer from:

Experimenter/researcher expectancy and reliability, participant expectancy, guessing, social desirability, desire to please, hostility …	to the extent that …	The experimenter/ researcher knows expected results, participants are able to respond to any consequent cues given, participants can get information from demand characteristics, are motivated to distort behaviour and/or are wise to psychological findings

expected to *react* to being studied. It could be argued that the closeness of the researcher, and the awesome surroundings, make reactive measures more distorting in the traditional laboratory experiment.

REMOVING BIAS – BLINDS AND DOUBLE BLINDS

Investigators usually do not want their participants to be aware of the experimental aim. Deception may well have to be employed to keep them in the dark and the moral implications of this are discussed in the chapter on ethics. Keeping participants in the dark is known as the employment of a 'single blind' procedure. But it has been argued here that experimenters may transmit cues. Hence, it makes sense to keep experimenters in the dark too. The employment of a 'double blind' procedure does just that

Table 5.3 *Comparison of laboratory and field experiments*

Field experiment	COMPARISON POINT	Laboratory experiment
Natural	Environment	Artificial
Controlled	Independent variable	Controlled
Random	Allocation of participants to conditions	Random
Participants *may* be unaware of study (if so, can't guess design, try to look good, etc.)	Awareness of aims by participants	Participants (except very young children) must be aware of being in experiment (though *not* what the design really is)
Weaker	Control of extraneous variables	Tighter
Higher	Realism	Lower
Harder	Replication	Easier
Usually higher	Expense & time	Usually lower
To real-life field setting – good To *other* real-life settings – probably weaker	Generalisation (ecological validity)	To real life – often very weak
Perhaps can't be brought to field situation	Equipment	Can be complex and only usable in the laboratory
OTHER DISADVANTAGES		
More confounding possible because of researcher's need to negotiate with field setting personnel and managers		Narrow IV and DV → low construct validity
		Setting more likely to create apprehension, wariness of strange surroundings, etc.

– experimenters, or those who gather results directly from the participants, are not told the true experimental aims. Where a placebo group is used, for example, neither the participants, nor the data gatherers may know who has received the real treatment.

THE HUMANIST OBJECTION

I pointed out in Chapter 1 that people involved in psychology experiments have traditionally been referred to as 'subjects', though this is now changing. Humanist psychologists have argued that this is a reflection of the experimentalists' attitude to humans and human research. It implies that the researcher holds, perhaps implicitly, a 'mechanistic' model of humans. Heather (1976) has claimed that 'Human beings continue to be regarded by psychologists as some kind of helpless clockwork puppet, jerked into life only when something happens to it.' Hampden-Turner (1971) states '. . . power over people in a laboratory can *only* lead . . . to a technology of behaviour control' (italics in original). Such objectors to the experimental method would normally be found in the qualitative research method 'camp' already introduced and discussed more thoroughly in Chapter 11.

There is, of course, a composite position, well put by Baars (1980): 'Without naturalistic facts, experimental research may become narrow and blind: but without experimental research, the naturalistic approach runs the danger of being shallow and uncertain.'

GLOSSARY

Study of the extent to which one variable is related to another, often referring to non-manipulated variables measured outside the laboratory	_____ _____	correlational study
Features of a study which help the participant to work out what is expected of him/her	_____ _____	demand characteristics
Procedure in an experiment where neither participants *nor* data gatherer (experimenter or assistants) know which 'treatment' participants have received	_____ _____	double blind
Participants' concern about being tested, which may affect results	_____ _____	evaluation apprehension
Study in which an independent variable is manipulated	_____	**experiment**
Experiment carried out in a natural setting outside the laboratory	_____ _____	field experiment
Experiment carried out in controlled conditions in experimenter's own habitat	_____ _____	laboratory experiment
Experiment which exploits the occurrence of a naturally occurring independent variable	_____ _____	natural experiment
Experiment in which experimenter does not have control over the allocation of participants to conditions	_____-_____	quasi-experiment
Tendency for experimenter's knowledge of what is being tested to influence the outcome of research	_____ _____	experimenter expectancy
The extent to which the results produced by two or more experimenters are related	_____ _____	experimenter reliability

Research where *pre-existing* and non-manipulated variables among people are measured for difference or correlation	_ ____ _____ _____	*ex post facto* research
An enquiring experimental or non-experimental piece of research	_____	investigation
Study in which people are not aware that they are part of the study in any way	__-_____ _____	non-reactive study
Research which simply measures characteristics of how people are or behave but doesn't intervene or (more narrowly) research in which the main data gathering technique involves looking directly at behaviour as it occurs and categorising or measuring it	_____ _____	observational study
Tendency of participants to act in accordance with what they think the experimenter would like	_____ ___ _____	pleasing the experimenter
Study in which participants are required to respond in some way; they are therefore aware of being the subject of assessment	_____ _____	reactive study
Procedure in an experiment where participants do not know which 'treatment' they received	_____ _____	single blind
Tendency of participants in research to want to 'look good' and provide socially acceptable answers	_____ _____	social desirability

EXERCISES

1 State whether the following are laboratory experiments, natural experiments, field experiments whether they are true or quasi-experiments or whether they are *ex post facto* studies:

   a) A ladder is placed against a street wall to see whether more males or females will avoid it

   b) Boys with no brother and boys with two brothers are observed under laboratory conditions to see which group exhibits greater aggression

   c) A researcher, dressed either casually or smart, approaches passengers at a station to ask for directions. The aim is to see whether smart dress elicits greater help

   d) Under laboratory conditions, people are asked to make a speech, contrary to their own view, first alone and then in front of others

   e) The study described in **b** is extended. Half of each group of boys is subjected to frustration and then observed again for level of aggression

f) Drug addicts are compared with a control group on their tolerance of pain, measured in the laboratory

g) Researchers visit various grades of worker at their place of employment and take them through a questionnaire on their attitude to authority. It is thought the more highly paid will express greater respect for authority

h) One of two very similar homes for the elderly passes from local government to private control. Workers in each are compared on job satisfaction over the following year, using informal interviews

i) Children in one class at a school are given a six-month trial of an experimental new reading programme using a multi-media approach. A second class of children receive special attention in reading but not the new programme. Improvements are compared

2 Of the designs outlined in **1**:
  a) Which are not likely to be affected by demand characteristics?
  b) Which might involve looser procedures?
  c) Which are subject to researcher bias?
  d) In which could 'blind' procedures be employed?

3 You are discussing with a colleague two methods of measuring 'conformity'. One involves recording how often people will answer a simple question wrongly when several other people in the room have already answered wrongly (laboratory study). The other involves stopping people in the street who have infringed a traffic light or litter regulation and taking those who agree to do so through a short questionnaire (field study). Find arguments for and against each proposal – I hope you can think of at least three for and three against each. Pages 69 to 72 of this chapter should provide the general information you need.

6

THE EXPERIMENTAL METHOD II

Experimental designs

This chapter introduces the basic experimental designs that can be used in psychological research along with their various strengths and weaknesses. The following main points are discussed:

Experimental design	Weaknesses	Solutions
Repeated measures	Order effects	Counterbalancing; randomisation
Independent samples	Participant (subject) variables	Random allocation to conditions; pre-testing; representative allocation
Matched pairs	Problems with matching	Limit matching to what is relevant
Single participant (subject)	Lack of generalisation	Use where generalisation not main criterion

Julie: It really infuriates me. I drive really smoothly on my own, completely in control; then Susie gets in and I do stupid things like crash gears and stall.

Pete: Yeah?

Julie: Right! I'm sure people perform worse when someone important's watching them.

Pete: Well I'm not. I play pool better when Nikki's around.

Julie: Perhaps it depends on what you're like. Perhaps extraverteds (or whatever you call 'em) do better and intrawhatsits do worse. I wonder if people in the middle aren't affected.

(Julie went on to take 'A' level psychology and a degree!)

Let's suppose we decide to check out Julie's first hypothesis. It predicts that people perform sensori-motor tasks worse in the presence of an audience. Let's set up a laboratory experiment.

We need to operationalise. We need: a sensori-motor task
an audience
a measure of performance

We could ask people to move a metal ring along one of those wiggly wire contraptions you see at village fêtes. They have to avoid touching the wire with the ring as they move. If they do touch, a buzzer sounds and an error is recorded – this is our measure of performance by which we can assess 'improvement' quantitatively. We can define our DV, then, as the number of errors recorded. Let's suppose we run the experiment with everyone doing the test in condition A first – in front of an audience of 12 observers. In the second condition (B) they perform the task in a quiet, soundproof room, alone. Let's also assume that we find significantly less errors in the second condition.

REPEATED MEASURES DESIGN

The design above would be known as REPEATED MEASURES in the language of experimental design. The measure (of doing the wiggly wire test) is *repeated* on each person under the various conditions of the IV. If the participants are the same for both conditions, and all other variables are controlled, any differences, we assume, (though we could be wrong), must be the effect of the IV.

> Just to check, what is the independent variable in the experiment described above?

Well, the recommendation in the last section was to look for the conditions which were varied. In this case then, the IV must be the variation between conditions: presence or not of an audience.

RELATED DESIGNS

The repeated measures design is one of a set known as RELATED DESIGNS – (see Table 6.1) – 'related' because, when results are presented, a value in one condition is directly related to a value in the other condition.

What we do in related designs is to answer the possible criticism that any difference found is caused by differences between the people in our two groups. Instead of a control group to compare experimental results with, in the repeated measures design we use the same people as their own control, so any differences between conditions *can't* be because the people in conditions were different from one another. For this reason, the repeated measure design is often called a 'within subjects' or 'within groups' design, since differences *between* participants have been eliminated as a source of difference and differences between conditions must be because the same people differed in the two circumstances.

Table 6.1 *Related and unrelated designs*

	In each condition:	
Design	**Same people**	**Different people**
Related	Repeated measures	Matched pairs
Unrelated	Single participant	Independent samples

WE'VE PROVED IT, PETE!

Suppose we report our result to Pete. He is unimpressed. He says 'Well, the way you did it, I'm not at all surprised they did better in the second condition.'

> What is he on about? What has he spotted? What might be responsible for people's improvement in condition B other than the absence of the audience?

ORDER EFFECTS

You probably realised that there is a possible confounding variable at work here. People might improve on the second condition because they've had some practice (and they may be less anxious about learning a new task). If they had performed worse on the second go this might have been through becoming disheartened by failure, through boredom or through fatigue.

Constant error caused by the order in which people participate in conditions is known as an ORDER EFFECT. This is one of the major disadvantages of a repeated measures design.

> Can you make a list now of some solutions to this problem? How can a researcher design an experiment which avoids the contamination of order effects?

DEALING WITH ORDER EFFECTS

1 Counterbalancing

If all participants' performances on condition B could be improved because of the experience in condition A, it makes sense to have half of them perform condition B first. This is known as COUNTERBALANCING the conditions.

Would this in fact *eliminate* the order effect? Well, no it wouldn't. Practice, if it is effective, will still produce improvement, but this will improve half the scores in condition A and half in condition B. Hence the improvements should cancel each other out overall. Suppose that each person improves by making five less errors on average in the condition they took second. We could imagine that what is going on is as shown in Figure 6.1 overleaf.

When participants take the with-audience condition first, the overall reduction from condition A to condition B – shown as X below – contains an extra component (d) which is the result of practice (we are assuming here). When participants take the alone condition first, the reduction of practice causes the overall difference, with this order of conditions, to be smaller than it should be if only the IV has any effect. So, condition A followed by B shows an exaggerated effect, whilst condition B followed by condition A shows a lessened effect. However, these two should cancel each other out, leaving, we hope, only the true effect of the IV as a difference overall. This is because the two *observed* (but distorted) differences – X and Y – are equal to what we assume *would* have occurred without the practice effect. These two *hypothetical* differences are $X - d$ and $Y + d$. Adding these: $(X - d) + (Y + d) = X + Y$.

Warning for tests and exams! It is easy to get fooled into thinking that, because the design involves splitting participants into two groups, we have an independent samples design (see below). The splitting is solely for the purpose of counterbalancing. For each participant we still have a pair of scores which are therefore related – one for each condition. Each participant is still taking both conditions.

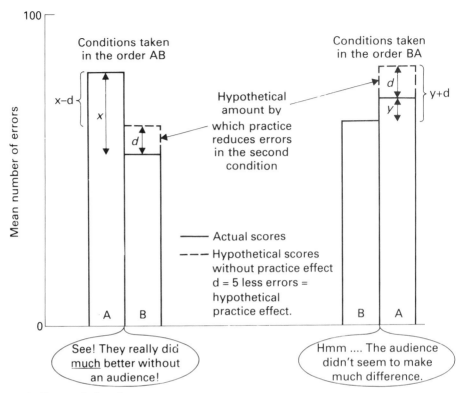

Figure 6.1 *Counterbalancing*

ASYMMETRICAL ORDER EFFECTS – This neat arrangement of counterbalancing may be upset though if the practice effect occurring in the A–B order is not equivalent to that produced in the B–A order.

For instance, suppose that in the alone condition it is possible to concentrate on improvement and that this transfers to the audience condition. However, when the audience is present in the first condition, all one's concentration goes on coping with the audience and no improvement in technique is transferred to the alone condition. Counterbalancing now loses its evening-out effect and we have the constant error of practice affecting the with-audience condition only. If this were the case we would end up with an artificially small difference overall.

Note: 'asymmetrical' just means 'not symmetrical' – the effect is not evenly balanced between the two groups.

2 Complex counterbalancing

a) ABBA

(Not an ageing Swedish pop group!) All participants take conditions in the order ABBA. Their score on A is taken as the mean of the two A conditions and likewise for B. This arrangement can still suffer from an asymmetrical effect, though it should be weakened.

b) Multi-condition designs

If an experiment has three conditions we might divide participants into six groups and have them take part in the following orders of condition:

ABC   ACB   BAC
BCA   CAB   CBA

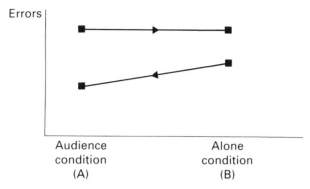

Figure 6.2 *Asymmetrical order effect – effect on practice*

3 Randomisation of condition order

Some experiments involve quite a number of conditions. For instance, a sensori-motor task may be performed under six different lighting conditions. Each participant would be given the conditions in a different random order.

4 Randomisation of stimulus items

This is an elegant way to deal with possible order effects in a two-condition experiment. Suppose we want to see whether concrete words are easier to recall than abstract words. Instead of giving the same group of people a list of concrete words to learn and recall, then a list of abstract words, we can give them just one list with concrete and abstract words randomly mixed together. Note that this could be a way to mix even three conditions together but either the list gets rather long or we have less of each item in the list. We might then present several such mixed lists in several trials.

5 Elapsed time

We can leave enough time between conditions for any learning or fatigue effects to dissipate.

6 Using another design

We may have to give up the idea of using the same group for each condition. We could have separate groups. We would then move to an 'independent samples design', described below, but, since this design has important disadvantages we might try to resist this more drastic solution to the problem of order effect.

OTHER DISADVANTAGES WITH REPEATED MEASURES DESIGN

- If each participant experiences both conditions of, say, a memory experiment using word lists, we have to use a different list in each condition. This creates the problem of choosing words for each list which are equivalent. It is possible to obtain lists which give the frequency of occurrence of words in the written English language, obtained through literature surveys.
- The aim of the experimental research may become obvious to the participant and this makes 'pleasing the experimenter' (or screwing up the results) much more likely.
- Participants must be available for both conditions. If conditions are weeks apart some may be lost.

When *not* to use a repeated measures design:

1 When order effects cannot be eliminated or are asymmetrical.

2 Often, people must be naïve for each condition. In 'VIGNETTE' studies, for example, a person is shown one of two alternatives, with all other material the same. For instance, people may be asked to rate an article having been told that either a teacher or a student is the author. A baby is presented as either a boy or a girl and people are asked to describe it. Lewis et al. (1990) sent vignettes which varied the sex and race of a fictitious client to 139 psychiatrists. When the client was African-Caribbean the following differences in ratings occurred compared with when the client was supposedly white. The illness was of a shorter duration, less drugs were required, the client was potentially more violent and criminal proceedings were more appropriate. Significantly more 'cannabis psychosis' was also diagnosed.

In these sorts of study, obviously the same participants cannot be used in both conditions, since, only then, could participants work out what the research aim is. When discussing such studies, conducted as class practicals, people often think from the vantage point of the experimenter. But it is important to 'empathise' with participants in such cases in order to see how difficult it would really be to work out what your experimenter is after when you only take part in *one* of the conditions.

3 Some studies involve an independent variable which is a category of persons, such as male/female, working class/middle class or extrovert/introvert. In this case we are comparing the performances of two different groups of people and a repeated measures design is obviously not possible.

4 We might pre-test a group of children, apply a programme designed to increase their sensitivity to the needs of people with disabilities, then test again to measure improvement. To check on internal validity (the children might have changed anyway, irrespective of the 'treatment') we need to compare their changes with a control and/or placebo group.

INDEPENDENT SAMPLES DESIGN

Suppose then that we organise two groups of people (from whom we can get – student colleagues on our course and the biology course who share statistics classes). One group do the with-audience condition, the other group do the task alone. Again, the alone condition errors are significantly lower.

We are now conducting what is known as an INDEPENDENT SAMPLES design experiment. This title says just what it means. An entirely different group of people take each condition (there could be three conditions or even more). It belongs to a category known as UNRELATED DESIGNS, since the scores from one group of participants, who undergo just one condition of the IV, are quite unrelated to the scores from another group who participate in the other condition of the IV.

Examples of independent samples designs would be:

1 One group are given a list of words and asked to repeat each word several times ('rehearse') before receiving the next item. A second group are asked to form vivid mental images of each item and to make links between each item and its successor. Both groups are tested for retention in a free recall task.

2 Beltramini (1992) investigated the effect of randomly allocating a company's business customers into those who would receive a gift and those who would not. The gift increased positive perception of the company but not intention to contact it again!

This design also comes with the titles: INDEPENDENT GROUPS, INDEPENDENT SUBJECTS and BETWEEN GROUPS. This last title is commonly used when the statistical analysis is ANOVA (see Chapter 20).

IT WORKED AGAIN PETE!

So what could doubting Pete say this time? He certainly has something to say. Before we hear it . . .

> What might now be responsible for the difference between conditions? What might cause one group to do worse, other than the fact that they performed in front of an audience? Also list any other disadvantages you can see in this design.

Pete says, 'Who did the experiment?' We tell him. He smirks, 'Ah! Remember you said, Julie, that introverts might be worse performers in front of an audience? Well, you know how introverted the biology mob are. Did you make sure you had equal numbers of them in each group?'

PARTICIPANT (OR SUBJECT) VARIABLES

Pete is referring to the variations among people which may be unevenly spread across our two groups. This is a major weakness of independent samples designs. Differences found might not be caused by the IV but by this uneven splitting into samples. Suppose, in example 1, above, we accidentally placed more good memorisers into the imagery group. It seems as though using imagery has caused the difference found but actually the DV difference is produced by variation between the people in the two groups.

DEALING WITH PARTICIPANT VARIABLES

In an independent samples design it would always be difficult to rule out participant variables as a possible source of variation in our results, but there are certain steps we can take to reduce the likelihood that they were the cause of differences found:

Random allocation of participants to conditions

This follows the classic line of experimental design. In biology, a researcher would randomly split a set of beans and subject one group to the treatment and use one as a control group. In psychology, the same line is followed. When results are in, the null hypothesis holds that any differences between the two groups are simply the result of chance variation between the two groups of people, not the effect of the IV. If there *is* a significant difference, we can at least reject this hypothesis. Here, of course, Pete has a point. Even student practicals should avoid obvious non-random differences between two sets of participants.

Notice that in the Beltramini study mentioned above, customers were allocated at random to the receiving gifts or control group. Random allocation is what makes a study a field experiment rather than a quasi-experiment (as we saw in the last chapter).

Pre-test of participants

We can show that both groups were similar in relevant performance before the experimental conditions were applied. For instance, in the memory study, both groups could be pre-tested on the same stimulus list, different from that used in the experimental trial. There still could be a participant variable problem. Though both groups might perform equally well on the pre-test list, the list for the experiment trial might contain words more familiar to people in one of the groups. There might, say, be several geographical terms and more geography students in the imagery group.

Representative allocation

We can ensure that each group contains half the males, a similar age range, a fairly similar range of educational backgrounds and so on. It might not strike us, however, to ensure an equal number of geography students. Inspection of the list might alert us to this possible confounding variable, but we can't balance the groups for every conceivable variable.

We must decide intuitively, given the nature of the research topic and aims, which variables are going to be the most important to balance for. Pete thinks we should have paid attention to his stereotype of the biology students. Within each relevant category chosen (male, female, psychology student etc.) allocation of half the category to one condition and half to the other would be performed on a random basis. The reasoning and method here are similar to that of stratified sampling.

OTHER DISADVANTAGES OF INDEPENDENT SAMPLES DESIGN

- To obtain as many scores in each condition we have to find and test twice the number of people as in repeated measures. This can be costly and time consuming. We do have the advantage (over repeated measures design), however, that we can't lose participants between conditions and we can run the two conditions simultaneously rather than having to wait until practice effects have worn off.
- If there is too much difference between the statistical variances of the two groups, we may not be able to proceed with a parametric test – the most powerful of statistical tests (see Chapters 12 and 17).

MATCHED-PAIRS DESIGN

We can actually do more than just ensure that the two groups for our research are roughly equivalent on relevant variables like extroversion. We can *pair* one person in the audience condition with a person in the alone condition. The two people can be *matched* for extroversion score, age, sex, occupation and any other variable thought to be relevant to wiggly-wire performance.

This compromise between the two designs so far discussed is known as the MATCHED-PAIRS design.

On a random basis, members of the pairs are each allocated to one of two groups. We pair people on the basis of relevant variables, the choice of what is relevant being, as before, based on the nature of the research. We now avoid order effects by having different groups in each condition, but we are also, we hope, keeping participant variables to a minimum.

We might, for example, pair each child who is to receive an experimental preschool programme with a child in a control group on the basis of, say, exact age, sex, ethnic group, social and economic background of parents and number of children in family. However, sample totals will limit the extent of what can be matched.

The matched-pairs design falls into the category of related designs since each score or rating in one group can be related to a score in the other group. This obviously can't be done where two sets of scores come from two unmatched groups.

One of nature's most useful gifts to psychological researchers is, some believe, the existence of identical (monozygotic) twins. These represent the perfect matched pair – when they're just born at least – and create the perfect natural experiment. Any differences between them later in life can fairly safely be attributed to differences in environmental experience. The converse is not true, however. Similarities cannot be easily attributed to common genetic make-up, since identical twins usually share fairly similar environments too.

SINGLE PARTICIPANT DESIGN

To hear of just one person being used for experimental research can make the scientifically minded recoil in horror. Surely this must produce quite unrepresentative results, impossible to generalise with? Quite rightly, they assume, one turns to objective psychological research in order to avoid the many generalisations which the lay person often makes from their own limited experience.

However, consider a physical scientist who obtains just one sample of weird moonrock from a returning space mission. The rock could be tested for amount of expansion at different temperatures, in a vacuum and in normal atmosphere, in order to detect significant changes in its behaviour. This would yield valuable scientific knowledge in itself.

Further, from our general knowledge of the world of rocks, we could fairly safely assume that similar rock would exist on the moon. In the same way there are some sorts of things which people do which, we know for good reason, are likely to vary according to the same *pattern* (but not necessarily at the same level) for almost everyone. An example of this might be the experimental situation in which someone has to make decisions from an increasing number of alternatives – sorting cards according to colour, then suit and so on.

Ebbinghaus carried out an enormous number of memory experiments on himself using a wide variation of conditions and lists of nonsense syllables. The introspectionists gave intense training to help people to report on feelings, sensations and mental processes.

RELATED OR UNRELATED?

A set of results for a single participant in an experiment, which measures reaction times as the DV, might appear as in Table 6.2.

Is this data produced from a related design? Contrary to our probable first conclusion, the answer is in fact 'no'! Each score in condition A has no *particular* partner in condition B. A particular score in A is related to *all* the scores in B to an equal degree, since the same person produced them all. But, in a related design, the first score in A (0·579) would be *uniquely* related to the first in B (0·713) because this was the only B score which the same person produced or because the B score was produced by the person matched with the first A person. Another way of seeing this is

Table 6.2 *Single participant design*

Condition A	Condition B
0.579 secs	0.713 secs
0.621	0.615
0.543	0.792
....	....
....	....

that it would be quite possible to have more scores in condition B than there are in condition A. The design *would* be related if we were somehow linking trial 1 in one condition to trial 1 in the other. This might happen if, say, we were correlating (see Chapter 18) equivalent trials under the two conditions to show that improvement takes a similar course under both.

Box 6.1 *Summary of advantages and disadvantages of the various experimental designs*

Design	Advantages	Disadvantages	Remedy (if any)
Repeated measures	Participant variables eliminated	Order effects	Counterbalance/ randomise conditions
	More economical on participants	May not be able to conduct second condition immediately	Leave long time gap between conditions
		Need different stimulus lists etc.	Do independent samples instead
			Randomise stimulus materials
	Homogeneity of variance not a problem (see Chapter 16)	Participants not naïve for second condition and may try to guess aim	Deceive participants as to aim (or leave long time gap)
	Need fewer participants	Loss of participants between conditions	
Independent samples	No order effect	Participant variables not controlled	Random allocation of participants to conditions
	Participants can't guess aim of experiment	Less economical on participants	
	Can use exactly the same stimulus lists etc.	Lack of 'homogeneity of variance' may prevent use of parametric test (Chapter 16)	Ensure roughly equal numbers in each group (see p. 280)
	No need to wait for participants to 'forget' first condition		
Matched pairs	No order effects	Some participant variables still present	Randomly allocate pairs to conditions
	Participant variables partly controlled	Hard to find perfect matches and therefore time consuming	
	No wait for participants to forget		

	Can use same stimulus lists etc.	Loss of one member of pair entails loss of whole pair	
	Homogeneity of variance not a problem		
Single participant	Useful where few participants available and/or a lot of time required for training participant	Can't generalise to other categories of people with confidence	
		Retraining required if original participant leaves project	Treat participant very nicely!

GLOSSARY

Half participants do conditions in a particular order and the other half take the conditions in the opposite order. This is done to balance (not eliminate) any order effects	_____	counterbalancing
Order effect which has greater strength in one particular order and where, therefore, counterbalancing would be ineffective	_____ _____ _____	asymmetrical order effect
		designs
Two or more separate groups take the various conditions of the IV	_____ _____	independent samples
" "	_____ _____	(between groups)
" "	_____ _____	(independent groups)
	_____ _____ _____	(independent subjects)
Each participant in one group/condition is paired on specific variable(s) with a participant in another group/condition	_____ _____	matched pairs
Each participant takes part in all conditions of the independent variable	_____ _____	repeated measures
" "	_____ _____	(within groups)
" "	_____ _____	(within subjects)
Design in which scores in one condition are paired with scores in other conditions	_____	related

Design in which particular scores in one condition cannot be paired (or linked) in any way with particular scores in any other condition	_____	unrelated
A confounding effect caused by experiencing one condition, then another, such as practice or fatigue	_____ _____	order effects
Random mixing together of items from both/all levels of the independent variable in order to avoid order effects	_____	randomisation
Study in which participants are given a short account of a person or deed and where just one aspect of the person or deed is varied across conditions	_____ _____	vignette study

EXERCISES

1 In Fantz's famous 'looking-chamber' experiment, a baby is shown two patterns and the researcher records how much time is spent looking at either pattern. The idea is to see whether the baby prefers complex patterns to simpler ones. What is the IV, the DV and what sort of design is this?

2 In one version of the 'visual cliff' experiment, infants are observed while their mothers try to entice them to come to them across a glass sheet with a large drop beneath it. What condition can be added to make this a true experiment and what sort of design would the experiment then be?

3 Your tutor conducts an experiment on your class. Each student is given a set of anagrams to solve and the time to solve each one is taken. You find that some of the anagrams were of concrete words and the others were of abstract words, in no particular order. This was the IV. What design was this, and what special precaution, associated with this design, has your tutor wisely taken and why?

4 Again your tutor conducts an experiment. Students are in pairs. You time your partner while she learns a finger maze, first with the left hand, then with the right. She then times you while you learn first with the right, then the left. What design is this? What special precaution is taken and why?

5 A researcher looks for families in which there are two brothers or two sisters born within a year of each other and where one sibling has suffered a certain illness before four years old. They are tested at eight years old to see whether the illness child is poorer than the other on number and reading skills. What sort of design is being employed here?

7

OBSERVATIONAL METHODS

The chapter covers most methods which are best classed as observation. In a sense, *all* data from people are gathered through some form of observation but, for instance, data gathered through questionnaire or interview deserve separate treatment.

Distinctions made are between:
- observation as a *technique* and as an overall research *design*
- participant (where observer is part of the observed group) and non-participant
- disclosed (people know what the observer is doing) and undisclosed
- structured and non-structured
- controlled (often in the laboratory) and naturalistic (observed's own environment)

Further topics are:
- role-play and simulation
- diaries
- advantages, difficulties and ethics of participant observation
- indirect observation (e.g. records, media)
- content analysis (treatment, often quantitative, of qualitative reports, writings)
- verbal protocols (verbal reports of participants' thoughts or silent speech)

INTRODUCTION

We have seen that there can be fairly serious problems with the use of the experimental method in psychology, particularly in the laboratory where a very narrow, and perhaps artificial, selection of behaviour may be studied, where 'demand characteristics' may distort the procedure and where persons studied are 'dehumanised'. A set of methods which can avoid some, but not always all, of these criticisms is the set known generally as 'observational methods'.

In a sense, behaviour is observed in every psychological study. A researcher makes observations on the participants' reaction times, answers to a questionnaire, memory performance and so on.

The emphasis, in using the term 'observational' however, is on the researcher observing *a relatively unconstrained segment of a person's freely chosen behaviour*.

There is ambiguity in the use of the term 'observational' in research literature. It can refer to the use of observation as a *technique* for gathering data about behaviour within an experimental design. On the other hand, 'observational' might describe the overall *design* of a study, in contrast to a controlled experiment.

OBSERVATION AS A TECHNIQUE OR AS AN OVERALL DESIGN

As technique

Observation may be used as a *technique* within a traditional experimental design, as in Milgram's (1963) work on obedience where, in addition to mechanical recordings of participants' responses, film record was made in order to observe changes in emotional reactions. We have previously described Bandura's (1965) studies on children's imitations of models for aggression. Using observation as a technique for measuring the DV of aggression, Bandura was able to manipulate a variety of IVs, including the status or role of the model, the consequences of the model's behaviour and the degree of frustration experienced by the child just prior to observing the aggressive model.

The two examples above employ observational techniques in a laboratory setting. Field experiments very often use observation as a technique. Friedrich and Stein's (1973) study, described earlier, is a good example. Observation may also be employed within a role play or simulation study, described later.

As overall design

If an investigation is given the title 'observational', this is usually in order to *contrast* it with other designs, particularly the experimental. In this case, the researcher has chosen to observe naturally occurring behaviour and *not* to experiment with it, i.e. no IV is manipulated. A hypothesis concerning an IV may nevertheless be tested, as when, for instance, an investigator observes the fantasy play of middle- and working-class children and predicts differences in amount or content.

WEAKNESS OF PURE OBSERVATIONAL STUDIES

Where the overall design is observational we have the weakness, outlined earlier, that if we discover a relationship between different sets of data we are not usually in a position to establish cause-effect relationships with any confidence, since manipulated IV has not led to changes in the DV.

Suppose we observe higher levels of aggression among children who choose and watch more violent television programmes. Does the television promote their aggression or does their aggression (arising from some other cause) affect their choice? A controlled experiment might provide enlightenment.

In an earlier chapter we saw that Friedrich and Stein (1972) assigned children to three experimental conditions – violent, pro-social and neutral television viewing programmes. After a month's viewing it was observed that the violent programme group were significantly more aggressive in nursery-school play. Interestingly, the impact was greatest on those children who were initially highest in aggression. An experiment, then, can back up a hypothesis formed from observation, by showing a fairly clear-cut causal effect.

PARTICIPANT AND NON-PARTICIPANT OBSERVATION

A PARTICIPANT OBSERVER is to some extent a part of the group of individuals being observed, whereas a NON-PARTICIPANT OBSERVER observes from a distance and should have no effect on the behaviour being observed. This is a 'dimension', since there are varying degrees of participation and these are described later on. There is also a dimensional aspect to DISCLOSURE in that persons observed can be more or less aware of the exact extent to which, or reasons for which, they are being observed.

The discussion of indirect, structured and controlled observation which follows is related entirely to non-participant studies. Participant observation is largely a qualitative approach and will be discussed later in the chapter.

STRUCTURED (OR 'SYSTEMATIC') OBSERVATIONS

DATA GATHERING DEVICES

Records of behaviour can be made using any or a mixture of the following devices:

- Film or video recording
- Still camera
- Audio tape (to record spoken observations)
- Hand-written notes, ratings or coding 'on the spot'

Visual recording has the advantage that behaviour can be analysed (rated or coded) after the event at any required pace.

All the methods above might be used discreetly such that the participant is either completely unaware of the recording process (in which case ethical issues arise) or at least unable to see or hear the equipment during the observation session. This can be achieved with the use of screens or 'one-way' mirrors, which act as a mirror for the participant but a window for observers or camera.

DATA GATHERING SYSTEMS

Observers may often work to a specific 'grid' of behavioural categories. On the chart in Table 7.1, observers of children's behaviour during a free-play nursery session, might record the amount of time or frequency that each child spent in each of the particular activities categorised (in columns).

Table 7.1 *Chart for data gathering*

Child	Inactive	Reading	Playing alone	Looking on	Playing with others		
					Different activity	Same activity	Cooperative activity
A							
B							
C etc.							

In addition to simply recording what behaviour occurs, and how often, observers may be required to:

RATE behaviour according to a structured scale – for instance one to 10 on 'showing interest'

CODE behaviour according to a set of coding categories – for instance, graphic symbols which represent the positions of parts of the body

In each case, some degree of standardisation would normally be sought by giving observers, intensive training prior to commencement of observation sessions.

To exemplify some of these points we can look at a study by Halliday and Leslie (1986) in which acts of communication between mother and child (both ways) were coded from video recordings made over a period of six months' data gathering. The researchers sought to extend Bruner's ideas and show that children do more than just make requests or references in their interactions. They were interested in how these other actions might contribute to language acquisition as the child increasingly finds non-verbal methods inadequate. The researchers identified a set of 42 different actions, shown in Table 7.2, during *pilot* sessions with a couple of mother–child pairs. In the main study, an average of 12 half-hour sessions were recorded with 12 mother–child pairs. Each of these video sessions was coded using the 42 categories. There could be as many as five actions from the mother, and five from the child, in any five-second interval. I quote the detail here to give you some idea of the mountain of coding and analysis which goes on in such a study. The success of standardisation was estimated by finding the number of occasions upon which two observers agreed

Table 7.2 *Complete list of codes with short definitions (from Halliday et al. 1986)*

Verbal categories

A	Demands attention	ON	Orders not to
D	Describes, gives information	PR	Praises
ET	Gives detailed label	PT	Prompts
F	Corrects	Q	Questions
I	Imitates completely	QT	Questions about a label
IP	Imitates partially	S	Tells story or recites
IQ	Imitates as question		rhyme
IS	Imitates as sentence	T	Labels, names
N	Says 'no'	TH	Says 'thank you' or 'ta'
NU	Count	Y	Says 'yes'
O	Orders, gives positive commands	Z	Adds tag

Non-verbal categories

a)	*Vocal*	**b)**	*Non-vocal*
B	Babbles (with intonation)	GO	Gives object
G	Laughs, giggles	H	Holds, takes hold of
QN	Makes questioning noise	L	Looks around
V	Makes monosyllabic vocalisation	LO	Looks at object
V2	Makes two-syllable vocalisation	LP	Looks at mother
		LI	Lifts child
VE	Makes an emotional noise	OB	Obeys
VN	Makes an object-specific noise	P	Points
		PL	Plays
VS	Vocalises one-syllable continuously	R	Reaches
		TO	Touches
W	Cries		
YN	Makes affirmative noise		

on 15% of the tapes. The figure was 76.7% and this is a form of *reliability* check (see below).

TIME, POINT AND EVENT SAMPLING

It may not always be possible or appropriate to record complete sequences of behaviour and interaction using video. If a session must be observed 'live', several observers might be required, one or two for each person observed. Where only one or a few observers are available, TIME SAMPLING techniques can be employed, in which observations of each individual are made for several short periods in say, a two-hour session. In some cases, the short periods of, say, 15 seconds, are consecutive, so that a picture of the frequency of behaviour is built up.

In POINT SAMPLING an observer concentrates on each individual in a group just long enough to record the category of their current behaviour before going on to observe the next person.

In EVENT SAMPLING observations are made of a specific event each time it occurs, for instance, each example of a 'fight', however this is operationally defined for the research in progress.

RELIABILITY OF OBSERVATIONAL TECHNIQUES

Observers need to produce reliable observational records. The reliability of observers can be established by correlating (Chapter 18) their records with those of another observer or team. Such comparison will produce a measure of INTERRATER RELIABIL-ITY, 'rater' being another term for an observer who 'rates' behaviour.

Reliability may be low because of OBSERVER BIAS. From the psychology of perception we know that each person's view of a situation is unique and that our perceptions can be biased by innumerable factors. An untrained observer might readily *evaluate* behaviour which the researcher wants reported as objectively as possible. Where the trained observer reports a hard blow, the novice might describe this as 'vicious'.

There may be human error in failing to observe some bits of behaviour at all. One is reminded of the 'blind' soccer referee or ice-skating judge. In the study of animals it is easy to 'see' human characteristics in animal behaviour. This is known as 'anthropomorphism' and occurs, for instance, when birds are said to be 'talking' or a cat to be 'smiling'. In human studies, it could be falsely assumed that Jason 'follows' an adult (and is perhaps insecure) when he happens to be walking in the same direction. Or Jenny might be mistakenly described as 'copying' when she looks into a box to see what it was Sarah was looking at.

The problem may not lie with the human observers, however, but with the rating scale they are given which could be too vague or ambiguous. Reliability is enhanced by specifying in advance precisely what behavioural acts are to count in particular categories. Observers have to decide, for instance, when a push counts as aggressive or when a child is 'demanding'. Observers are usually trained to a standard of reliability and accuracy *before* the observational study proper begins.

CONTROLLED OBSERVATION

Observations can be controlled through structure as outlined above. Control can also be exercised over the environment in which observations take place. A high degree of environmental control can be exercised in the laboratory, though the participant need not be acutely aware that the environment *is* a 'laboratory'. Discussion groups may be observed in a comfortable 'seminar room', for instance. Mary Ainsworth (1971), mentioned earlier, conducted a programme of research into infants' stranger and separation anxiety. In this study, the floor of a carefully organised playroom was marked into squares and trained observers recorded on film (and by speaking onto audiotape) the movements of a child when its mother left and a stranger entered the room. The infants' behaviour was also filmed and the results were related to events of sensitivity in mothers' interactions with their children.

OBJECTIONS TO CONTROL – NATURALISTIC OBSERVATION

Studies in the laboratory do not escape many of the criticisms of laboratory experiments made earlier, in the sense that the laboratory can provide a highly artificial, possibly inhibiting atmosphere. Behaviour in the normal social context cannot be observed here. Some researchers, in order to record more usual, everyday behaviour, go out into the field and make 'naturalistic' observations in, say, the home, the nursery or the workplace. The method was inherited by psychology largely from the ethologists (Lorenz, Tinbergen) who studied animals in their natural habitat but nevertheless made very detailed and accurate recordings of what they showed to be instinctive patterns of behaviour.

The early 'baby biographers', whom we shall encounter when discussing the 'diary method' below, were carrying out naturalistic observations, as did Piaget on his own children. Perhaps these studies also incorporated a certain amount of participative involvement on the part of the observers, however!

Because the behaviour observed in these studies, so long as the observer is discreet, would have occurred anyway, realism and aspects of ecological validity are likely to be high. In some studies, however, people are aware that they are being observed. This can mean a video camera following them around the house for instance. In this case we still have the problem of possibly distorted behaviour. As Shaffer (1985) describes:

> Consider the experiences of one graduate student who attempted to take pictures of children's playground antics. What he recorded in many of his photos was somewhat less than spontaneous play. For example, one child who was playing alone with a doll jumped up when the student approached with the camera and informed him that he should take a picture of her 'new trick' on the monkey bars. Another child . . . said 'Get this' as he broke away from the kickball game and laid a blindside tackle on an unsuspecting onlooker

What researchers *can* do is to become a predictable and familiar part of the environment. For instance, Charlesworth and Hartup (1967) made several visits to a nursery school, interacted with the children, learnt their names and so on. This also gave them the opportunity to test out and improve the reliability of the observation scheme they were going to employ.

Examples of research studies, from the general literature, which used naturalistic observation would be:

Brown et al. (1964)   – study of Adam, Eve and Sarah's speech productions in the home with parents every one or two weeks for several years

Caldwell & Bradley (1978) – developed the Home Observation for Measurement of the Environment (HOME) inventory, which observes parent–child interaction and provision of play materials, to be correlated with levels of intellectual development.

List the advantages and disadvantages of naturalistic observation as you understand it.

Box 7.1 *Advantages and disadvantages of naturalistic observation*

Advantages	Disadvantages
The behaviour which occurs is more natural and is (if the target is unaware of the observer) unaffected by anxiety or the target's need to impress	Extraneous variables are poorly controlled, if at all
Study is realistic and likely to produce higher ecological validity	There is greater potential for observer bias, since both extraneous variables and the observed behaviour are more unpredictable
This approach is useful where:	It is difficult to transport and use discretely some of the technical equipment required for good recordings
It would be unethical to experiment with, or intervene in the lives of, children or animals	It is difficult sometimes for observers to remain hidden
Individuals would be unlikely to cooperate with interview or questionnaire methods	Thorough replication is harder to achieve
The researcher decides that the full social context is necessary for the observed behaviour to carry meaning	If it uses a structured data gathering system it has the disadvantages of structured observation outlined below

OBJECTIONS TO STRUCTURED OBSERVATION

Because observation can be so structured and rigid, it would be considered inadequate by groups of (usually social) psychologists who argue against the reduction of behaviour to artificially isolated units. What *is* the smallest unit we can work with? To describe a person as 'lifting an arm' may be objective *physically* but is stripped of social meaning compared with 'she waved', 'he made a bid' or 'she threatened the child'. Reduction to the simplest units of behaviour (the 'molecular' level) can create observations which are numerous, separated and meaningless.

The attempt to categorise interactions or assess responses by number can produce data at the 'reliable but not rich' end of the data-gathering spectrum. This positivist approach would be criticised by, for instance, humanists and phenomenologists, who promote a 'holistic' view of the person in psychology.

Diesing (1972) states that the holist (psychologist) studies a 'whole human system in its natural setting', and says:

> The holist standpoint includes the belief that human systems tend to develop a characteristic wholeness or integrity. They are not simply a loose collection of traits or wants or reflexes or variables of any sort . . .; they have a unity that manifests itself in nearly every part . . . This means that the characteristics of a part are largely determined by the whole to which it belongs and by its particular location in the whole system.

Something is lost, it would be argued, by pigeon-holing responses and simply counting them, or by giving them a rating-scale value. It is more important to record events observed such that the social meaning of actions is preserved for analysis. This may mean recording as much as possible of the social context in which actions occurred. It may also mean making a comprehensive record of an individual's behaviour, such that specific actions are understood and perceived within the pattern of that person's unique experiences and motivation. It is not possible to do this using a highly constraining 'grid' or other pre-constructed framework for observation. We now turn to methods which attempt to generate a richer account of human behaviour in initially unquantified, descriptive form; that is, qualitative data.

QUALITATIVE NON-PARTICIPANT OBSERVATION

In Ainsworth's study, described above, some of the observers produced a running commentary on each child's behaviour by speaking into a tape recorder as they watched. The same technique has been used by observers following the interactions of mothers and children in their own home. This generates a lot of raw data in qualitative form. These studies however are not usually conducted under the holistic banner. Rigid structure may be imposed on the data, during analysis, by independent raters trained in the ways already mentioned.

Some studies of this sort, though, do go further along the qualitative route. The unquantified, descriptive data may not be simply categorised or coded. The data may also be analysed for illuminative insights leading to fresh research topics. Or they may be presented alongside quantitative analysis in order to illustrate qualitative differences and issues which numerical reports cannot portray. It is even possible that the *sorts* of observation made might change as the study progresses as a result of FORMATIVE revision of method, where feedback from early observations informs the researcher on optimum ways to proceed. The more the aim of the study tends away from purely positivist analysis, the more the data gathered become susceptible to the qualitative methods outlined in Chapters 11 and 25.

ROLE-PLAY AND SIMULATION

Discussion of these methods is situated here because, although some observations of role-play have been relatively pre-structured, the tendency has been to develop categories and models from fairly free-flowing, unrestricted participant behaviour and speech. In some cases, participants *observe* role-plays (non-active role), but, by and large, it is participants' role-playing which is observed (active role).

The techniques have been used for a long time in psychological research, particularly in the area of social psychology, but their use became highlighted when they were advocated as an alternative to the use of gross experimental deception during the 1970s.

ACTIVE ROLE

The study might require active role-playing within a simulated social setting, such as being asked to get to know a stranger. Participants may take on a specific role – being chairperson of a group making risky decisions. Participants have been asked to role-play in juries of various sizes, under varying pressures, whilst dynamics of the situation are recorded. These may be, for instance, the informal rules which are developed in the group (Davis et al., 1975).

People have been asked to simulate various emotional feelings and accompanying behavioural expressions.

In all these cases observations may be made at the time or behaviour filmed for subsequent detailed analysis.

NON-ACTIVE ROLE

Participants may be asked to watch a role-play or simulated performance and then be asked to report feelings, reactions or suggestions as to how the depicted scene might continue. They may be asked how they would behave in the continuing situation.

In this case, the simulation simply serves as material for what is basically a question-asking method belonging in the next chapter. One approach, the one which started the controversy over experimental deception, is worth mentioning. Mixon (1979) was analysing Milgram's famous studies on 'destructive obedience' (for an account of this experimental paradigm, see Chapter 26). Mixon's objection was partly moral but also that the true social situation, for the participant in Milgram's experiment, had not been thoroughly understood.

Milgram described the experiment to many other people, very few of whom said they would expect anyone to continue obeying the experimenter in giving electric shocks to an obviously suffering 'learner'. Mixon argued that Milgram made it obvious to these people that the experiment was really about 'destructive obedience'. Mixon gave his participants scripts of the experiment to read *with no clue* given to the real experimental aims. He asked them to describe how they thought the experiment would continue. He then altered the scripts with different groups. Only when the script included the experimenter seeming a little concerned for the victim did all participants say that they expected Milgram's participants to discontinue obedience. Mixon argues that the social context of Milgram's experiment gives strong messages that the norms of scientific professionalism are in place and that no harm can come to the victim (though, obviously, pain is occurring).

In a few cases the participant can be actor *and* audience. Storms (1973) had people engage in a two-person interaction which was filmed. They then viewed the film either seeing only their partner or only themselves. This had significant effects upon their attributions of cause to the behaviour observed.

PURPOSES OF ROLE-PLAY AND SIMULATION

Ginsburg (1979) argues that these methods can be used for discovery and verification. In discovery, general observations might be made which lead to more specifically testable hypotheses or models. In verification, hypotheses such as Mixon's can be tested.

Ginsburg thinks that the most valuable use is for illuminating what he calls the 'role/rule framework' under which actions occur. They will not tell us a lot about individuals but perhaps a lot about the rules people assume or invent, and follow, given certain social situations. They may show us how people go about negotiating such rules. They may tell us about sequences and hierarchies of social action.

WEAKNESSES OF ROLE-PLAY AND SIMULATION

Critics, early on, argued that role-play was non-spontaneous and passive; that people would act in socially desirable and superficial ways; and that what people said they would do and what they would do were very different matters.

Proponents argued back that experiments, too, can produce artificial, superficial behaviour and that deception itself, of the Milgram variety, introduced unreal conflict, for participants, between what seemed to be happening and what could be expected to happen in a humane, scientific establishment.

On the issue of spontaneity, several studies are cited as producing very great personal commitment and lack of pretence, perhaps the most dramatic being that of Zimbardo (1972), described briefly in Chapter 26, which had to be ended after five of its planned 14 days because students acting as 'prison guards' were being so ruthless and callous, whilst 'prisoners' were becoming so submissive and dejected.

THE DIARY METHOD

Towards the end of the nineteenth century, some academics began to realise that they could not argue endlessly about whether children were born with innate tendencies, 'inherently good' as Rousseau would have claimed, or with Locke's 'tabula rasa' for a mind. They realised that a scientific approach was necessary. The first steps towards this were taken by the 'baby biographers', of whom Charles Darwin (1877) is probably the most notable. Data were in the form of a diary of daily observations on the growth and development of his own son. Most diaries were developmental records of the observers' own children. The studies were therefore 'longitudinal' (see Chapter 10).

A problem with these diary accounts was that each biographer had their own particular perspective to support and tended to concentrate on quite different aspects of their child's behaviour from other diarists. They also tended not to standardise the intervals between their recordings.

Later, as child development study became a well-established discipline, Piaget kept diaries of the development of his children. He had a thorough model of cognitive development and his observations were used to exemplify aspects of the theory (*not* to 'prove it true'). He developed tests or demonstrations of some characteristics of children's thought at various ages – such as egocentricity – which he then used with other children, employing the CLINICAL METHOD (see Chapter 8).

Diaries are also kept during most participant observation studies. Where observation is covert these will be constructed, where possible, at the end of each day, either completely from memory or from any discreetly jotted notes recorded where opportunities have arisen.

In both these uses, the diary method has the great advantage that the observed persons are acting quite naturally, particularly so in the case of babies, since they are at home with their own parents. This must be a source of some of the richest, most genuine and intimate data in the business!

Jones and Fletcher (1992) asked couples to keep a daily diary of mood, stress and sleep variation over a period of three weeks. They found significant correlations (see

Chapter 18) overall, between partner pairs, on each of these three variables, supporting the view that occupational stress is transmitted from one partner to the other, although individual couples varied very much in the extent to which their stress levels were comparable.

A further, unusual use of diaries has occurred in participative research (see Chapter 11) where participants themselves keep diaries of their activities and perceptions throughout a study. The researcher then subjects the diary content to some form of content analysis. Rajesh Tandon (1981) did this in a study aimed at improving peer group organisation and initiative taking in a rural agricultural training and modernisation programme. He found that questionnaire data gathered was often at odds with the diary records, the latter being far more congruent with the researcher's own field notes.

Box 7.2 *Advantages and disadvantages of the traditional diary method*

Advantages	Disadvantages
Rich, genuine information	Observer bias can be high
Natural surroundings	Comparison with other diary studies difficult because of variation in emphasis
Observed participant completely relaxed	
Simple to conduct if in observer's own home	Commitment to quite long-term study

PARTICIPANT OBSERVATION

It follows from the line of argument above that a more authentic observation of people can be made by being involved in their day-to-day interactions within their normal network of human group relationships. The meaning of their behaviour should then be more accessible to the observer for ecologically valid recording. Whether these objectives can be achieved in a manner which would still count as scientific is a matter of heated debate and one which will be evaluated later on.

The degree to which an observer can participate in the group being studied is a continuum according to Patton (1980). He distinguishes between the following:

Full participant

The observer's true research role is hidden ('undisclosed') and members take her/him as an authentic member of the group. Hence, secrets may well be disclosed. However, Douglas (1972) argues that a respected and trusted, *known* researcher may be handed secrets that a real member might not receive for fear that the real member could use these against the divulger.

Participant as observer

The participant's observational role is not hidden but 'kept under wraps'. It is not seen to be the main reason for the participant's presence. Members relate to the participant mainly through roles and activities central to the group. An example here might be that of a researcher who effectively becomes a temporary member of a school's teaching staff in order to conduct research of which other staff are aware in general terms. Alternatively, a teacher might conduct research for a further qualification and use her work setting as a study.

Observer as participant

Here the observer role is uppermost and members of the group *accept* the observer in their midst as researcher. If valued, the researcher may be given quite intimate information but will be constrained in reporting it when such information is offered as secret.

Full observer

The role of uninvolved observer which we've already discussed as 'non-participant observation'.

UNDISCLOSED PARTICIPANT OBSERVATION

Classic examples of these studies are:

Festinger et al. (1956) – Joined a religious sect which believed the world would end on a certain date. He and his colleagues followed developments up to and just past the fateful moment, observing reactions during the last moments of life and the subsequent 'reprieve'. An interesting account can be found in Brown (1965).

Whyte (1943) – Studied an Italian street gang in Chicago by joining it. It was obvious Whyte was not a normal gang member. His 'cover' was that he was writing a book about the area. Most famous for his statement that 'I began as a non-participating observer. As I became accepted into the community, I found myself becoming almost a non-observing participant'.

Frankenburg (1957) – Studied a Welsh village and is often cited for his initiative in solving the problem of not 'blowing cover' yet taking good notes by becoming secretary of the local football club.

Rosenhan (1973) – A still controversial study which promoted criticism of the medical establishment's handling, labelling and diagnosis of psychiatric manifestations. Researchers presented themselves at hospital out-patients' departments complaining of hearing voices making certain noises in their heads. During their subsequent voluntary stays in a psychiatric ward they made observations on staff and patient behaviour and attitudes towards them. Patients often detected the 'normality' of the researchers well before the staff. An excellent example of seeing behaviour as pathological because of its producer's 'label' was the fact that a nurse recorded a researcher's note-taking as 'excessive writing behaviour'. To be fair, the nurse was dutifully carrying out strict instructions to observe and record anything unusual in patients' behaviour.

ETHICAL ISSUES IN UNDISCLOSED PARTICIPANT OBSERVATION

One of the reasons humanists, for instance, object to many psychological experiments (such as Milgram's (1963) or Asch's (1956)) is that they involve DECEPTION of participants. Participant observation which is undisclosed obviously suffers this criticism too. The researcher has also to decide what, if anything, can be published without the group's or any individual's consent. A particular hazard is that, when the observer 'comes clean' and declares the research role, any one individual studied may not be able to recall what they have divulged, or how they have behaved, since the research began. The individual should be allowed to view material for publication and to veto material which they object to where anonymity does not protect against the nature of the material identifying them.

Lack of consent-seeking leads to a greater mistrust of the distant and elite research body. An answer to the problem of deception is, of course, to disclose one's research role and objectives. These ethical issues are more fully discussed in Chapter 26.

DISCLOSED PARTICIPANT OBSERVATION

An example would be the study of Becker (1958) whose observers joined a group of medical students in lectures and laboratory sessions and engaged in casual conversation both in work time and in the social atmosphere of their dormitories. They also joined in ward rounds and discussion groups and spent some time simply watching the students' various activities.

In a strong sense, it could be argued that Whyte's study is disclosed since, for the gang members, writing a book about them and doing some research on them could hardly be distinguished. The studies of anthropologists, such as those of Margaret Mead (1928, 1930), whose work contributes to psychological debate and evidence, are disclosed participant observations in which the observer lives for a long period in a culture other than their own (see Chapter 10).

> What strengths and weaknesses can you see in the use of participant observation? List the advantages and disadvantages of disclosure.

STRENGTHS OF PARTICIPANT OBSERVATION

Flexibility

A pre-set structure for observation, interview or survey questionnaire imposes the researcher's framework, assumptions and priorities on those who are to be studied. What is relevant in the target group's social world has already been decided. Participant observation is flexible. What is to be included as data in the study is not set in concrete at the outset. Indeed, the extent to which the observer will participate may not be the same throughout the study, as Whyte's famous statement above makes clear. Whyte also found that through participant observation 'I learned the answers to questions I would not have had the sense to ask had I been getting my information solely on an interviewing basis.'

Relationship with observed group

Specific groups in the local environment, such as gangs or strongly-identifying cultural groups, are likely to see an establishment researcher as an authority figure and to be consequently suspicious. Methods for research, other than participant observation, such as interviewing or survey by questionnaire, do not give the researcher long enough to establish trust and to dissipate such suspicions. The research encounter is too brief to ensure genuine cooperation. Participant observation may sometimes be the only way to discover what truly makes such groups 'tick' and to find out which expressed attitudes stem from prior and perhaps deeper values and beliefs.

Kidder (1981) argues that the *longer* the participant observer spends in a research setting, where their aims and purpose are disclosed to group members, the *less* likely it is that their presence will influence or distort the behaviour of the observed persons. This seeming paradox is explained by pointing out that, although group members may wish to appear in a certain light to the observer, if this behaviour is unnatural for them they will not be able to sustain it for long among friends and relatives. Even if the observer does not recognise artificiality, friends and co-workers will, and the observer is likely to hear about it. Kidder adds that it is much easier for experimental, one-day participants, whose identities remain anonymous, to distort reality by behaving quite uncharacteristically.

Other advantages are summarised below.

DIFFICULTIES WITH PARTICIPANT OBSERVATION

The presence of a participant observer must change group behaviour to some degree, if only marginally since, unless the researcher remains mute and passive (and therefore *doesn't* participate), interactions must occur which wouldn't have occurred otherwise. Here is a statement from one of the members of Whyte's gang:

> You've slowed me down plenty since you've been down here. Now, when I do something, I have to think what Bill Whyte would want me to know about it and how I can explain it. Before I used to do these things by instinct.

Pretty damning for the researcher who claims their presence to be unobtrusive and non-influential. However, researchers like Whyte argue that they blended into and became a part of the activities of the group, rather than changing what happened substantially, supporting Kidder's view above.

As Whyte's statement on page 104 testifies, the researcher obviously becomes socially and emotionally involved in the group and this must cast doubt on their eventual objectivity in reporting. The participant observation supporter would argue, however, that the attempt to be totally objective leads to the artificiality and rigidity we discussed earlier.

The participant researcher can't usually make notes at the time of observation. Most have to rely on diary-keeping after the day's events. Frankenburg, as we noted earlier, found a crafty way to record notes under cover of being a club secretary, but this method would not be available to the observer of street-corner gang life. Necessarily then, most participant observers are prey to the psychological factors of memory loss and distortion.

Since the researcher is the only observer present and since events observed are unique, there is none of the usual opportunity to verify results objectively. Conclusions can only be loosely generalised to similar situations and groups.

INDIRECT OBSERVATION

Some events have already occurred but can serve as empirical evidence for social science theories. Durkheim, a sociologist, made ground-breaking studies of relative rates of suicide, comparing these with varying social conditions.

Many events, like suicide, are of interest to psychologists and are either unpredictable or do not occur often enough for thorough scientific research. Governmental elections are relatively infrequent and make the study of voting behaviour somewhat inconvenient. Behaviour cannot be observed directly in events such as earthquakes and suicide.

Psychological researchers might, instead, use observed social statistics as data. These can be drawn from historical sources ('ARCHIVAL DATA'), government information or the media. Television programmes might, for example, be observed for

Box 7.3 *Advantages and disadvantages of observational study types*

	Advantages	Disadvantages
Non-participant		
Laboratory	More flexible behaviour than that studied in laboratory experiment	Behaviour can be quite artificial with low ecological validity
	Stricter variable control	Participants can guess what researcher is expecting to see
	Can be part of experiment indicating cause-effect direction	Participants may be affected by knowledge that they are being observed
Naturalistic	Higher ecological validity likely than in a laboratory	
	Can be used where unethical to experiment, where verbal reports not available and where direct questioning would be rejected	Rarely possible to use in experiment indicating cause-effect direction
		Higher potential for observer bias
	Participants can be unaware of being observed and therefore behave naturally in social context	Difficult to hide observer or equipment
		Thorough replication less likely
Participant	Higher ecological validity likely than in laboratory	Researcher has to rely on memory
	Much richer information from intense and lengthy interaction	Emotional involvement makes objectivity less easy to maintain
	Meanings of actors' behaviour more available	Problem of keeping cover if required
	Lack of formality and presence of trust gives insights unavailable from any other method	Researcher's behaviour alters that of group members
		May be un-replicable and no one can check validity of data gathered
		May be difficult to generalise any result

examples of gender stereotyping. The fact that young black people obtain fewer interviews and less jobs compared with white youngsters might be attributed to black youngsters having lower qualifications. A researcher can eliminate this hypothesis with an observation of employment statistics which show that this discrepancy occurs among black and white youngsters with *equal* qualifications. This could also be called a survey of labour statistics. The common use of 'survey' is discussed in Chapter 8.

Note that, although indirect, these studies do make observations on the behaviour of people and, through some interpretation, prevailing attitudes. Notice that this is a perfectly legitimate way to test and eliminate hypotheses about causal factors in social phenomena. The observation of electronic or printed media coverage could be subjected to CONTENT ANALYSIS.

CONTENT ANALYSIS

Originally, the formalised approach called 'content analysis' was a specific method devised for sampling and analysing messages from the media and other recorded material, such as literature, famous people's speeches, or wartime propaganda.

Attempts to analyse media messages can be dated back to the turn of the century, when various writers were concerned about standards, about validity and about the influence of the press on society, crime and morals. In the 1930s and 1940s, however, content analysis 'took off', first because 'weighty' social psychological theory turned towards it for supporting evidence, second because propaganda became a serious threat before and during the war, and third, because the electronic media (radio, TV, film) could no longer be considered an extension of the press.

In this use it was seen as a quantifying instrument for descriptive information, as this definition demonstrates:

> ... content analysis broadly describes a heterogenous domain of techniques which are focused upon the (more or less) systematic, objective and quantitative description of a communication or series of communications.
> (Crano & Brewer (1973))

This, then, is another way of observing, not people directly, but the communications they have produced. The communications concerned were originally those already published, but some researchers conduct content analysis on materials which they *ask* people to produce, such as essays, answers to interview questions, diaries and verbal protocols (described later).

Examples of analysis of existing materials

SHNEIDMAN (1963) – Analysed the speeches of Kennedy and Nixon in their televised presidential debates, demonstrating differences in their logical argument.

OGILVIE ET AL. (1966) – Analysed real and simulated suicide notes with some success in discriminating between the two. In this case the simulated notes did not exist naturally but were written by persons matched for the real note-writers' characteristics.

BRUNER AND KELSO (1980) – Reviewed studies of 'restroom' graffiti spanning 30 years. Most studies analysed the material either at a superficial level – the overt content of statements – or at an interpretive, often psychoanalytic level. Bruner and Kelso analysed the messages 'semiotically', concluding that women's graffiti were more interpersonal and interactive, tending to contain questions and advice about love, relationships and commitment. Men's graffiti tended to be egocentric and competitive, concentrating on conquests and prowess. Their messages served the function of confirming a position of control and the maintenance of power, whereas women's messages reflected the cooperation and mutual help strategies of the dominated.

MANSTEAD AND MCCULLOCH (1981) – Content analysed 170 British television advertisements for gender role portrayal and found several differences in accordance with traditional stereotypes. For a detailed discussion of this study, and the limitations of content analysis as a method, see Gross (1994).

CUMBERBATCH (1990) – Analysed over 500 prime-time advertisements over a two-week period in 1990 involving over 200 character appearances. 75% of men but only

25% of women were judged to be over 30 years old. Men outnumbered women 2:1 and 89% of voice-overs, especially for expert/official information, were male. 50% of female voice-overs were categorised as 'sexy/sensuous'. The ratio of women to men rated as 'attractive' was 3:2. Men were as likely to be engaged in housework for friends as for their family, whilst females predominantly worked for their family and never friends.

Analysis of specially produced materials

KOUNIN AND GUMP (1961) – Asked children about bad school behaviour. They were in two groups, those of punitive and of non-punitive teachers. As predicted, content analysis of the interview protocols showed that children of punitive teachers were more concerned with aggression. Here, content analysis was used in a traditional hypothesis-testing design.

Content analysis has been used on plays, folklore, legend, nursery rhymes and even popular music in order to demonstrate differences between cultures and subcultures and within cultures over time. The preoccupations of various magazines, newspapers and journals have been linked, through content analysis, with the various political leanings of such publications. Changes in content have been used as indicators of change in public attitude (although they *could* indicate changes in the politics of the newspaper owner).

THE PROCESS OF CONTENT ANALYSIS

SAMPLING – The researcher has the problem of deciding just what material to sample from all that exists. For newspapers, this will mean making a decision based on political leaning, price, target readership and so on. For visual media, a representative sampling of programmes, times, advertising slots and so on, must occur. Advertising is often linked to the content of adjacent programmes.

CODING UNITS – These are the units into which the analysed material is to be categorised. These can be as shown in Box 7.4.

It became common in the 1980s to investigate children's literature and both children and adult television programmes for evidence of stereotyping, negative images or sheer omission of women or members of minority ethnic groups. Try the following exercise:

> Imagine that you are going to conduct a practical exercise in which the aim is to investigate cultural stereotyping in children's books, old and new. We are interested in the extent to which, and ways in which, black people are portrayed. What units (words, themes, characters) might you ask your coders to look out for?

Here are some possible units:

black person in picture
black person in leading role
black person in subsidiary role
European features; face made darker
disappearance from story pictures of black person who appeared earlier
success/failure/trouble – black and white characters compared
inappropriate words: 'coloured', 'immigrant'
portrayed as foreign/savage/'primitive' etc.
portrayed as comic, troublesome or problematic

Note: content analysis can highlight the *omission* of items, themes and characters.

Box 7.4 *Coding units*

Unit	Examples
word	Analyse for sex-related words in different magazines
theme	Analyse for occasions, in children's literature, on which boy/girl initiates and gets praised
item	Look for whole stories e.g. article on Northern Ireland
character	Analyse types of character occurring in TV cartoons
time and space	Count space or time devoted to particular issue in media

PROCEDURE

In the traditional model, the researcher will present coders with a preconstructed system for categorising occurrences. This means that the researcher will have to become very familiar with the sort of materials likely to be encountered prior to the start of the content analysis exercise.

As with observation, coders may be asked to *categorise* only, thus producing *nominal level* data. Or they may be asked to *rank* items, for instance, a set of open-ended responses on self-image, ranked for 'confidence'. Alternatively, each item might be *rated*: children's drawings could be scored for 'originality'. In the last two cases the measurement level would be *ordinal*. Nominal and ordinal data are levels of measurement introduced in Chapter 12. In the interests of removing researcher bias the coding might now be entirely completed by assistants who are unaware of the research hypothesis, if there is one. It has also been common to test for inter-coder reliability using correlational techniques (see Chapter 18).

VERBAL PROTOCOLS

In the last decade or so there has been an increase in use of VERBAL PROTOCOLS. These are the recorded product of asking participants to talk or think aloud during an activity. They may report on the thoughts they have whilst trying to solve a mental arithmetic problem, or 'talk through' the reasons for their decisions whilst operating a complex piece of machinery, such as the control-room instruments in a nuclear power installation. The method is closely linked with the practice of KNOWLEDGE ELICITATION.

The interesting development has been this generation of basically qualitative data in the heartland of experimental method – cognitive psychology. Ericsson and Simon (1984) made a strong case for the use of verbal reports as data. Good theories of problem-solving should produce rules from which problem-solving by humans can be simulated. Verbal protocols can then be compared with the simulation in order to verify the theory. Ericsson and Simon argued that asking participants to talk while they work does not necessarily impair their performance. It depends on what the verbalising instructions are. These could be:

1 Verbalise your silent speech – what you would say to yourself anyway whilst solving this problem (doing this task) – known as a 'talk aloud' instruction.

2 Verbalise whatever thoughts occur to you whilst doing this task – a 'think aloud' instruction.

3 Verbalise your thoughts and decisions and give reasons for these.

In analysing the results of many studies they found that only type **3** instructions seriously affected performance – not surprising really, since the participant is being asked to do so much in addition to the task. Type **2** instructions did not seriously affect accuracy but did slow down solution times. Type **1** instructions had little effect on time or accuracy. In addition, they found that *concurrent* verbal reports (produced as a task is performed) were more valid than retrospective ones. 'Implicit' knowledge (Broadbent et al., 1986) produces greater distortion than 'explicit' knowledge, the latter being more readily available, such as the easily stated verbal rules used to solve a problem. Implicit knowledge is often in non-verbal form and hard to articulate.

Knowledge elicitation work has generated 'expert systems' – bodies of knowledge about procedures, for instance in medical diagnosis, derived from the verbal protocols of experts. In addition, the difference between experts and novices has been the subject of research, either for practical uses, in the reduction of life-threatening work errors for instance, or as pure academic research on expertise in problem-solving. A further academic use is in the investigation of people's 'mental models' of everyday systems (e.g. your central heating) or laboratory produced simulations (e.g. launching a space ship).

Corcoran (1986) used verbal protocols with six expert and five novice nurses to investigate their approach to three cases of differing complexity. Novices were less systematic with the low complexity case, compared with experts.

Martin and Klimowski (1990) attempted to investigate the mental processes employed by managers as they evaluated their own and their subordinates' performance. It was found that they used more internal attributions when evaluating others than when evaluating themselves. An internal attribution occurs when we see behaviour as largely caused by a person's enduring characteristics, rather than blaming the surrounding situation.

GLOSSARY

Data obtained from existing records	_____ ____	archival data
System used to categorise observations	_____	coding
Analysis of content of media sources. Now also often used to quantify content of diaries, descriptions, verbal reports etc. through coding, categorisation and rating	_____ _____	content analysis
Data-gathering method where participant makes regular (often daily) record of relevant events	_____ _____	diary method
Letting people know that they are the object of observation	_____	disclosure
Observation and recording of specific events defined for the study	_____ _____	event sampling

Approach to observation in which the focus of observation may change as the study progresses and early data are analysed	_____ _____	formative approach
Gathering data which is assumed to form the observed person's knowledge and understanding of a specific system, often using verbal protocols	_____ _____	knowledge elicitation

		observation types
Observation in which many variables are kept constant	_____	controlled
Observations not made on people directly but upon data previously recorded or created by people	_____	indirect
Observation without intervention in observed people's own environment	_____	naturalistic
Observation in which observer does not take part or play a role in the group observed	___-_____	non-participant
Observation in which observer takes part or plays a role in the group observed	_____	participant
Observation which uses an explicitly defined framework for data recording	_____ _____	structured observation

Study which is solely observational and does not include any experimentation	_____ _____	observation design
Study using observation in some way and which may or may not be an experiment	_____ _____	observation technique
Effect causing unwanted variations in data recorded which are produced because of characteristics of the observer	_____ ____	observer bias
Extent to which observers agree in their rating or coding	_____ _____	observer (or inter-rater) reliability
Observation of one person long enough to record one category of behaviour before moving on to next individual to be observed	_____ _____	point sampling
Assessment of behaviour observed by choosing a point along a scale	_____	rating
Study in which participants act out parts	____-____	role-play
Study in which participants recreate and play through, to some extent, a complete social setting	_____	simulation

Observation of individuals for set lengths of time	_____ _____	time sampling
Recording of participants' talk when they have been asked to talk or think aloud	_____ _____	verbal protocol

EXERCISES

1 Outline a research study which would use observation to investigate the following hypotheses:

  a) During exploratory play, mothers allow their sons to venture further away from them than their daughters

  b) When asked personal, or slightly embarrassing questions, people are likely to avert their gaze

  c) Women are safer drivers than men

  d) There are common patterns of behaviour among individuals in groups which are asked to produce volunteers for an unpopular task

Ensure that: variables are operationalised;

the *exact* method of data gathering is described, including the location, sample selection, data collection method and equipment used.

2 A student decides to carry out participant observation on her own student group. She is interested in the different ways her classmates cope with study demands and social commitments. Discuss the ways she might go about this work, the problems she might face and the ways in which she might surmount difficulties.

3 Describe ways in which Bandura's hypotheses, including those which investigate the influence of different types of child and adult model, could have been investigated using naturalistic observation rather than the laboratory.

4 A researcher is concerned that the rating scale in use is not producing good inter-rater reliability. The observations of two observers are as follows:

Observation for child X: altruistic acts in 5-minute intervals:								
	0–5	6–10	11–15	16–20	21–25	26–30	31–35	36–40 41–45
Observer A	1	3	4	2	5	12	9	4 8
Observer B	2	10	8	7	1	3	5	5 6

Would you say this represents good reliability or not? What statistical procedure could tell us the degree of reliability (see Chapters 9 and 18)?

5 Work with a colleague and decide on a variable to observe in chidren or adults. Make the variable something which is likely to occur quite frequently in a short observation period (10 minutes), such as one person smiling in a two-person conversation in the college refectory. Make your observation of the same person at the same time separately and then compare your results to see whether you tend to agree fairly well or not.

8

ASKING QUESTIONS I

Interviews and surveys

This chapter introduces general principles concerning the asking of questions. Methods can be **disguised** or not, and they can be more or less **structured**.

- Advantages and disadvantages of structure are discussed as the dimension of interview techniques across the structured–unstructured dimension are introduced. The **clinical method** is included in these. In general, less structured studies generate more rich and genuine, but more local and less generalisable data.
- The general possible effects of **interpersonal variables** (gender, ethnicity, roles, personality, cues to interviewer's aims) in the face-to-face questioning situation are discussed.
- Advantages and disadvantages of the individual or group **case-study** are considered along with some research examples. The case-study provides unique information, unavailable by any other method, which may trigger more general and structured research.
- Techniques to **achieve and maintain support** are introduced, with the underlying assumption that good rapport produces more valid data from interviewees.
- **Types and sequencing of questions** are covered along with a short discussion of recording techniques.
- Finally, **surveys** are introduced as fully structured interviews. Surveys can be used purely to gather descriptive data *and/or* to test hypotheses. Surveys can be conducted face to face, by post or telephone. **Panels** and **focus groups** are briefly described as methods of assessing opinion on an issue.

INTRODUCTION

So far we have seen that the psychologist who needs information can set up experiments to see what people do under different conditions or use observation techniques to record segments of behaviour in more or less natural circumstances. Perhaps the reader has asked by now 'Why don't psychologists just go and ask people directly about themselves?' So far, it looks as though only the participant observer might have done that. A general term used for any method which asks people for information about themselves is SELF-REPORT METHOD.

There are in fact many ways in which psychological researchers ask questions about individuals. This can occur as part of an experiment or observational study, of course. The interviews conducted by Asch and Milgram after their celebrated demonstrations of seemingly bizarre human behaviour give some of the most fascinating and rich data one can imagine and certainly formed the springboard for a huge volume of further illuminating and productive research. Here, however, we are concentrating on studies where the gathering of information through FACE-TO-FACE questioning is the primary research mode.

STRUCTURE

These methods range across two major dimensions. A questioning method can be formally STRUCTURED, in which case every RESPONDENT (person who answers questions) receives exactly the same questions, probably in the same order. Alternatively, the method can tend towards the UNSTRUCTURED, in which case validity may be high though reliability suffers. (This is similar to the difference between controlled and unstructured observation covered in the last chapter.) In the unstructured study, objective comparison of cases and generalisability are weak but the researcher has the advantage of flexibility towards the respondent and of asking questions in a more formal, relaxed atmosphere in which genuine and complete answers may be more forthcoming.

However, the more unstructured the interview, the greater the skill required by interviewers and the more the success of the research depends on implementation of these skills. Also greater are the chances of researcher bias and selectivity.

THE KALAMAZOO STUDY

Questionnaires may be more or less structured too. The importance of giving respondents the freedom to say what they really think is demonstrated by the results of a piece of applied psychological research conducted by Peronne et al. (1976) who were evaluating a new accountability system set up by the Kalamazoo Education Association in its schools. The system had been heavily criticised. Teachers were asked to complete a questionnaire with fixed-choice questions – 'agree' or 'disagree'. The researchers also set a couple of open-ended questions to which staff could respond in their own words at any length.

School board members were prepared to dismiss the quantitative results from the fixed-choice questions as somehow biased but, on publication of the qualitative results they could hardly ignore the clear statements of fear, concern and frustration which dominated replies to the open-ended questions and they were influenced strongly enough to make substantial changes.

DISGUISE

A factor which might further enhance production of honest answers will be that of DISGUISE. The ethical principles involved in deceiving persons will be dealt with later, but obviously an aid to obtaining truthful information will be the disguising of the researcher's real aim where information sought is highly sensitive, potentially embarrassing or otherwise felt as a threat to the interviewee if disclosed. Interviewees may also try to 'look good' if they know what exactly is the focus of the study.

A matrix of assessment techniques which fall into four categories formed by these two variables, structure and disguise, is shown in Box 8.1. However, it must be remembered that each variable represents a dimension, not a pair of exclusive opposites. Some methods are only partially disguised and/or only relatively structured. In Hammond's technique, respondents were asked factual questions about days lost through strikes, for instance, and had to tick an answer from two, one of which was far too high and one far too low. Without it being obvious to the interviewee, attitude to trades unions was said to be measured.

Levin (1978) used psychoanalytic techniques to assess women's degree of 'penis envy'. The women she studied reported anything they thought they saw in Rorschach ink blots (see Chapter 9).

Eysenck's questionnaire on extroversion and neuroticism gives the respondent some idea of its aim but is not completely transparent.

We have mentioned the Kalamazoo study and we shall mention the Hawthorne studies in a short while. These were relatively undisguised.

A further way to disguise research aims is to ask questions about the topic of interest and simultaneously record the respondent's galvanic skin response (GSR), an indicator of anxiety if high.

The bogus pipeline disguise

In a cunning but deceitful exploitation of the GSR indicator, and as a way of dealing with interviewees who hide their true attitudes and wish to 'look good', Jones and Sigall (1971) introduced the 'bogus pipeline' technique. Participants are hooked up to a machine which, they are assured, can detect signs of anxiety – a form of 'lie detector'. The researcher already has some attitude information about each participant obtained clandestinely. The participant is asked to lie to a few of some questions the researcher actually knows the answer to. The machine therefore seems to work when the researcher 'detects' the false answers. Apparently, people tend to be more embarrassed at being found to be a liar than they do about revealing unpopular attitudes. This does seem to work but, as you'd imagine, the technique has come in for some ethical criticism (see Chapter 26).

EFFECTS OF INTERPERSONAL VARIABLES

This chapter is about asking people questions mostly to gather information. We have seen that some research designs, particularly the laboratory experiment, have been criticised for their artificiality and for producing *demand characteristics*. But when we ask people questions, however informally, so long as they are aware that there is a research aim, there may be an element of artificiality and distortion. There is an interaction of roles – interviewer and interviewee. Characteristics of the interviewer's style and presentation will affect the quality of information obtained. Demand characteristics may well operate in that the interviewee may use cues from the interviewer, or from the questionnaire, to try and behave according to perceived research aims. Researcher bias may also operate where the interviewer is aware of expected or desired results.

> The relationship and interaction between interviewer and interviewee will affect the quality and amount of information obtained in an interview. Make a list of all the ways in which you think this could happen.

My list would include all the following points:
In particular, the class, sex, culture or race, and age of either person in the interview may make a lot of difference to proceedings. Cultural difference, here, doesn't have

Box 8.1 *Matrix of assessment techniques*

	Structured	**Unstructured**
Disguised	Hammond's (1948) 'error choice technique'	Use of projective tests as in Levin (1978)
	Eysenck and Eysenck's (1975) EPQ questionnaire	Roethlisberger and Dickson (1939 Hawthorne studies)
Undisguised	Peronne et al. (1976) Kalamazoo study	
	Most attitude questionnaires	Most qualitative studies

to be great. It could be the difference between Londoner and Scot or northerner and southerner.

Gender

That gender is an important variable is demonstrated in a study by Finch (1984) where young mothers gave her access to views which a man would have been highly unlikely to obtain. A woman interviewee can assume common understanding with a woman interviewer, as when one of Finch's mothers said '. . . fellas don't see it like that do they?'

Ethnicity

That race or ethnic group creates differential interviewing behaviour was shown by Word et al. (1974). They observed the behaviour of white interviewers with white and black interviewees. With white interviewees, the interviewers showed significantly higher 'immediacy' – which includes closer interpersonal distance, more eye contact, more forward lean and so on. They followed this up with a demonstration that 'job applicants' in the study reciprocated the low-immediacy behaviour of the interviewers and received significantly poorer ratings for their interview performance.

Formal roles

The differences above may have greater effect if the interviewee also views the researcher as an authority figure. This perception will partly depend upon the style the researcher adopts but even a highly informal style may not deter the interviewee from seeing her or him as very important. Interviewees' answers then, may lack fluency because they are constrained by a search for 'correct' language or content. On the other hand, some respondents may feel quite superior to, or cynical about, the interviewer and consequently their answers may be somewhat superficial and cursory.

Personal qualities

Interacting with these major differences will be other personal qualities and characteristics of both people. The interviewer, instructed to be informal, may find this quite difficult with some people and may therefore behave rather artificially, this being detected by the interviewee. There may be something else about the interviewer that the interviewee just doesn't like.

Social desirability

A common problem in asking questions is that of SOCIAL DESIRABILITY. This is the tendency to want to look good to the outside world and to be seen to have socially desirable habits and attitudes. To an esteemed researcher, then, people may give a quite false impression of their attitudes and behaviour. It is notoriously difficult, for instance, to measure prejudice openly. When asked, many people will make statements like 'I believe we're all equal' and 'Everybody should be treated the same', whereas, in their everyday life, and in conversation with friends, other, more negative attitudes towards some groups may well emerge. At least, some aspects of their behaviour may belie their professed beliefs. On issues like child-rearing practice or safe driving people know what they ought to say to an interviewer.

Randomised response – *a way round social desirability* and *confidentiality*

An extremely cunning technique, which increases validity and deals with the issue of privacy for respondents on sensitive issues, is the 'randomised response' technique, discussed by Shotland and Yankowski (1982). The participant is asked two questions simultaneously as, say, item 8 on the questionnaire. Only the participant knows which of the two is being answered and this is decided on the toss of a coin. One question is the issue on which information is sought and could be sensitive. Let's say the question is 'Have you ever experienced sexual feelings towards a member of your own sex?' The second question is innocuous, say 'Do you drive a car to work?' The researchers already know the expected response, from large samples, to the second question. Let's say this proportion is 60%. From 200 people then, about 100 will answer the driving question and about 60 of these should answer 'yes'. For all 200 people, the number answering 'yes' to item 8, *above 60*, is an estimate of the number answering 'yes' to the sensitive question. This way, the participant retains privacy, yet a fair estimate of attitude or behaviour on a sensitive issue may be obtained.

Evaluative cues

It is unusual to be asked for one's opinion, in a situation where no criticism or argument can be expected. The interviewer has to be careful not to inadvertently display behaviour, however subtle, which might get interpreted as either disagreement or encouragement since the interviewee may well be searching for an acceptable or desired position. Not all researchers agree with this passive role – see Box 8.2.

INTERVIEWS

Face-to-face interviews range in style across the range of structure from fixed to open-ended questions. Answers to open-ended questions will often be coded by placing them into categories, such as 'left wing' or 'right wing' for political questions, or by rating them on a scale of perhaps one to ten for, say, aggressiveness. In some surveys, interviewers code answers on the spot as they are received. In the less structured type of interview, response analysis is a long, complicated and relatively subjective process. In qualitative research studies there may be no interest in quantifying responses at all beyond basic categorising. The emphasis will be on collating, prioritising and summarising all information acquired (see Chapter 25) and perhaps suggesting areas and strategies for action. The setting and procedure for interviewing may also be more or less structured and we will consider five categories of interview, starting at the relatively unstructured end of the continuum.

Box 8.2 *The discourse analysis view of interview bias*

There is a view quite contrary to the conventional research 'law' that interviewers should not engage or lead the respondent as one would in normal conversation. It is bound up with the discourse analysis approach which is discussed in more detail in Chapter 11. Potter and Wetherell (1987) explain that the entire focus of discourse analysis is on the ways in which people use language, in conversation, to *construct* and 'negotiate' a view of the world. They argue that we cannot assume some 'pure' truth in people's heads which we can get at if only we remove all possible bias and distorting influences. Their interest is in the ways people use discourse to promote certain versions of events, often those which serve their interests best or put them in the best light. Hence, for the discourse analytic interviewer, the interview should be naturalistic to the extent of promoting this everyday discursive use of language. The diversity which traditionally structured interviews try to minimise, in order to get 'consistent' responses from interviewees, is positively encouraged by the discourse approach. Consistency, for Potter and Wetherell, is a sign that respondents are producing only limited, probably compatible interpretations. They see the interview as 'an active site where the respondent's interpretive resources are explored and engaged to the full ...' and as a 'conversational encounter' (Potter and Wetherell, 1987). The interview is therefore conducted on an 'interventionist and confrontative' basis – not as a dispute but as a situation in which the interviewer is prepared to come back to areas obviously difficult or ambiguous for the interviewee in order, perhaps, to elicit some alternative construction. The interviewer will also be prepared to use probes and follow-up questions in fruitful areas. This makes the interview something similar to the 'informal but guided' type below with elements, also, of the 'clinical method', discussed later.

TYPES OF INTERVIEW

1 Non-directive

Some psychology practitioners use interviews in which the interviewee can talk about anything they like and in which the psychologist gives no directing influence to the topics but helps and guides discussion. The main aim would be to help the 'client' increase self-awareness and deal with personal problems. This method would be used by psychotherapists and counsellors and would not count, therefore, as research in the sense generally used in this book. But, of course, clients do, in a sense, research their own personality and the psychologist may need information, gathered in this manner, in order to help them.

This approach may be used in collecting information which forms part of a CASE-STUDY, a topic discussed later on.

The insights derived from such studies often get drawn together into an overall psychological theory, model or approach which adds, in time, to the pool of knowledge and ideas which is a stimulus for further research by other means. Freud's insights, for instance, influenced Bandura in his development of social learning theory which he supported mainly by controlled observation studies.

2 Informal

An informal interview has an overall data gathering aim. At the non-structured extreme the session is similar to the non-directive approach just described. This was employed in a large-scale and now famous study of industrial relations at the Western Electric company's Hawthorne works in Chicago, starting back in 1927. Early structured interviews were not successful. Employees went off the topics set by the interviewers' questions. The 'indirect approach' which the researchers then developed involved interviewers listening patiently, making intelligent comments, displaying no authority, giving no advice or argument and only asking questions when necessary i.e. to prompt further talking, to relieve anxiety, to praise, to cover an omitted topic and to discuss implicit assumptions if thought helpful. 'Rules of orientation' for the interviewer took into account many of the points made strongly today by the discourse analysts (Box 8.2 and Chapter 11). They found employees became far more articulate and, as an overall outcome of the study, management realised that seemingly trivial complaints were only the external symptoms of much deeper personal and social problems, requiring more than the superficial response to employee complaints they had originally envisaged (Roethlisberger and Dickson, 1939).

In the relaxed atmosphere of the informal, non-directive interview, interviewees can talk in their own terms. They don't have to answer pre-set questions which they might find confusing or which they just don't wish to answer. They are not constrained by fixed-answer questions which produce rather narrow information.

This approach has been used in social science research for some time and has more recently, largely in the 1980s, become popular in areas of applied research, particularly by the proponents of qualitative approaches.

Qualitative workers would argue that the attempt at objectivity, through being a cool, distant, impersonal and anonymous interviewer is only likely to instill anxiety. Interviewees grasp at clues to what is really expected from them and how their information will promote or hinder 'success'. I have been interviewed for research and remember feeling desparate to know what the context was so I could manage my answers more effectively, and perhaps recall more relevant ideas and experiences. I also remember the interviewer's '. . . well, I shouldn't strictly say this now but . . .' and similar straying from the structure at several points. Realistically, most interviews run like this. Dropped comments and asides may well form some of the most memorable and insight-producing information.

Box 8.3 *Summary of advantages and disadvantages of the informal interview*

Advantages	Disadvantages
Interview can be moulded to individual, situation and context	Unsystematic and therefore different information from different individuals
Richer, fuller information likely on interviewee's own terms	Difficult to analyse variety of information gathered
Interviewee feels relaxed and not under pressure of assessment	Strongly influenced by interpersonal variables
Realistic	Relatively unreliable/ungeneralisable

3 Informal but guided

One way to retain the advantage of the informal approach is to keep the procedure informal, not to ask pre-set questions in exactly the same order each time, but to provide interviewers with a guide which is an outline of topics to be covered and questions to be asked. The guide leaves the interviewer to decide, on the spot, how to work in and phrase questions on the various topics. In other words, with specific data requirements, the interviewer 'plays it by ear'.

Box 8.4 *Summary of advantages and disadvantages of the informal but guided interview*

Advantages	Disadvantages
Increase in consistency of information	Different question wording will create varying interpretations and emphasis
Data analysis simpler, more systematic	
Information genuinely given	Interviewer may miss important topics
Interviewer can still be flexible	Substantial influence by interpersonal variables
Fairly rich information	
Realistic	Low reliability/generalisability

4 Structured but open-ended

To avoid the looseness and inconsistency which accompany informally gathered interview data, the interview session can use a standardised procedure. The interviewer gives pre-set questions in a predetermined order to every interviewee. This keep the multiplicity of interpersonal variables involved in a two-way conversation to a minimum and ensures greater consistency in the data gathered. The respondent is still free to answer, however, in any way chosen. Questions are open ended. For instance, 'How do you feel about the company's sales policy?' might be asked, rather than 'Do you approve of the company's sales policy?'

Box 8.5 *Summary of advantages and disadvantages of the structured, open-ended interview*

Advantages	Disadvantages
Responses far more easily compared	Flexibility of interviewer being able to respond to different individuals, situations and contexts is lost
Data more easily analysed	
No topics missed or fleetingly covered	Question wordings may reduce richness
Reduction of interpersonal bias	Answers less natural
Can be used by several interviewers at the same time	Coding of answers may not be high in reliability
Can be reviewed by other researchers	
Respondents not constrained by fixed answer	Limits to generalisation

5 Fully structured

In this type of interview, as with the last, questions are fixed and ordered. In addition, the respondent may only answer according to a formal system. Three examples of structure, in increasing complexity, might be:

1 Answering questions with either 'yes' or 'no'.
2 Responding to a statement (not a question) with one of the following:
   Strongly agree   Agree   Neutral   Disagree   Strongly disagree
3 Selecting from several alternatives a suitable court sentence for a rapist.

In fact, this approach is hardly an interview worth the name at all. It is a face-to-face data-gathering technique, but could be conducted by telephone or by post (which would reduce bias from interpersonal variables still further). The structured method is usually in use when you're stopped on the street by someone with a clipboard. Responses can be counted and analysed numerically but can often be difficult to make because the respondent wants to say 'yes' (for this reason) but 'no' (for that reason) or 'I think so' or 'sometimes'. A sensitive structured system has a list for choosing responses including alternatives such as 'sometimes', 'hardly ever', or, 'certain', 'fairly confident' and so on. The method just described is often that used in a SURVEY.

Box 8.6 *Summary of advantages and disadvantages of the fully structured interview*

Advantages	Disadvantages
Very quick to administer	Respondent completely constrained by question and response system
Easily replicated	Information gained is narrow
Generalisable results	Information may be distorted by:
Data analysis relatively simple	ambiguous wordings
Quantification without bias	complex wordings
Low influence from interpersonal variables	inappropriate response choice list
High reliability	Suffers from all the difficulties associated with questionnaires

THE CLINICAL METHOD (OR 'CLINICAL INTERVIEW')

This method uses a semi-structured interview method in a particular manner. It is usually aimed at testing fairly specific hypotheses or at demonstrating a clear and limited phenomenon. However, it also recognises the unique experience of each interviewee. Initially, each person questioned will be asked the same questions, but further questions are tailored to the nature of initial replies. The method was extensively used by Piaget. Anyone who has tried to test a child on one of Piaget's conservation tasks will know that the specific language chosen, and the quality of the adult's interaction with the child, are all-important factors in determining the progress of such a test. It is easy to get a four-year-old child to give the 'wrong' (i.e. non-conserving) answer with an injudicious choice of question wording or with 'clumsy' conversation.

'Is there more liquid in this glass?' is a leading question which may well prompt the child into saying 'yes' to please. Anyway, after all, the column of liquid *is* taller (though narrower). The question 'Is there more in this glass, more in this other one, or are they both the same?' is rather demanding on the child's short-term memory!

The clinical method, then, uses a non-standardised procedure but heads for a definite goal. Standardised questions, rigidly adhered to by the interviewer can seem rather artificial to the adult respondent. The problem with children is greater. If they don't understand the particular form of words they may well 'fail' when an alteration in question form may well have revealed that the child has the concept sought after all. Piaget believed, therefore, that he could get the most accurate information about a child's thinking by varying the questioning in what seemed to the child a fairly natural conversation with an adult. Of course, we end up with the alleged weaknesses of unstandardised procedures.

Freud's methods too have been said to involve the clinical method, since the aim of some sessions was to test a specific hypothesis about the client's unconscious network of fears and ideas.

Box 8.7 *Summary of advantages and disadvantages of the clinical method*

Advantages	Disadvantages
Leads to accurate assessment of person's thinking and memory	Non-standardised method
Interviewer can vary questions in order to check person's understanding	Researcher's theoretical beliefs can influence questions asked and interpretations made of what person understands
Information gained fairly rich	
Interviewee relaxed	Difficulty in comparing one interview protocol with another

THE INDIVIDUAL CASE-STUDY

A case-study involves gathering detailed information about one individual or group. Typically this would include a comprehensive CASE HISTORY, usually, but not exclusively, gathered by interview. This would be the person's record to date in employment, education, family details, socio-economic status, relationships and so on, and might include a detailed account of experiences relevant to the issue which makes the person of particular research interest. This reason might be that the person has suffered severe social and physical deprivation, or that their life is particularly affected by, perhaps, illness or criminal background.

Information might also be gathered, as the study progresses, on all these variables. The person would be regularly interviewed, mostly in an unstructured manner, and may be asked to take psychological tests. A case-study may not use interviews exclusively. In some cases, particularly where the person is a young child, observation may play a large part in the collection of information, as when, for instance, the severely deprived child's play activities and developing social interactions are monitored for change.

In some instances the individual is selected for a forward-looking case-study because they are about to undergo a particularly interesting and possibly unique experience. Gregory and Wallace (1963) for instance studied the case of SB, blind almost from birth, who received sight through surgical operation at the age of 52. The researchers were able not only to study in depth his visual abilities and development, but also gathered qualitative data on his emotional reactions to his new experiences and progress. This included his initial euphoria and his later depressions, caused partly by loss of daylight and his disillusionment with impure surfaces (flaky paint, old chalk marks on blackboards).

A case-study, such as this one, though intrinsically valuable, can also shed light on general psychological issues such as the nature–nurture debate in perception. However, since SB had spent a lifetime specialising senses other than vision, his perceptual learning experiences cannot be directly compared with those of a young infant.

Freud developed his comprehensive psychoanalytic theory of human development using, as fuel and illustration, his records from dozens of patients' case histories.

At the social end of the psychological research spectrum, we would find case-studies on groups of individuals such as those conducted by participant observers or the evaluative studies of establishments exemplified by the Kalamazoo work, described earlier.

De Waele and Harré (1979) recommend the construction of assisted autobiographies. In this method, the autobiographical account is conceived as a cooperative effort between the participant and a team of about a dozen professionals (psychologist, social worker, etc.). Their project involved prisoners who, though volunteers, were paid a salary as a research team member. The process involves continuous detailed negotiation among team members about various 'accounts' from the participant. The participant's own life and resources are at all times respected and the professional team must 'stand in a relation of humility' to it.

This method is, of course, extremely time consuming and enormously expensive, though intense in its production of rich, meaningful data. Harré belongs among the 'new paradigm' researchers described in Chapter 11 and this type of research project is an example of the collaborative approach.

THE VALUE OF CASE-STUDIES

Being a somewhat unstructured, probably unreplicable study on just one individual or group, the case-study design would seem to be of the rich but not generalisable type and to be rather suspect in its scientific use. Bromley (1986) has argued however, that case-studies are the 'bedrock of scientific investigation'. Many psychological studies, he argues, are difficult to replicate in principle and it is the interesting, unpredictable case which has traditionally spurred scientists towards changes in paradigm or theoretical innovation. Bromley feels that a preoccupation with the experiment and psychometrics has led to a serious neglect of the case-study approach by most psychologists. He points out that, as in most cases, psychological evidence can be valid and effective, yet remain unquantifiable. The case-study has a variety of specific advantages and useful points which follow.

1 Outstanding cases

A phenomenon may occur which is unique or so dramatic it could not have been predicted or studied in any pre-planned way. An example is the study of multiple personality by Osgood et al. (1976) in which the very rare but genuine experiences of a person with three quite separate psychological identities is recorded and analysed. Luria (1969) studied a man with astonishing memory capabilities who was originally noticed because he was a journalist who took no notes at briefing meetings.

Such cases may bring to attention possibilities in the human condition which were not previously considered realistic and may prompt investigation into quite new, challenging areas.

2 Contradicting a theory

One contrary case is enough to seriously challenge an assumed trend or theory of cause–effect relationship. It has been assumed that humans go through a 'critical period' where language must be heard to be learned, or where attachments must be formed and maintained in order to avoid later psychological problems. One case of an isolated child learning language, or of a maternally deprived child developing normal adult social skills, after deprivation during much of the critical period, is enough to undermine the critical period hypothesis quite seriously and to promote vigorous research seeking the crucial variables.

3 Data pool

In an effort to identify common factors or experiences, a mass of information from many case-studies may be pooled, sorted and analysed. The focus may be, for instance, psychiatric patients or children with a particular reading disability. As a result, quantitative studies may be carried out, once linking variables appear or are suspected.

4 Insight

Whether or not case-studies of special circumstances lead to later, more formal, structured and quantitative studies, the richness they provide is their unique strength. Very often we could not possibly imagine the special experiences of the person studied, and we could not possibly draw up the appropriate questions to find out.

These experiences may cause us to quite restructure our thoughts on a particular condition, allowing us to empathise more fully, for example, with the AIDS sufferer or to understand the full impact of unemployment on a family. This adds to our overall knowledge pool and comprehension of human psychology though it may not test any specific hypothesis.

DISADVANTAGES OF THE CASE-STUDY

1 Reliability and validity

There is an obviously high degree of unreliability involved. No two cases are the same. Many studies are quite unreplicable, indeed, their uniqueness is usually the reason for their being carried out in the first place. Their strength is in richness, their weakness in lack of generalisability.

Some check on reliability can sometimes be made, however, by comparing information gained from different sources; for instance, the person themselves in interview, close relatives' accounts, documentary sources, such as diaries and court reports. This is similar to the notion of 'triangulation' described in Chapter 25.

Realism is high. The experiences recorded by the researcher are genuine and complex. Historical material, however, often depends on just the person's own memory. Memory is notoriously error-prone and subject to distortion. Experiences which we claim to recall from childhood are often our original reconstruction from relatives' stories told to us about our life before memory was possible.

2 Interviewer–interviewee interaction

Any interview involves human interaction and information collection is prone to the interpersonal variables discussed earlier on. But the case-study necessitates a very close relationship between interviewer and interviewee over an extended period and many intimate interviews. Though the very depth of this relationship may promote an extremely rich information source, it may also seriously interfere with the researcher's objectivity. Some case-studies resemble a form of participant observation and suffer from the same criticism of subjectivity.

3 Subjective selection

There is another possible element of subjectivity. Rather than present everything recorded during a case-study, which might take as long as the study itself, the researcher must be selective in what information enters the final report. This may well depend upon the points of background theory or issues which the researcher wishes to raise or emphasise. Further, for every illustrative case-study, we do not know how many cases did not deliver the kind of information the researcher wished to present.

INTERVIEW TECHNIQUES

If the interview is completely structured, the interviewer will be using a questionnaire and the construction of these is outlined in Chapter 9. The techniques and procedures described in the following pages apply to any interview which is less structured and, in particular, to interviews in which open-ended, qualitative data is sought.

ACHIEVING AND MAINTAINING RAPPORT

In an unstructured interview, the quality and characteristics of the interviewer's behaviour are of utmost importance and not just the interesting 'extraneous variables' they are often considered to be in the structured interview or survey study. People provide a lot more information about themselves when they are feeling comfortable and 'chatty' than in a strained, formal atmosphere where suspicions are not allayed. An awkward, 'stiff' or aggressive interviewer may produce little cooperation and even hostility from the interviewee. How may rapport be established?

LANGUAGE

It is valuable to spend some time discovering terminology used by the group under study. They may have nicknames and use their own jargon, including sets of initials (such as 'SUDs' – standing for 'seriously underdeprived' i.e. upper-class children).

Interviewees will be most comfortable and fluent using their normal language mode (dialect, accent, normal conversational style) and must be made to feel that its use is not only legitimate but welcome and valued.

NEUTRALITY

Accepting the language style and any non-verbal behaviour of the interviewee will help to assure her/him that the interview is entirely non-judgemental. The interviewee must feel that no moral assessment of what they say is, or will be, involved.

GIVING INFORMATION

The interviewer can give full information at the start of an interview about the purpose of the research, who it is conducted for, what sorts of topics will be covered and how confidentiality will be maintained. Unlike the case with formal questionnaires, the interviewer can explain the purpose of any particular question. A natural questioning environment should encourage the interviewee to ask what the interviewer has in mind but *offering* this information is courteous and keeps the participant involved.

CONFIDENTIALITY

If interviewees are to be quoted verbatim (one of the principles of some qualitative research) there is the problem that individuals can be identified from particular statements. In the 1950s, the people of Springdale village, in the USA, vilified researchers (Vidich and Bensman, 1958) who, though using pseudonyms, made identification of individuals possible because their problems were analysed in the research report. The villagers held an effigy of 'the author' over a manure spreader in their 4th of July parade!

Participants should be reminded of their right to veto comments made throughout the project and should be aware of the final format in order to exercise discretion over information divulged.

TRAINING

In order to establish and maintain rapport, interviewers can undergo some degree of training which might include the following:

Listening skills

The interviewer needs to learn when *not* to speak, particularly if he or she is normally quite 'speedy' and talkative. There are various skills in listening, too numerous to detail here, which include:

- not trivialising statements by saying 'How interesting but we must get on'
- hearing that a 'yes' is qualified and asking whether the interviewee wants to add anything. What follows may well amount to a 'no'
- not being too quick or dominant in offering an interpretation of what the interviewee was trying to say

Non-verbal communication

The interviewer needs to be sensitive to non-verbal cues, though not to the point of awkwardness. In what position will an interviewee talk most comfortably? What interviewer postures are interpreted as dominating? What is a pleasant tone and manner for questioning? And so on.

Natural questioning

This is really the biggest factor of all. How can the interviewer make the discussion feel natural, and therefore productive, whilst getting through a set of major questions? If the interviewer has only four or five target questions then it should not be too difficult to insert these into a freely flowing conversation. With a larger list it may be necessary to use prompt notes but some formality can be avoided by listing these on paper used for note taking.

Interest

It is essential that the interviewer remains interested and *believes* that the interviewee's information, as well as sacrificed time, are valuable. The interviewee needs to feel this is the case. Patton (1980) urges that the concept of the bad interviewee should be ignored, arguing that it is easy to summon up stereotypes (of the hostile or paranoid interviewee, for instance). He suggests that it is the sensitive interviewer's task to unlock the internal perspective of each interviewee by being adaptable in finding the style and format which will work in each case. We are a long way here from the argument that scientific research demands completely unswerving standardised procedure!

One overall necessity here is practice. Interviews can be made more effective with thoughtful preparation and by practising with colleagues as dummy interviewees until stumbling points and awkwardness have been reduced or ironed out.

TYPES OF QUESTION

It is deceptively simple to ask poor or problematic questions. Some of the common mistakes to avoid are outlined in the principles of questionnaire design described in Chapter 9. Items to avoid are double-barrelled, complex, ambiguous, leading and emotive questions. In addition, the following points might be noted:

1 It is easy to ask two or more questions at once if the interviewer gets enthusiastic. 'So tell me about it. What was it like? How did you feel? Did you regret it?', for instance, puts a memory strain, at least, on the interviewee.

2 Questions like 'Are you enjoying the course?' may well receive a monosyllabic answer. Open-ended questions like 'Please can you tell me what you are enjoying about the course?' will be more likely to produce richer information.

3 'Why?' questions can be wasteful in time. Asking a student 'Why did you join the course?' will produce a variety of replies in quite different categories. For instance:

'It'll get me a decent qualification'
'To meet new people'
'It was nearer than London'
'My mother thought it was a good idea'

are all possible answers. We can decide, during the planning stage, what category of reply we would like and design questions accordingly. What should certainly be avoided is an implication that the answer given is unwanted by saying, for instance, 'No, I didn't mean that . . .'

4 Interest may not be maintained if too many personal background details are asked. This point is valid for surveys too, as mentioned below.

THE SEQUENCE AND PROGRESS OF QUESTIONS

FEELINGS AND REACTIONS

As with more formal questioning methods, the interviewee will feel more comfortable if the session does not kick off with emotionally charged or controversial items. Likewise, it will be hard to discuss feelings about or reactions towards an issue or event until the interviewee has had a chance to acclimatise by describing it. Early questions can be aimed at eliciting a description, and later questions can prompt feelings about or reactions towards events described.

HELPFUL FEEDBACK

An interview will run more smoothly if the interviewee is aware of the position reached and the future direction. In particular it might be useful to let the interviewee know:

1 When the interviewer is about to change topic. For instance, 'Now let's talk about the students on the course'.

2 That the next question is particularly important, complex, controversial or sensitive. For instance, 'You've been telling me what you like about the course. Now I'd like to find out about what you don't like. Can you tell me . . .'

3 About what the interviewer thinks the interviewee has just said, or said earlier, without, of course, reinterpretations which depart far from the actual words used.

This feedback allows the interviewee to realise they are making sense and being productive; also, that they are not being misrepresented. They can alter or qualify what they've said. This process also keeps the interviewee actively involved and confident.

But it is important not to summarise interviewees' statements in a language form which makes them feel that their own statements were somehow inferior and in need of substantial rephrasing.

RECORDING DATA

Interviewers have three common choices for saving data: note taking, audio-tape or video-tape recordings.

NOTE TAKING

Taking hand-written notes will obviously slow down the procedure. It could be useful to develop some form of personal shorthand – at least short forms of commonly used terms and phrases. The note book does have the handy advantage of being a place to store discreetly the interview questions or outline. If used, the interviewer needs to be careful not to give the impression that what the interviewee is saying at any particular moment is not important because it is not being recorded.

AUDIO RECORDING

Many people feel inhibited in the presence of a tape recorder's microphone. The interviewer needs to justify its use in terms of catching the exact terms and richness of the interviewee's experiences and in terms of confidentiality. The interviewee has to be free to have the recording switched off at any time. The tape recorder has the advantage of leaving the interviewer free to converse naturally and encourage the greatest flow of information.

VIDEO RECORDING

A 'live' video camera in the room may dominate and can hardly help retain the informal, 'chatty' atmosphere which a loosely structured, open-ended interview is supposed to create. It is possible to acclimatise interviewees to its presence over quite a number of sessions, but this is costly in time. The great value, of course, is in the recording of non-verbal communication at a detailed level and the chance to analyse this at a comfortable pace. If this information is not required, however, then video is an unnecessary, intrusive gimmick.

Both video and audio recordings could be conducted unobtrusively by simply not revealing their presence to the interviewee, but, in this case, serious ethical issues must be addressed. Two answers to possible dilemmas here are:

1 Inform the interviewee of the recording process but keep equipment completely hidden

2 Give information about the recording only after the interview has taken place, but emphasise that recordings can be heard or viewed, sections omitted or the whole recording destroyed at the interviewee's request.

Option 2 is of course potentially wasteful and time consuming.

SURVEYS

A survey consists of asking a lot of people for information. In the informal, loosely structured interview, each respondent's answers form a small case-study. A survey can consist of a set of such small case-studies. Much more often, though, it would involve the use of a structured questionnaire, with answers open or closed, as described in interview types 4 and 5 on page 121. Each set of responses forms an equivalent unit in a large sample. Interviewers usually work as a team and procedures are therefore fully standardised. Each will be briefed on the exact introductory statement and steps to be followed with each respondent.

A survey may be used for two major research purposes: descriptive or analytical.

DESCRIPTIVE

Here the researcher wants accurate description of what people, in some target population, do and think and perhaps with what frequency. Bryant et al. (1980), for instance, studied child-minding in Oxfordshire and focused on the minders' behaviour and attitude towards their clients, as well as on the children's development. A more notorious and wide-ranging survey was that of Kinsey (1948, 1953) on American sexual behaviour. A recent, extremely comprehensive survey (Jowell & Topf, 1988) gathered information on current British social attitudes. The issues covered included: AIDS, the countryside, industry's and unions' influences on political parties, the government's current economic policies, education, the North–South divide and which household jobs should be shared – according to married and single persons' opinions.

ANALYTIC USE

Survey data can be used to test hypotheses. Hatfield and Walster (1981) interviewed 537 college men and women who had a regular partner. Those who felt their relationship was equitable were far more likely to predict its continuation over one to five years than were those who felt one partner received or gave too much. This tested hypothesis supported a theory of human interaction based on calculated gains and losses.

In Sears et al.'s (1957) wide-ranging study of child-rearing practices, using mothers from two suburbs of Boston, USA, many hypotheses were tested by correlating (see Chapter 18) rearing techniques with children's characteristic behaviour. Data was gathered by rating open-ended answers to structured questions given to the mothers. The raters assessed only from the interview recording and didn't meet the mother. The researchers found positive relationships between the use of physical punishment and a child's higher level of aggressive behaviour. Mothers who were rated as warm and used 'withdrawal of love' as a major disciplinary technique had children with stronger consciences. Both these variables, withdrawal of love and strength of conscience, were assessed indirectly from the interview data and are examples of constructs, operationally defined.

Often, from a large descriptive survey, hypotheses can be formulated or checked against further information from the same survey. For instance, in the second report of the National Child Development Study (Davie et al. 1972), a survey of a large sample of children born in 1958, it was found that children from social class V (unskilled manual) were at a particular disadvantage on reading tests, compared with other manual and non-manual classes. Why might this be? Well, from the same survey data it was found that overcrowded homes and homes lacking basic amenities were related to serious reading retardation irrespective of a child's social class, sex, area of the UK or accommodation type. Children from social class V were more likely to live in such homes. So, reading deficiency could be related to factors only indirectly related to, but more prevalent within, one class.

SURVEY DESIGN

In survey work there are three major areas of decision-making necessary before initiating the contact with respondents. These are the sample, mode of questioning, and the questions themselves. The first two areas will be dealt with now. I shall leave dealing with the actual content of questions until the next section on questionnaires and tests in general.

THE SAMPLE

Of all methods, the survey throws particular emphasis on the sample since the aim, very often, is to make generalisations about a relatively large section of the population, if not all of it. If the sample *is* the whole population then the survey is known as a CENSUS.

Box 8.8 *Advantages and disadvantages of the survey over the in-depth interview*

Advantages	Disadvantages
Many respondents can be questioned fairly quickly	Structured questions miss more informative data
Can be a lot less expensive than in-depth interviews (which have a lot of information to be transcribed)	Large-scale surveys can be expensive in assistants
Less influence from dynamics of interpersonal variables	More influenced by superficial interpersonal variables; respondent has no time to trust and confide in interviewer
Less bias in analysing answers, since questions are structured	More likely to produce 'public responses', not respondent's genuine ideas
	Possibility of social desirability effect is higher

We have dealt with the main methods and issues of sampling in an earlier chapter. Survey work has produced two other forms of sample not used elsewhere. These are the PANEL and the FOCUS GROUP.

The panel

This is a specially selected group of people who can be asked for information on a repetitive basis. They are much used by market research companies, government survey units and audience research in broadcasting. It is easier and more efficient to rely on the same, well-stratified group to provide information each time it is required.

One problem can be that panel members become too sophisticated in their reviewing and can become unrepresentative in, say, their viewing habits since they feel they must watch all the programmes mentioned in their questionnaire.

Focus groups

The idea here is to bring together a group of individuals with a common interest and to conduct a form of collective interview. Discussion among members may provoke an exchange of views and revelations providing information and insights less likely to surface during a one-to-one interview. Though not providing much in the way of reliable, quantifiable data, such groups can be a starting point for research into a specific area, as an aid to exposing and clarifying concepts.

THE MODE OF QUESTIONING

There are three obvious ways of communicating with respondents: face-to-face, telephone and letter. Of these, telephones are used rarely, though they will often be used for making initial contact.

The privacy of the postal method is likely to produce more honest answers. Interpersonal variables, discussed above, are reduced to a minimum in postal surveys though the respondent may make assumptions about the researcher from the style of the covering letter. The method is also a good deal cheaper and less time consuming.

The disadvantages are first, that the questionnaire must be exceptionally clear, and unambiguous instructions for its completion must be carefully written. Still, respondents may answer in an inappropriate way that a 'live' interviewer could have changed. Second, the proportion of non-returners is likely to be higher than the number of refusals by other approaches. This matters a lot when, for instance, it is reported that 75% of respondents (300) agreed that government should continue to finance higher education substantially if it is also true that only 400 out of 1000 persons contacted bothered to complete and return the form. Can we count the missing 600 as neutral or not bothered?

GLOSSARY

Record of person's important life events gathered and analysed in a case-study	____ _____	case history
In-depth study of one individual or group, usually qualitative in nature	____-_____	case-study
Survey of whole population	_____	census
Interview method using structure of questions to be asked but permitting tailoring of later questions to the individual's responses; also seeks to test specific hypothesis or effect	_____ _____	clinical method
Dimension of design which is the extent to which interviewees are kept ignorant of the aims of the questioning	_____	disguise

Interview in which researcher and interviewee talk together in the same physical location	____-__-____	face-to-face
Group with common interest who meet to discuss an issue in a collective interview in order for researchers to assess opinion	_____ _____	focus group
Interview item to which interviewees can respond in any way they please and at any length	____-_____ _____	open-ended question
Stratified group who are consulted in order for opinion to be assessed	_____	panel
Person who is questioned in interview or survey	_____	respondent
A general term for methods in which people provide information about themselves	____ _____	self-report
Dimension of design which is the extent to which questions and procedure are identical for everyone	_____	structure
Relatively structured questioning of large sample	_____	survey

EXERCISES

1 Without looking back at the text, try to think of several advantages and disadvantages the survey has compared with the informal interview.

2 Suppose you decide to conduct a survey on attitudes towards the environment in your area. Outline the steps you would take in planning and conducting the survey, paying particular attention to:

- the sample and means of obtaining it
- the exact approach to respondents you would use
- the types of question you would ask

To answer this last point in detail you will need to read the next section on questionnaires, at least briefly.

3 A researcher wishes to investigate specific instances of racism (abuse, physical harassment, discrimination) which members of minority ethnic groups have experienced. Four assistants are employed to conduct informal, guided interviews starting with individuals recommended by local community leaders.
   a) What kind of sample is drawn?
   b) One interviewer records far fewer instances than the other three. Can you give at least five reasons why this might be?
   c) Another interviewer argues that the study should follow up with a structured questionnaire over a far wider sample. Why might this be?

4 You are about to conduct an interview with the manager of the local, large supermarket. He is 43 years old, quite active in local politics and is known to be fairly friendly. Make a list of all the variables, especially those concerning your own personality and characteristics, which might influence the production of information in the interview.

5 A researcher wishes to survey young people's attitudes to law and order. Interviewers complete questionnaires with sixth formers who volunteer from the schools which agree to be included in the study. Families are also selected at random from the local telephone directory. Young people are also questioned at the local youth club. Discuss several ways in which the sample for the complete study may be biased.

ASKING QUESTIONS II

Questionnaires, scales and tests

The chapter looks at a variety of procedures for gathering data using some form of test, rather than the interview approaches covered in the last chapter. However, there is overlap, since some interviews consist of going through a structured questionnaire with the respondent.

- The first important matter is to consider carefully how people will, in reality, respond to certain types of question which are, for instance, difficult, embarrassing or controversial. Questions can be **fixed** or **open-ended** (in the latter the respondent has freedom in type and length of response).
- The attitude scales of **Thurstone**, **Likert**, **Bogardus**, **Guttman** and Osgood's **semantic differential** are covered. Likert's is probably the most popular and with this, decisions must be made about how many points to use (often five) and how the 'neutral' mid-point will be interpreted or dealt with. Items should vary in direction to avoid **response acquiescence**.
- Specific points about the pitfalls of question/item construction are described.
- **Projective** tests assume that unconscious forces can be assessed from the way people respond to ambiguous stimuli such as the **Rorschach** and **thematic apperception tests**
- **Sociograms** produce a graphic display of people's 'sociometric choices' – their preference choices of others in their group.
- **Psychometric tests** are intended to be standardised measurement instruments for human personality and ability characteristics. They can suffer from cultural content bias and have been extremely controversial in the area of intelligence or mental ability testing. Tests are validated and made meaningful to some extent using **factor analysis** which investigates correlation 'clusters' and provides statistical support for theories about what underlying 'factors' cause results to be so arranged on tests or sections of tests.
- Methods for checking a test's **reliability**, and **validity** are detailed. Reliability is consistency *within* a test or between repeated uses of it in the same circumstances. Validity concerns whether a test measures what it was created to measure. **Standardisation** involves adjusting raw scores to fit a normal distribution which makes comparison to norms possible but sometimes controversially assumes something we often don't actually know about the nature of human characteristics.

QUESTIONNAIRES AND ATTITUDE SCALES

Questionnaires, attitude scales and tests are instruments for gathering structured information from people. Questionnaires used in surveys are usually constructed for the specific research topic and tend to test for current opinion or patterns of behaviour. Attitude scales are usually intended to have a somewhat longer life span. They are seen as technical measuring instruments and therefore require STANDARDI-SATION and a more thorough preparation in terms of reliability and validity. It is usually intended that they tap a more permanent aspect of the individual's cognition and behaviour, such as attitude towards religion or authority.

However, many of the features of attitude scale construction can be employed by the student who wishes to create a measure of people's views on a current issue, such as preservation of the environment or on treatment of animals. A thorough assessment of attitude would involve at least two measurements, at differing times, since a defining feature of an attitude is its relatively enduring nature.

Questionnaires, scales, psychometric and projective tests can all be used as measures of experimental effects as well as in the field. One group might be assessed for 'self-esteem' before and after a 'treatment' in which they are made to feel successful. This can be compared with a control group's assessments.

QUESTIONNAIRES

In the section on attitude scales we will discuss in some detail the issues to be considered when developing scale items. Most of the points included there apply to survey questionnaires as well. If you are constructing a simple opinion questionnaire, it would make sense to check the general points made below and then go on to the section on 'Questionnaire or scale items'.

SOME GENERAL PRINCIPLES

The following principles are part of the common 'lore' of survey questionnaires. They apply particularly to the situation in which strangers, or people little known to the interviewer, are being asked a big favour in stopping to answer a few questions.

1 Ask for the minimum of information required for the research purpose

A respondent's time is precious so why ask for information obtainable elsewhere? Personal details may be available from company or school records. The respondent's time spent answering questions has a bearing on mood, and mood will certainly be altered if the interviewer asks what sex the respondent is! Other details, such as whether married and number of children may well be drawn from an introductory relaxing chat and, if not, during final checking.

A further argument concerns the principle of *parsimony*, that is, limiting effort to the necessary whilst maintaining efficiency. Too much information may not be useful. Some questions may have been included only because they 'seemed inter-esting', which is too vague a basis for inclusion.

2 Make sure questions can be answered

'How many times have you visited a doctor this year?' may be quite difficult for many people to answer at all accurately.

3 Make sure questions will be answered truthfully

The question in point **2** is unlikely to be answered truthfully because of its difficulty. Other difficult or wide-ranging questions are likely to receive an answer based more on well-known public opinion than on the individual's real beliefs. Questions on child-rearing, for instance, if not phrased very explicitly, are well known for producing, where wide error is possible, answers more in accord with prevailing 'expert' views on good practice.

4 Make sure questions will be answered and not refused

Some sensitive topics will obviously produce more refusals. Most respondents will continue on a sensitive topic, once started, but may baulk at a sensitive question turning up suddenly in an otherwise innocuous context, for instance a sex-life question among political items. The interviewer has to provide a context in order to justify sensitive points, or else avoid them.

FIXED AND OPEN-ENDED QUESTIONS

At the least structured extreme, survey questionnaires have open-ended questions. Most questionnaire items are fixed choice, however, where respondents are asked to select an answer from two or more alternatives. Open-ended questions have several advantages, some of which we alluded to earlier.

1 They deliver richer information.
2 The respondent does not feel frustrated by the constraint imposed with a fixed choice answer.
3 There is less chance of ambiguity, since the respondent says what he or she thinks and doesn't have to interpret a statement and then agree or disagree with it.
4 The questioning is more realistic. We rarely have simply to agree or disagree, or say how strongly, without giving our reasons.

However, open-ended questions are also difficult to code or quantify, whereas fixed-choice items make numerical comparison relatively easy. Chapter 25 on qualitative data, discusses methods of dealing with open-ended answers.

Here are a few examples of fixed-choice items:

1 I voted in the last election   YES/NO
2 I would describe my present dwelling as:
   a) Fully owned by me
   b) Owned by me with a mortgage
   c) Owned by me as part of a housing association
   d) Rented from the local council
   e) Rented from a private landlord
   f) Provided by employer
   g) Other (please state)
3 My age is: **a)** Under 16 **b)** 16–21 **c)** 22–35 **d)** Over 35
4 At what age did your baby start crawling? .... months

The questionnaire constructor has to be careful to phrase questions clearly and unambiguously, such that the respondent is in no doubt which answer to give. The supreme ideal is that all respondents will interpret an item in the same way. Some questions will permit the respondent to tick or check more than one item but if this is not desired (one response only should be unique to each respondent) then possible overlap must be carefully avoided.

> Is it possible to check more than one answer in any of the items given above? If so, which one(s) and why?

I would think there might be confusion if I were just 35 and answering item **3**. In item **2 e)** and **f)** might overlap.

FEATURES OF GOOD QUESTIONNAIRES AND MEASUREMENT SCALES

Where survey questionnaires are requesting purely factual information (such as occupation, number of children at school, hours of television watched, and so on) the following principles are not so crucial, though all measures should be reliable ones. (Factual questionnaires usually have 'face' validity – see later this chapter.) Where scales and tests attempt to measure psychological characteristics, the following are extremely important:

1 They should DISCRIMINATE as widely as possible across the variety of human response. They shouldn't identify a few extreme individuals whilst showing no difference between individuals clustered at the centre of the scale. This is referred to as DISCRIMINATORY POWER.

2 They should be highly RELIABLE.

3 They should be supported by tests of VALIDITY.

4 They should be STANDARDISED if they are to be used as general, practical measures of human characteristics.

A questionnaire, scale or test will normally be piloted, perhaps several times, before the researcher is satisfied that it meets these criteria. Even an unambitious questionnaire, constructed by students as part of course practical work, should be piloted at least once to highlight pitfalls and possible misinterpretations. Tests for the criteria are dealt with later in this chapter.

ATTITUDE SCALES

Attitude scales are quite like questionnaires but do not usually use questions. Most use statements with which the respondent has to agree or disagree.

Remember that questionnaires can vary along the dimension of DISGUISE and that the purpose of the scale could therefore be disguised from the respondent, as in Hammond's technique, mentioned in the last chapter. Some attitude scales give clues to their purpose while others are transparent, as in the case where a limited topic, such as dental hygiene, is involved.

We will look at the techniques of five popular types of attitude scale, along with their advantages and disadvantages.

EQUAL APPEARING INTERVALS (Thurstone, 1931)

To construct a Thurstone-type scale:

1 Produce a large set of statements, both positive and negative towards the attitude

object. If the attitude object were equal opportunities, one item might be: 'Companies should provide more crèche facilities'.

2 Engage a panel of judges to rate each item on a scale of one (highly negative on the issue) to 11 (highly positive on the issue). They are urged to use all of the scale and not to bunch items into a few categories.

3 Take the mean value, for each item, of all the judges' ratings. Our item above might get an average rating of 8.7 for instance. This is its SCALE VALUE.

4 In the interests of reliability, reject items which have a high variance (see Chapter 13). These items are those on which judges are least in agreement.

5 In the finished scale, a respondent now scores the scale value of each item agreed with. Hence, people favourable to equal opportunities measures will tend to score only on items above the average value and thus end up with a high overall score.

A sample of items which might appear in a Thurstone type scale is shown below, along with each item's scale value. The values, of course, would not be visible to the respondent.

Please tick if you agree

Women are less reliable employees because they are likely to leave through pregnancy. (2.1)

Interview panels should scrutinise all questions before interviewing to ensure that none are discriminatory. (5.8)

Companies should provide more crèche facilities. (8.7)

Box 9.1 *Weaknesses of the Thurstone method*

> 1 The judges themselves cannot be completely neutral, although they are asked to be objective. In an early debate on this issue, Hinckley (1932) was severely criticised for rejecting judges as 'careless' because they sorted a majority of items into a few extreme categories, against the exhortation mentioned in item 2 of the construction process above. It turned out that most of these judges were black (or pro-black whites) who rated as fairly hostile certain statements seen as relatively neutral by white judges unaware of, or unconcerned by, black issues
>
> 2 There is a difficulty in choosing the most discriminating items from among those with the same scale value

SUMMATED RATINGS (Likert, 1932)

To construct a Likert-type scale:

1 Produce an equal number of favourable and unfavourable statements about the attitude object.

2 Ask respondents to indicate, for each item, their response to the statement according to the following scale:

5	4	3	2	1
Strongly agree	Agree	Undecided	Disagree	Strongly disagree

3 Use the values on this scale as a score for each respondent on each item, so that the respondent scores five for strong agreement with an item favourable to the attitude object, but one for strong agreement with an unfavourable item.

4 Add up the scores for each item to give the respondent's overall score.

5 Carry out an item analysis test (discussed later) in order to determine the most discriminating items – those on which high overall scorers tend to score highly and vice versa.

6 Reject low discriminatory items, keeping a balance of favourable and unfavourable items.

Step 5 here is the Likert scale's greatest strength relative to other scales. It means that, unlike in a Thurstone scale, an item does not need to relate obviously to the attitude issue or object. It can be counted as DIAGNOSTIC if responses to it correlate well with responses overall. For instance, we might find that respondents fairly hostile to equal opportunities issues also tend to agree with 'Women have an instinctive need to be near their child for the first two to three years of its life'. This could stay in our attitude scale since it might predict negative equal opportunities attitude fairly well.

Box 9.2 *Weaknesses of the Likert method*

> 1 For each respondent, scores on the scale only have meaning *relative* to the scores in the distribution obtained from other respondents. Data produced is therefore best treated as ORDINAL (see Chapter 12) whereas Thurstone considered intervals on his scale to be truly equal
>
> 2 The 'undecided' score, 3, is ambiguous. Does it imply a neutral position (no opinion) or an on-the-fence position with the respondent torn between feelings in both directions?
>
> 3 Partly as a consequence of 2, overall scores, central to the distribution (say 30 out of 60) are quite ambiguous. Central scores could reflect a lot of 'undecided' answers, or they could comprise a collection of 'strongly for' and 'strongly against' answers, in which case, perhaps the scale measured two different attitudes

THE SOCIAL DISTANCE SCALE (Bogardus, 1925)

Bogardus' scale was originally intended to measure attitudes towards members of different nationalities. Respondents had to follow this instruction:

> According to my first feeling reactions, I would willingly admit members of each race [respondents were given several races or nationalities] (as a class, and not the best I have known, nor the worst members) to one or more of the classifications under which I have placed a cross.

They were then given this list to tick, for each race:

1 To close kinship by marriage

2 To my club as personal chums

3 To my street as neighbours

4 To employment in my occupation

5 To citizenship in my country

6 As visitors only in my country

7 Would exclude from my country

It is claimed that, in practice, it is unusual for respondents to accept the race or nationality at a higher level than one at which rejection has occurred, for instance, accepting in one's street, but not to one's occupation. This is known as a 'reversal'.

It is possible to adapt this technique to test attitudes towards any category of people. The classifications themselves will of course need altering to fit the particular categories of person.

On the equal opportunities theme, it would be possible to grade types of occupation into which respondents felt female workers should be encouraged. Modification, however, will require restandardisation in order to avoid too many reversals.

Box 9.3 *Weaknesses of the Bogardus method*

> **1** Reversals cannot be entirely eliminated. Some people are more protective about their employment than their streets, particularly in cities, I would suspect
>
> **2** The overall scale for scoring is narrow, leaving less room for sensitive statistical analysis

CUMULATIVE SCALING (Guttman, 1950)

Roughly speaking, the principle of the Bogardus scale is here extended to any attitude object, not just person categories. On a Bogardus scale, if we know a person's score we know just how far up the scale they went, assuming no reversals. Hence, we can exactly reproduce their scoring pattern. This last achievement is the ideal criterion of a Guttman scale. A clear (but not particularly useful) example would be a scale checking height, where you would tick all those items below which are true for you:

> **1** I am taller than 1 m 20
> **2** I am taller than 1 m 30
> **3** I am taller than 1 m 40
> **4** I am taller than 1 m 50
> **5** I am taller than 1 m 60
> **6** I am taller than 1 m 70

A positive response to item 4 logically entails a positive response to items 1, 2 and 3 also. In the same way as this scale measures a unitary dimension (height), so a true Guttman scale is supposed to only measure one finite attitude and is known as a 'undimensional scale'.

In practice, when measuring attitudes rather than height, it is never possible to reproduce perfectly a respondent's exact answering pattern from their overall score. As we shall see below, items can very often be interpreted differently by respondents and it is rarely possible to isolate attitudes such that answers reflect a undimensional scale. For instance, one respondent, who is a member of a particular minority ethnic group, might disagree with 'members of all ethnic groups should be treated equally' since, in his or her view, the group has been treated pretty unequally in the past and requires compensatory action. Hence, from the tester's point of view this person's answers may seem inconsistent, since they are otherwise strongly favourable to minority ethnic groups, yet a negative response on this item is taken as hostility. Here, we can see the importance of producing a scale through pilot trials *and* qualitative interviewing.

Box 9.4 *Weaknesses of the Guttman method*

1 Reversals cannot be eliminated

2 Guttman himself was criticised for not dealing with the problem of representativeness in selecting items. He claimed this could be achieved through intuitive thinking and experience

THE SEMANTIC DIFFERENTIAL (Osgood et al., 1957)

The original intention behind this scale was to use it for measuring the *connotative* meaning of an object for an individual, roughly speaking, the term's associations for us. Thus, we can all give a denotative meaning for 'nurse' – we have to define what a nurse is, as in a dictionary. The *connotation* of a nurse may, however, differ for each of us. For me, a nurse is associated with caring, strength and independence. For others, by popular stereotype, he or she may be seen as deferential and practical.

On a semantic differential the respondent is invited to mark a scale between bipolar adjectives according to the position they feel the object holds on that scale for them. For 'nurse' on the following bipolar opposites, I might mark as shown:

good	√	—	—	—	—	—	— bad
weak	—	—	—	—	—	√	— strong
active	—	√	—	—	—	—	— passive

Osgood claimed that factor analysis (see later in this chapter) of all scales gave rise to three general meaning factors, to one of which all bipolar pairs could be attached.

'Active' (along with 'slow–fast', 'hot–cold') is an example of the ACTIVITY factor. 'Strong' (along with 'rugged–delicate', 'thick–thin') is an example of the POTENCY factor. 'Good' (along with 'clean–dirty', 'pleasant–unpleasant') is an example of the EVALUATIVE factor.

Adapted to attitude measurement, the semantic differential apparently produces good reliability values and correlates well with other attitude scales, thus producing CONCURRENT VALIDITY (see page 153).

Box 9.5 *Weaknesses of the semantic differential*

1 Respondents may have a tendency towards a 'position response bias' where they habitually mark at the extreme end of the scale (or won't use the extreme at all) without considering possible weaker or stronger responses. This can occur with a Likert scale too, but is more likely here since the scale points lack the Likert verbal designations (of 'strongly agree' etc.)

2 Here, too, we have the problem of interpretation of the middle point on the scale

QUESTIONNAIRE OR SCALE ITEMS

WHAT TO AVOID IN STATEMENT CONSTRUCTION

What do you think is unsatisfactory about the following statements, intended for an attitude scale?

1 'We should begin to take compensatory action in areas of employment and training where, in the past, members of one ethnic group, sex or disability type have suffered discrimination or experienced disadvantages as a direct result of being a member of that category.'

2 'Society should attempt to undo the effects of institutional racism wherever possible.'

3 'Immigrants should not be allowed to settle in areas of high unemployment.'

4 'Abortion is purely a woman's choice and should be made freely available.'

5 'It should not be possible to ask a woman about her spouse's support, when husbands are not asked the same questions.'

6 'The present Tory government are callously dismantling the welfare state.'

7 'Do you agree that student grants should be increased?'

8 'Do you have a criminal record?'

1 Complexity

Not many respondents will take this in all in one go. The statement is far too complex. It could possibly be broken up into logical components.

2 Technical terms

Many respondents will not have a clear idea of what 'institutional racism' is. Either find another term or include a preamble to the item which explains the special term.

3 Ambiguity

Some students I taught used this item once and found almost everyone in general agreement, whether they were generally hostile to immigrants or not. Hence, it was not at all discriminating. This was probably because those positive towards immigrants considered their plight if new to the country *and* unemployed. Those who were hostile to immigrants may well have been making racist assumptions and either mistakenly thinking most immigrants were black, or equally incorrectly, thinking most black people were immigrants.

4 Double-barrelled items

This quite simple item is asking two questions at once. A person might well agree with free availability – to avoid the dangers of the back-street abortionist – yet may not feel that only the woman concerned should choose.

5 Negatives

In the interests of avoiding response set (see below), about half the items in a scale should be positive towards the object and about half negative. However, it is not a good idea to produce negative statements simply by negating a positive one. It can be confusing to answer a question with a double negative, even where one of the negatives is camouflaged, as in:

'It should not be possible to reject a candidate's application on the grounds of disability.'

This could be rephrased as 'A candidate's disability should be completely ignored when considering an application.'

The item in the exercise has two overt negatives in it and this can easily be confusing.

6 Emotive language

A statement such as this may not get an attitude test off to a good start, particularly in affluent constituencies. If there are emotive items at all it might be best to leave these until the respondent is feeling more relaxed with the interviewer or with the test itself.

7 Leading questions

As I said, most attitude tests don't have actual questions in them. Should this sort of question occur, however, it carries with it an implication that the respondent should say 'yes'. If you don't feel this is so, just try to imagine a friend or colleague opening the day's conversation with such a question. To the respondent it can seem hard to disagree, something which people would usually rather not do anyway. One might begin with 'Weeell. . .'. Respondents may well say 'Yes, but . . .' with the 'but' amounting to disagreement, even though the response is recorded as agreement.

8 Invasion of privacy

This is private information, along with sex life and other obvious areas. Many people will find questions about attitude quite intrusive. Certainly the student conducting a practical exercise should be very careful about such intrusion.

ORGANISATION OF ITEMS

1 Response set or bias

An effect called RESPONSE ACQUIESCENCE SET often occurs when responding to questionnaires. This is the tendency to agree rather than disagree ('Yeah saying'). To avoid a constant error from this effect, items need to be an unpredictable mixture of positive and negative statements about the attitude object. This has the effect either of keeping the respondent thinking about each item or of giving the inveterate yeah sayer a central score, rather than an extreme one. There is also some evidence of a smaller bias towards *disagreeing* with items.

2 Respondent's interpretation

With any questionnaire or scale, it is a good idea to make it clear that both positive and negative items will appear. There are several reasons for this.

Respondents are likely to view the interviewer as believing the statements made. A set of statements all contrary to what the respondent thinks may well set up strong emotional defences. We have said already that, for the same reason it would be best to start with less extreme statements.

There are also demand characteristics (see Chapter 5) associated with responding to a questionnaire. The respondent may well try to interpret the aim of the research or questions. Again, if all initial items are in the same direction the respondent may form an impression of the interviewer's aims or personality which can distort the respondent's later answers.

3 Social desirability

Defined in Chapter 5, this factor involves respondents guessing at what is counted as a socially acceptable or favourable answer and giving it in order to 'look good'. A further reason for guessing might be to 'please the researcher' by giving the results it is assumed are required. Some questionnaires attempt to deal with this problem by including items which only an angel would agree or disagree with. If too many such items are answered in the 'saintly' manner, the respondent's results are excluded from the research. Eysenck calls his set of items a 'lie scale', though an excluded respondent is not necessarily lying. They may be near perfect or they may be distorting the truth just a bit.

RELIABILITY AND NUMBER OF ITEMS

The number of items used in a questionnaire needs to be kept manageable in terms of time and the respondent's patience, but enough items should be chosen for reliability to become acceptably high. With a larger number of items, random errors, from respondents' individual interpretations and misunderstandings, should cancel each other out.

Box 9.6 *Steps in constructing an attitude scale*

1 Produce a substantial number of items which are balanced for:
   a Strength (some 'weak' statements, some 'hard')
   b Breadth: is the whole area covered?
   c Direction: in a Likert-type scale, some items should be 'pro' the issue and as many 'anti'; half of each of this set should be weak and half strong
2 Pilot this first batch of items for ambiguity, misunderstanding etc.
3 Replace deleted items by new ones, still keeping a balance
4 Repeat 2 and 3 until all items are unproblematic
5 Arrange items in a random or alternating order which will discourage response bias or hostility build up
6 Pilot this arrangement on good-sized sample and conduct item analysis on results
7 Test for reliability. Do item analysis and remove low discrimination items. Retest for realiability. If reliability still unsatisfactory, or if too few items left after item analysis, add new items and repeat cycle(s) until realiability is satisfactory
8 Inspect or test final version for validity. Do items still cover main issues? Do some topics now dominate? Do scores on test relate to an external criterion? If validity unsatisfactory, repeat cycles again

PROJECTIVE TESTS

These tests have been developed out of the psychoanalytic tradition of research and therapy. They are based on the Freudian notion that when we are confronted by an abstract or ambiguous picture, some of our inner thoughts, protected because they produce anxiety, are partially revealed by the way we *project* our interpretations onto the display.

The *Rorschach* ink blot test is a set of abstract designs rather like children produce with 'butterfly' paintings. (See Figure 9.1). The test-taker reports what he or she feels they can see in the picture.

Similarly, the *Thematic apperception test* (TAT) is a picture, often of people with their emotional expressions ambiguous or hidden, about which, the test-taker is asked, 'What is happening?'

These tests belong in the unstructured, disguised section of the quadrant formed by these two dimensions. It is claimed that their open-endedness produces richer information and that their disguised nature provides genuine data, unbiased by people guessing the researcher's (or therapist's) intent.

It is argued that the tests can be used to measure such factors as the affective, usually hidden, component of attitudes. They have very often been used to assess concealed aggression, hostility, anxiety, sexual fantasy and so on in hypothesis testing work. Levin's study, mentioned in Chapter 8, used Rorschach tests.

Box 9.7 *Weaknesses of projective tests*

1 Being open-ended and initially qualitative, the tests are suspect for their reliability. Some users take great care in checking agreement between raters who code and categorise responses, ignorant of the research hypothesis. The researcher provides a comprehensive and subtle coding scheme. In Levin's study, agreement between Rorschach scorers, ignorant of the research aim, was between 84% and 91%

2 It is quite possible for coders to be highly consistent, compared with one another, yet for the measures to be quite unrelated to any theoretical psychoanalytic principle. A person in Levin's study who said of people seen in the Rorschach blot 'I can't quite tell if they're male or female' may not *actually* be confused about their sexual body-image, for instance. Since the tests are also *disguised* measures of hypothetical concepts, the problem of validity is serious

Figure 9.1 *Rorschach ink blot*

SOCIOMETRY

Sociometry is specifically aimed at analysing the interconnections between people in smallish groups. Typically, group members are asked who their best friends are, with whom they would prefer to work on a problem or with whom they would share a room, and so on. Questions can also ask about least preferred group members or about who should be leader.

Table 9.1 *Sociometric matrix*

Solution matrix		Chosen				
		A	B	C	D	E
Chooser	A		0	1	1	1
	B	1		0	1	1
	C	1	0		1	0
	D	0	0	1		0
	E	0	0	0	1	

Information generated, then, is in the form of person choices, positive or negative. These choices can be represented on a SOCIOMETRIC MATRIX, as shown in Table 9.1. '1' represents being chosen and '0' not. It is possible to subject these matrices to mathematical analysis. Out of this can come measures of group cohesiveness or predictions of internal conflict.

A more obvious and direct product of the matrix is the SOCIOGRAM or, in more general methematical terms, the DIRECTED GRAPH. An example of the sociogram resulting from Table 9.1 is given in Figure 9.2.

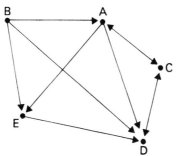

Figure 9.2 *Sociogram or directed graph*

From this diagram it is immediately obvious that B is an 'isolate', D is very popular, though chooses colleagues carefully, and C only chooses people who reciprocate the choice.

The sociogram tends only to be used in practical applications, rather than in research studies, where interactions are usually too numerous for charts, and detailed mathematical processing is required.

APPLICATIONS

Research applications include the study of classroom interactions. Teachers, for instance, have been found to prefer the children most chosen by their classmates, and vice versa. The effect of direct praise to pupils can be assessed in terms of increased popularity among peers.

In general, comparisons can be made between group structures and group effectiveness. For popular individuals, links can be sought with other measures of liking and attraction. The relationship of 'isolates' and 'cliques' to the rest of the group can be further investigated.

Box 9.8 *Weaknesses of sociometric method*

> 1 Although small group studies can use the sociogram for illustration, larger studies, and any seeking statistical analysis, require specialised mathematical methods
>
> 2 Choices made alone and on paper can differ markedly from those made in real situations with all group pressures present. On the other hand, the anonymity and distance of the choice might just disclose real attractions, suppressed in the practical group setting

PSYCHOMETRIC TESTS

Psychologists have developed many tests which were intended to be standardised instruments of measurement for human psychological characteristics. These are known as PSYCHOMETRIC TESTS and their use as PSYCHOMETRY. The tradition goes back to Galton who began the measurement of mental abilities in the 1890s by testing thousands of people on many sensory and cognitive tasks (many of the people tested paid Galton a fee for the privilege!). Although some attitude scales have become highly refined, and even projective tests are sometimes called 'psychometric', if well standardised, it is intelligence and personality tests which have undergone a high degree of standardisation and scrutiny for validity. This is partly because such tests are used in professional practice where people's life chances can be affected.

These tests have also undergone much periodic revision, since they are highly sensitive to bias from cultural, class and other social factors. It is on these grounds that their validity has been most seriously challenged and thoroughly investigated.

For instance, to the question 'What should you do if you find a stamped addressed envelope in the street?', it might be 'intelligent', in a very poor area, where petty crime is unremarkable, to steam off the stamp – a response which gained no mark in one famous test. A picture depicting a boy holding an umbrella at the wrong angle to falling rain was said by Puerto Ricans to be incorrect, not because of the angle but because the boy was holding the umbrella at all. This is considered highly effeminate in Puerto Rican society!

It is beyond the scope of this book to cover intelligence and personality testing in depth, along with all the weaknesses and criticisms of the tests. This is covered very well in other available texts, in particular Gross (1992)[1]. The examples given above simply demonstrate the need for standardisation and constant revision from a

---

[1] More specilialist texts include:

Anastasi, A. (1988) *Psychological Testing* Macmillan
Chronbach, L. J. (1984) *Essentials of Psychological Testing* Harper & Row
Kline, P. (1993) *Handbook of Test Construction* Routledge
Murphy, R. M. & Davidshofer, C. O. (1991) *Psychological Testing; principles and applications* Prentice-Hall

research method's point of view. They also show the reader, I hope, what is meant by class and cultural bias.

In studying research methods, however, it is important to recognise that any research, including experimental, might include, as data, results of psychometric tests. Most tests will be beyond the scope of student use, since they are closely guarded as technical instruments of the psychological profession. They also usually have quite complex scoring manuals which are even more closely monitored.

FACTOR ANALYSIS

Researchers often support the development and use of psychometric tests by employing a form of 'construct validity' (explained later in this chapter), which involves a complex statistical procedure known as FACTOR ANALYSIS. The aim is to find factors (hypothetical constructs) which might explain the observed relationships between people's scores on several tests or subtests. The steps involved are these:

1 A large sample of people are measured on several tests or subtests.
2 Correlations (see Chapter 18) are calculated between every possible pair of tests or subtests and arranged in a matrix as shown in Table 9.2 below.
3 The matrix of correlations is fed into the factor analysis programme which looks for 'clusters' – groups of tests or subtests which all correlate well together.
4 The researcher sets the programme to solve the matrix for a particular number of 'factors'. Factors, at this point, are nothing real, just mathematical concepts which will 'account for' as much as possible of the correlation found. The programme then gives the best configuration of this number of factors to account for all the correlations.
5 Alternatively, the programme will offer a solution in the best possible number of factors, with the least amount of variation unaccounted for. The whole 'explanation' is purely statistical accounting for the numerical relationships.
6 The researcher might ask the programme to solve for a higher number of factors if the amount 'unexplained' is too high.

To make the concept of factor analysis a little clearer, I hope, imagine the following. We select a few hundred people of average fitness and subject them to various athletic events. We correlate the results of every event with every other, producing a table, part of which might look like Table 9.2:

Table 9.2 *Correlations between various athletic events*

	100 Metres	200 Metres	3000 Metres	5000 Metres	Shot	Discus	Long Jump
100 Metres		0.87	0.24	0.31	−0.65	−0.32	0.47
200 Metres			0.19	0.28	−0.61	−0.29	0.39
3000 Metres				0.91	−0.16	0.03	0.13
5000 Metres					−0.08	0.11	0.09
Shot						0.65	0.14
Discus							−0.02
Long Jump							

As we'll see in Chapter 18, if people tend to score similarly on two variables, these variables are said to 'positively correlate' and we'd expect a value close to $+1$. If there is a tendency to be high on one variable whilst being low on the other we'd expect a value approaching -1. No relationship at all is signified by a value close to zero.

As we'd expect from common-sense prediction, there is a strong correlation between 100 and 200 metres, and between 3 000 and 5 000 metres. There is a moderate correlation between discus and shot put and between 100 metres and long jump, whereas that between 100 metres and shot put is moderately negative.

Intuition might suggest that the underlying factors responsible for these relationships are *sprinting ability*, *stamina* and *strength*. If we asked the factor analysis programme to solve for just two factors it would probably tell us that, no matter which way the matrix was solved, a lot of relationship between variables was left unaccounted for. For three variables it might well give us a good solution with little variation unexplained. But it is important to note that *it would be up to us to name the factors and to debate what real processes they are an indication of*.

Roughly speaking, this is what factor analysts do with the scores of large samples on personality and intelligence tests and subtests. The factors emerging are recognised and named intuitively. They are also validated against existing tests and known factor arrangements. The factors are said to be responsible for the participants' variations in performance across the tests.

It is important to recognise that factor analysis does not 'prove' that such factors exist. It simply provides supporting evidence which allows the researcher to claim that intelligence or personality could be organised in a particular way and that the factor analysis results don't refute this. Factor analysis is a purely statistical process. As with all statistical results, researchers, with particular views and theories to defend, interpret and present statistics in a way which gives them the best support.

There is a more extensive discussion of factor analysis and its limitations in Gross (1992, pp. 841–7 and 886–7). An extensive and severe criticism of the use of factor analysis to support models of intellectual structure is provided by Block and Dworkin (1974).

RELIABILITY, VALIDITY AND STANDARDISATION

It is common in psychological research to attempt the measurement of variables for which there is no universally agreed measure. Examples are attitude, motivation, intelligence. Some variables even appear as invented constructs, examples being: extroversion and introversion or ego-strength. The tests which psychologists construct in order to measure such variables often serve as operational definitions of the concept under research. The attitude scales and psychometric tests which we have discussed would all need to be checked formally for their reliability and validity. They would also need to be standardised for general use. We'll discuss methods for each of these checks in turn.

RELIABILITY

Any measure, but especially one we have just invented, must be queried as to its accuracy in terms of producing the same results on different occasions. A reliable measurement instrument is one which achieves just this performance. Consider a practical example. If you have kitchen scales which stick, you won't get the same reading for the same amount of flour each time you weigh it. The measure given by your scales is unreliable. We can also say that your scales have poor reliability.

A difference between kitchen scales and instruments used for human characteristic measurement is that psychologists often use tests with many items whereas weight is measured by just one indicator – the dial reading. Psychological tests of, for instance, political attitude can be queried as to their INTERNAL RELIABILITY, meaning 'is the test consistent within itself?' This is usually measured by checking whether people tend to answer each item in the same way as they answer all others. Like scales and other instruments, though, these tests can also be checked for their reliability in producing similar results at different times. Cronbach (1960) has discussed these two rather different uses of the term reliability applied to a psychological measure. Using Cronbach's terms, INTERNAL CONSISTENCY and STABILITY, the difference might be pictured as follows.

Imagine you were giving a statement to the police. Your statement might be found to be unreliable in two distinct ways:

1 Internal consistency – you may contradict yourself within the statement
2 Stability – you may alter important details when asked to remake the statement some time later

Internal consistency is the same as internal reliability. Stability may be called EXTERNAL RELIABILITY: does the test produce similar results on (at least two) different occasions?

METHODS FOR CHECKING INTERNAL RELIABILITY

Split half method

A psychological test which consists of several items or questions can be split so that items are divided randomly, or by odds and evens, into two sets comprising half the complete test each. If the test is reliable then people's scores on each half should be similar and the extent of similarity is assessed using correlation (Chapter 18). Correlations achieved here would be expected to exceed 0.9.

Item discrimination methods

These methods take into account people's performance on each item. The KUDER–RICHARDSON method is used for 'yes/no' or 'pass/fail' type items and has the effect of calculating the average of all possible split half correlations for a set of items. For items answered along a scale of response ('strongly agree', 'agree', etc.) CRONBACH'S ALPHA coefficient is used.

Item analysis

Items will produce higher reliability in a questionnaire if they *discriminate* well between individuals. There are two common methods for checking the discriminatory power of items.

1 For each item in the test or questionnaire, the correlation is calculated between each person's score on the item and their score on the test as a whole.
2 Looking at individuals' scores overall on the test, the highest 10% and the lowest 10% of scores are identified. This 10% is not fixed and could be 15% or 20% if desired. The scores of these two groups of people are then totalled for each item

in the test. If these two extreme groups scored very differently then the item is highly discriminative. If not, it is low in discriminating between the two groups and may be discarded.

Both these systems may be accused of some circularity since we are using overall totals to decide for each item, *contributing to that total*, how good it is at discriminating. The totals themselves will change as each poor item is removed. That is, the test for reliability uses scores on an as yet probably unreliable test.

CHECKING EXTERNAL RELIABILITY

Test–retest reliability

To check that a psychological test produces similar results each time it is used, we would have to use it on the *same* people on each occasion, otherwise we have no comparison. 'Test–retest' means that a group of people are tested once, then again some time later. The two sets of scores are *correlated*, to see whether people tend to get the same sort of score on the second occasion. If they do, the test has high reliability. Correlations achieved here would be expected to be at least around 0.75–0.8.

> There are several reasons, however, why people may not score the same, second time around, on the same test. Can you think of a few?

1 People may answer differently the second time *because* they took the test before and now wish to alter the image they feel they made.

2 They may also recall what they answered on the first occasion and not answer according to their current perceptions.

3 Some external event may have had a significant impact on attitudes. If the questionnaire is on capital punishment and a serious terrorist incident has occurred between first and second test, attitudes may have hardened. Of course, if everyone hardened their attitude to the same extent, correlation would not be affected, but effects are rarely this simple.

4 The research may have included an attempt to change attitude between first and second test, in which case the attitude scale should have *already* been tested for reliability.

VALIDITY

A test or effect may well be rated as excellent on reliability but may not be measuring what was originally intended. This criticism is often levelled at tests of intelligence which, though quite reliable, measure only a narrow range of intellectual ability, missing out, for instance, the whole range of creative thought which the public language definition would include. The validity of a psychological measure is the extent to which it *does* measure what it is intended to measure.

Suppose you gave some seven-year-old children a list of quite difficult words to remember and recall. You may actually be testing their reading ability or word knowledge rather than their memory. Early experiments on perceptual defence, which seemed to show that people would take longer to recognise 'taboo', rude or

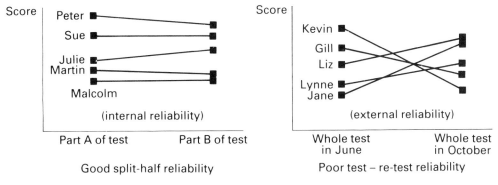

Figure 9.3 *Split-half and test-retest reliability*

emotional words, were criticised for the validity of the effect on the grounds that what may well have been demonstrated was people's unwillingness to report such words to a strange experimenter or their disbelief that such words could occur in a respectable scientific experiment. The effect was quite reliable but confounded, so that the variable actually measured was later held to be (conscious) embarrassment and/or social expectation.

There are various recognised means by which validity of tests can be assessed.

FACE VALIDITY

The crudest method for checking a test's validity is simply to inspect the contents to see whether it does indeed measure what it's supposed to. This is possible when devising a mathematics test, for example, for clearly the test should contain problems at the intended level and with sufficient breadth. It should not, inadvertently, involve use of higher level mathematics procedures in some of the problems.

CONTENT VALIDITY

A researcher may ask colleagues to evaluate the content of a test to ensure that it is representative of the area which it is intended to cover. They will carry out this task using their expertise in the topic area to judge whether the collection of items has failed to test certain skills or is unduly weighted towards some aspects of knowledge compared with others.

Content validity is, in fact, simply a more sophisticated version of face validity.

CRITERION VALIDITY

The validity of a test of neuroticism might reasonably be established by using it on a group of people who have suffered from a neurotic condition and comparing scores with a control group. Use of the neurotic group would be an example of what is called a KNOWN GROUPS CRITERION. There are two types of criterion validity differing only in terms of the timing of the criterion test:

Concurrent validity

If the new test is validated by comparison with a currently existing criterion, we have CONCURRENT VALIDITY. Very often, a new IQ or personality test might be compared with an older but similar test known to have good validity already. The known group example above is also a case of concurrent validity.

Predictive validity

A prediction may be made, on the basis of a new intelligence test for instance, that high scorers at age 12 will be more likely to obtain university degrees or enter the professions several years later. If the prediction is born out then the test has PREDICTIVE VALIDITY.

Both these methods are in fact predictive since, in science, the term 'predict' does not mean 'forecast'. A social scientist may well predict a relationship between *past* events. Used in this sense, then, there is virtually no difference between these two concepts except for the point in time of the prediction.

CONSTRUCT VALIDITY

This takes us back to our discussion of variables which are not directly observable and the psychologist's tendency to propose hypothetical constructs (Chapter 2) and the discussion of construct validity in Chapter 4. Constructs require some form of validation, otherwise, why should we continue to take them seriously? Typical of such constructs would be: achievement motivation, extroversion, dogmatism, dependency, ego-strength.

In each case there is no direct evidence for such constructs having any kind of real existence. Construct validity entails demonstrating the power of such a construct to explain a network of research findings and to predict further relationships. Rokeach (1960) showed that his test for dogmatism predictably distinguished between different religious and political groups, as well as having relationships with approaches to entirely new problems and acceptance of new artistic ideas. Eysenck (1970) argued that extroversion was related to the activity of the cerebral cortex and produced several testable hypotheses from his theory.

Intelligence factors and personality variables are supported as valid by the use of factor analysis, as explained earlier, which is an elaborate part of construct validation. If a construct is sound then it should be possible to support the argument for its existence with a variety of measures of its effects on, or relationships with, other variables. If cognitive dissonance, for instance, is a genuine, common psychological process, then we should be able to predict effects from a variety of different sorts of experiment, in the laboratory and field, with a variety of different groups of people performing a number of qualitatively different tasks.

This might all sound a bit magical. Why can't we just observe nice concrete events and objects like physicists do? Well, this is a misconception of the way physicists work with theory.

No physicist has ever seen an atom directly. What are observed are the effects of what is *assumed* to be an atom. Although the theory of atomic elements is beyond dispute, the construct of an atom is defined mathematically, is difficult for the lay person to understand and keeps changing in exact definition. Its validity as a construct is supported by a plethora of experimental support.

STANDARDISATION

The process of standardising a test involves adjusting it, using reliability and validity tests to eliminate items, until it is useful as a measure of the population it is targeted at, and will enable us to compare individuals with confidence. To make such comparisons the test must be used on a large sample of the target population, from whom means and standard scores (see Chapter 13) are established. This will tell us what percentage of people tend to fall between certain scores and what is the value which most of the population centre around.

Psychometric tests are used in research but also on an applied basis in decisions about people's life chances and opportunities. These may be related to education, psychotherapeutic treatment or job selection. Therefore, it is of the utmost importance that these tests do not discriminate, in a particular way, against some groups of people, which anyway reduces their scientific value. Standardisation has, therefore, both scientific and ethical importance.

STANDARDISATION TO A NORMAL DISTRIBUTION

Many tests are adjusted until testing of a large sample produces a score distribution which approximates very closely to the normal distribution (see Chapter 13). One reason for doing this is that the properties of the normal distribution allow us to perform some extremely powerful statistical estimates.

The fact that an IQ test can be devised and adjusted until it produces a normal distribution on large group testing has led some researchers to argue that the test therefore measures a largely innate quality since many biological characteristics are indeed normally distributed through the working of many random genetic processes together.

Critics have argued that the adjustment of the test to normal distribution is artificial and that many biological characteristics are not normal in distribution. Certainly, some psychological phenomena need not be normally distributed. Attitudes to some issues on which people are somewhat polarised in position (for instance, on nuclear weapons or abortion) will be spread, as measured by questionnaire, in a bi-modal (two-hump) fashion (Chapter 13).

An extremely important point here is that a test standardised on a particular population can obviously not be used with confidence on a different population. This criticism has been levelled at those who claimed a difference existed between white and black populations in intelligence. There *was* a difference in IQ score but, until 1973, the Stanford–Binet test had not included black persons in its sample for standardisation. Hence, the test was only applicable, with any confidence, to the white population.

GLOSSARY

		attitude scales
Scales on which, theoretically, the range of items the respondent would agree with is identifiable from their score – the point on the scale at which their agreement with items ended; the items concern persons of a certain category	_____	Bogardus
Similar to the scale just described but items can concern any attitude object	_____	Guttman

Scale on which respondent can choose from a dimension of responses, usually from strongly against/disagree to strongly for/agree	_____	Likert
On a Thurstone scale, the average rated value of an item; respondent is given this score if they agree with it	_____ _____	scale value
Scale measuring meaning of an object for the respondent by having them describe it using a point between the extremes of several bi-polar adjectives	_____ _____	semantic differential
Scale in which raters assess the relative 'strength' of each item and respondents agreeing with that item receive the average rated value for it	_____	Thurstone

Item not obviously or directly connected to the attitude object yet which correlates well with overall scores and therefore has discriminatory power	_____ ____	diagnostic item
An alternative term for 'sociogram' – see below	_____ _____	directed graph
Extent to which items, or the test as a whole, separate people along the scoring dimension	_____ _____	discriminatory power
Statistical technique, using patterns of test or subtest correlations, which provides support for theoretical constructs by locating 'clusters'	_____ _____	factor analysis
Tests which attempt to quantify psychological variables: skills, abilities, character etc.	_____ _____	psychometric tests

Consistency and stability of a test	_____	**reliability**
A generalised Kuder–Richardson type test of item discrimination/reliability for a response scale with several points (e.g. a Likert-type scale)	_____ _____	Cronbach's alpha
Stability of a test. Its tendency to produce the same results when repeated	_____	external
Consistency of a test. Extent to which items tend to be measuring the same thing and not in opposition to one another	_____	internal

Checking each item in a scale by comparing its relationship with the total scores on the scale	_____ _____	item analysis
A test of item discrimination/reliability which effectively gives the average of all possible split-half coefficients which could be calculated on a yes/no answer scale	_____–_____	Kuder–Richardson
Comparing scores on two parts formed by a random and equal division of the items in a test	_____ ____	split half

Tendency for people to agree with test items as a habitual response	_____ _____	response acquiescence
A table showing preferences of individuals in a group for each others' company, friendship (etc.); can be turned into a 'sociogram'	_____ _____	sociometric matrix
A visual representation of a sociometric matrix	_____	sociogram
Adjusting test until scores on it form a normal distribution; also calculation of norms for the distribution	_____	standardisation

Extent to which a test measures what was intended	_____	**validity**
Extent to which test results conform with those on some other measure, taken at the same time	_____	concurrent
Extent to which test results support a network of research hypotheses based on the assumed characteristics of a theoretical psychological variable	_____	construct
Extent to which test covers the whole of the relevant topic area	_____	content
Extent to which test scores can be used to make a specific prediction on another measure	_____	criterion
Extent to which the validity of a test is self-evident	____	face
Test of criterion validity involving groups between whom scores on the test should differentiate	_____ _____	known groups

Extent to which test scores can predict scores on another measure in the future	_____	predictive

EXERCISES

1 A scale measuring attitude towards nuclear energy is given a test–retest reliability check. It is found that correlation is 0.85. However, it is also found that scores for the sample have risen significantly.
   a) Should the test be used as it is?
   b) What might explain the rise in sample scores?

2 A student friend has devised a test of 'Attitude towards the British' which she wants to administer to a group of international students just about to leave the country.
   a) How could the test be validated?
   b) How could the test be checked for reliability?

3 A friend says 'My cat hates Whitney Houston's music. I've put the record on ten times now and each time she goes out'. Is this a reliable test, a valid test, or neither?

4 Comment on any flaws in the following potential attitude scale or questionnaire items:
   a) Do you feel that the government has gone too far with privatisation?
   b) What do you think is the best way to punish children?
   c) How many times were you late for work in the last two months?
   d) People from other countries are the same as us and should be treated with respect.
   e) It should not be possible to avoid taxation and not be punished for it.
   f) Women are taking a lot of management posts in traditionally male occupational areas (in a scale to measure attitude to women's rights).
   g) Tomorrow's sex role models should be more androgynous.

5 A researcher administers Rorschach tests to a control and experimental group of psychiatric patients. She then rates each response according to a very well-standardised scale for detecting anxiety. Could this procedure be improved?

COMPARISON STUDIES

The chapter looks at studies which are comparisons, either of the same people as they mature over longish periods, or of several groups of different ages (or sometimes class, occupation etc.) at the same moment. It also includes studies which compare samples from more than one culture (**cross-cultural studies**).

- **Longitudinal studies** follow a group ('cohort', if a large group) through a longish period of time, possibly comparing with a control group if the first group is receiving some 'treatment'.
- **Cross-sectional** studies capture several groups, usually of different ages, at one specific point. The general goals are to map developmental stages or the enhanced effect of a 'treatment' over time.
- There is a very serious and strong issue of ethnocentrism involved in **cross-cultural study** and recognition of this has mostly replaced older studies which had a highly Euro/American-centred and/or colonial flavour, sometimes bearing clear signs of racism. More recent studies take on the political issues and attempt to avoid ethnocentrism. There is some development of 'indigenous psychologies' – psychology originated by and geared to the socio-political needs of people within several cultures (e.g. India, Philippines).
- The student reader is warned of the need to clarify concepts of race, ethnicity and discrimination, through discussion and reading, before embarking on a possibly sensitive practical project which includes race issues. Attention to one's own stereotypes, received views and language is important.

CROSS-SECTIONAL STUDIES

Both these and longitudinal studies can give information on changes in a psychological variable over time. A cross-sectional study does this by taking groups of children or adults from different specified age bands and comparing them at the same moment in time. Comparisons may well highlight age-related changes and developmental trends. Cross-sectional data are often used to support developmental theories such as those of Piaget or Freud.

Two specific examples of cross-sectional studies are:

1 Williams et al. (1975) interviewed five-, seven- and nine-year-old children. She asked the children to guess the sex of heavily stereotyped story characters. Five-year-olds showed some stereotyping but seven- and nine-year-olds showed far more.

2 Kohlberg (1981) developed his theory of changes in the style of children's moral reasoning from a study of ten-, 13- and 16-year-olds' attempts to solve several moral dilemmas.

A cross-sectional study can also compare groups defined other than by age. A cross-section of classes might be studied, or of occupational or ethnic groups but always comparing the samples at the same time.

LONGITUDINAL STUDIES

The big disadvantage of cross-sectional studies is that of comparability, a problem encountered in any study using independent samples. We can't ever be sure that our two or more groups are similar enough for fair comparison. The longitudinal approach surmounts this difficulty since it employs repeated measures on the same group of people over a substantial period, often a number of years. In this way genuine changes and the stability of some characteristics may be observed. If intervals between observations are not too large, major points of change can be identified. In some longitudinal studies, such as Kagan's, below, a control group is used for comparison where the 'treatment' group is receiving some form of intervention programme or (as in Kagan's) there is a naturally differing independent variable. Examples of longitudinal studies are:

1 Kagan et al. (1980) showed that infants in day care during the working week were no worse developed on any measure than home-reared children, so long as care facilities were good.

2 Eron et al. (1972) demonstrated a correlation between longer viewing of television violence at age nine and higher aggressiveness at age 19, by following through a study with hundreds of boys.

3 Kohlberg also carried out longitudinal studies, one lasting for 20 years, on groups of children and their moral reasoning.

Every so often, huge longitudinal studies are carried out on a large section of the population, often children, in order to give some idea of national trends. In such cases the large sample of children is known as a COHORT. An example would be Davie et al. (1972) who followed almost 16 000 children from birth (one week in 1958) to the age of 11.

EVALUATION OF LONGITUDINAL AND CROSS-SECTIONAL STUDIES

The longitudinal approach can show genuine changes in the children studied. If the sample is small, generalisation has to be tentative, but with larger samples or replicated studies, researchers can be more confident that changes are common to the population sampled from.

Changes inferred from a cross-sectional study could be the result of variation between groups in, for instance, education or local cultural environment. Samples in cross-sectional studies can also be biased by age discrimination. A sample of 14-year-old village children may not include those at boarding school whereas their nine-year-old equivalents are present at the time of the study.

Where the cross-sectional age difference is large (say 20 years), the different social changes experienced by the two groups may interfere with direct comparison on the variables studied. This is known as the COHORT EFFECT. We can make cohort effects the object of research by selecting a group of 16-year-olds, for instance, in the years 1995, 2000 and 2005. This is known as TIME LAG study. Here we obviously can't make longitudinal comparisons (different people) or cross-sectional comparisons (same age, different time) but we can see whether attitudes have altered, or abilities improved, in the culture studied so long as we have confidence that the samples are all representative enough of 16-year-olds in that year.

Because of the expense and time involved, longitudinal research tends to use relatively fewer people. Of these, some may get sick, move or otherwise drop out of the study. The remaining sample might consequently be unrepresentative.

Events of one era, such as war, massive unemployment or a dramatic rise in divorce rate, might have a specific effect on one generation of children in a longitudinal study such that their particular pattern of development is not characteristic of other generations. This is known as the CROSS-GENERATIONAL PROBLEM.

Decisions made at the start of a longitudinal study are irreversible once the study has begun, unless the study is relatively unstructured (for instance, a case-study). A cross-sectional study can sooner be modified and replicated within the same generation.

Both longitudinal and cross-sectional studies may be confounded by maturational changes in children's general development. For instance, difficult questions will be more easily answered by nine-year-olds than by seven-year-olds. We might falsely conclude that the younger children don't have the knowledge or concept which certain questions ask about. Older children might be more capable of guessing what a researcher is after.

CROSS-SECTIONAL, SHORT-TERM LONGITUDINAL STUDY

This is a compromise design for the study of age comparison. Three groups, say of 13-, 15- and 17-year-olds may be studied over two years on the effects of a programme designed to reduce drug addiction. Each group would be compared with a control group, as in a longitudinal study using one age group. But here we can determine the age at which the programme has maximum effect whilst investigating the range 13 to 19 in just two years. An example is Halliday and Leslie (1986) who studied mother–child communications with children ranging from 9–29 months at

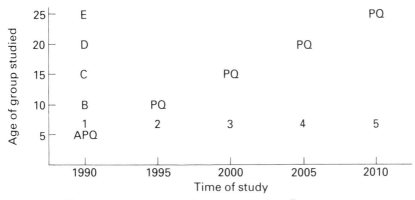

A – E = cross-sectional study on groups A to E
PQ   = longitudinal study on group P, control group Q
1 – 5 = time lag study on groups 1 to 5, all aged 7

Figure 10.1 *Different kinds of comparison study (adapted from Lewin, 1979)*

the start of the study, to 15–36 months at the end, so the age range of 9 to 36 months was covered in six months' recording.

Box 10.1 *Advantages and disadvantages of longitudinal and cross-sectional studies*

	Cross-sectional	**Longitudinal**
Advantages	Cross-sectional groups are studied at same historical moment so cross-generational problem avoided	The development of specific individuals is recorded
	Few people lost during study	No variation between groups can confound age and stage comparisons
	Relatively inexpensive and less time consuming. Support for theories, modification or replication all achieved more quickly	Useful where the effect of some 'treatment' or programme is to be followed through and results compared with those of a control group
Disadvantages	Cohort problem if age difference between groups is large	Samples smaller and people may be lost during study
	Non-equivalent groups may confound results	Once started, modification can be difficult or 'unscientific'
	Does not provide information on the development of specific individuals	Time consuming. Results only after a long period. Replication and modification difficult or impossible
		Relatively expensive
		Cross-generational problem possible when development of one generation compared with another

CROSS-CULTURAL STUDIES

Psychologists who discover reliable effects or who demonstrate strong developmental trends within one culture (an 'intra-cultural' study) may well be interested in whether these may be found in cultures other than that of the original study. If the trends appear elsewhere, the case for universal psychological factors is strengthened. Aspects of grammar development, for instance, seem to occur in stages recognisable in all cultures so far studied, though debates arise about more specific details.

There are massive academic and political problems in attempting to generalise findings and theories from one culture to another. Fortunately, not many psychologists have been as overtly racist as C. G. Jung (1930) who claimed:

'The inferior (African) man exercises a tremendous pull upon civilised beings who are forced to live with him, because he fascinates the inferior layers of our psyche, which has lived through untold ages of similar conditions'. Africans, he argued, had a 'whole evolutionary layer less', psychologically speaking.

It is staggering to me that anyone can, as people very often do, discuss, in one sweep, the 'African mind' or the 'Indian character', given the size and huge variety of the areas. Even talk of the 'Irish temperament' seems, to me, to be spoken from the wrong end of some very powerful binoculars. However, this book is about methods and statistics so what's the relevance of the politics? Simply, that it seems impossible to separate method from a vast dimension of possible cultural bias on the part of the tester or the test used. Jung's comments above demonstrate the frightening effect of having no objective method for comparison at all. However, also dangerous is the *impression* of objectivity lent by the scientific aura of psychological instruments and methods when these are exported unquestioningly to cultures they were not developed with or standardised upon.

Cross-cultural studies compare samples from two or more cultures on some psychological variable. Differences found are attributed either to broad socialisation processes or to genetic factors. By far the greater number of recent studies emphasise the social environment as cause. Studies conducted earlier in the twentieth century often had a distinctive colonial or Euro-centred flavour. The 'natives' were interesting to study, whole societies were described as 'primitive' and the term 'negro' was commonplace, though this latter term occurred uncritically as late as the 1980s in some psychology texts.

Typically, psychologists tested members of a tribal community on visual illusions or counting tasks. The emphasis was often on what tribes 'lacked', and the studies tended to be ETHNOCENTRIC. An example of ethnocentrism is to describe a tribe's religious beliefs as 'superstitious' whilst not recognising that one's own religious beliefs qualify for the same analysis. Westerners, who greet with a firm handshake and full eye contact, tend to describe non-Western greetings which involve a bowed head and no eye contact as 'deferential' or as exhibiting a 'shy' cultural personality. This is an ethnocentric description which assumes that Western interpretations are somehow true and that their greetings are a neutral norm with which to compare others. Such value judgements are solely from the Westerner's point of view and have no universal validity.

Ethnocentrism very easily leads to false alternative interpretations of behaviour. In Mozambique I was told of an educational psychologist who got children to do the 'draw a man' test, a projective test (see Chapter 9) whose procedure is obvious. Their tiny drawings in one corner of the page were interpreted as demonstrating the poor self-image of Mozambican children still present just after, and caused by, centuries of Portuguese colonialism. It was pointed out to her that Mozambican school children were under strict instructions not to waste paper in times of great shortage and weak economy!

Nisbet (1971) argued that the cross-cultural method was just another way, seemingly scientific and respectable, of placing European cultures at the top of a graded hierarchy. Campbell (1970) argued that some protection against ethnocentrism could be gained by carrying out a design in which a researcher from culture A studies cultures A and B (a common cross-cultural design) whilst a second researcher from culture B *also* studies cultures A and B.

To find fairly non-ethnocentric work, it is useful to turn to the work of the social anthropologists, who tend to conduct intense participant observation studies as a member of a village community for many months if not years. These researchers have studied the community in its own right, not as a comparison with the West. They would attempt to record the interrelationship of local customs, norms, taboos and social interactions such as marriage and trade.

Classic examples include Margaret Mead's studies of female adolescence in

Samoa and of sex-role differences in New Guinea. Ruth Benedict (1934) used the term CULTURAL RELATIVITY to underline her view that an individual's behaviour and thinking must be viewed through, and can only be understood using, that person's own cultural environment.

This point has been subscribed to by many psychologists who argue that the independent and dependent variables of controlled studies are difficult or impossible to compare across wide cultural gaps. Several studies, for instance, found rural African tribespeople significantly more affected than Westerners by some visual illusions, and less affected by others. This was explained with the 'carpentered world' hypothesis that a highly structured, sharp-cornered Western environment is responsible for the differences. A fierce debate arose when other research highlighted Western-style education as the crucial variable, with its emphasis on the interpretation of printed, two-dimensional graphic materials. Several illusions have been found to work similarly on members of non-industrialised cultures when presented using local artistic materials.

RESEARCH EXAMPLES

Cross-cultural studies in psychology have increased markedly since the late 1960s. Issues in the field, in particular ethnocentricity and related research methods problems, as well as recent research and numerous applications, can be found in Berry et al. (1992). A further modern source is Brislin (1990) for applied examples.

The studies now conducted have lost a lot of the early ethnocentrism. In the modern period, an early start was Ainsworth's (1967) comparison of attachment behaviour in the USA and in Uganda. Kohlberg's stages of moral development were confirmed in studies conducted in Taiwan, Turkey, Mexico, India and Kenya. However, recent studies by Miller et al. (1990) have suggested that Kohlberg's theory of stages is culture bound. Initially they found that (Asian) Indians tended to give moral priority to *social duties* whereas Americans were more individualistic, concentrating on a person's *rights*. In 1990, they found that Indians and Americans were similar in serious, say life-threatening, examples but Indians had a broader view of moral responsibilities and obligations, emphasising personal need more than the American sample.

Ma (1988) found two Chinese samples (Hong Kong and People's Republic) to be more altruistic than an English sample.

Joe (1991) provides a good example of using support of the null hypothesis as evidence. She studied Papiamento-speaking and Creole English-speaking children in the Caribbean. The first language is 'tonal', meaning that the same sounds, spoken in different pitches, indicate different meanings. A general theory has been that the use of a tonal language affects certain cognitive abilities but Joe found no general differences.

Williams and Best (1982) asked 2 800 people in 30 countries across four continents to report on the general view (not their own) of men and women in their culture. There were interesting cross-cultural differences. The female stereotype was valued most highly in Italy and Peru; females were seen as most active in Japan and the USA and most passive in France and India; males rated lowest on 'strength' in the USA and Venezuela. However, on 'activity' and 'strength' there was no overlap, the highest country's score for females not reaching the lowest country's score for males. In 1990 a further study in 14 countries found that women, in almost all countries, held a more 'egalitarian' sex-role ideology than did men (on a measure going from 'traditional' to 'egalitarian'), and where samples were more 'traditional' as a whole, the male stereotype was more highly valued.

A very important area of application for cross-cultural studies is in the area of 'acculturation', the process of becoming used to another culture, and perhaps having one's own culture change as a result, either through choice (e.g. emigration) or force (e.g. refugees). Williams and Berry (1991) argue that psychologists have enough knowledge now to implement programmes which would greatly reduce the stress involved. In Europe, at present, this could be very useful knowledge indeed.

INDIGENOUS PSYCHOLOGIES

In the same way as women found it unacceptable that a majority of men should define all psychology, including the study of gender, (see next chapter) so members of non-Western cultures have seen the imposition or model of Western psychology as inappropriate to their needs and understanding of themselves. Sinha (1986) characterised the early stages of the development of Indian psychology as very much 'tied to the apron strings of' Western principles and an almost reverent repetition of Western studies. The 'final' stage, 'indigenisation', meant the transformation of methods to suit Indian economic and political realities and needs. Enriquez (1990) is even more radical and promotes the development of an entirely separate Filipino psychology from its own fundamental roots. This movement has three primary objections: 'it is against a psychology that perpetuates the colonial status of the Filipino mind; it is against the imposition on a Third World country of psychologies developed in, and appropriate to, industrialised countries; and it is against a psychology used for the exploitation of the masses.' (Berry et al. 1990) As with feminist psychology, these movements, have, to some extent, identified strict positivism with a Western approach and, without complete rejection, have generally favoured a more qualitative approach, more closely integrated with general socio-economic development and policy. Quantitative methods also exist and these have moved towards development of 'home-grown' assessment methods and scales rather than the import and restandardisation of existing Western measures.

ETHNICITY AND CULTURE WITHIN ONE SOCIETY – DOING A 'RACE' PROJECT

Research projects on differing cultures within one society are referred to as 'intra-cultural' studies. Students very often choose to do such a project on 'prejudice' or 'race', mostly for the best of possible reasons – they are concerned about racism and injustice or, more positively, fascinated by a different perspective within their society. Such studies, however, are fraught with the dangers of ethnocentrism, stereotyping and misunderstanding. I am not impartial on this matter. A fence-sitting position can easily support racism. I do not believe it is possible to be reared in the UK (white or black) without subtly absorbing the images and themes which make up our past – a colonial country in which the vast majority of people would not have thought twice about Jung's statement, certainly when I was a child in the late fifties.

I would recommend that students *do* concern themselves with race issues but, in choosing to do what might have seemed a simple project, there would need to be a lot of preparation and groundwork on cultural perspectives and the language of racism. For instance, I am very concerned when a student says, quite innocently, that she wishes to get the attitudes of 'coloured' people in her study. Will she use this term with the participants and possibly alienate the majority, giving psychology a worse name than it sometimes has anyway? The researcher needs to investigate his or her *own* sense of ethnicity first – white people often don't think of themselves as 'ethnic' in any way, the term having become a euphemism for the earlier euphemism of 'coloured', meaning 'not naturally uncoloured like us'! The issue of language is crucial, since it is the conveyor of subtle, historically interwoven and politically tangled concepts. The student/researcher should seek advice on all the terms to be used in, say, a questionnaire or vignette. Deeper still, students/researchers should study thoroughly their own politics on the relationship between their own ethnic group and another. Are they 'culture/colour blind' host integrationists who believe that somehow, some day all this bother should go away and eventually black people will be and live 'just like us'? Or do they accept the similarity of people, but also recognise the valuable richness of cultural diversity in a land which, like many others, often tries to ignore the differences at the expense of the minorities, in an unhealthy attempt to pretend that the 'majority' culture is one, united, homogenous group? (see bottom of Box 10.2)

This is a book on methods and statistics which could attempt to be 'politically neutral' on these matters and argue that science and numbers are science and numbers. In an important sense this is true and much of this book supports the position. However, when people investigate people they interact and deploy the strength of opinions. A teacher claiming that the variety of children in her class are 'all the same colour' is *not* politically neutral. A researcher's stance and attitudes will undoubtedly flavour any research involving race. To *find out* about another group one must be prepared to destroy stereotypes; one cannot enter with a hidden belief in superiority, however subtle; only valuing and empathising with the group will produce validity and this involves homework on one's self.

READING ON RACE

As I write this morning there is an old controversial hot potato in the news which will be interesting to follow. It is the re-emphasis on just why black people in the UK are overrepresented in some psychiatric categories and receive higher levels of physical medication (as opposed to psychotherapy). This is not a new issue and the reader can get a flavour of race issues in psychology via arguments in psychiatry in Littlewood (1989). A lively, readable introduction to the ways in which television and film subtly portray racial and cultural images, along with good history, arguments and data blowing any myth that 'young people just don't have race prejudice these days' is John Twitchin's (1988) *The Black and White Media Book* (coupled with his programmes of the same name and obtainable as training material from the BBC).

COMPARISON STUDIES ARE DESIGN FRAMEWORKS

A research study can have a longitudinal, cross-sectional or cross-cultural design and still be either experimental or not. Given the nature of the comparison designs, and what they are most useful for, most studies using them are non-experimental. They tend to be observational or make use of some test, scale or interview technique in order to compare existing measured variables. If the independent variable focused on is the two (or more) different cultures then the design is *ex post facto*, since the investigator cannot manipulate the variable of cultural difference. The samples studied would preferably be randomly selected. Equivalence of samples is, of course, a huge issue and one I'll leave you to ponder about since there is not room here to go further. It would be easier to get two representative samples of university students,

Box 10.2 *Advantages and disadvantages of cross-cultural studies*

Advantages	Disadvantages
Can demonstrate universal development trends and effects	Can support disguised ethnocentric assumptions
Gives insight into quite different cultural systems, beliefs and practices	Extremely costly and time consuming
	Variables may not be culturally comparable
Can provide reassessment of 'home' society's norms in culturally relative terms	Difficulties of communication. Subtle differences between 'equivalent' terms may make large difference
Rich data	Can ignore the fact that the 'home' culture is not homogeneous. British society comprises many identifiable cultures which include Afro-Caribbean, Indian (several separable cultures), Pakistani, Scots (highland and lowland), Irish, Welsh (north and south), Geordie, Liverpudlian, and Cornish, to name a few

say, than two samples of working people or 'villagers', for instance.

A true experiment occurs when one group of randomly selected children are given a 'treatment' (say, special reading training), organised by the investigator, and another group serves as control, whilst both are followed up over several years.

GLOSSARY

Large sample of people, often children, identified for longitudinal or cross-sectional study	_____	cohort
Confounding in cross-sectional study when two different age groups have had quite different experiences	_____ _____	cohort effect
Confounding occurring when one longitudinally studied group is compared with another who have generally had quite different social experiences	_____-_____ _____	cross-generational problem
View that a person's behaviour and characteristics can only be understood through that person's own cultural environment	_____ _____	cultural relativity
Bias of viewing another's culture from one's own cultural perspective	_____	ethnocentrism
Psychological methodology developed by and within one culture, not imported from another	_____ _____	indigenous psychology

		types of study
Comparative study of two or more different societies, or social subgroups	_____-_____ _____	cross-cultural study
Comparative study of several groups captured for measurement at a single time point	_____-_____ _____	cross-sectional study
Comparative study of several age groups, followed through over a relatively short period	_____-_____, _____-____, _____ _____	cross-sectional, short-term, longitudinal study
Comparative study of one group over a relatively long period (possibly including a control group)	_____ _____	longitudinal study
Comparative study in which a sample of a specific age is selected each time the study is run. It is run at relatively long intervals	____-___ _____	time-lag study

II

NEW PARADIGMS

This chapter presents a summary of recent strengthening in the use of methods often known as '**qualitative**' or, to emphasise fundamental disagreement with the traditional methods, 'new paradigm'. Here, methods are not just an alternative set of procedures but incorporate a fundamental philosophical critique of the traditional 'positivist', hypothetico-deductive paradigm within psychological research. Positivism is the philosophy which sees only (numerically) measurable events as worthy of scientific study.

- Traditional quantitative methods have often produced relatively artificial and sterile results, inapplicable to the realities of everyday human life.
- The alternative approaches presented here emphasise closeness to participants and the richness of information produced when unstructured data gathering methods are applied.
- **Action research** involves intervention aimed at change; **endogenous** or **collaborative** approaches aim to help participants evolve their own research and processes of change, the former in communities, the latter often in organisations.
- **Feminist psychology** emphasises qualitative and participative research methods relatively neglected by the male establishment which has dominated psychological research development.
- **Discourse analysis** focuses on the ways people construct individual versions of events through their conversation.
- **Reflexivity** demands that readers of research reports are made aware of the relative nature of scientific views of the world through the author's discussion of their work with the reader by some appropriate 'reflexive' mechanism.

POSITIVISM

There is a debate which has raged on and off within psychology for a long time. It started as far back as 1894 when Dilthey criticised the experimental psychology of the time for copying the natural science model and for consequent reductionism in explaining mental processes. It sometimes dies down but has been particularly potent during the last ten to 15 years. It concerns whether psychological research should follow closely the example of the natural and physical sciences which have been so successful in advancing our understanding of natural phenomena. Their method has involved careful observation, accurate numerical measurement and the assumption that what cannot be so measured is not amenable to scientific investigation – a position amounting to POSITIVISM for want of a better term, though not everyone agrees on the precise meaning of this label. The overwhelming paradigm has been use of the *hypothetico-deductive method* described in Chapter 1. A 'paradigm' is the generally accepted method for conducting research and theory development. In practice, if you don't follow it you're less likely to get research grants or have your work taken seriously.

DOUBTS ABOUT POSITIVISM

In a nutshell the issue is: if we carry out research using the highly controlled procedures and exact quantification of variables recommended by traditional science and by most psychological textbooks, including this one in many parts, will we not be gaining only very narrow, perhaps artificial, perhaps sometimes useless knowledge of human behaviour and experience? Consider the following fictitious table of results from an experiment where the independent variable was 20 common or uncommon words in a list, presented one per second via computer screen, and the dependent variable was the number of words recalled, order irrelevant, in each condition during 60 seconds after exposure of the last item.

Table 11.1 *Number of common/uncommon words recalled*

Participant	Number of words recalled:	
	Common	**Uncommon**
1	12	5
2	13	10
3	7	6
4	5	4
5	18	12
6	15	12
6	12	6
7	18	10
8	14	7
9	7	3
10	12	6

This provides us with the not unsurprising information that infrequently met words are harder to recall. The empiricist argues that, nevertheless, (and in the spirit of the points made in Chapter 1 about 'armchair certainties') the research is required to back up what is otherwise only an unsupported, casual observation. A critic might argue as follows: only in psychology experiments and party games do people have to learn a list of 20 unrelated words. How can this relate to the normal use of human memory which operates in a social, meaningful context? The results of the experiment may be significant but they tell us little of relevance. The study gives us no information at all about the participants' experiences. They all, no doubt, used personally devised methods and found their own unique meanings in the combination of words presented. This information is powerful and 'belongs' to the participants, yet is unused and is not asked for, which could even constitute something of an insult to 'subjects' who participated in what, for them, was to be 'an interesting experiment'.

It is also argued that memory experiments using unconnected words out of context, or even sets of nonsense syllables, which restrict the use of natural capacities, give rise to unnecessarily simplistic models of the person and of the nature and operation of cognitive processes.

EXAMPLES OF NARROWNESS AND ARTIFICIALITY

Similarly, many studies measure attitude using a scale of the kind we looked at in Chapter 9. On this, each participant ends up with a single numerical value. On political attitude, for instance, a person's position may be represented as 34, where 40 is the highest value a 'conservative' (right-wing) person could score, the other end of the scale being 'radical' (left wing). Using this system, we are assuming political attitudes to lie along a unitary dimension, whereas, in fact, if we asked people in depth about their ideas and principles, we would uncover various unique combinations of left- and right-wing views which couldn't, meaningfully, be averaged down to a midpoint on the scale.

Consider the measurement of your intelligence, and all that it means to you, as a number not too far from 100. Think of the task of judging an anonymous person on a five point scale, knowing only that the person possesses characteristics in the form of single words like 'confident' written on a piece of card.

Harré (1981) argues that orthodox (positivist) research methods have led to a great deal of irrelevance in, for instance, social psychological research. He analyses an experiment in which women had to sit and look at themselves on a TV monitor for one minute. The IV was then applied in that they heard a lecture on venereal disease either straight away or four minutes later. They were then asked whether they would contribute to a venereal disease remedial programme under certain circumstances. The aim was to test the idea that heightened 'self-focus' would facilitate 'helping behaviour'. Harré argues that the 'self-focus' measure (watching themselves) completely trivialised the complex concept of self originally proposed by G. H. Mead.

THE ESTABLISHMENT PARADIGM

Working under syllabus requirements for students to produce strictly quantified data and analyses, I have often been instrumental in helping narrow an originally rich concept down to an empirically measurable one. For example, two teenage students, intensely interested, understandably, in researching the self-concept among teenagers, have ended up counting how many more times girls used social terms to describe themselves compared with boys, because this was a numerically verifiable test of a hypothesis.

My own training taught me to treat all non-quantitative evidence with suspicion approaching the hostile, and that information gathered without a prearranged numerical scoring system and rigidly adhered to procedure had to be wide open to vagueness, subjectivity and irrelevance.

Some would argue that this is an example of the establishment imposing the traditional paradigm right from the start. Others argue that this focusing is necessary in the interests of objectivity, clarity of thought and replicability. But it certainly seems possible to achieve the requisite clarity of thought without a knee-jerk reduction to numbers. Astronomers chemists and biologists don't always count – they look for patterns. So did Freud, Piaget, Bartlett, and many other psychologists whose insights do not always fundamentally depend on strictly quantified data.

THE MAJOR OBJECTIONS TO THE TRADITIONAL PARADIGM

Some of these have already been touched on in covering the more qualitative aspects of interviewing and observing, as well as in the case-study section. However, let's put together the general case 'against'.

1 Traditional research treats people as isolatable from their social contexts. It even treats part of people (e.g. their memory or attitude) as separable. 'Subjects' are to be treated as identical units for purposes of demonstrating the researcher's preconceived notions about humans which they cannot challenge. They are manipulated in and out of the research condition.

2 Whereas we all realise that to know and understand even one's good friends one has to stay close, the researcher, in the interests of objectivity, strains to remain distant. The researcher's attitudes and motives are not recognised, revealed or seen as relevant to the research process.

3 This objectivity is seen as mythical. The attempt to stay coolly distant, and the quantitative paradigm, blind the researcher to his/her own influence and active role in the research process which is a social context. When students administer structured questionnaires to peers, for instance, the respondents usually want to know what the student thinks and whether they *believe* all those statements which the respondent had to check.

4 The experimental situation or survey interview can only permit the gathering of superficial information. In the study of person perception and interpersonal attraction, for instance, mainly first impressions have been researched with traditional methods.

5 Experimental procedures restrict the normal powers of 'subjects' to plan, react and express appropriate social behaviour in the context of the research topic. Yet the investigator uses the results to make statements about human nature on the same topic. The resulting model of the person is simplistic and mechanistic.

6 Deception can only falsify the research context and give quite misleading results, besides treating the participant with contempt.

7 The relationship between experimenter and 'subject' is like that of employer–employee. It is dominating and elitist. Hence, behaviour exhibited will mirror this particular social context. This will also contribute to the resulting model of the person.

8 Highly structured research methods predetermine the nature of resulting information. Theoretical frameworks are imposed on the participants. Questionnaires, for example, singularly fail to extract the most important information from people. Information obtained is narrow, rarefied and unrealistic.

9 Highly structured coding and categorising systems lose sight of the wholeness of the individual.

SO WHAT DO NEW PARADIGMS PROPOSE?

Thomas Kuhn (1962) made the term 'paradigm' popular when he discussed ways in which science goes through radical changes in its overall conception of appropriate models and methodology. A 'paradigm shift' occurred when Einsteinian physics replaced Newtonian.

The paradigm which 'new paradigm' psychological researchers are seeking to replace is the positivist one, which embraces the traditional scientific (hypothetico-deductive) model. But there is not just one new paradigm. The term crops up in several contexts. The term is used by several people and groups with varying backgrounds, principles and aims but with most of the objections above in common. They also would agree with most, if not all of the following points:

1 Psychological research should concentrate on the meanings of actions in a social context, not on isolated, 'objective' units of behaviour – holism, not atomism.

2 The emphasis should also be upon interaction. Attribution, for instance, is not the work of one person, but the result of negotiation between observer and observed, the latter attempting to control or contradict attributions.

3 Meanings and interactions belong to social situations and contexts and can't be sensibly isolated from these.

4 Research is therefore mostly naturalistic and qualitative.

5 Research is conducted as closely as possible *with* the person(s) studied. A quote from Hall (1975) makes this point:

> Social science research often appears to produce a situation in which a medical doctor tries to diagnose a patient's symptoms from around the corner and out of sight. The social scientist uses his 'instruments' to measure the response of the patient as though they were a kind of long stethoscope. The focus of the researcher has been on developing a better and better stethoscope for going around corners and into houses when the real need is for the researcher to walk around the corner, into the house and begin talking with the people who live there.

6 Participants' own terms and interpretations are the most central data. To quote De Waele and Harré (1979):

> By taking participants' interpretations seriously we gained the falsification of reality which occurs when self-reports are confined to the replies to questionnaires etc., which have been devised in advance by the investigator . . . Participants, if allowed to construct their own interpretations, often present a range of meanings and reveal implicit theories sometimes widely at variance with those imposed by the investigators.

This approach is exemplified in Marsh's (1978) work on the accounts given by football fans of the 'rules' of football terrace behaviour. Marsh used an approach developed from Harré's 'ethogenic' perspective, the perspective outlined above.

7 Some version of INDUCTIVE ANALYSIS is preferred to the hypothetico-deductive approach. In the former, theories, models and hypotheses *emerge* from the data-gathering process rather than being confirmed by it. (Ironically, this is close to the philosophy of the early empirical method, where one was supposed to gather data from the natural, physical world with no preconceptions.)

Medawar (1963), however, has argued forcefully against the naïve assumption that one can approach any phenomenon, in order to study it, with absolutely no preconceptions as to its modes of functioning – certainly not in the social world anyway.

Inductive analysis also involves the process of constantly refining emergent categories and models in the light of incoming data.

The value of this approach is particularly seen in its ability to permit categories, processes, even hypotheses to emerge which might not have been envisaged as present before research began, whereas traditional research strictly defines variables and dimensions before data collection, such that data may be distorted to fit the prearranged scheme.

8 Emergent theories are likely to be local, rather than massive generalisations about the nature of human thought or personality.

9 For the more radical departures from the traditional paradigm there is a high degree of participation by those researched in some or all of the development, running and analysis of the research project. The extreme version of this approach involves the target group acting as collaborative researchers with the original researcher as a form of consultant and data organiser/analyst. Any findings or interpretations are discussed and modified by the group as a whole in its own terms. Reality is 'negotiated'.

10 At the very least, though, most methods under the 'new paradigm/qualitative' umbrella involve the notion of a 'research cycle', gone round several times, in which an integral step is to consult with participants as to the acceptability and accuracy of emergent theories, models and categories.

QUALITATIVE APPROACHES

I had originally intended to head this chapter 'qualitative approaches' and take you through a distinct set of methods. As it turned out, it made more sense to deal with the quantitative–qualitative dimension as we went through observation, interview and the like. The methods we have encountered so far which could count as qualitative include:

• Open-ended questionnaires
• Unstructured interviews
• Semi-structured observation
• Participant observation
• The diary method
• The clinical method (to some extent)
• Role-play and simulation (depending on particular research)
• Individual case-studies

Although these methods gather qualitative data, they are not all what one might call 'qualitative' in outlook, by which is meant that the research aim is to use the data in their qualitative form and not extract from them just that which can somehow be represented numerically. The data are retained in the form of meanings. In Chapter 25 we look at ways in which qualitative data can be dealt with. To the extent that data are strictly categorised, coded or content analysed, the approach tends to be positivistic rather than qualitative in outlook.

But it would be tempting to assume that all approaches which are qualitative in outlook would automatically fall into this category of new paradigm. However, the subterfuge and secrecy of much participant observation runs counter to several of the principles outlined above. The people studied are often not participants in the research, only the researcher is. The presentation of results can tend to deliver the message 'what fascinatingly strange people, and they're organised too.'

PARTICIPATIVE RESEARCH

The idea of people participating in research and collaborating with the researcher in evolving the project is not new. Here is a quote from Madge (1953):

> The techniques of experimentation which have so far been discussed are based on those evolved in the natural sciences. Can it be that a radically different approach is required in social science? Can the human beings who constitute the subject-matter of social science be regarded, not as objects for experimental manipulation, but as participants in what is being planned? If this can be so, it requires a transformed attitude towards social experiment. Traditionally, attention is concentrated on the precautions needed to objectify results, and this entails treating the participants as lay figures to be observed before and after subjection to a series of external stimuli. In contrast, the new approach entails the acceptance and encouragement of conscious co-operation by all concerned. There are then no longer an investigator and his passive subjects, but a number of human beings, one of whom is more experienced than the others and has somewhat more complex aims, but all of whom are knowingly collaborating in a research project.

What has increased in the 1980s and 1990s is the actual practice of such research and the recognition of people as active enquirers in the research process, so much so that even the establishment body for academic psychology, the British Psychological Society has recommended that the term 'subjects' be dropped in favour of 'participants'. The message has so far had little effect – as mentioned in Chapter 1, there was just one use of the term 'participants', in over 30 opportunities in the *British Journal of Psychology* from 1992 to mid-1993. However, these are early days for this change.

This is not to say that there weren't always *some* researchers using participative techniques with a philosophy, not just an analysis of data, which was broadly qualitative. Here are some research influences or strands of the general qualitative or 'new paradigm' perspective.

ACTION RESEARCH

First proposed by Kurt Lewin in the mid 1940s, this approach basically called for research to be applied to practical issues occurring in the everyday social world. The idea was to enter a social situation, attempt change and monitor results. This might be setting up or contributing to a programme designed to raise awareness on dietary needs or the dangers of smoking. The approach has been used extensively in the area of occupational psychology concerned with organisational change. Associated examples come from the work of the Tavistock Institute and their concentration on 'socio-technical systems'. The emphasis here is on facilitation of a work-group in developing human systems which counteract the otherwise dehumanising influence of machinery and technology. A guiding principle is that the researcher involves representatives of, if not all, the work-group in the process of change. There are examples as far back as Trist and Bamforth (1951) who reorganised workers in the Durham coalfields and Rice (1958) who did the same in Ahmedabad, India. Obviously, here is an area where the research aim and area lend themselves to a qualitative and participative approach.

ENDOGENOUS RESEARCH

This is an import from anthropology, the originators of participant observation on a big scale. In this approach, rather than living with a community for a year or so, coming away, then publishing a report, the researcher involves members of the community in a research project on their own customs, norms and organisation in their own terms.

COLLABORATIVE RESEARCH

Roughly speaking, putting the last two approaches together, we get the basis for collaborative research, in which participants are involved as fully as possible in research on their own group organisation. The researcher may have to lead at the beginning but as participants realise the nature of the game they become more centrally involved in the progress of research. In some cases the research is initiated by an already existing member of the organisation or group.

This is particularly suitable where a group is planning or undergoing change and requires evaluation. Participants take up data-gathering ideas, develop their own, consider the researcher's findings or analyse their own, and debate progress, directions and results in group meetings. Collaborative research is not without confrontations, but the idea is to build on these natural differences constructively. The idea is also to end up with participants directing their own change, rather than an outside expert's research findings, about what is wrong and what might be changed, arriving after research has been done *on* people.

Sims (1981) set out to study 'problem-generation' in health service teams and found that, as the participants became interested in the issues, they took on their own lines of investigation. This caused them to consider group dynamic issues they'd never thought about and created an atmosphere of awareness raising and constructive change. They were able to develop, with the researcher, many categories of processes in problem construction which could be transferred (not without addition and modification) to other group situations.

OTHER ROOTS AND SOURCES

Influences on this direction of research philosophy are numerous. Prominent among them would be: humanism; phenomenology; existentialism; Marxism; the psychoanalytic tradition; Kelly's repertory grid work; sociology's ethnomethodology.

The approaches in general tend to be somewhat interdisciplinary, borrowing many ideas from sociology and anthropology in particular. The areas tend to be social psychology and, to some extent, the study of personality. The emphasis is always completely practical and the approaches are at their best applied to problems or challenges within the fields of educational, organisational, clinical or criminological psychology (i.e. in *applied* settings).

A COMPLETE ALTERNATIVE?

Patton (1980), an evaluation researcher who advocates the use of a wholly qualitative approach, argues that the hypothetico-deductive method is not bad or wrong, but has simply overwhelmed research in psychology to become not just a major paradigm, but the *only* paradigm of which new researchers are aware. In advocating the qualitative approach he argues that the new paradigm is a 'paradigm of choice' between the traditional hypothetico-deductive and the alternative holistic, inductive one.

Latour (1987) argues that quantification is only one example of a more general process of deriving order and meaningful abstractions from data in science which can be transferred. Quantitative and qualitative procedures are just different forms of the analytic practice of 're-representation' in science. In other words, whether I measure what you say numerically, or re-describe it, what results is my summarised *version* of what you actually said.

A FEMINIST PERSPECTIVE

A further and more recent new force within psychological research methods has been the arrival of serious challenges to the traditional research paradigm from the point of view of the politics and ideology of the women's movement.

It is about as stunningly inappropriate that a male should author research on *The Psychology of Women* (I still have the Penguin paperback!) as that white psychologists should conduct studies on 'the negro' (as they once did).

The early stages of women's research involved studies, under a conventional paradigm, which destroyed (or should have) traditional stereotypes of women's nature or deficiencies relative to men. Research literature now contains a fair amount of stereotype challenging and consciousness-raising work. This stage also challenged the lack of female authorship and visible presence within the research community. Parallels with racism occurred in that, even where women had produced scholarship, this had somehow become marginalised or obscured. The overwhelmingly male-oriented and -dominated research community had edged such work to the periphery.

The content-oriented phase just described, however, though continuing, has led on to a realisation by women involved in the research process that the conventional methods which they have been using to develop the content are themselves largely the product of a male research network and thought-base.

This is not to say that women would think, reason and conduct their research *utterly* differently, given the opportunity. It would fall back onto old stereotypes to suggest that women didn't *tend* to use quantification or feel happy testing hypotheses statistically. The logic underlying chess, computer programming and the statistical tests in this book are in a major sense neutral. But they have been 'owned' and promoted for so long by men that it is hardly surprising that when women came to assess their values in the research process they were alerted to methods and research relationships neglected or never taken up by male researchers, and felt by many female researchers to be more valid in representing women's experience. The position is exemplified in Sue Wilkinson's *Feminist Social Psychology* (1986).

Recognised as characteristic of a male approach to research and understanding the world are: preoccupation with quantifying variables; an emphasis on control, mastery and manipulation; a tendency to remain distant rather than be involved with the subjects of research; a preference for gadget-oriented research over naturalistic enquiry; competition and ego building. In particular, Reinharz (1983) challenges the conventional researcher's pose of neutrality, where personal attitudes are hidden and deemed irrelevant, and argues that researchers' attitudes should be fully discussed and their values revealed and clearly located.

DISCOURSE ANALYSIS (DA)

An influential but controversial approach to research has been presented through the 1980s by Potter, Edwards, Middleton and Wetherell (Potter & Wetherell, 1987; Edwards & Potter, 1992; Middleton & Edwards, 1990) which, as with most approaches mentioned here, extends beyond specific method to an over-arching research paradigm, this one called 'Discursive Psychology' (the 1992 publication title). The approach wholeheartedly treats psychological topics, such as memory and attribution theory (two mainstream heartland topics), as processes of *discourse* between people. Memories are *not* close, or not so close, attempts at recalling 'the facts' but are motivated constructions by people with a 'stake' in producing an 'account' which may, for instance, suit their defences against blame or accountability. What people say, when memorising, cannot be taken as a rather opaque window onto cognitive memory processes. The scientific chase after these processes is seen as producing much arid theory and artificial results.

Much of the controversial debate is beyond the scope of this book. The debate, at times, carries the image of David and Goliath. The flavour of the toing and froing of debate can be gained from a read of *The Psychologist*, October 1992. The reason for giving the issue some prominence here is that DA specifically discredits the *methods* used, particularly in experimental psychology, and blames these for what they feel is a distorted model of human cognition and social judgement. They place language as *action* ahead of language as *representation*. They don't believe that we can treat psychologists' language as a trusty, objective route to 'what they really think'. DA treats language as the constructor of *versions* of truth *as the language occurs*. There are an infinite number of ways in which I can describe to you my (negative) views on, for instance, traditional behaviourism or privatisation of welfare services. DA's view is not that these are all versions of some ultimate reality inside my head but that I would redefine and negotiate my view each time I attempted to explain it, dependent on the challenges I receive, my listeners' views, who else can hear, how formal we are and so on. Above all, my production is *social action*.

Whereas traditional psychology would look at all the factors I just mentioned and say 'that's role theory' or 'there are plenty of experiments looking at how we change our tone dependent on the listener', DA's emphasis is entirely on the *discourse* involved in my production and how I handle it whilst trying, for instance, to maintain credibility. In the 'Discursive Action Model (DAM)' (Edwards & Potter, 1992), remembering and making attributions become redefined as action in the form of reports (versions, accounts) along with accompanying inferences. The focus is not on these activities as the reflection of inner mental cognitions. When we remember and attribute *in real life*, as opposed to the psychology experiment, our accounts attend to blame, defence, accountability, explanation and so on. What we often do is to present rememberings as fact when they are really constructions. The constructions use devices, highlighted by DA researchers, which serve the purpose of undermining alternative constructions. One device, for example, is that of the 'extreme case formulation' – 'Everyone gives their child a little smack once in a while, don't they?' would serve the purpose of justifying hitting children, a device Freud called 'projection'. As we speak we often justify, whilst keeping the appearance objective.

The DA writers talk of 'stake' or 'interest' and that speakers have a dilemma of trying to 'attend to interests without being undermined as interested' (Edwards & Potter, 1992). It is often important to get one's 'account' accepted as 'fact' hence the use of impersonal language by authorities – using 'one' and the passive voice. We need only think of the way politicians or 'big chiefs' phrase their accounts on television to understand this. Much of the 1992 book, above, deals with Nigel Lawson, Margaret Thatcher and the media.

One of DA's major points against highly controlled experimental approaches is that the materials often used (word lists in memory; 'vignettes' in social perception – see p. 86) take away the very essence of what people normally *do* when remembering or judging – we engage in discourse with others or even with ourselves. It is not that DA sees everyone as little Machiavellis, constantly plotting and creating self-interested accounts. Their emphasis is on studying memory and other traditional topic areas as *the way things are done*. We normally memorise or attribute with a *purpose* in a *context* that matters to us.

It is doubtful whether a movement spearheaded by DA will eventually supplant or seriously challenge the current mainstream on its home territory, for instance the cognitive heartlands of perception, memory, attention, problem-solving and so on. The approach has however quite healthily rattled the establishment (see *The Psychologist* articles) and produced innovative work, with valuable human applications, hardly likely to have appeared but for its approach – for instance, the reminiscence work with the elderly of Middleton, Buchanan and Suurmond (1993).

There are strong criticisms of the DA approach, many in too complex a philosophical form to present here but in practical research terms the following are important. The use of 'verbal protocols' (see p. 110) (e.g. Ericsson & Simon 1984) is an example of qualitative data already used in cognitive psychology. DA's emphasis is entirely on language yet eye-witness testimony research has a lot to do with non-verbal remembering. Many criticisms centre around the common concern about reliability and validity. How is one researcher's 'reading' of a piece of discourse checked against another's? DA supporters argue that this is done, as elsewhere, by persuasive argument, but the conventional system *also* has an agreed set of validating 'rules' (significance and all that) which this approach appears to lack. Baddeley (1992) wonders whether DA *may* be producing 'common sense dressed up as jargon', and whether all answers in DA are treated as equally true since none is perfectly true. Hyman (1992) questions possible researcher and design bias and fears that discourse approaches may end up as just 'a researcher's ideas with examples'. Hitch (1992) argues that DA is valuable but should be seen as complementary, not an overthrowing alternative, answering its own questions about memory in ways that other researchers should recognise along with their own. My own view, as an analogy here, is that whilst DA appears to be concentrating on how the traffic manages to get by and why it goes where it does, much (but not all) traditional memory research has been geared towards understanding the engine (and physiological psychology has a go at stripping it!). One worrying aspect of the DA versus conventional debate is DA writers dealing with criticism as more discourse to be analysed rather than answered. This is similar to Freudian theorists dealing with criticism on an *ad hominem* basis by analysing it in terms of their opponents' unconscious and aggressive defences – thus creating an irrefutable 'circular' theory.

REFLEXIVITY

One of the strong currents within DA and similar approaches, which to some extent protects it from the criticism of irrefutability, is its strong relationship and commitment to the self-critical theme of REFLEXIVITY. This is a term developed within modern sociology in the area of studies of scientific knowledge, but some of its effect is felt in psychology. The philosophy behind the term is recognised, if not fully accepted, by most qualitative or new paradigm researchers. This philosophy is of the type we have been discussing – opposition to positivism or 'scientism' and a 'relativist' view of knowledge. That is, sociologists studying the process of 'doing' natural science (producing theories, studies, conferences, journals, etc.) concluded that the notion of an individual studying and discovering natural, objective 'facts' was an illusion and that any body of scientific knowledge is the product of social, cultural, historical and political processes. To get the flavour of this somewhat rarefied 'coffee-at-two-in-the-morning-ain't-it-a-strange-world' idea of scientific theory, consider this. Recently, as an MSc student, I argued that facts were sometimes facts (I was feeling a bit realist at the time) with a lecturer delivering the relativist point of view. I said, if there was a pool of petrol on the floor and I held a lighted match, our actions would instantly demonstrate complete agreement about theory, prediction and fact. Actually this was a bit unfair. What the lecturer perhaps should have done was to follow with, 'But if I should ask you *why* does the petrol explode (after all we're discussing how people attempt to go *beyond* immediate perception) what would happen? Personally, I haven't a *clue* why petrol explodes but I can imagine a group of people, some more scientifically wise than others, having a discussion about it. It's no use saying 'because it's volatile' – this is a *re-description* of what happens. I can list things that explode, and when they do, but this isn't *explanation*. Someone, who's done some chemistry A level, might tell us about molecular 'vibration' or 'collision', but then tell us that lay people don't properly understand what the scientist 'really means' by 'collision'. You can imagine the breadth of possible explanations and emphases which might emerge here, and (this is the heart of the argument) the social forces which might lead to one view being better accepted by the group than another. How much more so if the group were debating causes of aggression. Think what 'evidence' people generally have ready for such disputes. The relativist (or 'constructionist') view is that much the same process goes on, but very much writ large, in the world of real scientists. Scientists, they argue, don't discover pure, cold, unarguable facts at a distance; rather, they construct *versions* of the facts according to a host of schemata, pressures, socially accepted values and so on.

Having analysed the discourse and thinking of *natural* scientists in this way there was an inevitable consequence. Rather like the animal in *Yellow Submarine* which sucks up its own tail and thence itself, the spotlight fell on the construction of social science as well. Writers became sensitive to their own construction of knowledge *as they produced and wrote it*. They became acutely self-conscious about the process of writing and analysing because they could see that they were just as 'guilty' of appearing to produce compartmentalised and 'objective' knowledge, with the stamp of authority, whereas their own knowledge must be just as 'relative' as any other. One technique to prevent readers accepting as fact what was being socially produced was to make readers aware of this as they read. Texts were then produced which carried markers to highlight this process and overall philosophy. Latour (1988) defines a reflexive text as one which, '. . . takes into account its own production and which, by doing so, claims to undo the deleterious effects upon its readers of being believed too little or too much.'[1]

A general principle, then, is to take 'methodological precautions' which ensure somehow that readers are aware of your own role in constructing what they are reading, of your own possible 'stake' and so on. Mentioned above, Reinharz's

---

[1] Latour (1988) argues that even the Bible was meant to be read this way, and was, until readers in the age of empiricism started taking it literally.

emphasis on researchers revealing and labelling their attitudes reflects this reflexive philosophy as a strong theme in feminist psychological research.

The method by which texts become reflexive are several. My own humble example of the common 'second voice' technique is in Box 11.1. Texts also include commentaries by the authors or peers after each section. The relevance to psychology here is that some research in this vein, often fieldwork and practically applied, is presented reflexively. Along with their raw data or analysis, researchers submit a diary of their thoughts as they gathered data, analysed it and constructed theory. They comment on their own attitudes and possible biases in coming to this or that conclusion or in proceeding this or that way in the research process. Rather than footnotes, or doubts admitted to trusted colleagues in the pub, this material is seen as equivalent in importance to the raw, summarised and analysed data.

One of the difficulties with the development of this approach has been deciding when enough reflexion is enough. There has been a tendency to reflect upon reflexion and upon these reflexions and so on ('meta-reflexivity'), creating the obvious possibility of an infinite regress. A further difficulty is that, if a writer is telling you about such constructionism in academic texts, their own text is included in the analysis, and the position becomes something like that of trying to deal with the Cretan liar: if *all* Cretans are liars, and a Cretan tells you this, what are you to believe?

THE CURRENT STATE OF PLAY

The philosophical issues surrounding the qualitative research debate are having an effect for certain. It is difficult to see at this stage how far-reaching the effect will be. It is combined with, but not the same as, a strong trend towards humanistic considerations in conducting conventional research. In fact, the most interesting thing will be to see how the promoters of the radical views themselves cope with becoming conventionalised. How will students be stopped from mere journalism? How will radicalism in research be graded? Will the tables turn (as with long and short hair) so that students will soon be rebuked for having too *precise* a hypothesis? And so on. The experimental and quantitative approach will no doubt 'prevail' for some time, especially in its strongholds and where quantification is clearly useful and productive. We need to know whether a child's language is seriously delayed, for instance, or whether perceptual task performance is affected in such and such an environment, and what to do about it, without having someone constantly demanding that we constantly reflect on our definition of 'delayed' and then comment on our definition and so on. While this is happening the child may be disadvantaged still further.

In general, though, the debate will not just die away. There is an increasing use of qualitative approaches within psychological research to the extent of warranting a review in the *British Journal of Psychology* (Henwood & Pidgeon, 1992). This article starts with the fundamental point that the qualitative–quantitative debate is *not* just about preferable methods for varying research contexts. It engages all the debate about experimentation, positivism, artificiality, political power of the establishment mainstream and the wrongness of 'natural science envy' which has been aired often but increasingly by humanists, new paradigm researchers and others. This author would prefer to see a less adversarial atmosphere in which each side agrees to work with and appreciate the value of the other. Both sides seem to succumb far too easily to simple, insular stereotypes and old-fashioned, non-academic, supremely counter-productive hostility.

Box 11.1 *A reflexive 'second voice'*

COLLEAGUE:	So why are you dabbling in this reflexive stuff, Hugh?
HUGH:	I wanted to show readers/students what it looks like, how it runs.
COLLEAGUE:	Why not use an existing example then, like Woolgar's or Edwards and Potter's?
HUGH:	Well, that wouldn't work because it has to be *live*, that is, connected with the ordinary text you're currently reading.
COLLEAGUE:	While we're at it . . .
HUGH:	Oh oh, here comes an argument.
COLLEAGUE:	. . . how can you publish a traditional methods and stats text including 'radical qualitative' material as well? Surely the two are mutually incompatible – either you ally with one or the other?
HUGH:	Not me. I've talked in the classroom for ages about the narrow nature of many traditional studies. I didn't discover the refreshing alternatives till a few years ago. However, even though I know the qualitative, discursive or reflexive approaches aren't just same level, amicable alternatives, I still believe you can't jump into them without an understanding of the quantitative, traditional method and all its weaknesses. Controlled study has its place, anyway, in the study of, say, vigilance or pattern recognition, or to dispute wild claims about the number of single-parent children who become criminals.
COLLEAGUE:	Hang on, you're getting into a long speech there that's turning into just another way of lecturing your readers. Aren't you kind of saying that the qualitative approach only has its place in 'soft' areas?
HUGH:	I hope not. I take the discursive psychology point that, as Bartlett said, we *construct* memory as an *action*. I understand that, in real contexts, as opposed to the laboratory, we *use* memorising to explain, blame, self-justify and so on. For me, though, I'm also fascinated as to how that works *inside our heads*, how well we do this or that sort of material, perhaps even what chemistry is responsible. To say that you can't get at memory processes through people's talk, and that therefore we should concentrate *entirely* on what people *do* sounds depressingly like the old behaviourist approach, as Neisser suggested – although Potter denies that discourse analysis is a positivist approach.
COLLEAGUE:	Well, that *was* a speech!
HUGH:	Yup! I don't think I'm much good at this reflexive style . . .
COLLEAGUE:	Well . . . Edwards' view in *Discursive Psychology* seemed to be that at least a 'reflexive box' made readers aware that what they're reading *is* discourse; there's no neutral language of description; in this textbook, as in any other, you're constructing and manipulating; your knowledge is 'localised' . . .
HUGH:	Meaning?
COLLEAGUE:	You have no absolute claim to the truth; you construct it as you see it. Your first version of this box distorted some of the DA arguments. You rely partly on colleagues' views, on personal communicators about your first edition, on textbooks more expert and complex than your own, on journals, on friends, students and others' comments, etc.
HUGH:	OK OK! Doesn't everyone?

COLLEAGUE:	Sure, but they don't always write or produce books as if this were true ...
HUGH:	What about prefaces, acknowledgements, brackets, footnotes and all that?
COLLEAGUE:	Yes, but you must admit, most textbooks do very little self-reflection and mostly appear to carry THE TRUTH.
HUGH:	I suppose so. There certainly are a lot of unrecognised politics behind several seemingly scientific texts I've seen on the nature–nurture, race and intelligence issue. But I still believe many practical issues require evidence ('facts' if you like) which is relatively incontravertible, accessible and independent of slightly varying individual constructions.
COLLEAGUE:	Hmm ... when I've got more time I'd really like to give you examples of the irrational but powerful ways even 'hard' scientists dismiss 'good' evidence ...

RECOMMENDED FURTHER READING

Edwards, D. and Potter, J. (1992) *Discursive Psychology*, London: Sage.

Henwood, K. and Pidgeon, N. (1992) Qualitative research and psychological theorising. *British Journal of Psychology*, 83, 97–111.

Potter, J. and Wetherell, M. (1987) *Discourse and Social Psychology: beyond attitudes and behaviour*, London: Sage.

Reason, P. and Rowan, J. (eds) (1981) *Human Enquiry: a sourcebook in new paradigm research*, Chichester: Wiley.

Ussher, J. M. (1991) *Women's Madness: misogyny or mental illness?*, London: Harvester/Wheatsheaf.

Wetherell, M. and Potter, J. (1993) *Mapping the Language of Racism: discourse and the legitimation of exploitation*, London: Harvester/Wheatsheaf.

Wilkinson, S. (1986) *Feminist Social Psychology*, Milton Keynes: OUP.

GLOSSARY

Practical intervention in everyday situations, often organisations, using applied psychology to produce change and monitor results	_____ _____	action research
Research in which participants are fully involved to the extent of organising their own processes of change	_____ _____	collaborative research
Qualitative analysis of interactive speech which assumes people use language to construct the world as they see it and according to their interests	_____ _____	discourse analysis
Research involving group members in study of their own customs, organisational norms and so on	_____ _____	endogenous research

Emphasis on women's perspective and on methods suitable to research which integrates gender politics	_____ _____	feminist psychology
Work with qualitative data which permits theory and hypotheses to evolve from the data rather than hypothetico-deductive *testing* of hypotheses set before data is obtained	_____ _____	inductive analysis
A prevailing agreed system of scientific thinking and behaviour within which research is conducted	_____	paradigm
Research in which participants are fully involved	_____ _____	participative research
The scientific belief that hard facts in the world can be discovered only through measurement of what is observable	_____	positivism
Work (research or theoretical text) which includes self-criticism and alerts the reader to the human subjective processes involved in production of the text; it warns the reader that knowledge is relative to the writer's perspective	_____	reflexivity
Belief that objective facts are an illusion and that knowledge is constructed by each individual	_____	relativism

PART THREE

Dealing with data

MEASUREMENT

Precision in many areas of research requires quantitative measurement which is carried out at various levels. There is a strong debate about whether any variable, properly so-called, can escape some form of quantitative measurement. Qualitatively different events can at least be counted or categorised and, strictly speaking, a variable must vary in some quantitative manner.

- The levels at which data can be measured are: **nominal**, **ordinal**, **interval** and **ratio**. The latter is a specific form of interval scaling.
- **Nominal** level is simple classification. At **ordinal** level, cases are ranked or ordered. **Interval** scales should use intervals equal in amount. **Ratio** scales are interval but include a real zero and relative proportions on the scale make sense.
- Attempts are made to convert many psychological scales to interval level using **standardisation**.
- Many scales used in psychology can be called **plastic interval** because numerically equal appearing intervals on the scale do not measure equal amounts of a construct.
- All variables can be classified according to whether they are **categorical** or **measured**.
- **Measured** variables may be measured on a **discrete** or a **continuous** scale. Many variables in psychology are measured on discrete scales, where there are only a limited number of separated points, but are treated as continuous for statistical purposes.
- Higher levels of measurement give greater amounts of information about the original data or phenomenon measured.
- Level of measurement limits choice in treatment of data, especially in terms of the statistical significance tests which may legitimately be carried out.

MEASUREMENT ASSUMPTIONS IN 'COMMON-SENSE' STATEMENTS

Let's start with two 'common-sense' statements which any two people might make over the dinner table:

> I think attractive people are more successful because they're more likely to be selected at interviews and to be given more attention generally.

> No. It could be that more attractive people develop better social confidence earlier on in life and that's what gets them through interviews and the like.

Inside both persons' heads there must be a concept (perhaps vague) of what counts as attractive. It isn't a concept held uniquely by each individual since they are claiming that people in general, and fairly consistently, respond to the attractive qualities. To prove their points through psychological research, each would need to *operationalise* their concept of 'attractiveness' (and perhaps of 'success' and 'self-confidence'). In some way or other, values must be attached to different levels of attractiveness with which we will be able to make comparisons. Many people will baulk at the idea of reducing concepts like 'attractiveness' to 'mere numbers', yet numbers measure quantity and quality; quantity or quality differences are implied in such statements as:

- Helen is more artistic than Clare
- George is a contemplative type whereas Rick is practical, energetic and impulsive
- Taureans are down-to-earth people
- Jason is far more intelligent than Jonathan

> Try specifying just what measurements you might try to make in order to support the statements made just above.

QUANTITATIVE AND QUALITATIVE DIFFERENCES

It may appear that a difference of quality, such as that expressed about George, does not need numerical values to confirm it, but how exactly do we know Rick is 'energetic' or 'impulsive'? We must be comparing some things he does (how strongly and how often) with their occurrence in others. We must define what counts as energetic and impulsive and show that Rick is like this more often or to a greater degree than is George. Hence, to demonstrate a difference, we would need some numerical measure. This might be achieved by counting how many people assess George or Rick as energetic, for instance.

Some would argue that the differences between people on some characteristics just *cannot* be meaningfully measured numerically. Differences in artistic quality, for instance, need to be exemplified by contrasting pieces of work, not by counting how often a masterpiece is produced. The hard-line quantitative view here is that, nevertheless, there must be *some* quantification in any contrast, if only to say Jane is like this and Robert isn't (scores, or 'codes', of 1 and 0 if you like). A variable can't be a *known* variable unless its changes are somehow noticeable and measurable.

NOMINAL LEVEL OF MEASUREMENT

Categories

For some differences of quality we do not need to count in order to distinguish one item from another. For instance:

- male and female
- red, green and blue objects
- Roman noses and other noses

Here we do not need to count anything to decide which object goes into which category. We simply compare each item with some learnt concept – what counts as green, a Roman nose (shape) or a male. On occasion we may count number of features present before categorising, for instance, when deciding whether to categorise a car as 'luxury' – how many luxury features does it have?

What matters for such categorisation is that we must be able to place each item in just one category, for purposes of comparison. We might decide to categorise people as 'energetic', 'average' and 'slow' for instance. A person is either male or female and can't, when we use a nominal scale, be included in both categories because he/she is a bit of both. Difficulties may arise in categorising a person as smoker or non-smoker, extrovert or introvert, optimist or pessimist, but on a nominal scale categories are *mutually exclusive*. People and things are bunched together on the basis of a common feature – Jason is not the same as Jonathan but they have maleness in common. All irrelevant differences are ignored for the measurement purpose at hand.

Labels for categories

If we were conducting a survey which investigated use of the college canteen, we might like to count the number of people using it and categorise these. Table 12.1 might be used:

Table 12.1 *Frequencies of people using the canteen*

Category	1	2	3	4	5
	Students	Teaching staff	Non-teaching staff	Visitors	Other
	650	34	43	17	2

The numbers given to the categories here are NOMINAL – 'in name only'. Number 1 (students) is not half of number 2 (teaching staff) or in any way prior to or less than the others in quantity. The numbers are simply convenient but arbitrary labels for identifying each type of person. We could have used 'A', 'B', 'C' etc. We are using numerals (the figures 1, 2, 3 etc.) as labels only and not as real numbers – they don't in any way stand for *quantities*. Likewise, numbers on office doors don't represent quantity but places to find people in.

The numbers *within* each category are known as FREQUENCIES or FREQUENCY DATA. They represent the number of times an event in category 1, for instance, occurred – presence of a student. These numbers *are* being used to count, they do stand for quantities and are known as 'cardinal' numbers. Note that, from the description of nominal data above, each person counted can only go in one category. Hence, a member of staff also undertaking a course as a student at the college can only go in one category, student *or* staff.

Some examples of psychological data gathered on a nominal scale are:

Table 12.2 *Number of children (average age 4.5 years) engaged in type of play*

non-play	solitary	associative	parallel	cooperative
8	5	17	23	6

Table 12.3 *Oldtown by-election: number of voters by political party*

Communist	Conservative	Labour	Lib. Dem.	Other
243	14678	15671	4371	567

Table 12.4 *Number of people smoking an average of N cigarettes per day*

N =	None	1–5	6–10	11–20	21–30	31–40	41+
	65	45	78	32	11	4	3

This last example is deceptive. The category titles do form a progressive scale (1–5, 6–10) etc. The essential point, however, is that data are represented in the form of *frequencies* in separate, exclusive categories, and there is no distinction between persons within each category.

Comparison of the nominal level with other levels

Suppose I made a rather foolish claim that brown horses run faster than grey horses. Suppose we observed a race in which there were 20 browns and 20 greys. We could present the results of the race as in Table 12.5:

Table 12.5 *Nominal level race results*

	Colour of horse	
	Grey	Brown
Finished in top ten	3	7
Finished in last ten	7	3

These are data presented at a nominal level. Each horse appears in one discrete category, along with other horses. The columns represent a nominal scale with two values – grey and brown, and the rows have the two values – 'in top ten' and 'in last ten'.

The result shows us that the browns did better overall but the differences aren't convincing enough to rule out the possibility that the greys might be the superior group next time. Suppose the greys had come first, second and third? We don't have enough information. We need to be able to *compare* the performances of the horses in the top and last ten places.

The nominal level of measurement provides the *least* amount of quantitative information. In a strict sense, there is no real measurement going on, simply the classification of items into categories.

ORDINAL LEVEL OF MEASUREMENT

Ordinal numbers represent position in a group. They tell us who came 1st, 2nd, 3rd and so on in a race or test. They do not tell us how far ahead the winner was from the second placed. They tell us nothing at all about distances between positions. It may be annoying to be beaten by one-tenth of a second in a cycle race when you and the leader were ten kilometres ahead of the rest of the 'bunch', but what goes on your record is just 'second'. To the punter it doesn't matter by what margin Golden Girl won – it won!

HOW TO RANK DATA

Giving ranks to scores or values obtained in research is very easy but must be done in a precise, conventional manner, otherwise the various significance tests based on ranks will give quite wrong results. Suppose we have to rank the scores of eight people on a general knowledge test shown in Table 12.6.

Table 12.6 *General knowledge scores*

Person	Score	Rank of score
1	18	5.5
2	25	7
3	14	1
4	18	5.5
5	15	3
6	15	3
7	15	3
8	29	8

The score of 14 is lowest and gets the rank one. In competitions we usually give the winner 'first' but in statistics it is less confusing to give low scores low ranks.

Persons five, six and seven 'share' the next three ranks (of second, third and fourth). In sport we might say 'equal second', but in statistical ranking we take the *median* value (see next chapter) of the ranks they share. If the number is odd, this is just the *middle* value. From 2 3 4 the middle value is 3. If the number is even we take the number midway between the two middle ranks shared. Persons one and four share the ranks 5 and 6. The point midway between these is 5.5. If four people shared 6 7 8 9, the mid point shared would be 7.5.

Here we have converted data which was at a higher, more informative level (RATIO data, which we will discuss below), into ordinal level data. The *scores* are ratio level, the *ranks* are ORDINAL.

Comparison of ordinal level with other levels

If we presented the results of the grey vs. brown horse race at an ordinal level, they might look like this:

Table 12.7 *Ordinal level race results*

Colour of horse	Grey	Brown
	1	4
	2	5
	3	6
		7
	11	8
	12	9
	13	10
	14	
	15	18
	16	19
	17	20

Now the superiority of the brown horses is very much in doubt. With seven out of the top ten places *and* something in the top three we might have been convinced, but we now know the first three were greys. We certainly can't say the browns are faster overall. Of course, all the first 10 horses might have come in very close together, in which case, coming first, second and third doesn't demonstrate substantially greater speed. What we need *now* is the actual *times* the horses took to run the course. This will tell us whether the first three greys were well ahead of the browns or not.

Ordinal level of measurement provides *more* information than the nominal scale (it tells us what order individuals can be placed in) but *less* information than an interval scale (we do not know how far apart the people at various rank positions are).

INTERVAL LEVEL OF MEASUREMENT

At the interval level of measurement we can talk meaningfully about distances between points on the scale which, ideally, are all equal for equal units. That is, 10 to 15 minutes is the same interval as 20 to 25 minutes and 30° to 35° is the same interval as $-10°$ to $-5°$. We must be careful what we mean though, by saying that intervals are the *same*. In the temperature example, what we mean is that the measuring system used, expansion of mercury say, changes by equal amounts for equal numerical units. What we *can't* say with temperature is that 30° is twice as hot as 15°. This is because the scale is not at the RATIO level – to be dealt with in a moment. Notice, first, that many scales *appearing* to be numerical and interval are not anything of the sort. Take, for instance, the marking of essays in college. In many institutions, 40 is a pass mark and very few people get more than 70. It is not possible to claim that the distance from 0 to 40 is the *same* as the distance from 40 to 80, or that 35 to 40 is the same size interval as 70 to 75, especially where, as is often the case, *all* fails are given between 38 and 40! There are even cases of these marks then being added and averaged as if they measured uniform amounts. In fact, what is really happening to work a lot of the time is that it is being *ordered* relative to present or past equivalent work. Some departments now have complex grading criteria but it is usually difficult to discover what *exactly* were the grounds for an essay achieving 63, say, rather than 67, other than that the one marked 67 was somehow *better*.

This problem of making artificial, judgement-based measurement systems appear as interval scales is acute in psychology. Philosophical problems occur around the issue of whether psychological scales measuring such variables as intelligence, strength of attachment or achievement motivation are really the interval scales they appear to be at first glance. If these were true interval scales, it ought to be the case that, for instance:

a) Two children scoring five and eight respectively on an achievement scale are as far apart in motivation to achieve as two children scoring nine and 12.
b) Jane, whose IQ is 100, is as far ahead of John (IQ 80) in intelligence as Jackie (IQ 120) is ahead of Jane.

In practice, these ratios don't make sense for most psychological scales but it is the goal of PSYCHOMETRISTS (those who construct psychological scales of measurement) to approach the criterion of equal intervals for their scales. In part, this approach is made through the process of *standardisation* explained earlier. By contrast, a true interval scale is exemplified by temperature. There is a regular underlying physical change for each change of 10° on our thermometer although, of course, each regular change is not felt as equal by us. It might be argued that the underlying change for IQ is the number of items answered correctly and that therefore the interval from 80 to 100 *is* equal to that from 100 to 120.

There are two arguments against this:

1 From a score of 80 you don't necessarily need twice as much extra intelligence to score 120 as you do to score 100. In the same way you don't need twice the arm length or twice the muscle to throw a ball twice the distance someone else did. This is a point where we can see the danger of REIFICATION of the concept of intelligence as if, because we can apply numbers to it, it must exist as something with quantity.

2 It cannot be assumed that all items in the test are equally hard to answer, so can we claim that your score of 110 is equal to my score of 110? Likewise, it is sometimes argued, one person's score of 15 words recalled in a verbal memory test cannot equal another person's score of 15 because some words are harder to retain and recall than others and some combinations may have special meaning for one person.

This is a somewhat hair-splitting argument. Generally speaking, psychologists use statistical tests and treatments which require interval level data even when they are measuring intelligence, achievement and the like. It is assumed that the measurements are on a scale with *approximately* equal intervals and that the researcher will be able to recognise when the assumption of equal intervals is affecting the treatment of results in a serious way.

PLASTIC INTERVAL SCALES – A useful term for the scales that abound in psychological research, where some numerically equivalent intervals are almost certainly not the same *size* as others, is PLASTIC INTERVAL. I discovered the term in Wright (1976) and it suits those data where you can say: 'Well, it *looks* like interval data but obviously it isn't since we've invented the scale, it's not standardised and you can't say that distances at the extremes, measured by 1 to 2 or 9 to 10, are the same in size as distances in the middle, say 5 to 6'.

When research produces data which are a human estimate, especially if based on an arbitrary scale, it is *safer* to assume that ratings are plastic interval and should be reduced to an ordinal level.

Scores given to individuals should be placed in rank order. This will then mean that a less sensitive statistical test must be used, called 'non-parametric' (see Chapters 15 and 16).

Here are some examples of human estimates on an arbitrary scale:

People are asked to estimate how masculine or feminine they are on the following scale:

1 **Feminine**   **Neutral**   **Masculine**
  10..9..8..7..6..5..4..3..2..1..0..1..2..3..4..5..6..7..8..9..10

2 Observers rate, on a scale of one to ten, the level of intimacy displayed by two people in a conversation.

THE LIMITATION OF SOME INTERVAL SCALES

I said above that we can't say that 30° is twice as hot as 15°. Of course the *number* 30 is twice 15. But just consider what happens when we convert to Fahrenheit. Now the values are 86°F and 59°F. The proportions of heat haven't changed, only the system of measurement has. Each scale has a different and somewhat arbitrary zero point, dependent upon the physical change used to measure temperature. Likewise, 100 is arbitrarily chosen to represent the average IQ of large populations and people score somewhere between 0 and 24 on Eysenck's (1975) extroversion and neuroticism dimensions. It doesn't make sense to say that someone scoring zero has *no* extroversion or anxiety, or that someone can have 'zero intelligence' as measured by an IQ test.

RATIO LEVEL OF MEASUREMENT

Scales with a true zero are known as RATIO SCALES. Examples are: time, distance, and most measures of physical qualities. Don't worry that time appears here again. All ratio scales are interval scales first. In our horse race, if Golden Girl completed the distance in eight minutes whilst Jim's Choice took 16 minutes then it certainly makes sense to state that Golden Girl ran twice as fast as Jim's Choice. Remember that it wasn't sensible to say that 30°C was twice as hot as 15°C. In this case all the horses are timed from zero minutes and this is the real zero mark. Similarly, if you recall 15 items from a word list and I recall just five, then your performance on this task (not necessarily your memory in general) is three times better than mine. On a ratio scale, negative numbers have no meaning. You can't recall minus three items and the time of 3.29 p.m. is irrelevant to timing horses from 3.30 p.m. The hallmark of a ratio scale is its possession of a *true zero point*.

In practice, as a student of psychology, you will not need to worry about the difference between interval and ratio scales except to state what the difference is. For the purposes of choosing an appropriate statistical test, covered in Chapter 24, they can be treated as the same thing and you need only justify your data as being at *least* interval level status.

Comparison of interval/ratio level data with other levels

Results of our horse race might look like Table 12.8 if presented at a ratio level of measurement:

Table 12.8 *Time taken to cover course (in seconds)*

Colour of horse	
Grey	**Brown**
120	123
121	124
122	126
	127
	128
	129
	130
137	
138	
139	
140	
141	145
142	146
144	147

Now we have the fullest information we can get on how fast the two groups of horses covered the race distance.

Notice that, as the level increased from nominal to ratio, we gained more specific information at each level. I hope Figure 12.1 makes this clear. The additional

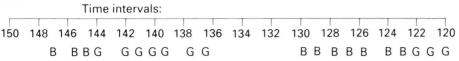

A Interval/ratio level

Time intervals:

| 150 | 148 | 146 | 144 | 142 | 140 | 138 | 136 | 134 | 132 | 130 | 128 | 126 | 124 | 122 | 120 |

B B BG   G GG G   G G   B B B B B   B BG G G

B Ordinal level

Final positions:

B B B G G G G G G G B B B B B B B G G G

C Nominal level

Categories:

	Bottom 10		Top 10	
	B B B	B B B B B B B
	G G G G G G G	G G G

B = brown
G = grey

Figure 12.1 *Levels of measurement and information obtained*

information might have enabled us to be more confident about my original hypothesis. As it is, we are now, I hope, not at all convinced.

Interval and ratio levels of measurement give us the *greatest* amount of information in measuring a variable. We need at least interval-level data in order to conduct PARAMETRIC TESTS.

Reducing data from interval/ratio to ordinal level

On inspection of a table of data you will often find two columns of figures, one the interval or plastic interval level data, and the other being the set of ranks to which the first (interval) set has been reduced. This has occurred in Table 12.9. The data on the left were truly interval; those on the right were unstandardised. *Plastic* interval data, as these intimacy ratings probably are, are best reduced to ordinal data since an ordinal level test is more appropriate for them.

Table 12.9 *Reduction of data (interval to ordinal level)*

Reaction time (sec.)	Rank	Intimacy rating (max. 10)	Rank
0.067	1	7	4
0.078	3	6	2.5
0.091	5	5	1
0.089	4	6	2.5
0.076	2	9	5

It is easy to spot the column which is of ordinal data. It will usually have the title 'rank(s)' at the top of it. Anyway, the column of ranks is the ordinal data set.

Reducing data from interval/ratio to nominal level

It is quite common to reduce data like that shown in Table 12.10 to a nominal level by grouping together those above and below the overall mean for the whole sample

Table 12.10 *Data prepared for reduction*

No. of anxiety indicators observed	
High competitive children	**Low competitive children**
14.0	10.0
21.0	6.0
7.0	13.0
13.0	5.0
18.0	11.0
Mean 14.6	Mean 9.0
Mean for whole group = 11.8	

and comparing this with another variable, in this case, high and low competitiveness. The data, reduced to nominal level, are shown in Table 12.11.

Table 12.11 is obtained by noting that four children in the high competitive group are above 11.8 (the average anxiety score for all ten children) and only one below.

Table 12.11 *Reduction of data (interval to nominal level)*

	Level of competitiveness	
	High	**Low**
Anxiety indicators		
Above mean	4	1
Below mean	1	4

CATEGORICAL AND MEASURED VARIABLES – A CATEGORICAL VARIABLE is what we have introduced in talking of a nominal scale – one in which there are discontinuous, qualitatively different categories into which we can simply count instances (frequencies). In this contrast, *all* variables which can at least be ordered are, in some sense, MEASURED, but these, in turn may be divided into those which are *truly* continuous and those which are discrete – see below.

CONTINUOUS AND DISCRETE SCALES OF MEASUREMENT

All the scales mentioned can be divided into two categories: continuous or discrete. On discrete scales each point is entirely separate from the next. It is not possible to have two-and-a-half children, for instance. In a memory experiment you can only recall a discrete number of words – although the *mean* may take a non-existent individual value of 14.3. Both these scales of measuring individual cases would be DISCRETE – see Figure 12.2. On CONTINUOUS scales there is no limit to the subdivisions of points which can occur. It is theoretically possible to measure your height to the nearest thousandth of an inch: technically this might be difficult and in practice, hardly likely to be useful.

Interval and ratio scales can be either continuous or discrete. Nominal scales can only be discrete. Ordinal scales generally have 0.5 as the smallest unit.

In general, psychological scales, such as IQ, and measures like number of words recalled from a 20-word list, are treated as continuous for statistical purposes, but an

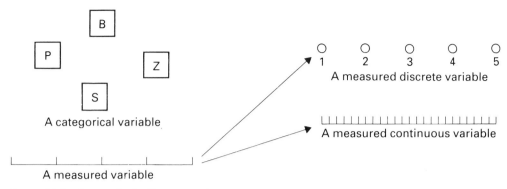

Figure 12.2 *Categorical, discrete and continuous variables*

important difference is that with a truly interval scale we avoid the issue of measuring to the nearest thousandth of an inch or whatever by using *intervals*. We say that someone's height is between 174.5 and 175.5 cm rather than that they are exactly 175 cm tall (explained further under 'Range' in the next chapter). There would rarely be anyone *exactly* 174.50000 cm tall, falling precisely on the interval boundary, so, should this rare event occur, we could place them in this interval, or the preceding one, by the toss of a coin.

GLOSSARY

Variable not measurable on a linear scale and which has only discrete values	_____ _____	categorical variable
Data presented as numbers of cases in specific categories	_____ ____	frequency data
Variable which is at least ordered	_____ _____	measured variable
Person who develops psychological measures and attempts to standardise the scales up to an interval level of measurement	_____	psychometrist
Difference between cases in *kind* and not numerically measurable, though *being different* can be counted	_____ _____	qualitative difference
Difference between cases measurable by number	_____ _____	quantitative difference
		scales/levels of measurement
Scale on which it is always (theoretically) possible to subdivide units of measurement	_____	continuous
Scale containing only separated values of the variable measured	_____	discrete

Level at which each unit measures an equal amount	_____	interval
Level at which numbers, if used, are mere labels; labels on the scale identify discrete categories of a categorical variable into which cases are sorted	_____	nominal
Level at which cases are arranged in rank positions	_____	ordinal
Scale which appears to be interval but on which equal numbers do not measure equal amounts	_____ _____	plastic interval
Level at which each unit measures an equal amount and proportions on the scale are meaningful; a real zero exists	_____	ratio

EXERCISES

1 Find one example of each level of measurement from any text books (on psychology) you have available.

2 When judges give their marks in an ice-skating contest for style and presentation, what level of measurement is it safest to treat their data as?

3 A set of surgical records classifies patients as 'chronic', 'acute' or 'not yet classified'. What level of measurement is being used?

4 At what level are the measurements in Table 12.12 being made?

5 Which of the boxes, **a** to **d**, in Table 12.12, contains the most sensitive or informative level of measurement?

Table 12.12 *Exercise 4*

a) Placings of top five riders in Tour de France, 13 July, 1993		b) Time taken so far on whole race	c) Popularity rating (max. 20) (fictitious)	d) Riders still in race	Riders so far dropped out
					(fictitious)
Indurain	1	35 h 29 m 25 s	12	121	77
Breukink	2	35 h 31 m 0 s	15		
Bruyneel	3	35 h 31 m 55 s	18		
Bugno	4	35 h 31 m 57 s	10		
Riis	5	35 h 31 m 59 s	13		

6 Your daughter argues that, since she came top in each of the three maths tests held in her class this year, she must be *far* better than all the other pupils. What might you point out to her? (Would you dare?)

7 Think of three ways to measure driving ability, one using nominal level data, one ordinal and one interval/ratio.

8 Can you change the data in Table 12.13 first to ordinal level, then to nominal level? The blank tables are for you to fill in. For ordinal level, treat all the scores as *one* group.

Table 12.13 *Exercise 8*

a) Time taken to read (seconds)		b) Ordinal level		c) Nominal level
Consistent story	Inconsistent story	Consistent story	Inconsistent story	
127	138			
136	154			
104	138			
111	117			
152	167			
111	117			
127	135			
138	149			
145	151			
Mean of all times: ($\bar{x}$) = 134.3				

9 Below are several methods for measuring dependent variables. For each measure decide what level of measurement is being used. Choose from:

1 Nominal   **2** Ordinal   **3** Interval   **4** Ratio

a) People are interviewed in the street and, on the basis of their replies, are recorded as either: pro-hanging, undecided, or anti-hanging
b) Stress questionnaire for which various occupational norms have been established
c) Photographs organised by participants according to level of attractiveness as follows:

Photos: F C B G E A H D
Most attractive ←   → Least attractive

d) Participants' estimates of various line lengths
e) Time taken to sort cards into categories
f) Number of people who read: *The Sun*, *The Times*, or *The Guardian*
g) Participants' sense of self-worth, estimated on a scale of 1–10
h) Participants' scores on Cattell's 16PF questionnaire
i) Distance two participants stand apart when asked to take part in an intimate conversation, measured from photos
j) Critical life events given positions 1–10 according to their perceived importance to each participant.

DESCRIPTIVE STATISTICS

This chapter concerns the ways in which data can be described. Sample statistics usually include a measure of **central tendency** (**mean**, **median**, **mode**) and a measure of **dispersion** (**range**, **semi-interquartile range**, **mean deviation**, **standard deviation** and **variance**, the last two being most common for interval level data).

- Sample **statistics**, at interval level, are often used to make estimates of population **parameters**. This is a powerful technique employed in **parametric tests**.
- The appropriateness of the statistic depends upon the **level of measurement** of the data.
- Large sets of data form a **distribution** and these may be represented in several ways. They may be divided into categories and presented as a **frequency table**. Statistics of distributions include **percentiles**, **quartiles** and **deciles**.
- A frequency distribution may be represented graphically as a **histogram**, where *all* data in a set are displayed by adjacent columns. In a **bar chart** only discrete categories of data are presented for comparison and this must be done fairly, without visual distortion.
- Other graphical forms include the **frequency polygon**, **line chart** and **ogive**. In recent years the techniques of **exploratory data analysis** have been promoted with an emphasis on thorough examination of patterns before submitting data sets to tests of statistical significance. Two methods are included here: **stem and leaf** diagrams, and **box-plots**.
- The **normal distribution** is an extremely important distribution shape. Data approximating to this shape can be tested with the most powerful significance techniques and estimates of underlying population **parameters** can be made from sample **statistics**.
- z-scores are **deviations** measured in numbers of standard deviations and on the normal distribution they cut off known percentages of the whole distribution.
- Distributions with substantially more scores at the high end of the measurement scale are said to be **positively skewed**. The opposite is a **negatively skewed** distribution. If a skewed distribution shows bunching at the top end because too many people score the maximum or very near it, then the variable measure shows a **ceiling effect**. Its opposite is a **floor effect**.
- Distributions with two distinct 'humps' (higher frequencies) are known as **bi-modal**.

STATISTICS ARE A SELECTION

In this section, we are looking simply at the ways in which statistical information can be presented. Statistical information follows from organising the numerical data gathered during quantitative research. Most research gathers far too much information for every little bit of it to be presented. When a survey of voting preference is conducted, or an experiment is run on 35 participants, it is not useful to be given just the RAW DATA, that is, every individual's answers or scores. We expect to be given a *summary* of the data which highlights major trends and differences. However, it is important to note that the very act of summarising introduces distortions. We will be given what the researcher decides is the most important information and this will be presented in what is believed to be the most appropriate manner. Politicians and companies, among others, are renowned for presenting data in the best possible light. A psychologist should be looking at the best way to present data *only* in terms of what gives the clearest, least ambiguous picture of what was found in a research study.

BUT I CAN'T DO SUMS!

As with many ideas in this book, the things we will study are based on everyday common-sense notions you have undoubtedly used before. Even if you hate maths, dread statistics and have never done any formal work in this area, you have undoubtedly made statistical descriptions many times in your life without necessarily being aware of it. You may believe that only clever, numerically minded people do this sort of thing, but consider this. Imagine you have just come home from your first day on a new college course and I ask you what your class is like. You would not proceed to tell me the exact age of each class member. This could take far too long. You'd be likely to say something like 'Well, most people in the class are around 25 years old but there are a couple of teenagers and one or two are over 40.' You have in fact summarised the class ages statistically, albeit rather loosely too. First you gave me a rough AVERAGE, the typical age in the group, then you gave me an idea of the actual *variation* from this typical age present in the group. Let's look at these aspects of description in a little more detail. Have a look at the data in Table 13.1.

Table 13.1 *Number of seconds five-year-old nursery class children spent talking in a ten-minute observation period, by sex*

Child	Male	Child	Female
1	132	6	332
2	34	7	345
3	5	8	289
4	237	9	503
5	450	10	367

Before looking at the comments, see what conclusions you can come to about the talking of girls and boys.

Overall, the girls speak just about twice the amount that boys do. We could see this by looking at the *average* for each group. But not only this, the boys' times vary *very* widely compared with the girls', from as little as five seconds to nearly the highest girl's time.

We shall now introduce two formal terms which are used to describe these two aspects of group data description.

CENTRAL TENDENCY   This is the value in a group of values which is the most *typical* for the group, or the score which all other scores are evenly clustered around. In normal language, this is better and more loosely known as 'the average'. In statistical description, though, we have to be more precise about just what sort of average we mean.

DISPERSION   This is a measure of how much or how little the rest of the values tend to *vary* around this central or typical value.

MEASURES OF CENTRAL TENDENCY

THE MEAN

In normal language we use the term 'average' for what is technically known as the ARITHMETIC MEAN. This is what we get when we add up all the values in a group and then divide by the number of values there are. Hence, if five people took 135, 109, 95, 121 and 140 seconds to solve an anagram, the mean time taken is:

$$\frac{135 + 109 + 95 + 121 + 140}{5} = \frac{600}{5} = 120 \text{ seconds}$$

Calculation of the mean
Term used: $(\bar{x})$

Formula: $\bar{x} = \dfrac{\Sigma x}{N}$

Procedure: 1 Add up all values
            2 Divide by total number of values (N)

This is our first use of a 'formula' which is simply a set of instructions. You just have to follow them faithfully to get the desired result, rather like following a recipe or instructions for Dr Jekyll's magic potion. The formula above tells you to add up all the scores (ΣX) and divide by the number of scores in the sample (N). There is a section at the end of this chapter on notation (e.g. Σ) and the rules for following a formula. I hope this will help you if it's some time since you did any 'sums' or hated them (or thought they were pointless). Rest assured that the *only* mathematical operations you need to perform, in going through this book, are the four junior school operations ($+ - \times \div$) and squares (which are multiplication anyway) and square roots (which are always found at the touch of a button). All work *can* be done on the simplest of calculators but, of course, and certainly towards the end of the book, computer programmes can make life a lot easier.

Advantages and disadvantages of the mean

ADVANTAGES – The mean is the statistic used in estimating population parameters (see page 211) and this estimation is the basis for PARAMETRIC TESTS (Chapter 17) which are powerful tests used, among other things, to show whether two means are significantly different from one another.

Very often the mean is not the same value as any of the values in the group. It acts like the fulcrum of a balanced pair of scales sitting exactly at the centre of all the DEVIATIONS from itself, as I hope Figure 13.1 illustrates, using the anagram time scores from the previous example. A 'deviation' is the distance of a score from its group mean.

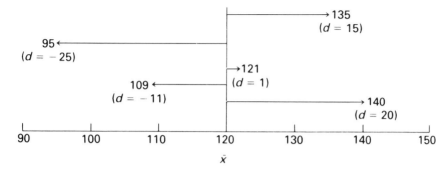

$(d = \text{distance from the mean})$

Figure 13.1 *Position of the mean*

The positive and negative distances from the individual scores to the mean exactly cancel out. ($[-25] + [-11] + 1 + 15 + 20 = 0$) This can only happen because the mean takes an exactly central position on an interval (and continuous) scale. This makes it the most sensitive of the measures of central tendency covered here.

DISADVANTAGES – This very sensitivity, however, can also be something of a disadvantage in certain circumstances. Suppose we add a sixth person's value to our set of anagram solving times. This person had a bad night's sleep and doesn't particularly like doing word games, having had an exceptionally competitive sister who always won at Scrabble. This person sits and stares at the anagram for exactly eight minutes before getting the answer. Our mean for the six values now becomes:

$$\frac{600 + 480}{6} = \frac{1080}{6} = \textbf{180 seconds}$$

180 seconds is just not representative of the group in general. It is a highly misleading figure to describe what most of the group did. Five out of six people took a lot less time than this to solve the anagram. A single extreme score in one direction (an 'outrider') can distort the mean (see Figure 13.2) (whereas extremes in both directions tend to cancel each other out).

THE MEDIAN

Using the median gets us around the difficulty for the mean outlined just above. The median is the *central* value of a set. If we have an odd number of values in our set then this couldn't be easier to find. The central value of our first five anagram solution times above is the third one. To find this we must first put all five in numerical order. This gives:

95, 109, 121, 135, 140   The median is **121**   (1)

If there is an even number of values, as with our sixth person's time added, we take the mean of the two central values, thus:

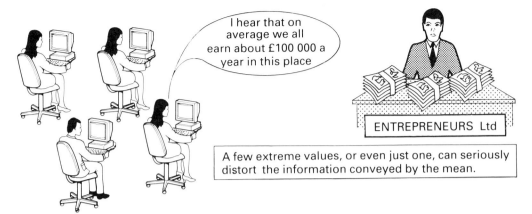

Figure 13.2 *One rogue value can distort the mean*

$$95, 109, 121, 135, 140, 480 \qquad \text{The median is } \frac{121 + 135}{2} = \mathbf{128} \qquad \mathbf{(2)}$$

Notice that this value is still reasonably representative of the group of values.

Calculation of the median

PROCEDURE

1 Find the MEDIAN POSITION or LOCATION. This is the *place* where we will find the median value. This is at

$$\frac{N+1}{2}$$

2 If N is odd this will be a whole number. Above (**1**) we would get

$$\frac{5+1}{2} = 3$$

The median is at the third position when the data are ordered.

3 If N is even the position will be midway between two of the values in the set. In (**2**), above, we get

$$\frac{6+1}{2} = 3.5$$

The median is midway between the third and fourth values when the data are ordered.

If there are a very large number of scores, putting these in order can be very tedious and the following formula for ties could be used instead.

WHEN THERE ARE TIES – Things are a little tricky when ties fall at the median position, although many textbooks omit to mention it, obviously concluding that ignoring ties will make little practical difference, which is true. However, the formula below is also useful for large data sets.

Consider the following set of values: 7, 7, 7, 8, 8, 8, 9, 9, 10, 10

The eights are assumed to be contained somewhere in the interval 7.5 to 8.5. (For clarification on this point, see the remarks just under the heading *The range*, below, and on page 197.) The median is a point within this interval which would leave two of the eights below it and one above. The best way to estimate this point is to take a value two-thirds of the way along this interval. The interval is one unit so two-thirds along is 0.66. Add this to 7.5, the lower limit of the interval, and we get 8.16 as the median. There is a formula for calculating this value exactly when necessary. It is:

$$\text{Median} = L + \frac{N/2 - F}{f_m} \times h$$

where:

L	= exact lower limit of interval containing median
F	= total number of values below L
f_m	= number of values in interval containing median
h	= size of class interval
N	= number of values

So, substituting here we get:

$$7.5 + \frac{10/2 - 3}{3} \times 1 = \mathbf{8.16}$$

This formula is particularly useful when data are grouped into categories which spread across several values. This occurs in Table 12.4, in the previous chapter on measurement, where smokers are grouped into categories based on how many cigarettes per day smoked. The categories 1–5, 6–10, 11–20 etc. are called CLASS INTERVALS. Notice that in this example they are not all the same size. Here, it is difficult to see where the median could be. There are 238 cases altogether so the median is the value above and below which 119 of all cases fall. This must be somewhere in the 6–10 category. We assume that values in this category are evenly spread throughout it. This is what our formula is based on. So L is 5.5, F is 110, f_m is 78, h is 5 and N is 238. The median is 6.08.

Advantages and disadvantages of the median

Advantages:	Easier to calculate than the mean (with small groups and no ties)
	Unaffected by extreme values in one direction, therefore better with skewed data than the mean (see later this chapter)
	Can be obtained when extreme values are unknown
Disadvantages:	Doesn't take into account the exact values of each item
	Can't be used in estimates of population parameters
	If values are few can be unrepresentative; for instance, with 2, 3, 5, 98, 112 the median would be 5

THE MODE

If we have data on a nominal scale, as with categories of play in Table 12.2, we cannot calculate a mean or a median. We can, however, say which type of play was engaged in most, i.e. which category had the highest frequency count. This is what is known as the MODE or MODAL VALUE. It is the most frequently occurring value and therefore even easier to find than the mean or median.

The mode of the set of numbers:

1, 2, 3, 3, 3, 4, 4, 4, 5, 5, 5, 5, 5, 5, 6, 6, 7, 7, 7, 8

is therefore 5 since this value occurs most often. For the set of anagram solving times there is no single modal value since each time occurs once only. For the set of numbers 7, 7, 7, 8, 8, 9, 9, 9, 10, 10 there are two modes, 7 and 9, and the set is said to be bi-modal (see Figure 13.21). For the table of play categories, the modal value is parallel play. Be careful here to note that the mode is not the number of times the most frequent value occurs but that value itself. Parallel play occurred most often.

There are special occasions when the mode is far more informative about reality than either the mean or the median. Suppose we asked people how many masculine or feminine traits they thought they possessed. The distribution we'd be likely to obtain may well be U-shaped and bi-modal, men scoring more masculine traits and women scoring more feminine ones, and relatively few people scoring in the centre. The mean and median here would give us the impression that the average person thought they were midway between male and female. Philosophically, perhaps we are, but it is unlikely most people in a survey would respond this way.

Advantages and disadvantages of the mode

Advantages: Shows the most important value of a set
Unaffected by extreme values in one direction
Can be obtained when extreme values are unknown
More informative than mean when distribution is U-shaped

Disadvantages: Doesn't take into account the exact value of each item
Can't be used in estimates of population parameters
Not useful for relatively small sets of data where several values occur equally frequently (1, 1, 2, 3, 4, 4)
Can't be estimated accurately when data are grouped into class intervals. We can have a modal interval – like 6–10 cigarettes in Table 12.4 – but this may change if the data are categorised differently

LEVELS OF MEASUREMENT AND CENTRAL TENDENCY MEASURES

Interval   The *mean* is the most sensitive measure but should only be used where data are at the interval level of measurement. Otherwise, the mean is calculated on numbers which don't represent equal amounts and the mean is misleading.

Ordinal   If data are not at interval level but can be ranked then the *median* is the appropriate measure of central tendency.

Nominal   If data are in discreetly separate categories, then only the *mode* can be used.

The mode *may* be used on ordinal and interval level data.
The median *may* be used on interval level data.

Measures of dispersion

THE RANGE

Think back to the description of new college classmates. The central tendency was given as 25 but some 'guesstimate' was also given of the way people spread around this central point. Without knowledge of spread (or more technically, dispersion) a mean can be very misleading. Take a look at the bowling performance of two cricketers shown in Figure 13.3. Both average around the middle stump but (a) varies much more than (b). The attempts of (a) are far more widely *dispersed*. Average wages in two companies may be the same but distribution of wages may be very different. Now let's see how we can summarise the dispersion of times spent talking by children in Table 13.1. There, we saw that, as well as talking less overall, the boys *varied* amongst themselves far more than did the girls. The simplest way to measure the variation among a set of values is to use what is called the RANGE. This is simply the distance between the top and bottom values of a set.

high variability   low variability

Figure 13.3 *Dispersion in bowlers' deliveries*

Calculation of the range

Formula: $(X_{top} - X_{bottom}) + 1$

Procedure: **1** Find top value of the set
 2 Find bottom value of the set
 3 Subtract bottom value from top value and add 1

For Table 13.1 this gives: Boys $(450 - 5) + 1 = $ **446**
 Girls $(503 - 289) + 1 = $ **215**

Why add 1?
The addition of 1 may seem a little strange. Surely the distance between 5 and 450 is, straightforwardly, 445? The addition of 1 allows for possible measurement error. When we say that a child spoke for 5 seconds, if our lowest unit of measurement is 1 second, then we can only claim that the child spoke for something between 4.5 and 5.5 seconds, the limits of our lowest measurement interval. If we had measured to *tenths* of a second then 4.3 seconds represents a value between 4.25 and 4.35. Hence, the range is measured from the lowest possible limit of the lowest value to the highest limit of the highest value, in the case of boys' talking times, 4.5 to 450.5

Advantages and disadvantages of the range

Advantages: Easy to calculate
 Includes extreme values
Disadvantages: Distorted by, and unrepresentative with, extreme values
 Unrepresentative of any features of the distribution of values between the extremes. For instance, the range doesn't tell us whether or not the values are closely grouped around the mean

THE SEMI-INTERQUARTILE RANGE

This deals with the last disadvantage of the range. It is a measure of the central grouping of values. It concentrates on the distance between the two values which cut off the bottom and top 25% of scores. These two values are known as the 25th and 75th percentiles, or the first and third quartiles respectively. (We shall deal with these more precisely in a while.) The semi-interquartile range is, in fact, half of the distance between these two values.

In the following set of values:

$$3, \ 3, \ 4, \ 5, \ 6, \ 8, \ 10, \ 13, \ 14, \ 16, \ 19$$

4 is the first quartile and 14 the third quartile. The distance between these is 10 and half this, the semi-interquartile range, is 5.

Calculation of the semi-interquartile range

Formula: $\dfrac{Q_3 - Q_1}{2}$

Procedure: **1** Find the first quartile (Q_1) and the third quartile (Q_3). A formula for finding percentiles is given later and the first and third quartiles are the 25th and 75th percentiles respectively
 2 Subtract Q_1 from Q_3
 3 Divide the result of step two by 2

Advantages and disadvantages of the semi-interquartile range

Advantages: Is representative of the central grouping of values
 Fairly simple to calculate
Disadvantages: Takes no account of extreme values
 Inaccurate where there are large class intervals

THE MEAN DEVIATION

In Figure 13.1, we encountered the concept of DEVIATION VALUE. This is the difference between any particular value and the mean. It is a measure of how far that value deviates from the mean. In formal terms:

$$d_i = x_i - \bar{x}$$

where x_i means the ith value of the set. x_1 is the first value, x_2 is the second and so on. Technically speaking, all formulae like these should include the little subscripts but, in the interests of clarity and simplicity, these are not used in this book unless terms could be ambiguous.

If five people, including yourself, took an IQ test and these were the resulting values:

Hugh	Helga	Harry	Helena	You
85	90	100	110	115

the mean would be 100 and your personal deviation score would be $115 - 100 = 15$. This is how much you *deviate* from the mean of the group.

The range took no notice, and the semi-interquartile range took only some notice, of the way values deviate from the mean. A sensible way to report dispersion might seem to be, therefore, to report the average (mean) of all the deviations in the set. The set of deviations for the set of IQ scores above is shown in Table 13.2:

Table 13.2 *IQ score deviations*

Score		Mean		Deviation (d)
85	–	100	=	– 15
90	–	100	=	– 10
100	–	100	=	0
110	–	100	=	10
115	–	100	=	15

The sum of these deviations is zero and therefore the mean of the deviations would also be zero. This isn't what we wanted. If you look back to Figure 13.1 you can see why this has happened. The means sits precisely in the centre of all the deviations around it. If we use the plus and minus signs to represent direction away from the mean then all the pluses and minuses will cancel each other out when we add the deviations. The answer is to take the mean of all the deviation *sizes*, and to ignore any minus signs. This is known as taking the ABSOLUTE VALUE and is represented mathematically by two vertical bars (|) either side of a number. So, for the absolute value of a deviation score we would write $|x - \bar{x}|$ or $|d|$.

Calculation of the mean deviation

Formula: $\text{MD} = \dfrac{\Sigma |x - \bar{x}|}{N}$ or $\text{MD} = \dfrac{\Sigma |d|}{N}$

Procedure: 1 Find the mean ($\bar{x}$)
2 Subtract the mean from each value $[(x - \bar{x}) = d]$ to obtain a set of deviations
3 Add up all these deviations taking no notice of any minus signs i.e., find $\Sigma |d|$
4 Divide result of step three by N

Using this on our IQ data we get:

$\Sigma |d| = 15 + 10 + 0 + 10 + 15 = 50 \qquad \text{MD} = \dfrac{50}{5} = \mathbf{10}$

Advantages and disadvantages of the mean deviation

Advantages: Takes account of all values in the set
                     Relatively simple to calculate
Disadvantages: Not possible to use in making estimates of population parameters

THE STANDARD DEVIATION AND VARIANCE

Another way out of the problem of having all the deviations sum to zero is to take the square of each deviation (d^2). This will also make the minus signs all disappear, but, of course, if we take the mean of all these values ($\Sigma d^2/N$) we will have a number which is rather large and not at all representative of the set of deviations. This value is known as the VARIANCE of the set of values. What the standard deviation then does is to take the square root of the variance in order to return us to the level the deviations are at.

Calculation of the standard deviation

1 For a group of scores treated solely as a group ('uncorrected')

2 For a sample used as an estimate of the population standard deviation ('unbiased')

$$S = \sqrt{\frac{\Sigma d^2}{N}}$$

$$s = \sqrt{\frac{\Sigma d^2}{(N-1)}}$$

Variance: In each case the variance is the value *before* the square root is found above:

e.g. estimate of population variance: $s^2 = \dfrac{\Sigma d^2}{(N-1)}$

You'll see that there are two formulae to cope with here. The reason is that researchers and statisticians are rarely interested in the variability within a group for its own sake. If we *are* only interested in the specific group variation we use equation 1 above. Most of the time, however, the standard deviation or variance is used as an *estimate of the variation in the underlying population* and equation 2 is used. Computer programmes generally give you the equation 2 version. **Throughout this book assume that s is the $N-1$, population estimate version, i.e. equation 2.** If we *have* the whole population in front of us then equation 1 would be used (there's now no need to estimate) and the symbol used is σ or σ^2.

Procedure for calculation of standard deviation and variance

(using IQ data in Table 13.3)

	Whole group version (N)	Population estimate version ($N-1$)
1 Calculate the sample mean ($\bar{x}$)	= 100	= 100
2 Subtract the mean from each value ($x - \bar{x}$) to obtain a set of deviations	see Table 13.3	see Table 13.3
3 Square each deviation (d^2)	see Table 13.3	see Table 13.3
4 Find the sum of the squared deviations	= 650 see Table 13.3	= 650 see Table 13.3
5 Divide the result of step **4** by N (for just the group variance) or $N-1$ for the population estimate	$S^2 = \dfrac{650}{5} = 130$	$s^2 = \dfrac{650}{4} = 162.5$

You have now found the variance. The standard deviation is found by taking the square root:

6 Find the square root of step **5** $\qquad S = \sqrt{130} = 11.4 \qquad s = \sqrt{162.5} = 12.75$

There is a version of equation 2 (for variance) which avoids the calculation of deviations and for which you only need the set of scores and their total:

$$s^2 = \left(\frac{\Sigma x^2 - (\Sigma x)^2 / N}{N-1} \right)$$

Table 13.3 *Deviations of IQ scores*

Score	Mean	Deviation (d)	Squared deviation (d^2)
85	100	-15	225
90	100	-10	100
100	100	0	0
110	100	10	100
115	100	15	225
			$\Sigma d^2 = 650$

(The standard deviation would include the square root step.)

In later work this is a highly important equation, especially in the whole area of significance testing using Analysis of Variance (Chapters 20–22). **Beware of the difference between Σx^2 and $(\Sigma x)^2$.**

POPULATION PARAMETERS AND SAMPLE STATISTICS

Equation 2, above, introduces a central notion in statistical work. Measures of a *sample*, known as STATISTICS, are very frequently used to *estimate* the same measures of a *population*, known as PARAMETERS. The measures concerned are most often the *mean* and *variance* (which is just the square of the standard deviation). These estimates are used in conducting PARAMETRIC TESTS (to be met in Chapter 17) which are very powerful tests and most likely to give us an accurate assessment of whether or not we should accept differences as significant, given certain assumptions about our data.

When these estimates are made it is assumed that the population mean is the same as our sample mean. Since the sample mean will always be a little different from the population mean, the difference is known as SAMPLING 'ERROR'. The sampling error is estimated using the variance of the sample so that we can state our confidence in how far the population mean is likely to be different from the sample mean. This is similar to what happens at election time when people estimate, from a sample of voters, not just the number of seats to be won by a party but also, the likely possible extremes of variation *from* this figure.

To make this estimate of how close our sample mean is likely to be to the real population mean however, our *sample* variance must be a good estimate of the *population* variance. The accuracy of *this* estimate depends on the size of our sample and *the larger the sample the less the likely sampling error*. With low N, in particular, the estimate of population variance, based on our sample, is said to be 'biased' because:

- our estimate of variance in the population is based on the *sample* mean
- a better estimate of the population variance would be obtained if we used the arrangement of our scores around the *population* mean
- we don't *know* the population mean so we *have* to use the sample mean
- the population mean will always be slightly different from the sample mean
- the effect of this difference is that the 'uncorrected' estimate of variance will always be smaller than the estimate based on the population mean. (This is

because the sample mean is in the exact centre of all the scores; it's the balancing point of all the deviations around it, whereas the population mean won't be.)

To compensate for this, the estimate from the sample is made larger by reducing the bottom of the equation by 1. For large N this difference will become trivial.

Advantages and disadvantages of the standard deviation and variance

Advantages: Can be used in population parameter estimates
Takes account of all values
Is the most sensitive of measures covered
Can be calculated directly on many calculators

Disadvantages: Somewhat more complicated to calculate (if you don't have an appropriate calculator!)

DISTRIBUTIONS

When we wish to communicate the nature of our results to others, be it to our tutor, class colleagues or for official publication, we would usually present at least the central tendency and dispersion of any set of numerical data. We might wish, for instance, to report that the mean age at which 'telegraphic' utterances were first noticed by parents was 18.3 months but that there was a wide variation from this shown by a standard deviation of 5.02.

Where possible, we'd usually like to go further than this and present a table of our results, such as Table 13.4.

Table 13.4 *Result table for small sample*

Child	Mean age at which telegraphic utterances first noticed (n months)
A	18
B	21
C	26
D	13
E	11
F	19
G	20
	$\Sigma x = 128$
	$\bar{x} = 18.3$
	$s = 5.02$

Now we can refer to individual variations and oddities, such as the child who doesn't produce until 26 months and the rather suspicious report of 11 months.

This method of displaying results is useful when the sample taken is relatively small. Had we questioned about 300 parents, however, this approach would be inappropriate and would consume too much space. The individual results – known as the 'raw data' – would be kept safe by the researcher but, for public display, they would be collated into a table known as a FREQUENCY DISTRIBUTION.

We might now end up with a table looking like Table 13.5.

Table 13.5 *Frequency distribution showing ages at which parents report first noticeable telegraphic utterances*

Age (months)	13	14	15	16	17	18	19	20	21	22	23	24	25	26	27	Total
No. of children reported		1	0	5	12	37	64	59	83	17	41	12	0	4	5	0	340

PERCENTILES, DECILES AND QUARTILES

There are 340 cases in this distribution. We may be interested in finding the age by which 10% of the children were reported as using telegraphic speech. If so we would want to find the tenth PERCENTILE, which is the point which cuts off the bottom 10% of the distribution in the same way that the median cuts off the bottom 50%. The median is in fact the 50th percentile. It is also the fifth DECILE, because deciles cut off the distribution in 10% units; the third decile cuts off the bottom 30% for instance. The median is also the second QUARTILE because quartiles cut off in 25% (or quarter) units.

In the distribution above, the tenth percentile will be the point on the age scale below which 34 children fall (10% of cases). This is somewhere in the 17-month category. Proportionally it must be 16 cases into this category which, in all, contains 37 cases. Hence it's about just under half-way between 16.5 and 17.5 months. We calculate this using a formula which is a general version of that for calculating the median of frequency distributions, seen earlier:

$$\text{Percentile} = L + \frac{(Np/100) - F}{f_m} \times h$$

where p is the relevant percentile required and the other symbols are the same as for the previous median calculation.

> Try calculating the tenth percentile for this distribution. You should get an answer of 16.93 months.

CLASS INTERVALS AND CUMULATIVE FREQUENCY

Where the scale in use has many points, we can compress the data into class intervals as shown in Table 13.6. This table also introduces the idea of CUMULATIVE FREQUENCY, where the column with that heading shows us how many values fall below the upper limit of the particular class interval.

Notice that we can tell at a glance how many children uttered 39 utterances or less, say, because we have the cumulative total of 61 in the table, not just how many children were in the 29.5 to 39.5 interval.

Notice, also, that the point about measurement intervals is here again. Even though, in this case, the scale is discrete and there are no decimal values, we may as well stick to the formal method so that you're ready for times when there *are*.

Table 13.6 *Number of children and number of daily telegraphic utterances*

No. of telegraphic utterances	No. of children	Cumulative frequency	Utterances less than:	
0– 9	3	3	9.5	(These are the
10–19	0	3	19.5	upper limits of
20–29	15	18	29.5	each class
30–39	43	61	39.5	interval)
40–49	69	130	49.5	
50–59	17	147	59.5	
60–69	24	171	69.5	
70–79	4	175	79.5	

$$N = \Sigma = 175$$

GRAPHICAL REPRESENTATION

To demonstrate to our readers the characteristics of this distribution more clearly, we could draw up a pictorial representation of the data. One of the advantages of doing this is that the mode will be immediately apparent, as will other features, such as the rate at which numbers fall off to either side and any specially interesting clusters of data. A graphical presentation can also be justified by its immediate appeal to the eye.

The histogram

A histogram of our distribution would look like Figure 13.4. The width of each column is the same and represents one class interval. Class intervals are represented by their midpoint at the centre of each column. Again, the measurement interval point gives rather odd numbers, but 24.5, for instance, is the exact mid-point of the 19.5 to 29.5 interval and we know exactly who should go in there. If class intervals are

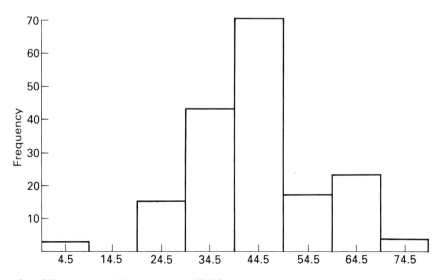

Figure 13.4 *Histogram of distribution in Table 13.6*

combined – it might have been desirable to start with 0–19.5 since there are so few in this bracket – the interval must be of appropriate width. Hence, 0–19.5 would be two columns wide. In a histogram, unlike a bar chart, all intervals are represented, even if empty, as for 9.5–19.5 above.

The height of each column represents the number of values found in that interval – the frequency of occurrence. Frequency is usually shown on the y- (vertical) axis and the scale or class intervals on the x-axis, although some statistical programmes (like Minitab™) present the categories on the vertical axis and the frequencies increasing from left to right, horizontally. Since columns are equal in width, it follows that the area of each column is proportional to the number of cases it represents throughout the histogram. It also follows that the total of all column areas represents the whole sample. If we call the whole area one unit (which is the convention), then a column which represents 10% of the sample will occupy 10% of the total area, that is 0.1 units. The column representing 59.5–69.5 utterances represents 24 of the 175 cases. Therefore its area will be 24/175 = 0.137 of the total area (or 13.7%).

FEATURES OF THE HISTOGRAM
- All categories represented
- Columns are equal width per equal category interval
- No intervals missed because empty
- Column areas proportional to frequency represented and these sum to the total area of one unit

The bar chart

The histogram displays a continuous variable. A bar chart displays a *discrete* variable. This is usually placed on the horizontal (x) axis.

- Because the variable has discrete values the columns of a bar chart should be separated, although several computer programmes (especially spreadsheets) don't show this.
- Not all the values of the discrete variable need be shown on the horizontal axis. We may only show, for instance, by way of contrast, the number of psychological articles published on AIDS in 1983 and 1993.
- The columns of a bar chart can represent frequencies or single statistics, such as the mean of a sample, or a percentage or other proportion.

The chart in Figure 13.5 shows the results of Duncan's (1976) experiment in which

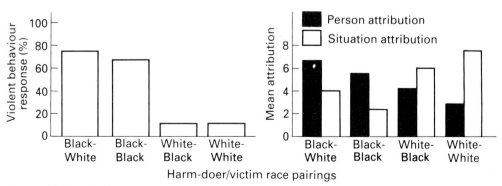

Figure 13.5 and Figure 13.6 *Description and attribution of intraracial and interracial behaviour (based on Duncan, 1976)*

White participants were asked to categorise the behaviour of a person who pushed another after a heated argument. The pusher could be Black or White, as could the person pushed, thus producing four experimental conditions. The height of each column represents the percentage of participants calling the behaviour 'violent' rather than alternatives such as 'playing around'.

COMBINED BAR CHARTS – A bar chart can display two values together. Duncan also asked participants to explain the pusher's behaviour as either caused by the person's enduring personality characteristics or more likely to have been induced by the particular situation – what is known as 'internal or external attribution'. The 'legend' or key to the combined bar chart in Figure 13.6 tells us, for each pusher/pushed condition, the mean attribution score to person or situation.

MISLEADING BAR CHARTS – It is very easy to mislead with unfairly displayed bar charts. Newspapers do it very frequently. Take a look at the charts in Figure 13.7 representing numbers of violent crimes in London for 1987 and 1988. The left-hand chart is correct. The right-hand one, by chopping off the scale from 0 to about 18 000, for convenience, makes the rise in one year look far steeper than it really is. It's the chart to present if you want to scare Londoners into paying more for their police force – but it's an unfair chart and shouldn't be used at all. The convention for avoiding this possible misrepresentation, when you need to economise on space in your diagram, is shown in the chart produced by David et al. (1986) – Figure 13.8. Notice that the vertical scale has been chopped between 0 and 15 but this is made obvious to the reader.

Frequency polygon

If we redraw our histogram (Figure 13.4) with only a dot at the centre of the top of each column we would get what is known as a FREQUENCY POLYGON when we joined up the dots, as in Figure 13.9.

This is particularly useful for showing the comparison between progress in two or more conditions of a study. For instance, where two groups of children receive different training-to-read programmes and progress is measured in error frequency over several months of continuous recording. Here, the columns are omitted, as shown in Figure 13.10.

If the horizontal scale ('months from start of programme') were not continuous then we would have a similar diagram known as a LINE CHART. The horizontal axis might carry the values of several trials in an experiment or testing of children at, say, two months, four months, six months etc. from the start of a programme.

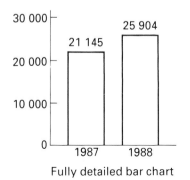

Fully detailed bar chart

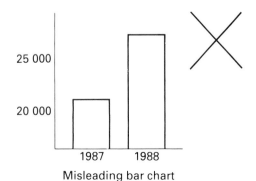

Misleading bar chart

Figure 13.7 *Correct and incorrect bar charts*

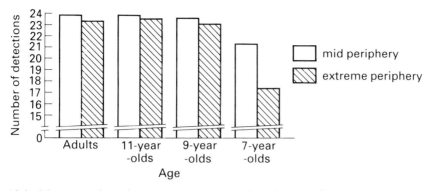

Figure 13.8 *Mean number of apparent movement detections made by the four age groups in mid and extreme periphery (from David et al., 1986)*

Ogive

This is obtained by plotting a cumulative frequency distribution as shown in Figure 13.11. The dots show the number of cases (61, vertical axis) which are below the scale point (39.5, horizontal axis). It is therefore possible to read off the number of cases above or below any scale point, by following this example. The shape of Figure 13.11 would be particularly 'S' shaped if the histogram for the distribution were 'normal' – a special curve which we shall spend some time on fairly soon.

EXPLORATORY DATA ANALYSIS

Within the last two decades the emphasis on good, informative display of data has increased, largely due to the work of Tukey (1977) whose book introduced the title of this section. Tukey argues that more than the traditional exploration of data should occur before submitting them to more sophisticated significance tests. He has introduced a number of techniques, too many and too complex for this book, but two of the most common will be demonstrated here. The main aim is to present data in visually meaningful ways *whilst retaining as much as possible of the original information.*

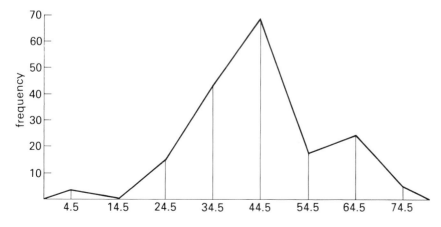

Figure 13.9 *Frequency polygon*

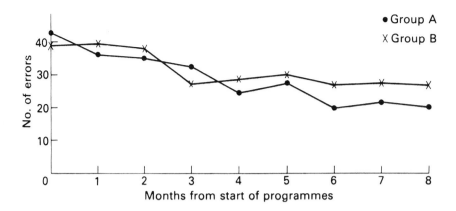

Figure 13.10 *Frequency polygon for two groups*

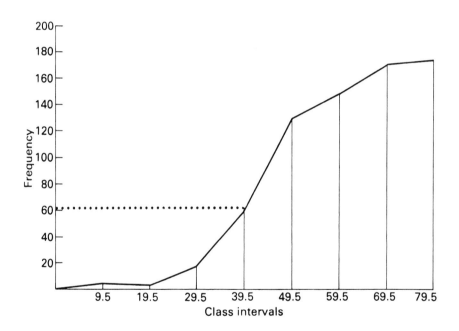

Figure 13.11 *Cumulative frequency – number of telegraphic utterances*

The stem and leaf display

One way to achieve this aim is with this highly cunning, horticultural sounding diagram. We may as well look at one straight away and then discuss it. Have a look at Figure 13.12.

Cum	Stem	Leaf	
I	0	5	
I	I		Data for the 30–39 stem:
4	2	129	
II	3	3445569	33 34 34 35 35 36 39
25	4	00122235667778	
47	5	0112223333444556677889	
65	6	000112456677777899	
72	7	1344578	
74	8	01	

Figure 13.12 *Stem and leaf display of exam results for 74 students*

- The *stem* is the tens digit of each score (but this could differ with different scales).
- The *leaves* are the units of each score. Hence, there was a 21, a 22 and a 29 in the set.
- The diagram takes up the shape of a sideways histogram with the same intervals.
- Note that we obtain this general histogram-like shape but retain each of the original individual scores which are lost in a traditional histogram.
- The column headed 'cum', which is not always included, gives the cumulative frequency of cases – there are 25 people with 49 or less.
- If there are too many data for each stem, *or* if the data are limited to only three stems, so the display would have only three lines, we can use * to represent the 0 to 4 leaves of each stem to 'flesh out' the chart into more detail. Figure 13.13 shows a stem and leaf diagram for our telegraphic utterances data in Table 13.6.

Cum	Stem	Leaf
2	0*	13
3	0	6
3	I*	
3	I	
II	2*	00123344
18	2	5567899
38	3*	0011112233333444444
61	3	55555555566777888999999
96	4*	00000000001111111111122222222233334444
130	4	555555556666666677777777888899999
137	5*	1223334
147	5	5556677789
161	6*	000111122233444
171	6	5566678899
174	7*	001
175	7	5

Figure 13.13 *Stem and leaf chart for telegraphic utterance data (Table 13.7)*

BOX PLOTS

These are based on *ordinal* measurements of the set of data. They give us a graphical display of what approximates to the interquartile range – the spread of the middle section of the data – whilst also giving us a view of the extremities. The following

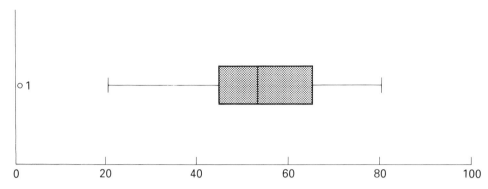

Figure 13.14 *Box-plot of data in Figure 13.12*

values have been calculated from the data in Figure 13.12 and produced the box plot shown in Figure 13.14:

Median position   = $(N+1)/2 = (75+1)/2 = \mathbf{37.5}$
Median   = Mean of 37th and 38th scores $= (54+54)/2 = \mathbf{54}$ (we needn't worry about complete accuracy of the true median with tied values since this is a chart, not calculation)
Hinge position   = (Median position $+ 1)/2 = (37+1)/2 = \mathbf{19}$ (we drop decimal values)
Lower hinge   = 19th lowest score $= \mathbf{45}$
Upper hinge   = 19th highest score $= \mathbf{66}$
Hinge spread   = upper hinge $-$ lower hinge $= 66 - 45 = \mathbf{21}$
Outer fences   = low: lower hinge $- 1.5 \times$ hinge spread $= 45 - (1.5 \times 21) = \mathbf{14}$
                       high: upper hinge $+ 1.5 \times$ hinge spread $= 66 + (1.5 \times 21) = \mathbf{97}$
Adjacent values: lower ($=$ first *inside* low outer fence, nearer to median) $= \mathbf{21}$
                       upper ($=$ first *inside* high outer fence, nearer to median) $= \mathbf{81}$

Explanatory notes

The box represents, roughly, the middle 50% of scores, shows the median, and is bounded by the two 'hinges'. The hinge spread is the *range* from lower to upper hinge. The 'fences' are $1\frac{1}{2}$ times the hinge spread away from the hinges. The 'adjacent values' are those scores furthest from the median yet still inside the fences. These are shown on the plot by the 'whiskers' at the ends of the thin lines coming away from the hinges. Finally, any extreme values are shown where they fall or, when showing them would make the plot awkwardly squashed because of a huge scale, they are simply given at the edges with their actual values. Extreme values are probably obvious from the raw data without inspection of a box plot. Here, perhaps the extremely low score of 5 represents someone who was sick at the start of the exam or who had 'spotted' the wrong questions in advance – a very dangerous practice!

THE NORMAL DISTRIBUTION

Earlier in this chapter, I pointed out that a measurement value, such as a person's height of, say, 163 cm, is really a statement that the value falls within a class interval. We are saying that the person, for instance, is closer to 163 cm than 162 or 164 cm, rather than that they measure 163 cm exactly. They are in the interval between 162.5

and 163.5 cm. In effect, if we measure to the nearest cm we are placing individuals in class intervals 1 cm wide. It happens that if we take a large enough random sample of individuals from a population and measure physical qualities such as height (or weight, or length of finger), especially if we use a fine scale of measurement (such as to the nearest millimetre), we get a distribution looking like Figure 13.15.

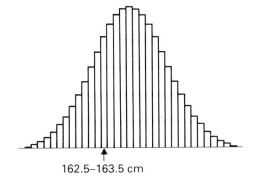

162.5–163.5 cm

Figure 13.15

The curve which typically results from such measurements *closely approximates* to a very well-known 'bell-shaped' mathematical curve, produced from a shockingly complicated formula (which you or I need not bother with) devised by Gauss. The curve is therefore known as 'Gaussian' but in statistical work we more commonly refer to it as a NORMAL DISTRIBUTION CURVE (Figure 13.16).

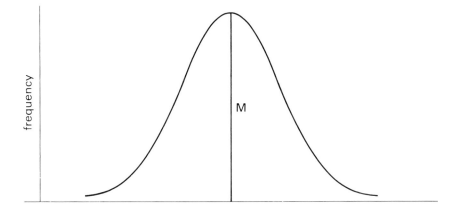

Figure 13.16 *A normal distribution curve*

Characteristics of a normal distribution curve

1 It is symmetrical about the mid-point of the horizontal axis
2 The point about which it is symmetrical (the line marked 'M' in Figure 13.16) is the point at which the mean, median and mode all fall.
3 The 'asymptotes' (tail ends) of the perfect curve never quite meet the horizontal axis. Although for distributions of real large samples there are existing real limits, we can always hypothesise a more extreme score.

4 It is known what area under the curve is contained between the central point (mean) and the point where one standard deviation falls. In fact, working in units of one standard deviation, we can calculate *any* area under the curve.

Approximations to the normal curve

It's very important to remember, in all that follows, that when psychological variables are said to be normally distributed, or standardised to fit a normal distribution, that we are *always* talking about approximations to a pure normal curve. This matters, because, when we come on to testing significance, for some tests, the statistical theory assumes a normal distribution and if there isn't really anything like a normal distribution in the population, for the variable measured, then the conclusions from the test may be seriously in error.

Normal curves and normal people

It's also important not to be morally outraged by the use of the term 'normal' or to baulk against calling people 'normal' or not. The curve is called 'normal' for purely *mathematical* reasons (you may remember the use of the term 'normal' as meaning 'perpendicular' in geometry).

AREA UNDER THE NORMAL DISTRIBUTION CURVE

Suppose we devise a reading test for eight-year-olds and the maximum score possible in the test is 80. The test is standardised to a normal distribution such that the mean score, for a large, representative sample of eight-year-olds, is 40 and the standard deviation is 10. I hope it is obvious, for starters, that 50% of eight-year-olds will therefore be above 40 and 50% below. The area for the top 50% is *all* the shaded area in Figure 13.17.

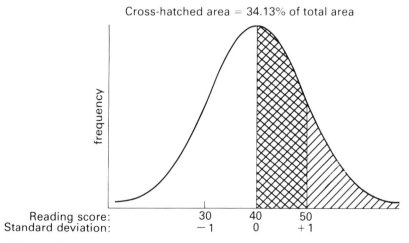

Figure 13.17 *Reading test distribution curve*

What we know, from the theory of the normal curve, is that one standard deviation, on any normal distribution curve, falls at the position shown by the line above 50 on Figure 13.17. This is the point where the downward curve inflects from an inward to an outward direction. We also know that the area trapped between the mean and this point is 0.3413 of the whole, shown cross-hatched. Hence we know that 34.13% of children score between 40 and 50 points on this test, since the standard deviation is 10 points. Figures worth noting are that:

34.13% of all values fall between $(\bar{x})$ and $+1$ (or -1) standard deviations (area = 0.3413)
47.72% of all values fall between $(\bar{x})$ and $+2$ (or -2) standard deviations (area = 0.4772)
49.87% of all values fall between $(\bar{x})$ and $+3$ (or -3) standard deviations (area = 0.4987)

The positions of these standard deviations are shown in Figure 13.18. Note the values above are doubled for areas between $-n$ and $+n$ standard deviations.

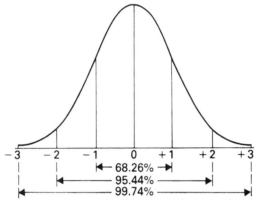

Area between $-n$ and $+n$ standard deviations on the normal curve.

Figure 13.18 *Positions of standard deviations*

Z-SCORES (or standard scores)

In the reading test example above, a child with a score of 50 lies one standard deviation above the mean. We could say that the number of standard deviations she is from the mean is $+1$ (the '$+$' signifying 'above'). Thus a child who is -1.5 standard deviations from the mean has a score of 25, because $1\frac{1}{2}$ standard deviations is 15 and this we subtract from the mean of 40. If we measure number of standard deviations from the mean in this way we are using Z-SCORES or STANDARD SCORES. The formula for calculating a z-score is:

$$z = \frac{x - \bar{x}}{s}$$

where s = standard deviation and $x - \bar{x}$, you'll notice, is the deviation score.

Dividing the deviation score by the standard deviation answers the question 'How many standard deviations is this deviation from the mean?' A z-score is the number of standard deviations a particular score is away from the mean. If the mean for shoe size in your class is 6, with a standard deviation of 1.5, then, if your shoe size is 9 your z-score is 2, or if your size is $4\frac{1}{2}$, your z-score is -1. You probably followed the example of the child with 25 points in your head but, in effect, you were using the formula shown. Let's check using the formula:

$$z = \frac{25 - 40}{10} = \frac{-15}{10} = -1.5$$

The formula is needed, of course, when scores aren't as convenient as the ones we've been using as examples.

z-scores cut off various known proportions of the area under the normal curve. Therefore we know the percentage of the population enclosed between the mean and any z-score. For instance, consulting Table 2 in Appendix 2 the area between the mean and the z-score of $+1.5$ is 0.4332 of the whole, shown by the right-hand shaded pattern in Figure 13.19:

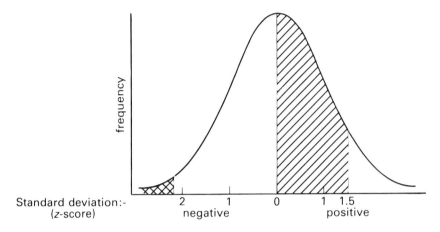

Figure 13.19 *Area between the mean and z-score of 1.5*

A z-score of -2.2 traps 0.486 of the area between it and the mean on the left-hand side. Since the *whole* of the left-hand side of the mean is 0.5 of the area, then only 0.014 $(0.5 - 0.486)$ is left at the left hand extreme after -2.2 standard deviations. This is shown by the cross-hatching in Figure 13.19, and by consulting the right-hand column of the table.

Standardisation of psychological measurements

This relationship between z-scores and area under the normal curve is of crucial importance in the world of testing. *If* (and it is a big 'if') a variable can be assumed to distribute normally among the population, *and* we have a test standardised on large samples, then we can quickly assess the relative position of people by using their raw score (the initial score on a test) converted to a z-score. This is valuable when assessing, for instance, children's reading ability, general intellectual or language development, adult stress, anxiety, aptitude for certain occupations (at interview) and so on. However, always recall that the 'if' is big and much work must go into the justification of treating a test result as normally distributed.

Psychologists have often argued that variables like intelligence, extroversion and the like are normally distributed. However, unlike the case of height, this is *not* based on research which simply *uncovers* this as a fact. In creating and standardising intelligence tests the assumption is made *before starting out*, that intelligence will be normally distributed. It is seen as a human quality produced by myriad random factors including, for some, genetic forces. Height is like this and is consequently normally distributed. Hence, the argument goes, why shouldn't intelligence be similar? It must always be recognised, then, that psychologists have not *discovered* that intelligence has a normal distribution in the population. The tests were created to *fit* a normal distribution, basically for research purposes and practical convenience. Usually, an IQ test is standardised (raw scores are adjusted) to produce a mean of 100 and a standard deviation of 15 points.

SKEWED DISTRIBUTIONS

Some distributions obtained from psychological measures which might be expected to be normal, in fact turn out SKEWED. That is, they are 'lop-sided', having their peak (mode) to one side and a distinctive tail on the side where more than half the values occur. Have a look at Figure 13.20.

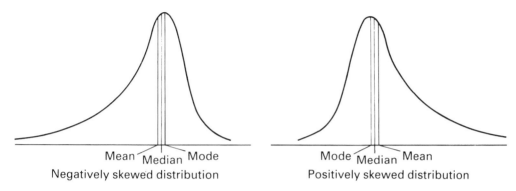

Mean ⌐Median⌐ Mode   Mode ⌐Median⌐ Mean
Negatively skewed distribution   Positively skewed distribution

Figure 13.20 *Positive and negative skews*

> Suppose we were measuring reaction time to respond to words displayed one at a time on a computer screen. You have to decide as quickly as possible whether the word is real or non-English. The reaction time, on the majority of trials, is around 0.7 seconds. Over many trials, which sort of skewed curve might be produced?

It is possible to be very much slower than the majority of scores, but is it possible to be very much faster, when the majority of scores are around 0.7 seconds? This is like the situation in athletics where times can be quite a bit slower than the current good standard but not a lot faster. We would get a positively skewed distribution then. Notice that a positive skew has its tail up the positive end (higher values) of the horizontal axis.

> How would you construct a test which produced a negative skew – make it very easy or very hard to answer?

A negatively skewed distribution can be produced where a test is relatively easy. It produces what are known as 'ceiling effects'. People can't score much *higher* than the mean if the mean is, say, about 17 out of 20, but a substantial number of people can score a lot *lower* than the mean. The opposite phenomenon is known as a 'floor effect'.

Central tendency of skewed distributions

Notice where the mean, median and mode fall on each distribution. The mode obviously still falls at the top, where the majority of scores are. In each case the mean is furthest from the mode – not surprising really, since we said that it was the most affected by extreme scores in one direction.

BI-MODAL DISTRIBUTIONS

Some distributions are known as BI-MODAL and, like some camels, have two distinct humps. We noted in the section on standardisation in Chapter 9 that some measures of psychological variables may well produce such a distribution. Attitude measurement on a controversial issue (like privatisation of health services) where not many people are neutral might produce bi-modal distributions. So might a measure of job satisfaction in a company where there are a large number of well-paid white collar workers along with a similar number of poorly paid manual workers.

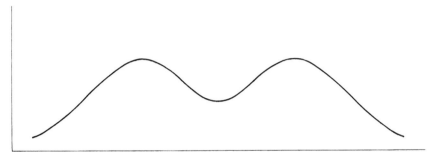

Figure 13.21 *A bi-modal distribution*

GLOSSARY

Value of a number, ignoring its sign; a number treated as positive even if it is originally negative	_____ _____	absolute value
Common language term for central tendency	_____	average
Chart in which one axis (usually the horizontal) represents a categorical or at least discrete variable	__ _____	bar chart
Chart showing central spread of data and position of relative extremes; type of exploratory data analysis	__ ____	box plot
Formal term for any measure of the typical or middle value in a group	_____ _____	central tendency
Categories into which a continuous data scale is divided in order to summarise frequencies	_____ _____	class interval
Interval of 10% on a continuous scale	_____	decile
Amount by which a particular score is different from the mean of its set	_____ ____/_____	deviation value/score

Technical term for any measure of the variation or spread of a sample of data or a population	_____	dispersion
		distributions
Distribution with two prominent frequency peaks	__-_____	bi-modal
Distribution showing total numbers above or below each class interval	_____ _____	cumulative frequency
Distribution showing how often certain values occurred	_____	frequency
Distribution which is not symmetrical about the vertical centre and which contains a lot more lower than higher values, relative to the mode	_____ _____	negative skew
Continuous distribution, bell-shaped, symmetrical about its mid-point and the result of a variable affected by many random influences	_____	normal
Distribution which is not symmetrical about the vertical centre and which contains a lot more higher than lower values, relative to the mode	_____ _____	positive skew
Close examination of data by a variety of means, including visual display, before submitting them to significance testing – recommended by Tukey	_____ _____ _____	exploratory data analysis
Chart showing only the peaks of class intervals	_____ _____	frequency polygon
Chart containing whole of continuous data set divided into proportional intervals	_____	histogram
Measure of central tendency – sum of scores divided by number of scores	____	mean
Measure of dispersion – mean of all absolute deviations	____ _____	mean deviation
Measure of central tendency – mid-point of data set	_____	median
Place where median is to be found in the ordered data set	_____ _____/_____	median position/location
Measure of central tendency – most frequent value	____/_____ _____	mode/modal value
Chart showing cumulative frequencies	_____	ogive
Statistical measure of population	_____	parameter (of population)

Point on continuous distribution which cuts off certain percentage of cases	_____	percentile
Point on continuous distribution which cuts off one of the quarters (i.e. one block of 25%)	_____	quartile
Measure of dispersion – top minus bottom plus one	_____	range
Untreated value obtained directly from measuring process used in study	___ ____/_____	raw data/score
Difference between a sample mean and the true population mean, assumed to be random in origin	_____ _____	sampling error
Statistical measure of a sample	_____ _____	sample statistic
Half distance between first and third quartile in a continuous distribution	_____-_____ _____	semi-interquartile range
Measure of dispersion – the square root of the sum of all squared deviations divided by N (or $N-1$)	_____ _____	standard deviation
Same as z-score	_____ _____	standard score
Measure of dispersion – square of standard deviation	_____	variance
Measure of individual deviation – number of standard deviations a particular score is from its sample mean	_-_____	z-score

EXERCISES

1 Find the mean and median of the two sets of talking times in Table 13.1.

2 Consider the following set of times, measured in 1/100ths of a second:

62 65 71 72 73 75 76 77 79 80 82 83 92 100 106 117 127

65 70 72 72 74 75 76 77 79 80 82 88 93 102 110 121 128

65 70 72 73 74 76 76 78 80 81 83 90 95 103 112 122 135

a) Sketch a distribution for the data and decide which would be the most appropriate measure of central tendency for it. Calculate this measure and also a measure of dispersion.

b) Design a stem-and-leaf chart for this data.

3 Draw a histogram for the data in Table 13.5. Calculate the mean for this data.

4 Sketch two roughly normal distributions which have the same mean but quite different standard deviations. Also sketch two normal distributions with the same standard deviation but different means.

5 You are told that a set of data includes one score which is 0.8. The standard deviation for the set is 0. Can you give the mean of the set and say anything else about the six other scores in the set?

An introduction to significance testing

PROBABILITY AND SIGNIFICANCE

- Probability of events occurring is measured on a scale of 0 (not possible) to 1 (must happen). **Logical probability** is calculated from first principles as the ratio of the number of ways our predicted outcome can happen divided by the number of possible outcomes. **Empirical probability** uses the same ratio but puts the number of relevants which *have* happened on top of the equation, and the total number of relevant events on the bottom.

- Differences (or correlations) need to be submitted to a **test of significance** in order for a decision to be made concerning whether the differences are to be counted as showing a genuine effect or dismissed as likely to represent just chance fluctuation.

- Social scientists reject the null hypothesis, that differences occur at a chance level only, when the probability of this being true drops below 0.05. This is often called the '**5% significance level**'. If the null hypothesis is true but has been rejected because $p < 0.05$ it is said that a **type I error** has been made. A **type II error** occurs when the null hypothesis is retained, because $p > 0.05$, yet there is a real underlying effect.

- When the hypothesis tested is controversial, either theoretically or ethically, it is usual to seek significance with $p < 0.01$ or still better. A result with $p < 0.1$ might warrant further investigation, tightening of procedures, altering of design and so on.

- If the hypothesis investigated was directional then a **one-tailed test** of probability is used. Otherwise the test is **two-tailed**. Results tested with a one-tailed test are more likely to reach significance but if the direction is opposite to that predicted, even if the difference is past the significant critical value, the null hypothesis must be retained.

- A **probability distribution** is a histogram with columns measuring the likelihood of occurrence of the event they represent. The normal distribution is a probability distribution and probabilities can be read off using z-scores to measure the deviation of a score from the mean.

PROBABILITY

Before you get fed up, in this chapter, with the idea of tossing coins or picking cards, please keep in mind that the chapter has a sole purpose – to demonstrate the means by which researchers decide that a difference or association between variables is unlikely to have been the result of mere chance coincidence. We want to know how to evaluate claims that group A did 'better than' group B. When should we agree to take this difference seriously – and when should we dismiss it as just meaningless chance variation? Remember, there will *always* be differences when measuring people even on the same (psychological) thing twice. The question is, when are differences significant?

Let's set out with a practical problem to solve:

> Suppose a friend said she could reliably forecast the sex of unborn babies by swinging a stone pendulum above the mother's womb. Let's assume she guesses your baby's sex correctly. Would you be impressed? Your personal involvement might well cause you to react with 'amazing!' or at least, 'well it is interesting; there *might* be something in it.' Stepping back coolly from the situation you realise she had a 50–50 chance of being correct. Nevertheless most people would begin to think she had something going if she managed to go on to predict correctly the sex of two or three more friends' babies. Suppose she has ten babies' sexes to guess. How many would you expect her to predict correctly in order for you to be impressed that she's not just guessing and being lucky? For instance, would 7 out of 10 convince you? Or would you want more or would less do?

When teaching research methods and statistics in psychology, I always tell my students that they already have many of the important concepts framed in their heads, perhaps somewhat vaguely, developed through years of worldly experience. My job is to illuminate, clarify and name these concepts. This is particularly true of the concept of probability and yet it is the area which causes a relatively higher degree of anxiety and confusion. Most people do have a very good sense of how probable various events are and yet many people are also loathe to get involved in giving such probabilities a numerical value, either because it seems complicated or because one then seems committed to mysterious 'laws of chance'. A recent conversation with my friend's 11-year-old son, whilst giving him and his family a lift to the airport, is a good example:

> 'But planes do crash.' 'Yes, but you only hear about the accidents. Thousands of flights run safely and the odds of you crashing are hundreds of thousands to one.' 'I know but it still *could* be our plane.'

. . . and so on, as if this were an argument when, really, we were both saying the same thing but with different emphasis and personal involvement (I was staying behind to finish this second edition – in the first edition this was a *fictitious* conversation!). Here is someone who *seems* to agree with what I'm saying about probability:

> Probability is an obvious and simple subject. It is a baffling and complex subject. It is a subject we know a great deal about, and a subject we know nothing about. Kindergarteners can study probability, and philosophers do. It is dull; it is interesting. Such contradictions are the stuff of probability. (Kerlinger, 1973)

It is often said that there are three types of probability:

- logical probability
- empirical probability
- subjective probability

The first two we shall be tackling in a little while. Subjective probability refers to the *feeling* of likelihood one gets about certain events, no matter what the statisticians or mathematicians tell you. My 11-year-old friend's qualms above are an example. It's hard to be convinced that a plane, *when you're in it*, is many times safer than travel by road. Gamblers may ruin their lives betting on what they *think* will happen. Take a look at Box 14.1 for a light-hearted account of the testing of subjective probability.

Probability works out in peculiar ways. What do you think are the chances of four tossed coins all coming up tails? How many people do you think would have to be in one room before there is a 50–50 chance that two people among them have the same birthday? The answer to the first question is 1 in 16 yet many people respond initially with 1 in 4. The answer to the second is that, surprisingly, just 23 people will do.

Box 14.1 *Sod's law*

Do you ever get the feeling that fate has it in for you? At the supermarket, for instance, do you always pick the wrong queue, the one looking shorter but which contains someone with five unpriced items and several redemption coupons? Do you take the outside lane only to find there's a hidden right-turner? Sod's law (known as Murphy's law in the USA), in its simplest form states that whatever can go wrong, will. Have you ever returned an item to a shop, or taken a car to the garage with a problem, only to find it working perfectly for the assistant? This is Sod's law working in reverse but still against you. A colleague of mine holds the extension of Sod's law that things will go wrong even if they can't.

An amusing *QED* TV programme tested this perspective of subjective probability. The particular hypothesis, following from the law, was that celebrated kitchen occurrence where toast always falls butter side down – doesn't it? First attempts engaged a University Physics professor in developing machines for tossing the toast without bias. These included modified toasters and an electric typewriter. Results from this were not encouraging. The null hypothesis doggedly retained itself, buttered sides not making significantly more contact with the floor. It was decided that the human element was missing. Sod's law might only work for human toast droppers.

The attempt at greater ecological validity was made using students and a stately home. Benches and tables were laid out in the grounds and dozens of students asked to butter one side of bread then throw it in a specially trained fashion to avoid toss bias. In a cunning variation of the experiment a new independent variable was introduced. Students were asked to pull out their slice of bread and, just before they were about to butter a side, to change their decision and butter the other side instead. This should produce a bias away from butter on grass if sides to fall on the floor are decided by fate early on in the buttering process. Sadly neither this nor the first experiment produced verification of Sod's law. I don't recall the exact figures but results were out of 300 tosses each time and were around 154 butter side, 146 plain, and 148–152. Now the scientists had one of those flashes of creative insight. A corollary of Sod's law is that when things go wrong (as they surely will – general rule) they will go wrong in the worst possible manner. The researchers now placed expensive carpet over the large lawns. Surely this would tempt fate into a reaction? Do things fall butter side down more often on the living room carpet? (*I'm* sure they do!)

I'm afraid this was the extent of the research. Results were yet again around the

148–152 mark. (Incidentally what test would be done on these frequencies? see page 265–6.) Murphy, it turned out, was a United States services officer testing for space flight by sending service men on a horizontally jet propelled chair across a mid-Western desert to produce many Gs of gravitational pressure. I'm still not convinced about his law. The psychologists suggest the explanation might lie in selective memory – we tend to remember the annoying incidents and ignore all the unnotable dry sides down or whizzes through the supermarket tills. But I still see looks on customer's faces as they wait patiently – they seem to *know* something about my queue . . .

GIVING PROBABILITY A VALUE

Have a look at the statements below. For most of them, you'll find you have some idea of how likely or not it is that these events will occur. Try to give a value between zero (not at all likely) and 100 (highly likely) to each statement, depending on how likely you think it is to occur:

1 It will rain on Wednesday of next week

2 You will eat breakfast on the first day of next month

3 Your psychology tutor will sneeze in the next lesson

4 You will be given a million pounds next year

5 The sun will rise tomorrow morning

6 You will think about elephants later today

7 Someone will bump into you later today

8 A coin tossed fairly will come down showing tails

9 Two coins tossed fairly will both come down tails

For number one, if you live in the UK, whatever the time of year, you may have answered with 50, whereas if you live in Bombay, and the month is October, you'd say about 3. Numbers two and seven depend on your habits and the time of day it is. I would be interested in what happens with number 6, now I've said it!

Now divide all the values you gave by 100. So, if you answered 20 to number seven, for instance, then divide 20 by 100 and you get 0.2.

Probability is always officially measured on a scale of:

$$0 \longleftarrow \text{to} \longrightarrow 1$$

NOT possible   MUST happen

. . . usually in decimal values, like 0.3, 0.5 and so on. I shall try to explain now why this makes sense.

LOGICAL PROBABILITY

Your answer to number eight in the exercise above should have been exactly 50 which converts to 0.5. If you answered 25 (converts to 0.25) to number nine, you can already calculate probability (probably!).

Statements eight and nine are quite different from the rest. We can calculate the probability involved from *logical* principles. The reasoning for statement eight runs as follows:

There are two possible outcomes – a head or a tail. (We discount occasions when it falls on its edge!)

One of these is the outcome we want.

There is therefore one chance in two that tails will come up.

The formula for logical probability is:

$$p = \frac{\text{number of ways desired outcome can occur}}{\text{total number of outcomes possible}}$$

where *p* stands for 'probability' when all events are equally likely.

When we toss one coin then, using the above formula and what we just said about outcomes:

$$p = \frac{1}{2}$$

(or 0.5) for the probability of getting a tail (or a head). Notice that the probability of getting a tail (0.5) *added* to the probability of getting a head (0.5) = 1. This makes sense because we know the probability of what *must* happen is 1 and either a tail *or* a head must happen. This leads to one of two probability rules:

Probability rule 1:   the probability of event A *or* event B happening is
(the 'or' rule)   p(A) + p(B) where p(event) is the probability of an
                           event occurring

We may as well introduce rule 2 now as well. Suppose you tossed two coins. What are the chances of getting two tails from two independent tosses (question **9**, above)? Well, one way to answer this is to use rule 2:

Probability rule 2:   the probability of event A *and* event B happening is
(the 'and' rule)   p(A) × p(B)

According to *this* rule our answer is 0.5 × 0.5 = 0.25 (or $\frac{1}{4}$). Let's do this the long way, using our fundamental formula for probability above, and check that we agree with the multiplication result. How many possible events are there? Well, these are listed in Table 14.1

Table 14.1 *The possible events that could have occurred in tossing two coins*

1st toss	2nd toss
H	H
H	T
T	H
T	T

H = head   T = tail

There were four possible outcomes and we were interested in just one of these. The values for the probability equation then, are 1 on top and 4 underneath, giving $\frac{1}{4}$ (0.25).

> If there were 20 students in your class and the tutor was about to pick one of you to talk about this week's reading, how likely is she to pick you (assuming her choice is random)? How likely is it that she will pick someone else?

The tutor has 20 possible choices and you're just one of them. Your chances of being picked are therefore $\frac{1}{20}$, which is 0.05, fairly close to zero. The chances of someone else having to talk are $\frac{19}{20}$ since there are 19 ways she can make this happen. This comes out at 0.95 (note that the two probabilities added together make 1 – she's going to pick *someone*!).

Although fractions like $\frac{1}{4}$ and $\frac{1}{20}$ can be read as 'one in four' (chances), most probability figures will not be so simple. In fact, for interpreting statistics in psychology, you will need to be fairly agile in converting between decimal values (like 0.05) and *percentage values* (like 5%, the equivalent, on a scale of 0–100, of 0.05 on the scale of 0 to 1). This is what you were doing in the exercise just above. For those who really get muddled commuting between one and the other, Box 14.2 should help you.

Box 14.2 *% decimal conversion*

From percentage to decimal
5% to $p = 0.05$

1 Remove the '%' sign ($= 5$)
2 Put decimal point after the whole number ($= 5.$)*
3 Move the decimal point *two* places to the left, inserting zeros as you go where necessary (i.e. first move 0.5, second move 0.05)

*If there already *is* a decimal point, leave it where it is, and go straight to step **3**, e.g.
2.5% → 2.5 → 0.25 → 0.025

From decimal to percentage
$p = 0.05$ to 5%

1 Move the decimal point *two* places to the right (005.)
2 Lose any zeros to the left of the first left hand whole digit ($= 5.$)
3 Lose the decimal point if there is nothing to the right of it ($= 5$)
4 Add the '%' sign ($= 5\%$)

e.g. for 0.025:
0.025 → 00.25 → 002.5 → 2.5 → 2.5%

EMPIRICAL PROBABILITY

In the case of tossing coins it is relatively simple to work out what should happen according to the 'laws' of probability. With real life events, such as the chance of an earthquake, a plane crash or of England beating Australia in cricket, we can't make such calculations. There are just too many variables to account for. Instead, in these circumstances, statisticians rely on 'actuarial' data – that is, data which are already available. The process is backward rather than forward looking. We say, to estimate the probability of X happening, 'how many X-type events have happened so far out of the total number of relevant events?' For instance, the probability of your tutor sneezing next lesson might be estimated at:

number of lessons in which tutor has sneezed so far

total number of tutor's lessons so far

We can use empirical probability to back up our 'analytic' calculation of the likelihood of obtaining two tails from two tosses of a coin. I asked my computer to 'toss two coins' 1000 times. It took about four seconds and came up with 238 cases of two tails. 238/1000 = 0.24 – not a bad estimate of our logical figure of 0.25. In fact, the *distribution* the computer came up with is shown in Figure 14.1.

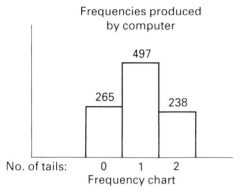 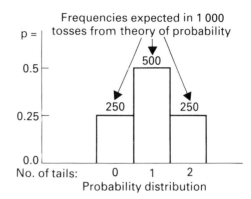

Figure 14.1 *Tossing two coins 1 000 times*

PROBABILITY DISTRIBUTIONS

On the right-hand side of Figure 14.1 is shown the PROBABILITY DISTRIBUTION expected for throwing two coins. Notice that, although I've put expected frequencies out of 1 000 on the columns, the chart is really one of probabilities for each event. It doesn't show what *has* happened – it shows the expected proportion of things which *should* happen using the 'laws' of probability. These can be turned into expected frequencies when you know how many events are going to occur together, in this case 1 000. If the probability of obtaining two tails is 0.25 then we'd expect 0.25 × 1 000 cases of two tails. We expect 250; we got 238.

The second column on the right of Figure 14.1 shows that the probability of getting a head and a tail is 0.5. If you look at Table 14.1 you'll see that there are two ways of getting a head and a tail. You can get a head followed by a tail or a tail followed by a head. The top of the probability equation is therefore 2 and the bottom is 4 as before. For every time we get two tails we'd expect twice as many results containing one head and one tail. Finally, of course, we'd expect as many times two heads as we get two tails.

COMBINATIONS

What we've just started talking about is the topic of *combinations of events.* We said that for the tossing of two coins there are four possible combinations as outcomes and we stated what these were. If you now think back to our sex-guessing friend, it would help if we knew how many *possible* outcomes from 10 guesses there are (*bottom* of the probability equation) and then work out how many ways there are to get seven right, eight right and so on (the *top* of the equation). We can work towards this goal by considering *three* coins. Don't forget, if she's guessing, then her choices of boy or girl are equally likely and this is exactly the same as tossing a coin. We are only working out the probability of events with two equally likely outcomes.

For three events you might like to look at Figure 14.2. Imagine a ball bearing is placed at the top of the diagram at the 'choice' point. It 'chooses' to go left or right

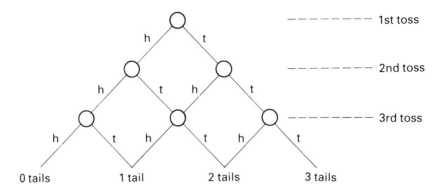

Figure 14.2 *Possible outcomes of tossing three coins*

purely at random. Having done this it meets another random choice point and goes left or right again at random, and so on. What we're interested in is what proportion of ball bearings would 'choose' to end up at the far right. In terms of coins, if we tossed three, very many times, how many outcomes would be three tails? Rather than turn to my smoking computer again, let's work it out formally from first principles. How many possible combinations are there? How many ways can three coins fall? If you trace down Figure 14.2 you'll see that there are three ways (routes) to get two tails or one tail but only one way to get 0 tails or three tails. These outcomes are listed in Table 14.2. The probability of getting three tails is one event in eight $= \frac{1}{8} = 0.125$. To get two tails and a head is three times more likely – three events out of eight – $\frac{3}{8}$ or 0.375, and so on. We now know that if our friend guessed three babies' sex correctly in succession the probability of this happening by chance would be 0.125.

Table 14.2 *Outcomes from tossing three coins*

		$p =$
TTT	one way to get three tails	0.125
TTH THT HTT	three ways to get two tails + one head	0.375
THH HTH HHT	three ways to get two heads + one tail	0.375
HHH	one way to get three heads	0.125
Total possible outcomes = 8		

Figure 14.3 shows the probability distribution for three and four coins. How did I get the values for four coins? Fortunately, we don't have to keep going back to first principles, or an increasingly larger Figure 14.2, to count out the possible combinations. Take a look at Pascal's triangle in Figure 14.4. If you look at the second and third lines down you'll see the frequencies for two and three coins which we expected from probability theory. Each number in the triangle is obtained by adding together the two numbers above it, so, theoretically, we could go on generating this figure ad infinitum, but the numbers would soon get rather large. For the fourth line, the

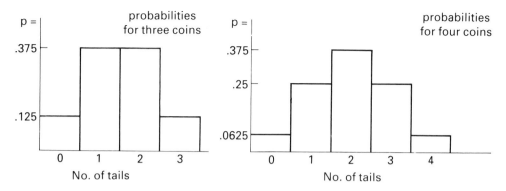

Figure 14.3 *Probability distributions for tossing three and four coins*

frequencies are 1 4 6 4 1 – one way to get all four tails, four ways to get three tails and one head, and so on, with 16 possible combinations altogether. The probability of getting four tails can be immediately calculated as $\frac{1}{16} = 0.0625$. For three tails and one head (in any order) the probability is $\frac{4}{16}$ (or 0.25) and so on. Note that the probabilities for all the columns will still add to 1.

```
                                                              [Total]
                          1                                      1
                       1     1                                   2
                     1    2    1                                 4
                   1    3    3    1                              8
                 1    4    6    4    1                          16
               1    5   10   10    5    1                       32
             1    6   15   20   15    6    1                    64
           1    7   21   35   35   21    7    1                128
         1    8   28   56   70   56   28    8    1             256
       1    9   36   84  126  126   84   36    9    1          512
     1   10   45  120  210  252  210  120   45   10    1      1024
```

Figure 14.4 *Pascal's triangle*

We know now that if, say, our friend guessed correctly the sex of three babies out of four, the probability of this occurring by chance was 0.25. Note that the probability of her guessing three out of four *or better* (i.e. three *or* four correct out of four) is 0.25 *plus* 0.0625 (= 0.3125). We can now make a quick leap to calculating the probability that our baby sex-guessing friend might guess all 10 babies correctly. Line 10 of Pascal's triangle shows us that there are 1 024 combinations possible, of which, only one covers getting all 10 guesses correct (like throwing 10 tails), so the probability is $\frac{1}{1024}$ or 0.001. However many coins we toss there is always only one way to get all of them falling one way. *Every* coin must fall that way and we follow the outside edge of the diagram in Figure 14.2. You'll see that Pascal's triangle starts and ends with a 1 for all lines.

We can also see that the probability of our friend guessing just nine sexes correctly is $\frac{10}{1024}$ (0.01) and eight correct would be $\frac{45}{1024}$ (0.044). This is all very well. I think most of us would accept that if the chance of our friend guessing all 10 babies correctly is less than one in a thousand we would reject the idea that she's just guessing. In formal terms this, as we said in Chapter 1, would be a case of 'rejecting the null hypothesis' that her results vary only at the level of chance. We would accept that *something* was going on, though of course we could remain cynical about the stone pendulum. Perhaps she uses body shape or has access to the hospital's scanner records!

SIGNIFICANCE IS THE PROBLEM NOW

There is always some cynical person in a class who doesn't even accept that $\frac{1}{1000}$ (p = 0.001) is good enough to rule out chance. Like my 11-year-old friend, they say 'ah but it *could* happen by chance still', with which I am forced to agree. To this I add, 'Yes, but we have to think *forwards*. If I *predict* that X will happen, as a result of a theory, and it does, with less than $\frac{1}{1000}$ probability of it happening by chance, in everyday life we usually accept that I have some sort of control or understanding. For instance, imagine I ask a member of the audience to select a number between 1 and 1 000. I then ask *you* to pick a number from 1 000 raffle tickets, already checked and shuffled in a bag. If I "get" you to pick the same number you'd think I was a pretty good conjuror, *not* just lucky!' We can rely on extremes of probability so much that, at a recent village fete, a local garage safely offered a free new car if anyone threw seven 6s with seven dice.

SIGNIFICANCE

We are often faced with informal significance decisions in everyday life. Suppose you received 62% for your last essay and 60% for the one you've just had marked. Are you doing worse or is this just forgettable fluctuation in your tutor's grading? If you got 45% next time, you'd know there was a difference which mattered. The current difference, however, is unlikely to bother you. So, we are often certain that a difference indicates a real change and often certain that it doesn't. That's the easy part. When do we change from one decision to the other? How far below 62% indicates a real drop in your standard? What we are looking for now is a system for making a decision of STATISTICAL SIGNIFICANCE.

A common television advertisement shows the promoted washing-up liquid dealing with far more tables of crockery than an unnamed competitor. The viewer isn't given the chance, though, to discover whether the difference is statistically significant. Similarly, we often see just one person successfully choosing the promoted margarine rather than its anonymous rival. How many people would you want to see making this rather fortunate choice before you were convinced that the result you see is not a fluke? For situations like these we need a formal test.

There will always be some difference between the results of two conditions in an experiment or investigation. It is not enough to show that a difference occurred in the direction we wanted or predicted, which is all the television advertisements do. We have to show that the difference is *significant*. Have a look at the results of the two memory experiments in Table 14.3.

THE 'EYEBALL TEST'

An EYEBALL TEST is an inspection of results prior to formal testing. Without yet knowing the formal rules of significance decisions we can come to some pretty safe conclusions about the results in Table 14.3. On the right, we can see that the difference between means is quite unimpressive. Note, for issues later in this book, that you intuitively take into account the *variation* between individual scores in each sample in order to decide that 12.75–12.5 is obviously an unimpressive difference. On the left, it seems equally obvious that something has happened. Surely these differences could not be caused by chance fluctuation alone?

One can never rely *only* on an eyeball test. A formal statistical test must always be applied to the main data. It is useful, though, where several differences have been hypothesised, and some of these can be ruled out as unworthy of testing because obviously insignificant.

What we are seeking now, however, is a formal cut-off level. How unlikely does a difference have to be before we can call it a 'significant' one?

Table 14.3 *Memory experiment results*

No. of words recalled out of 20:		No. of words recalled out of 20:		
Pt	Common words	Uncommon words	Pt	6-letter words	7-letter words
1	15	10	1	14	13
2	14	7	2	13	14
3	10	6	3	10	12
4	18	11	4	15	13
5	16	4	5	9	7
6	12	7	6	11	15
7	9	2	7	12	13
8	16	9	8	16	15
	Mean = 13.75	Mean = 7		Mean = 12.5	Mean = 12.75
	Difference between means = 6.75			Difference between means = 0.25	

At the start of the chapter I asked you to think about how many successful sex choices, out of 10, would convince you that our baby-sexing friend was not just guessing. Some of you will have said 10, some nine some lower. If you said five, you're accepting what she would get most often if she *were* just guessing. So the number we should settle on to convince us that her result is *significant* lies somewhere between six and 10, unless you're really a cynic. The issue of where to draw the decision line, between luck or real effect, is known as SIGNIFICANCE TESTING.

SIGNIFICANCE LEVELS

Social scientists have several levels at which they reject null hypotheses. They calculate the probability that differences in their results could have occurred by chance alone. If this probability is less than the set level they reject the null hypothesis that the results did occur by chance alone and they claim support for the research hypothesis. They say that the results are *significant* and the significance level is a measure of how confident they are that the results are not a fluke.

There is, however, one level of probability which is a standard. If the probability of a difference occurring were higher than this value then, by convention, no researcher would claim significance for the result. Now what is this level? Should probability for a difference always be below 0.001 ($\frac{1}{1000}$), 0.01, 0.05 or what?

Let's see if you already have a sense of where this limit might lie. Suppose I hand you a pack of cards. There are only two possibilities: *either* all the red cards are on top *or* the pack is randomly shuffled. The second alternative is equivalent to the null hypothesis. Your job is to decide which of these two alternatives is the truth by turning over one card at a time from the top. There is a catch. You start with £1000. Every time you turn over a card this amount halves. If you take a guess after turning over two cards, then, you stand to win £250. After turning over how many red cards would you decide, fairly confidently, that the reds are all on top? If you wait till 17 reds are turned over, you'll win just 1p! Even after ten reds you'll only get £1. Make your choice now.

The probability of drawing a red card off the top of a full, shuffled pack is 0.5 (there are two possible colours, equally represented, and we want one of these). Doing this four times in succession, replacing each time, gives 0.5^4 $(0.5 \times 0.5 \times 0.5 \times 0.5)$ $= 0.063$ $((\frac{1}{2})^4 = \frac{1}{16})$. Actually, to be absolutely accurate, we should calculate without replacement, since that's how the problem was set above. This would be

$$\frac{26}{52} \times \frac{25}{51} \times \frac{24}{50} \times \frac{23}{49} = 0.055$$

since there are 26 reds to start with but one less each time a red is drawn. A large number of people say that by four reds they feel pretty confident that the pack is fixed, not shuffled (and even more agree by five). In other words, they reject the (null) hypothesis that this run could have occurred by chance.

The 5% significance level

Social scientists call a difference significant, and reject the null hypothesis of no difference, when the probability of the null hypothesis being true drops below 0.05. This is popularly known as the 5% SIGNIFICANCE LEVEL. You can see from the little exercise above that, if we replaced the cards each time, a run of five reds would be significant but a run of four would not. If we just drew the cards and didn't replace, however, a run of four reds would very nearly count as significant. In other words, when you're dealing from a full, shuffled deck of cards, you'll get four consecutive reds just about 1 time in 20. Would you like to try it? This would make a nice little programming exercise if you're doing computer studies. Otherwise, please just trust the theory! The point is that many people make a decision intuitively at around the 5% level that a sequence of events wasn't a fluke.

SIGNIFICANCE DECISIONS

We have come to an absolutely fundamental principle underpinning all social science research – the notion of rejecting the null hypothesis at a certain level of significance. Official theory says that, before we conduct a study, we state what level we will take as a criterion for rejecting our null hypothesis. In practice, the level of $p \leq 0.05$ is the golden standard, the general yardstick by which differences or relationships are counted as significant or not. To summarise:

- If a result is significant ($p \leq 0.05$) the null hypothesis is rejected
- If a result is not significant ($p > 0.05$) the null hypothesis is retained

By 'result is significant' I mean the rather long winded statement 'If the difference (or relationship) is unlikely to have occurred by chance at the level set'.

It is usually said that, if your results reach this level, you qualify for publication. However, as I said in Chapter 1, there are times when support for a null hypothesis is what our theory predicts – the finding of *no* difference can be very important. But in that case, the level used to make the decision would still be $p \leqslant 0.05$, except under special circumstances.

But couldn't it still be a fluke?

About one time in 20 you *will* deal four red cards off the top of a shuffled pack. I can hear students going home, playing snap with their younger sister or brother and saying, 'There! Four reds! . . . and that Coolican says it's rare.' Well, we *expect* you to get this result around one time in 20, remember. So now you can hear a little voice (like my 11-year-old friend) saying, 'Well that means, if social scientists accept results less likely than 0.05 by chance, that one time in 20 they're accepting fluke results!' And the voice is right! (In a way.) Let's think about this:

> What steps can be taken to ensure that, when a researcher finds results significant at $p \leqslant 0.05$, the pattern of results is not a fluke occurrence?

What researchers do is to *replicate* studies. If an effect is taken as significant, and therefore published, someone else would try to obtain the same results in a repeat of the original study. The probability of two predicted significant differences both occurring by chance is less than the chance of just one occurring by chance.

CRITICAL VALUE

We need to apply what we've just covered to our baby sex-guesser. We want to know the number of correct predictions she must make in order for the probability of her efforts occurring to drop below 0.05. We already know the odds of her getting none right, one right and so on, by using Pascal's triangle. The various possibilities are listed in Table 14.4. You'll see that the values we already calculated are shown beside 10, 9 and 8 correct predictions. To make things simpler for the first statistical test in the next chapter, can we just switch to thinking about how many she can get *wrong* and still have her result count as significant? The values are just the same. If she gets *none* wrong, the probability is 0.001. If she gets one wrong $p = 0.01$; for two wrong $p = 0.044$. Let's suppose she got two wrong. I wonder how many readers are saying 'that's still pretty good'?

We did not predict that our friend would get *exactly* two wrong. What we want is the probability that she would do this *well*. In other words, we want the probability that she would get two wrong *or less*. This is the probability for none, one and two wrong *added together*. This is $0.001 + 0.01 + 0.44$ and this gives 0.055. Unfortunately, this value is just over the probability value we can allow for making a decision of significant effect i.e. we can't reject the null hypothesis that her performance produced chance level results. However, had she got just one wrong (nine correct) the resulting probability would be $0.001 + 0.01$ and this is a mere 0.011. If you thought nine correct choices would convince you then your thinking was the same as a psychologist's would be with these results. If you accepted eight or less then you were a little generous and likely to be accepting mere guesses. If you wanted 10 (or even more) then you were erring on the side of caution, being a little 'conservative' with significance.

Table 14.4 *Probabilities from Pascal's triangle*

No. of correct predictions (N)	Probability of N occurring by chance (guessing) alone	
	Fraction	Decimal
0	1/1024	0.001
1	10/1024	0.01
2	45/1024	0.044
3	120/1024	0.117
4	210/1024	0.205
5	252/1024	0.246
6	210/1024	0.205
7	120/1024	0.117
8	45/1024	0.044
9	10/1024	0.01
10	1/1024	0.001

In terms of the number our friend can get *wrong* then, we would talk of a CRITICAL VALUE of just 1. If she gets one wrong, no more, we can reject the null hypothesis that her results are just chance level. But she got two wrong. We must retain the null hypothesis. This doesn't mean that she's a fraud. We don't say the null hypothesis is *true*, only that, as yet, we do not have enough evidence to reject it. She could always try again with another 10 babies.

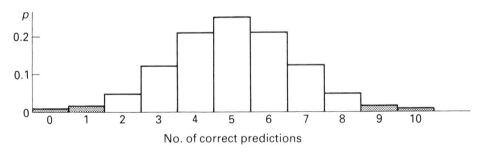

Figure 14.5 *Probability distribution for 10 predictions of two equally likely outcomes*

The probability distribution for 10 events (coin tosses, sex guesses and so on) is shown in Figure 14.5. I hope you'll see that this is a graphical representation of the numbers in line 10 of Pascal's triangle. The most likely event to occur (on a chance basis) is five correct and five wrong, flanked closely by six correct, four wrong and four correct, six wrong. If you look at the areas involved you can see just how likely it is that the number of correct guesses will fall somewhere between three and seven, and just how unlikely it is that the result will fall out towards what are known as the 'tails' of the distribution.

ONE-TAILED AND TWO-TAILED TESTS

Suppose our friend had got every single prediction wrong. Would we say she was a hopeless baby-sex guesser? Or would this be a fascinating result? After all, the probability of her doing *this* by chance alone is also 0.001. We might suspect that she has indeed got a valid method but that she has her instrument round the wrong way or is reading it incorrectly!

A DIRECTIONAL HYPOTHESIS is made when we predict the *direction* of our results. For instance, we might predict that subjects will recall more common than uncommon words. A test of this hypothesis is known as a ONE-TAILED TEST.

A NON-DIRECTIONAL HYPOTHESIS is made when we predict a difference but do not state any expected direction. We might predict that males and females will differ in their attitude to male homosexuality, but we do not make a statement about who will be more positive. The test of this hypothesis is TWO-TAILED.

If we conduct a one-tailed test and the results go in the opposite direction to that predicted, we cannot reject the null hypothesis, *even* if the probability of their occurrence is below 0.05. With a two-tailed test we can reject the null hypothesis whichever direction the results take, so long as the probability of their occurrence is below 0.05. So why not always make two-tailed predictions then?

One reason is that the one-tailed hypothesis will usually be a specific prediction from a theory. If results are extreme in the opposite direction from that predicted we do not have support for our theory and must return to the drawing board to look for one of several things: a confounding variable in the design or procedure, a fault in our logic predicting the result, or a way to revise our theory to take account of conflicting results.

Another reason is that significance with two-tailed predictions is harder to achieve as I shall try to explain.

TAILS OF A DISTRIBUTION

Figure 14.6 shows an expanded version of the right-hand 'tail' of the probability histogram in Figure 14.5. For significance, we already calculated that a result must be in the shaded area. If the sex guesser made only eight correct predictions, the area involved would be (0.055) 5.5% of the total – just too much for significance.

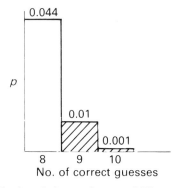

Figure 14.6 *Expansion of right-hand three columns of Figure 14.5*

Suppose we were interested in the probability that our friend would either do extremely well *or* extremely poorly. We predict, in other words that her result will depart significantly from the null hypothesis of mere guessing, *in either direction*. We are making a non-directional hypothesis. The probability of our sex guesser getting *either* nine or more of her predictions right *or* nine or more wrong is the addition of the following probabilities:

$$10 \text{ right} \qquad p = 0.001$$
$$9 \text{ right} \qquad p = 0.01$$
$$10 \text{ wrong} \qquad p = 0.001$$
$$9 \text{ wrong} \qquad p = 0.01$$
$$\text{Total} \qquad p = 0.022$$

We have added the probabilities at each tail of the distribution. Even if we'd predicted that she'd get a lot right *or* a lot wrong, her result of nine or ten correct would count as significant, because the probability of this occurring is 0.022 and still well below 0.05. But in other cases this doubling of probabilities for a two-tailed test would cause total probability to rise above 0.05 and leave the result non-significant. In other words, if you hedge your bets, probability rises. A bookie lowers your odds if you change your prediction from 'first' to 'first or in the first three'.

In Figure 14.5 you can see that the area into which results must fall, for significance in a two-tailed test, is darkened. The left end is the mirror image of the right end in Figure 14.6. Results falling in any other columns are not significant.

THE NORMAL PROBABILITY DISTRIBUTION

You can see in Figure 14.5 that a histogram of probability for 10 equally likely events forms a symmetrical 'organ pipe' pattern. Imagine what this would look like if we tossed, say, 32 coins very many times. We'd get the pattern shown in Figure 13.15 in the last chapter. Instead of showing actual frequencies however, we could show expected probabilities of occurrence for 0 tails, 1 tail etc. up to 32 tails. If you now generalise this pattern, I hope you can see that, for very many events, the shape would end up looking pretty much like a normal curve (you can see a naturally occurring probability distribution of this shape when you look at very old stone or wooden steps – why do they curve down in the middle?). We can use the normal distribution as a probability curve in much the same way as we used Figure 14.5 for 10 events. For instance, think back to z-scores and deviations in the last chapter. In the reading test example (p. 222) I hope it's obvious that the probability that any child, selected at random, has a reading score higher than 40 is 0.5. We also know that 68.26% of all scores fell between a z-score of $+1$ and -1. The area under the curve for this section is 0.6826. We can say therefore, that the probability that any child, selected at random, will have a z-score between $+1$ and -1 (that is, a reading score between 30 and 50 in that example) is 0.6826.

This is the great value of the normal distribution curve and why, in the last chapter, the area under the curve was emphasised. The whole thinking here is immensely important when we come to using significance tests to decide when two means, for instance, are significantly different from one another. We can go through an example of a 'one sample' test right now as an example of what we can conclude with this curve.

A simple significance test

Suppose we discovered some children, reared on a commune where all 'schooling' had been done within the small community as a part of daily living. Reading had not been 'taught' in lessons but integrated into normal activities. An educational visitor is impressed and wants to compare the children with the national mean. Assume that our test, in Chapter 13, is nationally standardised. The mean for the population, then, is 40. Our children average 61. The deviation is $61 - 40 = 21$. To get a z-score we divide the deviation by the standard deviation. This is: $21/10 = 2.1$. If we look up a z-value of 2.1 in Table 2 we find it cuts off the remaining 0.0179 of the right-hand end of the area under the curve. In other words, our children would appear to be better, on average, than all but 1.79% of the population and well within the top 2.5%. This can be seen in Figure 14.7. A z-score of 1.65 cuts off the top 5% of the whole distribution and a z-score of 1.96 cuts off 2.5%. So the children's mean seems to be genuinely unusual, not a chance fluctuation from average.

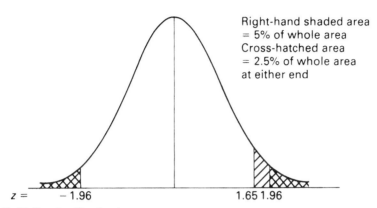

Right-hand shaded area
= 5% of whole area
Cross-hatched area
= 2.5% of whole area
at either end

Figure 14.7 *Tails of a distribution*

In significance testing in general, with a two-tailed test, any result must be associated with a z-score of *either* more than 1.96 *or* less than -1.96 in order to count as significant at 5%. For a one-tailed test the z must be higher than 1.65, *in the direction predicted*. But we can't have our cake and eat it too. If we commit ourselves to a one-tailed test we need only get this lesser z value, but should our obtained z be a *minus* value – results went in the opposite direction to that expected, no matter by how much – we just can't claim any significance. It's arguable whether the test on our commune children should be one or two-tailed but, either way, they end up significantly above average.

OTHER LEVELS OF SIGNIFICANCE

If the baby sexer had got all ten predictions correct it would seem necessary to say that she didn't produce a result which was *just* significant at 5%. Her result was less likely than $p = 0.001$, which is 0.1%. When this happens, psychologists point out the level obtained in their final report. There is a tendency to use the following language in reporting results:
Significant at 5%   'Results were significant'
Significant at 1%   'Results were highly significant'

The 10% level ($p \leqslant 0.1$)

A researcher cannot be confident of results, or publish them as an effect, if the level achieved is only 10%. But if the level is in fact close to 5% (like the sex guesser's results if she gets eight predictions correct) it may well be decided that the research is worth pursuing. Procedure would be tightened or altered, the design may be slightly changed and sampling might be scrutinised.

The 1% level ($p \leqslant 0.01$)

Sometimes it is necessary to be more certain of our results. If we are about to challenge a well-established theory or research finding by publishing results which contradict it, the convention is to achieve 1% significance before publication. A further reason for requiring 1% significance would be when the researcher only has a one-off chance to demonstrate an effect. Replication may be impossible in many field studies or 'natural experiments'. In any case, significance at 1% gives researchers greater confidence in rejecting the null hypothesis.

Lower than 1% (p < 0.01)

In research which may produce applications affecting human health or life changes, such as the testing of drugs for unwanted psychological or behavioural effects, we'd want to be even more certain that no chance effects were being recorded.

Above 5% (p > 0.05)

Yes, it seems we covered this with the 10% level. But the emphasis here is different. A researcher may be replicating a study which was a challenge to their work. It may be that showing there *isn't* a difference is the research aim. This would be the case with a lot of modern studies aimed at demonstrating a *lack* of difference between men and women on various tests and tasks. In this case the prediction is that the null hypothesis will be retained. The probability associated with results must now fall in the less extreme 95% area under the probability curve.

CRITICAL VALUES AT VARIOUS SIGNIFICANCE LEVELS

Notice that for significance at 1% (one-tailed) z would have to be 2.33 or above, because a z-value of 2.33 leaves just 0.01 of the area lying on the right-hand side of the distribution. Check in Table 2, Appendix 2, using the right-hand 'area left' column.

Just to make sure you've got a fair understanding of what critical levels are and how they work, try the following exercise. If you find it tricky, please don't bang your head against the wall, give up psychology or feel inadequate. Most people find this fairly tricky at first. Do the exercise with a friend, stick at it and/or pester your tutor for examples until you get the hang of it!

What is the critical value of z which obtained z-scores would have to beat if results were to be counted as significant at the following levels:

Two-tailed	10%	2%	1%
One-tailed	2.5%	1%	0.01%

Answers: Two-tailed   10%   = 1.65   2% = 2.33   1%   = 2.58
One-tailed   2.5% = 1.96   1% = 2.33   0.1% = 3.11

TYPE I AND TYPE II ERROR

When we have finished analysing research results, and we have tested for significance, we make a statement that we must accept or reject the null hypothesis at the set level of significance, usually $p < 0.05$.

We may be right or wrong. We can never be *absolutely* certain that an apparent effect is not a fluke. Sometimes it seems crazy to challenge. Say, for instance, we ran an experiment in which there were two conditions: recall of common words, like 'cat', and recall of uncommon words, like 'otiose'. A significant difference at $p < 0.001$ would appear unassailable. However, within psychological research, results are rarely as unambiguous as this, though high levels of significance are what good research aims at.

If a researcher claims support for the research hypothesis with a significant result when, in fact, variations in results are caused by random variables alone, then a TYPE ONE ERROR would be said to have occurred.

Through poor design or faulty sampling, researchers may fail to achieve significance, *even though the effect they were attempting to demonstrate actually does exist.* In this case it would be said that they had made a TYPE TWO ERROR. These outcomes are summarised in Table 14.5

Table 14.5 *Type one and Type two errors*

	Null hypothesis is:	
Null hypothesis is actually:	Accepted	Rejected
True	✓	Type one error
False	Type two error	✓

Obviously, if we set a stringent (low) significance level, such as 1%, we may well make a type two error. At 10%, a type one error is much more likely.

GLOSSARY

Value with which a statistic, calculated from sample data, can be compared in order to decide whether a null hypothesis should be rejected; the value is related to the particular level of probability chosen	_____ _____	critical value
Prediction which states in which direction differences (or correlation) will occur	_____	directional hypothesis
Informal test of data made simply by inspection and mental calculation plus experience of values	_____ ____	eyeball test
Prediction which does not state in which direction differences (or correlation) will occur	___-_____	non-directional hypothesis
Test made if the research hypothesis is directional	___-_____ ____	one-tailed test
A numerical measure of pure 'chance'	_____	**probability**
A measure of probability based on existing data and comparing number of target events which have occurred with total number of relevant events	_____	empirical

A measure of probability calculated from analytical formulae and first principles	_____	logical
A measure of probability made on the basis of human internal, and often emotional assessment	_____	subjective
A histogram or table showing the probabilities associated with a complete range of possible events	_____ _____	probability distribution
Levels of probability at which it is agreed that the null hypothesis will be rejected	_____ _____	**significance levels**
Significance level generally considered too high for rejection of the null hypothesis but which might merit further investigation	___	10% (p<0.1)
Conventional significance level	___	5% (p<0.05)
Significance level preferred for greater confidence than the conventional one and which should be set where research is controversial or unique	___	1% (p<0.01)
Test performed in order to decide whether the null hypothesis should be retained or rejected	_____ ____/_____	significance test/decision
Test made if the research hypothesis is non-directional	___-_____ ____	two-tailed test
Mistake made in rejecting the null hypothesis when it is true	____ __ _____	type I error
Mistake made in retaining the null hypothesis when it is false	____ __ _____	type II error

EXERCISES

1 State whether the following values of z (on a normal distribution) are significant or not ($p < 0.05$) for:
   a) One-tailed tests
      1.32   1.75   −1.9   −0.78
   b) Two-tailed tests
      −2.05   1.89   −1.6   1.98

2 State whether tests of the following hypotheses would require one- or two-tailed tests:
   a) Diabetics will be more health conscious than other people
   b) Extroverts and introverts will differ in their ability to learn people's names
   c) Job satisfaction will correlate negatively with absenteeism
   d) Self-esteem will correlate with outward confidence

3 A student sets out to show that attitude change will be greater if people are paid more to make a speech which contradicts their present attitude. Her tutor tells her that this runs directly counter to research findings on 'cognitive dissonance'.
  a) What would be the appropriate significance level for her to set?
  b) If she had originally intended to use the 5% level, is she now more or less likely to make a type two error?

4 A z-score is significant (two-tailed), with $p \leqslant 0.05$ because it is greater than the critical value of 1.96 for $p \leqslant 0.05$. This is why the first line of the table below is marked 'true'. Can you complete the rest of the table with ticks or crosses?

	z	One- or two-tailed test	$p \leqslant$	True or false
a)	2.0	Two	0.05	true
b)	1.78	One	0.05	
c)	2.3	Two	0.025	
d)	2.88	One	0.002	
e)	3.35	Two	0.001	
f)	2.22	One	0.01	

Simple tests of difference – non-parametric

USING TESTS OF SIGNIFICANCE – GENERAL PROCEDURE

Significance tests are used when you've collected and organised your data and have come to a point where you're asking questions like, 'Well, we got a difference just as we predicted but is it a big enough one not to be a fluke?' or, 'It obviously worked [the independent variable], but where do I go from here?' Writing the statistical test section of practical reports is one of the hardest tasks for new students of psychology, often because the full logical process hasn't been completely absorbed, so I would recommend that you turn to this section whenever, in the early days, you want to organise this part of your practical write-up.

Let's look at what we did in the last chapter in brief terms.

	right	wrong

1 We obtained a difference. A description of our raw data was: 8   2

2 We calculated the maximum number wrong (with this form and quantity of data) that would give a result less likely to occur than five times in 100. This value was 1.

3 We compared our friend's result with this 'critical value'.

4 We decided which side of the critical value our result was on – the non-significant side, because we wanted 1 for significance but obtained 2 (known as s in the sign test below).

5 We consequently reported significance or not at the level of probability set (0.05). Officially, this level should be set before testing but $p \leqslant 0.05$ is the traditional maximum. This is a way of stating how confident we are that the null hypothesis is incorrect. If results are not significant we are not confident enough to reject the null hypothesis.

This is the logical sequence behind *any* test of significance, no matter how complicated they get. In fact, one aspect of the above sequence is even easier. We don't *calculate* the critical value – we look it up in tables. You'll see from the calculation of the SIGN TEST below, that the value of 1, which we worked out in the last chapter, is given directly by tables at the back of this book. If you're using a computer program you will usually be given the exact probability of the null hypothesis being correct and you won't even have to consult tables. Table 15.1 opposite puts the whole process in formal terms.

The first tests covered in this book are called 'non-parametric'. They get this title because they do not make any assumptions about underlying population parameters (see Chapter 17). That is, they do not rely on estimates of the mean and standard deviation of the population in order to see how far the data we have obtained are from those estimates. This is what happens in the parametric tests to be dealt with in later chapters.

Table 15.1 *Standard procedure in conducting and reporting results of a statistical test of significance*

Choose appropriate statistical test	When we've covered all the tests, Chapter 24 will help you through this step
Calculate test statistic	In our sex-typing case this was 2, the number our friend got wrong. In all cases the statistic will be denoted by a letter, for instance t or U. In our test, $s = 2$
Compare test statistic with critical value in tables Take account of:	Tables are provided at the back of the book for all the tests introduced. In calculating our critical value, we took account of:
1 Number of cases in sample or df	**1** $N = 10$
2 Whether one- or two-tailed test	**2** One-tailed test
3 Maximum probability level acceptable	**3** $p \leqslant 0.05$
	Critical value was 1
Decide which side of the critical value your result is on – pay attention to instructions accompanying the table	Our result was on the non-significant side of the critical value
Report the decision – whether to retain or reject the null hypothesis and at what level of confidence (significance)	We retained the null hypothesis. We found a probability >0.05 that it was true. Therefore we didn't have sufficient confidence to reject it

TESTS AT NOMINAL LEVEL

This Section introduces tests of significant difference. It is extremely important to understand and use the conventional manner and logic of reporting steps in the significance decision process. The general set of steps, for *any* significance decision, are given and related to **rejection** or **retention** of the **null hypothesis**.

The tests presented in this Chapter are '**non-parametric**', meaning that they do not rely on assumptions about underlying population parameters (mean, variance) as is required for parametric tests. The tests covered are at the **nominal** level of measurement. The tests are:

- Binomial sign test (better known as just 'sign test')
- Chi-squared (χ^2) – test of association between two variables
  - 2×2
  - $R \times C$ (more than two rows or columns)
  - Goodness of fit
  - One variable, two levels

There are limitations on the use of χ^2: data must be frequencies, not ratios, means or proportions, and must belong exclusively to one or another category, i.e. the same case (person) must not appear in more than one 'cell' of the data table.

There is statistical debate about what to do when expected cell frequencies are low. The best thing is to avoid low cell frequencies where possible, but with overall sample sizes above 20 the risk of a type I error becomes acceptably low without using Yates' correction (as was traditional).

RELATED DATA – THE BINOMIAL SIGN TEST (USUALLY SHORTENED TO 'SIGN TEST')

CONDITIONS FOR USE

- Differences or correlation   Differences
- Level of data   Nominal
- Type of design   Related

DATA

A psychotherapist wishes to assess the therapeutic process. One way is to ask clients

Table 15.2 *Therapy data*

	A	B	C	D
		Rating		
Client No.		After three	Difference	Sign of
(N = 10)	Pre-therapy	months' therapy	(B − A)	difference
1	3	7	4	+
2	12	18	6	+
3	9	5	−4	−
4	7	7	0	
5	8	12	4	+
6	1	5	4	+
7	15	16	1	+
8	10	12	2	+
9	11	15	4	+
10	10	17	7	+

whether, after three months of therapy, they feel better about themselves. They are asked to rate their self-image by giving a score out of 20, before and after the three months of therapy (see Table 15.2).

Procedure	**Calculation on our data**
1 Calculate the difference between A and B, always subtracting in the same direction. If a one-tailed hypothesis has been made, it makes sense to subtract the score expected to be lower from that expected to be higher. Enter difference in column C.	See column C.
2 Enter sign of difference in column D. Ignore any zero values (i.e. cases where there is no difference in score pairs).	See column D. N becomes 9 because one result is zero.
3 Add up the number of times the less frequent sign occurs. Call this 's'.	Negative signs occur less frequently, so $s = 1$.
4 Find the relevant line of critical values from Table 3, Appendix 2 where N = total number of positive and negative signs (not zeros). Decide whether to pay attention to one- or two-tailed 'p' values.	Consult table and look at the horizontal line next to N = 9. Since therapy was supposed to *improve* people's self-image, we are conducting a one-tailed test.
5 Compare s with the critical value shown for the significance level set. s must be equal to or lower than the	Our s is 1. The critical value under the column headed '$p < 0.05$' (one-tailed) is 1. Therefore, our result matches the

critical value for results to be considered significant.	conditions required for significance.
6 Make statement of significance.	We reject the null hypothesis. The probability that we are wrong to do so is $p < 0.05$ (but see Box 15.1).

SUMMARY

The test looks only at the *direction* of differences. The critical value tells us the maximum number of differences in the unwanted direction we can have and still call our results significant at a particular level.

EXPLANATORY NOTES

The level is nominal because, for each result, all we know is whether there was a difference and the direction of that difference. We started with plastic interval level data but we reduced it to just sign of difference, thereby losing any information about *sizes* of difference. For each result we have just three possible categories: '+', '−' or '0'. In our test we use only two of these, ignoring any zeros. The null hypothesis here is that the pluses are no more numerous than what we'd expect by chance. Underlying this is the interpreted view that our 10 clients rate themselves no differently from any other 10 similar people asked to rate their self-image either side of a three-month interval and no therapy. We reject this view because we are rejecting the statistical null hypothesis. Another, purely statistical way to look at the reasoning is that, drawing samples of nine at random (we ignored zeros), and with replacement, from a barrel containing equal numbers of pluses and minuses, we would get a distribution this extreme (8:1) less times than 1 in 20.

Box 15.1 *Setting the significance level before or after the results are in*

There is a long-running debate between statistical 'purists' and practical researchers. Purists argue that the 'rules' of the significance testing game say that you should state *before testing* what level is acceptable and that is the only level you can then legitimately report. For instance, assume you state that you will reject the null hypothesis if the probability of a type I error (being wrong about rejecting the null hypothesis) is less than 0.05. If it turns out that your result is really extreme – it 'beats' the critical value for $p < 0.001$ for instance, according to this view you can't report anything other than that your results were significant at the level set (0.05). However, in practice, most students, *and* research psychologists, would report the 'better' value obtained. For instance, in the sign test just calculated, the researcher might report that the difference was significant with $p < 0.025$ because, if you look at the tables again you'll see that 1 is also the critical value in the 0.025 (one-tailed) column. I think I'm not a purist on this. It seems to me there is no harm in saying, 'Our result was, in fact less likely to occur by chance than $2\frac{1}{2}$ times in 100'. It's important to remember, however, that a result significant at $p < 0.001$ is not necessarily 'better' than one at $p < 0.05$. A highly *significant* effect can nevertheless be quite *weak*, if the sample is very large. This is a further argument against over-large samples and is explained more fully in the correlation chapter.

	+		−
	8		1

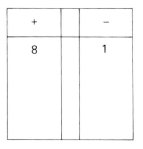

Figure 15.1 *The sign test gives the probability of drawing plusses and minuses at random*

UNRELATED DATA – THE χ^2 TEST (ALSO WRITTEN AS 'CHI-SQUARE' AND PRONOUNCED 'KY SQUARE')

CONDITIONS FOR USE

- Differences or correlation   Differences (tested by 'association')
- Level of data   Nominal
- Type of design   Unrelated
- Special note   Data must be in the form of frequencies. Although we are usually looking for differences in the effect of the IV, the test actually looks at the *association* between row categories and column categories.

There are other limitations on the use of χ^2, outlined at the end of this chapter.

DATA

The results in Table 15.2a were actually obtained at a psychology workshop by

Table 15.2a *Observed frequencies*

	Sex of driver		
	Female	Male	Total
Driver stopped	90 A	B 88	178
Driver didn't stop	56 C	D 89	145
Total:	146	177	323

Table 15.2b *Expected frequencies*

	Sex of driver		
	Female	Male	Total
Driver stopped	80.46 A	B 97.54	178
Driver didn't stop	65.54 C	D 79.46	145
Total:	146	177	323

students observing male and female drivers at a pedestrian traffic light. They observed whether a driver stopped or not when approaching the light as it turned to amber. These are *frequencies* (see Chapter 12).

Procedure	*Calculation on our data*

1 Give the raw data (OBSERVED FREQUENCIES) a letter for each cell

See Table 15.2a

2 Calculated corresponding EXPECTED FREQUENCIES as follows:

Formula: $E = \dfrac{RC}{T}$ where:

R = total of row cells
   (A + B) or (C + D)
C = total of column cells
   (A + C) or (B + D)
T = total of all cells
   (A + B + C + D)

Cell A: $E = \dfrac{178 \times 146}{323} = 80.46$

Cell B: $E = \dfrac{178 \times 177}{323} = 97.54$

Cell C: $E = \dfrac{145 \times 146}{323} = 65.54$

Cell D: $E = \dfrac{145 \times 177}{323} = 79.46$

3 Call data in observed cells 'O' and expected cells 'E' and put values into the following equation:

$\chi^2 = \sum \dfrac{(O-E)^2}{E}$ by operating as follows:

a) Subtract E from O
b) Square the result of step **a**
c) Divide the result of step **b** by E

Cell	Step a $(O-E)$	Step b $(O-E)^2$	Step c $(O-E)^2/E$
A	$90 - 80.46$ = **9.54**	9.54^2 = **91.01**	$91.01 \div 80.46$ = **1.13**
B	$88 - 97.54$ = **−9.54**	-9.54^2 = **91.01**	$91.01 \div 97.54$ = **0.93**
C	$56 - 65.54$ = **−9.54**	-9.54^2 = **91.01**	$91.01 \div 65.54$ = **1.39**
D	$89 - 79.46$ = **9.45**	9.54^2 = **91.01**	$91.01 \div 79.46$ = **1.15**

d) Add the results of step **c**

$\chi^2 = 1.13 + 0.93 + 1.39 + 1.15 = $ **4.6**

4 Find DEGREES OF FREEDOM as follows:
$df = (R-1)(C-1)$
where R is number of rows and C is number of columns

$df = 1 \times 1 = 1$

5 Using the *df* found, consult Table 4 (Appendix 3) and find the relevant critical value

Using $df = 1$ we find that a value of 3.84 is required for significance with $p < 0.05$.

6 Make significance decision

Our obtained value is higher than the critical value required. Note that, with χ^2, obtained values must be *higher* than the critical value. Always check the instructions with the tables. Note, also, that we could not have reported significance at any higher level. We did not 'beat' the critical value for $p < 0.01$, which is 5.41.

NOTE 1: ONE- AND TWO-TAILED TESTS WITH χ^2 – Always use two-tailed values except in one special case to be discussed later. Don't worry! χ^2 is the only test which doesn't follow the usual pattern of one- and two-tailed tests. It doesn't matter in which direction we predicted here, we still use two-tailed values.

NOTE 2: DEGREES OF FREEDOM – This is a very complicated notion to explain fully. For several tests in this book, before checking for the critical value in tables, you need to know what the degrees of freedom are. In the χ^2 test it is calculated as shown above. One way to think about the concept is to ask, 'How many of the cells (A, B, C and D) in a 2×2 frequency table are free to vary?' If we know what the row and column totals are, then once we've filled in one cell, all the others are automatically fixed. In Table 15.2a, once we know there are 90 female drivers who stopped, given the row and column totals, the values 88, 56 and 89 follow automatically – they *couldn't* be different. Hence, we get just 1 degree of freedom in a 2×2 table because just one cell is free to vary.

NOTE 3 – Some textbooks, and the first edition of this one, still cling to a conservative version of the χ^2 formula when $df = 1$, using what is known as 'Yates' correction'. In line with most modern practice, however, this use has been dropped in this second edition. There is still some danger, with low overall frequencies, of rejecting the null hypothesis when $p > 0.05$. This will be discussed further on in this section.

Quick 2×2 formula

This can be used only where there are two columns and two rows, as in the example above. It saves the labour of calculating expected frequencies and, if you're handy with a calculator, you'll find this can be done in one move from the cell totals:

$$\chi^2 = \frac{N(AD - BC)^2}{(A + B)(C + D)(A + C)(B + D)}$$

where N is the total sample size.

SUMMARY

The test looks at the variation between observed frequencies and expected frequencies – those expected if, given row and column totals, there was absolutely no association between the vertical and horizontal variables, i.e. no systematic relationship between the DV and levels of the IV.

EXPLANATORY NOTES

If you consider our data, it is obvious that, of the 177 males observed, just 50% of them stopped on amber, whereas 62% of females (90 out of 146) stopped. The χ^2 test looks at these relative proportions. Let's consider a convenient but fictitious example.

Assume 50 high extroverts and 50 high introverts were asked whether they would feel comfortable on a nudist beach. The results might run like those in Table 15.3a.

Table 15.3a *Observed frequencies*

	Extroverts	Introverts	
Would feel:			Total
comfortable	40	10	**50**
uncomfortable	10	40	**50**
Total	**50**	**50**	**100**

Table 15.3b *Expected frequencies*

	Extroverts	Introverts
Would feel:		
comfortable	25	25
uncomfortable	25	25

Note that, of all 100 people asked, 50 said they would be comfortable and 50 said they wouldn't. But these 50 aren't evenly spread between the two types of person. A large proportion of extroverts would feel comfortable. Statistically, since 50 out of 100 people *in all* said they'd feel comfortable, we'd expect half the introverts, as well as half the extroverts, to say this *if* there is no relationship between extroversion/introversion and feeling comfortable on a nudist beach. If you agree with that point then, in your head, you actually performed a version of the expected cells formula

$$E = \frac{RC}{T}.$$

You agreed that 1/2 (50/100) of each 50 should appear in each cell, i.e.

$$\frac{50}{100} \times 50.$$

Imagine we took very many samples this size in a purely random manner. We would get many results close to those shown in Table 15.3b. The null hypothesis here is that our *observed* data (the results we actually got – Table 15.3a) do not differ significantly from those in Table 15.3b. The job of χ^2 is to tell us how unlikely this is to be true. Let me present one more imaginary example which, I hope, will explain graphically what χ^2 does.

Suppose we dropped ball bearings onto the centre spot in the equipment shown in Figure 15.2 which is supposed to be a box divided into four equal compartments. The ball bearings bounce away from the spot in a random manner. We stop when all rows and columns add to 50 – which makes the whole process non-random, but this is only an illustrative example. Each time we did this we'd get results not varying too much from those in Table 15.3b. Now and again, however, under probability 'laws', freak variations quite far from these frequencies would occur. The χ^2 calculation tells us just how often, in terms of probability, we could expect a result as extreme as the one actually observed.

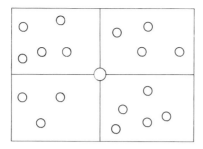

Figure 15.2 *Balls bouncing into a box*

In fact, the calculation of χ^2 on the extrovert/introvert data shows a very large deviation of the observed from the expected data. χ^2 is 33.64 and the probability of this value occurring was: $p < 0.0001$. Hence, we could safely assume, if these results were real, that the null hypothesis can be rejected and this therefore would support (*not* prove!) the theory that feeling comfortable with nudists *is associated with* extroversion. The χ^2 test is, in fact, often called a **TEST OF ASSOCIATION** between two variables.

Returning to our original real data then, the expected frequencies show that, since 178 drivers in all stopped, out of a total of 323, then we'd expect 178/323 of the 146 female drivers to stop *if* sex is not associated with stopping on amber. This expected value is 80.46. In fact, 90 females stopped. Male drivers stopped *less* frequently than the expected totals would predict on the null hypothesis. The χ^2 being significant at $p < 0.05$, we assume that (female) sex *is* associated with stopping on amber.

Warning for tests and exams!

It is very easy to get the idea of expected frequencies wrong. When asked what they are, many people answer that they are 'what the researcher expects' or similar. I hope you see that they are the *opposite* of what the researcher (usually) wants to happen. *The expected frequencies are what is expected to occur (most often) under the null hypothesis* (i.e. if 'nothing's going on').

THE $R \times C \, \chi^2$ TEST

We can extend this test to situations where either of the two variables being tested for association has more than two values. There can be R rows and C columns. For instance, four different colleges might be compared for their students' performances in a psychology A level exam:

Table 15.4 *Four by two frequency table*

	College A	College B	College C	College D	Total
Passed	32	46	34	23	135
Failed	5	12	18	1	36
Total	37	58	52	24	171

The test will tell us whether these ratios of pass and fail are significantly different among the four colleges. Degrees of freedom here are $(R-1)(C-1) = (2-1)$ $(4-1) = 3$. You can see that, once 3 cells are known, the rest are fixed, given the row and column totals. I haven't included the calculation, since it follows the earlier method exactly. The χ^2 result is 11.14 and $p < 0.02$.

χ^2 'GOODNESS OF FIT' TEST

A special use of χ^2 occurs when we want to investigate a set of data measured on only one variable. For instance, suppose we weren't interested in sex differences for stopping at an amber light. However, we are interested in how all drivers behave at a variety of traffic stopping points. Consider this table:

Table 15.5 *'Failure-to-halt' offences for county of Undershire*

A	B	C	D	E	
Roundabout	Junction stop sign	Traffic light	Pedestrian crossing	Police controlled junction	Total
47	17	19	12	3	98

An 'eyeball test' of this data surely leads us to suspect that drivers are far more careless or disrespectful of driving laws at roundabouts than elsewhere (and, of course, obedient with police officers!). We can treat this as a $R \times C$ test with just one row but five columns. We have to calculate degrees of freedom from first principles because $R - 1 = 1 - 1 = 0$, which isn't allowed! But, there are five cells and, knowing the row total, four of these are free to vary before the last is fixed. So degrees of freedom for a 'goodness of fit' test are given by $C - 1$.

Calculation

1 Calculate expected frequencies on the basis of the null hypothesis that all cells should be equal

$98 \div 5 = \mathbf{19.6}$

2 Using the observed values from Table 15.5 and the expected frequency calculated, use the χ^2 equation as before:

O: 47   17   19   12   3
E: 19.6 19.6 19.6 19.6 19.6

3 **a** $(O - E)$ **b** $(O - E)^2$ **c** $(O - E)^2/E$

	a $(O-E)$	b $(O-E)^2$	c $(O-E)^2/E$
Cell A	$47 - 19.6 = 27.4$	$27.4^2 = 750.76$	$750.76/19.6 = 38.30$
Cell B	$17 - 19.6 = -2.6$	$-2.6^2 = 6.76$	$6.76/19.6 = 0.34$
Cell C	$19 - 19.6 = -0.6$	$-0.6^2 = 0.36$	$0.36/19.6 = 0.02$
Cell D	$12 - 19.6 = -7.6$	$-7.6^2 = 57.76$	$57.76/19.6 = 2.95$
Cell E	$3 - 19.6 = -16.6$	$-16.6^2 = 275.56$	$275.56/19.6 = 14.06$

$$\chi^2 = \mathbf{55.67}$$

4 Find critical value using *df* and two-tailed values

df = 4
critical value for $p < 0.001$ is 18.46

5 Make significance decision   Assume we can reject null
                                                     hypothesis of no difference with
                                                     $p < 0.001$ of a type one error

Our result is far higher than the maximum table value given so there is an extremely significant 'lump' in the distribution of scores. Notice that the calculation of cell E contributes quite a lot to the overall χ^2 value, but nothing like that contributed by cell A. Roundabout misbehaviour is far *further* from the average number of misdemeanours per category than is obedience at police-controlled crossings.

'GOODNESS OF FIT' AND NORMAL DISTRIBUTIONS

This test can be used to decide whether a large sample closely approximates to a normal distribution or not. In this case, our expected frequencies would be calculated according to Table 2 (Appendix 3) which shows what proportion of a normally distributed population falls between different z-scores. For instance, for a normal distribution we expect 34.13% of all values to fall between the mean and one standard deviation ($z = +1$) and 13.59% should fall between one and two standard deviations from the mean (between $z = +1$ and $z = +2$). χ^2 'goodness of fit' compares the proportions of our actual distribution with these ideal proportions.

ONE VARIABLE – TWO CATEGORIES ONLY

This is a special case of the 'goodness of fit' χ^2 where we have data measured on just one variable and have only split it into two cells. Suppose, for instance, we told people that a fictitious person was 'warm' and asked them to decide whether the person would also be happy or unhappy. We might ask them to rate several such 'bi-polar opposites' but let's just deal with one result shown in Table 15.6.

If people are choosing at random (the null hypothesis) then we should get about half the total in each cell, that is, 25. So expected frequencies are 25 for each cell. The calculation then proceeds as normal.

Table 15.6 *'Warm' ratings*

	Happy	**Unhappy**	Total
No. of participants choosing	42	8	50

The χ^2 value in this case would be 23.12. I hope you'll find this very highly significant.

This is the 'special case' referred to earlier when we can take the test to be one-tailed, if our hypothesis correctly predicted the direction of any difference.

LIMITATIONS ON THE USE OF χ^2

Observations must appear in one cell only. For instance, if we looked at male and female swimmers and hurdlers, one person could appear in both the swimmers *and* the hurdlers category if they enjoyed both sports. This would make use of χ^2 invalid.

Actual frequencies must appear in the cells, not percentages, proportions or numbers which do anything other than count. For instance, the mean of an interval scale variable cannot appear.

Low expected frequencies

One limitation on which the current generation of A level psychology tutors (including myself), will most likely have been reared is that one should not proceed with a χ^2 test where expected frequency cells fall below 5. In the first edition of this book, I recommended the rule of thumb which I had inherited, and which comes from Cochran (1954) which was that *no more than 20% of expected cells should fall below 5*. This would rule out any 2×2 in which at least one expected cell was less than 5.

Table 15.7 *Handedness*

	Preferred hand		
Better ear	Left	Right	Total
Left	2	1	3
Right	0	17	17
Total	2	18	20

Table 15.8

Age	Conserved	Didn't conserve	Total
5 years	2	6	8
7 years	6	2	8
Total	8	8	16

I hadn't realised the size of the hornets' nest I was mixing with. Having received several conflicting communications, I was prompted to investigate further. The most uncontroversial position in contemporary research seems to be that *with a total sample of more than 20*, the test can tolerate expected frequencies as low as 1 or 2 in one or two cells. In a 2×2 design – which many student practicals use – to obtain *three* cells with expected frequencies less than 5 there would have to be something quite lop-sided about the sampling. A typically useless set of data, statistically speaking, might occur with a poorly thought out project where, as shown in Table 15.7, it had been decided to see whether, from an available class of students, left-handers also had better left-ear hearing. You don't really need a statistics course to see that no strong conclusion can be drawn from this data.

For total sample sizes less than 20 and two expected cells below 5, the risk of a type I error is too high. For instance, the data shown in Table 15.8 give a χ^2 of 4.0 (which is 'significant' for one *df*) yet it's easy to see, again, without much formal statistical training, that the result was relatively likely to occur – only two children in each age group needed to move away, in opposite directions, from the expected frequencies of four in each cell for these results to occur. From first principles (working out all the possible combinations) the probability of these results occurring comes out sub-stantially higher than 0.05. If you have these sort of data it doesn't take too long to work from first principles but it's far better to make sure your analysis will be valid by taking a large enough sample, with a sensible design. Even with tables larger than

2×2, if several expected frequencies fall below 5 *and* the row or column totals are quite severely skewed, the possibility of a type I error increases.

Fisher's exact test

If the row *and* column totals are fixed, before the study is begun, then this test can be employed. However, this is rarely the case in psychological research. An example might be where you decided to select 20 girls and 20 boys, *and* ensured that 20 of these liked guns and 20 didn't, *then* looked at the association of sex of child with gun preference.

GLOSSARY

Number of cells in frequency table which are free to vary if row and column totals are known. Also used in other tests where it defines the number of individual values free to vary when a group total is known	_____ __ _____	degrees of freedom
Frequencies theoretically expected in table if no relationship exists between variables	_____	expected frequencies
Frequencies actually obtained and submitted to a significance test using Chi-square	_____	observed frequencies
The figure calculated at the end of a statistical test which is then compared with critical value tables	____ _____	test statistic

		tests
Test of association between two variables, using unrelated data at nominal level	___-_____	Chi-squared
Frequency level test used to decide whether a given distribution is close enough to a theoretical pattern	_____ __ ___	goodness of fit
Nominal level test for differences between two sets of related data	____ ____	sign test (binomial)

EXERCISES

I Carry out a χ^2 test on the following data:

	pro-hanging	anti-hanging
politics		
left	17	48
right	33	16

2 Should a χ^2 test be carried out on the following data?
7	1
2	7

3 A (fictitious) survey shows that, in a sample of 100, 91 people are against the privatisation of health services, whereas nine support the idea.
- **a)** What test of significance can be performed on these data?
- **b)** Would this test be one- or two-tailed if the results are in the predicted direction?
- **c)** If, for a large sample, we knew *only* that 87% of people were against the idea and 13% were for it, could we carry out the same test to see whether this split is significant?
- **d)** Calculate the χ^2 value and check it for significance.

4 A field study produced the following table of results:

	Observed frequencies			**Expected frequencies**		
	Taste preferred					
	A	**B**	**C**	**A**	**B**	**C**
Age						
Under 14	3	8	4	2.5	5.25	7.25
14–30	4	6	2	2.0	4.2	5.8
Over-30	3	7	23	5.5	11.55	15.95

- **a)** How many degrees of freedom are involved here?
- **b)** Does it look safe to conduct a χ^2 test on these data?

5 Nine people are sent on an interpersonal skills training course. They are asked to rate their opinion of the need for this type of course both before and after attendance. Seven people rated the need lower having attended, one rated it higher and one didn't change in opinion. Using a sign test, decide whether this apparent negative effect of the course is significant.

TESTS AT ORDINAL LEVEL

Tests presented here are at the ordinal level of measurement. In this case data, which may originally have been at interval (or 'plastic' interval) level, are given ranks and these are the values used by the tests. The tests are:

- **Wilcoxon signed ranks** – Related data
- **Mann–Whitney *U*** – Unrelated data
- **Wilcoxon rank sum** – Unrelated data (simpler to calculate than Mann–Whitney)

Formulae are provided for when *N* is large, where the ordinal level test statistic can be converted into a *z*-score and checked in normal distribution tables.

RELATED DATA – THE WILCOXON (*T*) SIGNED RANKS TEST

This is one of two major tests used at the ordinal level for testing differences. One is for *related* and the other for *unrelated* designs. There are two points to be careful of:

1 The Wilcoxon statistic is known as '*T*' and this is extremely easy to confuse with the (little) '*t*' test to be met later as a parametric test.

2 There is also a Wilcoxon 'rank sum' test which works on unrelated data and can be used instead of the Mann–Whitney test, which we'll look at after this one.

CONDITIONS FOR USE

- Differences or correlation   Differences
- Level of data   Ordinal; data must be meaningfully rankable[1]
- Type of design   Related
- Special notes   Don't confuse this with:
  1 The little *t* test
  2 Wilcoxon's rank sum test for unrelated data
  Where *N* is large (>20) see 'When *N* is large', below

---

[1] It is not legitimate to rank data where one difference is not meaningfully higher than another. This can occur where there are ceiling (or floor) effects. For instance, if Jane improves from 10 to 15 points on a reading test, but Jason increases from 17 to the test maximum of 20, it is not reasonable to claim that Jane's increase is 'better' or greater, since Jason has no chance to show his potential increase.

DATA

Students were asked to assess two teaching/learning methods, experienced for one term each, using a specially devised attitude questionnaire.

Table 16.1 *Student assessment data*

Student (N = 15)	Rating of traditional lecture A	Rating of assignment based method B	Difference (B − A) C	Rank of difference D
Abassi	23	33	10	12
Bennett	14	22	8	9.5
Berridge	35	38	3	3
Chapman	26	30	4	5
Collins	28	31	3	3
Gentry	19	17	−2	1
Higgs	42	42	0	
Laver	30	25	−5	6
Montgomery	26	34	8	9.5
Parrott	31	24	−7	8
Peart	18	21	3	3
Ramakrishnan	25	46	21	14
Spencer	23	29	6	7
Turner	31	40	9	11
Williams	30	41	11	13

Procedure

1 Calculate the difference between the pairs of scores (in columns A and B), always subtracting in the same direction. As with the sign test, with a one-tailed hypothesis it makes sense to subtract in the direction differences are predicted to go, i.e. predicted smaller from predicted larger value.

2 Rank the differences in the usual way (see page 190). Ignore the sign of the difference. For instance, Laver's difference (−5) is given rank 6 because it is the next largest, in absolute size, after the value (+)4. Also ignore any zero values. These results are omitted from the analysis.[1]

3 Find the sum of the ranks of positive differences, and the sum of ranks of

Calculation on our data

See Table 16.1

See Table 16.1. Note that Higgs' results are dropped from the analysis

Sum of ranks of negative signed differences (−2, −5, and −7) will negative differences. The *smaller* of these[2] is T. If the sum of one set of ranks is obviously smaller, you need only add these.

4 Find relevant line (using N which doesn't include zero differences) in Table 7 (Appendix 2) and decide whether to pay attention to one- or two-tailed values.

5 Find lowest critical value which T does not exceed. If T exceeds all critical values, results are not significant.

6 Make statement of significance.

obviously be smaller. Therefore add their ranks: $1 + 6 + 8$. Hence, $T = 15$

Relevant line is $N = 14$ (remember one result has been dropped). Assume preferred teaching method not predicted. Therefore two-tailed test is appropriate.

T does not exceed 25 or 21 or 15, but it does exceed 6. 15 is therefore the relevant critical value. It is under $p < 0.02$.

Differences are significant ($p < 0.02$).

SUMMARY

The Wilcoxon test looks at the differences between related pairs of values. It ranks these according to absolute size, ignoring the direction of the difference. Statistic T is calculated by adding the ranks of the positive and negative differences and taking the smaller sum. Critical values are the maximum value T can be for the particular significance level. In a sense it asks 'How likely is it that differences this size, relative to all other differences, would occur in the 'wrong' direction?'

EXPLANATORY NOTES

Like the sign test, the Wilcoxon looks at differences between paired values. The sign test looked only at the probability of the *number* of differences in the less frequent direction being so low. The Wilcoxon also looks at the rank of these differences relative to the other differences. If we've made a one-tailed prediction that scores in one condition will be higher than scores in the other, we can say, loosely, that the smaller sum of (negative) differences is 'unwanted'. The test asks, in effect, 'what positions in the whole set do these unwanted differences take relative to the wanted ones?'

Suppose we asked several people to recite the alphabet both forwards and backwards and timed their performance. We would surely predict a set of positive differences if we subtracted forwards time from backwards? Random sampling may

---

[1] Almost all writers tell you to ignore zero differences so you'll be in safe company if you do. However, a small bias is incurred and Hays (1973) advises the following: with *even* numbers of zero differences, give each the average rank that all the zeros would get (they rank below 1) and arbitrarily give half a negative sign. Do the same with an *odd* number, but randomly discard one of them first. This might make some results significant that wouldn't otherwise be. Notice, this has no effect on our calculation above because, with *one* zero difference the methods are the same.

[2] Some textbooks say T is the sum of the ranks of the least frequent sign. This is because that *usually* is also the smaller sum of ranks. When it isn't, you can be sure that differences were not significant at 5%. If you want to know the exact probability of occurence (with a little error for small samples) then you can use the formula on page 276 to convert to a z-score. Using one sum of ranks will give you the same z value as the other, except with an opposite sign. Oddly, MINITAB™ always gives you the sum of the positive ranks! (but it also gives you the exact probability of T occurring at this value).

have introduced a poor English speaker or a person who has developed reverse alphabet recital as a party trick or even someone who just loves fouling up psychology experiments. This sort of participant might produce a faster reverse time. Some participants might take the task really carefully in both directions, in which case differences could be marginally in favour of reverse or forwards. But, overall, we should find most differences in the direction of forwards faster. We can tolerate a small number of large differences in the other direction, or a large number of more moderate ones. The table for critical values of T will reflect this.

For instance, with $N = 10$, T must be less than or equal to 11 for significance at 5%, one-tailed. Therefore the *lowest* score (rank 1) and the *highest* score (rank 10) can be in the unwanted direction (and only these). T will then be 11 and we still have significance. On the other hand, the scores ranking 2, 3 and 6 can be in the wrong direction, as can those ranking 1, 2, 3 and 5, since, in each case, T is just 11 and therefore significant.

This demonstrates the weakness of ordinal data where we do not take into account the *amount* of difference involved. Have a look at the data in Table 16.2.

Table 16.2 *Therapy data*

	Decrease in aggressive responses after therapy	Rank	Increase in cooperative responses after therapy	Rank
Archie	17	8	16	7.5
Bill	13	2.5	2	3
Colin	−12	1	−14	5
Derek	18	9	1	1.5
Eric	13	2.5	1	1.5
Francis	15	6	4	4
George	14	4.5	19	10
Hugh	14	4.5	18	9
Ian	16	7	16	7.5
John	−43	10	−15	6

In both cases $T = 11$ and makes the result significant. The negative sign means the child has gone in the opposite direction to the trend. John and Colin have increased in aggressiveness and decreased in cooperation. John's increase is far more than anyone's decrease in aggression but the ordinal level of data just puts him 10th in absolute size of change.

Whereas a Wilcoxon T would lead us to reject the null hypothesis for both these results, a parametric (t) test would not, thus suggesting that to reject the null hypothesis would be a type one error, since parametric tests are the more powerful tests.

UNRELATED DATA – THE MANN–WHITNEY (U) TEST

CONDITIONS OF USE

- Differences or correlation   Differences
- Level of data   Ordinal; data must be meaningfully rankable

- Type of design   Unrelated
- Special notes   Where N is large (>20) see 'When N is large', below

DATA

Children's tendency to stereotype according to traditional sex roles was observed. They were asked questions about several stories. The maximum score was 100, indicating extreme stereotyping. Two groups were used, one with mothers who had full time paid employment and one whose mothers did not work outside the home.

Table 16.3 *Sex-role stereotyping*

Scores of children whose mothers:			
had full-time jobs **$N = 7$**	**Rank**	**had no job outside home** **$N = 9$**	**Rank**
17	1	19	2
32	7	63	12
39	9	78	15
27	4	29	5
58	10	35	8
25	3	59	11
31	6	77	14
		81	16
		68	13
Rank totals	40 (R_A)		96 (R_B)

Note that, since the design is independent samples, there is no requirement for samples to be equal in size.

Procedure	*Calculation on our data*
1 If one group is smaller call this group A	The full-time job mothers are group A
2 Rank all the scores as one group	See Table 16.3
3 Find the sum of the ranks in group A (R_A) and group B (R_B)	See Table 16.3 $R_A = 40$; $R_B = 96$
4 Use the following formula to calculate U_A: $$U_A = N_A N_B + \frac{N_A(N_A + 1)}{2} - R_A$$	$$U_A = 7 \times 9 + \frac{7 \times (7 + 1)}{2} - 40$$ $$= 63 + \frac{56}{2} - 40 = 63 + 28 - 40$$ $$= \mathbf{51}$$
5 Then calculate U_B from: $$U_B = N_A N_B + \frac{N_B(N_B + 1)}{2} - R_B$$	$$U_B = 7 \times 9 + \frac{9 \times (9 + 1)}{2} - 96$$ $$= 63 + \frac{90}{2} - 96 = 63 + 45 - 96$$ $$= \mathbf{12}$$

6 Select the smaller of U_A and U_B and call it U	Since $12 < 51$ then $U = 12$
7 Check the value of U against critical values in Table 5, Appendix 2.	Our two sample sizes are 7 and 9. We'll treat the test as one-tailed. For $p < 0.01$ the U has to be equal or to less than ($\leq$)9. Our value is not this low. The $p < 0.025$ critical value is 12 so our U just reaches this level.
8 Make statement of significance	We would report the result as significant with $p < 0.025$. If the test had been two-tailed we would report $p < 0.05$.

If there are many tied ranks you should use the formula given under the heading 'When N is large' further on.

SUMMARY

The test looks at differences between the sums of two sets of ranks. The value U is calculated from the two rank sums. The critical value gives the value of U, for the particular numbers in each group, below which less than 5% (or 1% etc.) of Us would fall if members of each group acquired their rank on a random basis.

EXPLANATORY NOTES

This test can be related to a very familiar situation in which we look at the performance of two teams. Suppose you were in a five-person school cross-country team, competing against a local school. You would have to be impressed if the other school took, say, the first four places with the last of their team coming seventh. The sum of their places is $1 + 2 + 3 + 4 + 7 = 17$. The total sum of places (1 to 10) is 55. Our rank sum must be $55 - 17 = \mathbf{38}$.

Imagine, instead, that members of the two teams each drew from the numbers one to ten placed in a hat. The Mann–Whitney, in a sense, looks at all the combinations of rank sums which are possible when doing this. By comparing our result (for U) with tables, we know whether our split in rank sums (17 against 38) is one which would occur less than 5% of the time, if we repeated the number drawing many times. In other words, the critical value is the point below which we start saying 'The other school's apparent superiority was not a fluke!', something which of course we would rush to admit!

Again we have the weakness that the test deals only with relative positions and not absolute scores. If all the first eight runners were neck and neck at the tape (rare in cross-country), then we would not feel so ashamed, at least, not in front of those watching the race. This is the point made in the chapter on 'Measurement', page 192.

As we said above, the weakness is that we are losing information in dealing with ordinal, rather than interval level data. If we know the runners' times, we could carry out a more sensitive test of significance. The tests which deal with interval level data are known as PARAMETRIC and we shall look at these in Chapter 17.

Figure 16.1 *The B team position looks good! – the logic of the Mann-Whitney test*

THE WILCOXON RANK SUM TEST

(Conditions of use are the same as for the Mann–Whitney.)

The procedure here is the same as for the Mann–Whitney up to and including the ranking of the data. From this point we simply take the lower rank sum (40 in our example of children and stereotyping), call this T and check this against the critical values in Table 6 (Appendix 2) for $N_1 = 7$ and $N_2 = 9$. We find, for a one-tailed test at $p < 0.05$ our T needs to be under 43, and for $p < 0.025$, our rank sum just matches the critical value ($N_1 = N_A$; $N_2 = N_B$).

Beware of getting this test mixed up with the Wilcoxon SIGNED RANKS test! If you remember there's only one of these two Wilcoxon tests in which signs are relevant, you should be OK.

When N for either sample is greater than 20, use the z-score conversion for large samples shown below.

Mann–Whitney or Wilcoxon Rank Sum?

Obviously the Wilcoxon test just given is a lot simpler than the Mann–Whitney. Is one preferable to the other? Not really. The reason Mann–Whitney is included is that it is popular, being the only test mentioned or included in several syllabuses and computer programmes.

WHEN *N* IS LARGE

Non-parametric rank tests use tables in which N, for either group, only goes up to a modest value of 20 or 25. For larger values there is usually a conversion formula which gives a z-score. For large samples, the values of Mann–Whitney U and Wilcoxon T, if performed many times on two sets of randomly produced ranks, would form normal-like distributions. For any particular U or T, we can find out where it would fall on that distribution in terms of a z-score. We want to achieve a z-score which cuts off the last 5% (one-tailed) or 2.5% (two-tailed) of the distribution. From the normal distribution table in Appendix 2 (and see Figure 14.7, on page 249), I hope you'll agree that a z-score of 1.65 does the former and 1.96 the latter.

The relevant formulae are:

Mann–Whitney

$$z = \frac{\dfrac{U - N_A N_B}{2}}{\sqrt{\left(\left[\dfrac{N_A N_B}{N(N-1)}\right] \times \left[\dfrac{N^3 - N}{12} - \Sigma T\right]\right)}}$$

where N = the sum of N_A and N_B and

$$T = \frac{t^3 - t}{12}$$

each time a number of values are tied at a particular rank and t is the number of times the value occurs. For instance, for the data in Table 17.2, the score 8 appears three times. $t = 3$ and $T = (3^3 - 3)/12 = 2$. This would then be repeated for 9, which occurs twice. This time $T = (2^3 - 2)/12 = 0.5$. This would be repeated for 10, 12 and so on.

Wilcoxon signed ranks (related)

$$z = \frac{N(N+1) - 4T}{\sqrt{\left(\dfrac{2N(N+1)(2N+1)}{3}\right)}}$$

where T is Wilcoxon's T calculated in the usual way.

Wilcoxon rank sum (unrelated)

$$z = \frac{2T - N_A(N+1)}{\sqrt{\left(\dfrac{N_A N_B(N+1)}{3}\right)}}$$

where T is calculated as explained in the rank sum method, N_A is the number of values in the smaller sample and N_B is the number in the larger sample.

GLOSSARY

Ordinal level test for differences between two sets of unrelated data – using U	____-_____	Mann–Whitney
Ordinal level test for differences between two sets of unrelated data – using T	_____ ____ ___	Wilcoxon rank sum
Ordinal level test for differences between two related sets of data – using T	_____ _____ _____	Wilcoxon signed ranks
Feature of data when scores are given identical rank values	____	ties (tied data)

EXERCISES

I Find out whether the following test statistics are significant, and at what level, for the one- or two-tailed tests indicated. You can put the probability value (*p*) achieved in the blank columns under 'sig'.

No. in each group N=	N=	U=	Sig. One-tail	Two-tail	T (WRS)=	Sig. One-tail	Two-tail	N=	T (WSR)=	Sig. One-tail	Two-tail
(a) 15	14	49			158			(c) 18	35		
(b) 8	12	5			68			(d) 30	48		

note: WRS = Wilcoxon rank sum   WSR = Wilcoxon signed ranks

2 Carry out the appropriate test (either Mann–Whitney or Wilcoxon signed ranks) on the data in:

a) Table 17.1 (in Chapter 17)
b) Table 17.2 (in Chapter 17)

and test the results for significance using one-tailed values.

Simple tests of difference – parametric

17

TESTS AT INTERVAL/RATIO LEVEL

Parametric tests are more **power efficient** (better at detecting genuine differences) but this is paid for by there being certain restrictions on what data can safely be submitted to these tests. The restrictions (i.e. assumptions) are:
- At least interval level data
- Homogeneity of variance (matters mainly where sample numbers are quite different in an unrelated design)
- Samples are drawn from a **normally distributed population**

The tests are also **robust**, meaning they can withstand some divergence from these assumptions and still remain reliable. The tests are:
- *t*-test for related data
- *t*-test for unrelated data

The related *t* test assumes the difference between means comes from a normally distributed population of difference means whose mean is 0. The variance of the differences between pairs of scores is used to estimate the variance in the difference mean population. *t* is the number of standard deviations (or 'standard errors') the obtained difference mean would be from the hypothetical mean of zero.

In the unrelated cases it is assumed that both samples come from the same population. The hypothetical underlying population referred to is a distribution of differences between two sample means estimated using the combined ('pooled') variance of the two obtained samples. The obtained difference between two means is compared with the standard error of this hypothetical distribution. Again, *t* is a measure of standard errors from the hypothetical mean of zero difference between two sample means. Critical values are in the same tables as for the related test.

PARAMETRIC TESTS

Some way back we discussed 'parameters'. Perhaps you'd like to try and remember what these are before reading any further, or to remind yourself by looking back to page 211. Here, anyway, is a redefinition. Parameters are measures of populations, in particular the mean and variance. Remember that the variance is the square of the standard deviation. Parametric tests are so called because *their calculation involves an estimate of population parameters made on the basis of sample statistics*. The larger the sample, the more accurate the estimate will be. The smaller the sample, the more distorted the sample mean will be by the odd, extreme value.

POWER

Parametric tests are said to have more POWER. Power is defined as *the likelihood of the test detecting a significant difference when the null hypothesis is false*, i.e. there really *is* a difference associated with the independent variable. Put another way, it is the probability of *not* making a type II error. Non-parametric tests require more data (more sets of scores, so more participants in the study) to reach the same power as parametric tests. Several things affect the power of tests:

• Type of test	Parametrics are more sensitive
• Making more accurate measurements	This, again is the emphasis on a tight procedure and clearly defined and measured dependent variable
• Having a one-tailed hypothesis	This lowers the critical value required for equivalent levels of significance

The comparison of the power of, say, a parametric and non-parametric test is known as POWER EFFICIENCY and is expressed as a ratio. You would encounter the mathematics behind this in a more advanced text. Non-mathematically speaking, efficiency is, in a sense, the savings made by the more powerful test in terms of finding more differences that are non-random differences and in, therefore, helping to dismiss 'no difference' assumptions.

It is important to remember, however, that parametric tests can't undo damage already done. If data has been collected poorly and/or there are just too few data (N is very low) then the greater sensitivity of the parametric test will not compensate for this. Very often the slight advantage of the parametric test can be neutralised, using a rank type test like those in the last chapter, by simply taking a few more participants for testing. Non-parametric tests also have the advantages of being usually easier to calculate and being more widely usable. As we shall see in a moment, parametric tests can only be used on special types of data.

You can see an example of the superior power of parametric tests at the end of this chapter on page 290.

The greater power of parametric tests comes from their greater sensitivity to the data. This in turn is because they use *all* the information available. They look at *size* of differences and values involved, not just ranks (order of sizes). They are more subtle, then, in their analysis of data.

This power and accuracy, however, has to be paid for. The tests make estimates of underlying population parameters. These estimates are made on the assumption that the underlying population has certain characteristics, mainly that it has a normal distribution. Such a distribution only occurs if the level of measurement we are using is at least interval. With interval-level data, certain sophisticated mathematical operations can be carried out which can't be done on ordinal data (ranks). These are the assumptions we must satisfy before proceeding with a parametric test:

ASSUMPTIONS UNDERLYING THE USE OF PARAMETRIC TESTS

1 The level of measurement must be at least interval
2 The sample data are drawn from a normally distributed population
3 The variances of the two samples are not significantly different – this is known as the principle of HOMOGENEITY OF VARIANCE.

Notes on assumption number:

1 We must make a decision about our dependent variable. Is it truly interval level? If it is an unstandardised scale, or if it is based on human estimation or rating, would it be safer to make it ordinal? Remember, data don't often get collected *as* ordinal. They often appear interval-like (plastic interval) but we *reduce* them to ordinal by ranking them.

2 This principle is often written in error as 'the sample must be normally distributed'. This is not so. Most samples are too small to look anything like a normal distribution, which only gets its characteristic bell-like shape from the accumulation of very many scores. A largish sample can be tested for the likelihood that it came from a normal distribution using the χ^2 'goodness of fit' test covered in chapter 15.

   In practice, for small samples, we have to assume that the population they were drawn from is a normal distribution on grounds of past experience or theory. It may be known, from other research, that the variable tested is normally distributed, or it may be possible to argue that, given what we do know, the assumption is reasonable.

3 Statisticians have further investigated this requirement, which used to demand very similar variances. Fortunately, we can now largely ignore it when dealing with *related* samples, without any great risk of distortion in our result. For *unrelated* samples we need to be more careful *where sample sizes are quite different*.

   A simple check for variance difference between two samples can be made by checking the two ranges. A thorough check involves use of the *F*-test, (see Chapter 20) which tests for the difference between two sample variances in much the same way as a *t*-test (see below) checks for a significant difference between the two means. Even this test is considered unsafe when the populations depart from normal distributions. (See Howell, 1992, from which you can get pretty complicated but reliable tests by O'Brien or Levene.) Hence, the safest thing is to try to get almost identical sample sizes in your project!

PARAMETRIC TESTS ARE ROBUST

The principles above are not set in concrete. One can do a parametric test on data which don't fit the assumptions exactly. The fact that the tests, under such conditions, still give fairly accurate probability estimates has led to them being called ROBUST. They do not break down, or produce many errors in significance decisions, unless the assumptions are quite poorly met.

COMPARISON OF PARAMETRIC AND NON-PARAMETRIC TESTS

Parametric	*Non-parametric*
More power; higher power-efficiency compared with non-parametric tests	Power often not far from parametric equivalent
	May need higher N to match power of parametric test
More sensitive to features of data collected	Simpler and quicker to calculate
Robust – data can depart somewhat from assumptions	No need to meet data requirements of parametric tests at all

PARAMETRIC TESTS AND THEIR NON-PARAMETRIC EQUIVALENTS

	Related design	**Unrelated design**	**Correlation**
Parametric	Related (or 'correlated')* t-test	Unrelated (or 'uncorrelated')* t-test	Pearson product-moment correlation coefficient
Non-parametric equivalent	Wilcoxon signed ranks	Mann–Whitney U (or Wilcoxon rank sum)	Spearman rho (ρ)

* Tests on related samples (repeated measures or matched pairs) are often referred to as 'correlated', because a value in one group is *co-related* with a value in the other group. The values come in related pairs. It is important *not* to let the use of this term fool you into thinking that a *correlation* test (see next chapter) is being performed.

THE *t*-TEST FOR RELATED DATA

CONDITIONS FOR USE

- Differences or correlation   Differences
- Level of data   Interval or ratio
- Type of design   Related
- Special note   Data must satisfy parametric assumptions

DATA

Participants were given two equivalent sets of 15 words to memorise under two conditions. In condition A they were instructed to form visual imagery links between each item and the next. In condition B they were instructed only to rehearse the words as they heard them. Participants had two minutes immediately after list presentation, to 'free recall' the words (recall in any order).

JUSTIFICATION OF USE OF *t*-TEST

- The data are of interval level status
- It is commonly assumed that recall totals in a free recall task such as this would form a normal-like distribution

- The standard deviations are quite different. However, this is a related design and therefore the homogeneity of variance requirement is not so important.

FORMULA

$$t = \frac{\Sigma d}{\sqrt{\left(\dfrac{N\Sigma d^2 - [\Sigma d]^2}{N-1}\right)}}$$

Note: There are several variations of this formula so don't get worried if you find another which looks different. This is the easiest to work with on a simple calculator. On the following page there is a version which is even easier if your calculator gives standard deviations, or you have them already calculated.

Table 17.1 *Word recall data*

Participant number	Number of words recalled in: Imagery condition (A)	Rehearsal condition (B)	Difference d	d^2
1	6	6	0	0
2	15	10	5	25
3	13	7	6	36
4	14	8	6	36
5	12	8	4	16
6	16	12	4	16
7	14	10	4	16
8	15	10	5	25
9	18	11	7	49
10	17	9	8	64
15	12	8	4	16
12	7	8	−1	1
13	15	8	7	49

$\bar{x}_A = 13.38$ $\bar{x}_B = 8.85$ $\Sigma d = 59$ $\Sigma d^2 = 349$

$s_A = 3.52$ $s_B = 1.68$ $(\Sigma d)^2 = 3481$

Mean of differences ('difference mean') $\bar{d} = 4.54$

$s_d = 2.60$

Procedure

1 Calculate the mean of the scores in each condition

2 Arrange the final results table such that the first column has the higher mean and call this group (or column) A. Call its mean $\bar{x}_A$. Call the other mean $\bar{x}_B$ and the group (or column) B (see note below)

Calculation on our data

See Table 17.1

See Table 17.1

3 Subtract each participant's B score from their A score. Call this d

See Table 17.1

4 Square the d for each participant

See Table 17.1

5 Add up all the ds (Σd) and all the d^2s (Σd^2)

$\Sigma d = 59$ $\Sigma d^2 = 349$

6 Square Σd. Note this is $(\Sigma d)^2$. *Be careful to distinguish between Σd^2 and $(\Sigma d)^2$!*

$(\Sigma d)^2 = 3481$

7 Multiply N (the number of pairs of scores there are) by Σd^2

$13 \times 349 = 4537$

8 Subtract $(\Sigma d)^2$ from the result of step **7**

$4537 - 3481 = 1056$

9 Divide the result of step **8** by $N - 1$

$1056 \div 12 = 88$

10 Find the square root of step **9**

$\sqrt{(88)} = 9.381$

11 Divide Σd by the result of step **10** to give t

$59 \div 9.381 = 6.289$ $t = 6.289$

12 Find degrees of freedom (df). For a related design this is $N - 1$ where N is the number of *pairs of values*

$13 - 1 = 12$

13 Find the largest value of t in Table 8, Appendix 2, given the degrees of freedom and appropriate number of tails, which does not exceed our obtained value of t. Make significance statement

Critical value for $p < 0.01$ is 3.055, assuming a two-tailed test. The table goes no higher than this. Our value of 6.289 easily exceeds it. Therefore, the probability of our t value occurring by chance alone is at least as low as 0.01 and probably a lot lower. The difference is therefore highly significant.

Note on step 2: if your hypothesis is one-tailed (you already *expect* one mean to be higher than the other from your research theory and aims) then there is no need to arrange the columns this way. Just take the values you predict to be lower from the other values. If you're wrong, and the results, in fact, go the other way (the *other* mean is the higher) then your t value will arrive with a negative sign (and you can't, anyway, have a significant result).

PROCEDURE WITH AUTOMATIC CALCULATION OF STANDARD DEVIATION

If your calculator gives you the standard deviation of a set of values directly there is a far easier route to t. This is:

$$t = \frac{\bar{d}}{\sqrt{s^2/N}}$$

1 Find the standard deviation of the differences, using the population estimate version. In the example above $s = 2.60$

2 Find s^2 (This is the *variance* of the differences) ($= 6.76$)

3 Divide s^2 by N ($= 0.52$)

4 Find the square root of step **3** (= 0.721)

5 Divide the mean of the differences ($\bar{d}$) by the result of step **4** (t = 6.297)

EXPLANATORY NOTES

The basis of this test can be understood by assuming the position of the null hypothesis. This says, in effect, that there is no difference between sample means. Let's look at what would happen if there really *were* no difference. Then we can see whether our result looks similar to those expected when there is no difference between conditions.

   Since this is rather a complex argument, I would suggest that you take it in small steps, stopping every so often to review where we've got to.

   1 First, let's find a situation where a null hypothesis *is* true. We have two equally difficult word lists. We test a sample of people on their ability to learn and recall both lists, using counterbalancing of course.

   2 If there is no difference between the lists, then people's performance should theoretically be exactly the same on each. But in real life there are always minor differences (random errors). We find that list one is recalled marginally better. We show this by looking at the mean of the differences, (from now on we'll call this a 'difference mean') just as in Table 17.1. Theoretically, the difference mean should be zero.

   3 We take a second group and test them. This time there is a minor difference in the opposite direction. The difference mean is negative instead of positive.

   4 We repeat this process over and over again on perhaps 200 samples of people. (Don't worry, this is statistical talk – no one ever really does this or needs to. We work from estimates!) Very many of the difference means will be small, half one side and half the other side of zero. Fewer will be large but these will still occur evenly either side of zero.

   5 We plot the distribution formed by all the difference means and obtain the curve shown in Figure 17.1. This is called a SAMPLING DISTRIBUTION of difference means.

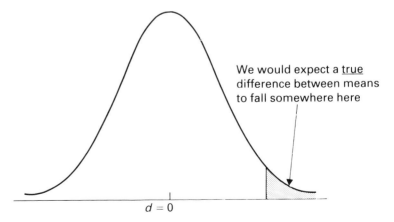

Figure 17.1 *Sampling distribution of difference means*

   6 The standard deviation of a sampling distribution is known as the STANDARD ERROR. If we knew this value we could compare any particular difference mean with it and get something similar to a *z*-score. We could see how many standard deviations (or 'errors') our particular difference mean was from the theoretical mean of zero.

7 Statisticians reckon they can *estimate* theoretically the standard error of such a distribution, from a particular sample, by taking the square root of s^2/N, where s^2 is the sample variance. This is what we did in the quick formula for *t* above, in fact. The operation there went on to divide *our* difference mean by the standard error to give *t*. *t* is therefore *the number of standard errors our difference mean is from zero* in the middle of the theoretical distribution.

8 As you may well have guessed, the objective, when we test a hypothesis, is to see whether our particular difference mean falls within the most extreme 5% of difference means which could be expected. For a one-tailed test, that's the right-hand 5% of the curve in Figure 17.1.

9 Suppose for every one of the 200-odd samples we took the calculated *t*. These values (which are quite like *z*-scores) would themselves form a distribution. The curve formed would be a familiar shape. If *df* for our samples was fairly large, the curve would look normally distributed. For lower *df* the curve would be a bit flatter and a bit wider. The important thing is that the *t*-curve is the same shape and has the same values, no matter what value the actual variables measured were. It's shape depends solely on *df*. It is, after all, based only on a *ratio* between standard deviations and particular deviations.

We are indebted to William Gosett for the theory behind *t* and its distributions. He worked for Guinness who, at that time, did not permit its workers to publish findings connected with their company work. Hence, he published under the pseudonym of Student and the distribution statistic is known as Student's *t*.

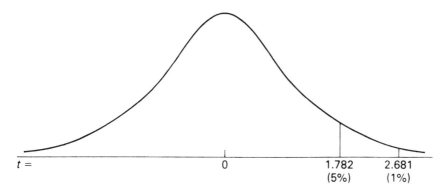

Figure 17.2 *t-curve for df* = 12

10 The *t*-curve for *df* = 12 will look something like Figure 17.2, with the one-tailed values for 5% and 1% significance shown on it. We simply want to compare our *t* with this as we would a *z*-score on a normal distribution. The job is one of consulting tables rather than actual curves, however. The values for *t* with different *df* are given in Table 8 in Appendix 2. Notice how similar the values for *t* are to *z* when *df* becomes relatively large.

The table shows us the distribution expected when the null hypothesis is true. *t*-tests for people performing on our two equivalent lists should fall into this pattern. However, if, as in our imaginery experiment, we are predicting that the operation of an independent variable will create a significant difference between two recall conditions, our *t* must simply be *larger* than the critical value at the 5% or 1% end of the distribution.

THE *T*-TEST FOR UNRELATED DATA

CONDITIONS FOR USE

• Differences or correlation	Differences
• Level of data	Interval or ratio
• Type of design	Unrelated
• Special note	Data must satisfy parametric assumptions

DATA

12 participants were asked to use visual image linking in memorising a list of 15 words. 13 participants were asked to use only rehearsal on the same list of words. Participants used free recall to demonstrate retention.

Table 17.2 *Imagery/rehearsal recall data*

Number of words correctly recalled in:			
Group A (N = 12) (score = x_A)	x_A^2	**Group B** (N = 13) (score = x_B)	x_B^2
12	144	12	144
18	324	9	81
12	144	12	144
10	100	8	64
10	100	10	100
14	196	8	64
14	196	7	49
18	324	13	169
12	144	16	256
8	64	11	121
14	196	15	225
14	196	13	169
		9	81
$\Sigma x_A = 156$	$\Sigma x_A^2 = 2128$	$\Sigma x_B = 143$	$\Sigma x_B^2 = 1667$
$\bar{x}_A = 13$		$\bar{x}_B = 11$	
$(\Sigma x_A)^2 = 24336$		$(\Sigma x_B)^2 = 20449$	
$s_A = 3.015$		$s_B = 2.799$	

JUSTIFICATION OF USE OF *T*-TEST

• The data are of interval level status
• It is commonly assumed that recall totals in a free-recall task such as this would

form a near normal distribution
• The standard deviations are not very different. Even if they were, sample numbers
  are very close and therefore the homogeneity of variance requirement is not so
  important.

FORMULA

Unrelated $t =$

$$\frac{|\bar{x}_A - \bar{x}_B|}{\sqrt{\left[\frac{\left(\sum x_A^2 - \frac{(\sum x_A)^2}{N_A}\right) + \left(\sum x_B^2 - \frac{(\sum x_B)^2}{N_B}\right)}{(N_A + N_B - 2)}\right] \left[\frac{N_A + N_B}{(N_A)(N_B)}\right]}}$$

This is about the most complex formula with the greatest number of steps, in the
book, so do try to be careful and patient!

Procedure	*Calculation on our data*
1 Add up all the scores (x_A) in group A to give Σx_A	See Table 17.2
2 Add up all the squares of group A scores (x_A^2) to give Σx_A^2	See Table 17.2
3 Square the result of step **1** to give $(\Sigma x_A)^2$. Again, be careful to distinguish this from Σx_A^2	See Table 17.2
4 Divide the result of step **3** by N_A (number of results in group A)	$24336 \div 12 = 2028$
5 Subtract result of step **4** from result of step **2**	$2128 - 2028 = 100$
Steps **6–8** Repeat steps **1** to **3** on the group B scores to give: Σx_B (step **6**), Σx_B^2 (step **7**) and $(\Sigma x_B)^2$ (step **8**)	See Table 17.2
9 Divide the result of step **8** by N_B (number of results in group B)	$20449 \div 13 = 1573$
10 Subtract result of step **9** from result of step **7**	$1667 - 1573 = 94$
11 Add the results of steps **5** and **10**	$100 + 94 = 194$
12 Divide the result of step **11** by $(N_A + N_B - 2)$	$194 \div (12 + 13 - 2) = 194 \div 23 = 8.435$
13 Multiply the result of step **12** by $\dfrac{N_A + N_B}{N_A \times N_B}$	$8.435 \times \dfrac{(12 + 13)}{12 \times 13} = 8.435 \times \dfrac{25}{156}$ $= 8.435 \times 0.16 = \mathbf{1.35}$
14 Find the square root of the result of step **13**	$\sqrt{1.35} = 1.162$

15 Find the difference between the two means: $\bar{x}_A - \bar{x}_B$	$13 - 11 = 2$
16 Divide the result of step **15** by the result of step **14** to give t	$2 \div 1.162 = 1.721$ Therefore $t = \mathbf{1.721}$
17 Calculate degrees of freedom when $df = N_A + N_B - 2$	$12 + 13 - 2 = 23$
18 Consult Table 8, Appendix 2 and make significance statement as for related t	For a one-tailed test, with $df = 23$, the critical value of t is 1.714 for significance with $p < 0.05$. Hence, our result is significant (by the narrowest of margins!). Note, for a two-tailed test significance would not be achieved.

EXPLANATORY NOTES

Much of the reasoning here is similar to that for the related t. It might help to clarify the reasoning behind the unrelated t with a concrete, non-psychology example.

Suppose you have recently bought two lots of a dozen or so screws from a local shop. You suspect that the second lot are, on the whole, shorter than the first lot. You return to the shopkeeper who assures you that the two lots are from the same stock. This position is that of the null hypothesis. It proposes that the difference between the means of the two samples is caused by random fluctuations in screw length alone, all screws being from the same population. Your position is like that of the experimental hypothesis which holds that the second lot of screws came from a population with a lower mean. The t-test result tells us to what extent our two samples need to differ in order to reject the null hypothesis.

Suppose we did this many times:

1 Take two random samples from one population of screws (i.e. all those in one stock carton)

2 Take the mean of each sample

3 Take the difference between these two means taking the second from the first mean

4 Repeat steps **1** to **3** very many times, always taking the second from the first mean

Figure 17.3 *How not to decide significance – calculate a* t *test and use tables instead!*

If we plotted all the differences between the two means we would obtain a *sampling distribution of the difference between two means*, looking pretty much like Figure 17.1, again.

The differences would mostly be small, rarely large, and could be in either direction, negative or positive. They would centre around zero then. The distribution has a standard error, estimated from the pooled variances of the two samples. The difference we obtained is divided by this to find out how many standard errors our difference is from the hypothetical mean difference of zero. This division gives us our *t* statistic. Again, we reject the null hypothesis when *t* is large enough. If you look at the rather nasty unrelated *t* formula, you can see that the difference between means is on top and therefore, underneath is the estimate of standard error for the hypothetical distribution.

If the null hypothesis is rejected, after carrying out a test on the two shop samples, we assume that the two samples do indeed come from two separate distributions arranged something like Figure 17.4.

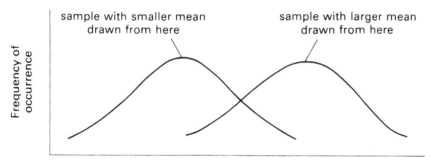

Figure 17.4 *Two separate populations*

We might now question our shopkeeper further and he might of course claim that your discrepancy is 'just one of those things'. It might be a coincidence, of course, but we have shown the probability of it being so is less than 0.05. If the shopkeeper plays by the rules of social science a further investigation might be made. Perhaps an assistant made a mistake. Perhaps a newly opened carton really does have a lower mean than the previous carton. We could take another sample from here, and one from the old one, in a replication attempt.

SUMMARY – RELATED *T*-TEST

This looks at the mean of differences (difference mean) between pairs of related values. Using the variance of the differences, it estimates the standard error of a sampling distribution of similar difference means. The null hypothesis assumes that the mean of this sampling distribution would be zero. The *t*-value given is the number of standard errors the obtained difference mean is from zero. The critical value from tables is the value *t* must reach or exceed for significance.

SUMMARY – UNRELATED *T*-TEST

This looks at the difference between the two means of two sets of unrelated values. It estimates, using the pooled variance of both sets, the likely standard error of a sampling distribution of differences between two means drawn from the hypothetical distribution implied by the null hypothesis, which has a mean of zero. *t* is the number of standard errors away from zero the obtained difference between means is on this distribution. The critical value from tables is the value t must reach or exceed for significance.

POWER EFFICIENCY REVISITED – COMPARING OUR *T*-TEST RESULT WITH A NON-PARAMETRIC TEST

We looked at power efficiency earlier in the chapter. We said that parametric tests had greater power and that the probability estimates given by them have greater validity. Where the margin of significance is quite small (our obtained value only just exceeds the critical value), the non-parametric test equivalent may not show significance, hence we may make a type two error with the latter test.

If you rank the values in Table 17.2, and then add the ranks up for each group, you will find that the lower of these two sums is 140. If you look in the tables for the Wilcoxon rank sum test, with smaller N being 12 and larger N being 13, you'll find that we must not exceed 125 for significance at $p = 0.05$, one-tailed. Yet the t-test we conducted told us that the result was just significant.

In some circumstances it is also possible for a non-parametric test to show significance when a parametric test wouldn't.

As an exercise for the end of this chapter, try conducting the appropriate t-test and a Wilcoxon rank sum test on the table of data shown here which is for two unrelated samples.

13.4	13.1
13.6	13.1
13.2	13.1
13.7	13.6
13.7	13.4

You'll find that here the non-parametric test gives significance where the t value just fails to reach the critical value. What kind of error would a researcher be making if the (true) null hypothesis were rejected after use of the Wilcoxon?[1]

Notice that this error is possible because the rank test doesn't 'know' that the actual values are so close. Again we see the value of interval level data in taking account of actual distances between values, rather than mere positions.

GLOSSARY

Assumption to be satisfied by data before proceeding with a parametric test; this condition occurs when the two variances are not significantly different	_____ __ _____	homogeneity of variance
Relatively powerful significance test for data at interval level or above. The tests make estimations of population characteristics and the data tested must therefore satisfy certain assumptions	_____ ____	parametric test

---

[1] Type one error.

Likelihood of a test detecting a significant difference when the null hypothesis is false	_____	power (of test)
Comparison of the power of two different tests of significance	____ _____	power efficiency
Parametric difference test for related data	_____ _-____	related (correlated) t-test
Tendency of test to give satisfactory probability estimates even when data assumptions for the test vary somewhat from the ideal	_____	robustness
Hypothetical population distribution (often of means or differences between means) which can be estimated from sample statistics	_____ _____	sampling distribution
Standard deviation of a hypothetical sampling distribution	_____ ____	standard error
Parametric difference test for unrelated data	_____ _-____	unrelated (uncorrelated) t-test

EXERCISES

1 Comment on the wisdom of carrying out a t-test on the following two sets of data:

a)
17 23
18   9 (unrelated data)
18 31
16 45
    16
    18
    17
     6

b)
17 23
18 11 (related data)
18 24
16 29
12 19
15 16

For each of **a)** and **b)**, what is an appropriate non-parametric test?

2 A report claims that a t-value of 2.85 is significant ($p < 0.01$) when the number of people in a repeated measures design was 11. Could the hypothesis tested have been two-tailed?

3 At what level, if any, are the following values of t significant? The last three columns are for you to fill in. Don't forget to think about degrees of freedom.

	t =	N	Design of study	One- or two-tailed	$p \leqslant$	Significant at (%)	Reject null hypothesis?
a)	1.750	16	related	1			
b)	2.88	20	unrelated	2			
c)	1.70	26	unrelated	1			
d)	5.1	10	unrelated	1			
e)	2.09	16	related	2			
f)	3.7	30	related	2			

4 Two groups of children are observed for the number of times they make a generous response during one day. The researcher wishes to conduct a parametric test for differences between the two groups and their 'generosity response score'. A rough grouping of the data shows this distribution of scores:

	Number of generous responses						
	0–3	**4–6**	**7–9**	**10–12**	**13–15**	**16–19**	**20–22**
Group							
A	2	16	24	8	3	0	1
B	5	18	19	10	5	1	3

Why does the researcher's colleague advise that a *t*-test would be an inappropriate test to use on this occasion?

Correlation

18

CORRELATION AND ITS SIGNIFICANCE

Correlation is the measurement of the extent to which pairs of related values on two variables tend to change together. It also gives a measure of the extent to which values on one variable can be predicted from values on the other variable. If one variable increases with the other, the correlation is **positive** (near to $+1$). If the relationship is inverse, it is a **negative** correlation (near to -1). A lack of any correlation is signified by a value close to zero. Two major calculations for correlation are introduced:

- **Pearson's product moment correlation** – based on variance in two sets of scores. *r* is high when large deviations are paired with large deviations.
- **Spearman's rank correlation** – ranks the values on each variable and a special case formula uses differences between these pairs of ranks. The general case is to calculate Pearson's *r* on the pairs of ranks and this should be done when there are tied ranks.

Important points about correlations are:

- **Cause** cannot be inferred from the existence of a strong correlation between variables.
- **Strength** is a measure of association but **significance** assesses how unlikely such an association was to occur. This assessment depends on the size of *N*. When *N* is large, quite small correlation coefficients can be significant.
- **Scattergrams** can demonstrate the strength of correlation and whether the relationship has any peculiar properties.
- **Sampling** weaknesses may artificially increase or decrease a correlation coefficient.
- **Common uses** of correlation in psychology are:
  - *ex post facto* studies on two measured variables
  - reliability testing of scales, tests and questionnaires
  - factor analysis
  - twin studies
  - in **multiple regression** where several correlations are used as predictors of a target variable

Correlations for **dichotomous variables** are covered briefly (point biserial correlation and the Phi coefficient).

THE NATURE OF CORRELATION

POSITIVE AND NEGATIVE CORRELATIONS

Have a look at the following statements:

1 The older I get, the worse my memory becomes
2 The more you give kids, the more they expect
3 Taller people tend to be more successful in their careers
4 The more physical punishment children receive, the more aggressive they become when they're older
5 Good musicians are usually good at maths
6 People who are good at maths tend to be poor at literature
7 The more you practise guitar playing, the less mistakes you make

These are all examples of relationships known as CORRELATION. In each statement it is proposed that two variables are correlated, i.e. they go together in the sense that either:

   a) as one variable increases so does the other. For instance:

   The further you walk, the more money you collect for charity.
   The more papers you have to deliver, the longer it takes you.

or **b)** as one variable *increases* the other variable *decreases*. For instance:

   As temperature increases, sales of woolly jumpers decrease.
   The more papers you have to carry, the slower you walk.

The correlations of the type stated in **a)**, are known as POSITIVE and those in **b)** as NEGATIVE (someone once suggested the following memory 'hook' for negative correlation: 'as rain comes down so umbrellas go up', a common enough *negative* experience for British people!). There is a more graphic example in Figure 18.1 – but the seesaw will only be a negative experience for some readers.

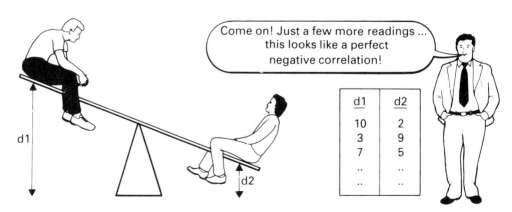

Figure 18.1 *A perfect negative correlation between d1 and 2 ... but is it a negative experience?*

Decide which of the proposed correlations (1–7) above are positive and which are negative.

Think of other examples of positive and negative correlation, in particular, two of each from the research you have studied so far.

SETTING UP A CORRELATIONAL STUDY

It is fairly easy to see how we could check out the validity of statement **6** above. We could have a look at school class-test grades or exam results for people who have taken both subjects. To test statement **3** we have a straightforward measure of variable one (height) but how do we go about measuring the second variable, 'career success'? Do we measure only salary or should we include a factor of 'job satisfaction' – and with what sort of weighting? We would need to operationalise our variables.

Describe *specifically* the two variables to be compared in each of statements **1** to **7** above, and how exactly you would *operationalise* them for precise measurement.

MEASUREMENT OF A CORRELATION

Statements like 'there is a correlation between severe punishment and later delinquency in young boys' or 'severe punishment and delinquency in young boys tend to correlate' are often made in theoretical literature. Actually the golden word 'significant' is missing from the first statement and 'significantly' from the second. Both fail to report the *strength* of the relationship. We can actually calculate the strength of correlation between any two measurable variables under the sun so long as there is some way of pairing values. Values may be paired because they belong to the same individual (for instance, maths and literature mark in class), or to larger or more abstract units (for instance, resources of school and exam passes, average temperature for the week and number of suicides in that week). When a correlation is announced in the loose manner above, however, it is assumed that the relationship is not coincidental or likely by chance alone.

The *calculation* of correlation between two variables is a *descriptive* measure. We measure the 'togetherness' of the two variables. Testing the correlation for significance is inferential.

The STRENGTH of relationship between two variables is the degree to which one variable *does* tend to be high if the other variable is high (or low, for negative correlation). This strength of relationship is expressed on a scale ranging from -1 (perfect negative) through zero (no relationship) to $+1$ (perfect positive). The figure arrived at to express the relationship is known as a CORRELATION COEFFICIENT or COEFFICIENT OF CORRELATION. This figure can be calculated for the relationship between any two variables and, as explained above, when it is stated that there *is* a correlation, what is meant is that the coefficient calculated is strong enough not to be considered likely by chance alone. Oddly enough, a fairly weak coefficient, as low as 0.3, can be counted as significant if the number of pairs of values is quite high, a point to be explained below.

It is not possible to obtain a coefficient less than -1 or greater than $+1$. If you do obtain such a value there is a mistake somewhere in your calculations (but this can't indicate an error in your raw data). The interpretation of the correlation coefficient scale is, in general:

Figure 18.2 *Scale of correlation*

Something might jar here. How can something getting more negative be described as getting stronger? Well it can. The sign simply tells us the *direction* of the relationship.

Warning for tests and exams!

It is very easy to call a *negative* correlation 'no correlation', probably because the two terms 'negative' and 'no' sometimes are equivalent. Here, beware! To assess strength of correlation *ignore the sign*. Negative correlation means the two variables are *inversely* related. *Zero* correlation means there is no relationship at all.

SCATTERGRAMS

One way to investigate the relationship between two variables is to plot pairs of values (one on variable A, the other on variable B) on a SCATTERGRAM, so named because it shows the scattering of pairs. The extent to which pairs of readings are not scattered randomly on the diagram, but do form a consistent pattern, is a sign of the strength of the relationship. I hope the scattergrams in Figures 18.3–18.11 will demonstrate this. The first three represent data from one person taken after each trial on a simulated driving task:

Data	
Number of trials	Points scored
1	27
2	54
3	78
4	105
5	120
6	149

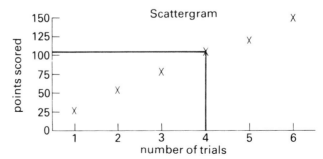

Figure 18.3 *Driving task-points*

In the first example (Figure 18.3) you'll see that the cross for the pair of values 4 trials/105 points is placed on a vertical line up from 4 on the 'trials' axis and on a horizontal line from 105 on the 'points' axis. All points are plotted in this way. For trials/points we get a picture of a strong positive correlation, for trials/time taken (Figure 18.4) a strong negative, and for trials/number of words spoken throughout

Data	
Number of trials	Time to complete route (secs.)
1	127
2	118
3	106
4	98
5	85
6	76

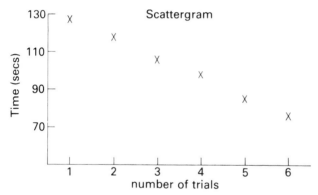

Figure 18.4 *Driving task-time*

Data	
Number of trials	Number of words spoken
1	20
2	4
3	13
4	24
5	5
6	15

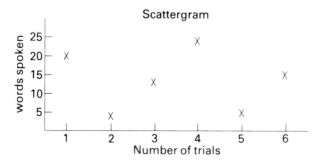

Figure 18.5 *Driving task–words spoken*

the trial (Figure 18.5) we get no relationship at all. Perfect correlations would take the shapes shown in Figures 18.6 and 18.7.

If there were no relationship at all between two variables, we could end up with

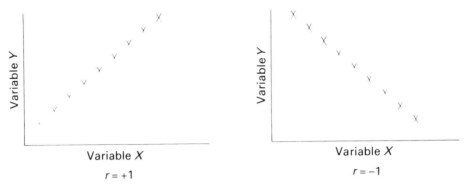

Figure 18.6 *Perfect positive correlation*   Figure 18.7 *Perfect negative correlation*

scattergrams as shown in Figures 18.8 and 18.9.

In Figure 18.8 we have no relationship because variable Y does not change in any way that is related to changes in variable X. Another way of putting this is to say that changes in Y are not at all predictable from changes in X.

In Figure 18.9 we have no relationship because variable Y stays the same value no matter what changes occur in variable X. If X were time and Y were body temperature, this is the relationship we might expect in a healthy, calm and motionless person.

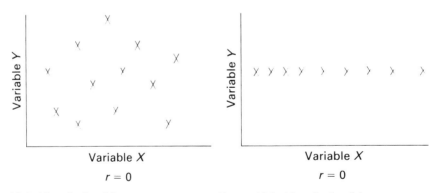

Figure 18.8 *No relationship*   Figure 18.9 *No relationship*

DOES $r = 0$ ALWAYS MEAN NO RELATIONSHIP?

Why bother to plot the values if the size of r tells us the strength of the relationship? There are several patterned relationships which might show up on a scattergram when our calculation of r gives us near zero. Look, for instance, at Figures 18.10 and 18.11:

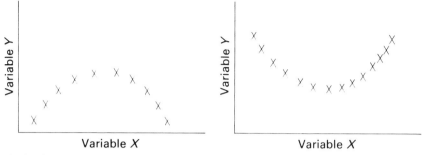

Figure 18.10 *Curvilinear relationship*   Figure 18.11 *Curvilinear relationship*

These are called CURVILINEAR relationships for obvious reasons. What might show this relationship? What about temperatures and months of the year? Is there a good psychological example? Fr.ud argued that the more one was *under*-gratified or the more one was *over*-gratified, the more likelihood there was of fixation at a psychosexual stage. People perform worse on memory tasks both when there has been extreme sensory deprivation and with sensory overload. One's interest in a task might increase then wane with increasing practice.

1 Draw the scattergrams for the other tables of data in this chapter (Tables 18.1, 18.4 and 18.5).

2 Can you think of other relationships between variables which might be curvilinear?

CALCULATING CORRELATION COEFFICIENTS

The two most frequently used coefficients are:

Name	Symbol	Level of data used with
Pearson	r	Interval/Ratio (PARAMETRIC test)
Spearman	ρ*	Ordinal (NON-PARAMETRIC test)

*pronounced 'ro', this is the Greek letter rho and is also often written as r_s.

CALCULATING CORRELATION

PEARSON'S PRODUCT–MOMENT CORRELATION COEFFICIENT

CONDITIONS FOR USE

- Differences or correlation Correlation
- Level of data Interval/ratio
- Type of design Related (correlations are by definition)
- Special note Data must be in the form of related pairs of scores

The grand title of this coefficient might make you feel that this could just be a little complicated . . . and you'd be right! There is, however, a simple way of starting out. One formula for Pearson's *r* is:

$$r = \frac{\Sigma(z_x z_y)}{N-1}$$

where z_x is the standard score (or z-score) for the first value (variable X) in each pair, and z_y is the z-score for the second value (variable Y).

Suppose we were testing the validity of a new reading test by comparing it with an older version. We expect children to score roughly the same on both tests.

Table 18.1 *Reading test results*

Child No.	Score on old test (X)	Deviation from mean (d)	z_x*	Score on new test (Y)	Deviation from mean (d)	z_y	$z_x z_y$
1	67	10.4	0.87	65	5.7	0.41	0.36
2	72	15.4	1.29	84	24.7	1.78	2.29
3	45	−11.6	−0.97	51	−8.3	−0.60	0.58
4	58	1.4	0.12	56	−3.3	−0.24	−0.03
5	63	6.4	0.54	67	7.7	0.55	0.30
6	39	−17.6	−1.48	42	−17.3	−1.24	1.84
7	52	−4.6	−0.39	50	−9.3	−0.67	0.26
	$\bar{X} = 56.6$ $s_x = 11.9$			$\bar{Y} = 59.3$ $s_y = 13.9$			$\Sigma(z_x z_y) = 5.6$

$$\text{Pearson's } r = \frac{5.6}{6} = 0.93$$

*Just to remind you: a z-score is the number of standard deviations a particular value is away from the mean. On the old test, the sd is 11.9, child number one's score of 67 is 10.4 points from the mean of 56.6 and this is 10.4/11.9 standard deviations. Think in units of 11.9 – how many 11.9s is it away from the mean? This gives the standard (z) score of 0.87

So Pearson's r just takes each pair of z-scores and multiplies them, adds this lot up and then divides by $N-1$. There is a complicated-looking formula for doing this which removes the problem of calculating z-scores, however, and which can be used straight away (with a calculator) from Table 18.2.

a) $$r = \frac{N\Sigma(XY) - \Sigma X \Sigma Y}{\sqrt{[N\Sigma X^2 - (\Sigma X)^2][N\Sigma Y^2 - (\Sigma Y)^2]}}$$

but if you have already calculated your deviations and standard deviations:

b) $$r = \frac{\Sigma(X - \bar{X})(Y - \bar{Y})}{(N-1)s_X s_Y}$$

is a lot easier. Note that s_X and s_Y are the population estimate forms of the standard deviation (using $N-1$ as denominator) as explained in Chapter 13.

Procedure using version a	*Calculation on our data*
1 Find ΣX and $(\Sigma X)^2$	See column A, Table 18.2
2 Add all X^2 to get ΣX^2	See column B, Table 18.2
3 Multiply ΣX^2 (step 2 result) by N	$23256 \times 7 = 162792$

Table 18.2 *Reading test values for calculating* r *by hand*

Column: Child number	A Score X	B (Score X)^2	C Score Y	D (Score Y)^2	E (X × Y)
1	67	4489	65	4225	4355
2	72	5184	84	7056	6048
3	45	2025	51	2601	2295
4	58	3364	56	3136	3248
5	63	3969	67	4489	4221
6	39	1521	42	1764	1638
7	52	2704	50	2500	2600

$\Sigma X = 396$ $\Sigma X^2 = 23256$ $\Sigma Y = 415$ $\Sigma Y^2 = 25771$ $\Sigma XY = 24405$
$(\Sigma X)^2 = 156816$ $(\Sigma Y)^2 = 172225$

4 Subtract $(\Sigma x)^2$ from step **3** result　　$162792 - 156816 = 5976$

5 to **8** Repeat steps **1** to **4** on the Y　　See columns C and D, Table 18.2
　　data　　$25771 \times 7 = 180397$
　　　　$180397 - 172225 = 8172$

9 Multiply step **4** result by step **8**　　$5976 \times 8172 = 48835872$
　　result

10 Take square root of step **9** result　　$\sqrt{48835872} = 6988.27$

11 Multiply ΣX by ΣY　　$396 \times 415 = 164340$

12 Find ΣXY (multiply *each* X by its Y　　See column E, Table 18.2
　　and add the results)

13 Multiply step **12** result by N　　$24405 \times 7 = 170835$

14 Subtract step **11** result from step **13**　　$170835 - 164340 = 6495$
　　result

15 Divide step **14** result by step **10**　　$6495 \div 6988.27 = 0.929 = 0.93$
　　result
For the significance check, $df = N - 2$.　　$df = 5$, $p < 0.005$, one-tailed

As an exercise, try checking that Formula b produces the same result.

SUMMARY

Pearson's correlation coefficient (r) shows the degree of correlation, on a scale of $+1$ to -1, between two interval level variables where each value on one variable has a partner in the other set. The higher the value of r, the more positive the correlation. The lower the value (below zero) the more negative the correlation.

EXPLANATORY NOTES

The correlation calculation is based on the idea of dispersion (check back to Chapter 13 to revise this notion). Think of all scores in terms of their distance from the group mean. If there is a strong correlation then if a person is far above the mean on one variable they should also be far above on the other. Similarly, anyone way below the mean should be way below on the other. In general, there should be a match between each person's distance from the mean on both variables. If we *multiply* these distances from the mean ('deviations') then the *maximum* result would occur when there is a strong relationship because high will be multiplied with high (and even where the two distances are negative, the *result* will be positive). Look at the arrangements in Table 18.3 and you can see this happening with the different totals of the multiplied deviations. Imagine deviations on the A variable are the same each time.

Table 18.3

PERFECT POSITIVE			PERFECT NEGATIVE		WEAK RELATIONSHIP	
Deviation			Deviation		Deviation	
A	B	$d_A d_B$	B	$d_A d_B$	B	$d_A d_B$
3	3	9	−3	−9	2	6
2	2	4	−2	−4	−1	−2
1	1	1	−1	−1	1	1
−1	−1	1	1	−1	−2	2
−2	−2	4	2	−4	−3	6
−3	−3	9	3	−9	3	−9
Totals		28		−28		4

For the perfect positive, the highest deviations are matched with the highest and vice versa, resulting in the maximum product possible of 28. For the perfect negative, the opposite occurs and the maximum product occurs of −28. These two results would produce the highest and the lowest possible *r* values respectively. A random mixing of deviations gives an intermediate value of 4 which would produce a very low value for *r*.

In fact, the Pearson formula doesn't just multiply deviation by deviation because, if variance for either or both group of scores were low, then *r* would be low. Pearson uses the *standard scores*, and these take account of the standard deviations in the samples as well.

SPEARMAN'S RHO

CONDITIONS FOR USE

- Differences or correlation   Correlation
- Level of data   Ordinal
- Type of design   Related (correlations are by definition)
- Special note   Data must be in the form of related pairs of scores

DATA

The following fictitious data give students' maths and music class test grades. Columns C and D give the results in rank order form.

Formula: $r_s = 1 - \dfrac{6 \Sigma d^2}{N(N^2 - 1)}$

Table 18.4 *Class test results*

Student	A Maths mark	B Music mark	C Maths rank	D Music rank	E Difference between ranks (*d*)	F *d*^{2}
John	53	34	5	2	3	9
Julia	91	43	7	3	4	16
Jerry	49	73	4	5	−1	1
Jean	45	75	3	6	−3	9
Jill	38	93	2	7	−5	25
Jonah	17	18	1	1	0	0
Jasmine	58	71	6	4	2	4
						$\Sigma d^2 = 64$

Before starting on the Spearman procedure take a look at the squared rank differences in column F. If we are expecting people to score about the same on both tests, what size would we expect these values to be, large or small? What size would we expect Σd^2 to be then, if there is to be a strong positive correlation?

I hope you agree that, if there is to be a strong correlation between pairs of values, each of the differences (*d*) should be small or zero. This will indicate that students are scoring at about the same *position* on both tests. Σd^2 should therefore be small. Let's see how Spearman's approach incorporates this expectation.

Procedure

1 Give ranks to values of variable *X*

2 Give ranks to values of variable *Y*

3 Subtract each rank on *Y* from each paired rank on *X*

4 Square results of step **4**

5 Add the results of step **4**

6 Insert the result of step **5** into the formula:

$$r_s = 1 - \frac{6\Sigma d^2}{N(N^2 - 1)}$$

where *N* is the number of pairs★

7 Calculate r_s and consult Table 9★★

8 r_s has to be equal to or greater than the table value for significance at the level consulted

9 Make significance statement

Calculation on our data

See column C, Table 18.4

See column D, Table 18.4

See column E, Table 18.4

See column F, Table 18.4

Total of column F = 64

$$r_s = 1 - \frac{6 \times 64}{7(7^2 - 1)} = 1 - \frac{384}{336} = -0.143$$

$r_s = -0.143$

Critical value for $p \le 0.05$, where $N = 7$ and test is two-tailed is 0.786

Coefficient is not significant★★★

* *Do* watch the figure 1 here. Students often report wonderfully 'successful' results, about which they are understandably pleased, only to find that their result of, say, 0.81 has yet to be subtracted from 1.

** Note that in all other tests, the test statistic (t, U, etc.) is used on the way to determining significance. Correlation coefficients are also often used as descriptive statistics to indicate the strength of the relationship and may be used in other calculations as well (e.g. candidate selection in applied psychology).

***If we'd made a *one-tailed* prediction that the correlation would be *positive*, there would be no point even consulting tables since the negative sign here tells us that, whatever the size, the relationship found is *inverse* (i.e. negative).

When there are tied ranks

The Spearman formula above is technically for use *only* when there are no tied ranks. If ties occur the statistic becomes a weaker estimate of what it is supposed to measure. In fact, the formula is just a special case of what is done generally to correlate ranked values. The general approach is to carry out a Pearson calculation on the pairs of ranks. This is what you should do, then, if any values are tied. In Table 18.4 we would calculate a Pearson correlation on columns C and D. The resulting coefficient is still referred to as Spearman's r. Actually, the difference between the Spearman formula and using Pearson on the ranks, when there are ties, is rather slight, especially with large samples. For instance, with $N = 40$ and 75% of values tied the difference between the formula calculation and using Pearson on the ranks is around 0.001 or less. Statisticians however, are correct in insisting that the formula for Spearman is not correct when ties occur. This will not trouble the computer user but means a bit more work with a calculator.

WHEN *N* IS GREATER THAN 30

The table of critical values for r_s stops at $N = 30$. If N is larger than 30, r_s (or Pearson's r) can be converted to a t value using:

$$t = r_s \sqrt{\left(\frac{(N-2)}{(1 - r_s^2)} \right)}$$

t is then checked for significance with $N - 2$ degrees of freedom.

SUMMARY

Spearman's Rho r_s or ρ shows the degree of correlation between two sets of paired ranks on a scale of $+1$ (perfect positive) to -1 (perfect negative).

EXPLANATORY NOTES

As with the Wilcoxon signed ranks test, we are looking here at differences between pairs of ranks, one recorded on each of two variables. With Spearman's correlation, however, we don't want positive differences to be large to show an effect. Here, we want *all* differences to be as small as possible if we wish to demonstrate a strong, positive correlation. Consequently, the sum of the *squared* differences will be small.

DOES THE FORMULA WORK?

If you look at the formula you'll see that Σd^2 is the only value that can change. 6 is a number and N is fixed by the number of pairs of ranks in the sample. If there are no differences between pairs of ranks, Σd^2 is zero and the value to be subtracted from 1, in Spearman's equation, becomes zero, because $N(N^2 - 1)$ divided into zero is zero. Hence we get the perfect correlation coefficient of $+1$.

Table 18.5 *Anagram-solving results*

Participant	Anagrams solved	Rank	Seconds to solve first anagram	Rank	Rank difference d	d²
1	19	5	8	1	4	16
2	17	3	24	3	0	0
3	18	4	15	2	2	4
4	15	1	45	5	−4	16
5	16	2	32	4	−2	4
					$\Sigma d = 0$	$\Sigma d^2 = 40$

Let's look at a perfect negative correlation. In Table 18.5 you'll see that the *more* anagrams people solved the *less* time they took to solve the first one. Inserting Σd^2 into the formula we get:

$$r_s = 1 - \frac{6 \times 40}{5 \times 24} = 1 - \frac{240}{120} = 1 - 2 = -1$$

The perfect negative correlation gets the value -1.

ADVANTAGES AND DISADVANTAGES OF SPEARMAN'S RHO

The disadvantages are that the test is *non-parametric* and therefore suffers the associated weaknesses of these tests outlined in the last section.

The advantages are that it is easy to calculate and can be used on non-interval data.

SIGNIFICANCE AND CORRELATION COEFFICIENTS

Now we turn to a familiar theme. Consider the results for maths and music results in Table 18.4 and the reading test results in Table 18.1 above. I hope you'll agree that, whereas for maths and music it's pretty obvious (by an 'eyeball test') that nothing at all is going on in terms of a relationship, for the test scores above it's equally obvious that there *is* a relationship. The scattergrams in Figure 18.12 show this too.

The theme is that we can tell when a correlation is obviously significant (just as you could tell when the baby-sexer was successful) and you can tell when there is obviously nothing going on. How do we decide when a coefficient of correlation becomes significant? We need to know, for a particular number of score pairs (i.e. $N = 7$ in the two examples) the value of r above which just 5% of coefficients would occur if we were doing our calculations on randomly associated pairs. Let me clarify.

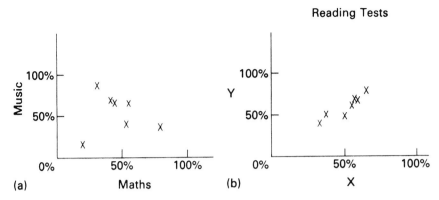

Figure 18.12 *Test score relationships*

Suppose we have obtained for some participants a piece of writing on 'Myself and my family'. You are to rate each piece for *self-confidence* whereas I will rate them for *warmth* in the feelings expressed by each participant towards their parents and siblings. We are predicting that the two ratings will be positively correlated. We rate by placing the pieces of writing in rank order on our two variables. We get the results shown in Table 18.6 with just three participants. We treat this as ordinal, ranked data.

Table 18.6 *Rankings of participants' writing*

	Self-confidence	Warmth
Participant A	1	1
Participant B	2	2
Participant C	3	3

The *strength* of the correlation is +1, perfect. But is it *significant*? How likely is it that my rankings would agree exactly with yours? In other words, what is the probability that I would produce my rankings by chance alone, for instance, by simply picking from a hat containing these three numbers?

Remember that probability is $\dfrac{\text{number of desired outcomes}}{\text{number of possible outcomes}}$

The rankings I *could* have produced are shown in Table 18.7.

The probability that I would produce the order I did (by chance) is therefore 1/6, because there were six possible rankings for me to produce.

Table 18.7 *Possible rankings on warmth paired with self-confidence*

	Your ranking on self-confidence	The possible rankings I could have produced:
Participant A	1	1 1 2 2 3 3
Participant B	2	2 3 1 3 1 2
Participant C	3	3 2 3 1 2 1

Expressed in the usual way, probability was therefore 0.167. This is not low enough to be significant. We require a value less than 0.05.

What happens if there are *four* participants and our two sets of rankings match perfectly? The ranks one to four can be arranged in 24 different ways. Therefore, the probability of a perfect match is now 1/24 and this gives $p = 0.042$ – a value low enough for significance.

In the case of five participants, the probability of a perfect match is 0.008. The probability of being just one rank out, as in Table 18.8, for instance, is $p = 0.033$.[1]

Table 18.8 *Five-participant correlation*

	Self-confidence	Warmth
Participant A	1	1
Participant B	2	2
Participant C	3	4
Participant D	4	3
Participant E	5	5
$N = 5$		$r_s = 0.9$

Probability of correlation of 0.9 = 0.033
Probability of correlation of +1 = 0.008

Therefore, total probability of either 0.9 or +1 occurring is: 0.041

Hence, the probability of getting either a correlation of +1 *or* of 0.09 is a total of 0.041. We can count the correlation in Table 18.8 as significant then, since the probability of it, or a higher correlation, occurring by chance is, in total, less than 0.05. The next possible value for the coefficient is 0.8 and the probability of this value occurring is far higher than 0.05.

The CRITICAL VALUE for Spearman's *r* when $N = 5$ then, is 0.09 (one-tailed).

When $N = 6$, tables give the critical value as 0.829 (one-tailed). If we had numbers one to six in two separate hats and drew one from each hat to create six pairs, the probability of achieving a correlation between these pairs of more than 0.829 is 0.05 or less. Another way of saying this is that if we were perverse enough to repeat this pairing operation very many times we would get a great number of low correlations and only 5% of results would be 0.829 or above.

For $N = 20$, however, the value which only 5% of results would exceed is as low as 0.38. As N increases so the distribution of the frequency of correlations lessens or 'bunches up', as I hope Figure 18.13 makes clear. The values for $N = 6$, particularly, would not form such a smooth curve in fact. There would actually be a discrete number of steps – values which r_s can take. But the rough outline of the shape the curves would take is as in Figure 18.13.

Notice that as N increases so the critical value for 5% significance decreases. This is, in itself, a negative correlation.

Note, too, that if, with $N = 6$, you predicted a negative correlation, as you might between say, self-confidence and feelings of dependence, then your calculated

---

[1] There are just four ways in which the warmth ranks can be arranged such that they are only one rank out from the self-confidence ranks. There are 120 ways of arranging ranks one to five altogether: 4/120 = 0.033.

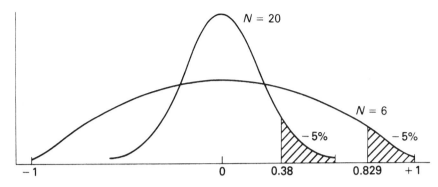

Figure 18.13 *Distribution of correlations when* N = 6 *and* N = 20

correlation coefficient must be *absolutely* greater than 0.829. For example, −0.93 would count as significant since it is more extreme, on the negative end of the curve, than −0.829.

BUT SURELY A *STRONG* CORRELATION MUST BE *SIGNIFICANT?*

Our natural inclination, I'm sure, is to feel this must be so. But reconsider what we've been looking at. It's *easy* to get a high-valued coefficient with low *N*. With three pairs we'd get +1 or −1 every one time in three trials so, by the rules of social science research and of common sense, we can hardly call these results *significant*, even though they're perfect in *strength*. On the other hand, as we saw just above, for the moderate sample size of 20, correlations above 0.38 will not be expected more than 5% of the time, and are therefore significant when they do occur, though weak.

THE GUESSING ERROR, VARIANCE ESTIMATE OR COEFFICIENT OF DETERMINATION

We have two problems now. One is that a rather low coefficient can tell us that two variables are significantly but only weakly connected. What does this weak relationship mean? What can we infer from it? The other problem is that correlation coefficients don't lie on a ratio scale. A correlation of 0.6 is not twice as 'good' or predictive as one of 0.3.

One way of converting these figures to a ratio scale is to square the value of the coefficient i.e. find r^2. Statisticians use this as a VARIANCE ESTIMATE, arguing as follows:

> Any set of scores (for instance, the set of reading test X scores) has a variation within it – what we know as the *variance*. The reading test Y scores also have a variance. Our r for these two sets of scores was 0.93 and r^2 would therefore be 0.86. It is now said that 86% of the variability in Y is predictable from the variability in X. The other 14% variability must be accounted for either by random performance errors or some difference between the new test and the old. The variance estimate is made using the COEFFICIENT OF DETERMINATION. This value is: $r^2 \times 100$, which is simply our value r^2 above, expressed as a percentage.

As another example of variance estimation, suppose you heard of a study which showed a correlation of 0.43 between amount of physical punishment given to a child (assessed by observation and interview, say) and a measure of aggression in the child.

You could assume that 0.18 (0.43 × 0.43) or 18% of the variation in aggression amongst the children studied was linked with ('explained by') the variation in the amount of physical punishment they had received. Remember though that we *can't* say that the punishment *causes* the aggression, only that the two are linked and aggression can be predicted, to a certain extent, from the punishment scores. All this is tied up with a topic known as REGRESSION which we'll discuss in Chapter 23 on the more complex statistical techniques available. Even if you're going to leave that chapter alone, it might be worth just reading the section on regression and prediction in order to understand the power and value of correlation more fully. In talking of the 'power' of correlation, let me just give you a flavour of how regression can be used. 18% predictability, above, may seem rather limited, especially when the coefficient of 0.43 seemed quite something. In MULTIPLE REGRESSION, however, it is possible to *add* the predictability power of *several* variables and thus get a far better predictive combination of variables. In predicting aggression, for instance, these might be, amount of violent television watched, attitudes of parents towards physical aggression, behaviour of siblings and so on.

WHAT YOU CAN'T ASSUME WITH A CORRELATION
CAUSE AND EFFECT

See if you can detect flaws in the following statements:

Research has established a strong correlation between the use of physical punishment by parents and the development of aggression in their children. Parents should not use this form of discipline then, if they don't want their children to end up aggressive.

There is a significant correlation between early weaning and later irritability in the infant, so don't hurry weaning if you want a good-tempered child.

Poverty is correlated with crime, so, if you can achieve a higher income, your children are less likely to become law-breakers.

In each case above it is assumed that one variable is the cause of another.

With any significant correlation there are several possible interpretations:

1 Variable A has a causal effect on variable B
2 Variable B has a causal effect on variable A
3 A and B are both related to some other linking factor(s)
4 We have type one error (i.e. a fluke coincidence)

A good example of situation **3** would be the perfect correlation of two adjacent thermometers, one in °C and the other in °F. The common factor is of course heat and one thermometer cannot affect the other. Similarly, physical punishment may be a method of control used to a greater extent by parents who are also those more likely to encourage or fail to control aggression *or* who tend to live in environments where aggression is more likely to flourish. There again, interpretation **2** is interesting. Perhaps aggression has a substantial hereditary base and children born with more aggressive dispositions *invoke* more physical methods of control from their parents – not an explanation I support, but simply a possibility which can't be dismissed.

When you are asked: 'A researcher concludes from a correlation result that . . . (A is the cause of B) . . . Could there be an alternative interpretation? – try B causes A as the alternative. Then try looking for common causes of both A and B. Visually, with the arrows representing causal direction:

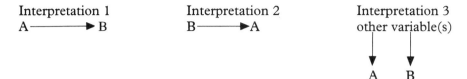

| Interpretation 1 | Interpretation 2 | Interpretation 3 |
| A ⟶ B | B ⟶ A | other variable(s) |

When cause is more likely

1 THE PRIOR VARIABLE – One variable may be *prior* to the other. For instance, if tall people were found to be more successful, success could hardly have affected their height. It may of course make them 'walk tall' and it certainly affects others' *perception* of their height as shown by American research indicating that people tend to significantly overestimate the winning candidate in presidential elections. But later success can't influence the genetic blueprint for the physical development of height.

A type **3** explanation is possible, however. Other genetic qualities of tall people might contribute to success in later life, not the height factor itself.

2 IN EXPERIMENTS – In a non-experimental correlation between two measured variables it is hazardous to claim that one of the variables is the cause of the other.

When a researcher conducts a highly controlled experiment in the laboratory, for instance on hours of food deprivation in rats and their errors in learning to run a maze, the independent variable can take several values and hence a scattergram of results like those shown in Figure 18.14 might emerge:

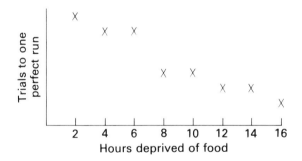

A positive or negative correlation?

Figure 18.14 *Scattergram of rats' learning results*

Notice, in Figure 18.14, that measurement of learning, by comparing errors made with time passed, typically produces a negative correlation shape as in this figure.

Similarly we might display words at varying brief intervals and measure the number correctly recognised each time. Here we can be more confident that A causes B, even though we've used a correlation. The correlation simply serves a statistical purpose – it demonstrates a *trend* between IV and DV. For the brief word display example, as display period increases, so do the number of words correctly recognised. The *design* is still experimental. We can make the same assumptions we make in a traditional two condition experiment about the independent variable affecting the dependent variable. Since the IV is altered first, the DV can't be causing changes in the IV, though, of course, a confounding variable could be.

The missing middle

By selecting certain groups to be included in a correlational study a researcher could appear to demonstrate a strong correlational effect. For instance, such a correlation might be announced between financial status and unwanted pregnancies, in that more unwanted pregnancies were reported from lower income households. This could be used politically *either* to blame the poor for a higher birth rate (along with the sin of being poor) *or* for a campaign against low incomes and for better sex education.

The actual facts, however, may have been obscured by biased sampling of only particularly low- and high-income families. Have a look at Figure 18.15:

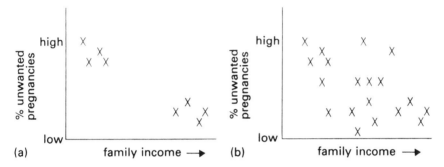

Figure 18.15 *Unwanted pregnancies/financial status*

The selective samples drawn (a) may show a strong correlation, but a more representative sample (b) won't.

An opposite effect may occur when the range is restricted in a different way, the 'range' meaning the whole possible continuum of scores on either variable. Suppose a company employed an occupational psychologist to assess candidates for posts using a battery of psychometric tests and also to compare these later with the productivity of those employed after one year in the job. Using the data shown in Figure 18.16 the psychologist might conclude that the test results aren't strongly related to later productivity, since the correlation calculated would use only that data on the 'selected' side of the diagram. Had it been possible to measure the productivity after one year of those *rejected*, however, the correlation now using *all* the data in the diagram, would have been a lot stronger.

Correlation when one variable is nominal

In general, if one variable is a purely nominal category type measure then correlation cannot be carried out, unless it is dichotomous, like male/female (see below). Consider the data in the first two columns of Table 18.9. Assume that we have asked separate people to rate different car owners for trustworthiness. The variable of car type is nominal. We can't *order* the car types meaningfully (unless value is relevant, in which case we could rank the values). The correlation of car type with average rating can't be carried out as the data stand.

Recall from Chapter 15 that χ^2 was called *a test of association*. As we've seen in this chapter already, correlation is *also* a measure of association between two variables. What we *can* do with nominal data, such as that on car ownership, is to reduce the *other*, continuous variable to nominal level and conduct a χ^2 test on the result. This is

Table 18.9

Car owned	% rating on trustworthiness	N	Number above mean	Number below mean
			(Trustworthiness mean = 58.99)	
Vauxhall	78	12	8	4
BMW	65	15	9	6
Rover	51	14	6	8
Citroen	62	17	9	8
Porsche	49	21	7	14
Jaguar	56	16	7	9
		95	46	49

only possible, however, where you have gathered several cases in each category. On the right-hand side of Table 18.9 imagine that 12 people assessed the Jaguar owner, 15 the BMW owner and so on. We can find the *overall* mean rating and, for each car category, record how many judgements were above this mean and how many were below. Then we can proceed with a standard 2×6 χ^2 test.

Correlation with a dichotomous nominal variable

The special case, mentioned above, is when the nominal/categorical variable has just two all-inclusive values. Examples would be male/female, car owner/non-car owner, pass/fail. Here, we are permitted to give an arbitrary value according to membership of the categories, e.g. 1 for female and 2 for male. The number can be any value, so 5 = pass, 10 = fail will do. We then proceed with the Pearson correlation as usual. The correlation is known as the *point biserial correlation* and is written as r_{pb}. This value can be turned into an ordinary t using the formula on page 304 which turned correlation into a t value. Significance is then found using $N - 2$ *df*. This may sound like a cheat because we emphasised earlier that Pearson's was parametric and that the usual assumptions about data needed to be made. This is true *only* if you want to make certain assumptions from your result about underlying populations which are mostly too complex for the level of this book. We will mention this again briefly though when looking at the assumptions underlying multiple regression.

To check this works, try finding out r_{pb} and the resulting t value, using the data in Table 18.9, and giving one value to each of the European cars (BMW, Porsche,

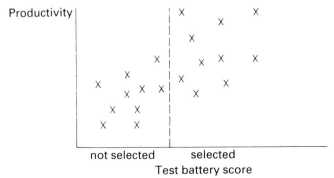

Figure 18.16 *Restricted range of test–productivity correlation*

Citroen) and another value to the remaining (sort of) UK cars. *Then*, calculate an independent t test on the same two groups. You should find that the t values are identical – not really surprising. Saying there is an *association* between type of car (the IV, measured in two groups) and trustworthiness scores (DV) is the same as saying there is a significant difference in trustworthiness rating between the two groups.

Truly or artificially dichotomous?

You might have reduced what was once interval level data down to a dichotomy, as we did above with the above the mean/below the mean calculation. Here the dichotomy is said to be 'artificial' because there is an interval scale lying underneath. If the dichotomies for two variables are both 'true' however (such as male/female), there is even a correlation for these, called ϕ.

The Phi coefficient

If *both* variables are truly dichotomous they can both be given two arbitrary values and a Pearson calculated again. The result is called ϕ, the PHI COEFFICIENT, and significance is even easier to test with this one because we get $\chi^2 = N\phi^2$ and we check in the usual way using $1df$. The resulting χ^2 is the same value we'd get from a $2 \times 2 \chi^2$ calculation on the data.

Why bother with association when difference tests give the same result?

Notice that a $2 \times 2\ \chi^2$ is like a collapsed correlation. Correlations and χ^2 are tests of association between two variables. In a 2×2 frequency table we simply don't have information about how the cases are separated (ranked or measured) *or* they *can't* be separated. The point of finding ϕ or r_{pb} is to look at the degree of *association* between our variables, on a -1 to $+1$ scale, rather than the differences (or the χ^2 value). Reassuringly, if we test *either* the association or the difference for significance we come to the same decision. There are also other, more advanced statistical reasons why these association statistics come in useful.

COMMON USES OF CORRELATION IN PSYCHOLOGY

Apart from the several uses already described, there are particular areas of research where a correlation is especially useful and popular.

Ex post facto studies

By far the most common use of correlation is in the sort of study where a sample is drawn and two variables are measured which already exist, i.e. the study is non-experimental. Examples have been given in this chapter but others might be: amount smoked and anxiety level; attitude on sexism and attitude on racism; locus of control and stress felt in job. This is why non-experimental studies are sometimes referred to as 'correlational' but, as I said in Chapter 5, this can be misleading because not *all* such studies use correlation, and correlation may be used in experiments.

Reliability

When testing for reliability, the test–retest method would involve taking a set of measurements on, say, 50 people at one time, then retesting *the same people* at a later date, say six months later. Then we perform a correlation between the two sets of scores. Tests between raters (people who rate) for their reliability of judgement would also use correlation, as would a comparison between two halves or two equivalent forms of the same test (see Chapter 9).

Factor analysis

This uses a matrix of all correlations possible between several tests (a 'battery') taken by the same individuals. Factors statistically derived from the analysis are said to 'account for' the relationships shown in the matrix.

Twin studies

Identical twins (and to some extent, fraternal twins) form an ideal MATCHED PAIRS design. Very often scores for twin pairs are correlated. This is of particular use in heritability estimates and was relied on very heavily in the IQ inheritance debate where a strong correlation between twins reared apart was powerful evidence for a genetic contribution. It was the *strength* of correlation for high numbers of twin pairs which first encouraged Leon Kamin to investigate Sir Cyril Burt's famous flawed data, but it was the uncanny coincidences in getting *exactly* the same coefficient, to three decimal places, with differing numbers of pairs, which led to allegations of fraud.

GLOSSARY

Relationship between two variables		**correlation**
Numerical value of relationship between two variables	_____	coefficient
Relationship between two variables which gives a low value for *r* because the relationship does not fit a straight line but a good curve	_____	curvilinear
Relationship where, as values of one variable increase, related values of the other tend to decrease	_____	negative
Relationship where, as values of one variable increase, related values of the other variable also tend to increase	_____	positive
Measure of whether a correlation was likely to have occurred by chance or not	_____	significance
Measure of the degree of matching measured by a correlation	_____	strength
Percentage of variability in one variable predictable from another using the correlation coefficient between them	_____ __ _____	coefficient of determination
Extent to which predictions of values of one variable are likely to be incorrect using values of another variable	_____ _____	guessing error

Technique in which the value of one variable is estimated using the correlation with several other variables	_____ _____	multiple regression
Parametric measure of correlation	_____ _____ - _____ _____	Pearson's product–moment coefficient
Measure of correlation between two *true* dichotomous variables	___ _____	Phi coefficient
Measure of correlation where one variable is dichotomous	___ _____ _____	point biserial correlation
Diagram showing placement of paired values on a two-dimensional grid	_____	scattergram
Non-parametric, ordinal level measure of correlation; correlation of ranks	_____ ___	Spearman's rho
Estimate of variability in one variable using variance of a correlated variable	_____ _____	variance estimate

EXERCISES

1 (From an article in the *Times Educational Supplement*, 3 June 1988)

> . . . teaching the sound and shape of letters can give preschool children a head start . . . children who performed best at the age of seven tended to be those who had the most knowledge and understanding of the three Rs at the age of four.
>
> In the case of reading, the strongest predictor of ability among seven-year-olds was 'the number of letters the child could identify at the age of four-and-three-quarters' . . . Tizard concludes that nursery teachers should give more emphasis to literacy and numeracy skills . . .

a) What conclusion, other than the researcher's, could be drawn here?

b) Briefly describe a study which could help us decide between these alternative interpretations.

c) What sort of correlation must the researchers have found between number of letters identified at four and number of reading *errors* at seven – *positive* or *negative*?

d) Suppose the correlation between adding ability at five and mathematical ability at seven was +0.83 (Pearson). How would you describe the strength of this coefficient verbally?

e) What level of significance would the correlation of 0.83 be at (one-tailed) if the sample of children had numbered 33?

2 Several students in your group have carried out correlations, got their results, know what significance level they need to reach, but have sadly forgotten how to check in tables for significance. They agree to do calculations on your data if you'll just check their results and tell them whether to reject or accept their null hypotheses. The blank column in Table 18.10 is for you to fill in.

3 Spearman's correlation can always be calculated instead of Pearson's. Is the reverse of this true? Please give a reason.

4 A researcher correlates scores on a questionnaire concerning 'ego-strength' with

Table 18.10 *Exercise 2*

	Coefficient obtained	$N =$	Significance level required	Direction Predicted	Accept or reject H_0?
a)	$r =$ 0.3	14	$p < 0.01$	+	
b)	$r = -0.19$	112	$p < 0.01$	−	
c)	$r_s =$ 0.78	7	$p < 0.05$	+	
d)	$r =$ 0.71	6	$p < 0.05$	+	
e)	$r_s =$ 0.9	5	$p < 0.05$	+	
f)	$r =$ 0.63	12	$p < 0.01$	no prediction made	
g)	$r =$ 0.54	30	$p < 0.05$	−	

measures of their anxiety level obtained by rating their verbal responses to several pictures. Which measure of correlation should be employed?

5 If a student tells you she has obtained a correlation coefficient of 2.79, what might you advise her to do?

Tests for more than two conditions

INTRODUCTION TO MORE COMPLEX TESTS

Three students are discussing a practical project which has to be of their own design. They've decided to investigate whether knowing a person's attitude to the environment affects our overall assessment of them, measured as 'liking'.

> *Tim*: So one group will hear that our fictitious person (let's call her Jane) cares about global warming and the other group will hear the opposite.
>
> *Helen*: Yes! erm, but . . . hold on a minute; wouldn't it be important, well, more interesting to have a control group, you know, a 'baseline measure' wow! Posh word!
>
> *Francesca*: OK, so the third group gets nothing at all . . . or should they have an alternative 'neutral' bit of information about Jane, nothing to do with the environment – like a placebo group? [Now level with Helen on Brownie points for jargon.]
>
> *Helen*: Maybe we should have the group with no information *and* the sort of placebo group . . . but hang on! How can we test for significance between more than two groups?

. . . and so on. Having more than two conditions in your research is pretty common. Very often it makes sense to have 'treatment' A, 'treatment' B, no 'treatment' at all and even the placebo 'treatment'. There are two problems which Francesca, Helen and Tim are going to face, one practical and one (more seriously) theoretical.

PROBLEM I – INCONVENIENCE

Think what test would be appropriate for testing for significant difference between assessment scores in the first two conditions which Tim mentions, before reading any further. The appropriate parametric and non-parametric tests are mentioned at the foot of this page[1]. Now, if the students are going to use this test for looking at significance between all their conditions just count the number of tests they'll have to conduct. The combinations of four conditions, taken two at a time, come to six, but they might also like to look at the difference between, say, the don't care-about-global-warming condition and all the other three together. Perhaps the other three are similar whereas the negative information produces lower evaluations of Jane.

---

[1] parametric = unrelated *t* test; non-parametric = Mann–Whitney or Wilcoxon Rank Sum

The first, and less important problem which the students face, then, is the sheer inconvenience and time involved in conducting so many *t* tests – not a huge problem if they can use a computer.

PROBLEM 2 – CAPITALISING ON CHANCE

The fundamental difficulty concerns what is often termed 'capitalising on chance'. If we conduct *several* significance tests we increase the probability that we will get a low probability (and seemingly 'significant') result by chance alone i.e., a Type I error. Suppose the null hypothesis is in fact true for a particular prediction. Changing the focus to sex differences in perception, let's assume males and females don't differ at all on colour recognition. If we select two random samples of males and females and test for difference, and repeat this process 20 times, we would expect to reach 5% significance on one of these tests. This is because that's just what our original significance estimate is based on – the critical value we have to reach (from tables) is calculated as that value which only 5% of tests would reach *if* the null hypothesis is true, that is, the samples only vary by chance from one another. We will discuss this issue a little further on under the heading of 'Error rates' on p. 337.

MULTI-LEVEL TESTS

All the tests we are going to mention in this section are designed to take this reasoning into account and to tell us when a *group* of samples (i.e. three or more) differ significantly among themselves. The tests we have already used for two samples are mostly just *special cases* of the more general tests introduced here. Some tests, properly called 'multi-variate tests', deal with the situation where a researcher uses more than one independent variable simultaneously. These 'factorial approaches' will be encountered in Chapters 21–23. For the non-parametric tests in Chapter 19 we will not dwell on the background theory for each test. We will simply learn how to use the tests and when they are appropriate. Readers wishing to go further should consult any of the commonly available books mentioned in the reference section at the end of Chapter 22. On page 379 there is a chart indicating the appropriate use of multi-level tests. Because ANOVA ('Analysis of Variance' – for parametric testing) is so widely and popularly used, I have included fuller explanations of the versions and calculations of this technique for investigating statistical differences among multiple samples and variables.

TRENDS

The fact of having three or more conditions in a research study introduces a new concept concerning the results. Not only might we wish to see whether the samples differ significantly among themselves, we might also wish to test the prediction that, as the level of the IV alters in one direction, so does the value of the DV. We might predict, for instance, that higher doses of coffee or amphetamines produce longer periods of staying awake or greater accuracy in vigilance tasks. We might predict that the therapy we are promoting produces more effective client improvement than, say, psychoanalysis, and that a control group with no treatment would fare worst of all. Such dependent variable relationships are known as *trends*.

Through most of this section we will work with the same set of data. Let's assume the students could test only four people in each condition. Obviously you would be advised to use more than this in your own investigations, but this low number will make all calculations a lot simpler to understand and learn from. Let's also assume the students used:

Condition A: person doesn't care about global warming
Condition B: no information about person's attitude on global warming given
Condition C: person does care about global warming

The data they obtained are displayed in Table 19.1.

Table 19.1 *Overall 'liking' assessment of Jane*
0 = negative (don't like at all)   12 = positive (like very much)

			Information given about Jane's attitude to global warming:		
Partici-pant No.	**Condition A** doesn't care	**Partici-pant No.**	**Condition B** no information	**Partici-pant No.**	**Condition C** cares
1	3	5	2	9	10
2	5	6	7	10	8
3	6	7	9	11	7
4	3	8	8	12	11
Sum	**17**		**26**		**36**
Mean	**4.25**		**6.5**		**9**

19

NON-PARAMETRIC TESTS – MORE THAN TWO CONDITIONS

This chapter introduces four new tests for non-parametric data categorised as follows:

- Unrelated
  - Differences: Kruskal–Wallis one-way analysis of variance
  - Trend: Jonckheere
- Related
  - Differences: Friedman
  - Trend: Page

The **difference** tests are used when we move beyond two sample designs. They will give the probability that two *or more* samples were drawn from identical populations (not populations with the same mean).

The **trend** tests assess the probability that the sample ranks increase significantly in the direction predicted.

All the rank tests lose a certain amount of power, weighed by the advantage that they are 'distribution free' – they can be used on data from any shape of distribution whereas parametric tests require a near-normal distribution pattern.

Unrelated designs

KRUSKAL–WALLIS – ONE-WAY ANALYSIS OF VARIANCE

CONDITIONS OF USE

- Differences or correlation   Differences
- Level of data   Ordinal
- Type of design   Unrelated
- Special note   Not to be confused with ANOVA – see next chapter

This is a generalised version of the Wilcoxon Rank Sum test, dealt with earlier. If we used the test, as described here, on the data in Table 16.3 we should come to the same conclusion about significance as we did when using the Rank Sum test. It will tell us whether *three or more* samples differ significantly among themselves. It tells us the probability that the samples were all drawn from the same population (the null hypothesis). If this probability is lower than the value we set (usually $p = 0.05$) we can reject the null hypothesis as likely to be false. Have a look at our data as arranged in Table 19.2:

Table 19.2

Partici-pant No.	1 Condition A (doesn't care)	2 Rank	Partici-pant No.	3 Condition B (no info)	4 Rank	Parti-pant No.	5 Condition C (does care)	6 Rank
1	3	2.5	5	2	1	9	10	11
2	5	4	6	7	6.5	10	8	8.5
3	6	5	7	9	10	11	7	6.5
4	3	2.5	8	8	8.5	12	11	12
Sum		$R_A = 14$			$R_B = 26$			$R_C = 38$

CALCULATION OF THE KRUSKAL–WALLIS TEST

Procedure

1 Rank all scores irrespective of sample

2 Add the ranks for each group and use them in the following equation:

$$H = \frac{12}{N(N+1)} \sum \frac{R_c^2}{n_c} - 3(N+1)$$

where $\sum \frac{R_c^2}{n_c}$ means take the sum of

ranks for each condition (R_c), square it, divide it by the number of values in that condition (n_c) and add the results of these operations together; N = total sample size

3 H can then be treated as a χ^2 value with
$df = C - 1$
C = no. of conditions

Calculation on our data

See columns **2, 4, 6** in Table 19.2

See the 'Sum' row in Table 19.2

$$H = \frac{12}{12(12+1)} \sum \frac{14^2}{4} + \frac{26^2}{4} + \frac{38^2}{4}$$
$$- 3(12+1)$$

$= (12/156 \times (49 + 169 + 361)) - 3 \times 13$

$= (0.07692 \times 579) - 39$

$= 44.525 - 39$

$= 5.537$

With 2 df (i.e. $3 - 1$), χ^2 must be $\geqslant 5.99$ for significance ($p < 0.05$). Hence we cannot reject the null hypothesis that all these samples come from the same population

JONCKHEERE TREND TEST

CONDITIONS OF USE

• Differences or correlation   Differences (trend across samples)
• Level of data   Ordinal
• Type of design   Unrelated
• Special note   Trend must be predicted

This is appropriate when we not only want to know whether three or more unrelated samples are likely to have come from different populations but also whether there is a significant TREND as the rank totals increase from lowest to highest. Of course, we need to predict here that the trend would go in a specific order and direction, i.e., lowest rating for 'doesn't care' and highest rating for 'does care'. We can't observe a trend *post hoc* (after the event) and then test for it. *It must follow from the theory we're attempting to support.* The calculations in this test involve you in quite a lot of simple counting and not a lot of difficult formula work.

Table 19.3

1 Partici-pant	2 Condition A	3 No. of greater values to right	4 Partici-pant	5 Condition B	6 No. of greater values to right	Partici-pant	Condition C
1	3	7	5	2	4	9	10
2	5	7	6	7	3	10	8
3	6	7	7	9	2	11	7
4	3	7	8	8	2	12	11
Sum		28			11		

CALCULATION OF THE JONCKHEERE TREND TEST

Procedure

1 For each score, count how many scores exceed it in any of the columns to its right. It's easier to start this process from the extreme left-hand column first. See columns **3** and **5**

2 The sums of these count columns are added to give a value called **A**

3 Now find the highest value that **A** could have been using the formula:

$$B = C(C - 1)/2 \times n^2$$

where

C = number of conditions and
n = number of people in each condition

4 Calculate: $P = 2A - B$

Calculation on our data

The first score, in column **2** is exceeded by 7, 9, 8, 10, 8, 7, 11 in columns **4** and **6**. The score of 7 in column **4** is exceeded only by 8, 10, 11 in column **6** – don't count the tied score of 7

Sum of columns **3** and **5**:
$$A = 28 + 11 = 39$$

$$B = (3 \times 2)/2 \times 4^2$$
$$= 3 \times 16$$
$$= 48$$

$$P = 78 - 48 = 30$$

Table 13 (Appendix 2) shows that with $C = 3$ and $n = 4$, P must be ≥ 24 ($p \leq 0.05$) so here we can *reject* the null hypothesis that the trend is a chance pattern, since our P is 30.

Unequal or large sample sizes

If the number of values in each condition is not always the same, or if n exceeds 10 you'll have to use the forbidding formula:

$$z = \frac{2A - \Sigma(n_i n_j) - 1}{\sqrt{\dfrac{1}{18}\{N^2(2N+3) - 3\Sigma(n^2) - 2\Sigma(n^3)\}}}$$

where N is the total of sample sizes, n is the total in any particular sample, and where $\Sigma(n_i n_j)$ means multiply all possible combinations of sample sizes, 2 by 2, and add the results. So, if the sample sizes were 4, 6 and 7 we would get $(4 \times 6) + (4 \times 7) + (6 \times 7) = \mathbf{94}$. Note, also, that here $\Sigma(n^2)$ would be $4^2 + 6^2 + 7^2 = 101$. z is a z-score and gets checked for significance, referring to normal distribution areas in the manner described in Chapter 14.

Related designs

FRIEDMAN

CONDITIONS OF USE

- Differences or correlation   Differences
- Level of data   Ordinal
- Type of design   Related
- Special note   Calculates a χ^2 known as Friedman's χ^2 or χ^2_F

This will be appropriate when the data are *related*. Assume that the data in Table 19.4 are from the *same* sample of three people but taken in three conditions. The test can be thought of as similar to the Wilcoxon signed ranks test but for three or more conditions.

Table 19.4

1 Partici- pant	2 Score on Condition A	3 Rank of column 2	4 Score on Condition B	5 Rank of Column 4	6 Score on Condition C	7 Rank of Column 6
1	3	2	2	1	10	3
2	5	1	7	2	8	3
3	6	1	9	3	7	2
4	3	1	8	2	11	3
Sum		$R_A = 5$		$R_B = 8$		$R_C = 11$

Procedure

1 Here, we first rank each person's scores across the three conditions. The first horizontal line (row) in the table represents the first person's scores and each row represents another person's set of scores

2 Find the sum of the columns of ranks

3 Insert the sums of the rank columns into the equation:

$$\chi^2_F = \left(\frac{12}{N_c(c+1)} \sum R_c^2\right) - 3N(c+1)$$

where c is the number of conditions, N is the number of rows (sets of related scores, e.g. people, in this case) and R_c is the sum of ranks in each condition

χ^2_F represents Friedman's χ^2

$df = c - 1$

Calculation

See columns **3, 5, 7**
Note: for person '1', their score of 2 (condition B) was lowest and gets rank 1, the score of 3 gets rank 2 and the 10 gets rank 3

See 'Sum' row in Table 19.4

$\Sigma R_A = 5 \quad \Sigma R_B = 8 \quad \Sigma R_C = 11$

$$\chi^2_F = \left(\frac{12}{4 \times 3(3+1)}[5^2 + 8^2 + 11^2]\right)$$

$- 3 \times 4(3+1)$
$= [12/48 \times (25 + 64 + 121)] - 48$
$= [0.25 \times 210] - 48$
$= 52.5 - 48$
$= \mathbf{4.5}$

$df = 2$, so the critical value required is 5.99 and our result is not significant for $p \leqslant 0.05$

PAGE TREND TEST

CONDITIONS OF USE

- Differences or correlation   Differences (trend across samples)
- Level of data   Ordinal
- Type of design   Related
- Special note   Trend must be predicted

This is appropriate when we not only want to know whether three or more *related* samples are likely to have come from different populations but also whether there is a significant *trend* as the rank totals increase from lowest to highest. As with the Jonckheere test, before it makes sense to conduct the Page test, the samples should have produced total rank scores which increase in the *predicted* order. Let's suppose we predicted that, in Table 19.4: *condition A scores < condition B scores < condition C scores*

Procedure

1 Rank data as in Table 19.4

2 Use the formula:

$L = \Sigma (R_c \times c)$

where R_c = the sum of a column of ranks and c is the predicted order

Calculation

From Table 19.4:

$L = \quad 5 \times 1$ (for column **3**)
$\quad + \quad 8 \times 2$ (for column **5**)
$\quad + 11 \times 3$ (for column **7**)

number of that column. We predicted condition **A** scores (and therefore rank total) would be the lowest, hence the predicted order for the **A** rank total is 1

$$L = \quad 5 + 16 + 33$$
$$\text{Total} = \mathbf{54}$$

From Table 14 (Appendix 2) we find that with conditions = 3 and $N = 4$ we need to equal or exceed 54 for significance ($p < 0.05$). So this trend test also just makes it to significance.

Notice here that L gets larger as it approaches significance because the higher numbered rank totals get multiplied by the higher numbered column numbers. If scores in column **2** had been, contrary to our expectation, higher than those in column **4**, then a relatively high rank total would have been multiplied by 1 rather than 2, thus lowering the possible value of L.

Large samples

if N is greater than 10 use:

$$z = \frac{12L - 3nc(c + 1)^2}{\sqrt{c^2(c^2 - 1)(c + 1)}} \quad \text{where:}$$

n = number in the sample and c = number of conditions.

GLOSSARY

Conducting several significance tests on the same data (or parts of it) so that the probability of obtaining at least one significant result increases above 0.05	_____ ___ _____	capitalising on chance
Test for significant differences between two or more related samples; data at ordinal level	_____	Friedman
Test for trend across three or more independent samples; data at ordinal level	_____	Jonckheere
Test for significant differences between two or more independent samples; data at ordinal level	_____-_____	Kruskal–Wallis
Test for trend across three or more related samples; data at ordinal level	_____	Page
Tendency for scores to rise in a predicted manner across several conditions	_____	trend

EXERCISES

I What non-parametric test is appropriate in the following circumstances?

a) A researcher wants to know whether there are significant differences between a group given a stimulant, a group given a placebo pill and a control group, in the number of errors they make in recognising briefly presented words.

b) Participants are asked to sort cards into category piles, first, when there are only two category piles, then when there are four categories and finally into eight categories. It is expected that time will increase across the three conditions.

c) Three groups of children are given sets of nonsense words, with typically French spellings, and later tested for recall. It is expected that French children will recall best, English children worst, with English children of one French parent falling in between these.

d) A group of participants are tested for hearing sensitivity in the morning, at midday and in the evening. Significant differences are expected between the sets of scores.

20

ONE-WAY **ANOVA**

The set of procedures generally known as **ANOVA** (analysis of variance) are powerful parametric methods for testing significance where more than two conditions are used, or even when several independent variables are involved. Methods with more than one independent variable are dealt with in Chapter 21 – 'Multi-factor ANOVA'.

One-way ANOVA is dealt with here and tests the null hypothesis that two or more samples were drawn from the same population by comparing means.

The test involves comparing the variance of the sample means (*between groups* variation) with the variance *within groups* (an average of the variances within each sample). If means differ among themselves far more than people differ within groups then the F ratio will be higher than 1 to a significant extent assessed from tables using the df associated with the 'effect' (the IV) and the df associated with the 'error' (the 'left over' variance within groups).

Tests of specific comparisons (such as A against C, or A and B *combined* against C) are either **a priori** ('planned' *before* testing because predicted from theoretical reasoning) or **post hoc** (tested only because the difference looks significant once results are in).

One or possibly two simple comparisons can be made using t tests and **linear contrasts** which make possible the testing of *combined* means where a set of coefficients must be calculated.

Making several tests on data raises the probability of obtaining a 'significant' result on a chance basis alone ('capitalising on chance') and the **family-wise error rate** must be attended to.

Either the significance level for *each* test can be lowered or several types of test, devised for multiple situations, can be resorted to. These include: **Bonferroni t tests**, the **Newman–Keuls test**, **Tukey's honestly significant difference** test, and **Scheffé's test**.

ANOVA MODELS – CONDITIONS OF USE

- Differences or correlation   Differences (between groups of means)
- Level of data measurement Interval/ratio
- Type of design[1]   Unrelated – between groups/subjects
                                                Related   – repeated measures; within groups/
                                                                    subjects
                                                Mixed   – between *and* within group variables

---

[1] The designs above are dealt with in this and following Chapters 20–22. This chapter deals only with an unrelated one-way design.

• Special notes   Greatest strength is use with more than one IV, each
                               with several values, when each IV could be related or
                               unrelated
                               Parametric assumptions need to be met

WHAT'S ANOVA ALL ABOUT THEN?

Suppose Helen recalled from her A-level learning that t tests were more powerful and
robust than non-parametric tests because they were 'parametric' and used interval
level data (at least). She might (quite correctly) assume that either of the two tests of
difference described in the last chapter (Kruskal–Wallis or Friedman), because they
use only ranked data, might not be powerful enough to show a significant difference
between sets of scores when in fact there is one (i.e. she suspects the danger of a type
II error). She is quite correct and would be well advised to turn to the extremely
popular set of methods which come under the general heading of ANALYSIS OF
VARIANCE (ANOVA for short), *so long as her data satisfy parametric assumptions*.

The thinking behind the most simple 'model' is relatively easy to comprehend. In
Table 19.1 all the scores, taken as one set, vary. They vary for two reasons – one,
because the groups differ and, two, because people differ *within* each group. In
ANOVA the variation of all the data values together is divided into the variation
between the conditions *and* the 'left over' variation – attributable to general random
error *within* each condition. If the means vary a lot, relative to the remaining
variation, then it is more likely that there is a real difference between conditions. This
section relies heavily on the concept of *variance* so, if you're a bit hazy about this at
the moment I strongly urge you to go back and refresh the concepts. Remember that
we're looking at the spread of scores around the mean.

Notice that the term 'variation' is used when talking about differences among data
values, rather than 'variance', except when a variance *calculation* is being referred to.
In general, 'variation' means (the non-technically defined) spread of scores or values
within a set.

The calculations in ANOVA can get rather complicated – a lot of number
crunching rather than anything mathematically sophisticated – and it is to be hoped
that the reader using this section will have access to one of the commonly used
computer programmes available these days, such as SPSS™ (for Windows™ or PC
or MAC™) and Minitab™. I have, however, included calculation of the simpler
models in recognition of the view that calculating the formulae of tests by hand leads
to greater understanding of what the test is actually doing. For the more complex
models I've provided an outline, but if you require the by-hand calculation, please
consult one of the texts indicated at the end of Chapter 22.

THE GENERAL THEORY UNDERLYING THE ANOVA APPROACH

If you look at the sample data we used earlier (Table 19.1) you'll see that, although
there is overlap between scores in our three groups, the condition C mean is greater
than the condition B mean which is, in turn, greater than the condition A mean. In
mathematical symbols: $\bar{x}_A < \bar{x}_B < \bar{x}_C$. As we have seen, the non-parametric difference
tests on these groups fell just short of significance, though the trend tests *were*
significant.

The null hypothesis tested by ANOVA is that the three samples in the table come
from populations with the same means and obviously, if we have a theory which
predicts differences between the groups, we are interested in being able to reject this

null hypothesis with confidence. We want a measure of the probability that this null hypothesis is true and we expect that probability to be very small.

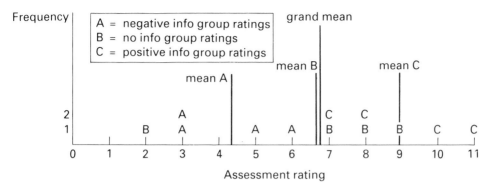

Figure 20.1 *Spread of data from Table 19.1*

If we plot the scores for the three groups in the manner shown in Figure 20.1 we can see the position of the means and the extent of the overlap between groups. I hope you can see that if the *variation* of the scores in each group is relatively large then the overlap of scores from the three groups will be greater than when variation is small.

ANOVA – THE FUNDAMENTAL CONCEPT

I hope it is fairly clear to you that we would be more certain that a group of means differed significantly the more the distribution of the scores around them approached the sort of pattern shown in Figure 20.2a where, *relative to the amount by which scores vary around their individual means* (the within groups, or sample variance), the means differ quite markedly. On the other hand, where the within groups variance is quite large, relative to the differences between the means, we would be ready to assume that all three samples come from the same underlying population (see Figure 20.2b). This can also be seen at the bottom of Figures 20.3a and 20.3b, where the thin horizontal bars represent deviations of individuals from their group means.

The ANOVA test makes a direct comparison between the amount by which sample means vary and the amount each sample varies around its own mean.

In fact, when we discussed the *t* test, we needed some measure of the expected variation of scores around the sample means. In Table 14.3 we agreed that the means in the right-hand table looked virtually no different. You couldn't *make* this decision unless you took into account the extent of variation in the sets of scores as a whole. Suppose **12.5** and **12.75** had been the means but scores in the first group, for example, were of the order of: 12.51, 12.48, 12.505 and so on, whereas in the second they were: 12.765, 12.745, 12.76. In this case, 12.5 and 12.75 look some way apart. Often in this book we've said you can 'intuitively' tell that a real difference exists between two sets of data, but in each case this depended on you being able, perhaps without consciously recognising it, to take into account the relative amount of variation *within* the samples.

HOW DOES ANOVA MAKE THE COMPARISON?

The heart of ANOVA calculations is the *F* ratio. In the simple 'one-way' case we are describing:

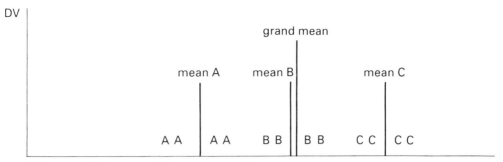

Variance within groups is low – strong effect

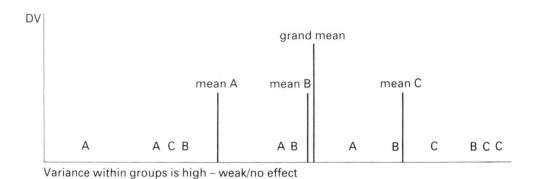

Variance within groups is high – weak/no effect

Figure 20.2a and b *Relationship between variance and significance of effect*

$$F = \frac{\text{variance estimate from sample means}}{\text{variance estimate from within groups}} = \frac{\text{between groups variation}}{\text{within groups variation}}$$

In fact, the top and bottom of the equation amount to two estimates of the population variance. The *bottom* one is an average of the variances of each sample. Since the test is *parametric* we would have assumed *homogeneity of variance* so all the samples combined should give us a fair estimate of population variance as explained in Chapter 13. The *top* of the equation uses the means we've obtained to estimate how much the population must vary to produce means as far apart as these. It is assuming the null hypothesis is true and that populations do indeed have the same means. The logic is the reverse of that in the *t* test where an estimate of population variance was used to estimate the likely variation of means. Here we *have* (a sample of) the variation in means.

The crucial point is, if the means vary a lot, *relative to average variation within groups*, then the top part of the equation will be large, *F* will be large, and we can reject, at some point, the idea that the population means are the same. For the situation depicted in Figures 20.2a, or 20.3b, we should get a high *F* and, when it is higher than the table critical value, we would reject the null hypothesis that the population means are equal.

THE VARIANCE COMPONENTS IN ONE-WAY ANOVA

Central to ANOVA thinking is the idea that the total variation of all values around their GRAND MEAN can be broken into several variation components. In a one-way

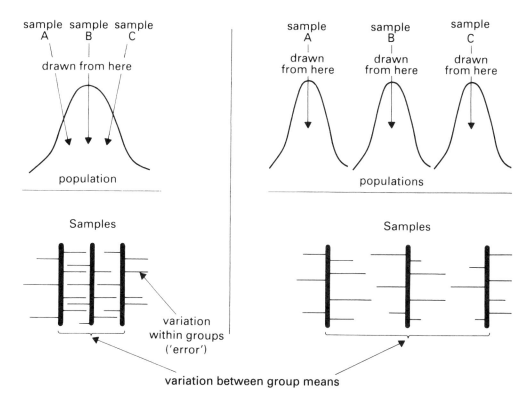

Figure 20.3a *If null hypothesis retained*   Figure 20.3b *If null hypothesis rejected*

ANOVA the two components are those described above – the variation of values around group means ('error') and the variation of the group means ('effect').

A way to understand this is to look at the way each individual's score can be broken up. Suppose we look at the variable of age and that we have taken two samples, one of 10 women the other of 10 men. Our sample of men has a mean age of 35 and one person (Andrew) in the sample is 47 years old. The mean age for the sample of women is 39. The 'grand mean' of all 20 ages is 37. We can summarise:

mean age for female sample	= 39
mean age for male sample	= 35
grand mean	= 37
Andrew's age	= 47
Andrew's deviation from the grand mean	= 10

and this is made up of:

Andrew's deviation from his sample mean	= 12
Deviation of Andrew's sample from the grand mean	= −2

Note that $12 + (-2) = 10$. This notion can be seen diagrammatically in Figure 20.4 – the route from Andrew's age to the grand mean is via his deviation from his group mean and his group mean's deviation from the grand mean.

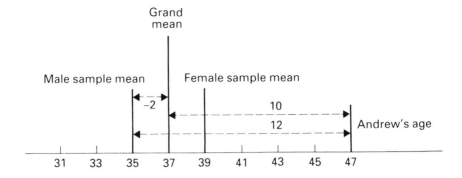

Figure 20.4 *Components of a score in deviations*

In ANOVA we can consider each score in a sample as broken down in a similar manner. Moving from the individual to the group, then:

For the individual:

Andrew's deviation from grand mean	= deviation of Andrew's group mean from grand mean	+ deviation of Andrew from his group mean

For the whole sample:

Total variation	**= between groups variation**	**+ error**

WHY 'ERROR'?

In a sense, ANOVA estimates the extent to which each person's deviation from the grand mean can be 'explained' by the deviation of their group's mean from the other group means. The remainder, the within groups variation, is known as 'error' because it's the amount of the total variation *not explained* by the variation between the group means. It's a measure of how much people vary *within* their groups, around their mean, as a result of unknown variables and *not* as a result of the IV. If every person, in each group, was a cloned robot then there would be no 'error' within groups. In each group everyone would perform at exactly the same level and total variation would be entirely made up of the between groups variation.

In order to calculate the various estimates of variation in the three components given above, using *variance*, a central step in ANOVA calculation is finding the SUM OF SQUARES. We move on to that most crucial stage right now.

SUMS OF SQUARES

In Chapter 13 we said that one equation for variance was very important in ANOVA work. This is:

$$s^2 = \frac{\Sigma x^2 - (\Sigma x)^2/N}{N-1}$$

In ANOVA terms the *top* part of the equation above is known as the SUM OF SQUARES, the *bottom* part is the DEGREES OF FREEDOM for the particular variance calculation being conducted.

Note that the top part isn't just the sum of squared xs but also includes what is known as a 'correction factor' which is *easy* to leave out when doing calculations by hand – be warned!

Calculation of the sum of squares components

Using the *top* part of the equation above:

1 **Total sum of squares** (SS_{total})

- x is each individual's score
- N is total number of scores
- $(\Sigma x)^2/N$ is the 'correction factor' or 'constant'

  It is used as the second part of *all* SS calculations

2 **Between groups sum of squares** (SS_{groups})

- Σx^2 becomes: $\dfrac{\Sigma T^2}{n}$, where T is the total of values in each group and n is the number in each group[1]

3 **Error sum of squares** (SS_{error}) (i.e. the variation *within* groups)

- Subtract **between groups SS** from **total SS** i.e. $SS_{error} = SS_{total} - SS_{groups}$

  This is not a fiddle! The full method is to find, *for each group*, $\Sigma x^2 - (\Sigma x)^2/n$ (where Σx and n refer only to the *group*), and to add these results up. But it can be shown with algebra that:

  $$SS_{total} = SS_{groups} + SS_{error}$$

  This is what we said earlier about the division of variation

'RULES' FOR ALL ANOVA CALCULATIONS

The calculations made in step **1** and **2** above are common throughout ANOVA. Step **1** is always made – it's the sum of *all* the squared scores in the entire data set *minus* what is known as the CORRECTION FACTOR: $(\Sigma x^2)/N$. Other calculations of SS, as in step **2** always have the same form (when samples are equal in size):

T is the total of each of the groups (or samples or conditions or 'cells') which are the focus of interest for the calculation and n is the *number of values* which contribute to that total.

MEAN SUM OF SQUARES – THE VARIANCE ESTIMATE

The actual variance estimate for each component is known as the MEAN SUM OF SQUARES (MS) and is obtained by dividing the obtained sum of squares by the

---

[1] This is where we're finding the variation of the set of means. However, rather than putting $\bar{x}$ where x occurs in the equation, it's easier to work with *totals*. The division by n makes everything come out OK in the end but you need to watch carefully for what n *is* in each of the calculations, especially with more complex versions, later on.

appropriate degrees of freedom. It is the completion of the equation in the 'sums of squares' section, above.

CALCULATION OF ONE-WAY ANOVA ON DATA IN TABLE 19.1

1 Calculate SS_{total} (total sum of squares) using the formula:

$$\Sigma x^2 - \frac{(\Sigma x)^2}{N} \qquad (A)\star$$

Note the difference between Σx^2 and $(\Sigma x)^2$

$\Sigma x = 3+5+6+3+2+7+9+8+$
$\quad 10+8+7+11$
$\quad = 79$

$SS_{total} = 3^2+5^2+6^2+3^2+2^2+7^2+9^2$
$\quad +8^2+10^2+8^2+7^2+11^2 -$
$\quad ((79)^2 \div 12)$
$\quad = 611 - 6241/12$
$\quad = 611 - 520.08$
$\quad = \mathbf{90.92}$

2 Calculate SS_{groups} (between groups sum of squares) using:

$$\frac{\Sigma T^2}{n} - \frac{(\Sigma x)^2}{N} \qquad (B)\star$$

where T is the total number of values in each group and n is the number of values per group. Note that n is *always* the number of values in any set whose total is T. Check below if sample numbers are unequal

$\star$ these two equations will be referred to as 'A' and 'B' throughout the ANOVA calculations from now on

$SS_{groups} = (17^2 + 26^2 + 36^2)/4 - 520.08$
$\quad = (289 + 676 + 1296)/4$
$\quad\quad - 520.08$
$\quad = 2261/4 - 520.08$
$\quad = 565.25 - 520.08$
$\quad = \mathbf{45.17}$

3 Calculate SS_{error} (error sum of squares) using:

$SS_{error} = SS_{total} - SS_{groups}$

$SS_{error} = 90.92 - 45.17 = 45.75$

4 Calculate df for

$\quad$ total $= N - 1$
$\quad$ groups $= C - 1$
(where C = number of conditions)
$\quad$ error $=$ total $-$ groups

$df_{total} = 12 - 1 = 11$
$df_{groups} = 3 - 1 = 2$

$df_{error} = 11 - 2 = 9$

5 Calculate each mean sum of squares by dividing the sum of squares by df

$MS_{total} = 90.92/11 = 8.26$
$MS_{groups} = 45.17/2 = 22.59$
$MS_{error} = 45.75/9 = 5.08$

6 Calculate $F = \dfrac{MS_{groups}}{MS_{error}}$

$F = \dfrac{22.59}{5.08} = \mathbf{4.45}$

7 Look up significance of F in Table 11 as described in the paragraph below

df for numerator (between groups) $= 2$
df for denominator (error) $= 9$
checking for significance with $p < 0.05$:
critical value for $F_{0.05}(2,9)$ $= \mathbf{4.26}$[1]

FINDING THE SIGNIFICANCE OF F

We need to consult F ratio tables (pp. 465—6) and use these as follows. First go to the table for $p < 0.05$, since this is the highest value for probability with which we can claim significance. To find the critical value we must use the degrees of freedom for the effect concerned – this is the *numerator* (since it goes on the *top* of the F ratio equation) and the degrees of freedom for the error variance estimate – this is the *denominator* in the equation. As usual, if we achieve significance with $p < 0.05$ we could consult further to see whether our F value is greater than critical values for smaller values of p. In the F tables this means moving to the next whole page of table values (but see p. 258).

ANOVA TABLE OF RESULTS

It is conventional to lay out the results of an ANOVA test as in Table 20.1

Table 20.1   *ANOVA test results*

Source of variation (one-way unrelated)	Sum of squares	df	Mean sum of squares	F ratio	Probability of F
Between groups*	45.17	2	22.59	4.446	$p < 0.05$
Error	45.75	9	5.08		
Total	90.92	11			

* Often referred to as the variation for the 'effect'.

CONCLUSION FROM OUR TEST (INTERPRETING THE ANOVA RESULT)

Using ANOVA we are justified (by the narrowest of margins, assuming $p < 0.05$ is acceptable) in rejecting the null hypothesis that the sample means are of groups with identical population means.

INTERPRETING THE F TEST RESULT IN ANOVA

What we know from this result is that *at least one mean differs significantly from at least one other mean.* We don't know which means these might be but we can see from the group means (group A: **4.25** group B: **6.5** group C: **9**) that the most likely significant difference is between group A and group C, with the next likely contender being the difference between group B and group C. In order to decide which groups differ significantly from which, without *capitalising on chance* (see p. 318) and just conducting several t tests, we need to consider what are known as A PRIORI and POST HOC COMPARISONS.

---

[1] Note the way of writing our critical values where the *df* in brackets are for the effect (numerator) first then the error variance estimate (denominator).

A PRIORI AND POST HOC COMPARISONS

Have a look at the results (Table 20.2) from a fictitious study on memory where the cell means represent mean recall of items from a 25-word list by different groups of participants being tested on Monday to Friday.

Table 20.2 *Mean recall per condition (day of week)*

(a) Monday $\bar{X}_m$ 16.71	(b) Tuesday $\bar{X}_t$ 14.56	(c) Wednesday $\bar{X}_w$ 10.45	(d) Thursday $\bar{X}_{th}$ 13.78	(e) Friday $\bar{X}_f$ 14.23

Let's suppose that the 'complete' null hypothesis is true and that, for the population sampled, recall does not differ significantly across days of the week ($\mu_1 = \mu_2 = \mu_3 = \mu_4 = \mu_5$). In other words, the theoretical means for each day of the week are all the same value. Suppose *also* that on this particular occasion of testing we had a fluke result where the mean for Monday *does* differ significantly from the mean for Wednesday, using an unrelated t test. On this occasion a type I error has occurred *if* we reject the null hypothesis that these two means come from populations with the same means.

POST HOC COMPARISONS

Post hoc comparisons are those we make *after* inspecting the results of our ANOVA test. Suppose, having obtained the overall results in Table 20.2 we decided to make all possible tests between pairs of means and count any significant differences as justification for rejecting the null hypothesis. In this case we would be *bound* to make a type I error, since we are bound to test Monday and Wednesday's means along with all the others.

A PRIORI COMPARISONS

On the other hand, if we had decided, on the basis of our general theory, that only Monday's and Friday's means should be tested, because we believed people would, say, be more tired at the end than at the beginning of the week, we would not make this type I error. *Whatever our prior prediction had been*, we only had a 1 in 10 ($p = 0.1$) chance of making a type I error given the results occurred as they did. There were 10 possible predictions to make (one with 2, 3, 4, 5; two with 3, 4, 5; three with 4, 5; four with 5) and only one of the results that we could have predicted was 'significant'. This assumes that the prediction concerned just two means (known as PAIRWISE COMPARISON). A priori ('PLANNED') comparisons, then, are comparisons we can make, having made a specific prediction, based on theoretical argument, *before* conducting our ANOVA test. This *should* remind you of one and two-tailed tests because, in the simple two condition experiment, a one-tailed hypothesis is an a priori planned comparison.

Making all possible comparisons produces a far higher probability of making a type I error than occurs if we make selected and predetermined a priori comparisons. In fact, deciding, in advance, to make all possible comparison tests is the same thing as conducting post hoc tests. The latter involves inspecting everything and testing what looks likely. The former amounts to the same thing because the prior plan is to test everything and see what turns up as 'significant', unless there is good theoretical argument for all possible differences being significant.

FAMILY-WISE ERROR RATE

We have said before that if you make 20 tests of significance on randomly arranged data you are more than likely to get one 'significant' difference. That is the logic of significance testing. We look for results which would only occur five times in 100 by chance and count them as significant if we predicted them before testing. If we set significance at $p = 0.05$, then, and make multiple tests on randomly arranged data, we know that there is a 0.05 chance that any comparison we make will be wrongly assumed to be significant; i.e. we will have made a type I error. We are said to be working with an ERROR RATE PER COMPARISON of 0.05. If we are making several tests on our data it is possible to calculate something known as the FAMILY-WISE ERROR RATE which is the probability of making *at least one* type I error when making multiple tests.

TESTS FOR A PRIORI COMPARISONS

If you have *justifiably* predicted just one significant difference ('planned one comparison') then there is no problem in testing this with a special t test (as used by 'linear contrasts' – see below), since you have a 0.05 chance of a type I error. If you make two tests your chance of making *at least one* type I error rises to near 0.01. You can compensate by setting your significance level, *prior to testing*, at 0.025. The new test will be:

$$t = \bar{x}_1 - \bar{x}_2 \left/ \sqrt{\frac{MS_{error}}{n_1} - \frac{MS_{error}}{n_2}} \right. \text{using } df_{error} \text{ and}$$

where MS_{error} comes from the overall ANOVA result and n_1 and n_2 are sample numbers.

BONFERRONI *T* TESTS

Rather than doing this however, you can use these tests. They are only recommended though if you are making a *few* comparisons. If you want to test *all* possible comparisons then you should use one of the tests required for post hoc comparisons. These tests are not dealt with here but will be found on computer programs, such as SPSS^{TM} running ANOVA.

LINEAR CONTRASTS – TESTING COMBINATIONS OF MEANS

There may be occasions when you want to test for significance between *combinations* of means, for instance, in our days of the week and recall example, between the combined mean for Monday and Tuesday against the combined mean for Thursday and Friday. When this occurs you need to make use of the LINEAR CONTRAST approach. The mathematics is not covered in this text but, assuming you are using a commercial statistics package (such as SPSS^{TM}), the only tricky calculation you'll have to perform is to provide a set of COEFFICIENTS to let the program know, using numerical codes, which combinations of means you wish to test between. The tests themselves will use the F ratio on relevant sums of squares. You can also use linear contrasts to test simple comparisons between just two means – basically a t test.

RULES FOR DETERMINING CONTRAST COEFFICIENTS

1 All coefficients must sum together to zero.

2 The sum of coefficients for one mean or combination of means must equal the sum of coefficients for the other mean or combination of means but have the opposite sign.

3 The coefficient for any mean not tested must be zero.

Table 20.3 *Coefficients used for means*

Test of:	Mon	Tues	Wed	Thur	Fri	Explanation using rules
$\bar{X}_m$ against $\bar{X}_w$	1	0	−1	0	0	Rule **1** – numbers sum to zero Rule **2** – 1 and −1 sum to zero Rule **3** – other numbers are 0
$\bar{X}_m + \bar{X}_t$ combined against $\bar{X}_{th} + \bar{X}_f$	1	1	0	−1	−1	Rule **2** – the two means marked will be taken together and contrasted with the two marked −1. Other rules as above
$\bar{X}_m + \bar{X}_t$ combined against $\bar{X}_w$	−1	−1	2	0	0	Rule **2** – −1 + −1 = −2; Wed has +2 and will be contrasted with the other two together

Choosing coefficients is something of an intuitive task. There is no one right answer. For instance, in the third row, Table 20.3 we *could* have chosen: 0.5 0.5 −1 0 0

TESTS FOR POST HOC COMPARISONS

These would be used in either of two situations:

1 Where *all* possible comparisons are desired, decided a priori.

2 Where comparisons are only being made *after* examination of the ANOVA results and *not* because of any theoretical prediction.

There are several tests, each with variations and complications, for carrying out post hoc comparisons. I am just going to mention two of the most popular, with their associated characteristics.

NEWMAN–KEULS TEST

This alternative is generally controversial because, under certain circumstances, the family-wise error rate gets high. This can occur when *several* pairs of means do not, in fact, differ significantly, i.e. where several null hypotheses are, in fact, true. This will only happen in studies with quite a lot of conditions, and, for studies involving only three conditions the Newman–Keuls gives a greater chance of showing real significant differences, with only slightly more risk of making type I errors than the Tukey$_a$ test. Again, the calculations for the Newman–Keuls and Tukey's test, below, are not dealt with here but will be found in SPSS^{TM} and similar.

TUKEY'S$_a$ (HONESTLY SIGNIFICANT DIFFERENCE) TEST

This engagingly titled test is generally considered the safest you can use if you wish to carry out all possible 'pairwise' (two means at a time) comparisons and keep the family-wise error rate down to 0.05. The price you pay is that the test is 'conservative' – you might miss real differences in keeping your interpretations safe.

EXAMPLES OF TUKEY$_a$ RESULTS

If we had conducted a Tukey HSD on our sample data, following the ANOVA result in Table 20.1 we would have obtained the result below (Figure 20.5), which is part of the SPSS^{TM} (Windows^{TM}) output:

Homogeneous subsets (highest and lowest means are not significantly different)

					G G G
Subset 1					
Group	Grp 1	Grp 2			r r r
					p p p
Mean	4.2500	6.5000			1 2 3
			Mean	Condition	
Subset 2					
Group	Grp 2	Grp 3	4.2500	Grp 1	
			6.5000	Grp 2	
Mean	6.5000	9.0000	9.0000	Grp 3 *	

Figure 20.5 *Result of Tukey test in SPSS^{TM}*

This shows us that the means for group 1 and group 3 *are* significantly different but that no other difference is. This means that groups 1 and 2 can be assumed to belong in the same 'subset' – their means do not differ significantly. This is also true of groups 2 and 3 taken as a pair. But, as we know, it is too unlikely that all *three* come from the same population.

Whether group 2 'belongs' in reality with group 1 or group 3 we can't say on this occasion, but look at the data in Table 20.4. Here, again, the ANOVA result is significant. Here the Tukey result tells us that groups 1(A) and 2(B) belong together and their means are *both* significantly different from group 3(C)'s mean.

Table 20.4 *SPSS^{TM} result (Tukey)*

	Group A	Group B (scores)	Group C	Homogeneous subsets		
	12.00	14.00	16.00	Subset 1		
	14.00	15.00	20.00	Group	Grp 1	Grp 2
	13.00	14.00	18.00	Mean	13.2500	14.7500
	14.00	16.00	19.00	Subset 2		
Means	13.25	14.75	18.25	Group	Grp 3	
				Mean	18.2500	

General options for comparisons in ANOVA

- For one *planned* comparison (or possibly two, lowering the significance level) between pairs of means ('pairwise') use *individual (special) t tests* or *linear contrasts*
- Where these one (or two) comparisons involve the means of *combinations* of groups, use *linear contrasts*
- If several planned comparisons are to be made (pairwise or with combinations) use a *Bonferroni t test method*
- If you want to compare all possible pairs of means, or make more than two pre-planned comparisons where there are several groups use *Newman–Keuls* (or *Tukey's HSD* for safety)
- If you want to compare all possible pairs of means where there are quite a few groups (five or more) use *Tukey's HSD*
- If you want to make all possible contrasts (i.e. not just 'pairwise' but including all possible combinations of means against others) use the *Scheffé* test (not described here)

WHERE ARE ALL THESE ALTERNATIVES?

There are other specific alternatives depending on the particular design of the study and on your specific purposes. The above comparisons are all found in statistical programmes like SPSS^{TM} but you really should check in one of the advanced texts mentioned at the end of Chapter 22 before proceeding, in order to know that your analysis is valid.

Unequal numbers in the samples

Usually it's safest to attempt to get the same number of people in each sample but sometimes one is stuck with unequal numbers – we couldn't know, in advance, how many would answer a questionnaire in a certain way, for instance. People's results may be unusable or they may fail to show up for testing. In the case of one-way ANOVA this isn't *too* difficult. In step **2** of the one-way ANOVA calculation above, we don't find the sum of all T^2, *then* divide by n. We divide *each* T^2 by its associated n. In the case of multi-way ANOVA tests, to be dealt with later, it is beyond the scope of this book to provide the relevant calculations. You could either consult one of the more detailed texts referenced at the end of the chapter, or check that your software deals with different numbers in each sample. SPSS^{TM} just steams ahead and copes.

Glossary

Differences between means, or combinations of means, which were predicted from theory before the data were collected	_ _____ _____	a priori comparisons
Statistical technique which compares variances within and between samples in order to estimate the significance between sets of means	_____ __ _____	analysis of variance

Sum of squares of deviations of group means from the grand mean; used to calculate the variance component related to the 'effect', i.e. distance between group means	_____ _____ ___ __ _____	between groups sums of squares
Procedure for testing several *planned* comparisons between (groups of) means	_____ __ _____	Bonferroni t tests
$(\Sigma x)^2/N$ – the second term in all ANOVA equations	_____ _____	correction factor

error rates

Given the significance level set, the likelihood of an error in *each* test made on the data	__ _____	(error rate) per comparison
The probability of having made *at least one* type error in all the tests made on a set of data	_____-_____	family-wise (error rate)

Sum of all the squares of deviations of each score from its group mean, for all scores in a set of data where there are two or more groups; used to calculate an estimate of the 'unexplained' variance with which to compare the 'explained' variance of group means around the grand mean	_____ ___ __ _____	error sum of squares
Comparison of two variances by dividing one by the other; used in all ANOVA tests	_ ____	F test
Mean of all scores in a data set, irrespective of groups	_____ ____	grand mean
Values to be entered into an equation for calculating 'linear contrasts' – see below	_____ _____	linear coefficients
Procedure for testing between individual pairs of means or combinations of means when planned comparisons (see below) have been made	_____ _____	linear contrasts
Sum of squares divided by degrees of freedom; a particular component's variance estimate in ANOVA	____ ___ __ _____	mean sum of squares
Procedure for testing all possible pairs of means in a data set for significance, so long as number of groups is relatively low	_____-_____ ____	Newman–Keuls test

Comparison of just two means from a set of means	_____ _____	pairwise comparison
Tests which it was intended to make, because of theoretical predictions, *before* data were collected	_____ _____	planned comparisons
Tests between means, or groups of means, only decided upon after inspection of data	____ ___ _____	post hoc comparisons
Procedure for testing all possible pairs of means from a data set where there are a relatively large number of groups; with low number of groups, considered rather conservative	_____ (___) ____	Tukey's$_a$ (HSD) test
Procedure for testing all possible combinations of means	_____ ____	Scheffé test
Alternative name for the *F* test – see above	_____ _____ ____	variance ratio test

EXERCISES

1 Produce three samples of eight values by using the random numbers in Table 1, Appendix 2 (start anywhere, for each sample, and select the next eight numbers in any direction). Calculate a one-way ANOVA (unrelated) and check the *F* ratio for significance. If it is significant, tell your tutor you're a little more sceptical about the 5% significance level convention!

2 Imagine that you conduct an experiment with five people in one condition, six in a second condition and eight in a third condition, and that you are going to conduct a one-way ANOVA analysis. Produce the outline 'source of variance' table, including the degrees of freedom for each component.

3 In the experiment in question **2**, if the null hypothesis has already been rejected and you *now* decide to test all the paired comparisons, what test would be appropriate? Tukey *or* set alpha at 0.01 and do *t* tests?

4 Suppose, in the experiment of question **2**, you had predicted in your introduction that only the first and third conditions would differ. What test might it now be legitimate to conduct?

5 In the experiment in question **2**, we wish to use a linear contrast to test for a difference between conditions one and two *together* against condition three. What would be the simplest set of coefficients to use?

MULTI-FACTOR ANOVA

The chapter deals with multi-factor ANOVA where more than one IV is involved. Each IV is known as a **factor** and each condition of one IV is known as a **level** of that factor.

A design where all factors are between groups is known as **unrelated**. When at least one factor is repeated measures, the design is **mixed**, unless *all* factors are repeated measures, in which case the model is **repeated measures** or **within subjects**.

The use of more than one factor raises the possibility that each factor may have no overall effect but that a factor may have significant effects when *individual levels* of the other factor(s) are taken into account. This effect is known as an **interaction effect**. An example might be that one factor, sex of author, may have no overall effect on the rating of an article's quality, and a further factor, male or female-oriented content of article, may also have no effect. However, a female author may be rated lower on the 'male' article and a male author may be downrated on the 'female' article.

Effects of one level of one factor across levels of another (e.g. effect of male content across male and female author) are known as **simple effects**. The effect of one factor over all levels of another factor taken together is known as a **main effect**.

Total variation in a multi-factor ANOVA analysis, is divided into:
- **Between groups** variation (the 'explained' variation) which divides into:
  - **Between groups variation** – for *each* factor plus
  - **Interaction variation** – a component for *every possible combination* of factors
- **Error** – the 'unexplained', within-groups variation

USING TWO OR MORE INDEPENDENT VARIABLES

THE STUDENT PROJECT EXPANDS

Let's suppose Tim, Helen and Francesca (remember them?) have pushed their ideas even further. One of them has realised that the people they tested, being students, were likely to hold strong views about global warming. Helen suggests that if they'd tested people who don't care about global warming then perhaps the results would have been different. Perhaps people who don't care would have viewed rather negatively the person who did care and seen the person who didn't care as positive since that person thinks as they do. They realise that what they should have done was to take samples from among a group known not to care and a group known to care about global warming in order to test this more complicated hypothesis.

The example of ANOVA which we have already considered involved the manipulation of just *one* IV (with three values). Very often, researchers test the effect of *two* independent variables at the same time.

Suppose we had tested the sex stereotyping hypothesis that people will rate an article more highly on writer's expertise when they are told the author is male than when they are told the author is female. We may well find no rating difference for the male and female authors. But suppose we investigate further by adding another condition – one article is about a traditionally 'male' topic, say car maintenance, and the other is on a traditionally 'female' topic, say baby care – remember we're talking about *stereotypes* here, not reality! Now, what we might find is that ratings of the male and female author do not differ overall, nor do the ratings of the two articles. What *might* occur is that the male author is rated higher on the 'male' article and the female higher on the 'female' article. This is known as an INTERACTION EFFECT. Results of multi-factor studies, such as this one, are often displayed in a diagram like that in Figure 21.1 where, in this fictitious case, a typical interaction effect is shown. There are, however, no overall differences between participants given a 'male' or 'female' author, nor between those given the car or the baby article. It is said that there are no MAIN EFFECTS. These two 'effect' terms I shall attempt to explain more fully in a moment.

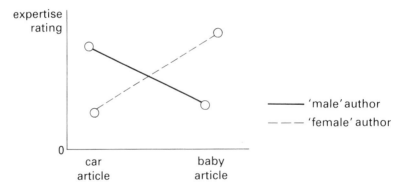

Figure 21.1 *Interaction between author factor and type of article factor*

FACTORS AND LEVELS

In multi-factor ANOVA designs we introduce some new terminology. Each IV is known as a FACTOR and each of these has several LEVELS. For instance, in the author assessment example, one factor is the described sex of author, with levels of 'male' and 'female', whilst the other factor is type of article – 'male oriented' or 'female oriented'.

Designs are often referred to by their factor structure. The sex of author design is an example of a *2 × 2 factorial design* (two sexes of author; two types of article).

I shall now describe a fairly recent, slightly more complex design. In 1986, Alexander and Guenther reported a study in which they manipulated the moods of three groups of participants by getting them to read statements. These led to states described as either 'elated', 'depressed' or 'neutral'. They then read them a list of equal numbers of positive and negative personality traits to see whether mood affected the type of trait recalled. Apparently it did. This is an example of a *2 × 3 factorial design* (two types of trait; three types of mood).

(*Note*: this, along with suitably doctored versions of the male/female author or place-dependent memory studies would make interesting topics for student projects.)

Designs can become very complicated indeed. A 1984 study by Samuel and Bryant (discussed in Gross 1994) involved testing four ages of child (factor 1) on three types of task (factor 2) using three types of material (factor 3) – a $4 × 3 × 3$ design, David et al. (1986) used a $4 × 2 × 16$ design in the investigation of road accidents and Gulian and Thomas (1986) used a $2 × 2 × 3 × 4$ design where males and females were tested in high or low noise, under three different sets of instructions about the noise across four different periods of testing! There is no limit to the complexity of designs which can be used apart from the researchers' patience with data analysis and the size of the willing participant pool.

UNRELATED AND RELATED DESIGNS

If *all* the factors of a complex ANOVA design are between groups, i.e. independent samples for each 'level' – it is known as an UNRELATED design. If *all* participants undergo *all* combinations of conditions (appear in every 'cell' of the data table) it is a related or REPEATED MEASURES design. If at least one of the factors is unrelated, and at least one a repeat measure, then we refer to a MIXED design.

> The designs of our 'global warming' attitude study, and of the mood manipulation one just described, are outlined in Table 21.1. See if you can fill in the information required for the other designs in the table. Answers are in the 'Answers to exercises' section (question 1), Appendix 3.

Table 21.1 *ANOVA designs*

Description of study	Levels	Factorial design
1 Effect on perception of a person of knowing whether they are concerned or unconcerned about global warming and when no such information is given	level 1 – knowing person is unconcerned level 2 – knowing person is concerned level 3 – no information	one way unrelated ANOVA; three levels of single IV
2 Effect of mood (depressed, neutral, elated) on recall of positive or negative traits	Factor 1: Mood (unrelated) level 1 – depressed level 2 – neutral level 3 – elated Factor 2: Trait type (repeat measure) level 1 – positive level 2 – negative	3 × 2 ANOVA mixed design
3 Investigation of different times taken by same people		

to name colours of colour
patches, non-colour words
or colour words

4 Effect of psychoanalysis,
humanist therapy or
behaviour modification on
groups of male and female
clients

5 Effect of age (old vs. young)
on recall performance using
three different memorising
methods on each group of
participants

6 Effect of coffee, alcohol or a
placebo on performance of
a visual monitoring task
under conditions of loud
noise, moderate noise,
intermittent noise and no
noise – all groups have
different participants

7 Extroverts and introverts are
given either a stimulant,
placebo or tranquiliser and
observed as they perform an
energetic and then a dull
task

8 People with either high or
low race prejudice observe
either a black or a white
person performing either a
pro-social, neutral or hostile
act. Their ratings of the
person observed are
compared

INTERACTION

An important feature of 'factorial' designs (two-way or more) is the possibility of detecting interaction effects. Very often, in testing the effect of a single variable, one is drawn to the speculation that an apparent lack of effect may be obscuring a difference in performance between types of people or on different sorts of tasks. Here are some examples:

1 Are people better in the morning or in the afternoon at performing tasks requiring good attention? No significant difference might be obtained yet, if Eysenck (1970) is correct, we might expect to find that extroverts perform better in the afternoon and introverts in the morning.

2 Students were given arguments to convince them that their college should initiate

a new, harder exam system. They were given either three or nine strong or weak arguments. This produces four conditions. Overall, nine strong arguments produced greater agreement than did three, *but* nine weak arguments produced even *less* agreement than did three (Petty and Cacioppo 1984 – see Figure 21.2).

3 In a dramatic study, Godden and Baddeley (1975) showed that people tested for memory did better if they recalled in the same place as they had been when they had learned the original material – either on land or under water – they used scuba divers! Here, one IV is place of learning and the other is place of recall. Interaction occurred in that words were not better recalled under water or above ground and it didn't matter, overall, where the words had originally been learned. The two groups who did best were those both learning and recalling in the same place.

An interaction effect, then, occurs when the effect of one factor is dependent upon which levels of other factors are considered. In example **3**, just above, differences in performance associated with learning under water or on land depend on whether recall is performed under water or not. In example **2**, the effect of three rather than nine arguments needs to be considered along with the *strength* of the arguments since weak arguments create opposite effects to strong ones.

MAIN EFFECTS

These are our familiar effects from a single IV. A MAIN EFFECT occurs when one of the IVs, irrespective of any other variable, has an overall significant effect. For instance, in example **2** above, strong arguments produced significantly more agreement by students *overall* (disregarding number of arguments given).

SIMPLE EFFECTS

A SIMPLE EFFECT occurs when we extract a *part* of a multi-factor ANOVA result and look at just the effect of *one* level of one IV across one of the other IVs. For instance, there may be a simple effect of time of day on extroverts, or of female author assessment across the two types of article. Simple effects *can* be investigated for significance using *t* tests, planned contrasts or even a one way ANOVA. For instance, if, in the mood and memory study, we predicted that positive traits would be recalled most by elated, less by neutral, and least by depressed participants, we could conduct a one-way ANOVA across these three conditions. *But simple effects can only be investigated without 'capitalising on chance', as with all other comparisons and contrasts, as explained on page 318.*

Various kinds of interaction and main effect are possible. Have a look at Figure 21.3 and try to interpret what has happened. Note that it is possible to have main and interaction effects occurring together.

DATA IN A TWO-WAY UNRELATED ANOVA DESIGN

Let's assume that our students *did* originally think of this more complex design and that the data they obtained from 24 people, 12 who care about global warming and 12 who don't, are arranged as shown in Table 21.2. They can't just go and get a further group of non-caring people, test them in the three conditions, add these to the

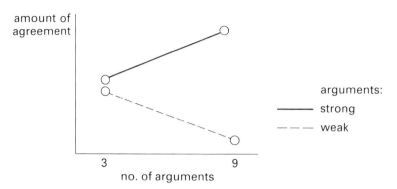

Figure 21.2 *Agreement after three or nine strong or weak arguments (after Petty and Cacioppo, 1984, in Atkinson et al., 1993)*

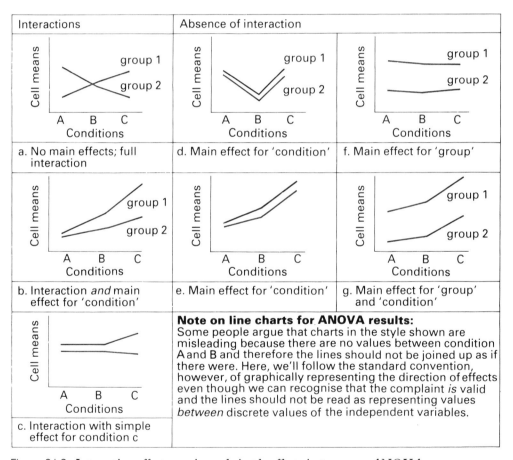

Figure 21.3 *Interaction effects, main and simple effects in two-way ANOVA*

data pool and conduct a two-way ANOVA because they'd be 'capitalising on chance'. The two groups must be randomly selected from their populations.

Each of the six sections in Table 21.2, below, which contains a set of data and a mean (A1B1, A1B2 etc.) is known as a 'cell' of the table (one group).

PARTITIONING THE SUMS OF SQUARES

When we calculated the sums of squares for the one-way ANOVA we had three terms: **1** SS_{total} **2** SS_{groups} and **3** SS_{error}.

For two-way ANOVA, we divide the sums of squares up as shown in Figure 21.4.

Here, just think of the between groups SS in the one-way example being split up into variation for the two conditions *plus* variation for the interaction *between* the two conditions. What's left ('error') is, again, the variation of people *within* their groups.

As I said earlier, I would hope that readers will not need to calculate tests at this level or higher *by hand*. Most would, I hope, be using a computer program. Consequently, I have included here a step-by-step approach to the calculation of two-way ANOVA, with explanation, but excluding all the arithmetic detail. The calculations are, in any case, already familiar, since the same formula for calculating variance components is used throughout. What the reader *does* need to pay attention to is the meaning of each of the components and their role in the overall analysis.

Table 21.2 *Overall assessment rating of Jane (0 = negative; 12 = positive)*

| | **Jane's attitude to global warming (Factor A):** | | | |
	doesn't care (condition A1)	is neutral (condition A2)	cares (condition A3)	**Group totals**
Factor B ↓ **Participant (group):**	Group A1B1	Group A2B1	Group A3B1	T_{group} ↓
very concerned about global warming (Group B1)	3 5 6 3	2 7 9 8	10 8 7 11	
	$T_{cell}(A1B1) = 17$ $\bar{X}_{A1B1} = 4.25$	$T_{cell}(A2B1) = 26$ $\bar{X}_{A2B1} = 6.5$	$T_{cell}(A3B1) = 36$ $\bar{X}_{A3B1} = 9$	79
	Group A1B2	Group A2B2	Group A3B2	
not bothered about global warming (Group B2)	5 4 7 7	6 5 6 5	5 3 5 4	
	$T_{cell}(A1B2) = 23$ $\bar{X}_{A1B2} = 5.75$	$T_{cell}(A2B2) = 22$ $\bar{X}_{A2B2} = 5.5$	$T_{cell}(A3B2) = 17$ $\bar{X}_{A3B2} = 4.25$	62
Totals for conditions T_{cond}→	40	48	53	141

$$\Sigma x^2 = (3^2 + 5^2 + 6^2 \text{ etc.}) = \mathbf{947}$$

CALCULATION OF TWO-WAY (RANDOMISED) ANOVA

Calculation of two-way ANOVA on data

1 Calculate SS_{total} as before, using the formula opposite

$$\Sigma x^2 - \frac{(\Sigma x)^2}{N} \qquad (A)$$

$$= \mathbf{118.625}$$

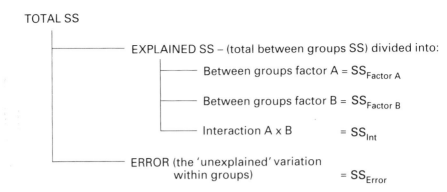

Figure 21.4 *Division of variation in a two-way unrelated ANOVA design*

Note that $\dfrac{(\Sigma x)^2}{N}$ is the same as before, the square of the sum of all scores $(141)^2$, divided by the total number of participants (24); this value is also used in equation (B) below

2 Calculate $SS_{factorA}$ (information condition) using equation (B), as before
T is the total of each condition (T_{cond})
n is the number in each condition $= 8$

$$\frac{\Sigma T^2}{n} - \frac{(\Sigma x)^2}{N} \qquad (B)$$

$SS_{info} \qquad = \mathbf{10.75}$

3 Calculate $SS_{factorB}$ (participant attitude group) using equation (B) above. T is now T_{group}; n is the number in each group $= 12$

$SS_{group} \qquad = \mathbf{12.042}$

4 Calculate SS_{cells} – the variation produced by all the *cell totals* around their mean. Here, T is T_{cells}, the values 17, 26, etc., which are the totals of scores in each cell shown in Table 21.2; n is the number in each cell $= 4\star$

$SS_{cells} \qquad = \mathbf{62.375}$

5 Calculate $SS_{factorA \times factorB}$ – the interaction SS using:

$SS_{factorAfactorB} = SS_{cells} - SS_{factorA} - SS_{factorB}$

Calculate SS_{error} using:

$SS_{error} = SS_{total} - SS_{cells}$

$SS_{info} \times _{group} = 62.375$
$\qquad\qquad\ \ - 10.75$
$\qquad\qquad\ \ - 12.042$
$\qquad\qquad\ \ = \mathbf{39.583}$

$SS_{error} \qquad = \mathbf{56.25}$

6 Calculate *degrees of freedom*.
For each *factor* this is (levels -1)
For the *interaction effect*, multiply together the *df* for each of the components of the interaction (i.e., in this case, information and group)

Degrees of freedom:
Total $\qquad\quad = N - 1 \qquad\qquad\qquad\qquad\quad = 23$
Factor A (info) $\ = 3 - 1 \qquad\qquad\qquad\qquad\quad = 2$
Factor B (group) $= 2 - 1 \qquad\qquad\qquad\qquad\quad = 1$
Interaction $\qquad = 2 \times 1 \qquad\qquad\qquad\qquad\quad = 2$
Error $=$ total *df* $-$ effects *df* $= 23 - 5 \qquad\qquad = 18$

7 Calculate *mean sums of squares* as for the one-way example by dividing each sum of squares by its appropriate *df*; results are shown in Table 21.3

8 Calculate *F* for all effects as before by dividing each effect (two mains and one interaction) by the error term; results are in Table 21.3

* Calculating the SS_{cells} value is a short cut to get the value for the interaction SS and is always used from now on. Taking the *main* effects from the 'cells' value leaves a residual amount which is an estimate of the variation related to the interaction of the two independent variables.

Table 21.3

Source of variation (two-way unrelated)	Sum of squares	df	Mean sum of squares	F ratio	Probability of F
Between groups:					
Information	10.75	2	5.375	1.72	NS ($p > 0.05$)
Group	12.042	1	12.042	3.853	NS ($p > 0.05$)
Interaction (info × group)	39.583	2	19.79	6.333	$p < 0.01$
Error	56.25	18	3.125		
Total	118.625	23	5.156		

Finding the significance of F

We need to consult *F* ratio tables as explained for the one-way example. Here, we consult for *all* our effects – that's the three *F* values shown in Table 21.3. In each case the effect MeanSS is the *numerator* and the error MeanSS is the *denominator*. For our example:

Effect	Obtained value	df	Critical value	p
Main effect – information	1.72	2,18	$F_{0.05}(2,18) = 3.55$	<0.05
Main effect – group	3.853	1,18	$F_{0.05}(1,18) = 4.41$	<0.05
Interaction (info × group)	6.333	2,18	$F_{0.01}(2,18) = 6.01$	<0.01

INTERPRETING THE RESULT

It appears that neither IV had a significant effect, taken in isolation, across all of its levels, irrespective of levels of the other IV (there was no 'main effect'). That is, varying the information about Jane's global warming attitude had no consistent effect on all the people tested taken as an undivided group. Nor did the concerned group's attitude toward Jane differ significantly from the unconcerned group's attitude if we ignore the division of this group according to what information they were given about her.

There *is*, however, a significant *interaction effect* (see Figure 21.5). The two groups of participants *do* differ in attitude to Jane when we take into account the separate conditions of attitude to global warming factor. It appears that the strongest effect comes from the difference between the two groups when they are told that Jane is extremely concerned about global warming. If predicted, the *simple effect* of 'knowing Jane is concerned' could be tested across the two participant types – do care and don't care – as a simple comparison.

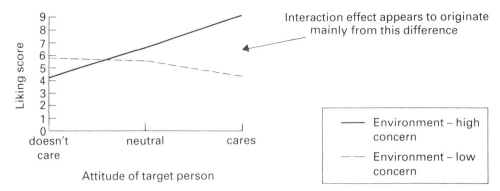

Figure 21.5 *Environmental attitude and perception of person whose environmental attitude is known*

THREE-WAY ANOVA CALCULATION

I hope you would never be unfortunate enough to find yourself needing to calculate a three-way unrelated ANOVA by hand (not a likely event in the twenty-first century). I will list here the components that would need to be found, however, so that you can understand what a computer printout is telling you. It's important to lay out your data clearly *even if* you're using a computer, since otherwise you'll get in a mess wondering what all the components of the results table are. Imagine that our dogged students originally used a further condition (C) which is a new 'public' condition where participants either do or don't have to declare their ratings to an audience of students! In this three-way design you'd need to find the following components:

TOTAL SS ——— Between Groups SS ——— $SS_{\text{Factor A*}}$ 1

——— $SS_{\text{Factor B}}$ 2

——— $SS_{\text{Factor C}}$ 3

——— $SS_{\text{Interaction AB}}$ $(SS_{\text{cells AB}} -1 -2)**$ 4

——— $SS_{\text{Interaction AC}}$ $(SS_{\text{Cells AC}} -1 -3)$ 5

——— $SS_{\text{Interaction BC}}$ $(SS_{\text{cells BC}} -2 -3)$ 6

——— $SS_{\text{Interaction ABC}}$ $(SS_{\text{cells ABC}} - 1-2-3-4-5-6)***$

——— Error SS $(TOTAL\ SS - SS_{\text{cells ABC}})$

Figure 21.6 *Division of variation in a three-way unrelated design*

*   Use overall totals of condition A *ignoring* the other two factors

** SS_{cellsAB} is found using the totals of conditions A and B ignoring C as a factor, i.e. the totals of A1B1, A1B2, A1B3, A2B1, A2B2, A2B3

*** SS_{cellsABC} uses the total of *all* cells, A1B1C1, A1B1C2 etc.

GLOSSARY

An ANOVA design using only unrelated samples in all factors (IVs)	_____ ____	unrelated design
One of the IVs in a design with more than one IV	_____	factor
A research design involving more than one IV	_____ _____	factorial design
Effect of one factor which is significant but which depends upon only certain level(s) of other factor(s)	_____ _____	interaction effect
The different values (conditions) of an IV	_____	levels
Effect of one factor which is significant, across all its levels taken together, irrespective of any other factors	____ _____	main effects
An ANOVA design using at least one repeated measure IV and at least one unrelated IV	_____ _____	mixed model
One level of a factor only has a significant effect across levels of the other factor(s)	_____ _____	simple effect

EXERCISES

1 Do the exercise on page 345 if you haven't done it already!

2 Imagine that two groups of students, one vegetarian, the other meat-eating (Factor 1 – groups 1 and 2) are asked to memorise animal words, vegetable words and flower words (Factor 2 – conditions A, B and C). There's no research I know of to predict any particular result so suppose, in each example below, that the stated results occurred. Pick out the diagram from Figure 21.3 which you think best depicts the result obtained. To avoid repetition, assume that 'differences' when mentioned are significant.

   a) Vegetarians and meat-eaters differ. No other effect.
   b) Vegetarians and meat-eaters differ and there are differences across conditions as a whole. No interaction.
   c) There are overall differences across conditions only.
   d) There is a difference between groups on one condition only and no other effects.
   e) There is *only* an interaction effect between eating style and memory condition. There is no overall difference between eating styles or between memory conditions.
   f) There is an overall difference across conditions but this is significantly more extreme for one of the groups.

3 Suppose the following data were obtained from a study of the sociability of boys and girls with no siblings who have or haven't attended preschool of some kind before starting school. Calculate the two-way ANOVA and comment on the effects.

	Preschool children Sociability scores					**No preschool children Sociability scores**				
Boys	45	23	25	56	49	12	14	21	18	9
				42	39					
Girls	35	48	45			35	34	35	38	48

4 Suppose we measure people on a variable called 'sociability' – 'S' for short. We then investigate their performance on a wiggly-wire task where touching the wire with a ring-on-a-stick causes a buzzer to ring and records an error. Suppose it is true that high S people perform well in front of an audience but poorly alone and that low S people perform quite the other way round. Overall, high and low S people tend to perform at about the same level. What effects would you expect from ANOVA? Sketch the expected effects or choose the appropriate diagram from Figure 21.3.

REPEATED MEASURES ANOVA

This chapter deals with one-way or multi-factor ANOVA when at least one of the factors is **repeated measures**.

The one-way repeated measures model **partials out** the variation which is assumed to relate to variation among the individuals in the sample.

It may be that individuals differ very much from one another. This variation is known as the **between subjects** variation. If, nevertheless, they all differ in the same way *across* conditions, i.e. **between conditions**, then *most* of the **total** variation will be accounted for by the **between conditions variation** and the **between subjects variation**, leaving very little residual **'error'** (which is actually the **interaction** of subjects with conditions, as if conditions were one factor and total for individuals in the sample were levels of another factor). Thus, a high value of *F* will occur.

In **multi-factor repeated measures** designs, each main effect, and each interaction, has its own associated error term, calculated from the interaction of individual totals with the main or interaction effect.

In a **mixed design** unrelated factors are dealt with much as in the unrelated randomised model. Their **main effects**, plus **interaction for the unrelated factors** only, plus **error** together make up the **between subjects variation**. The **within subjects** variation is made up of the **main effects of the repeated measures factors** plus their **interaction** plus their **interactions with the unrelated factors**, plus the residual **error for within subjects**.

At the end of this chapter some recommended further and more technical reading on ANOVA procedures is included.

Up till now we've worked in detail on designs which use only independent samples throughout, known as 'unrelated designs'. Suppose we now look at a design which includes a *repeated measure*. In this case, a group of participants is tested at least twice in different conditions (levels) of an IV. For instance, let's look at a fictitious experiment based on an investigation of 'levels of processing' and as originally conducted by Craik and Tulving, (1975). Participants are asked one of three possible questions about each of a set of presented words:

1 Is it in capitals?

2 Does it rhyme with _____ ?

3 Does it fit into the sentence _____ ?

These three conditions are known as 1 'physical', 2 'phonetic', 3 'semantic', based on the assumed type of processing the participants have to perform on the presented word for each type of question. There are 45 words altogether, 15 for each type of question. The conditions are presented in a randomised manner (see Chapter 6). The hypothesis is that participants will recall significantly more at each level, i.e. $mean_1 < mean_2 < mean_3$. The data in Table 22.1 might have been produced by such an experiment.

Table 22.1   *Number of words recalled correctly*

Participant	Conditions Physical (1)	Phonetic (2)	Semantic (3)	T_{subs}
1	5	8	9	22
2	3	5	10	18
3	4	8	12	24
4	6	6	11	23
5	5	4	10	19
T_{conds}	23	31	52	$\Sigma x = 106$

RATIONALE FOR REPEAT MEASURES ANOVA

If you think back to Chapter 20 you'll recall that the one-way ANOVA is based on comparing the variation *within* samples with the variation *between* them (between their means). Above, we have three samples of scores (but each sample consists of the same people). As before, the more the scores vary *within* each condition, the less confident we are that the condition means differ significantly. **But**, in a repeated measures design, such as this one, the variation *within* each condition is *related to the variation in all the others*. Rather than the variation in each condition being thought of as three separate samples of the variation in the general population, we know that *part* of the variation in each column is predictable from knowing the variation in the others, because it's coming from the differences *between the same people*. These *overall* differences between people (in the 'T_{subs}' column in Table 22.1) are known as the BETWEEN SUBJECTS variation.

Please note here that I have kept to the use of the term 'subjects' because much other work you conduct with ANOVA will use this term and I wouldn't want to confuse people more than ANOVA tends to anyway. It is a generic term referring to animals or even plants (in biology) as much as to human results. *Some* computer software refers to 'cases', but not in a medical sense!

BETWEEN SUBJECTS VARIATION

Have a look at the fictitious and extremely idealised data in Table 22.2b. In a crudely simplistic way, what repeat measures ANOVA does is to say, we *know* participant 4 (let's call her Sally) is better than the rest. Her score causes variation *within* each condition. But we can ignore this variation because it's completely regular – it is accounted for by the *between subject variation*. We want to know if she varies *between conditions* like the rest.

Table 22.2a

Participant	Condition			
	A	B	C	
1	2	4	6	**12**
2	2	4	6	**12**
3	2	4	6	**12**
4	2	4	6	**12**
	8	**16**	**24**	48

Total SS = 32
Between subs SS = 0
Between conds SS = 32
Error SS = 0

Table 22.2b

Participant	Condition			
	A	B	C	
1	2	4	6	**12**
2	2	4	6	**12**
3	2	4	6	**12**
4	4	6	8	**18**
	10	**18**	**26**	54

Total SS = 41
Between subs SS = 9
Between conds SS = 32
Error SS = 0

Table 22.2c

Participant	Condition			
	A	B	C	
1	2	4	6	**12**
2	2	4	6	**12**
3	2	4	6	**12**
4	8	6	4	**18**
	14	**18**	**22**	54

Total SS = 41
Between subs SS = 9
Between conds SS = 8
Error SS = 24

Imagine that Table 22.2 represents three *different* sets of results which might occur with four participants. In Table 22.2a we have the persons-as-robots experimental dream result which scientific minds would adore! Each person performs at exactly the same level and only the 'treatment' (IV) has any effect on performance – the effect being perfectly regular. Here, the *total* variation (assessed, as always from sums of squares) is *completely* accounted for by the variation BETWEEN CONDITIONS. In Table 22.2b participant 4 performs two points better than the others, but is affected by the treatment conditions just the same. So here the variation *between conditions* and *between subjects together* completely explain overall variation in the 'cells' of the table. There is still no 'unexplained' error.

Finally, in Table 22.2c, a trifle more like reality, subject 4 performs as in Table 22.2b *except* that the scores are in the reverse order. There is *interaction* between people and conditions here. This is *exactly* like the concept of interaction in the previous two-way unrelated example – see the exercise just below. Note that *between subjects SS* is unchanged from Table 22.2b, but the *between conditions SS* is very much reduced. We can have little faith in the now narrow difference across conditions, especially considering the 'unexplained' variation (sometimes called 'RESIDUAL'), left in the 'error' SS and unaccounted for by overall subject or condition differences. It is produced by the *unsystematic* ways in which people have varied across the conditions (in this case there's just one 'deviant' actually!).

One-way related ANOVA can be understood by comparing it with the two-way unrelated design earlier. Think of there being *two* factors – conditions and subjects – and the 'cells' are the individual scores by each person on each condition.

> As an exercise, and if you have the time and patience (or computer software), take each of the tables in Table 22.2 in turn and try calculating the two-way, unrelated ANOVA which would result from treating the data as produced by *two* variables, one called 'conds' and the other called 'subs', with only one result for each combination (or 'cell') – hence there are twelve cells. You *should* obtain the sums of squares shown above under each table of data, with the error SS above becoming the *interaction* between 'conds' and 'subs'. Note, there is no *further* error left after calculating this interaction, as there would be in a two-way unrelated ANOVA, since there is only one value per conds X subs cell and there can be no variation within this!

THE POWER OF REPEATED MEASURES DESIGN

This technique demonstrates the true power of the repeat measures design. We are able to reduce the value of the *bottom* portion (denominator) of the F ratio – the estimate of population variance from within sample variation – by extracting variation within conditions which we can attribute to differences *between* people. The smaller the denominator, the larger is F and the better estimate we have of the likelihood of the difference *between conditions* being a chance fluctuation; i.e. there is a lower probability of a type II error. In the one-way unrelated example each score in each sample was in no way related to scores in the other samples. Hence, *all* the variation *within conditions* was 'error' or unexplained variation from any number of random variables. However, in the repeat measures design *some* of that variability, attributable to individual differences, is accounted for.

THE DIVISION OF VARIATION – 'BETWEEN SUBJECTS' AND 'WITHIN SUBJECTS' VARIATION

The *total variation* in related ANOVA is split into the BETWEEN SUBJECTS *variation*, which is said to be '*partialled out*', and WITHIN SUBJECTS *variation* which consists of:

1 *Between conditions variation* – how the individuals differ as a result of the different conditions, irrespective of any differences between the individuals themselves
and:

2 *Error* remaining – the *interaction* of 'subjects' with conditions, that is, the extent to which different people respond unsystematically across the conditions. This is the residual or 'unexplained' variation and, the smaller it is, the greater confidence we can have in the effectiveness of the IV.

```
TOTAL SS
    ├──── BETWEEN SUBJECTS ──── Between subjects SS
    │
    └──── WITHIN SUBJECTS ──── Between conditions SS
                          ──── Error SS
                               (the 'left over' SS, as before, but
                               with between subjects SS removed)
```

Figure 22.1 *Division of variation in a one-way related ANOVA design*

CALCULATIONS FOR REPEATED MEASURES ANOVA

As with the two-way unrelated, I shall include the calculation steps and explanatory notes but not the number crunching arithmetic steps:

Calculation of one-way repeated measures ANOVA on data in Table 22.1

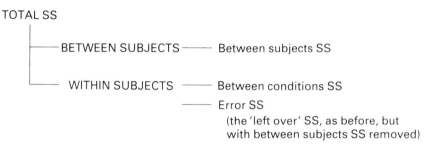

1 Calculate SS_{total} using formula (A) as before

Note: N is the total number of values *not* the number of people. Each provides three, hence, it is 15 (three conditions $\times$ 5) here

$$\Sigma x^2 - \frac{(\Sigma x)^2}{N} \qquad (A)$$

$$SS_{total} \quad = \textbf{112.93}$$

2 Calculate SS_{subs} (between subjects) using, as ever, equation (B)

Here T is T_{subs} and N is the number of conditions for each $T_{sub} = 3$. Note: n is *not* the number of people here; it is the number of values making up each T_{sub}

$$\frac{\Sigma T^2}{n} - \frac{(\Sigma x)^2}{N} \qquad (B)$$

$$SS_{subs} \quad = \quad \textbf{8.93}$$

3 Calculate SS_{conds} (between conditions) using equation (B), as for SS_{groups} or SS_{factor} earlier.

T is T_{conds}; n is the number in each condition = 5

$$SS_{conds} \quad = \quad \textbf{89.73}$$

4 Calculate SS_{error} by using:

$SS_{error} = SS_{total} - SS_{subs} - SS_{conds}$

$$SS_{error} = 112.93 - 8.93 - 89.73$$
$$= \quad \textbf{14.27}$$

5 Calculate *degrees of freedom*.

Total = $N - 1$	=	14
Between subjects = $(5 - 1)\star$	=	4
Between conditions = $(3 - 1)$	=	2
Error = total − between subjects − between conditions	=	8

$\star$ treat 'subjects' as a factor with five levels

6 Mean squares and F ratios are calculated as before and the results are shown in Table 22.3. Note that we are only interested in the F value for *between conditions* (our IV) and the error MS is divided into the within conditions MS.

Table 22.3

Source of variation (repeated measures – one-way)	Sum of squares	df	Mean sum of squares	F ratio	Probability of F
Between subjects	8.93	4	2.23		
Within subjects	104	10			
Between conditions	89.73	2	44.87	25.21	$p < 0.001$
Error	14.27	8	1.78		
Total	112.93	14			

INTERPRETING THE RESULT

Here, our hypothesis that the mean numbers of words recalled in each of the three conditions of processing would differ significantly is strongly supported by our repeated measures analysis.

Two-way (related) design

For this, and the mixed design which follows, the calculations get rather complicated and it is difficult to conceptualise how the variation components are being accounted for. Here, then, I haven't included the equations, since they are the same as those used before. I again hope you'll have access to computer calculations of ANOVA. Though you might wish to check the calculations, the important point is to understand what the different components are doing, as I emphasised earlier. If you can understand what you have to do in these two models, and the three-way unrelated, then you can manage and interpret all other possible combinations of ANOVA model (in terms of within or between subjects variables).

In this design, the *same* group of participants undergo *all* levels of *all* factors – if they have the energy and stamina! Although this is often not covered in introductory texts it is, in fact, quite a common design in projects, where people may be hard to come by and you can get your friends and/or family to do, say, two versions of the Stroop test under two conditions, say fast presentation and slow.

Imagine that the fictitious data in Table 22.4, below, are from a hypothetical study in which *one* group of air traffic controllers performs both a simple and a complex vigilance task under both quiet and noisy conditions. Values shown are errors. Counterbalancing would be employed, of course, to even out order effects.

Table 22.4

	Simple task (A1)			Complex task (A2)					
	Quiet (B1) A1B1	Noisy (B2) A1B2	A1 total	Quiet (B1) A2B1	Noisy (B2) A2B2	A2 total	B1 total	B2 total	Subs totals
Participant									
1	3	4	7	7	12	19	10	16	26
2	5	5	10	3	13	16	8	18	26
3	9	4	13	5	15	20	14	19	33
4	7	8	15	9	21	30	16	29	45
Totals	24	21	**45**	24	61	**85**	**48**	**82**	**130**

What is new in the two-way related ANOVA calculation is the existence of an error term for *each* of the effects (main and interaction). We do with *each* factor what we did with the *single* factor, in the one-way. We look at the *interaction* of subjects with the factor – how far their scores vary across the conditions in a way contrary to how the condition *totals* vary.

For each effect (main and interaction) we consult the relevant interaction cells as we would for the three-way unrelated design. In calculating the error for factor A (SS_{errorA}), for example, we consult the *factor A × subjects* interaction cells. These are the eight values in the columns labelled 'A1 total' and 'A2 total' in Table 22.4. We are looking for the error or 'leftover' variation not accounted for by subject variation and condition variation – just as in the one-way example. Hence we calculate SS_{cells} for these cells. There are *two* values per cell total (from the two B conditions) so *n* here is 2. We then subtract the SS for factor A and the SS between subjects, as we did in the one-way version.

Calculation of two-way repeat measures ANOVA on data in Table 22.4

1 Calculate SS_{total} using formula (A) as before SS_{total} = **371.75**
   Note: *N* is the total number of *values* = 16

2 Calculate SS_{subs} as before SS_{subs} = **60.25**

3 Calculate $SS_{factorA}$. Use totals for A (45 and 85) $SS_{factorA}$ = **100**
   in Table 22.4. *n* = 4

4 Calculate SS_{errorA} by finding $SS_{cellsAS}$ – see $SS_{cellsAS}$ = **173.75**
   explanation above. Then SS_{errorA} = **13.5**
   $SS_{errorA} = SS_{cellsAS} - SS_{factorA} - SS_{subs}$

5 Calculate $SS_{factorB}$. Use totals for B in $SS_{factorB}$ = **72.25**
   Table 22.4. *n* = 4

6 Calculate SS_{errorB} as for SS_{errorA} but this time $SS_{cellsBS}$ = **142.75**
   use cells for B × S. These will be the eight SS_{errorB} = **10.25**
   totals in columns B1 and B2.
   $SS_{errorB} = SS_{cellsBS} - SS_{factorB} - SS_{subs}$

7 Calculate $SS_{factorA\,factorB}$ – the interaction factor. For this, put the totals of A1B1, A2B2, A2B1 and A2B2 into the standard equation to find $SS_{cellsAB}$. n will be 4

$$SS_{AB} = SS_{cellsAB} - SS_{factorA} - SS_{factorB}$$

$$SS_{cellsAB} = 272.25$$
$$SS_{AB} = 100$$

8 Calculate the error term for the interaction –

$$SS_{errorAB} = SS_{total} - SS_{subs} - SS_{factorA} - SS_{factorB} - SS_{errorA} - SS_{errorB} - SS_{AB}$$

$$SS_{errorAB} = 15.5$$

9 Degrees of freedom:

Total	$= N - 1 = 16$ values $- 1$	$= 15$
Between subjects	$= 4 - 1$	$= 3$
Between conditions (A)	$= 2 - 1$	$= 1$
$Error_A$	$= 1 \times 3$*	$= 3$
Between conditions (B)	$= 2 - 1$	$= 1$
$Error_B$	$= 1 \times 3$	$= 3$
Interaction (AB)	$= 1 \times 1$	$= 1$
$Error_{AB}$	$= 3 \times 1 \times 1$	$= 3$

* $Error_A$ is the interaction of factor A with subjects; hence we multiply df for A $\times$ df subjects.

Source of variation (two-way repeat measures)	Sum of squares	df	Mean sum of squares (SS/df)	F ratio	Probability of F
Between subjects	60.25	3	20.08		
Within subjects					
Factor A (task)	100	1	100	22.22*	$p < 0.02$
$Error_{factorA}$	13.5	3	4.5		
Factor B (noise level)	72.25	1	72.25	21.13	$p < 0.02$
$Error_{factorB}$	10.25	3	3.42		
$Interaction_{AB}$ (task $\times$ noise)	100	1	100	19.34	$p < 0.05$
$Error_{AB}$	15.5	3	5.17		
Total	**371.75**	15			

*Each effect is divided by its associated error MS.

INTERPRETING THE RESULT

We have significant main effects for both factors (task complexity *and* noise) and a significant interaction effect. In fact, it is the interaction which requires scrutiny since it appears to be the much worse performance by controllers on the complex task in noisy conditions, relative to all the other conditions, which has produced the significant results.

ANOVA MIXED DESIGN – ONE REPEAT MEASURE AND

ONE UNRELATED FACTOR

In the example below, assume that we now have *two* groups of participants doing the experiment described in the one-way repeated measures test. One group have the items presented visually, the others listen to them. Note that, in the calculations, an *error* term is found for *both* the between and within subjects effects. Note, also, that any effect which includes the repeat measure factor is also counted as 'within subjects'. In this example, therefore, the *interaction* between groups and conditions gets counted as *within*, since it includes the within subjects conditions factor.

Table 22.6 *Number of words recalled correctly*

	Conditions			
	Physical	**Phonetic**	**Semantic**	(= 'levels')
GROUP 1 (Visual)				
Participant				T_{subs}
1	5	8	9	22
2	3	5	10	18
3	4	8	12	24
4	6	6	11	23
5	5	4	10	19
T_{cells}	**23**	**31**	**52**	$T_{group1} = 106$
GROUP 2 (Auditory)				
Participant				
6	5	3	4	12
7	4	9	3	16
8	9	7	7	23
9	3	6	6	15
10	6	8	5	19
T_{cells}	**27**	**33**	**25**	$T_{group2} = 85$
T_{conds}	**50**	**64**	**77**	$\Sigma x = 191$

Note: the calculation for between (unrelated) conditions, below, produces exactly the result which would occur if we conducted a one-way ANOVA on the two group results for auditory vs. visual, *ignoring* the existence of the repeat measures conditions.

Calculations for mixed design – one between subjects and one repeat factor

1 SS_{total} is found by using equation (A) as in previous tables. Note that N is total number of values again, not people SS_{total} = 186.97

2 SS_{subs} is found using equation (B) as previously. T is T_{subs}; n is total for each $T_{sub} = 3$ SS_{subs} = 46.97

3   SS_{unrel} is found using equation B. T is T_{group}; n is number of *values* per group $= 15$ $SS_{vis/aud}$ $= 14.7$

4   $SS_{error/between}$ is $SS_{subs} - SS_{unrel}$ $SS_{error/between}$ $= 32.27$

5   SS_{within} is found from: $SS_{total} - SS_{subs}$ SS_{within} $= 140$

6   SS_{rep} is found using equation (B). T is T_{conds}; n is the number per condition $= 10$ SS_{levels} $= 36.47$

7   SS_{cells} is found using equation (B). T is T_{cells}; n therefore $= 5$ SS_{cells} $= 111.37$

8   $SS_{unrel \times rep}$ is found from: $SS_{vis/aud \times levels}$ $= 60.2$

    $SS_{cells} - SS_{unrel} - SS_{rep}$

9   $SS_{error/within}$ is found from: $SS_{error/within}$ $= 43.33$

    $SS_{within} - SS_{rep} - SS_{unrel \times rep}$

10 Degrees of freedom:

    Total $= N - 1 = 30$ values $- 1$ $= 29$

    Between subjects $=$ Subjects $- 1$ $= 10 - 1$ $= 9$

      Between (unrelated) conditions $=$ conds $- 1$ $= 2 - 1$ $= 1$

      Error/between $=$ between subs $-$ between (unrel) conds $= 9 - 1$ $= 8$

    Within subjects $=$ total $-$ between subjects $= 29 - 9$ $= 20$

      Between (related) conditions $=$ conds $- 1$ $= 3 - 1$ $= 2$

      Interaction (unrel $\times$ rel) $=$ unrel conds $\times$ rel conds $= 1 \times 2$ $= 2$

      Error/within $=$ within subs $-$ bet conds(rel) $-$ int $= 20 - 2 - 2$ $= 16$

Table 22.7

Source of variation (mixed model: 2(unrelated) × 3(related))	Sum of squares	df	Mean sum of squares (SS/df)	F ratio	Probability of F
Between subjects	46.97	9			
vis/aud	14.7	1	14.7	3.648	Not sig
error/between	32.27	8	4.03		
Within subjects	140	20			
level of processing	36.47	2	18.24	6.731	$p < 0.01$
interaction vis/aud × level	60.2	2	30.1	11.107	$p < 0.001$
error/within	43.33	16	2.71		
Total	**186.97**	**29**			

INTERPRETING THE RESULT

It looks as though levels of processing has an effect but that this effect is limited to the visual presentation group only. There is a *main effect* for levels but also a significant *interaction* and, by inspection, we can see the progression upwards of words recalled for the visual but not for the auditory presentation group. These *are* fictitious data – if

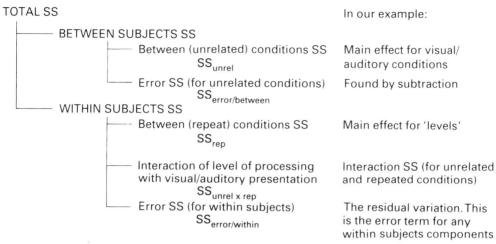

Figure 22.2 *Division of variation in a mixed design (one related and one unrelated factor)*

anyone actually *does* this study, please let me know the result! Note that there is no main effect for presentation type, the auditory group not doing worse overall than the visual group.

MORE COMPLEX ANOVA DESIGNS

We've reached a point where it makes sense to stop. You now have the principles for any more complicated design. As I've said once or twice, I doubt you'll be calculating at this level by hand. You should now be able to interpret the terms produced when submitting your data to software analysis. Should you need to carry out more complicated calculations, the principles are just more of those presented. In a two-unrelated plus one-repeat measure design, for instance, you'll need to work out the SS for two unrelated factors, *and* their interaction, and subtract these from the between subjects SS, before proceeding to find the within conditions factor SS and the SS *for all* the interactions of it with the unrelated factors. The calculations are obviously lengthy, but if you are careful to lay out the data accurately and follow each step in the manner already explained you should get there in the end. If you require further theoretical understanding or need to check more detailed calculations then please consult one of the texts I've referred to below. The last mentioned, by Winer, is treated by many, in awe, as the 'bible' for ANOVA theory. Howell's is deep at times, but excellent, modern and uses actual research examples throughout.

FURTHER READING ON ANOVA TECHNIQUES AND THEORY

Hays, W. L. (1974) *Statistics for the Social Sciences*, New York: Holt Rinehart Winston
Hays, W. L. (1988) *Statistics*, New York: Holt Rinehart Winston
Howell, D. C. (1992) *Statistical Methods for Psychology*, Boston: PWS-Kent
Winer, B. J. (1971) *Statistical Principles in Experimental Design*, New York: McGraw-Hill

Glossary

Variation associated with the differences between participants' overall totals in a repeat measures design; this variation is partialled out of the overall error which would be used in an unrelated design	_____ _____ _____	between subjects variation
Variation, calculated in a repeat measure design, which comes from how scores between the conditions vary when the variation between participants' overall totals has been removed	_____ _____ _____	between conditions variation
A term for the remaining variation in a repeat measures design when variation between subjects and between conditions has been removed; the remaining 'unexplained' variation	_____	residual

Exercises

1 As in Chapter 20, use random number tables to generate three sets of eight scores. This time, assume that the three sets are from the same eight people and conduct a one-way repeat measures ANOVA. Again, complain to your tutor if the results are significant!

2 Produce an outline 'source of variation' results table for a mixed design where there is one repeated measures factor with three levels and one unrelated factor with four levels, eight people in each. As in Chapter 20, put values into the 'degrees of freedom' column.

3 Below in Table 22.8 is an incomplete fictitious results table for a two by three ANOVA. For each statement below choose between true/false or choose the correct answer:

a) There was a significant main effect for *groups*.   T/F
b) There was a significant main effect for *conditions*.   T/F
c) There was a significant interaction effect between *groups* and *conditions*.   T/F
d) The design was fully unrelated.   T/F
e) Total degrees of freedom were: 36   41   42 (choose an answer)
f) There were three groups.   T/F
g) There were three conditions.   T/F
h) The number of participants was: 7   21   14

Table 22.8 *Fictitious data for question 3*

Source of variation	SS	df	MS	F	Significance of F
Between subjects		13			
Groups	14.88	1	14.88	4.55	0.054
Error between	39.24	12	3.27		
Within subjects					
Conditions	16.33	2	8.17	1.32	0.286
Groups × conditions	48.90	2	24.45	3.94	0.033
Error within	148.76	24	6.20		

OTHER USEFUL COMPLEX MULTI-VARIATE TESTS – A BRIEF SUMMARY

This chapter gives a very brief look at some other more complex statistical techniques which might be useful in project work of some kinds but which really necessitate the use of a personal computer.

MANOVA is a method for conducting analyses of variance on *several* DVs together, taken as a combination.

Analysis of co-variance (ANCOVA) adjusts the means of samples according to the extent to which scores on the variable measured correlate with another variable, known as the **co-variate**. The example used is that one group may start a training programme lower overall in numeracy than a second group. Scores on the final test for both group are known to correlate with initial numeracy level. Thus initial numeracy level **confounds** the real change in ability by the group originally lower on numeracy. ANCOVA takes the numeracy-final score correlation into account and gives, in a sense, the difference between means estimated to occur if the groups started out equal.

Multiple regression uses the correlations of *several* **predictor variables** with a **criterion variable**. It *adds* the predictive power of each variable until the optimum level of prediction of the criterion variable is achieved using some or all of the predictor variables. R^2 is a measure of the overall prediction of variance in the criterion variable. An example of the use of the method in practice is for the selection of personnel using a battery of tests and other obtained measures, knowing the correlation of each of these with overall performance.

The method uses the basic method of **regression**. This estimates the best fit of a line through a scatter of related score pairs such that **residuals** (the distances between *actual* score on *Y* and scores predicted by the regression line) are minimised.

Almost as an afterthought, because this book has gone as far as it really ought with advanced tests, I would just like to mention three more sophisticated forms of analyses, mainly because quite simple student projects sometimes generate data on which these techniques can be used if a computer program is available.

MANOVA – MULTIVARIATE ANALYSIS OF VARIANCE

Put simply, this is a set of statistical procedures which tests the significance of *multiple DVs* as a set. Suppose you had gathered data evaluating your college course where students assessed usefulness, interest, enjoyment and so on. With MANOVA it is possible to test these DVs as a set across the various conditions of the IV, which, in this case, might be part-time, full-time and evening students. It would be possible here to conduct a one-way ANOVA for *each* of the assessment scores separately, or *t* tests if only two types of student were involved. MANOVA does this but also estimates the significance of any difference across levels of the IV *taking all assessments (DVs) together*.

ANCOVA – ANALYSIS OF CO-VARIANCE

This will be easier to explain using an example first. Suppose we conduct a quasi-experiment using two groups of students, one a day-time class and one a part-time evening group. These are the only two groups available and we want to see whether a group using a new interactive computer package for learning statistics and research methods, with less traditional teacher contact, does as well as a conventionally taught group. The trouble is that the groups did not start off equal on competence in numeracy. The evening group, who used the computer package, contained more adults returning to education after several years and were generally weaker, though there is a lot of overlap between the two groups and the range within each group is wide. In addition, when we investigate end-of-year test results as a whole, we find that initial numeracy level correlates quite strongly with 'final achievement', no matter what class the student was in. We suspect that the independent learning package did help the evening group but the difference between groups is not significant. Our results are confounded by the initial numeracy available. There are several other variables which could be responsible for the final difference between the

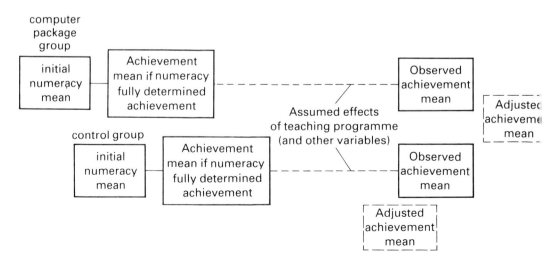

Figure 23.1 *Observed and adjusted means in ANCOVA*

two groups – evening students are more mature, perhaps more committed, and so on. These are the usual problematic uncontrolled variables differing between any two groups, especially when they are not the result of random allocation, as in this case. However, we *do* have an element of control over the numeracy variable because we happen to know how it correlates with final achievement scores. ANCOVA permits us to 'partial out' the effect of the numeracy differences (known as the CO-VARIATE). It gives us an estimate of the means of the two groups which would occur *if*, in a sense, both groups started from equal positions on numeracy. The fictitious data in Table 23.1, and Figure 23.1 illustrate this approach.

Table 23.1

Groups		Student scores							Means observed	adjusted
Programme	Numeracy	23	45	33	18	65	72	54	44.29	
	Achievement	55	63	58	48	63	68	60	**59.29**	**62.64**
Control	Numeracy	81	78	45	23	78	65	59	61.29	
	Achievement	71	75	53	42	65	54	53	**59.00**	**55.64**

Difference between obtained means:	N/S
Difference between adjusted means:	$p = 0.029$
Correlation between numeracy and achievement	$= 0.794$

Notice that in the fictitious data, the two groups end up pretty equal on achievement, even though the programme group started out well behind on numeracy which has a lot of influence on achievement scores. It is important to note that ANCOVA does *two* things. First, if groups start out similar on the co-variate it only takes out the variance which is assumed to be caused by the co-variate. This reduces the error term of the standard ANOVA calculation. That is, we've reduced the 'unexplained' error in the bottom half of the F ratio calculation. This, in turn, gives a more accurate estimate of significant differences between means. Second, if the groups differ on the co-variate to start with, ANCOVA is used to conduct the analysis of variance on the estimate of what the means would be if they *didn't* differ on the co-variate.

MULTIPLE REGRESSION

Multiple regression can be used when we have a set of variables (X_1, X_2, X_3, etc.) each of which correlates to some known extent with a variable (Y) for which we would like to predict values. We may wish, for example, to predict likely satisfaction in a job from a number of selection measures: abilities, age, interests, qualifications and so on – see Figure 23.2.

To explain this complex method, it is first necessary to explain briefly what is meant by REGRESSION. We need to think back to correlation (Chapter 18). Remember that we can plot the relationship between two sets of paired scores on a scattergram. The

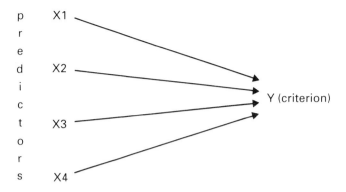

Figure 23.2 *The concept of multiple regression*

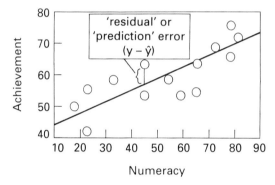

Figure 23.3 *Scattergram of correlation between numeracy and achievement*

correlation pattern for numeracy and achievement score, from the ANCOVA example above, is plotted in Figure 23.3. The idea behind regression is that, if we know scores on one variable (the PREDICTOR VARIABLE) we can, to an extent dependent on the size of r^2, predict scores on the other variable (the CRITERION VARIABLE). This is done by using a regression line, which is the line of 'best fit' placed among the points shown on our scattergram. What is meant by best fit? Well, if we're estimating scores on Y from scores on X it makes sense to find the line which creates the lowest differences between what we would predict for Y ($\hat{Y}$) and what the Y values actually were. This 'prediction error' (also called a 'RESIDUAL') is the vertical distance between each point on our scattergram and the regression line, when we've decided where it should fall. In other words, the regression line minimises these vertical distances – all the values ($Y - \hat{Y}$). The mathematics involved is somewhat complex and involves the use of calculus. However, for those readers with a vague memory of school algebra, you might remember that the equation of a straight line can be written as: $\hat{Y} = bX + a$. Here, b is the *slope* of the line and a is the point where it cuts the Y axis (i.e. when $X = 0$). Statistical programmes will kindly calculate a and b for us. In our example, a takes the value 42.5. b is 0.318. Substituting one more value for X gives us two points with which to draw the line shown in Figure 23.3.

MULTIPLE PREDICTIONS

So far so good. We have looked at a way in which values of a variable may be *predicted*, to some extent, from known values on another variable, if we have conducted a correlation calculation on a decent-sized sample (prediction errors will be much greater, the smaller the sample used). The interesting part comes when we ask, 'If we were partly able to predict achievement because we knew students' initial numeracy scores, could we make a *better* prediction of achievement if we had information on *other* correlating variables?' This is the nub of multiple regression. We do what we did above for all the variables for which we have correlations with achievement and we *combine* these individual correlations to obtain an improved prediction of achievement. Take a look at Figure 23.4.

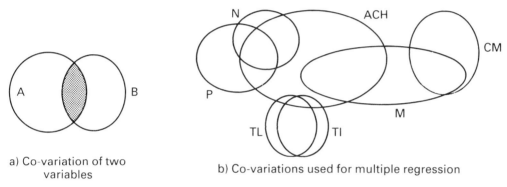

a) Co-variation of two
variables

b) Co-variations used for multiple regression

Figure 23.4 *Multiple regression – concept of co-variation*

In Figure 23.4a we see a representation of the situation when two variables, A and B, vary together to some extent. The shaded portion represents the amount of correlation, or rather, the variance which they share in common. Remember that the *square* of the correlation coefficient is used to estimate how much variance in one variable is 'explained' by variance in the other. In Figure 23.4b the big circle, labelled 'ACH', represents the variance of our students' scores on the end-of-year test ('achievement'). Other variables might also correlate with achievement score, such as teacher liking (TL), teacher interest (TI) and motivation (M). There are two more variables on Figure 23.4b. One is 'P' which stands for scores on a test which measures people's ability with patterns (recognising them when rotated, imagining abstract relationships visually, and so on). We will assume that numeracy and pattern recognition are somewhat correlated and that both correlate with achievement, numeracy more strongly. CM stands for career motivation and for the sake of this example we'll assume that, whilst motivation in general *does* correlate with achievement, career motivation does not at all. Teacher liking and teacher interest turn out to be almost the same thing in terms of their correlation with one another and achievement. Assume we have test assessments of our students for *all* these variables.

In multiple regression *a statistical prediction of one variable is made using the correlations of other known variables with it*. The extent that *each* predictor variable predicts values of the criterion (achievement, in this case) is known as its REGRESSION COEFFICIENT. Here, N is a good predictor of ACH, and so is P to a slightly lesser extent. The very important point however, is the issue of how much *extra* P contributes to the prediction of ACH. This is the amount of variance it shares with ACH *but not with N*. You'll see that TL doesn't tell us much more about ACH than TI does. M's contribution is unique. What is CM appearing for then? Well, the motivation test will have variance to do with career motivation and (we are assuming) career motivation has nothing to do with achievement on the end-of-year test. Hence, if we set up a test of career motivation we can assess the contribution of this to overall motivation and then subtract this out of the contribution in variance that motivation makes to test achievement. Career motivation is known as a 'SUPPRESSOR VARIABLE' because, if not accounted for, it suppresses the amount by which we can predict achievement from motivation as a whole. The regression coefficient for each predictor variable is related to its correlation with the criterion variable but *also* takes into account these inter-correlations between all the predictors.

In multiple regression then, there is an equation which predicts Y, not just from X as in simple correlation and regression, but from the regression coefficients of X_1, X_2, X_3 . . . and so on, where the Xs are predictor variables whose correlations with Y are known. The equation would take the form:

$$\hat{Y} = b_0 + b_1X_1 + b_2X_2 + b_3X_3 \ldots \text{ and so on,}$$

where the bs are the regression coefficients for each of the predictors (Xs) and b_0 plays the role of a in the simple regression equation.

Programmes for multiple regression calculate R, the MULTIPLE REGRESSION COEFFICIENT (you can, of course do this by hand!). R is a measure of the correlation between **1** $\hat{Y}$, using the *combined* regression coefficients, and **2** the *actual* values of Y. The more predictors we have, which share some *unique* variance with Y, the more variance in Y we can account for. As with simple correlation, R^2 is an estimate of the amount of variance in Y which we have 'explained', this time using a combination of predictors, not just one X variable. This technique is typically employed when occupational psychologists are attempting to construct predictive measures of job performance by combining the predictive power of variables such as: years of experience, age, qualifications, test scores and so on. In the same context, it is also used in the construction of a single test to decide which combination of many items are the best predictors of a criterion. A 'stepwise' program will offer the value of R^2 as each extra item is added to the overall predictive equation. We might find, for instance, that item 23 of a test of computing aptitude (potential) is the strongest predictor, on its own, of test results after one year of computer training. Item 19 adds more predictive power, so do items 12, 6, 28 and so on, whereas, later on in the analysis we find additional items adding virtually nothing of significance (in the technical sense) to the prediction of Y. It is important to remember that this does *not* make item 19 the 'second-best predictor' because this is only true in the context of taking item 23 first. Multiple regression calculations take into account the inter-correlations between all predictor variables. Also, it does not mean that any *one* individual's score can be predicted to the level of general accuracy found. As ever, with psychological variables, the predictive accuracy refers to samples as a whole. A large company may well decide, though, that over large numbers, they would be fairer and more efficient in their selection if they used this form of analysis of their selection resources.

Glossary

Statistical procedure used to investigate differences between two means which may be adjusted to allow for the fact that the two groups differ on a variable which correlates with the DV (the 'co-variate')	_____	ANCOVA
A variable which correlates with the DV and on which two groups, who are being investigated for difference, differ. The biasing effect of this confounding variable can be adjusted for in ANCOVA	__-_____	co-variate
Variable which is being predicted in regression procedures	_____ _____	criterion variable
Statistical procedure for testing the effects of one or more IVs *on more than one DV*	_____	MANOVA
Statistical procedure in which the correlations of several predictor variables with a criterion variable are *summed* to give a better prediction of that variable	_____ _____	multiple regression
A value indicating the strength of prediction of the combined set of predictor variables being used in multiple regression	_____ _____ _____	multiple regression coefficient
Variable being used to predict a criterion variable in regression procedures	_____ _____	predictor variable
Procedure of predicting a criterion variable $(\hat{Y})$ from a predictor variable (X) using the 'line of best fit' around which correlated pairs of X and Y scores are arranged	_____	regression
Value indicating the extent to which each predictor variable predicts scores on the criterion variable in multiple regression procedures	_____ _____	regression coefficient
Difference between an actual score and what it would be as predicted by a predictor variable using a regression procedure $(Y - \hat{Y})$	_____	residual
Variable whose common variance can be partialled out of the variance of a predictor variable so that the latter can more accurately predict values of a criterion variable (in multiple regression procedures)	_____ _____	suppressor variable

What analysis to use?

CHOOSING AN APPROPRIATE TEST

Trying to choose an appropriate test can leave you with a floundering feeling, since there are so many tests and there can be a lot of data and several hypotheses. The first golden rule is *not to panic*! Stay calm. Next . . .

- Take one hypothesis at a time
- Choose the test for this hypothesis
- Calculate the test
- Decide whether the result is significant

TESTS FOR TWO SAMPLES

Most tests covered in detail in this book assume you have just *two* samples and that you want to test for a difference or a correlation between them. If this is your position then just ignore the bottom part of Figure 24.1 on page 378, below the section titled 'More than two samples'. Tests for more than two samples are dealt with after the general system for making decisions has been outlined.

MAKING A CHOICE

So how do we choose the appropriate test? This really should be quite simple if you follow the three steps in Box 24.1 and use the flow chart in Figure 24.1. Notice that the decision you have to make at each step is indicated on the flow chart.

PARAMETRIC TEST ASSUMPTIONS

Remember (from Chapter 17) these are:

1 Interval level data required
2 Samples drawn from a normally distributed population
3 Homogeneity of variance (. . . with some divergence from these allowed)

Box 24.1 *Steps in choosing the appropriate test*

Decision 1 Does the hypothesis predict difference or correlation?

Decision 2 At what level of measurement are the data?

> *Note:* If the level is interval and you wish to conduct a parametric test, check that your data satisfy the parametric test assumptions before proceeding. If the assumptions cannot reasonably be met, you will have to convert your data to ranked data.

Decision 3 Is the design related or unrelated?

EXAMPLES OF CHOOSING A TEST

Take a look at Table 24.1. The data were produced by asking male and female 17-year-olds to estimate their own IQ, by measuring their actual IQ, measuring their height and measuring their mothers' IQs.

Table 24.1 *Male and female IQ data*

Males				Females			
Estimated IQ	Measured IQ	Height (cm)	Mother's IQ	Estimated IQ	Measured IQ	Height (cm)	Mother's IQ
120	107	160	100	100	97	155	105
110	112	181	105	95	92	165	97
95	130	175	102	90	104	177	115
140	95	164	97	110	112	162	96
100	104	163	120	85	130	173	100
120	92	158	131	100	95	159	120
110	97	172	115	105	107	164	102
105	101	171	96	100	101	165	131

Assume that mother and offspring can be treated as matched pairs.
Assume that estimated IQ cannot be treated as interval data.
Assume that this researcher will treat measured IQ as interval level data (though as explained earlier, there is debate about this).

Using the decision chart (Figure 24.1), try to select the appropriate test for each of the following hypotheses:

1 Male IQ estimates are higher than female estimates

2 Female measured IQs are higher than male measured IQs

3 The taller people are, the higher their IQ

4 Female measured IQs are higher than their mothers' measured IQs

Hypothesis 1   Decision 1: we are looking for a *difference*

Decision 2: we shall have to convert the estimated IQs to ranked, *ordinal* data

Decision 3: the design is *unrelated*; we have separate groups of males and females

Our choice is therefore **Mann–Whitney** (or **Wilcoxon rank sum**).

Hypothesis 2   Decision 1:   we are again looking for a *difference*
                     Decision 2:   these data are being treated as *internal* level
                     Decision 3:   the design is *unrelated*, as before

Our choice is therefore a ***t*-test for unrelated samples**.

Parametric assumptions must be met:
- The interval level data assumption has been made.
- IQ tests are standardised to ensure that scores for the general population are normally distributed on them. Hence, the samples must come from a normally distributed population.
- Using an 'eyeball' test, variances are not too different. This is not a big problem anyway, since although we have an unrelated design, the numbers in each group are equal.

Hypothesis 3   Decision 1: a positive *correlation* is predicted between height and IQ. We can treat male and female as one group
                     Decision 2: IQ is being treated as *interval*. Height is ratio level and therefore, at least *interval* level
                     Decision 3: correlations are automatically related designs

Our choice is therefore **Pearson's correlation coefficient**.

Parametric assumptions must be met:

- Arguments are the same as for **hypothesis 2** except that the design is related; height is known to be normally distributed.

Hypothesis 4   Decision 1: a *difference* is predicted
                     Decision 2: measured IQ is being treated as *interval* level data
                     Decision 3: matched pairs are a *related* design

Our choice is therefore a ***t*-test for related samples**.

Parametric assumptions must be met:

- Arguments are covered above.

For each of the cases where a parametric test is chosen you could of course have chosen a non-parametric test, if you just wanted to use a simpler but possibly less powerful test.

Here are some general hints to keep in mind when choosing tests:

- Correlations must always be, logically, related designs.
- χ^2 tests the *difference* between *observed* frequencies and *expected* frequencies. This is why it is placed where it is on the chart. However, the net result is to tell us whether there is a significant association between one variable (say, being a smoker [or not] and having poor health [or not]). It is called a 'test of association'.
- If data appear as frequencies, in categories, a χ^2 test is indicated. Even though the numbers in the categories are cardinal numbers, if it means that *all* you know is that, say 22 people are in one category, and you know no more about them and can't separate them in any way (by rank or score) the data are in frequency form and the categories concerned can be treated as a nominal scale.
- If a test or other psychological measure has been *standardised*, it can be treated as producing interval level data.

- If the results in question are in the form of scores or numbers produced by humans estimating or 'rating' events or behaviour, on some arbitrary scale, it is almost always safest to convert the numbers to ordinal level (by ranking them). The same goes for scores on an unstandardised questionnaire or opinion survey.
- Ordinal data appear as a set of ranks ('ord' for order).

TESTS FOR MORE THAN TWO SAMPLES

To discover which test is appropriate you need to go through the three decisions already described for two sample tests. When you use Figure 24.1, look below the section marked 'more than two samples'. What is important, if you have more than two samples, is that you don't just split your samples into sets of two and carry out a *t* test, say, on all the various combinations. Each time you carry out a test the probability level for significance is 0.05 and if you do *two* tests you obviously increase your chance of getting a 'significant' result by chance. This is known as 'capitalising on chance' and is discussed more fully in the introduction to Section 5.

Your decisions, in choosing a difference test for more than two samples, can be organised as follows:

Are parametric assumptions met?

YES: Use ANOVA method unless non-parametric method preferred

Single factorial	unrelated	– one-way unrelated
	repeat measures	– one-way repeated measures
Multi-factorial	all factors unrelated	– unrelated
	all factors related	– repeated measures
	at least one factor unrelated and at least one related	– mixed

NO:

Unrelated	differences	– Kruskal–Wallis
	trend	– Jonckheere
Related	differences	– Friedman
	trend	– Page

SOME INFORMATION ON COMPUTER PROGRAMS

Computers have taken the donkey work out of statistical description and testing, of that there is no doubt. In preparing this book I have been able to calculate tests in a few seconds which would have taken me several minutes a few years ago, armed only with a calculator. However, as any tutor will argue, it is only by calculating at least the easier tests that you come to realise just what the test is doing, *why* it shows what it does, what its limitations are and so on. By grappling (or playing) with numbers you get to realise what's going on. I would definitely recommend therefore that you calculate some tests to begin with *and* check for significance in tables. By just taking what the computer says you can end up with only a passive and superficial understanding of statistical testing, and simple mistakes can easily be missed because final results don't strike you as obviously impossible.

That said, once you *do* understand what's going on I see no point in masochism. Computers in this domain are doing just what they were intended for, not putting you out of work but leaving you free to concentrate on things which require new and

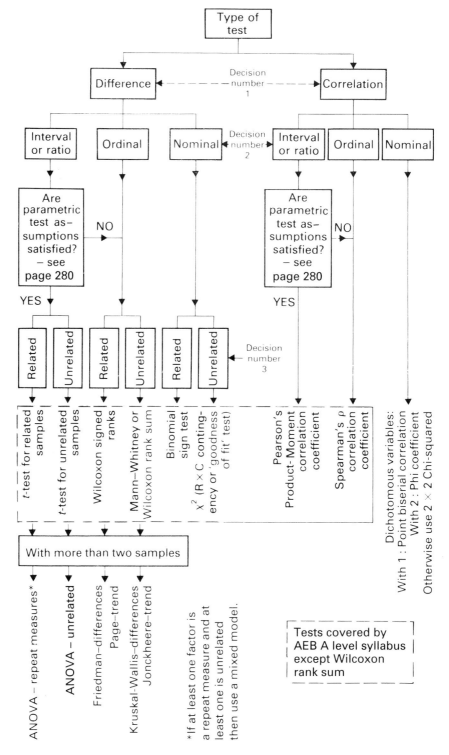

Figure 24.1 *Chart for choosing the appropriate test*

creative thought. Computers used to be a luxury. Now they're ubiquitous and even the poorest college department can afford the cheapest program which will be adequate for A-level work. Below then, I've given a brief description of a few programmes which I hope you'll find useful. They need to be approached with patience because they each use slightly different language, at times, for the same concepts.

SPSS™

This was unfriendly on mainframe but now comes as a MAC™ or MSDOS™ version or under WINDOWS™ with all the usual refinements of that environment. Data is entered in spreadsheet format but every row is always a 'case' (participant). It will do everything in this book and far beyond, including factor analysis, reliability tests, item analysis, multiple regression, multi-factor ANOVA and so on. It is now extremely friendly and 'talks' to other applications, such as word processors and spreadsheets. It can still be operated with the mainframe language if required. It produces wonderful editable charts though it does this rather slowly. The problem here is cost.

MINITAB™

This is an old favourite and also comes in spreadsheet format, though its old language can still be used, and has to be used for some procedures. It is difficult to see why some of the most common tests aren't on the menu system but the language isn't hard (for instance 'ttest c3' does a t test on a set of differences in column 3). If you enter any non-numerical data into a column by mistake it doesn't let you know until you go to calculate (having entered, say, 60 items) that your column is defined as 'alpha-numeric' and the only way to change this seems to be to wipe out the whole column and start again. Apart from these vagaries, it's pretty powerful, and does ANOVA, multiple regression, box-plots and so on. Its charts can't be edited as is possible in SPSS. The charm is the price in this case. There is a tutor version at around £70.00 and a student version at £40.00 from Addison-Wesley publishers. The student version doesn't have quite the complexity, but is more than adequate for A-level and early degree work.

STATPAK

Written by Concord Informatics Ltd. and distributed by the Association of Teachers of Psychology (your tutor should belong!), this is cheap, cheerful and written specifically for A-level psychology work. It can be obtained for the Amstrad™ PCWs or any IBM™ compatible PC. It uses all the A-level (AEB) tests (Wilcoxon signed-ranks, Mann–Whitney, t tests, Pearson's and Spearman's correlation and Chi-square). A speciality making it more useful for teaching than either of the others, is a print-out of the *calculation steps* in the test so you can see how the answer was obtained! It will mostly only work on two samples at a time but will hold up to 20 columns of data at once so you can do several tests – but beware of 'capitalising on chance'.

EXERCISES

The following exercises are all based on tests for two samples only. Exercises involving choice of more complex tests are included at the end of the relevant Chapters (19–22) and also in the text of the ANOVA Chapter – see p. 345.

What tests should be carried out on the following data? Where there is a choice, select the more powerful test. ·

I Height (in cm) of girls bred on:

All Bran	Bread and dripping
172	162
181	172
190	154
165	143
167	167

The researcher was interested in whether one of the diets tended to produce taller girls.

2

Table 24.2 *Snooker players – position in league table*

Smoking and drinking players		Abstemious players	
Terry Davis	2	Steve Griffiths	8
Alex Hendry	6	Steve Higgins	1
Fred Longpole	10	Chris Cushion	5
Alf Garnett	9	Betty Baulk	3
Bob Black	4	Susan Swerveshot	7

In this case, we want to know whether abstemious players get significantly higher placings.

3

	No. of businessmen standing on window ledges	No. of businessmen *not* standing on window ledges
Tokyo	46	598
New York	103	524

If this was what happened when the stock market crashed in 1987, was the crash significantly far worse in the USA? What test will tell us?

4 Students observe whether males or females do or don't walk under a ladder. They want to see whether one sex is more 'superstitious' than the other. What test do they need to use?

5 20 people perform a sensori-motor task in two conditions, one in a quiet room, alone, the other in a brightly lit room with a dozen people watching. An electronic timer takes an accurate record of the number of errors made in each condition.
  a) What test would be appropriate for investigating the significance of the differences in performance between the two conditions?
  b) Assume everybody deteriorates in the second condition. What test would be appropriate for seeing whether individuals tend to deteriorate by about the same amount?

6 A psychologist claims to have a very well standardised measurement scale. What statistical test would be used to check its test–retest reliability? What test would be used to check its validity on a criterion group who should score higher than a control group?

7 A set of photos of couples are rated for attractiveness by a panel of judges who rate the males separately from the females. The hypothesis tested is that people in couples tend to be of a similar level of attractiveness. What test would be used to compare the similarity of the two sets of ratings for male and female partners?

8 Question 4, Chapter 17, shows two distributions of scores (A and B). Suppose the researcher felt that these departed significantly from the pattern of a normal distribution. Which test could settle the matter?

9 Two groups of people are selected. One has a very high 'initiative-taking' score, the other group's score is quite low. They are asked to select just one of three possible activities which they would prefer to do. The choices are: rock-climbing, dancing or reading a book. What test would demonstrate significant differences between their choices?

10 The time is recorded for the same group of participants to read out loud a list of rhyming words and a list of non-rhyming words. What test is appropriate for showing whether the rhyming words take significantly less time to read?

11 A group of management personnel undergo an intensive course on race issues. Essays written before and after the course are content analysed and rated for attitudes to race. What test would be appropriate for demonstrating a significant change of attitude as expressed in the essays?

12 A group of people attempting to give up smoking have been assessed for their progress on two occasions separated by six months. Raw scores have been discarded and we only know for each client whether they have improved, worsened or stayed about the same. What test would show any significant change over the period?

ANALYSING QUALITATIVE DATA

This chapter gives a brief introduction to the methods employed by qualitative researchers who treat qualitative data as meaningful and an end in itself, rather than reducing originally qualitative data to frequencies or treating it as subsidiary to quantitative data gathered in the same research project.

Qualitative data is often organised into categories to some extent but the categories are analysed for their *meaning* and, often, for their unique qualities and insights provided. Analogies are employed as in early investigative work in any science.

Original quotations are used and are usually checked out with the participant before inclusion in the context proposed by the researcher.

Qualitative researchers often allow theory to develop *during* the research process rather than test preordained and fixed hypotheses as in the quantitative model. This principle of operation is basic to **grounded theory**.

Validity, for qualitative researchers, is established through several means:
- the naturalistic and realistic nature of the data obtained
- triangulation – use of several perspectives
- the fact that the research cycle is repeated; participants are re-interviewed and early hunches followed up further, for instance
- consultation and rapport with participants, reducing their wariness, reticence, or need to obscure true opinions and thinking

Qualitative data consists of any information, gathered during research, which has not (yet, at least) been quantified in any rigorous way.

QUALITATIVE DATA AND HYPOTHESIS TESTING

Because of the over-powering paradigm of natural science, it is often assumed that hypotheses can only be tested with quantified, empirical data. But we use qualitative data very often in supporting or contradicting our predictions and explanations.

Much of our reasoning about people's motivations and decision-making is based on qualitative evidence. We may explain the unusual or depressive behaviour of a friend in terms of her unique situation in being a single parent and having just lost a supportive parent.

We can predict that persistent young offenders will feel more alienated from middle-class society. We can demonstrate this with the sheer strength and animosity of the content of their accounts. We are not limited to simply counting the number of aggressive responses. No doubt it will be argued that 'strength and animosity' must come from comparison with other accounts, but what *informs* us here are the qualitative differences in content.

The positivist may well feel tempted to create a standardised questionnaire from the offenders' data for use on offenders elsewhere, or on a control group.

The point being made, however, is that some psychological researchers have argued forcefully for the need to use the qualitative content gained in their research. It is the unexpected *meaning* contained in offenders' accounts which will be of use, not the trivial but true fact that their accounts will somehow differ from non-offenders' accounts. It is what offenders say, and we may never have heard, which research uncovers and highlights for debate. The qualitative researchers might argue, too, that insights gained in interviewing a group of offenders can be generalised with as much validity as questionnaire results. A perspective on the world, quite novel and unexpected, may emerge from the interview and give another interviewer a new range of ideas to broach with different offenders, or with 'control' teenagers who don't share the ideas.

We have seen elsewhere that individual case-studies can add important information to the pool of knowledge and ideas which constitutes our understanding of humans and their behaviour. The value of Watson's study of 'Little Albert' was not that it was entirely quantitative. In a single-subject study we learnt just how easy it was to condition a child's fears and we acquired interesting information about how these generalised and failed to extinguish. It seems a bit futile to argue that we should compare with a control child to ensure that the stages Albert went through did not occur just by chance. There is extremely valuable qualitative information contained within many reports of even traditionally organised research. The interviews with Asch's participants, post testing, are illuminating and it was necessary to *ask* Milgram's participants why they seemed to chuckle as they thought they delivered fatal electric shocks to an innocent victim. The extent of their stress, which forced this nervous laughter, is far more readily got at through the interview process and discussion of the meaning of what participants said.

TWO APPROACHES TO QUALITATIVE DATA

Looking through the literature on qualitative data, two general views seem to emerge on what to do with it. These correspond to the positivist–non-positivist dimension but it must be stressed that this *is* a dimension – there are not just two views but a wide variety.

For the positivist, unquantified data is accepted in a subsidiary role. It is seen as having the following uses:

- it can illuminate and give a context to otherwise neutral and uninspiring statistics, as when Asch tells us *how* his conforming participants behaved and looked uncomfortable;
- it can lead us to hypotheses testable in quantitative terms, as with the children of unemployed parents mentioned in Chapter 4.

The qualitative researcher, however, sees qualitative data as meaningful in its own right. In fact, the use of the term 'qualitative method' usually indicates a commitment to publish the results of research in qualitative terms, remembering, of course, that such a researcher is not averse to looking at things quantitatively, should the opportunity arise and be found illuminating.

QUALITATIVE ANALYSIS OF QUALITATIVE CONTENT

We saw earlier that content analysis can be used to deal with originally qualitative information. The data is rigorously analysed and reduced to quantified units, susceptible to statistical significance testing.

The qualitative researcher too has to categorise data. The whole data set may have been produced from any of the following sources:

* Participants' notes and diaries
* Participant observer's field notes
* Informal or part-structured interviews
* Open-ended questions (interview or questionnaire)
* In-depth case-study (mixture of interviews, observations, records)

and might consist of speech, interactions, behaviour patterns, written or visual recorded material. They might also include the researcher's own ideas, impressions and feelings, recorded as the research project was progressing.

The set of data will need order imposing upon it. It has to be organised so that comparisons, contrasts and insights can be made and demonstrated. The qualitative researcher however, will not be categorising in order to count occurrences. Instead, data will be categorised in order to analyse and compare the various *meanings* produced in any one category. From interviews with drug addicts, for instance, on their experiences in trying to break the habit, various fears and perceptions of the 'straight' world may emerge which are unique and qualitatively different from others. Each has a special value in painting a picture of personal experience, invisible to non-addicts, but of great utility to a rehabilitation therapist. The Bruner and Kelso (1980) study described in Chapter 7 is another example of qualitative content analysis of this kind.

The richness of the unique qualitites of category items is therefore preserved in qualitative analysis. To use an analogy, at home I may file articles on 'travelling in India' in one category, but hardly because I need to count how many I have!

METHODS OF ANALYSIS

It is not possible to give precise guidelines on the analysis and presentation of qualitative data. There is no universally accepted paradigm. The decisions will be influenced by the theoretical background or model from which the researcher is working. Several quite specialised methods of analysis have been developed for different sorts of data (conversations (see Box 25.1), non-verbal communication, pedestrian behaviour and so on). What follows is a set of points applying to collections of data produced from the types of source mentioned above. After that, the reader will be directed to several specialised texts which have more to say on various qualitative or 'new paradigm' methods.

Categorising

The qualitative researcher will inevitably begin with a large quantity of written notes and material (audio and video recordings will have been transcribed).

As the notes are read and re-read it should be possible to start grouping items together. As a simple example, if you had asked student colleagues to discuss, during informal interviews, reactions to their college course, statements they make might fall into the following groupings:

Box 25.1 *Transcribing speech*

Edwards and Potter argue that how one chooses to report or display recorded speech (TRANSCRIPTION) will depend upon, not just technical decisions, but a theoretical position. If *only* words are recorded, making the speech appear as text in a book, then this displays a lack of interest in what people *do* with speech or in the difference between talk and text. In turn, this might reflect the position of a researcher who sees the speech as a fairly direct reflection of internal mental processes. Analyses of discourse may vary somewhat but many researchers now stick fairly close to a system devised by Jefferson (1985). What follows is partly quoted (* to *) from Edwards and Potter's 1992 text and partly condensed.

/ / signifies overlapping or simultaneous speech:
(*)

> *Dean:* That was the – impression that very//clearly came out.
> *Gurney:* In other words, your – your *whole* thesis

Alternatively, the start and end of overlapping speech may be marked with extended square brackets thus:

> *N:* Oh:: do:ggone I [thought maybe we could]
> *E:*   [I'd <u>like</u> to get   ] some little slippers but uh,

Numbers in round brackets indicate pauses, timed to tenths of seconds, while the symbol (.) represents a pause which is hearable but too short to measure:

> now Prime Minister (.2) how you res↑po::nd (.) to this claim of <u>blame</u>(.) may be of <u>crucial</u> significance

A break in the voicing of sound is marked by a single slash:

> as I reca::ll (1.0) with Mister Ghobanifa/r   (*)

:	single elongation of the previous sound
underline	added emphasis
↑/↓	upward/downward turn in intonation
-	abrupt stop
●hmm	● represents audible intake of breath before 'hmm'
</>	speeded up/slowed down pace of speech

social contacts	quality of teaching	available resources
link to career	timetable	facilities (canteen, etc.)

. . . and so on.

Some statements will fall into more than one category. Traditionally, the analyst would make several copies of all data so that items can be cut and pasted into various categories and clusters. The modern, labour-saving way is to use the computer and a flexible database system.

Indigenous categories

Prior to development of the researcher's own categories and groupings, the analyst usually looks at those used by the participants themselves. An example would be a group of students who call themselves 'the brains' whilst others get called 'the Neanderthals' by staff. Later on, the analyst might compare these titles and propose explanations of their derivation.

Researcher's categories

Some categories may emerge quite clearly on analysis or during data collection. In studying the organisation of a school, for instance, it might emerge that teachers are split into those who do and do not get involved in after-school activities. More likely, though, will be *dimensions* along which people vary, for instance, teachers in their attitude towards student discipline. These could range from the severe, through moderate to lax. This might sound like a quantitative dimension. However, the qualitative researcher is more interested in the *perspective* of each person. So the positions along the dimension from severe to lax are only roughly ordinal but are determined by specific reasons given. People are in a category along the dimension. 'Severe' would be those who say 'you have to show them who's boss' and the like. 'Moderate' teachers might say 'It's no good being the strict parent with them. They get enough of that at home and they don't respect it.'

Typologies

Where categories and dimensions are descriptions of people, some researchers may cross these in order to produce a matrix of 'types'. A teacher who is 'lax' on the discipline dimension, but also 'caring' rather than 'distant' may turn out to have an identifiable approach to students, different from all other staff, in that she particularly tries to raise self-esteem and enable students to take control of their own lives. Researchers sometimes give names to these types. In this case the type might be 'therapist'. It is important to remember, however, that the type is mere analogy. Any types created are products of the researcher's current scheme of looking at the data and not lasting realities.

All sciences use analogy and metaphor. In order to tell us what atoms are *like*, physicists describe electrons and neutrons as little balls. Electrical theory borrows the analogy of current 'flowing' like a river. Analogy is necessary in order to communicate under these circumstances. It tells us what something unique and novel is like, not what it *is*.

Creating the matrix of types, however, is useful in several ways. The reasons why a person fits none of the types created might well be worth investigating and lead to fresh insights. Conversely, a type might be produced which no one fits.

Quotations

The final report of qualitative findings will usually include verbatim quotations from participants which will bring the reader into the reality of the situation studied. At times, the researcher will, of course, be summarising the perspectives and understandings of participants in the study. But it is important that these summaries, which must, to some extent, be interpretive, or at least selective, are clearly identified as such. The quotes themselves are selections from the raw data which 'tell it like it is'. Very often comments just stick with us because they typify perfectly a perspective or stance in life. Here are a few:

> 'Everybody else out there seems to be having a great time except me'
> 'I just want everyone to like me'
> 'It's no use me speaking out. Nobody wants to listen and they'd tell me it was wrong anyway'
> 'Live for tomorrow, that's what I always say. You can't undo what's been done'

Most researchers see it as important that quotations, especially those intended for publication, are checked out first with the original speaker.

SEPARATING REPORT COMPONENTS

A qualitative research report will contain raw data and summaries of it, analysis, inference and, in the case of participant observation, perhaps feelings and reactions of the observer at the time significant events occurred. These are all valid components for inclusion but it is important that analysis, inference and feeling are clearly separated and labelled as such.

EARLY AND FINAL ANALYSIS

Most qualitative researchers agree that some analysis of data can occur *during*, rather than after, the collection stage. This can direct the researcher to areas and avenues of questioning not originally prepared for. Obviously it is important that such EARLY ANALYSIS does not produce blindness to some other areas. In comparison to quantitative research, however, it is possible to construct hypotheses *after* the data collection has begun rather than before it starts. Patton (1980), an evaluation researcher, states:

> The cardinal principle of qualitative analysis is that causal relationships and theoretical statements be clearly emergent from and grounded in the phenomena studied. The theory emerges from the data; it is not imposed on the data.

Grounded theory

Patton's statement is very close to the basic principles of 'GROUNDED THEORY' advocated by Glaser and Strauss (1967). This publication was a forceful presentation of the 'unstructured' approach to observations of human behaviour discussed in Chapter 7. These writers argued that observers should a) enter a research situation with no prior theoretical preconceptions, and b) create, refine and revise theory in the light of further data collected.

The result expected is that 'grounded' hypotheses, generated through actual observation, would be more true to life than those deduced by prior commitment to, say, behaviourism or Piagetian theory. In fact, grounded theory is an import from sociology, but several of the qualitative or 'new paradigm' social psychologists have incorporated its principles.

THE FINAL REPORT

The final qualitative research report, then, should give an account of early hypotheses that were formed and the extent to which these guided or changed the direction of further enquiry. Very often, in this sort of research, a point emerges in one interview and the researcher might think 'If only I could go back and ask all the other interviewees about this'. Where possible, this is just what does happen. To some extent, the final report can be a diary of insights and question development. To the extent that the researchers attempt reflexivity (Chapter 11) the report will also contain an account of the researcher's questioning of their own decisions along the way and may contain discussion of the researcher's self-assessment of bias, emotion, doubts and misgivings.

RELIABILITY AND VALIDITY

Qualitative researchers argue that their methods produce more valid data for reasons already discussed (Chapters 4 and 11). They would also argue that they have developed safeguards against lack of reliability. Some of these follow.

Triangulation

Borrowed from surveying, and used in evaluative research, this means comparing two different views of the same thing: interview with observational data, open with closed questions or one researcher's analysis with another's.

Analysis of negative cases

This is the consideration of why certain cases just don't fit the major patterns outlined as a result of analysis. The willingness to do this openly is held to be a validity check. Others can accept the proffered explanation or not, and can call for re-analysis, analyse raw data themselves or attempt some form of replication.

Repetition of the research cycle

Qualitative researchers go around the 'research cycle' several times. The researcher checks and rechecks the early assumptions and inferences made. As patterns and theories are developed, so the researcher goes back in again to gather more information which should confirm tentative hypotheses and/or help to further refine, deepen and clarify categories.

Participant consultation

Participants are consulted and provide feedback. Qualitative researchers 'at the non-alienating end of the [research] spectrum' (Reason, 1981) involve the participants in evaluation of tentative conclusions and refine these in the light of feedback from this process. Reason makes the point:

> Once we start to do research which does not conform to the general requirements of experimental method, we run the risk of being accused of being mere journalists; indeed we run the risk of *being* mere journalists.

Reason's answer to this criticism is an eloquent argument summarised in these last two safeguards. Journalists, he argues, tend to do one round, depart and write fairly impressionistic accounts, with little, if any, feedback process.

ON DOING A QUALITATIVE PROJECT – IT ISN'T EASY!

The last two points above are reasons why students may find a qualitative project harder than they might at first have thought. Students may well be drawn towards 'doing a qualitative project' because they feel unhappy with figures and are 'not mathematical'. This would be one of the worst reasons I can think of for doing a qualitative project. Because the methods are so tied up with the philosophy rejecting positivism, I believe that you can't really understand what qualitative research is trying to do without a good understanding of what it rejects in the quantitative approach. It would be silly, for instance, to start with a basically quantitative supposition (e.g. I believe smokers are more anxious than non-smokers) and then discount quantification for the sake of it or from number phobia. An understanding of quantitative weaknesses will strengthen a qualitative project, but the main reason I express caution is that doing a *good* qualitative project will be *hard*. The student will have to go through quite a few examples of the approach and much raw (verbal) data before getting some idea of how the work typically proceeds (there is no one right or accepted way, and that's a lot of the difficulty here). Having said that, if the student is prepared to put in the time and effort then I'm sure many tutors would be delighted to see more qualitative work coming their way. Just don't do it as an easy option!

Analysing discourse

To illuminate the point, above, that there is no one right way to analyse qualitative data, have a look at what Potter and Wetherell (1993) have to say on the non-similarity of discourse analysis to traditional quantitative methods:

> Analysis in those [quantitative] settings consists in a distinct set of procedures: aggregating scores, categorising instances, performing various sorts of statistical analysis and so on. It is sometimes tempting to think that in discourse work there is some analogous set of codified procedures that can be put into effect and which will lead to another set of entities known as 'the results'. To see things in this way would be very misleading, although, given the authority which accrues to these procedures, it is tempting to try . . . Much of the work of discourse analysis is a craft skill, something like riding a bike or chicken sexing, which is not easy to render or describe in a codified manner. Indeed as the analyst becomes more practised it becomes harder and harder to identify explicit procedures that could be called analysis. Nevertheless, there are a number of considerations that recur in the process of analysis

The procedures then highlighted are:

1 **Using variation as a lever**: variation *between* speakers is of obvious interest but variation *within* one speaker's discourse, even if only slight, can give great insight into what the person is *doing* with their speech. This is reminiscent of 'internal reliability' except that here, rather than treating this as a 'nuisance', as in quantitative measurement, it is treated as some of the most valuable information available.

2 **Reading the details**: rather than discount detail in the interests of generalisability, as is traditional, analysts might see almost innocuous details as indicators of the purpose behind utterances. Potter's example is the use of 'rarest' (rather than, say, 'uncommon') in referring to curable cancers, in a television programme whose aim was to cast doubt on the useful products of cancer research charities.

3 **Rhetorical organisation**: discourse is inspected for the way it undermines alternative perspectives on an issue, through argument, whilst preserving a seeming 'factual' orientation. Such rhetoric 'draws our attention away from questions about how a version relates to some putative reality . . . and focuses it on how a version relates to competing alternatives.

4 **Accountability**: aspects of discourse which are rhetorical usually relate to the individual's 'accountability'. This is not a theory of pure self-interest, irrespective of the truth. It suggests that, since there is rarely, if ever, a 'pure truth', discourse is constructed with counter-arguments in mind so that a more solid case can be presented.

5 **Other discourse studies**: this group of qualitative researchers (and most others) do not try to produce an alternative set of rigid procedures and conventions for studies to follow. Nevertheless they would argue that study of, and reference to

other researchers' work is a way to develop the 'analytic mentality'. More specifically, this may prompt fruitful lines of enquiry, in particular, where an attempt is made to reproduce earlier findings in new studies.

Potter and Wetherell are anxious not to claim that there are *no* common or 'mechanical' procedures for this sort of analysis, only that use of any such pre-ordained method will not automatically guarantee that 'interesting results will fall out in some way'.

FURTHER READING

Burgess (1984) discusses the taking and organising of field notes in great detail. Patton (1980) discusses in depth the content analysis of qualitative data. Potter and Wetherell (1987) include a step-by-step guide to discourse analysis. Bromley (1986) declared the partial aim of setting out rules of procedure for gathering and analysing case-study data.

Burgess, R. G. & Bryman, A. (eds) (1993) *Analysing Qualitative Data*, London: Routledge is a useful practical volume.

Edwards, D. and Potter, J. (1992) *Discursive Psychology*, London: Sage is very readable and contains the extract of analysed speech included in this chapter.

Hayes, N. J. (in press) *Introduction to Qualitative Research*, Hove: LEA is likely to be very useful since it will contain chapters by a variety of qualitative researchers exemplifying their approach through their own work in enough detail for the (student) reader to be able to use the method in their own project.

GLOSSARY

Formation of hypothesis and theoretical ideas *during* the acquisition of data	_____ _____	early analysis
Theory 'grounded in' specific observational data; patterns *emerge from* the data set and are not imposed on it before it is gathered	_____ _____	grounded theory
Analysis of reasons why single case does not fit patterns identified so far	_____ ____ _____	negative case analysis
Comparison of at least two views of the same thing(s) – events, behaviour, actions etc.	_____	triangulation
Written recording of directly recorded speech, as exactly as possible, but depending upon approach; usually often includes pauses, intonation etc.	_____	transcription

PART FIVE

Ethics and practice

ETHICAL ISSUES AND HUMANISM IN PSYCHOLOGICAL RESEARCH

The chapter deals with two major sets of responsibilities carried by professional psychologists, whether their work is applied or research oriented.

First, psychologists have responsibilities as a **research community** to publish only well-founded results with conventional support, open to analysis by colleagues.

They also need to pay attention to possible social effects of research results and assess these in the prevailing moral and political climate.

Second, they need to follow strict codes of conduct, devised by both the British Psychological Society and the American Psychological Association, when working with participants.

These codes cover: **confidentiality** (of results and those who produced them), **privacy**, **deception** (which has been held to lower the public's trust in psychological research), **debriefing** (informing participants and returning them to their pre-test state), **mental** and **physical stress** and **discomfort**, **recognition of participants' rights to withdraw** and the **special power of the investigator**, problems with **involuntary participation** and **intervention**.

There are various techniques which gain information but guarantee privacy and confidentiality and several have been suggested for avoiding the need to deceive, but psychology has the peculiar characteristic that informing people of what is being tested has the effect of altering their likely 'natural' behaviour.

The arguments **for** and **against animal research** are outlined.

INTRODUCTION

The British Psychological Society (BPS) and the American Psychological Association (APA) have both agreed guidelines on the ethical issues involved in psychological research. The BPS currently has a booklet of statements (1993), covering a wide range of issues, and also a code of conduct (1985) adopted through a postal ballot of all its members. The 1992 revision of the 1978 principles is entitled *Ethical Principles for Conducting Research with Human Participants* and introduces 'with' as well as changing 'subjects' to 'participants' – not trivial amendments. The APA (1987) has a more comprehensive set of ethical principles comprising ten major categories, each with several sub-principles. The general public can bring complaints to the ethics committee who then adjudicate. The psychologist concerned can be reprimanded, dismissed or required to alter behaviour or attend relevant training. This breadth of principles and disciplinary power reflects the far wider application of psychology to the general public as consumers in the USA. Most of the major principles are similar to those which are relevant in the doctor–patient relationship.

The 1992 (BPS) *Principles* cover the following areas: consent, deception, debriefing, withdrawal from an investigation, confidentiality, protection of participants, observational research, giving advice (to participants) and monitoring of colleagues in the profession. Section 2 of the *Principles*, entitled 'General', runs as follows:

> In all circumstances, investigators must consider the ethical implications and psychological consequences for the participants in their research. The essential principle is that the investigation should be considered from the standpoint of all participants: foreseeable threats to their psychological well-being, health, values or dignity should be eliminated. Investigators should recognise that, in our multi-cultural and multi-ethnic society and where investigations involve individuals of different ages, gender and social background, the investigators may not have sufficient knowledge of the implications of any investigation for the participants. It should be borne in mind that the best judge of whether an investigation will cause offence may be members of the population from which the participants in the research are to be drawn.

Both the British and United States' principles stress that psychological research should lead to better understanding of ourselves and to the enhancement of the human condition and promotion of human welfare. Both stress the need for an atmosphere of free enquiry in order to generate the widest, most valid body of knowledge. But both also stress that this free atmosphere requires a commitment to responsibility on the part of the psychologist in terms of competence, objectivity and the welfare of research participants.

Since 1987, the Royal Charter of the BPS has been amended, taking us some way towards the American model described above. The Society now maintains a 'register' of 'chartered psychologists'. These are people who practise psychology either in an applied or a research capacity. Members of the register use the formal letters 'C.Psychol', can be struck off for unprofessional behaviour and, it is hoped, will become recognised as bona fide 'trademarked' practitioners whom the general public can recognise and trust.

In the 1990s most research institutions now have an ethics committee to vet research proposals (of staff and students) for unacceptable procedures in any of the areas which we are about to consider.

PUBLICATION AND ACCESS TO DATA

Before taking a look at the rights and protection of individual participants, we can consider how psychologists are expected to commit themselves to freedom of information.

In general, a psychologist cannot claim to have demonstrated an effect and then withhold raw data or information on procedures and samples used. Persons who do this are generally considered to be charlatans. Where psychologists are prepared, as most are, to be completely open with their data, they would still not allow the alleged results of their work to affect people's lives, by policy formulation for instance, before the research community has thoroughly verified, evaluated and replicated results where possible. They should not 'rush to publish'.

There are occasions, in fact, when any scientist may feel that publication of results is potentially harmful or even dangerous. (One is reminded of the scientists who first became fully aware of the horrendous power of the nuclear fission process.) In such cases, the investigator is expected to seek the opinion of 'experienced and disinterested colleagues', an option recommended several times in the BPS statement for various dilemmas.

A significant example of the dangers avoided by these principles is that of Cyril Burt's work on separated identical twins which appeared to provide very strong evidence of a substantial genetic role in human intellectual abilities. The early findings played a part in the political debate which produced the British '11-plus' examination and a two (originally three) tier secondary education system, wherein the successful 20% of children passing the exam received a grammar school education. Only after Burt's death did Leon Kamin (1977) establish beyond doubt that Burt's data was inconsistent, to a degree way beyond acceptability and probably fraudulent. Kamin demonstrated that Burt was persistently vague about the exact tests in use and had not made it at all easy to check his raw data. The cult of the 'great expert' had also inhibited investigation of Burt's work by 'lesser' researchers.

Joynson (1989) has recently reopened this debate, arguing that these accusations are ill-founded and that Burt should be exonerated.

Findings on racial difference (in intelligence or personality, for instance) almost always stir up controversy, which is hardly surprising. For this reason some psychologists have been led to argue that a moratorium should be held on publication. They argue that, since race is always inextricably bound up with culture and socio-economic position, most responsible researchers would announce results with great qualification. However, they cannot then stop the lay racist or ignorant reader from using the unqualified information in discriminatory or abusive practices.

Psychologists have also discussed the problem of projective or personality tests being used by the lay selector for jobs or other positions.

They have also argued that professional psychological researchers should exercise integrity over the sources of their funding, increasingly likely to come from industry with an interest in the non-academic use of findings.

CONFIDENTIALITY AND PRIVACY

Apart from any ethical considerations, there is a purely pragmatic argument for guaranteeing anonymity for participants at all times. If psychologists kept publishing identities along with results, the general public would soon cease to volunteer or agree to research participation.

An investigator can guarantee anonymity or request permission to identify individuals. Such identification may occur, through the use of video recordings as teaching materials for instance, as in Milgram's film *Obedience to Authority*. Research participants who have been seriously deceived have the right to witness destruction of any such records they do not wish to be kept. If records are kept, participants have the right to assume these will be safeguarded and used only by thoroughly briefed research staff. Usually, though, results are made anonymous as early as possible during analysis by using a letter or number instead of a name.

There are very special circumstances where an investigator might contravene the confidentiality rule and these are where there are clear, direct dangers to human life. An investigator conducting participant observation into gang life would have a clear obligation to break confidence where a serious crime was about to be committed. A psychiatric patient's plan to kill himself or a room-mate would be reported. The ethical principles involved here are broader than those involved in conducting scientific research.

The participant obviously has the right to privacy, and procedures should not be planned which directly invade this without warning. Where a procedure is potentially intimate, embarrassing or sensitive, the participant should be clearly reminded of the right to withhold information or participation. Particular care would be required, for instance, where participants are being asked about sexual attitudes or behaviour (and remember the 'randomised response' technique in Chapter 8).

This principle is difficult to follow in the case of covert participant observation, and serious criticism has been levelled at users of this approach on these grounds.

Investigators would usually send a copy of the final research report to all participants, along with its justification and contribution to scientific knowledge and benefit to society in general. This procedure can be difficult where covert observation in a field situation has occurred, and expensive where a survey has used a very large sample.

MILGRAM – THE CLASSIC EXPERIMENT FOR ETHICAL DEBATE

Any discussion of ethical principles in psychological research inevitably throws up Milgram's famous demonstrations of obedience fairly early on in the debate. Several ethical issues are involved in this study so let me just describe it briefly and then ask you to think about what these issues are. Almost certainly you will have already heard about the experiment and fuller details are given in, for instance, Gross (1992).

> Volunteers were introduced to another 'participant' who was actually an experimental confederate. The volunteer became a 'teacher' who was asked to administer electric shocks, increasing by 15 volts for each mistake made by the confederate. 375 volts was described as 'Danger: severe shock'. A tape recording of screams and refusals deceived the teacher–participant into believing the confederate was experiencing great pain and wished to end the session. The teacher–participant was pressured into continuing by 'prods' from the experimenter such as 'The experiment requires that you continue' and 'You have no choice but to go on'. To Milgram's surprise, 65% of participants delivered shocks to the end of the scale (450 volts) even though the confederate had ceased responding at 315 volts. Milgram had consulted 'experienced and disinterested colleagues' – psychiatrists predicted that no more than 0.1% would obey to the end. The teacher–participant often displayed extreme anxiety. One even suffered a seizure. An observer wrote:
> I observed a mature and initially poised businessman enter the laboratory

smiling and confident. Within 20 minutes he was reduced to a twitching, stuttering wreck, who was rapidly approaching a point of nervous collapse. He constantly pulled at his ear lobe and twisted his hands. At one point he pushed his fist into his forehead and muttered, 'Oh God, let's stop it.' (Milgram (1974))

The results of this experiment were used to argue that many ordinary people are capable of behaving in a manner, under pressure, which is retrospectively considered cruel. Atrocities are not necessarily carried out by purely evil persons.

> List the aspects of this experiment which you consider to be unethical. Should the research have been carried out at all? Do the ends (scientific and surprising knowledge) justify the means?

DECEPTION

Milgram's participants were quite grossly deceived. Not only did they believe they were shocking an innocent victim and that the victim suffered terribly, but also the whole purpose of the research was completely distorted as concerning the effects of punishment on learning.

DECEPTION, or at least the withholding of information, is exceedingly common in psychology experiments. Menges (1973) reviewed about 1 000 American studies and found that 80% involved giving participants less than complete information. In only 3% of studies were participants given complete information about the IV, and information about the DV was incomplete in 75% of cases.

Some of this deception seems fairly innocuous. Some participants are told a baby is male, others that it is female, and their descriptions of it are compared. Participants performing a sensori-motor task, where the true aim is to record the effect of an observer on performance, are told that the observer is present to note details of the skilled behaviour involved. Children are told not to play with a toy because it belongs to another child who is next door. Students are told their experimental rats are 'bright'. Even the use of placebos is often a deception.

Some deception is more serious. Participants have been told that test results demonstrate that they are poorly adjusted. Female participants are given feedback that they are considered attractive or unattractive by the men who will later interview them. Bramel (1962) gave male participants false feedback about their emotional reaction to photographs of men such that their responses seemed homosexually related. Participants in Latané and Darley's (1976) experiments thought they were overhearing an authentic epilectic seizure. The DV was the speed or occurrence of reporting the seizure.

So what can the investigator do if deception is to be used?

First, the 1992 BPS *Principles* recommend that, wherever possible, consultation should be conducted with individuals who share the social and cultural background of the participants.

Second, in some cases it is possible to obtain permission to deceive. Volunteers can be asked to select what sort of research they would be prepared to participate in from, for instance:

a) Research on recognition of commercial products

b) Research on safety of products

c) Research in which you will be misled about the purpose until afterward

d) Research involving questions on attitudes

Third, debriefing should be very carefully attended to.

DEBRIEFING

In all research studies, the investigator has a responsibility to debrief each participant. The true purpose and aims of the study are revealed and every attempt is made to ensure that participants feel the same about themselves when they leave as they did when they arrived. Where participants have been seriously deceived, this responsibility incurs a substantial effort in reassurance and explanation. The DEBRIEFING itself may have to involve a little more deception, as when children are told they 'did very well indeed' whatever the actual standard of their performance and when any suspicion that a participant really is 'poorly adjusted' is not communicated to them.

Applying this to Milgram's experiments, participants who went to the end of the scale were told that some people did this quite gleefully, in order that they could then compare their own unwillingness to proceed, and felt anxiety, fairly favourably. (Milgram has never reported that any participant *did* proceed at all happily.) However, at least 26 out of 40 participants knew, when they left, that they were capable, under pressure, of inflicting extreme pain, if not death, on an innocent human being. It seems hardly possible that these people left the laboratory feeling the same about themselves as before they entered. In Asch's (1956) classic paradigm, too, participants find they have 'conformed' to silly answers to simple problems because a group of confederates answered first. These participants also exhibited great anxiety during the experimental sessions.

DOES DEBRIEFING WORK?

Milgram sent a questionnaire to his participants after the study and 84% said they were glad to have participated, whereas only 1% regretted being involved, the remainder reporting neutral feelings. 80% believed more research like Milgram's should be carried out. 75% found the experience meaningful and self-enlightening.

Some writers discounted this broad range of appreciative and illuminating comments as an attempt by Milgram to justify an ethically unacceptable study. Ring et al. (1970) decided to evaluate the consequences to the participant in a study which, even though the investigators were critical of Milgram, not only included the deceptions of the original study but also used a dishonest primary debriefing before a second honest one. They showed that an initial, superficial debriefing dramatically reduces any negative participant evaluation of the research. However, they also found that one third of participants reported residual anger and disappointment with themselves even after the second, complete debriefing.

The fact that even a few participants feel quite negative about themselves well after the experiment, and that many participants felt extremely upset during it, has led many researchers to the position that deception and stress this extreme are ethically unacceptable.

Besides the question of ethics, it is unwise of investigators to indulge in a great deal of deception. Students very often suspect that the manifest structure and explanation of a study in which they participate is false. Ring found that 50% of their participants claimed they would be more wary and suspicious of psychology experiments in the future.

As Reason and Rowan (1981) put it 'Good research means never having to say you are sorry.'

IF YOU WON'T DECEIVE, WHAT CAN YOU DO?

Several investigators, finding gross deception at the Asch or Milgram level quite unacceptable, have turned to role-play or simulation. A description of successful findings by Mixon, (1974) who used the heading above for his title, is given in Chapter 7.

Ring was among the advocates of role-playing, whereas Aronson and Carlsmith (1968) argued that essential realism would be lost. Horowitz and Rothschild (1970) conducted a replication of Asch's design using a 'forewarned' group, who were told that the experiment was a fake but were asked to play the part of a naïve participant, and a 'pre-briefed' group who knew the experimental aim in detail. The forewarned group 'conformed' at a similar level to the traditionally deceived group, whereas the fully informed group did not conform at all.

These latter participants seemed to behave in accordance with what most people believe would actually occur in the Asch set up. This is, after all, why Asch's study is so renowned, gripping and well-recalled by the psychology student. It defies common sense. The prognosis for role-play, on this evidence, in demonstrating such counter-intuitive effects, therefore, seems not so good. However, the capacity in normal students during role-play for aggressive authoritarianism and subservience, was demonstrated convincingly and against prediction in Zimbardo's classic study described briefly below.

This does not mean that deception of the Milgram intensity is therefore ethically acceptable. Both the BPS and the APA ask that the uncertain investigator seek opinion, again, from those 'experienced and disinterested colleagues' who are not fervently committed to the investigator's desire to confirm theory with the particular hypothesis to be tested.

STRESS AND DISCOMFORT

There is no argument against the principle that psychological investigators should guarantee the safety of their participants and that everything possible should be done to protect them from harm or discomfort. The difficulty comes in trying to decide what kind of stress or discomfort, physical or mental, is unacceptable. Humanists and others might argue that *any* traditional experimental research on 'subjects' is an affront to human dignity. At a lesser extreme, those who see value in the human experimental procedure have nevertheless criticised some investigators for going too far.

MENTAL STRESS

Examples of studies involving a possibly substantial degree of mental stress were given above. These involved deterioration of a person's self-image or the strain of feeling responsible for action in the Latané and Darley study. A further example, causing some dissent, is that in which a child was asked to guard the experimenter's pet hamster, which was removed from its cage through a hole in the floor when the child wasn't looking.

But not all mental stress emanates from deception. Participants may be exposed to pornographic or violent film sequences. Extreme psychological discomfort, in the form of delusions and hallucinations, was experienced by participants undergoing 'sensory deprivation' (deprived of sound, touch and sight) such that they often terminated the experience after three days. Zimbardo's (1972) simulation of authority and obedience had to be stopped after six days of the 14 it was supposed to run. Students played the part of aggressive, sadistic and brutal prison guards far too well. Their 'prisoners' (other students) became extremely passive and dependent. Within two days, and on the next few, participants had to be released, since they were exhibiting signs of severe emotional and psychological disorder (uncontrollable crying and screaming) and one even developed a nervous rash.

There is an obligation for investigators, not only to debrief, but also to attempt to remove even long-term negative effects of psychological research procedures. 40 of Milgram's participants were examined, one year after the experiment, by a psychiatrist who reported that no participant had been harmed psychologically by their experience. The 1992 BPS *Principles* urge investigators to inform participants of procedures for contacting them should stress or other harm occur after participation.

PHYSICAL DISCOMFORT

Many psychological experiments have manipulated the variables of, for instance, electric shock, extreme noise level, food and sleep deprivation, anxiety or nausea producing drugs and so on.

Watson and Rayner (1920), as is well known, caused 'Little Albert', a young infant, to exhibit anxiety towards a white rat he had previously fondled quite happily, by producing a loud disturbing noise whenever he did so. Apparently Albert even became wary of other furry white objects.

His mother moved away and so Albert was removed from the project before he could be deconditioned.

This procedure developed into that of 'aversive conditioning' which is intended to rid willing clients of unwanted or destructive behaviour.

The term 'willing' creates difficulties. In the sensitive case of gay men submitting themselves to aversive therapy, it has been argued that treatment is unethical, since the men are succumbing to a conventional norm structure which treats their preference as undesirable or 'sick'. In general research work, a 'willing' participant may act under social pressure. They may wish to sustain a 'real man' image, to bear as much as, or 'beat', their peers. They may feel they are ruining the experiment or letting down the experimenter (the special power of the investigator is discussed below).

For these reasons, the investigator has a set of obligations to participants to ensure they do not suffer unduly or unnecessarily. These are outlined in the following section. In any research where discomfort might be expected the investigator is expected to seek opinion and advice from professional colleagues before going ahead.

THE RIGHT TO NON-PARTICIPATION

The investigator is obliged to:

1 Give the participant full information as to the likely level of discomfort and to emphasise the voluntary nature of the exercise and right to withdraw at any time.

2 Remind the participant of this right to withdraw at any point in the procedure where discomfort appears to be higher than anticipated.

3 Terminate the procedure where discomfort levels are substantially higher than anticipated and/or the participant is obviously disturbed to an unacceptable level.

Now we can see one of the most objectionable aspects of Milgram's study. His experimenter flagrantly contravened all three of these principles. The duty to respect the participant's right to withdraw and to remind the participant of this right are both stressed by the APA. Yet, contrary to this, each participant wishing to stop was commanded to continue in the interests of the research programme. Continuance was 'absolutely essential' and the participant had 'no choice but to go on'. The APA even stresses special vigilance when the investigator is in a position of power over the participant. This was, of course, the very position forcefully exploited and examined in the Milgram study.

It is usual to obtain the informed consent of research participants. As we shall see below, this isn't always possible before the research is conducted, though for laboratory experiments consent can always be obtained. In research with children, the informed consent of parents must first be obtained. For obvious reasons, children cannot be subject to great stress, even in the unlikely instance that parents agree (though there was little Albert).

Two factors working against informed consent are the investigator's need to deceive on some occasions, and the significant power attaching to the investigator *role*.

THE SPECIAL POWER OF THE INVESTIGATOR

In general, then, the investigator is obliged to give the participant every chance not to participate, both before and during the experimental procedure. Working against this, as we have just said, is the position of influence, prestige and power of the investigator. Torbert (1981) says:

> . . . the unilaterally controlled research context is itself only one particular kind of social context and a politically authoritarian context at that. It should not be surprising that some of its most spectacularly well-conceived findings concern persons' responses to authoritarianism.

An additional dimension to this power emerges when we consider the common position of United States' psychology undergraduates who often face an obligatory participation in a research project of their choice. In some cases an exemption is offered but it costs one additional term paper, making the choice more apparent than real.

A further issue for ethical concern has been the practice of obtaining prison inmates or psychiatric patients for stressful experimental studies, where inducements, such as a pack of cigarettes or temporary release from daily routines, are minimal and would not normally 'buy' participation outside the particular institution.

The 1992 BPS *Principles* lay particular emphasis on the way in which consent is obtained from detained persons and also on the special circumstances of children and adults with impairments in understanding or communication.

INVOLUNTARY PARTICIPATION

In participant observation studies, and in naturalistic (covert) observation, the persons observed are quite often unaware of their participation. This seems fairly unobjectionable where completely unobtrusive observation is made and each observee is just one in a frequency count; for instance, when drivers are observed in order to determine whether more males or more females stop at a 'stop' road sign.

In participant observation people's private lives may be invaded. Humphreys (1970) investigated the behaviour of consenting homosexuals by acting as a public washroom 'lookout'. Persons observed were completely unaware of the study and of the fact that their car registration numbers were recorded in order to obtain more background information later on.

Some field studies carried out in the public arena involve manipulations which interfere with people's lives. A street survey obviously delays each respondent but here consent is always sought first. In Piliavin et al.'s (1969) studies on bystander intervention, a person looking either lame or drunk 'collapsed' in a subway train. In one version the actor bit a capsule which produced a blood-like trickle on his chin. Predictably, the 'lame' person got more help than the drunk, with the 'blood' condition having a lowering effect on helping. Piliavin's study, in fact, contravenes the principles of openness (no deception), stress avoidance and informed consent before participation.

Doob and Gross (1968) delayed drivers at a traffic light in either a very smart, new car or an older, lower status one. Effects were predictable in that it took drivers longer to honk at the smarter car.

If these results are fairly unsurprising, couldn't willing participants simply be asked to imagine the situation and consider their likely response? Would simulation work here? Doob and Gross used a questionnaire as well, and found no difference between the reports of how long independent samples of students thought it would take them to honk at each car. Oddly, of the 11 students who said they would not honk, all six of those who would not honk at the low status car were male, and all five of those not honking at the high status car were female.

The 'as if' findings were so different from actual behaviour that the defenders of field research seemed vindicated in their claim to more realistic data. However, by 1991, a computer simulation had been devised, and this produced results confirming the original findings.

INTERVENTION

Some aspects of brief INTERVENTION with naïve participants have been dealt with above. Several studies have involved intervention on a substantial scale but with willing participation. For instance, psychologists have worked with parents and children in the home in an effort to demonstrate the beneficial effects of parental stimulation on the child's learning and intellectual performance. In these studies a control group is necessary for baseline comparison. In hospital experiments with new drugs, trials are halted if success is apparent on the grounds that it would be unethical to withhold treatment from the placebo and control groups. Unfortunately, in psychological intervention research, even if success is apparent, there would not usually be the political power and resources to implement the 'treatment' across all disadvantaged families. Ethical issues arise, therefore, in selecting one group for special treatment.

Where intervention occurs for research purposes only, and involves the production of behaviour usually considered socially unacceptable, ethical principles need very careful consideration. Leyens et al. (1975), for instance, raised levels of aggression in boys shown a series of violent films. They were observed to be more aggressive in daily activities compared with a control group shown non-violent films. Several other studies have produced the same effect, some with adults. It is quite difficult to see how debriefing alone could leave the boys just where they were before the study began.

RESEARCH WITH ANIMALS

There is nothing more certain of producing a lively debate among psychology students than the discussion of whether or not it is necessary or useful to experiment on defenceless animals. Many students are far more emotionally outraged about animal research than about some of the more questionable human studies, on the grounds that humans can refuse whereas animals have no such chance.

One cannot deceive animals, though one can fool them. Nor can they give their informed consent, be debriefed or ask for a procedure to be terminated, though only the most callously inhumane experimenter could ignore severe suffering. Animals can, however, be subject to exploitation, extreme levels of physical pain and mental stress.

Many students spend the whole of an essay on ethics discussing the plight of research animals, though Milgram will often be a secondary focus of attention. I don't intend to go through the innumerable examples of animals in pitiful situations in the psychological research laboratory. To list the kinds of situation is enough:

- severe sensory deprivation
- severe to complete social deprivation
- extirpation or lesion of the nervous system or body parts
- use of extremely aversive physical stimuli including electric shock, noise, poisonous or otherwise aversive chemicals, mood or behaviour altering chemicals
- starvation

Why have psychologists found it useful or necessary to use these methods?

THE CASE FOR ANIMAL RESEARCH

1 Animals can be used where humans can't. For instance, they can be deprived of their mothers or reared in complete darkness. This point of course completely begs the question of whether such procedures are ethical.

2 Great control can be exerted over variables. Animals can be made to feed, for instance, at precise intervals.

3 The whole process of development can be observed.

4 Several generations can be bred where species have short gestation and maturation periods. This is useful in studying genetic processes.

5 An effect shown or insight gained in animal studies, although not directly applicable to humans, may lead to fresh and fertile theories about human behaviour. Animal studies have contributed ideas to the debate on human adult–infant bonding and maternal separation, for example.

6 Comparisons across the phylogenetic scale are valuable for showing what humans *don't* have or *can't* do – what we have probably evolved away from or out of. Comparison is invaluable in helping us develop a framework for brain analysis based on evolutionary history. A seemingly useless or mystical piece of the nervous system may serve, or have served, a function disclosed only through the discovery of its current function in another species.

7 At a very elementary, physiological level, animals and humans have things in common. The nature of the synapse, neural connections and transmission for instance, are similar among higher primates.

8 Skinner argued that elementary units of learning would also be similar across most higher species. Hence, he mostly used rat and pigeon subjects in his research work, arguing that patterns of stimulus–response contingencies, schedules of reinforcement and so on were generalisable to the world of human behaviour.

THE CASE AGAINST ANIMAL RESEARCH

Theorists have argued that too much extrapolation from animal to human has occurred. Here are some reasons why such extrapolation is considered inappropriate.

1 Seligman (1972) has argued for the concept of 'preparedness' which implies that some animals are born especially prepared, through evolutionary processes, to learn easily certain behaviour patterns of survival value to the species. Likewise, some patterns are difficult or impossible to learn at all – the animal is 'contra-prepared'. This makes comparison between one species and another hazardous, let alone comparison between human and animal.

2 Kohler (1925) demonstrated in apes what he referred to as 'insight' learning – solving a novel problem with a sudden reorganisation of detail, much like we do when we spontaneously solve one of those annoying match-stick problems. If apes can do what humans certainly can, then the validity of comparing human learning processes with those of the rat, who *doesn't* exhibit 'insight', seems questionable.

3 The ethologists have shown that quite a lot of behaviour, subject to cultural variation and slow developmental learning in humans, is instinctive in animals, demonstrated as 'fixed action patterns'. Mating preludes and territorial defence are quite rigidly organised in a large number of species yet quite ungeneralised across the breadth of human cultures.

4 The ethologists, among others, have also questioned the validity of having

animals do abnormal things in the laboratory and have concentrated on behaviour in the natural environment, only testing animals in the laboratory with variations of the stimuli which would be encountered normally outside it.

5 Language, strongly defined in terms of syntax and symbol, appears to be unique to humans. Language is the vehicle for transmission of cultural values, meanings and the individual's social construction of reality. Very much psychological research, consciously or not, assumes these values and meanings as integral to human awareness. The comparison with most animals seems at its weakest here.

The points above are all aimed at the rejection of animal research on *practical* grounds. It is argued that such research will not tell us what we want to know. Other arguments take a moral or humanitarian line.

6 Some argue that it is just categorically wrong to inflict pain and suffering on any living creature.

7 A more profound argument is that the experimenter's 'attack' on nature typifies the 'controlling' model of humankind associated with the psychologist as hard, objective, neutral scientist. This image of the scientist is currently rejected, not just by humanist and many other psychologists, but by many scientists across the disciplines who wish to project a model of environmental care.

Supporters of the points above would argue that kittens need not be deprived of visual experience in order to study the nature–nurture issue in perception. Field studies on children who unfortunately *happen* to have been so deprived would be considered more valid and more ethical. Likewise, monkeys do not need to be deprived of their mothers. Plenty of children have been. The great debate in attachment theory has been over the number and quality of bonds necessary for optimum child development and here, monkey studies can hardly help us.

Whatever the rationale for animal studies, or the fierce, impassioned objections, it seems likely they will continue as an adjunct to psychological research, though perhaps not at their earlier intensity.

British research is carried out under guidelines issued by the BPS (1985). In these the following points are made:

- Knowledge to be gained must justify procedure; trivial research is not encouraged; alternative methods are
- The smallest possible number of animals should be used
- No members of endangered species should ever be used
- Caging, food deprivation, procedures causing discomfort or pain should all be assessed relative to the particular species studied. A procedure relatively mild to one can be damaging to another
- Naturalistic studies are preferred to laboratory ones, but animals should be disturbed as little as possible in the wild
- Experimenters must be familiar with the technical aspects of anaesthesia, pharmacological compounds and so on; regular post-operative medical checks must be made

The guidelines also direct the psychologist to the relevant laws under which animal research is conducted and to the need for various licences.

CONCLUSION

All in all, it looks difficult to conduct much research at all without running into ethical arguments. Certainly it seems impossible to proceed with anything before considering possible ethical objections. But this is as it should be. Other sciences too have their associations and committees for considering social responsibility in scientific research. They argue about the use to which findings might be put or the organisations from whom it would not be prudent to accept sponsorship. They consider the likely impact of their work on society as a whole.

Similarly, psychology has to make these considerations. But, since humans, as individuals in society, are also the focal point of research, it is hardly surprising that psychology, as a research society, has to be far sharper on its toes in spotting malpractice, abuse, thoughtlessness and lack of professionalism. If psychologists prefer not to have people take one step backwards at parties and say things like 'I bet you're testing me' or 'Is this part of an experiment?', they need to reassure the public constantly that some excesses of the past cannot now happen and that deception really *is* only used when necessary.

The humanists and 'new paradigm' researchers appear to have gained the moral high ground on these ethical issues, not just because they put dignity and honesty first, but because they see their collaborative or non-directive methods as the only route to genuine, uncoerced information. As Maslow puts it:

'. . . if you prod at people like things, they won't let you know them.'

Well, what do you think? You'll probably discuss quite heatedly, with co-students or colleagues, the rights and wrongs of conducting some experiments. I can't help feeling that the information from Milgram's work is extremely valuable. It certainly undermined stereotypes I had about whole cultures being inherently cruel. But I also can't help thinking immediately about those participants who went all the way. Can we be so sure we'd be in the 35% who stopped? Not even all these stopped as soon as the victim was clearly in trouble. How would we feel the rest of our lives? Should we inflict such a loss of dignity on others? I haven't made any final decision about this issue, as about many other psychological debates and philosophical dilemmas. Fortunately, I'm not in a position where I have to vote on it. But what do you think . . . ?

GLOSSARY

Informing participants about the full nature and rationale of the study they've experienced and removing any harm to self-image or self-esteem	_____	debriefing
Leading participant to believe that something other than the true IV is involved or, at least, not giving full information to the participant about the IV, DV or overall procedure	_____	deception

Research which makes some alteration to people's lives beyond the specific research setting, in some cases because there is an intention to remove disadvantage or make improvements of some kind in people's overall condition	_____	intervention
Effect of research which intrudes on people's personal lives	_____ __ _____	invasion of privacy
Taking part in research without agreement or knowledge of the study	_____ _____	involuntary participation

27

PLANNING PRACTICALS

If you are going to be devising and running your own practical work in psychology, good luck! It is great fun, and highly satisfying, to be presenting a report of work which is all your own, rather than of a practical which your tutor sets up and sends you all off to do. However, beware! Your tutor almost certainly has a lot of experience in planning such exercises such that you do not waste all your efforts and end up with useless data or find yourself running a project with hopeless snags or a completely inappropriate design.

Below I have jotted down most of the things I can think of which need attention before you start your data gathering. I've almost certainly missed some things but I hope these will be of some help. *Nothing I've written, however can substitute for very careful planning, preferably in a small group, before you start your data collection.*

Remember that the 'practical' doesn't start when you actually begin running your trials and testing your participants. That is a tiny part of the whole process. There is a large portion of time to spend planning and another large portion to spend analysing and (dare I say it) writing up your report!

I have written these notes with the traditional, 'tight' hypothesis test in mind. Hence there is emphasis on strict definition of variables and thinking about the system of analysis before starting. This obviously runs counter to the tenets of qualitative and 'new paradigm' research. However, most students will find that, through syllabus requirements or other forces, they will need to be familiar with this traditional design. Besides, since the 'old paradigm' is hardly likely to disappear overnight, I believe it is necessary to understand the approach fully in order to understand its weaknesses and to be able to take off in other directions.

The student wishing to conduct something more qualitative in design would need to consult thoroughly with their tutor in order to avoid ending up with a report which is fascinating but is seen as the work of a 'displaced novelist' and mainly anecdotal.

THE OVERALL AIM

- Did the idea just pop up in your head? It is worth checking to see if there is *related theory*. This might give you firmer ideas. You will probably be working to a syllabus which wants you to 'embed' the research aims in some background theory. There is nothing wrong in principle, however, in testing a personal idea which came to you unaided. Creativity is encouraging. However, it is likely that there *is* some related work on it, though perhaps hard to find in your college library. You can always phone up or write to other institutions or libraries, however, such as your local university.
- *Now* is the time to state your hypotheses very carefully, not when you come to write up the report!

THE DESIGN

- Do you need to quantify your variables because there is no existing measure? Can this be done sensibly? How will 'self-concept', for instance, be measured?
- In thinking of variables it will be useful to think about any *statistical analysis* you are going to employ. For instance, if you have been asked to use correlation then it is almost certainly intended that you should use Pearson or Spearman where both your variables should be measurable on at least an ordinal scale. Otherwise, if you tried to 'correlate sex with driving speed', for instance, you would end up with the difference between males and females, since sex is a nominal variable – it only has two qualitatively different values. There are the special procedures mentioned in Chapter 18 but you can't get a conventional scattergram, using all of both axes, when one variable has only two distinct values. With such variables it makes sense to test for difference.

  Will you be able to develop a plausible rating scale for your variable(s)? Can people rate a photograph of a face on a scale of one to ten for 'happiness', for example? Using this approach, you will only be able to do a non-parametric test.

  If you measure driving ability by whether a driver stops or not, you can only achieve nominal level data. Is that what you want? Similarly, compare asking whether people passed their test first time with asking how long it took them to learn.

- Are you dealing with too many variables to keep statistical analysis simple enough? Say you wanted to see whether introverts improve on a task without an audience, whereas extroverts deteriorate. You'd like to see whether this is more true for males than for females and perhaps whether age has an effect too. Admirable thinking on interacting variables, but the statistical analysis will get very complicated. You'll need to use ANOVA. Do you understand the procedure? Can you easily get computer assistance?

- The last example would be very costly on participants. Could you get enough? In general, will you be able to get enough people for your chosen design? Remember, an unrelated design requires twice the number of people, to get the same number of scores as a repeated measures design. Will you be able to match pairs appropriately? You may not be able to obtain the information you need for this (e.g. social class). If you are going to use repeated measures, with tests on two different occasions, will everyone be available second time around?

- Have you got all the control conditions or groups you need? A pair of students once planned a test of the matching hypothesis. They wanted to see whether people tended to pair photos of couples when they didn't know, out of a set of 10 men and 10 women, who was married to whom. They conducted the test and reported how often each of their participants had been successful in making a match. It suddenly struck them that this wasn't a test of the hypothesis that 'people tend to marry people physically similar to themselves'. They had no baseline comparison. They got the people to do the matching test again, this time with the pictures face down. The expected chance 'hit' rate could have been calculated but there may have been cues in the different pieces of card used in their study.

  So, will you need a *condition for comparison*? Could you use a placebo group? Think of how you will statistically support your hypothesis.

- Is there a likelihood of any obvious confounding variables? If the general public are to be approached by researchers, will it matter that most of them are female? Some students I knew were going to say 'hello' to passers-by under two conditions, with and without a smile. It struck them that all of them were female and that there could be a differential response from male and female passers-by!

- Are conditions *equivalent*? If the experimental group have longer, more intricate instructions and introduction to their task, could this act as a confounding variable? Should the control group get equivalent but 'dummy' introduction and instructions, and/or equivalent time with the experimenters?

THE SAMPLE(S)

- Will you have to use the same old 'friends and acquaintances' or students in the college canteen? If so, will they be too much aware of your previous deceptions?
- Will they reveal the nature of the research to naïve participants you still wish to test?
- Even though the sample can't be truly random or representative, can you balance groups for sex, age etc.?
- Should you ask whether they've participated in this before? You can't ask beforehand, in many cases, such as, when you're showing an illusion. You'll have to ask afterwards and exclude them from the results if they weren't 'naïve'.
- If you suspected some participants of 'mucking around' or of already knowing the aim and perhaps trying to 'look good', you'll have to decide, having asked them afterwards, whether it is legitimate to drop their results. You can discuss this with colleagues.

THE MATERIALS

- Are they *equivalent* for both conditions? A group of students were doing a version of the Asch 'warm–cold' study. People in one group were shown a set of terms: *intelligent, shy, confident, warm, practical, quick, quiet*. The other group were shown the same terms except that '*cold*' was substituted for '*warm*'. The people had to judge other characteristics of the hypothetical person. One student had missed a class and had no '*cold*' forms, so she changed the word 'warm' in ink and photocopied. This gave a not-too-subtle clue to her second group as to what the important word in the set was.

  Can two memory word-lists be equivalent? Can you say that the words in each are equally frequent in normal language use, or that two sets of anagrams are equally hard to solve? You can use *pre-testing* of the materials to show there is no real difference.
- Are instructions to participants *intelligible*?
- Are there too many units in the material? Will it take too long to test all on each participant? Can they be shortened?
- If you want to construct a questionnaire, see Chapter 9. Remember, a test of an attitude is often made, not with questions but with statements for people to agree/ disagree with or say how far it represents their view. Don't say 'Do you believe in abortion/nuclear power/strikes?' These things exist! We want to know what people *think* about them.
- If you're unsure of the wording in the questionnaire, get the help of someone who's good with language. Respondents will not respect or take seriously a badly-written questionnaire.
- In all cases, *pilot*! Try out materials on friends and relatives.

It takes many years to train in the psychoanalytic interpretation of projective tests, such as the Rorschach and TAT. Their validity is very much questioned within the academic world. Therefore it would be unwise to attempt to incorporate the use of these instruments in a student practical.

If you are focusing on a specific group of people, such as a minority ethnic group, then please read 'doing a race project' in Chapter 10 and be extremely careful with your choice of language. If possible, check with members of the group concerned, other 'experts', your tutor and/or your classmates. This applies wherever a specific group is the focus, *whether members of that group will themselves be questioned or not* (e.g. a nationality, gay people, people with disabilities or specific illnesses or difficulties such as dyslexia, and so on).

THE PROCEDURE

- There may well be several of you going out to gather data. *Make sure you standardise your procedure exactly before you start.* The most common problem I have seen amongst a group of students doing a practical together is that they didn't have a final check that they had all got exactly the same steps of procedure. Don't be shy to ask your friends to do a final check before they rush off after a lot of hurried changes. Don't feel stupid if you don't feel confident about exactly what you have to do. Ask your friends or the tutor where appropriate. It's better to take a little more time, and admit you're not perfect, than to end up with results that can't be used or, worse, having to do things over again.
- Decide what *extra data* is worth recording (sex, age) because it might show up a relationship which wasn't part of the original hypotheses.
- *Record all the information on the spot.* If you decide to wait till later to record age or occupation of your interviewee, you may well forget. Then the result may be wasted.
- Be prepared to put participants at their ease and give an encouraging introduction.
- Work out the *exact* instructions to participants. Have a simulated run through with a colleague. What have you failed to explain? What else might people need/ want to know?
- Decide how you will answer questions your participants might ask. Will you have stock answers or will you ask them to wait until after the testing?
- If the study is an observation:
  i) Will the observations really be unobtrusive? Check out the recording position beforehand.
  ii) Will recording be easy? Does talking into a tape recorder attract too much attention for instance? Does the coding system work? Is there time and ample space to make written notes?
  iii) Will more than one person make records simultaneously in the interests of reliability?

ETHICS

As a student, it is unlikely that you have been trained sufficiently to be able to conduct satisfactory debriefing sessions. Professional research psychologists themselves often argue these days about the adequacy of debriefing in returning people to normal and 'undoing' any psychological harm done. It is also unlikely that you'll have the time or resources to debrief properly. You may not have the finances to send a copy of your report to each of your participants. Therefore it is extremely important that your proposed research project will not involve any of the following:

- Invasion of privacy
- Causing participants to lose dignity
- Causing participants to think less of themselves
- Deception which causes resentment or hostility (check that any deception used is absolutely necessary)
- Unnecessary withholding of information
- Pain or discomfort
- Breaking of local prohibitions (for instance, drinking alcohol on college premises)
- Anything at all about which participants feel uncomfortable.

Assure participants that anonymity will be maintained, and *maintain it*! It is discourteous and bad practice even to talk with close colleagues in the project, or very best friends, in a derogatory manner about participants, even if anonymous. It develops an elitist, manipulative approach to people who have tried to help you in your work.

Also assure participants that they will not feel or look stupid, or reveal anything they don't wish to about themselves. Assure them that they can have destroyed any record of behaviour, in particular any they feel very uncomfortable about. Remind them they can stop if they wish to.

On approaching unknown members of the public, tell them who you are, where you're from and the reason for doing research (part of your required coursework, for instance).

Make sure your tutor and college are happy about your approach to the public, since they will receive any complaints if you use the college name.

If you have any doubts at all discuss the proposal with your tutor and/or another responsible person whose opinions you respect.

NOW HAVE FUN!

28

WRITING YOUR PRACTICAL REPORT

If you carry out some practical work, you will find yourself faced with the onerous task of writing it all up. My first piece of advice is *don't put it off*! You'll find it much harder to come back to when any enthusiasm you had for the project will have worn off, and you won't be able to understand why certain precautions were taken or just what certain conditions were all about. You'll find essential details of data and analysis are missing and you may need the help of your class colleagues who've now lost their raw data or are too busy to help much.

WHAT IS THE PURPOSE OF A REPORT?

There are two main purposes, neither of which is to do with keeping your tutor happy. First, you are telling your reader just what you did, why you did it and what you think it adds to the stockpile of knowledge and theory development. Second, you are recording your procedures in enough detail for some of those readers, who are so inclined, to *replicate* your work. We have seen elsewhere why this is so important to scientific method.

Golden rule number one for report writing, then, is:

> **Make sure you write with enough depth and clarity for a complete stranger to repeat exactly what you did in every detail.**

WHAT ARE THE RULES?

There are none. However, your tutor will often act as if there are when commenting on your work. This is because there *are* conventions fairly generally accepted. Most of these make sense and work in the interests of good report organisation and communication between researchers. Have a look at some journals in your college library, if that's possible, or ask to borrow a copy of one volume from a local academic institution. Your tutor may well have copies of old student work, though very often only the poorer work gets left. (Why this systematic bias?) The Associated Examining Board (now part of the Southern Examining Group) will send examples of marked work. I have included one fictitious report, with commentary, at the end of this chapter.

What follows, then, is the generally accepted format, around which most articles vary just a bit. Qualitative, inductive work will follow much the same format but will not have a specific hypothesis to test. However, it will have overall aims clearly set out. Another major difference will be that the 'results' section will tend to merge with the discussion. Otherwise, reporting of procedures and evaluation of findings, overall design and method should all be similar.

Plagiarism

Perhaps I was wrong about rules above. Plagiarism is copying directly from another's work *or* paraphrasing it so closely that it is recognisably similar. In official publishing this is illegal and people can be sued for it. On college courses, if coursework counts towards final marks then plagiarism is exactly the same as cheating in an exam. On many courses the ruling is stiff – one substantial piece of copying fails the entire work. The main point is that coursework must be your *own* (or, in some cases, your group's) work. The educational point is that we learn very little from copying, as you'll know from your psychological studies of memory and learning processes. The ethical point is that copying is stealing. So be very careful not to copy from texts. Of course you can't invent your ideas. Learning is about appreciating what has gone before, then, hopefully, adding to it. The best procedure is to read, make notes, close any books, ask yourself questions to see how far you've understood, *then* attempt to write out the ideas as you now see them. This is just as important in the introduction and discussion sections of practical reports as in any essay.

Box 28.1 shows a skeleton scheme of the various sections of a report.

Box 28.1 *Sections of a practical report*

> Title
> Abstract/summary
> Introduction/aims
>   *Hypotheses*
> Method: Design
>   Participants
>   Materials/Apparatus
>   Procedure
> Results: Description/Summary
>   Analysis/Treatment
> Discussion
> Conclusion
> References
> Appendices

The title

This should be as concise as possible. You don't need 'An investigation to see whether . . .' or similar. You just need the main variables. Very often, in an experiment, you can use the IV and DV. For instance, 'The use of imagery and rehearsal methods in recall of verbal material' will adequately describe a (probably familiar) study. For a field investigation using correlation, 'The relationship between age and attitude to environmental issues' says enough.

Abstract

Also known as the 'summary'. But why on earth does a summary come at the *beginning*? Well, suppose you were interested in whether anyone had done work on your proposed topic: anxiety and jogging behaviour in red-bearded vegetarian East Londoners. As you flip through dozens of journals looking for related work, how much easier it is to see the summary of findings right at the beginning of the article, without having to wade through to the end. The abstract contains the main points of the research report, 'abstracted' from it. Most of this century, volumes have been produced each month called *Psychological Abstracts*, containing only abstracts from articles in a huge variety of research journals. This speeds up the job of finding relevant work. Nowadays, this process has been speeded up enormously by the use of a CD-ROM database called Psychlit™.

Your abstract should stand out from the rest of the report by being in a box, in a different colour, indented or in a different (typed/word processed) font.

Introduction

I like to think of this as a funnel.

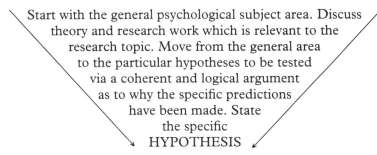

Start with the general psychological subject area. Discuss theory and research work which is relevant to the research topic. Move from the general area to the particular hypotheses to be tested via a coherent and logical argument as to why the specific predictions have been made. State the specific HYPOTHESIS

If you recall, way back in Chapter 1, we went through, very briefly, the reasons why a prediction was made that, when 'image linking' was used, more items from a word list would be recalled than when rehearsal only was used.

The introduction to a study testing this hypothesis need not contain a five-page essay on the psychology of memory, including Ebbinghaus' work and the performance of eye-witnesses in court. The hypothesis test belongs within a specialised area of memory research.

We can move our reader through the introduction in the following steps:

- The concepts of short- and long-term memory stores
- Outline of the two-process memory model
- Some evidence for the two-process model
- Phenomena the model explains, such as primacy and recency in free-recall tasks
- Focus in on the model's emphasis on rehearsal as the process by which material is transferred to the long-term store
- Introduce the 'cognitive' objection that humans always attempt to construct meaning out of incoming sensory data. Give examples of what this means
- From this theory it follows that an attempt to give an unconnected word list some 'life', by visualising the items and connecting them, should be more successful in storing the information than simple rote repetition of each word
- Additional support could be given here, referring to previous similar studies and the work on imagery in the literature

We have argued through to our specific prediction. It only remains to state the aims and hypothesis in the clearest terms so there can be no doubt over what exactly were the results we expected.

Stating aims

One aim of our research is to demonstrate our hypothesis to be valid, using a free-recall experiment under two conditions. An overall aim is to challenge the traditional two-store memory model. Aims are what the research project is *for*, what it is supposed to do. In qualitative projects, aims may be far more wide ranging and less specific than those in a hypothesis-testing project. For this reason, particular care would be taken to specify aims at this point in qualitative research.

The hypothesis

This must be very precisely stated. It is simply a clear statement of what is expected to happen. It helps here to concentrate on IV and DV again. I stated the hypothesis for the memory experiment in Chapter 1. What the hypothesis does *not* contain is any of the theory about *why* the prediction is made. It does contain variables precisely identified. Fuller definition of variables will follow in the report, such as the precise meaning of 'rating' in Exercise 7 of Box 28.2.

> Below, in Box 28.2 I have stated on the left the hypotheses from some of the exercises at the end of Chapter 24. I have, however, stated them too loosely. Try to write out your correct, precise version before checking my final versions on the right (cover the right-hand side up!)

Box 28.2 *Hypotheses from exercises (Chapter 24)*

Too loosely/Incorrectly stated	**Correctly stated**
Exercise no.	
4 'More people of one sex will avoid the ladder because they are superstitious'	'The difference between the number of men and the number of women not walking under the ladder will be significant'
5 'People will perform worse on the sensori-motor task in front of an audience'	'Participants will make significantly more errors on the sensori-motor task in front of an audience than when they are alone'
7 'Ratings on attractiveness will be similar for each member of a couple'	'There will be a significant, positive correlation between ratings of male and female partners on attractiveness'
10 'Non-rhyming words are harder to read'	'Times for reading non-rhyming words will be significantly longer than times for reading rhyming words'
11 'Participants will improve in their attitude to race as a result of the training course'	'Post-course essay ratings will be significantly higher than pre-course ratings'
12 'Smokers will have improved'	'Significantly more smokers will be assessed as "improved" than will be assessed as "worsened"'

THE NULL HYPOTHESIS – The research hypothesis is often given the symbol H_1 and the null hypothesis gets H_0. Further hypotheses being tested get numbered logically, H_2, H_3 etc., each with their accompanying H_0. The null hypothesis gets stated directly after each hypothesis.

Note: it is a good exercise, in early psychological studies, to specify precisely what it is you are testing. Most tutors will ask you to state H_0, and the exam boards usually mention it. In published research reports, in fact, the null hypothesis is rarely mentioned or explicitly stated. Even hypotheses are not as dogmatically expressed as I've recommended. However, writers *do* make clear exactly what they're testing using well-developed writing styles.

The method

It is customary and convenient, but not absolutely necessary, to break the method used down into the following four subheadings. Materials and procedure may often be one heading.

DESIGN – This describes the 'skeleton' outline of the study – its basic framework. For instance, is it an experiment or not? If it is, what design is used (repeated measures, etc.)? What conditions are there, and how many groups are used? What is the purpose of each group (control, placebo etc.)? How many participants are in each group (though this information can go in the 'participants' section below)? In many cases, describing the groups will be a way of describing the IV. In any case, both the IV and DV should be outlined here.

What controls have been employed? Is there counterbalancing and, if so, of what form?

In our experiment on imagery and rehearsal, we could say 'we used a repeated measures design with one group of 15 participants who were presented with a 20-item word list in two conditions, one with instructions only to rehearse each item, the other with instructions to use image-linking. Order of taking conditions was reversed for half the participants. The DV was number of items recalled under free recall conditions.' . . . and that's about enough.

You don't need to give any details of procedure or materials used, otherwise you'll find yourself laboriously repeating yourself later on.

If the study is non-experimental, its overall approach (e.g. observational) can be stated along with design structures such as longitudinal, cross-sectional etc. Again there may be (uncontrolled) IV and DV, for instance sex and stopping at an amber traffic light. Controls, such as measures of inter-observer reliability, may have been incorporated. Don't mention details here, just that the control was employed.

PARTICIPANTS – Give numbers, including how many in each group, and other details relevant to the study. If someone wishes to replicate your findings about 'adolescents' and their self-concepts, it is important for them to know exactly what ages and sex your participants were. These variables are less important in technical laboratory tasks, though general age range is usually useful and handedness may be relevant. Other variables, such as social class or occupation might be highly relevant for some research topics. Certainly important is how naïve to psychology participants were. Otherwise, keep details to a minimum.

How were participants obtained? How were they allocated to the various experimental groups (if not covered in your 'design')?

MATERIALS/APPARATUS – Again, apply the golden rule: ***give enough detail for a proper replication to be possible***. This means giving specifications of constructed equipment (finger-maze, illusion box) and source (manufacturer, make, model) of commercial items (tachistoscope, computer). Exact details of all written materials should be given here or in an appendix, including: word lists, questionnaires, lists people had to choose from, pictures and so on. You *don't* need to give details of blank paper or pencils!

In our memory study we would need two lists of words because we can't have people learning the same list twice without a mammoth confounding variable. We would state in this section how we justify our two lists being equivalent – selected from word frequency list, same number of concrete and abstract terms, etc.

It may be useful to include a diagram or photo of an experimental set-up or seating arrangements.

Procedure – The rule here is simple. Describe exactly what happened from start to finish in testing. This must be enough for good replication. Any standardised instructions should be included here or in an appendix, including any standard answers to predicted questions from participants.

The exact wording used in training participants to use imagery in our memory experiment should be included, together with any practice trials and words used for these.

It is very tempting to 'skim' the materials and procedure sections and give far too little detail. My advice if you're not sure you've written enough is:

GIVE IT TO A FRIEND OR RELATIVE TO READ!

If your mother or boyfriend can understand *exactly* what happened, if they could go off and do it, then it's clear and enough. (They might not get on too well with the other sections without some psychological knowledge.)

Results

Description – Large amounts of raw data go in an appendix. A summary table of these is presented in the results section, including frequencies, means, standard deviations or their equivalents. Any tables (appearing here *or* in the appendix) should be well headed. For instance, a table of our experiment starting like Table 28.1 is inadequate. What do the numbers stand for? We need a heading 'Number of words recalled in the stated condition'. If results are times, state 'seconds' or 'minutes'; if they are distance measurements, state the units.

Table 28.1 *Incorrect experimental results table*

Participant	Imagery	Rehearsal
1	12	8
2	15	12
etc.	etc.	etc.
:	:	:

You might wish to present a graphical representation of your data, such as a histogram or scattergram. Make sure these are clearly headed too, and that the vertical and horizontal axes have titles.

Tables and charts will need numbering for reference purposes.

Analysis or treatment – If there are several hypotheses to test, or different treatments, take one at a time and divide this section into subsections ((a), (b), etc.) with a heading for each one stating what hypothesis is being tested in each case.

State which statistical test is being applied and *justify* this using the decision procedures outlined in Chapter 24.

State the result clearly and compare this with the appropriate critical value. Justify the choice of this critical value including N or degrees of freedom, number of tails, and the corresponding level of probability ('$p < \ldots$'). Box 28.3 is a quick exercise in noting what can be missing from statements of significance.

Box 28.3 *Incomplete significance statements*

Statements	What's missing
'The *t*-test showed that differences were significant'	At what level? How many degrees of freedom? How many tails?
'There was a strong correlation between the two variables'	But was it significant, and at what level? Was the correlation positive or negative? Was the prediction one- or two-tailed?
'There was a significant difference between the two conditions at the 1% level'	How many degrees of freedom? How many tails?

State whether the null hypothesis is being rejected or retained.

Calculations of your tests, if you wish to include them, should appear only in the appendix. Many calculations these days will be performed by computer or dedicated calculator. The software used, and intermediary results, can be mentioned in an appendix.

If there are a number of test results, these could be presented in a clear summary table.

Discussion

The first step here is to explain in non-statistical language just what has happened in the results section. These results must then be related to the hypotheses you set out to test, and to the original aims of the research. These in turn are then related to the background theory, showing support or a need to modify theory in the light of contradictory or ambiguous findings.

Unexpected findings of 'quirks' in the results can also be discussed as a secondary issue. From time to time, such 'oddities' lead in novel research directions. You can try to offer some explanations of these if you have good reasons.

Evaluating the method

The conscientious researcher always evaluates the design and method, picking out flaws and areas of weakness. This isn't just to nitpick. A reader of the report might well come back and accuse the researcher of not considering such weaknesses. The researcher can forestall such criticism by presenting a good argument as to why the weakness should not have serious effect.

The emphasis of the evaluation depends partly on the outcome:

a If we got the result we expected, we should look carefully at the design for possible confounding variables producing a type I error. If we were predicting that the null hypothesis would be supported, we should look for ways in which the design and procedures may have hidden differences or relationships.

b If we failed to get what we predicted, we should look for sources of random variables (though research with a successful outcome may also have been affected by these). What aspects of the design, procedures and materials used did we find unsatisfactory? There could even be a confounding variable which *suppresses* our predicted effect.

c Not everything in an experiment or investigation can be perfect. There is no need to talk about not controlling temperature or background noise unless there is good reason to suppose that variation in these could have seriously affected results. Usually this is quite unlikely.

SUGGEST MODIFICATIONS – Most research leads on to more research. From the considerations made so far you should be able to suggest modifications of this design, or quite new directions, which will follow up on, or check the points made.

Conclusion

Part of the 'lore' of people teaching psychology is that the main report should end with a conclusion containing a summary of the main statistical conclusions. Looking through several copies of *The British Journal of Psychology*, I find that no one does this. There is no section called 'Conclusion', even though there is sometimes one called 'Final Comment'. This is probably the best thing to do – make some summarising comment in terms of overall findings, their relationship to the relevant model or theory and implications for the future. Avoid repeating the abstract or the beginning of your discussion, however. A verbal summary of statistical findings may be useful where several tests in the results analysis were talked about one by one in the discussion.

It is worth pointing out that actual journal articles never show calculations or include raw data and rarely justify the statistical test chosen. However, this information is always available through private correspondence. Students doing practical work are usually asked to substitute for the real-life situation by including these with their reports.

References

This is one of the most tedious aspects of writing a report, especially if you've referred to a lot of different research in your work. There is also often a lot of confusion over what exactly counts as a reference, what should be included.

Golden rule number 2 is:

> **If you referred to it directly somewhere in your text, include it. If you didn't refer to it, don't include it!**

If you wrote '. . . Gross (1992) argues that . . .'. this *is* a reference. The date means you're telling the reader where you got the information from. If you happened to read Gross' textbook whilst preparing your practical or trying to write it up – it may be where you got Bower (1977) from, for instance – then Gross is *not* a reference (but Bower will be, if you included it). Strictly speaking, if you read Bower *only* in Gross, you can say 'Bower (1977) plus reference details, as cited in Gross (1992) . . .' (etc.), giving the full Gross reference *and* page number(s). If you want to tell your reader what you read but didn't specifically refer to in your text, put these titles under 'Bibliography' if you like. In other words, your 'references' are what your text refers to, not what you read in total.

Write references in the way they appear at the back of this book. Notice that *journal articles* have the journal title in italics. The article is in ordinary print. For *books* the book title gets special treatment. There can be a few awkward ones which were articles in someone else's collection of articles, government reports and so on.

Appendices

These might contain: calculations, instructions given to participants, memory list items, questionnaires and so on. These continue your normal page numbering. Separate topics go in separate, numbered appendices ('Appendix 1', 'Appendix 2', etc.).

General presentation

It is useful to have page numbering throughout. You might find it convenient to refer to pages in your text.

A title page sets the whole project off well and a contents page helps the reader go to specific sections. If you have presented a set of projects together, it might help to begin the whole set with a contents page and to have a 'header' on each page telling the reader what particular practical we're in.

CHECKLIST FOR WRITING A PRACTICAL REPORT

(Note: some of these points will not apply to non-experimental or qualitative work)

TITLE – Does your title give a brief, but clear indication of the content?

CONTENTS – Have you numbered every page? Have you included a contents page listing main sections of the report?

ABSTRACT/SUMMARY – Does your summary cover the aims, IV, DV, participants, design, measures, main statistical results and conclusions of the research project? Does it convey a brief, essential impression of the research in less than 200 words?

INTRODUCTION – Have you given a brief general overview of the issues and concepts that are relevant to the topic which places the research in context? Is there an account of similar or related studies? Have you explained why your study was undertaken? Have you explained the main aims of the investigation? Are hypotheses (if any), including null, clearly stated in a straightforward, predictive form?

METHOD – Will your readers have enough detail to repeat the study exactly as you did it? Have you chosen a suitable set of subheadings which organise the information clearly?

DESIGN – Have you stated the main design form (field observation, repeated measures experiment, etc.)? Have you explained briefly why this design was selected? Have you explained the purpose of the different groups and given numbers in each? Have you identified the IV and DV and described conditions? Have you listed controls introduced ('blinds', counterbalancing).

PARTICIPANTS – Is it clear who they were and how they were chosen or obtained? Have you provided any additional information which may be relevant to the research (age, sex, first language, naïvety)?

MATERIALS/APPARATUS – Have you described these in sufficient detail for replication? Have you made use, where necessary, of drawings and diagrams? Have you described any technical apparatus? Have you included word lists, questionnaires etc?

PROCEDURE – Have you explained, in sequence, exactly what the experimenter/researcher did and what each participant experienced? Have you reported in full any important instructions given? (Copies in appendix.) Have you given a clear impression of the layout and arrangement of events?

RESULTS – Is there a summary table of results giving totals, means, standard deviations or their equivalents? Are lengthy, raw data in an appendix? Have you exploited opportunities for visual presentation? Are all tables, graphs and charts fully and clearly labelled and numbered? Have you given each a title and are units clearly shown? Have you clearly explained any coding or rating systems, scoring of questionnaires or other ways data were manipulated before final analysis?

Analysis/treatment – Have you explained and justified your choice of statistical test for analysis? Have you listed the results of the tests, their significance, the degrees of freedom, number of tails? Are calculations in the appendix, or an explanation of how they were done (e.g. computer)? Are statements made about rejection or not of each null hypothesis?

Discussion – Is there a verbal (not statistical) description of results? Do you explain how the results relate to your hypotheses and any background theory or prior research? Can you explain any unexpected results? Have you evaluated the design and procedures used? Have you considered alternative explanations of results? Have you suggested modifications, extensions or new research to deal with these last three points?

References – Have you listed *all* the studies which you referred to (with a date in brackets) in your text? Have you used the standard format for references? i.e. last name, initials (date) *book title*, place published: publisher *or* last name, initials (date) article title, *journal title*, Vol. pp.

Appendices – Have you labelled each appendix clearly? Do the appendices continue the page numbering? Are the appendices included on your contents page and referred to at appropriate points in the text?

COMMENTS ON A STUDENT PRACTICAL REPORT

What you see below is a *fictitious* student report. *It is not a good report*, so please use it carefully as a model, taking into account all the comments I've made beside it. My reasoning was this. If I include a perfect report the recent newcomer to psychology and its practical writing conventions would have little clue as to what typically goes *wrong* in report writing. To include *all* possible mistakes would be to produce an unreadable piece of work serving little purpose. The report below would be roughly in the mid-range at A-level, perhaps a little lower at first year degree level (I think) but its exact mark would depend upon the level or particular syllabus. Hence, I've refrained from assessing it formally. It contains quite a lot of omissions and ambiguities, but few outright mistakes. Too many of these might be misleading. I have coded comments as follows:

- ✓ a good point
- ✗ an error, omission, ambiguity; in general, a point which would count to lower the overall mark for the report
- ? an ambiguity or odd point which would not lower the mark on its own but could contribute to an overall lower mark if it were repeated. Also used for grammatical and conventional style points which, again, are not terribly bad on their own but which may accumulate into a feeling of 'not quite so good' (but this *does* depend on your level of study)

Assume that materials mentioned as in appendices *were* included (often they aren't!).

AN EXPERIMENT TO SHOW WHETHER PEOPLE ARE[1] AFFECTED BY KNOWING A WRITER'S SEX WHEN THEY JUDGE A PIECE OF WRITING

ABSTRACT

We[2] set out to see whether people make sexist assumptions about an author when they read their writing. We asked 39 participants to read an article and told half of them (19) that the author was a man and the others that it was a woman. We did this by making the writer's name 'John Kelly' for one article and 'Jean Kelly' for the other.[3] Because of stereotyping we expected the 'Jean Kelly' group to think worse of the article's quality.[4] Results were not significant[5] and the null hypothesis was kept. It was thought that the article was too neutral and women might have been voted lower on a technical article and men lower on a child-care article. If results were valid this could be interpreted as a change in attitude since Goldberg's (1968) work.[6]

INTRODUCTION

People use stereotypes when they look at other people. When we perceive people it's like looking at things in the world. We look through a framework of what we've learnt and we don't see the real thing but our impressions of it are coloured by what we expect and our biases. Bruner (1957) said we 'go beyond the information given';[7] we use what's there as 'cues' to what we interpret is really there. For example, when we see a car on the road and a mountain behind it, the mountain might look only twice as high as the car but because we know how far away the mountain is we can estimate what size it really is. When we take a picture of a pretty sight we often get telephone wires in the way because we've learnt not to see what isn't important. Also, we take a shot of Uncle Arthur on the beach and he comes out really small because we thought he looked much bigger in the viewfinder because he's important to us. Bruner and his friends started the 'new look' in perception where they experimented with perception to show that we're affected by our emotions, motivation and 'set'. In one experiment they showed sweet jars to children that were either filled with sand or sweets.[8] The children saw the jars with sweets as larger, so we are affected by our past experience and what we *want*. (Dukes and Bevan, 1951.)[9]

To show that a small bit of information affects our judgement of persons Asch (1946) gave some people some words to describe a person. The words were the same except that 'warm' and 'cold' were different. This even works when the person is real because Kelley (1950) introduced students to a 'warm' or 'cold' person and they liked the warm one more. The 'warm' person was seen quite differently from the 'cold' one.

Sex differences are a myth.[10] Condry and Condry (1976) showed people a film of a nine-month-old child reacting to a jack-in-the-box. If they were told he was a boy the reaction was thought of as 'anger' but for a 'girl' it was thought of as 'fear'. Deux (1977) reviewed several studies and found females often explain their performance as luck, even if they do well, but men say their ability helped them. This was where the task they did was unfamiliar. This means that men and women accept their

1 ? Don't need 'An experiment . . .'; title could be shorter, 'The effect of author's sex on assessment of an article'.

2 ? Conventional reports are written in passive not personal mode; e.g. 'The theory was tested that author's sex affects judgement of writing.' '39 participants were asked . . .'

3 ✓ IV is clearly described.

4 ✗ DV is not at all defined. How will 'thinking worse of' be measured?

5 ✗ Results very poorly reported. What test was used? What data were the test(s) on? What *was* the null hypothesis? What significance level was chosen to reject at? (e.g. $p < 0.5$)

6 ✓ Some brief statement of conclusions included.

7 ✓ Quotation is in quote marks and attributed to an author, with date – this *must* be referenced at the end of the report.

8 (Poor children! – you wouldn't think they'd let psychologists do that sort of thing!)

9 ✓ A broad start about factors which affect judgement in perception. The introduction should now go on to introduce *person* perception and narrow down to sex-role stereotype effects.

10 ✗ !!! A gigantic and unjustified assumption made here; there are *some* differences (e.g. reading development rate); the claim needs qualifying with the use of 'some', 'many' or examples.

stereotype and go along with it in their lives.[11] Maccoby and Jacklin's experiment[12] in 1974 showed that males describe themselves with independent terms (e.g. intelligent, ambitious) but females use more social terms (e.g. cooperative, honest).

A psychologist called[13] Goldberg (1968) got female students to read articles written by a man or a woman (they thought). The articles written by a man were rated as better. This is the experiment we're doing here.[14]

Hypothesis

People thinking an author is male will think some articles are better written than people thinking the author is female.[15]

H_0

There will be no difference between the male and female author conditions.

METHOD[16]

Design

The experiment was independent samples.[17] There were two groups. The independent variable was the sex of the author and the dependent variable was the way they judged the article.[18]

Participants

We used a random sample of 39 participants from the college canteen.[19] Originally there were 20 in the male author condition and 20 in the female author condition but the results for one in the male author condition went missing. The participants were all students except for one who was a friend of one of the students.

Materials

We used an article from *The Guardian Weekend* magazine about travelling in Tuscany. This is in Appendix 1. It was 908 words long and was printed on two sheets of A4 paper. We also used a rating sheet (in Appendix 2) where participants recorded their rating of the article for quality and interest on a 10-point scale.[20,21] This also had some questions on it to make sure the participants had noticed the name of the author.[22]

Procedure

We sat each participant down and made them feel at ease. We told them there would be no serious deception and that they would not be 'tested' or made to feel stupid in any way. We said we just wanted their opinion of something and that their opinion would be combined with others and their results would be anonymous.[23] We then gave them the instructions shown below. All this was done in a standardised way.[24]

> 'We would like you to read the article we are about to give you. Please read it once quickly, then again slowly. When you have done that, please answer the questions on the sheet which is attached to the article. Try to answer as best you can but please be sure to answer all questions *in the order given*.'[25]

If the participant's number was odd they received the female author where the article was written by 'Jean Kelly'. The other participants were given 'John Kelly' sheets. In one case this order was reversed by mistake.[26]

Participants were then left to read the article and no questions were answered by

11   ✗   Another grand assumption here, following a very specific result; needs qualification.

12   ✗   It wasn't an experiment; it was a review of mostly *ex post facto* studies.

13   ?   Don't need 'A psychologist called . . .'

14   ✗   The leap into the hypothesis is *far* too sudden here; we lurch from good background description straight into the hypothesis without some introduction to the (different) nature of the study being reported.

15   ✗   Hypothesis far too vague; should include reference to an expected significant difference between group means on the DV (which still hasn't been specifically introduced); in fact there will be *two* hypotheses tested – the differences between the means of both the 'quality' and 'interest' ratings; the null hypothesis should talk of there being no significant difference between means.

16   ✓   Good that all sections of the method are present and correctly titled.

17   ✓   Correct design and this *is* an experiment.

18   ✗   Again, DV not specified; it doesn't need complete description here but there should be an operational definition of the measure – 'quality was measured by scores given on a 10-point scale'. Other controls have not been specified.

19   ✗   Almost certainly not randomly selected from the canteen; no mention of the sex breakdown of participants and this might be important in this particular study.

20   ✓   Materials well described.

21   ✗   Notice that tucked away here is the first, and only, mention of the 10-point scale; we should have heard about this earlier; we still don't know which way the scale runs – is 10 high or low quality?

22   ✗   The technique of asking questions, including dummy ones, in order to ensure participants noticed the sex of the author deserves mention in the design (as types of 'control') and not to be tucked away in the materials section, along with the 10-point scale.

23   ✓   Ethical considerations well implemented here.

24   ?   Ambiguity; was the initial rapport session standardised, or just the instruction giving?

25   ✓   Exact instructions given are included.

26   ✗   This system of allocation of participants might have been mentioned in the
      ✓   design; good that the mistake was reported however.

the experimenters unless it did not concern the reading at all, for instance, if they wanted the light turned on or heater turned off. Questions about the reading were answered 'Please answer as best you can and we can talk about ("that problem") after you've finished. That way, all our participants do exactly the same thing. Thank you for your cooperation.'

The experimenters kept a watchful eye to ensure that instructions were followed in the correct order.

RESULTS

Data obtained

The results from the two groups were collected and organised into the table of raw data shown in Appendix 3. The averages and standard deviations were calculated and these are shown in Table 1.

Table 1[27]

	Author	
	Female	**Male**
Quality		
Mean	6.7	6.3
SD	1.5	2.3
Interest		
Mean	4.3	5.2
SD	1.1	1.3

You can see from this Table[28] that the male got a lower rating on quality but a higher rating on interest. This may be because people think men *can* write more interestingly, in general, but women are more likely to be accurate and are generally better with language and the rules of grammar.[29]

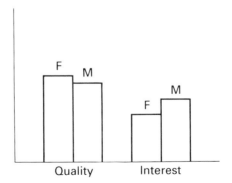

Figure 1[30]

Analysis

We decided to use an unrelated *t* test on this data to test for difference between the means. *t* tests are parametric and there must be a normal distribution from which the sample comes. Also, there must be homogeneity of variance and the level of measurement is interval.[31,32]

27 ✗ Table has no title; it does not state what the values 6.7 etc. *are*; should refer to 'points given by participants on a 10-point scale for the assessment indicated' or similar.

28 ? Should describe and summarise *for* the reader, not refer to them in this personal way.

29 ✗ Any interpretation or speculation should be conducted in the 'Discussion' section; here, just the factual results should be reported.

30 ✗ Chart has no title; 'M' and 'F' have no key (yes, it's obvious what they mean but clarity is the keyword here); the vertical scale has no values; the chart is correctly drawn as a bar chart (not histogram); hair-splitters may argue that, since male and female are qualitatively separate, there should be space between the M and F bars, but the approach used here is common and usefully illustrative.

31 ✓ Good that parametric criteria are recognised and described fairly well.

32 ✗ The *use* of the *t* test here has not been justified – there should be an answer to the criteria given here, showing that *these* data are therefore suitable for a *t* test.

The calculation for *t* is shown in Appendix 4.

Our *t* was 0.97 for quality and 1.43 for interest. Neither of these is significant and in both cases we retained the null hypothesis.[33,34]

DISCUSSION

As we see above, there were small differences between the male and female author groups but the tests showed there was no significance. It could be that there is a difference but our design has failed to show this.[35] Or else there really is no difference in the way people judge this article according to the sex of the author. If this is true then we have contradicted Goldberg's results but these were done in 1968. Perhaps things have changed since then and people no longer judge according to sex on writing. First we will look at the things that could be wrong with our design.[36]

We asked participants to answer some 'dummy' questions so that we could be sure they'd noticed the sex of the author before they rated the article.[37] When we thought about it afterwards, we decided perhaps we should have got them to do the questions (or some of them) *before* they read the article so that they would be aware of the sex *while* they were reading it. This might have made a difference and we could do another study like this sometime.[38] We didn't take any notice of the sex of our participants but obviously this might make a difference.[39] Perhaps males would downrate female authors and maybe vice versa. In a future study we could take groups of men and women separately. Another problem was that not everybody would use our scale in the same way. 'Good' might be 7 to one person and 9 to another. We could perhaps have standardised by getting them to rate something else first and then discussing the points on the scale with them.[40] Also, we should have used more participants[41] and participants may have guessed what was going on and there may have been demand characteristics.[42]

We felt that the article used was on a very neutral subject. Goldberg used a selection of articles. Some were on traditionally male subjects and some of the subjects would be more associated with females. We could do the study again using, perhaps, an article on car maintenance and one on child-care to see whether this made a difference.[43]

If our result is genuine then perhaps times have changed since 1968. These days there are female bus drivers, fire-fighters and even matadors.

Bem sees sex stereotypes as a 'straight-jacket'[44] (Gross, 1992) and argues that society would improve with a shift towards 'androgyny'. This is where a person has the strengths of both traditional sex-roles. In order to 'discover' androgyny, it was necessary to see masculinity and femininity as not mutually exclusive but as two *independent* dimensions and to incorporate this into a new sort of test which would produce two logically independent scores. Bem developed such a test (1974).[45] It has been shown that people scoring high on Bem's Sex Role Inventory report higher levels of emotional well-being than others (Lubinski et al., 1981) and show higher self-esteem (Spence et al., 1975). Perhaps, from our results, we have shown that people are less likely today to take sex into account when judging the quality of writing because androgyny is more acceptable.[46]

33 ✓ Doing calculations helps understand the test (in some cases – perhaps not here) and mental effort, in general, is usually rewarded; however, not strictly necessary for A-level and in many other syllabuses; check whether you *need* to show working.

34 ✗ Where are critical values? What level of probability was referred to ($p <$?)? Was the test one or two-tailed?

35 ✓ Recognition that a type II error could have occurred and that the alternative needs interpretation in the light of its contradiction of other work.

36 ✓ Deals with type II error possibility first, i.e. looks critically at the method.

37 ? Again, role of dummy questions should have been made clear earlier but we have already taken this weakness into account in our assessment – not a double penalty.

38 ✓ Suggests modifications based on an analysis of the present study's outcomes and weaknesses.

39 ✓ Good! This point from our earlier debits has now been picked up so we can balance this in our assessment.

40 ✓ This point has also been picked up but it's a pity the implications for a parametric test aren't spotted here; should the data have been accepted as interval level then? Really, this is a partial ✗

41 ✗ Should avoid this knee-jerk point, unless there is a good reason to include it; there were a fair number of participants and with no reason given this is rather an empty point, 'thrown in'.

42 ✗ A difficult one; is the point that people may have guessed *and* there could
   ? have been 'demand characteristics'? If so, there should be an explanation of *why* the effect of demand characteristics is suspected; in what way? If people's guessing was meant *as* a demand characteristic, is this *feasible*? It must always be remembered in independent samples designs of this kind that *you* know what the IV is but how can the participants know? Why should *they* suspect that another author will be a different sex? This is an example of 'ego-centrism' to some extent, and being wise after the event.

43 ✓ Good extension of study proposed – but looks dangerously like an ANOVA design! Are we ready for the testing involved? Remember, we can't just do several t tests (or Mann–Whitneys – see introduction to Part IV, Section 5).

44 ✓ Has quoted and acknowledged Gross's specific term here.

45 ✗ !!! This suddenly technical and academic sounding piece of text, compared to most of the rest of the report, should set alarm bells ringing for the tutor. Most tutors, after only a little experience, can spot this kind of change and will lurch for the most likely textbooks to check for plagiarism. It is, in fact, cribbed straight from Gross (1992) page 696. This really would be a shame in an otherwise adequate report.

46 ✓ Good attempt to feed the result into general context. Some of these results are up to 20 years old. However, in some colleges it's difficult to get hold of more up-to-date research to relate to but try, if you can, to include more recent work.

REFERENCES[47]

Asch, S. E. (1946) Forming impressions of personality, *Journal of Abnormal and Social Psychology*, 4, 258–90.

Bem, S. L. (1974) The measurement of psychological androgyny. *Journal of Consulting and Clinical Psychology*, 42(2), 155–62.

Bruner, J. S. (1957) Going beyond the information given. In *Contemporary Approaches to Cognition: a symposium held at the University of Colorado*, Cambridge, MA: Harvard University Press.

Condry, J. and Condry, S. (1976) Sex differences: A study in the eye of the beholder. *Child Development*, 47, 812–19.

Deux, K. (1977) The social psychology of sex roles, in L. Wrightsman, *Social Psychology*, Monterey, CA: Brooks/Cole.

Dukes, W. F. and Bevan, W. (1951) Accentuation and response variability in the perception of personally relevant objects, *Journal of Personality*, 20, 457–465.

Goldberg, P. (1968) Are women prejudiced against women?, *Transaction*, April, 1968.

Gross, R. D. (1992) *Psychology: The Science of Mind and Behaviour*, Sevenoaks: Hodder and Stoughton.

Kelley, H. H. (1950) The warm–cold variable in first impressions of people. *Journal of Personality*, 18, 431–9. Lubinski et al. (1981) as cited in Gross, R. D. (above)[48].

Maccoby, E. E. and Jacklin, C. N. (1974) *The Psychology of Sex Differences*, Stanford, CA: Stanford University Press.

Spence, J. T., Helmreich, R. L. and Stapp, J. (1975) Ratings of self and peers on sex-role attributes and their relation to self-esteem and concepts of masculinity and feminity. *Journal of Personality and Social Psychology*, 32, 29–39.

Atkinson, R. L., Atkinson, R. C., Smith, E. E. and Bem, D. J. (1993) *Introduction to Psychology*, Fort Worth: Harcourt Brace Jovanovitch[49].

47 ✓ Good references, put in conventional style and in alphabetical order.

48 ✓ Yes! This one isn't in my current printing of Gross (though, by the time you read this, it may be). This is the way to refer to works you don't have/ can't get the original reference for but which you've seen referred to by another author.

49 ✗ 'Allo, 'allo! What's this one doing here? It's not in alphabetical order and, much more important, it *wasn't* referred to in the text of the report at any time. It's probably been read to do the report but it *isn't* a reference. It could be included as 'background reading' or, sometimes 'bibliography'. (But beware! Sociologists use 'bibliography' as psychologists use 'references'!)

STRUCTURED QUESTIONS

The following structured questions will give the reader practice in answering exam-type questions whilst noting that marks available indicate where longer answers are required.

QUESTION I

A group of 20 five-year-old children on one housing estate have attended a special early-years education project since they were three years old. At the time their parents volunteered for the programme, a control group of 20 children was found by selecting every tenth family from a list of the 200 other families on the estate. The two groups were fairly similar in IQ score at the start of the project. The researchers predict that, among other things, the IQ scores of the project group will now be higher than that of the control group. The IQ of the two groups at age five, is measured using a standardised test. The mean of all 40 children is 100. The following results are found:

	Special project children	Control group children
Above mean	16	12
Below mean	4	8

QUESTIONS

		Marks
1	What is the *independent variable* in this study?	1
2	What is the purpose of the *control group*?	2
3	Has the control group been *randomly selected*? Give a reason for your answer.	2
4	Describe *one* important way in which the two groups differ. Why does this difference matter?	2
5	At what *level of measurement* are the data in the table?	1
6	What statistical test would be appropriate for deciding whether the project group are significantly higher in IQ? Give reasons for choosing this test.	3
7	When would it be unwise to use the statistical test you have chosen?	2
8	If we knew the individual IQ score for each child, **a)** what statistical test might then be more appropriate?	1

b) why would this test be preferable? 2

9 The researchers decide to *reject their null hypothesis* after analysing the results. What does this statement mean? 1

10 What would be meant if it were claimed that the researchers had made a 'type I error'? 1

11 **a)** What is meant by a test being '*reliable*'? 1
b) Describe how the IQ test would have been *standardised*. 2

12 The early-years project itself may not have been responsible for the difference in IQ. *Referring to the information given on the project,* state two reasons why the project group's IQ might have been higher than that of the control group at five years old. 2

13 What *ethical considerations* might be made before publishing the results of this research? 2

QUESTION 2

In a longitudinal study, a sample of 16 children were given an IQ test at ages three, nine and 15 years. The children were selected at random from all children attending a local playgroup who were likely to remain in the area for the duration of the study.

The researcher believed that IQ is a relatively stable factor across development.

The correlation between the children's IQ values at ages three and nine was 0.41.

The correlation between the children's IQ values at ages nine and 15 was 0.78.

QUESTIONS

Marks

1 State two important features of the design in this study. 2

2 Give one disadvantage for each of the features you have mentioned in question 1. 2

3 State one source of *bias* in the sample selected. 1

4 Why is it important for the children to stay in the same area, apart from convenience to the researcher? 1

5 The researcher tests all the children herself. Why might this introduce *error* in the results? How might this be easily avoided? 2

6 On the diagrams below, show *roughly* the shapes you would expect for a *scattergram* when the correlation is:

a) 0.78 1
b) −0.95 1

IQ 15 years | $r = 0.78$ | $r = -0.95$

IQ at 9 years

7 IQ scores for the test used are standardised so that the mean of a large sample tested is 100 and the standard deviation is 15.

    a) What would be a child's IQ score if they had a *z*-score of +1.5?   1

    b) How many children would score below 85?   1

8   The researcher chose to calculate *Pearson's correlation coefficient*. Can you   2
justify the choice?

9   Would the hypotheses of the study be *one-tailed* or *two-tailed*?   1

10   Below is a section of the table of critical values for Pearson's coefficient.
Use this to answer these questions:

    a) Is the correlation of 0.41 significant?   1

    b) At what level is the correlation of 0.78 significant?   1

df	Level of significance ($p<$) (one-tailed)			
$(= N-2)$	**0.05**	**0.025**	**0.01**	**0.005**
14	0.426	0.497	0.623	0.742
15	0.412	0.482	0.606	0.725
16	0.400	0.468	0.590	0.708

11   What would a correlation of -0.95, if found, indicate about the two   1
variables being correlated?

12   **a)** For the nine-year and 15-year comparison, state the *null hypothesis*.   1

    b) Would the null hypothesis you stated in **a)** be *accepted* or *rejected*, given   1
the results above?

13   Another researcher carried out a similar study and also obtained a   1
correlation of 0.78. However, in this case the result was not significant at
any level. What must be the difference between the new study and the one
described here?

14   In what way do the results support the researcher's theory and in what way   2
do they fail to support it?

15   Describe two common *weaknesses* of IQ tests   2

QUESTION 3

An experiment is conducted on a single participant who has to decide whether a
word, when it appears on a specially devised screen, is a real word or a nonsense
word. Presentation is arranged such that, on each trial, the word appears either only
in the left visual field or only in the right. The sequence of left and right side
presentations is randomly organised.

From past research it is predicted that words appearing to the right will be
recognised faster since they go directly to the left ('language specialised') brain
hemisphere.

Recognition speed is measured by the time taken to press a reaction timing switch
when the word has been judged real or not. If an error is made an extra trial is
given.

The results, over many trials, form a positively skewed distribution. Differences
are significant at 5%, but times for words appearing to the left are faster.

QUESTIONS

Marks

1 Give two advantages and two disadvantages of using a *single participant* 4
   design such as this one.

2 What are the *independent* and *dependent variables*? 2

3 What should the researcher take into account when choosing the real and 2
   nonsense words for stimulus display?

4 Can you think of a reason for giving an extra trial each time the participant 1
   makes an incorrect judgement?

5 **a)** Why are the left and right-side trials presented in a *random* order?
   b) How could a *random order* be *selected*? 2

6 At what *level of measurement* (nominal/ordinal/interval/ratio) would a set of 1
   reaction times be?

7 **a)** The researcher would like to conduct a *parametric test* but finally 1
   decides not to. Why might this be?
   b) Which *non-parametric test* would be used? 1

8 Roughly sketch a *positively skewed* distribution and mark on it where the 2
   mean and *median* of the scores would fall.

9 It is found that, for this participant, times for words appearing to the left
   are significantly faster than for those appearing to the right.

   a) What might explain this participant's times going contrary to 2
   prediction?
   b) What should happen to the *null hypothesis*? 1

10 The odd result causes the researcher to form a new hypothesis which runs 1
   contrary to established research theory in this area. What *significance level*
   should be set for the new hypothesis test?

11 For the new hypothesis, the researcher tests one group with right-side
   presentations and one group with left-side presentations.

   a) What type of *design* is this? 1
   b) Give one advantage and one disadvantage of this design. 2
   c) How should participants be allocated to the two conditions and why? 2

QUESTION 4

A psychologist carries out research in two teaching departments of a college. The
departments are of roughly equal size, one specialising in catering subjects and the
other in social work. The catering department is run on fairly traditional leadership
lines, where the Head of Department takes all major decisions and consults with her
senior staff who pass on management decisions to more junior lecturers. The social
work department is organised into small team units which take responsibility for
quite major decisions within their area of work.

The researcher is interested in job satisfaction and staff–management relationships. She uses the following methods:

• Unstructured interview with each member of staff.

- A structured questionnaire on job satisfaction just developed by the psychologist (top score = 50, lowest score = 0). Internal split-half reliability is measured as a correlation of 0.86.
- A week of participant observation in each department (she does a small amount of teaching for each department, but members of staff know her true purpose).

The researcher finds that there is no significant difference between departments in scores on the job satisfaction questionnaire. However, among the more junior lecturers in the social work department she finds there is strong resentment over taking responsibility and she concludes that this is because they do not feel there is adequate reward or recognition for their participation.

QUESTIONS

Marks

1 What advantages does the *interview* have over either of the other two methods used in this research? 2

2 What problems of *biased responding* might the questionnaire produce? 2

3 In what ways might the information from the participant observation method be unique and otherwise unavailable? 2

4 Can you give an alternative reason for the lecturers' resentment? 2

5 What is meant by the '*internal reliability*' of the questionnaire? 2

6 Describe how the questionnaire would be tested for *split-half internal reliability*. 2

7 The researcher decides to convert the questionnaire scores to *ordinal data*. How would this be done? 2

8 0.86 is a *correlation coefficient*. Which measure of correlation would be used? 1

9 What does the value of 0.86 tell you about the *reliability* of this questionnaire? 1

10 What other information would you need in order to decide whether a correlation of 0.86 is *significant*? 1

11 What is the difference between the *strength* and *significance* of a correlation coefficient? 2

12 How could the researcher's conclusions about the young lecturers be tested more objectively by further research? 2

13 Why might the questionnaires not have shown up the feelings of resentment? 2

14 What sort of *ethical* issues will the researcher face in publishing the results of her research? 2

QUESTION 5

15 volunteers are given Rorschach ink-blot tests. These are abstract patterns which participants are asked to look at. They are asked to report on what the shapes look

like to them. Their responses are analysed for aggressive content by two trained raters whose final rating score is on a scale from one to 25. A check is made that one rater is scoring at about the same level as the other.

The participants are then given tasks which are impossible to complete. This is intended to create frustration and increase aggression.

The Rorschach tests and ratings for aggression are then repeated and 'post-treatment' scores are obtained. It is expected that the frustration will increase aggression.

Differences between pre- and post-treatment scores are significant at the 5% level.

QUESTIONS

		Marks
1	In what way could this sample be *biased*?	1
2	**a)** What are *'demand characteristics'*? **b)** Make a brief comment on ways in which *demand characteristics* might occur in this study.	3
3	One rater's scores are compared with the other's in order to see whether they are both rating at about the same level. What sort of check is being carried out here and why?	2
4	What kind of *statistical test* would be used to compare the two raters' scores?	1
5	A colleague argues that scores might have risen even without the frustration task, because participants were annoyed by the time they were wasting. What could be added to the design in order to rule out this possibility?	1
6	The effect in question 5 would be a *confounding variable*. What is meant by this term?	2
7	The rating scale is not considered sensitive enough to count as *interval level* data. What level would it be treated as?	1
8	What *statistical test* would be performed to establish that the pre- and post-treatment scores are significantly different?	1
9	**a)** State the *hypothesis* in this study. **b)** Is the test of this hypothesis *one-* or *two-tailed*?	2
10	What is the probability that this researcher has made a *type I error*?	1
11	Describe two main weaknesses of *unstructured* and *disguised* tests like the Rorschach.	4
12	Outline another method by which aggression could have been assessed.	3
13	**a)** What is an *'operational definition'*? **b)** What is the researcher's operational definition of *'aggression'* in this study?	3

QUESTION 6

One group of 10 participants is asked to solve two sets of six anagrams. One set is of common words and the other set is of uncommon words. The sets of words for the anagrams are selected at random from larger sets of frequently and infrequently occurring words. The two conditions are counterbalanced. The time taken to solve each anagram was measured by stopwatch and recorded. Results appear in the table below.

Anagram results

Participant	Median solution time (in seconds) for six anagrams	
	Common words	Uncommon words
A	14	27
B	23	85
C	35	32
D	15	30
E	27	130
F	5	13
G	25	60
H	32	125
I	17	33
J	21	28

The researcher argues that when people solve anagrams they do not just passively rearrange letters until a word emerges. The theory is that people are *active* problem-solvers and that they *generate* possible words which might fit some of the letters before, and whilst arranging the letters. The research was designed to support this theory.

QUESTIONS

Marks

1 What are the *independent* and *dependent variables* in this experiment?   2

2 What kind of *experimental design* is being employed?   1

3 **a)** Why is *counterbalancing* carried out?   1
   b) How exactly would the counterbalancing be carried out?   2
   c) Assuming one group still takes both conditions, what other technique would have dealt with the problem for which *counterbalancing* was used?   1

4 If the researcher had used two different groups, one for each condition, why could this have been unsatisfactory?   1

5 Apart from changes in noise and lighting levels, suggest two *random variables* which might affect the participants' performances.   2

6 The researcher asked experimenters to use a *standardised procedure* which included explaining the task in exactly the same words to each participant. Give two reasons for this approach.   2

7 The times for one person on each of the six anagrams of uncommon words are as follows:

85 97 119 131 156 287

a) When values occur like this, why is the *median* preferable to the *mean*? 1
b) Which participant took these times? 1

8 At what *level of measurement* are the times shown in the table (nominal, ordinal, interval or ratio)? 1

9 a) Does the level of measurement permit a *parametric test*? 1
b) State two conditions, other than level of measurement, which must be satisfied before carrying out a *parametric test*. 2

10 Give *one* advantage of using a *parametric test*. 1

11 What parametric test would be used to test for a significant difference here? 1

12 What is meant by a '*level of significance*'? 1

13 Do you think that the difference between the two sets of times in the table will be shown to be significant? Give reasons. 2

14 The researcher argues that people produce guesses at the word, from among all the words they know, as they rearrange the letters. They are likely to produce less of the infrequent words as guesses. Can you think of any other theoretical explanation for the slower times? 2

QUESTION 7

A researcher predicts that younger teenage mothers will be more controlling with their children. Three representative samples of mothers are asked to participate in a cross-sectional study. The groups are 15, 19 and 23 years old. The researcher's assistants record on videotape a 30-minute play session, once a day, at exactly the same time, for a fortnight. The sessions are recorded in the mother's own home. Several 'raters', who do not know the research hypothesis, are given a rigorous coding system, and they analyse the videotape content in 10-second units.

The combined raters' scores for verbal control (items like 'Come here!' 'Leave it alone!') are shown for the 15- and 23-year-old groups in the table below. The ratings are out of a possible total of 100.

Verbal control ratings

15-year-olds	23-year-olds
78	45
56	34
65	56
89	56
68	78

Rank chart

Rank	1									10
Rating	34									89

QUESTIONS

Marks

1   Is this an *experiment*? Give a reason for your answer.   2

2   What is meant by a *'cross-sectional'* study?   1

3   Give one *advantage* and one *disadvantage* of cross-sectional studies.   2

4   What is one advantage and one disadvantage of carrying out a *field study* rather than a study in the *laboratory*?   2

5   What advantage does the use of videotape have over the method of coding behaviour on the spot, as it occurs?   1

6   **a)** Why is it important to draw a *representative sample*?   1
   b) What factors might be taken into account in trying to make these samples representative?   2

7   Why is it important that the recording sessions take place at the same time each day?   1

8   Why would the raters be kept unaware of the research hypothesis?   1

9   How could the *reliability* of two of the raters' judgements be tested?   2

10   It is decided not to treat the combined raters' scores as *interval level* data. Why might this be?   1

11   All 10 scores in the table need to be *ranked* as one group. Put the 10 scores into rank order using a table like that shown in the rank chart above. The highest and lowest have already been entered for you.   2

12   What test would be used to look for a *significant difference* between the two sets of ranks?   1

13   The result of this test shows the probability of the differences occurring by chance alone was about 0.07. Does this mean the research idea should be abandoned? Give reasons for your answer.   2

14   How could *interviews* be used to strengthen the research findings?   2

15   Two of the mothers speak to the researcher at the end of the study. One wishes to know exactly what the whole project was about. The other wishes to remove her video recordings from the results since some of the events were extremely embarrassing. In each case, what should the researcher say or do?   2

QUESTION 8

A researcher who is interested in stress wishes to test the hypothesis that individuals who are generally more anxious tend to have worse health records.

It is decided to administer two standardised tests to a sample of individuals in a variety of occupations who respond to a newspaper advertisement for participants.

One test is a measure of general anxiety level and a high score indicares high anxiety. The other test measures general state of health, including visits to doctors, days off sick, and so on. A high score on this test indicates good general health. The participants are tested alone in a small soundproof cubicle.

The questionnaires are scored by two pairs of assistants. One pair score only the health questionnaires and the other pair score only the anxiety questionnaires. Both are unaware of the nature of the hypothesis being tested.

After testing, each participant was given full information about the research and assured that their results would remain anonymous.

The data gathered are considered to be at interval level and to satisfy other parametric assumptions. The coefficient of correlation between the two measures is -0.32 and this value is significant with $p < 0.01$.

QUESTIONS

Marks

1 Would this research design count as an *experiment*? Give reasons for your answer. 2

2 Are the researchers studying a *random* sample of participants? Please justify your answer. 2

3 Why are the assistants who score each questionnaire

   a) not told about the research hypothesis? 1
   b) given only one questionnaire to score? 1

4 Why is it important that the participants were tested *alone*? 1

5 Why do *two* people rate each questionnaire? 1

6 What feature of the tests, in the information given above, permits the data gathered to be treated as *interval level* data? 1

7 To conduct a parametric test, data must at least be interval level. What are the other *two major assumptions* to be satisfied in order to conduct a *parametric test*? 2

8 Which test of correlation would have been used on this data? 1

9 What is meant by a *negative correlation*? 1

10 Explain why a *negative correlation* was expected from the use of the two tests in this study. 2

11 What is meant by the expression '*significant with $p < 0.01$*'? 2

12 When would a researcher be *expected* to achieve a significance level of $p < 0.01$? 1

13 Would you call the correlation found in this study '*fairly strong*' or '*fairly weak*'? 1

14 Why can a '*weak*' correlation still be called '*significant*'? 2

15 What is the point of *debriefing* all participants at the end? 2

16 The researcher assumes that high levels of anxiety are a cause of poorer health. What alternative explanation of the result is possible? 2

Question 9

A researcher wished to establish which of two new types of word-processing packages (Wordpal and Wordmate) was easier to learn and which seemed more 'friendly'. 37 experienced secretaries already using word processors were obtained by asking for volunteers in a wide variety of work settings. For technical reasons, only 12 were tested with Wordmate, whereas 25 were tested on Wordpal.

Using their previous word-processing knowledge, plus on-screen information, the secretaries were asked to produce a letter with the program they were given to use. Measures were taken of the total time taken to complete the letter perfectly and of their evaluation of the program using a previously piloted questionnaire.

The researchers calculated the standard deviation of the letter completion times and, from this, they found each secretary's *standard score*. The means and standard deviations are shown in the table below. The scores appeared to be drawn from a normal distribution.

	Wordmate	Wordpal
Mean completion time (mins)	36.1	19.834
Standard deviation	22.8	10.166

A non-parametric test of difference showed that the time taken to produce a letter with Wordpal was significantly lower than the time taken to produce the letter with Wordmate ($p < 0.05$). A test for difference between the two sets of evaluation scores was non-significant.

QUESTIONS

		Marks
1	Give *one* reason why the sample gathered can be considered biased.	1
2	**a)** What was the *independent variable* in this study?	1
	b) What were the two *dependent variables* in this study?	2
3	What *experimental design* is used here and what is one of its advantages?	2
4	**a)** Explain what is meant by '*piloting*' a questionnaire	1
	b) Why is it important that a questionnaire should be *piloted*?	2
5	Explain what is meant by '*standard deviation*'.	2
6	16% of secretaries take longer than 30 minutes to complete the letter using Wordpal. One secretary's *standard score* for completing a letter in Wordpal is 1.3. Explain how we know that this person took *longer* than 30 minutes.	2
7	The researchers used a *non-parametric* test of difference. Exactly what test could this have been?	1
8	State *one* assumption that must be made before proceeding with a *parametric test*.	1
9	What information above indicates that it might be unwise to use a *parametric test* in these circumstances?	2
10	Would the researchers have consulted *one-tailed* or *two-tailed* values in	2

determining the significance of the test result? Give a reason for your choice.

11 After the test of difference between the evaluations of the two programmes 2
the researchers said they would '*retain the null hypothesis*'. What did they mean?

12 Give some explanation of why the letter completion times may have 2
differed by so much, *apart from* the differences between the two word-processing programmes.

13 One secretary does so badly with the program used that she/he wants to 2
withdraw and have the results destroyed. How would you advise the researcher to proceed in these circumstances?

QUESTION 10

A group of 12 people with alcohol problems, attending a clinic, volunteer to take part in an experimental therapeutic programme. For each volunteer, a second alcoholic is selected who is like the volunteer on several important characteristics. After three months of the programme, both groups are assessed by two methods. One is a structured and standardised questionnaire, completed by participants. The other is a clinical interview, conducted by a therapist.

The treatment group show strong and significant improvement, as measured by questionnaire, but this improvement is not so marked as measured by the therapists' interview rating. Correlation between the questionnaire score and interview ratings is 0.87.

QUESTIONS

		Marks
1	**a)** What sort of *experimental design* is used here?	1
	b) State one *advantage* of the experimental design used.	1

2 What is a major weakness of the *clinical interview* when used for psycho- 1
logical measurement?

3 Describe *two* problems which might be encountered when constructing 2
any questionnaire?

4 Give two reasons why the *questionnaire* might have produced greater 2
evidence of improvement than the *interview*?

5 What can we learn from the *correlation* of interview ratings and ques- 2
tionnaire scores?

6 A *placebo group* could have been used in this research.

a) Why might this have been useful? 2

b) What *procedure* might have been used with the placebo group? 2

7 The questionnaire scores are treated as *interval level* data. Why might this 1
be?

8 What statistical test would be used to test for significant difference 1
between the questionnaire scores for the two groups?

9 Give one disadvantage of using a *non-parametric test*. 1

10 In accepting the questionnaire differences as significant the researcher is warned that a *type I error* might have occurred. What does this mean?   2

11 The correlation between questionnaire scores and interview ratings would be described as *positive*. What does this mean?   2

12 The correlation of 0.87 was significant with a sample of 12. When would 0.87 *not* be significant, if the sample were *smaller* or *larger*?   1

13 Give *two* reasons why the treatment group may have improved *other than* because of the programme itself.   2

14 After six months the programme shows obvious success. Ethically, what should now happen to the control group and why?   2

STATISTICAL TABLES

Table 1 *Random numbers*

```
03 47 43 73 86   39 96 47 36 61   46 98 63 71 62   33 26 16 80 45   60 11 14 10 95
97 74 24 67 62   42 81 14 57 20   42 53 32 37 32   27 07 36 07 51   24 51 79 89 73
16 76 62 27 66   56 50 26 71 07   32 90 79 78 53   13 55 38 58 59   88 97 54 14 10
12 56 85 99 26   96 96 68 27 31   05 03 72 93 15   57 12 10 14 21   88 26 49 81 76
55 59 56 35 64   38 54 82 46 22   31 62 43 09 90   06 18 44 32 53   23 83 01 30 30

16 22 77 94 39   49 54 43 54 82   17 37 93 23 78   87 35 20 96 43   84 26 34 91 64
84 42 17 53 31   57 24 55 06 88   77 04 74 47 67   21 76 33 50 25   83 92 12 06 76
63 01 63 78 59   16 95 55 67 19   98 10 50 71 75   12 86 73 58 07   44 39 52 38 79
33 21 12 34 29   78 64 56 07 82   52 42 07 44 38   15 51 00 13 42   99 66 02 79 54
57 60 86 32 44   09 47 27 96 54   49 17 46 09 62   90 52 84 77 27   08 02 73 43 28

18 18 07 92 46   44 17 16 58 09   79 83 86 16 62   06 76 50 03 10   55 23 64 05 05
26 62 38 97 75   84 16 07 44 99   83 11 46 32 24   20 14 85 88 45   10 93 72 88 71
23 42 40 64 74   82 97 77 77 81   07 45 32 14 08   32 98 94 07 72   93 85 79 10 75
52 36 28 19 95   50 92 26 11 97   00 56 76 31 38   80 22 02 53 53   86 60 42 04 53
37 85 94 35 12   83 39 50 08 30   42 34 07 96 88   54 42 06 87 98   35 85 29 48 38

70 29 17 12 13   40 33 20 38 26   13 89 51 03 74   17 76 37 13 04   07 74 21 19 30
56 62 18 37 35   96 83 50 87 75   97 12 25 93 47   70 33 24 03 54   97 77 46 44 80
99 49 57 22 77   88 42 95 45 72   16 64 36 16 00   04 43 18 66 79   94 77 24 21 90
16 08 15 04 72   33 27 14 34 90   45 59 34 68 49   12 72 07 34 45   99 27 72 95 14
31 16 93 32 43   50 27 89 87 19   20 15 37 00 49   52 85 66 60 44   38 68 88 11 80

68 34 30 13 70   55 74 30 77 40   44 22 78 84 26   04 33 46 09 52   68 07 97 06 57
74 57 25 65 76   59 29 97 68 60   71 91 38 67 54   13 58 18 24 76   15 54 55 95 52
27 42 37 86 53   48 55 90 65 72   96 57 69 36 10   96 46 92 42 45   97 60 49 04 91
00 39 68 29 61   66 37 32 20 30   77 84 57 03 29   10 45 65 04 26   11 04 96 67 24
29 94 98 94 24   68 49 69 10 82   53 75 91 93 30   34 25 20 57 27   40 48 73 51 92

16 90 82 66 59   83 62 64 11 12   67 19 00 71 74   60 47 21 29 68   02 02 37 03 31
11 27 94 75 06   06 09 19 74 66   02 94 37 34 02   76 70 90 30 86   38 45 94 30 38
35 24 10 16 20   33 32 51 26 38   79 78 45 04 91   16 92 53 56 16   02 75 50 95 98
38 23 16 86 38   42 38 97 01 50   87 75 66 81 41   40 01 74 91 62   48 51 84 08 32
31 96 25 91 47   96 44 33 49 13   34 86 82 53 91   00 52 43 48 85   27 55 26 89 62

66 67 40 67 14   64 05 71 95 86   11 05 65 09 68   76 83 20 37 90   57 16 00 11 66
14 90 84 45 11   75 73 88 05 90   52 27 41 14 86   22 98 12 22 08   07 52 74 95 80
68 05 51 18 00   33 96 02 75 19   07 60 62 93 55   59 33 82 43 90   49 37 38 44 59
20 46 78 73 90   97 51 40 14 02   04 02 33 31 08   39 54 16 49 36   47 95 93 13 30
64 19 58 97 79   15 06 15 93 20   01 90 10 75 06   40 78 78 89 62   02 67 74 17 33

05 26 93 70 60   22 35 85 15 13   92 03 51 59 77   59 56 78 06 83   52 91 05 70 74
07 97 10 88 23   09 98 42 99 64   61 71 62 99 15   06 51 29 16 93   58 05 77 09 51
68 71 86 85 85   54 87 66 47 54   73 32 08 11 12   44 95 92 63 16   29 56 24 29 48
26 99 61 65 53   58 37 78 80 70   42 10 50 67 42   32 17 55 85 74   94 44 67 16 94
14 65 52 68 75   87 59 36 22 41   26 78 63 06 55   13 08 27 01 50   15 29 39 39 43
```

Abridged from R. A. Fisher and F. Yates, *Statistical Tables for Biological, Agricultural and Medical Research*, (6th ed.) Longman Group UK Ltd (1974).

Table 2 *Areas under the normal distribution*

z	0 z	0 z	z	0 z	0 z	z	0 z	0 z
0.00	0.0000	0.5000	0.40	0.1554	0.3446	0.80	0.2881	0.2119
0.01	0.0040	0.4960	0.41	0.1591	0.3409	0.81	0.2910	0.2090
0.02	0.0080	0.4920	0.42	0.1628	0.3372	0.82	0.2939	0.2061
0.03	0.0120	0.4880	0.43	0.1664	0.3336	0.83	0.2967	0.2033
0.04	0.0160	0.4840	0.44	0.1700	0.3300	0.84	0.2995	0.2005
0.05	0.0199	0.4801	0.45	0.1736	0.3264	0.85	0.3023	0.1977
0.06	0.0239	0.4761	0.46	0.1772	0.3228	0.86	0.3051	0.1949
0.07	0.0279	0.4721	0.47	0.1808	0.3192	0.87	0.3078	0.1922
0.08	0.0319	0.4681	0.48	0.1844	0.3156	0.88	0.3106	0.1894
0.09	0.0359	0.4641	0.49	0.1879	0.3121	0.89	0.3133	0.1867
0.10	0.0398	0.4602	0.50	0.1915	0.3085	0.90	0.3159	0.1841
0.11	0.0438	0.4562	0.51	0.1950	0.3050	0.91	0.3186	0.1814
0.12	0.0478	0.4522	0.52	0.1985	0.3015	0.92	0.3212	0.1788
0.13	0.0517	0.4483	0.53	0.2019	0.2981	0.93	0.3238	0.1762
0.14	0.0557	0.4443	0.54	0.2054	0.2946	0.94	0.3264	0.1736
0.15	0.0596	0.4404	0.55	0.2088	0.2912	0.95	0.3289	0.1711
0.16	0.0636	0.4364	0.56	0.2123	0.2877	0.96	0.3315	0.1685
0.17	0.0675	0.4325	0.57	0.2157	0.2843	0.97	0.3340	0.1660
0.18	0.0714	0.4286	0.58	0.2190	0.2810	0.98	0.3365	0.1635
0.19	0.0753	0.4247	0.59	0.2224	0.2776	0.99	0.3389	0.1611
0.20	0.0793	0.4207	0.60	0.2257	0.2743	1.00	0.3413	0.1587
0.21	0.0832	0.4168	0.61	0.2291	0.2709	1.01	0.3438	0.1562
0.22	0.0871	0.4129	0.62	0.2324	0.2676	1.02	0.3461	0.1539
0.23	0.0910	0.4090	0.63	0.2357	0.2643	1.03	0.3485	0.1515
0.24	0.0948	0.4052	0.64	0.2389	0.2611	1.04	0.3508	0.1492
0.25	0.0987	0.4013	0.65	0.2422	0.2578	1.05	0.3531	0.1469
0.26	0.1026	0.3974	0.66	0.2454	0.2546	1.06	0.3554	0.1446
0.27	0.1064	0.3969	0.67	0.2486	0.2514	1.07	0.3577	0.1423
0.28	0.1103	0.3897	0.68	0.2517	0.2483	1.08	0.3599	0.1401
0.29	0.1141	0.3859	0.69	0.2549	0.2451	1.09	0.3621	0.1379
0.30	0.1179	0.3821	0.70	0.2580	0.2420	1.10	0.3643	0.1357
0.31	0.1217	0.3783	0.71	0.2611	0.2389	1.11	0.3665	0.1335
0.32	0.1255	0.3745	0.72	0.2642	0.2358	1.12	0.3686	0.1314
0.33	0.1293	0.3707	0.73	0.2673	0.2327	1.13	0.3708	0.1292
0.34	0.1331	0.3669	0.74	0.2704	0.2296	1.14	0.3729	0.1271
0.35	0.1368	0.3632	0.75	0.2734	0.2266	1.15	0.3749	0.1251
0.36	0.1406	0.3594	0.76	0.2764	0.2236	1.16	0.3770	0.1230
0.37	0.1443	0.3557	0.77	0.2794	0.2206	1.17	0.3790	0.1210
0.38	0.1480	0.3520	0.78	0.2823	0.2177	1.18	0.3810	0.1190
0.39	0.1517	0.3483	0.79	0.2852	0.2148	1.19	0.3830	0.1170

Table 2 *Continued*

z	0 z	0 z	z	0 z	0 z	z	0 z	0 z
1.20	0.3849	0.1151	1.60	0.4452	0.0548	2.00	0.4772	0.0228
1.21	0.3869	0.1131	1.61	0.4463	0.0537	2.01	0.4778	0.0222
1.22	0.3888	0.1112	1.62	0.4474	0.0526	2.02	0.4783	0.0217
1.23	0.3907	0.1093	1.63	0.4484	0.0516	2.03	0.4788	0.0212
1.24	0.3925	0.1075	1.64	0.4495	0.0505	2.04	0.4793	0.0207
1.25	0.3944	0.1056	1.65	0.4505	0.0495	2.05	0.4798	0.0202
1.26	0.3962	0.1038	1.66	0.4515	0.0485	2.06	0.4803	0.0197
1.27	0.3980	0.1020	1.67	0.4525	0.0475	2.07	0.4808	0.0192
1.28	0.3997	0.1003	1.68	0.4535	0.0465	2.08	0.4812	0.0188
1.29	0.4015	0.0985	1.69	0.4545	0.0455	2.09	0.4817	0.0183
1.30	0.4032	0.0968	1.70	0.4554	0.0446	2.10	0.4821	0.0179
1.31	0.4049	0.0951	1.71	0.4564	0.0436	2.11	0.4826	0.0174
1.32	0.4066	0.0934	1.72	0.4573	0.0427	2.12	0.4830	0.0170
1.33	0.4082	0.0918	1.73	0.4582	0.0418	2.13	0.4834	0.0166
1.34	0.4099	0.0901	1.74	0.4591	0.0409	2.14	0.4838	0.0162
1.35	0.4115	0.0885	1.75	0.4599	0.0401	2.15	0.4842	0.0158
1.36	0.4131	0.0869	1.76	0.4608	0.0392	2.16	0.4846	0.0154
1.37	0.4147	0.0853	1.77	0.4616	0.0384	2.17	0.4850	0.0150
1.38	0.4162	0.0838	1.78	0.4625	0.0375	2.18	0.4854	0.0146
1.39	0.4177	0.0823	1.79	0.4633	0.0367	2.19	0.4857	0.0143
1.40	0.4192	0.0808	1.80	0.4641	0.0359	2.20	0.4861	0.0139
1.41	0.4207	0.0793	1.81	0.4649	0.0351	2.21	0.4864	0.0136
1.42	0.4222	0.0778	1.82	0.4656	0.0344	2.22	0.4868	0.0132
1.43	0.4236	0.0764	1.83	0.4664	0.0336	2.23	0.4871	0.0129
1.44	0.4251	0.0749	1.84	0.4671	0.0329	2.24	0.4875	0.0125
1.45	0.4265	0.0735	1.85	0.4678	0.0322	2.25	0.4878	0.0122
1.46	0.4279	0.0721	1.86	0.4686	0.0314	2.26	0.4881	0.0119
1.47	0.4292	0.0708	1.87	0.4693	0.0307	2.27	0.4884	0.0116
1.48	0.4306	0.0694	1.88	0.4699	0.0301	2.28	0.4887	0.0113
1.49	0.4319	0.0681	1.89	0.4706	0.0294	2.29	0.4890	0.0110
1.50	0.4332	0.0668	1.90	0.4713	0.0287	2.30	0.4893	0.0107
1.51	0.4345	0.0655	1.91	0.4719	0.0281	2.31	0.4896	0.0104
1.52	0.4357	0.0643	1.92	0.4726	0.0274	2.32	0.4898	0.0102
1.53	0.4370	0.0630	1.93	0.4732	0.0268	2.33	0.4901	0.0099
1.54	0.4382	0.0618	1.94	0.4738	0.0262	2.34	0.4904	0.0096
1.55	0.4394	0.0606	1.95	0.4744	0.0256	2.35	0.4906	0.0094
1.56	0.4406	0.0594	1.96	0.4750	0.0250	2.36	0.4909	0.0091
1.57	0.4418	0.0582	1.97	0.4756	0.0244	2.37	0.4911	0.0089
1.58	0.4429	0.0571	1.98	0.4761	0.0239	2.38	0.4913	0.0087
1.59	0.4441	0.0559	1.99	0.4767	0.0233	2.39	0.4916	0.0084

Table 2 *Continued*

z	0 z	0 z	z	0 z	0 z	z	0 z	0 z
2.40	0.4918	0.0082	2.72	0.4967	0.0033	3.04	0.4988	0.0012
2.41	0.4920	0.0080	2.73	0.4968	0.0032	3.05	0.4989	0.0011
2.42	0.4922	0.0078	2.74	0.4969	0.0031	3.06	0.4989	0.0011
2.43	0.4925	0.0075	2.75	0.4970	0.0030	3.07	0.4989	0.0011
2.44	0.4927	0.0073	2.76	0.4971	0.0029	3.08	0.4990	0.0010
2.45	0.4929	0.0017	2.77	0.4972	0.0028	3.09	0.4990	0.0010
2.46	0.4931	0.0069	2.78	0.4973	0.0027	3.10	0.4990	0.0010
2.47	0.4932	0.0068	2.79	0.4974	0.0026	3.11	0.4991	0.0009
2.48	0.4934	0.0066	2.80	0.4974	0.0026	3.12	0.4991	0.0009
2.49	0.4936	0.0064	2.81	0.4975	0.0025	3.13	0.4991	0.0009
2.50	0.4938	0.0062	2.82	0.4976	0.0024	3.14	0.4992	0.0008
2.51	0.4940	0.0060	2.83	0.4977	0.0023	3.15	0.4992	0.0008
2.52	0.4941	0.0059	2.84	0.4977	0.0023	3.16	0.4992	0.0008
2.53	0.4943	0.0057	2.85	0.4978	0.0022	3.17	0.4992	0.0008
2.54	0.4945	0.0055	2.86	0.4979	0.0021	3.18	0.4993	0.0007
2.55	0.4946	0.0054	2.87	0.4979	0.0021	3.19	0.4993	0.0007
2.56	0.4948	0.0052	2.88	0.4980	0.0020	3.20	0.4993	0.0007
2.57	0.4949	0.0051	2.89	0.4981	0.0019	3.21	0.4993	0.0007
2.58	0.4951	0.0049	2.90	0.4981	0.0019	3.22	0.4994	0.0006
2.59	0.4952	0.0048	2.91	0.4982	0.0018	3.23	0.4994	0.0006
2.60	0.4953	0.0047	2.92	0.4982	0.0018	3.24	0.4994	0.0006
2.61	0.4955	0.0045	2.93	0.4983	0.0017	3.25	0.4994	0.0006
2.62	0.4956	0.0044	2.94	0.4984	0.0016	3.30	0.4995	0.0005
2.63	0.4957	0.0043	2.95	0.4984	0.0016	3.35	0.4996	0.0004
2.64	0.4959	0.0041	2.96	0.4985	0.0015	3.40	0.4997	0.0003
2.65	0.4960	0.0040	2.97	0.4985	0.0015	3.45	0.4997	0.0003
2.66	0.4961	0.0039	2.98	0.4986	0.0014	3.50	0.4998	0.0002
2.67	0.4962	0.0038	2.99	0.4986	0.0014	3.60	0.4998	0.0002
2.68	0.4963	0.0037	3.00	0.4987	0.0013	3.70	0.4999	0.0001
2.69	0.4964	0.0036	3.01	0.4987	0.0013	3.80	0.4999	0.0001
2.70	0.4965	0.0035	3.02	0.4987	0.0013	3.90	0.49995	0.00005
2.71	0.4966	0.0034	3.03	0.4988	0.0012	4.00	0.49997	0.00003

The left-hand column in each set of three shows the particular z-value. The centre column shows the area contained between the mean and this z-value. The right-hand column shows the area left in the whole distribution to the right of this z-value. The whole area is one unit and values shown are decimal portions of it. These are also the probabilities of finding a value within the area concerned. For percentages, multiply all area values by 100. For areas between −z and +z, double the values shown.

SOURCE: R. P. Runyon and A. Haber, *Fundamentals of Behavioral Statistics*, 3rd Ed. Reading, Mass.: McGraw-Hill, Inc. (1976) Used with permission. Artwork from R. B. McCall. *Fundamental Statistics for Psychology*, Second Edition, New York: Harcourt Brace Jovanovich, Inc. (1975).

Table 3 *Critical values in the Binomial Sign Test*

N	**Level of significance for one-tailed test**				
	0.05	0.025	0.01	0.005	0.0005
	Level of significance for two-tailed test				
	0.10	0.05	0.02	0.01	0.001
5	0	—	—	—	—
6	0	0	—	—	—
7	0	0	0	—	—
8	1	0	0	0	—
9	1	1	0	0	—
10	1	1	0	0	—
11	2	1	1	0	0
12	2	2	1	1	0
13	3	2	1	1	0
14	3	2	2	1	0
15	3	3	2	2	1
16	4	3	2	2	1
17	4	4	3	2	1
18	5	4	3	3	1
19	5	4	4	3	2
20	5	5	4	3	2
25	7	7	6	5	4
30	10	9	8	7	5
35	12	11	10	9	7

Calculated S must be EQUAL TO or LESS THAN the table (critical) value for significance at the level shown.

SOURCE: F. Clegg, *Simple Statistics*, Cambridge University Press, 1982. With the kind permission of the author and publishers.

Table 4 *Critical values of* χ^2

	Level of significance for a one-tailed test					
	0.10	0.05	0.025	0.01	0.005	0.0005
	Level of significance for a two-tailed test					
df	0.20	0.10	0.05	0.02	0.01	0.001
1	1.64	2.71	3.84	5.41	6.64	10.83
2	3.22	4.60	5.99	7.82	9.21	13.82
3	4.64	6.25	7.82	9.84	11.34	16.27
4	5.99	7.78	9.49	11.67	13.28	18.46
5	7.29	9.24	11.07	13.39	15.09	20.52
6	8.56	10.64	12.59	15.03	16.81	22.46
7	9.80	12.02	14.07	16.62	18.48	24.32
8	11.03	13.36	15.51	18.17	20.09	26.12
9	12.24	14.68	16.92	19.68	21.67	27.88
10	13.44	15.99	18.31	21.16	23.21	29.59
11	14.63	17.28	19.68	22.62	24.72	31.26
12	15.81	18.55	21.03	24.05	26.22	32.91
13	16.98	19.81	22.36	25.47	27.69	34.53
14	18.15	21.06	23.68	26.87	29.14	36.12
15	19.31	22.31	25.00	28.26	30.58	37.70
16	20.46	23.54	26.30	29.63	32.00	39.29
17	21.62	24.77	27.59	31.00	33.41	40.75
18	22.76	25.99	28.87	32.35	34.80	42.31
19	23.90	27.20	30.14	33.69	36.19	43.82
20	25.04	28.41	31.41	35.02	37.57	45.32
21	26.17	29.62	32.67	36.34	38.93	46.80
22	27.30	30.81	33.92	37.66	40.29	48.27
23	28.43	32.01	35.17	38.97	41.64	49.73
24	29.55	33.20	36.42	40.27	42.98	51.18
25	30.68	34.38	37.65	41.57	44.31	52.62
26	31.80	35.56	38.88	42.86	45.64	54.05
27	32.91	36.74	40.11	44.14	46.96	55.48
28	34.03	37.92	41.34	45.42	48.28	56.89
29	35.14	39.09	42.69	49.69	49.59	58.30
30	36.25	40.26	43.77	47.96	50.89	59.70
32	38.47	42.59	46.19	50.49	53.49	62.49
34	40.68	44.90	48.60	53.00	56.06	65.25
36	42.88	47.21	51.00	55.49	58.62	67.99
38	45.08	49.51	53.38	57.97	61.16	70.70
40	47.27	51.81	55.76	60.44	63.69	73.40
44	51.64	56.37	60.48	65.34	68.71	78.75
48	55.99	60.91	65.17	70.20	73.68	84.04
52	60.33	65.42	69.83	75.02	78.62	89.27
56	64.66	69.92	74.47	79.82	83.51	94.46
60	68.97	74.40	79.08	84.58	88.38	99.61

Calculated value of χ^2 must EQUAL or EXCEED the table (critical) values for significance at the level shown.

Abridged from R. A. Fisher and F. Yates, *Statistical Tables for Biological, Agricultural and Medical Research*, (6th ed.) Longman Group UK Ltd (1974).

Table 5a   *Critical values of U for a one-tailed test at 0.005; two-tailed test at 0.01 ★ (Mann–Whitney)*

n_1

n_2	1	2	3	4	5	6	7	8	9	10	11	12	13	14	15	16	17	18	19	20
1	—	—	—	—	—	—	—	—	—	—	—	—	—	—	—	—	—	—	—	—
2	—	—	—	—	—	—	—	—	—	—	—	—	—	—	—	—	—	—	0	0
3	—	—	—	—	—	—	—	—	0	0	0	1	1	1	2	2	2	2	3	3
4	—	—	—	—	—	0	0	1	1	2	2	3	3	4	5	5	6	6	7	8
5	—	—	—	—	0	1	1	2	3	4	5	6	7	7	8	9	10	11	12	13
6	—	—	—	0	1	2	3	4	5	6	7	9	10	11	12	13	15	16	17	18
7	—	—	—	0	1	3	4	6	7	9	10	12	13	15	16	18	19	21	22	24
8	—	—	—	1	2	4	6	7	9	11	13	15	17	18	20	22	24	26	28	30
9	—	—	0	1	3	5	7	9	11	13	16	18	20	22	24	27	29	31	33	36
10	—	—	0	2	4	6	9	11	13	16	18	21	24	26	29	31	34	37	39	42
11	—	—	0	2	5	7	10	13	16	18	21	24	27	30	33	36	39	42	45	48
12	—	—	1	3	6	9	12	15	18	21	24	27	31	34	37	41	44	47	51	54
13	—	—	1	3	7	10	13	17	20	24	27	31	34	38	42	45	49	53	56	60
14	—	—	1	4	7	11	15	18	22	26	30	34	38	42	46	50	54	58	63	67
15	—	—	2	5	8	12	16	20	24	29	33	37	42	46	51	55	60	64	69	73
16	—	—	2	5	9	13	18	22	27	31	36	41	45	50	55	60	65	70	74	79
17	—	—	2	6	10	15	19	24	29	34	39	44	49	54	60	65	70	75	81	86
18	—	—	2	6	11	16	21	26	31	37	42	47	53	58	64	70	75	81	87	92
19	—	0	3	7	12	17	22	28	33	39	45	51	56	63	69	74	81	87	93	99
20	—	0	3	8	13	18	24	30	36	42	48	54	60	67	73	79	86	92	99	105

★ Dashes in the body of the table indicate that no decision is possible at the stated level of significance.

For any n_1 and n_2 the observed value of U is significant at a given level of significance if it is *equal to or less than* the critical values shown.

SOURCE: R. Runyon and A. Haber (1976) Fundamentals of Behavioural Statistics (3rd ed.) Reading, Mass.: McGraw Hill, Inc. with kind permission of the publisher.

Table 5b *Critical values of* U *for a one-tailed test at 0.01; two-tailed test at 0.02* (Mann–Whitney)*

											n_1									
n_2	1	2	3	4	5	6	7	8	9	10	11	12	13	14	15	16	17	18	19	20
1	—	—	—	—	—	—	—	—	—	—	—	—	—	—	—	—	—	—	—	—
2	—	—	—	—	—	—	—	—	—	—	—	—	0	0	0	0	0	0	1	1
3	—	—	—	—	—	—	0	0	1	1	1	2	2	2	3	3	4	4	4	5
4	—	—	—	—	0	1	1	2	3	3	4	5	5	6	7	7	8	9	9	10
5	—	—	—	0	1	2	3	4	5	6	7	8	9	10	11	12	13	14	15	16
6	—	—	—	1	2	3	4	6	7	8	9	11	12	13	15	16	18	19	20	22
7	—	—	0	1	3	4	6	7	9	11	12	14	16	17	19	21	23	24	26	28
8	—	—	0	2	4	6	7	9	11	13	15	17	20	22	24	26	28	30	32	34
9	—	—	1	3	5	7	9	11	14	16	18	21	23	26	28	31	33	36	38	40
10	—	—	1	3	6	8	11	13	16	19	22	24	27	30	33	36	38	41	44	47
11	—	—	1	4	7	9	12	15	18	22	25	28	31	34	37	41	44	47	50	53
12	—	—	2	5	8	11	14	17	21	24	28	31	35	38	42	46	49	53	56	60
13	—	0	2	5	9	12	16	20	23	27	31	35	39	43	47	51	55	59	63	67
14	—	0	2	6	10	13	17	22	26	30	34	38	43	47	51	56	60	65	69	73
15	—	0	3	7	11	15	19	24	28	33	37	42	47	51	56	61	66	70	75	80
16	—	0	3	7	12	16	21	26	31	36	41	46	51	56	61	66	71	76	82	87
17	—	0	4	8	13	18	23	28	33	38	44	49	55	60	66	71	77	82	88	93
18	—	0	4	9	14	19	24	30	36	41	47	53	59	65	70	76	82	88	94	100
19	—	1	4	9	15	20	26	32	38	44	50	56	63	69	75	82	88	94	101	107
20	—	1	5	10	16	22	28	34	40	47	53	60	67	73	80	87	93	100	107	114

* Dashes in the body of the table indicate that no decision is possible at the stated level of significance.

For any n_1 and n_2 the observed value of U is significant at a given level of significance if it is *equal* to or less than the critical values shown.

SOURCE: R. Runyon and A. Haber (1976) Fundamentals of Behavioural Statistics (3rd ed.) Reading, Mass.: McGraw Hill, Inc. with kind permission of the publisher.

Table 5c *Critical values of U for a one-tailed test at 0.025; two-tailed test at 0.05* (Mann–Whitney)

n_1

n_2	1	2	3	4	5	6	7	8	9	10	11	12	13	14	15	16	17	18	19	20
1	—	—	—	—	—	—	—	—	—	—	—	—	—	—	—	—	—	—	—	—
2	—	—	—	—	—	—	—	0	0	0	0	1	1	1	1	1	2	2	2	2
3	—	—	—	—	0	1	1	2	2	3	3	4	4	5	5	6	6	7	7	8
4	—	—	—	0	1	2	3	4	4	5	6	7	8	9	10	11	11	12	13	13
5	—	—	0	1	2	3	5	6	7	8	9	11	12	13	14	15	17	18	19	20
6	—	—	1	2	3	5	6	8	10	11	13	14	16	17	19	21	22	24	25	27
7	—	—	1	3	5	6	8	10	12	14	16	18	20	22	24	26	28	30	32	34
8	—	0	2	4	6	8	10	13	15	17	19	22	24	26	29	31	34	36	38	41
9	—	0	2	4	7	10	12	15	17	20	23	26	28	31	34	37	39	42	45	48
10	—	0	3	5	8	11	14	17	20	23	26	29	33	36	39	42	45	48	52	55
11	—	0	3	6	9	13	16	19	23	26	30	33	37	40	44	47	51	55	58	62
12	—	1	4	7	11	14	18	22	26	29	33	37	41	45	49	53	57	61	65	69
13	—	1	4	8	12	16	20	24	28	33	37	41	45	50	54	59	63	67	72	76
14	—	1	5	9	13	17	22	26	31	36	40	45	50	55	59	64	67	74	78	83
15	—	1	5	10	14	19	24	29	34	39	44	49	54	59	64	70	75	80	85	90
16	—	1	6	11	15	21	26	31	37	42	47	53	59	64	70	75	81	86	92	98
17	—	2	6	11	17	22	28	34	39	45	51	57	63	67	75	81	87	93	99	105
18	—	2	7	12	18	24	30	36	42	48	55	61	67	74	80	86	93	99	106	112
19	—	2	7	13	19	25	32	38	45	52	58	65	72	78	85	92	99	106	113	119
20	—	2	8	13	20	27	34	41	48	55	62	69	76	83	90	98	105	112	119	127

*Dashes in the body of the table indicate that no decision is possible at the stated level of significance.

For any n_1 and n_2 the observed value of U is significant at a given level of significance if it is *equal to or less than* the critical values shown.

SOURCE: R. Runyon and A. Haber (1976) Fundamentals of Behavioural Statistics (3rd ed.) Reading, Mass.: McGraw Hill, Inc. with kind permission of the publisher.

Table 5d *Critical values of U for a one-tailed test at 0.05; two-tailed test at 0.10* (Mann-Whitney)*

n_2 \ n_1	1	2	3	4	5	6	7	8	9	10	11	12	13	14	15	16	17	18	19	20
1	—	—	—	—	—	—	—	—	—	—	—	—	—	—	—	—	—	—	—	—
2	—	—	—	—	0	0	0	1	1	1	1	2	2	2	3	3	3	4	4	4
3	—	—	0	0	1	2	2	3	3	4	5	5	6	7	7	8	9	9	10	11
4	—	—	0	1	2	3	4	5	6	7	8	9	10	11	12	14	15	16	17	18
5	—	0	1	2	4	5	6	8	9	11	12	13	15	16	18	19	20	22	23	25
6	—	0	2	3	5	7	8	10	12	14	16	17	19	21	23	25	26	28	30	32
7	—	0	2	4	6	8	11	13	15	17	19	21	24	26	28	30	33	35	37	39
8	—	1	3	5	8	10	13	15	18	20	23	26	28	31	33	36	39	41	44	47
9	—	1	3	6	9	12	15	18	21	24	27	30	33	36	39	42	45	48	51	54
10	—	1	4	7	11	14	17	20	24	27	31	34	37	41	44	48	51	55	58	62
11	—	1	5	8	12	16	19	23	27	31	34	38	42	46	50	54	57	61	65	69
12	—	2	5	9	13	17	21	26	30	34	38	42	47	51	55	60	64	68	72	77
13	—	2	6	10	15	19	24	28	33	37	42	47	51	56	61	65	70	75	80	84
14	—	2	7	11	16	21	26	31	36	41	46	51	56	61	66	71	77	82	87	92
15	—	3	7	12	18	23	28	33	39	44	50	55	61	66	72	77	83	88	94	100
16	—	3	8	14	19	25	30	36	42	48	54	60	65	71	77	83	89	95	101	107
17	—	3	9	15	20	26	33	39	45	51	57	64	70	77	83	89	96	102	109	115
18	—	4	9	16	22	28	35	41	48	55	61	68	75	82	88	95	102	109	116	123
19	0	4	10	17	23	30	37	44	51	58	65	72	80	87	94	101	109	116	123	130
20	0	4	11	18	25	32	39	47	54	62	69	77	84	92	100	107	115	123	130	138

* Dashes in the body of the table indicate that no decision is possible at the stated level of significance.

For any n_1 and n_2 the observed value of U is significant at a given level of significance if it is *equal to* or *less than* the critical values shown.

SOURCE: R. Runyon and A. Haber (1976) Fundamentals of Behavioural Statistics (3rd ed.) Reading, Mass.: McGraw-Hill, Inc. with kind permission of the publisher.

Table 6 *Critical values of T in the Wilcoxon Rank Sum test*

Number of scores in the larger sample (n₁)	Level of significance One-tailed	Two-tailed	1	2	3	4	5	6	7	8	9	10	11	12	13	14	15	16	17	18	19	20
3	0.10	0.20		3	7																	
	0.05	0.10			6																	
	0.025	0.05																				
	0.005	0.01				(4)																
4	0.10	0.20		3	7	13																
	0.05	0.10			6	11																
	0.025	0.05				10																
	0.005	0.01					(5)															
5	0.10	0.20		4	8	14	20															
	0.05	0.10			7	12	19															
	0.025	0.05			6	11	17															
	0.005	0.01				10	15	(6)														
6	0.10	0.20		4	9	15	22	30														
	0.05	0.10		3	8	13	20	28														
	0.025	0.05			7	12	18	26														
	0.005	0.01				10	16	23	(7)													
7	0.10	0.20		4	10	16	23	32	41													
	0.05	0.10		3	8	14	21	29	39													
	0.025	0.05			7	13	20	27	36													
	0.005	0.01				10	16	24	32	(8)												
8	0.10	0.20		5	11	17	25	34	44	55												
	0.05	0.10		4	9	15	23	31	41	51												
	0.025	0.05		3	8	14	21	29	38	49												
	0.005	0.01				11	17	25	34	43	(9)											

Number of scores in the smaller sample (n₂)

n			1	2	3	4	5	6	7	8	9	(10)	(11)	(12)	(13)	(14)	(15)
9	0.10	0.20	1	5	11	19	27	36	46	58	70						
	0.05	0.10	—	4	9	16	24	33	43	54	66						
	0.025	0.05	—	3	8	14	22	31	40	51	62						
	0.005	0.01	—	—	6	11	18	26	35	45	56						
10	0.10	0.20	1	6	12	20	28	38	49	60	73	87					
	0.05	0.10	—	4	10	17	26	35	45	56	69	82					
	0.025	0.05	—	3	9	15	23	32	42	53	65	78					
	0.005	0.01	—	—	6	12	19	27	37	47	58	71					
11	0.10	0.20	1	6	13	21	30	40	51	63	76	91	106				
	0.05	0.10	—	4	11	18	27	37	47	59	72	86	100				
	0.025	0.05	—	3	9	16	24	34	44	55	68	81	96				
	0.005	0.01	—	—	6	12	20	28	38	49	61	73	87				
12	0.10	0.20	1	7	14	22	32	42	54	66	80	94	110	127			
	0.05	0.10	—	5	11	19	28	38	49	62	75	89	104	120			
	0.025	0.05	—	4	10	17	26	35	46	58	71	84	99	115			
	0.005	0.01	—	—	7	13	21	30	40	51	63	76	90	105			
13	0.10	0.20	1	7	15	23	33	44	56	69	83	98	114	131	149		
	0.05	0.10	—	5	12	20	30	40	52	64	78	92	108	125	142		
	0.025	0.05	—	4	10	18	27	37	48	60	73	88	103	119	136		
	0.005	0.01	—	—	7	14	22	31	41	53	65	79	93	109	125		
14	0.10	0.20	1	7	16	25	35	46	59	72	86	102	118	136	154	174	
	0.05	0.10	—	5	13	21	31	42	54	67	81	96	112	129	147	166	
	0.025	0.05	—	4	11	19	28	38	50	62	76	91	106	123	141	160	
	0.005	0.01	—	—	7	14	22	32	43	54	67	81	96	112	129	147	
15	0.10	0.20	1	8	16	26	37	48	61	75	90	106	123	141	159	179	200
	0.05	0.10	—	6	13	22	33	44	56	69	84	99	116	133	152	171	192
	0.025	0.05	—	4	11	20	29	40	52	65	79	94	110	127	145	164	184
	0.005	0.01	—	—	8	15	23	33	44	56	69	84	99	115	129	151	171

Table 6 *Continued*

Level of significance (One-tailed / Two-tailed) against **Number of scores in the smaller sample (n_2)**

n_1	One-tailed	Two-tailed	1	2	3	4	5	6	7	8	9	10	11	12	13	14	15	16	17	18	19	20
(16) 16	0.10	0.20	—	8	17	27	38	50	64	78	93	109	127	145	165	185	206	229				
	0.05	0.10		6	14	24	34	46	58	72	87	103	120	138	156	176	197	219				
	0.025	0.05		4	12	21	30	42	54	67	82	97	113	131	150	169	190	211				
	0.005	0.01			8	15	24	34	46	58	72	86	102	119	136	155	175	196	(17)			
17	0.10	0.20	—	9	18	28	40	52	66	81	97	113	131	150	170	190	212	235	259			
	0.05	0.10		6	15	25	35	47	61	75	90	106	123	142	161	182	203	225	249			
	0.025	0.05		5	12	21	32	43	56	70	84	100	117	135	154	174	195	217	240			
	0.005	0.01			8	16	25	36	47	60	74	89	105	122	140	159	180	201	223	(18)		
18	0.10	0.20	—	9	19	30	42	55	69	84	100	117	135	155	175	196	218	242	266	291		
	0.05	0.10		7	15	26	37	49	63	77	93	110	127	146	166	187	208	231	255	280		
	0.025	0.05		5	13	22	33	45	58	72	87	103	121	139	158	179	200	222	246	270		
	0.005	0.01			8	16	26	37	49	62	76	92	108	125	144	163	184	206	228	252	(19)	
19	0.10	0.20	2	10	20	31	43	57	71	87	103	121	139	159	180	202	224	248	273	299	325	
	0.05	0.10	—	7	16	27	38	51	65	80	96	113	131	150	171	192	214	237	262	287	313	
	0.025	0.05		5	13	23	34	46	60	74	90	107	124	143	163	182	205	228	252	277	303	
	0.005	0.01		3	9	17	27	38	50	64	78	94	111	129	147	168	189	210	234	258	283	(20)
20	0.10	0.20	2	10	21	32	45	59	74	90	107	125	144	164	185	207	230	255	280	306	333	361
	0.05	0.10	—	7	17	28	40	53	67	83	99	117	135	155	175	197	220	243	268	294	320	348
	0.025	0.05		5	14	24	35	48	62	77	93	110	128	147	167	188	210	234	258	283	309	337
	0.005	0.01		3	9	18	28	39	52	66	81	97	114	132	151	172	193	215	239	263	289	315

Calculated *T* must be EQUAL TO or LESS THAN the table (critical) value for significance at the level shown.

SOURCE: Tate and Clelland, *Non-parametric and short-cut statistics*, Interstate Printers and Publishers Inc., Danville, Illinois (1957) by kind permission of the authors.

Table 7 *Critical values of* T *in the Wilcoxon Signed Ranks test*

	Levels of significance			
	One-tailed test			
	0.05	0.025	0.01	0.001
	Two-tailed test			
Sample size	0.1	0.05	0.02	0.002
N = 5	T ≤ 0			
6	2	0		
7	3	2	0	
8	5	3	1	
9	8	5	3	
10	11	8	5	0
11	13	10	7	1
12	17	13	9	2
13	21	17	12	4
14	25	21	15	6
15	30	25	19	8
16	35	29	23	11
17	41	34	27	14
18	47	40	32	18
19	53	46	37	21
20	60	52	43	26
21	67	58	49	30
22	75	65	55	35
23	83	73	62	40
24	91	81	69	45
25	100	89	76	51
26	110	98	84	58
27	119	107	92	64
28	130	116	101	71
30	151	137	120	86
31	163	147	130	94
32	175	159	140	103
33	187	170	151	112

Calculated *T* must be EQUAL TO or LESS THAN the table (critical) value for significance at the level shown.

SOURCE: Adapted from R. Meddis, *Statistical Handbook for Non-Statisticians*, McGraw-Hill, London (1975), with the kind permission of the author and publishers.

Table 8   *Critical values of t*

	Level of significance for a one-tailed test			
	0.05	0.025	0.01	0.005
	Level of significance for a two-tailed test			
Degrees of freedom	0.10	0.05	0.02	0.01
1	6.314	12.706	31.821	63.657
2	2.920	4.303	6.965	9.925
3	2.353	3.182	4.541	5.841
4	2.132	2.776	3.747	4.604
5	2.015	2.571	3.365	4.032
6	1.943	2.447	3.143	3.707
7	1.895	2.365	2.998	3.499
8	1.860	2.306	2.896	3.355
9	1.833	2.262	2.821	3.250
10	1.812	2.228	2.764	3.169
11	1.796	2.201	2.718	3.106
12	1.782	2.179	2.681	3.055
13	1.771	2.160	2.650	3.012
14	1.761	2.145	2.624	2.977
15	1.753	2.131	2.602	2.947
16	1.746	2.120	2.583	2.921
17	1.740	2.110	2.567	2.898
18	1.734	2.101	2.552	2.878
19	1.729	2.093	2.539	2.861
20	1.725	2.086	2.528	2.845
21	1.721	2.080	2.518	2.831
22	1.717	2.074	2.508	2.819
23	1.714	2.069	2.500	2.807
24	1.711	2.064	2.492	2.797
25	1.708	2.060	2.485	2.787
26	1.706	2.056	2.479	2.779
27	1.703	2.052	2.473	2.771
28	1.701	2.048	2.467	2.763
29	1.699	2.045	2.462	2.756
30	1.697	2.042	2.457	2.750
40	1.684	2.021	2.423	2.704
60	1.671	2.000	2.390	2.660
120	1.658	1.980	2.358	2.617
∞	1.645	1.960	2.326	2.576

Calculated *t* must EQUAL or EXCEED the table (critical) value for significance at the level shown.

SOURCE: Abridged from R. A. Fisher and F. Yates, *Statistical Tables for Biological, Agricultural and Medical Research*, (6th ed.) Longman Group UK Ltd (1974).

Table 9 *Critical values of Spearman's r_s*

| | **Level of significance for a two-tailed test** | | | |
	0.10	0.05	0.02	0.01
	Level of significance for a one-tailed test			
	0.05	0.025	0.01	0.005
n = 4	1.000			
5	0.900	1.000	1.000	
6	0.829	0.886	0.943	1.000
7	0.714	0.786	0.893	0.929
8	0.643	0.738	0.833	0.881
9	0.600	0.700	0.783	0.833
10	0.564	0.648	0.745	0.794
11	0.536	0.618	0.709	0.755
12	0.503	0.587	0.671	0.727
13	0.484	0.560	0.648	0.703
14	0.464	0.538	0.622	0.675
15	0.443	0.521	0.604	0.654
16	0.429	0.503	0.582	0.635
17	0.414	0.485	0.566	0.615
18	0.401	0.472	0.550	0.600
19	0.391	0.460	0.535	0.584
20	0.380	0.447	0.520	0.570
21	0.370	0.435	0.508	0.556
22	0.361	0.425	0.496	0.544
23	0.353	0.415	0.486	0.532
24	0.344	0.406	0.476	0.521
25	0.337	0.398	0.466	0.511
26	0.331	0.390	0.457	0.501
27	0.324	0.382	0.448	0.491
28	0.317	0.375	0.440	0.483
29	0.312	0.368	0.433	0.475
30	0.306	0.362	0.425	0.467

For $n > 30$, the significance of r_s can be tested by using the formula:

$$t = r_s \sqrt{\frac{n-2}{1-r_s^2}} \quad df = n - 2$$

and checking the value of t in Table 8.

Calculated r_s must EQUAL or EXCEED the table (critical) value for significance at the level shown.

SOURCE: J. H. Zhar, Significance testing of the Spearman Rank Correlation Coefficient, *Journal of the American Statistical Association*, 67, 578–80. With the kind permission of the publishers.

Table 10 *Critical values of Pearson's r*

df (N − 2)	Level of significance for a one-tailed test			
	0.05	0.025	0.005	0.0005
	Level of significance for a two-tailed test			
	0.10	0.05	0.01	0.001
2	0.9000	0.9500	0.9900	0.9999
3	0.805	0.878	0.9587	0.9911
4	0.729	0.811	0.9172	0.9741
5	0.669	0.754	0.875	0.9509
6	0.621	0.707	0.834	0.9241
7	0.582	0.666	0.798	0.898
8	0.549	0.632	0.765	0.872
9	0.521	0.602	0.735	0.847
10	0.497	0.576	0.708	0.823
11	0.476	0.553	0.684	0.801
12	0.475	0.532	0.661	0.780
13	0.441	0.514	0.641	0.760
14	0.426	0.497	0.623	0.742
15	0.412	0.482	0.606	0.725
16	0.400	0.468	0.590	0.708
17	0.389	0.456	0.575	0.693
18	0.378	0.444	0.561	0.679
19	0.369	0.433	0.549	0.665
20	0.360	0.423	0.537	0.652
25	0.323	0.381	0.487	0.597
30	0.296	0.349	0.449	0.554
35	0.275	0.325	0.418	0.519
40	0.257	0.304	0.393	0.490
45	0.243	0.288	0.372	0.465
50	0.231	0.273	0.354	0.443
60	0.211	0.250	0.325	0.408
70	0.195	0.232	0.302	0.380
80	0.183	0.217	0.283	0.357
90	0.173	0.205	0.267	0.338
100	0.164	0.195	0.254	0.321

Calculated r must EQUAL or EXCEED the table (critical) value for significance at the level shown.
SOURCE: F. C. Powell, *Cambridge Mathematical and Statistical Tables*, Cambridge University Press (1976). With kind permission of the author and publishers.

Table 11 *Critical values of F at the 5% level of significance*

| Degrees of freedom for the denominator | Degrees of freedom for the numerator ||||||||||||||||||| |
	1	2	3	4	5	6	7	8	9	10	12	15	20	24	30	40	60	120	∞
1	161.4	199.5	215.7	224.6	230.2	234.0	236.8	238.9	240.5	241.9	243.9	245.9	248.0	249.1	250.1	251.1	252.2	253.3	254.3
2	18.51	19.00	19.16	19.25	19.30	19.33	19.35	19.37	19.38	19.40	19.41	19.43	19.45	19.45	19.46	19.47	19.48	19.49	19.50
3	10.13	9.55	9.28	9.12	9.01	8.94	8.89	8.85	8.81	8.79	8.74	8.70	8.66	8.64	8.62	8.59	8.57	8.55	8.53
4	7.71	6.94	6.59	6.39	6.26	6.16	6.09	6.04	6.00	5.96	5.91	5.86	5.80	5.77	5.75	5.72	5.69	5.66	5.63
5	6.61	5.79	5.41	5.19	5.05	4.95	4.88	4.82	4.77	4.74	4.68	4.62	4.56	4.53	4.50	4.46	4.43	4.40	4.36
6	5.99	5.14	4.76	4.53	4.39	4.28	4.21	4.15	4.10	4.06	4.00	3.94	3.87	3.84	3.81	3.77	3.74	3.70	3.67
7	5.59	4.74	4.35	4.12	3.97	3.87	3.79	3.73	3.68	3.64	3.57	3.51	3.44	3.41	3.38	3.34	3.30	3.27	3.23
8	5.32	4.46	4.07	3.84	3.69	3.58	3.50	3.44	3.39	3.35	3.28	3.22	3.15	3.12	3.08	3.04	3.01	2.97	2.93
9	5.12	4.26	3.86	3.63	3.48	3.37	3.29	3.23	3.18	3.14	3.07	3.01	2.94	2.90	2.86	2.83	2.79	2.75	2.71
10	4.96	4.10	3.71	3.48	3.33	3.22	3.14	3.07	3.02	2.98	2.91	2.85	2.77	2.74	2.70	2.66	2.62	2.58	2.54
11	4.84	3.98	3.59	3.36	3.20	3.09	3.01	2.95	2.90	2.85	2.79	2.72	2.65	2.61	2.57	2.53	2.49	2.45	2.40
12	4.75	3.89	3.49	3.26	3.11	3.00	2.91	2.85	2.80	2.75	2.69	2.62	2.54	2.51	2.47	2.43	2.38	2.34	2.30
13	4.67	3.81	3.41	3.18	3.03	2.92	2.83	2.77	2.71	2.67	2.60	2.53	2.46	2.42	2.38	2.34	2.30	2.25	2.21
14	4.60	3.74	3.34	3.11	2.96	2.85	2.76	2.70	2.65	2.60	2.53	2.46	2.39	2.35	2.31	2.27	2.22	2.18	2.13
15	4.54	3.68	3.29	3.06	2.90	2.79	2.71	2.64	2.59	2.54	2.48	2.40	2.33	2.29	2.25	2.20	2.16	2.11	2.07
16	4.49	3.63	3.24	3.01	2.85	2.74	2.66	2.59	2.54	2.49	2.42	2.35	2.28	2.24	2.19	2.15	2.11	2.06	2.01
17	4.45	3.59	3.20	2.96	2.81	2.70	2.61	2.55	2.49	2.45	2.38	2.31	2.23	2.19	2.15	2.10	2.06	2.01	1.96
18	4.41	3.55	3.16	2.93	2.77	2.66	2.58	2.51	2.46	2.41	2.34	2.27	2.19	2.15	2.11	2.06	2.02	1.97	1.92
19	4.38	3.52	3.13	2.90	2.74	2.63	2.54	2.48	2.42	2.38	2.31	2.23	2.16	2.11	2.07	2.03	1.98	1.93	1.88
20	4.35	3.49	3.10	2.87	2.71	2.60	2.51	2.45	2.39	2.35	2.28	2.20	2.12	2.08	2.04	1.99	1.95	1.90	1.84
21	4.32	3.47	3.07	2.84	2.68	2.57	2.49	2.42	2.37	2.32	2.25	2.18	2.10	2.05	2.01	1.96	1.92	1.87	1.81
22	4.30	3.44	3.05	2.82	2.66	2.55	2.46	2.40	2.34	2.30	2.23	2.15	2.07	2.03	1.98	1.94	1.89	1.84	1.78
23	4.28	3.42	3.03	2.80	2.64	2.53	2.44	2.37	2.32	2.27	2.20	2.13	2.05	2.01	1.96	1.91	1.86	1.81	1.76
24	4.26	3.40	3.01	2.78	2.62	2.51	2.42	2.36	2.30	2.25	2.18	2.11	2.03	1.98	1.94	1.89	1.84	1.79	1.73
25	4.24	3.39	2.99	2.76	2.60	2.49	2.40	2.34	2.28	2.24	2.16	2.09	2.01	1.96	1.92	1.87	1.82	1.77	1.71
26	4.23	3.37	2.98	2.74	2.59	2.47	2.39	2.32	2.27	2.22	2.15	2.07	1.99	1.95	1.90	1.85	1.80	1.75	1.69
27	4.21	3.35	2.96	2.73	2.57	2.46	2.37	2.31	2.25	2.20	2.13	2.06	1.97	1.93	1.88	1.84	1.79	1.73	1.67
28	4.20	3.34	2.95	2.71	2.56	2.45	2.36	2.29	2.24	2.19	2.12	2.04	1.96	1.91	1.87	1.82	1.77	1.71	1.65
29	4.18	3.33	2.93	2.70	2.55	2.43	2.35	2.28	2.22	2.18	2.10	2.03	1.94	1.90	1.85	1.81	1.75	1.70	1.64
30	4.17	3.32	2.92	2.69	2.53	2.42	2.33	2.27	2.21	2.16	2.09	2.01	1.93	1.89	1.84	1.79	1.74	1.68	1.62
40	4.08	3.23	2.84	2.61	2.45	2.34	2.25	2.18	2.12	2.08	2.00	1.92	1.84	1.79	1.74	1.69	1.64	1.58	1.51
60	4.00	3.15	2.76	2.53	2.37	2.25	2.17	2.10	2.04	1.99	1.92	1.84	1.75	1.70	1.65	1.59	1.53	1.47	1.39
120	3.92	3.07	2.68	2.45	2.29	2.17	2.09	2.02	1.96	1.91	1.83	1.75	1.66	1.61	1.55	1.50	1.43	1.35	1.25
∞	3.84	3.00	2.60	2.37	2.21	2.10	2.01	1.94	1.88	1.83	1.75	1.67	1.57	1.52	1.46	1.39	1.32	1.22	1.00

Values of F that equal or exceed the tabled value are significant at or beyond the 5% level.

SOURCE: J. Radford & E. Govier Textbook of Psychology (2nd ed.) Routledge (Abridged from Table 18 of The Biometrika Tables for Statisticians, Vol. I, edited by Pearson, E. S. and Hartley, H. O. with the permission of E. S. Pearson and the trustees of Biometrika.)

Table 12 *Critical values of F at the 1% level of significance*

Degrees of freedom for the denominator		Degrees of freedom for the numerator

	1	2	3	4	5	6	7	8	9	10	12	15	20	24	30	40	60	120	∞
1	4052	4999.5	5403	5625	5764	5859	5928	5982	6022	6056	6106	6157	6209	6235	6261	6287	6313	6339	6366
2	98.50	99.00	99.17	99.25	99.30	99.33	99.36	99.37	99.39	99.40	99.42	99.43	99.45	99.46	99.47	99.47	99.48	99.49	99.50
3	34.12	30.82	29.46	28.71	28.24	27.91	27.67	27.49	27.35	27.23	27.05	26.87	26.69	26.60	26.50	26.41	26.32	26.22	26.13
4	21.20	18.00	16.69	15.98	15.52	15.21	14.98	14.80	14.66	14.55	14.37	14.20	14.02	13.93	13.84	13.75	13.65	13.56	13.46
5	16.26	13.27	12.06	11.39	10.97	10.67	10.46	10.29	10.16	10.05	9.89	9.72	9.55	9.47	9.38	9.29	9.20	9.11	9.02
6	13.75	10.92	9.78	9.15	8.75	8.47	8.26	8.10	7.98	7.87	7.72	7.56	7.40	7.31	7.23	7.14	7.06	6.97	6.88
7	12.25	9.55	8.45	7.85	7.46	7.19	6.99	6.84	6.72	6.62	6.47	6.31	6.16	6.07	5.99	5.91	5.82	5.74	5.65
8	11.26	8.65	7.59	7.01	6.63	6.37	6.18	6.03	5.91	5.81	5.67	5.52	5.36	5.28	5.20	5.12	5.03	4.95	4.86
9	10.56	8.02	6.99	6.42	6.06	5.80	5.61	5.47	5.35	5.26	5.11	4.96	4.81	4.73	4.65	4.57	4.48	4.40	4.31
10	10.04	7.56	6.55	5.99	5.64	5.39	5.20	5.06	4.94	4.85	4.71	4.56	4.41	4.33	4.25	4.17	4.08	4.00	3.91
11	9.65	7.21	6.22	5.67	5.32	5.07	4.89	4.74	4.63	4.54	4.40	4.25	4.10	4.02	3.94	3.86	3.78	3.69	3.60
12	9.33	6.93	5.95	5.41	5.06	4.82	4.64	4.50	4.39	4.30	4.16	4.01	3.86	3.78	3.70	3.62	3.54	3.45	3.36
13	9.07	6.70	5.74	5.21	4.86	4.62	4.44	4.30	4.19	4.10	3.96	3.82	3.66	3.59	3.51	3.43	3.34	3.25	3.17
14	8.86	6.51	5.56	5.04	4.69	4.46	4.28	4.14	4.03	3.94	3.80	3.66	3.51	3.43	3.35	3.27	3.18	3.09	3.00
15	8.68	6.36	5.42	4.89	4.56	4.32	4.14	4.00	3.89	3.80	3.67	3.52	3.37	3.29	3.21	3.13	3.05	2.96	2.87
16	8.53	6.23	5.29	4.77	4.44	4.20	4.03	3.89	3.78	3.69	3.55	3.41	3.26	3.18	3.10	3.02	2.93	2.84	2.75
17	8.40	6.11	5.18	4.67	4.34	4.10	3.93	3.79	3.68	3.59	3.46	3.31	3.16	3.08	3.00	2.92	2.83	2.75	2.65
18	8.29	6.01	5.09	4.58	4.25	4.01	3.84	3.71	3.60	3.51	3.37	3.23	3.08	3.00	2.92	2.84	2.75	2.66	2.57
19	8.18	5.93	5.01	4.50	4.17	3.94	3.77	3.63	3.52	3.43	3.30	3.15	3.00	2.92	2.84	2.76	2.67	2.58	2.49
20	8.10	5.85	4.94	4.43	4.10	3.87	3.70	3.56	3.46	3.37	3.23	3.09	2.94	2.86	2.78	2.69	2.61	2.52	2.42
21	8.02	5.78	4.87	4.37	4.04	3.81	3.64	3.51	3.40	3.31	3.17	3.03	2.88	2.80	2.72	2.64	2.55	2.46	2.36
22	7.95	5.72	4.82	4.31	3.99	3.76	3.59	3.45	3.35	3.26	3.12	2.98	2.83	2.75	2.67	2.58	2.50	2.40	2.31
23	7.88	5.66	4.76	4.26	3.94	3.71	3.54	3.41	3.30	3.21	3.07	2.93	2.78	2.70	2.62	2.54	2.45	2.35	2.26
24	7.82	5.61	4.72	4.22	3.90	3.67	3.50	3.36	3.26	3.17	3.03	2.89	2.74	2.66	2.58	2.49	2.40	2.31	2.21
25	7.77	5.57	4.68	4.18	3.85	3.63	3.46	3.32	3.22	3.13	2.99	2.85	2.70	2.62	2.54	2.45	2.36	2.27	2.17
26	7.72	5.53	4.64	4.14	3.82	3.59	3.42	3.29	3.18	3.09	2.96	2.81	2.66	2.58	2.50	2.42	2.33	2.23	2.13
27	7.68	5.49	4.60	4.11	3.78	3.56	3.39	3.26	3.15	3.06	2.93	2.78	2.63	2.55	2.47	2.38	2.29	2.20	2.10
28	7.64	5.45	4.57	4.07	3.75	3.53	3.36	3.23	3.12	3.03	2.90	2.75	2.60	2.52	2.44	2.35	2.26	2.17	2.06
29	7.60	5.42	4.54	4.04	3.73	3.50	3.33	3.20	3.09	3.00	2.87	2.73	2.57	2.49	2.41	2.33	2.23	2.14	2.03
30	7.56	5.39	4.51	4.02	3.70	3.47	3.30	3.17	3.07	2.98	2.84	2.70	2.55	2.47	2.39	2.30	2.21	2.11	2.01
40	7.31	5.18	4.31	3.83	3.51	3.29	3.12	2.99	2.89	2.80	2.66	2.52	2.37	2.29	2.20	2.11	2.02	1.92	1.80
60	7.08	4.98	4.13	3.65	3.34	3.12	2.95	2.82	2.72	2.63	2.50	2.35	2.20	2.12	2.03	1.94	1.84	1.73	1.60
120	6.85	4.79	3.95	3.48	3.17	2.96	2.79	2.66	2.56	2.47	2.34	2.19	2.03	1.95	1.86	1.76	1.66	1.53	1.33
∞	6.63	4.61	3.78	3.32	3.02	2.80	2.64	2.51	2.41	2.32	2.18	2.04	1.88	1.79	1.70	1.59	1.47	1.32	1.00

Values of F that equal or exceed the tabled value are significant at or beyond the 1% level.

Table 13 *Critical values of P in Jonckheere's Trend test*

		Number of samples (k)						
		3		4		5		6
Level of significance		0.05	0.01	0.05	0.01	0.05	0.01	0.05	0.01
2		10	–	14	20	20	26	26	34
3		17	23	26	34	34	48	44	62
4		24	32	38	50	51	72	67	94
5		33	45	51	71	71	99	93	130
6		42	59	66	92	92	129	121	170
7		53	74	82	115	115	162	151	213
8		64	90	100	140	140	197	184	260
9		76	106	118	167	166	234	219	309
10		88	124	138	195	194	274	256	361

Number of sample (n) labels the row values 2 through 10.

Values of P that equal or exceed the tabled value are significant at, or beyond, the level indicated.

For values of k and n beyond these tabled above, and/or where sample sizes differ, the significance of P can be tested using the formular in the text, see p. 323.

Taken from Jonckheere, A. R., 'A distribution-free k-sample test against ordered alternatives'. *Biometrika*, Vol. 41, pp. 133–145. With the permission of the trustees of Biometrika.

Table 14 *Critical values of L in Page's Trend test*

		Number of samples (k)							
			3		4		5		6
	Level of significance	0.05	0.01	0.05	0.01	0.05	0.01	0.05	0.01
	2	28	–	58	60	103	106	166	173
	3	41	42	84	87	150	155	244	252
	4	54	55	111	114	197	204	321	331
	5	66	68	137	141	244	251	397	409
	6	79	81	163	167	291	299	474	486
	7	91	93	189	193	338	346	550	563
	8	104	106	214	220	384	393	625	640
	9	116	119	240	246	431	441	701	717
	10	128	131	266	272	477	487	777	793

*(Row label, left margin, rotated: **Number of sample (n)**)*

Values of L that equal or exceed the tabled value are significant at, or beyond, the level indicated.

For values of k and n beyond these tabled above, and/or where sample sizes differ, the significance of P can be tested using the formular in the text, see p. 325.

Taken from Page, E. B. 'Ordered hypotheses for multiple trements: a significance test for linear rank.' *Journal of the American Statistical Association*, Vol. 58, pp. 216–230. With permission of the publishers.

ANSWERS TO EXERCISES AND STRUCTURED QUESTIONS

For the end-of-chapter questions only direct and specific answers are given. They are not included where the reader is asked to conduct an exercise or give an open-ended description.

CHAPTER 2

1   IV   DV

	IV	DV
a)	Type of propaganda	Strength of attitude
b)	Noise level	Work efficiency
c)	Time of day	Attention span
d)	Amount of practice	Level of performance
e)	Smile given or not	Smile received or not
f)	Level of frustration	Level of aggression
g)	Order of birth	Personality and intellectual level
h)	Presence or absence of crowd	People's behaviour

2 Examples:
   Noise: Use specific audio recording of mechanical noise. IV in terms of measured decibel levels.
   Attention span: Measured by number of 'blips' noticed on a radar-like screen.
   Smile: As recognised by rater who doesn't know research aim and lasting longer than one second.

3 a) IV: preschool education or not.
       DV: cognitive skills and sociability.
   b) e.g.: preschool children's parents more educationally concerned?
   c) Match parents (on educational concern) in both groups.

CHAPTER 3

1 Test participants (or equivalent control group) *without* the confederates.

2 e.g. area, number of children, age, etc.

3 Only volunteers; must read bulletin; no teetotallers.

4 Only *c.*

5 Placebo group; no special programme but with some attention, and where parents expect child to improve.

6 e.g. left side contained a 'clever' clique of students.

CHAPTER 4

1 **b)** Most likely to avoid distortion through knowledge of testing, for instance.
   d) Is probably the most reliable; less to change between measures.

2 **a)** Any study where the effect is statistically significant and genuine but where generalisation to other people or places is unlikely; for instance, using mental images improves list memory for almost everyone, anywhere, but the images themselves may not be the causal factor; the effort of creating the images may improve recall.
   b) Any study where the effect demonstrated extends to other people in other places but where there is a confounding variable responsible; for instance, using mental images improves list memory for almost everyone, anywhere, but the images themselves may not be the causal factor; the effort of creating the images may improve recall.
   c) A psychological test may always produce much the same data from the same people (it is *consistent*) yet may measure something quite different from what is intended. A reliable measure of 'authoritarianism' may actually measure 'assertiveness'.

4 As examples: the differences between one's love for a mother and a partner; the feelings of helplessness of a civil war refugee; nostalgia produced by long forgotten song.

CHAPTER 5

1 **a)** Field investigation – *ex post facto* because IV is sex
   b) Laboratory investigation; *ex post facto*
   c) Field experiment
   d) Laboratory experiment
   e) Laboratory quasi-experiment
   f) Laboratory investigation; *ex post facto*
   g) Field investigation
   h) Natural experiment
   i) Quasi field experiment

2 **a)** a and c
   b) g and h
   c) all
   d) all (in **(a)**, observer need not know that sex is the IV)

CHAPTER 6

1 IV – complexity of pattern. DV – time spent gazing. Design – repeated measures (with randomisation and simultaneous presentation of IV).

2 Add condition with same babies enticed over the shallow side – this gives repeated measures; *or*, have control group enticed over shallow side – independent samples.

3 Repeated measures. Randomisation of IV stimuli. Avoid order effects.

4 Repeated measures. Counterbalancing. Avoid order effects.

5 Matched pairs.

CHAPTER 7

4 The raters vary very much from each other. Correlation is used and gives -0.24. Reliability is far too low, the correlation is negative.

CHAPTER 8

1 See page 131

3 a) Non-random. Start of snowball sample.
  b) Initial interviewee unwilling to admit problem; initial interviewee gives fewer further contacts; interviewer doesn't see some incidents as 'serious'; interviewer doesn't want to record the incidents for personal political reasons; interviewer is a poor questioner, is aggressive, shows prejudice etc.
  c) Structured questionnaire more reliable; results more comparable; larger sample more representative.

5 The sixth-formers are volunteers. Only schools which agreed to the study can be sampled from. Those without telephones cannot be included. Those who use the youth club are more likely to be selected.

CHAPTER 9

1 a) It has been found reliable since the correlation is high, hence should be all right to use.
  b) Recent nuclear accident?

2 a) Compare results with interview data?
  b) Can't test the students again under similar circumstances so reliability will have to be checked only *internally*.

3 Reliable, not necessarily valid.

4 a) Question invites agreement.
  b) Assumes children *should* be punished.
  c) Is this easy to answer?
  d) Double barrelled – 'people *aren't* the same, but should be treated with respect' is a possible response.
  e) Double negative.
  f) Ambiguous responding. Extreme sexist *and* feminist might well agree.
  g) Technical term; will this be understood?

5 Use blind assessment using a different naïve researcher.

CHAPTER 12

2 Ordinal.

3 Nominal.

4 a) Ordinal
   b) Ratio
   c) Interval-like (or 'plastic interval') but treat as ordinal
   d) Nominal

5 Box b

6 'Top' is a measure on an ordinal scale. We don't know how far ahead of the others she was.

7 Nominal – did/didn't hit kerb; Ordinal – rate smoothness on one to 10 scale; Interval/ratio – measure speed in race.

8

Ordinal level	
Consistent	Inconsistent
6.5	11
9	17
1	11
2.5	4.5
16	18
2.5	4.5
6.5	8
11	14
13	15

Nominal level		
	Consistent	Inconsistent
above mean	4	7
below mean	5	2

9 a) Nominal
   b) Interval (because standardised)
   c) Ordinal
   d) Plastic interval – best to convert to ordinal
   e) Ratio
   f) Nominal (frequencies)
   g) Plastic interval – best converted to ordinal
   h) Interval, because scale is standardised
   i) Ratio if measured using rule
   j) Ordinal

CHAPTER 13

1 Males: mean = 171.6; median = 132. Females: mean = 367.2; median = 345

2 Data are skewed, therefore use median. Median = 79 (or 79.25 if the precise formula is used).

Stem and Leaf
6.2555
7.0012222334455666677899
8.000122338
9.0235
10.0236
11.027
12.1278
13.5

3 Mean = 19.403

5 Since there is absolutely no variation, all scores must be the same; all scores are therefore 0.8 and the mean is 0.8.

6 a) 75.3   b) 25.14%   c) 1.33

7 Negative skew.

8

Mean	SD	Specific value	Deviation	z-score	% above	% below
40	10	25	−15	−1.5	93.3	6.7
100	15	135	35	2.33	0.99	99.01
17.5	2.5	22.5	5	2	2.28	97.72
64	4	57	−7	−1.75	95.99	4.01
21	8	25	4	0.5	30.85	69.15
15.6	3.47	16.12	0.52	0.15	44	56

9   Median position: 26   Median = 79
     Hinge position: 13   Lower hinge: 73   Upper hinge: 95
     Hinge spread: 22   Low outer fence: 40   High outer fence: 128
     Outlier: 135   Adjacent value: 62   Adjacent value: 128

CHAPTER 14

1 a) 1.32 and −0.78 are not significant. 1.75 and −1.9 are.
   b) 1.89 and −1.6 are not significant. −2.05 and 1.98 are.

2 a) One   b) Two   c) One   d) Two

3 a) 1%   b) More likely

4 b) True   c) True   d) True   e) True   f) False

CHAPTER 15

1 χ^2 = 19.25

2 Unwise because all expected frequencies less than 5 and sample is very small overall.

3 a) 'Goodness of fit' Chi-square, one variable, two categories.
   b) One-tailed, if direction predicted.
   c) No. χ^2 cannot be performed on percentages. We require actual frequencies.
   d) χ^2 = 67.24, $p < 0.001$.

4 a) 4 *df*   **b)** More than 20% of expected frequencies are below 5 *and* data are skewed, but result is highly significant ($p < 0.01$). Hence, fairly safe conclusion of significance.

5 $N = 8$, $S = 1$. Result is significant at 5%, one-tailed only. We assume a negative evaluation wasn't predicted. Hence not significant (two-tailed).

CHAPTER 16

1 a) *U*: 0.01 (one-tail), 0.02 (two-tail); *T*(WRS): 0.025 (one-tail), 0.05 (two-tail)
  b) *U*: 0.005 (one-tail), 0.01 (two-tail), *T*(WRS): Not sig. (one- or two-tail)
  c) *T*(WSR): 0.025 (one-tail), 0.05 (two-tail)
  d) 0.001 (one-tail), 0.002 (two-tail)

2 a) Table 17.1 – use Wilcoxon signed ranks: $T = 1$, $N = 12$, $p < 0.001$.
  b) Table 17.2 – use Mann–Whitney or Wilcoxon Rank Sum.
  Mann–Whitney: $U = 49$; Wilcoxon: $T = 140$; both not significant ($p > 0.05$).

CHAPTER 17

1 a) No homogeneity of variance, unrelated design and very different sample numbers. Therefore very unwise. Mann–Whitney/Wilcoxon Rank Sum.
  b) Lack of homogeneity of variance but related design. Therefore, safe to carry on with *t* (non-parametric test would be Wilcoxon Signed Ranks).

2 No. $df = 10$. cv (two-tailed) at $p < 0.01 = 3.169$

3 a) NS, keep NH
  b) 0.01, 1%, reject NH
  c) NS, keep NH
  d) 0.005, 0.5%, reject NH
  e) NS, keep NH
  f) 0.01, 1%, reject NH

4 Distributions are skewed, contrary to normal distribution assumption. Since samples are large, the whole population may well be skewed too.

CHAPTER 18

1 a) Early number recognition *correlates* with reading ability at seven years old but may not *cause* the superior reading. It may be related to something else that is responsible for better reading ability *or* children may differ innately in letter recognition and reading ability, in which case the greater emphasis would make little difference.
  c) negative
  d) strong/very strong
  e) $p < 0.0005$

2 a) Accept **b)** Accept **c)** Reject **d)** Accept **e)** Reject **f)** Accept **g)** Accept (wrong direction)

3 No. For Pearson, data must meet parametric requirements.

4 Spearman. Data should be treated as ordinal because human judgement.

5 Check her calculations – highest possible is 1.

Chapter 19

1 Kruskal–Wallis' one-way analysis of variance.

2 Page's trend test.

3 Jonckheere's trend test.

4 Friedman's χ^2.

Chapter 20

2 Variance components: Total   Between groups   Error (Within groups)
   Degrees of freedom: 18   2   16

Rest of table (transposed) as for one-way example on page 335.

3 Tukey is safest, but for three conditions there are six possible t tests (1 v 2, 1 v 3, 2 v 3, (1 + 2) v 3, 1 v (2 + 3), (1 + 3) v 2) and $6 \times 0.01 = 0.06$ which is a rough estimate of the likelihood of a type I error and this is an almost acceptable level.

4 Special t test

5 1 1 − 2

Chapter 21

1 3) Factor: colour naming speed (three levels); one-way repeated measures.
   4) Factor 1: type of therapy (three levels); Factor 2: sex of client (two levels); 3×2 unrelated.
   5) Factor 1: age (two levels, unrelated); Factor 2: memorising method (three levels, repeat measure); 2×3 mixed design.
   6) Factor 1: stimulant (three levels); Factor 2: noise level (four levels); 3×4 unrelated.
   7) Factor 1: personality type (two levels, unrelated); Factor 2: drug (three levels, unrelated); Factor 3: task type (two levels, repeat measure); $2 \times 3 \times 2$ mixed design.
   8) Factor 1: prejudice level (two levels); Factor 2: race of target person (two levels); Factor 3: type of social act (three levels); $2 \times 2 \times 3$ unrelated.

2 **a)** f   **b)** g   **c)** d or e   **d)** c   **e)** a   **f)** b

3
Source of variation	Sum of squares	df	Mean square	F	Significance of F
Total	3582.950	19			
Main effects;					
School	1022.450	1	1022.450	13.601	0.002
Sex	806.450	1	806.450	10.728	0.005
Interaction:					
School × sex	551.250	1	551.250	7.333	0.016
Error	1202.800	16	75.175		

4 No main effects; significant interaction effect. Diagram **a** from Figure 21.3.

Chapter 22

2	SS	df	MS	Sig. of F
Total		95		
Between subjects		31		
Between conditions (unrelated)		3		
Error between		28		
Within subjects		64		
Within conditions		2		
Between × within conditions		6		
Error within		56		

3 **a)** False **b)** False **c)** True **d)** False **e)** 41 **f)** False **g)** True **h)** 14

Chapter 24

1 Unrelated t; simpler alternative – Mann–Whitney or Wilcoxon Rank Sum.

2 Mann–Whitney or Wilcoxon Rank Sum.

3 Chi-square.

4 Chi-square.

5 **a)** Related t; simpler alternative – Wilcoxon Signed Ranks.
   b) Pearson's correlation.

6 Pearson; Validity test – unrelated t.

7 Spearman correlation.

8 Chi-square – 'goodness of fit'.

9 Chi-square.

10 Related t; simpler alternative – Wilcoxon Signed Ranks.

11 Wilcoxon Signed Ranks.

12 Sign test.

Structured question I

1 Attendance at the project or not.

2 Provides baseline comparison so we can rule out the possibility that any changes or IQ values gained would have occurred irrespective of the project.

3 No. This is systematic sampling – every child does *not* have an equal chance of being selected.

4 Control group parents didn't volunteer. Project parents may be particularly interested in their children's education and therefore might stimulate their children more *outside* the project. Children know they are being specially treated.

5 Nominal (frequencies).

6 Chi-squared. Data are nominal, in frequency form. The test is of difference (or association). Design is unrelated.

7 With low N (near 20) and expected frequency cells less than 5. Conservatively, if more than 20% of expected cells are less than 5. Also, if frequencies in any cell are linked to frequencies in any other cell. Also, if cell values are proportions.

8 Mann–Whitney or Wilcoxon Rank Sum if arguing that IQ tests don't provide true interval level data. Unrelated t test if arguing that IQ tests are standardised and therefore close enough to interval. Either answer is acceptable. All these tests have greater power efficiency than χ^2 because they use more information from the data available.

9 Groups' scores are significantly different. Reject idea that they vary at chance level only.

10 They had rejected the null hypothesis when it was true.

11 a) It produces similar results on similar occasions i.e. is consistent.
   b) Tested on large sample of target population. Unreliable or non-discriminating items rejected. Norms for population established.

12 Reasons given in answer to question 4. Children might be aware of 'special' nature of study and try harder (or parents may push them). Children enjoy special attention given.

13 If project works well, are all the other children disadvantaged by not participating? Families shown information which might identify them; asked for permission to publish; asked to comment on report.

STRUCTURED QUESTION 2

1 Longitudinal; correlational; *ex post facto*.

2 Longitudinal – participants drop out; correlational and *ex post facto* – no control over extraneous variables.

3 Children not attending playgroup could not be selected. Only those staying a long time were selected.

4 So that children experience some similarity in environment over the period of the study and do not suffer school disruption (for instance) which might temporarily lower IQ scores.

5 Researcher bias. She knows their last result and may expect certain performances. Could use tester 'blind' to the previous scores of each child.

6

IQ 15 years   IQ at 9 years $r = 0.78$ $r = -0.95$

7 a) 122.5 b) 16% (or 15.87%)

8 Have to treat IQ scores as interval. Some would argue they're really ordinal. However, if standardisation is good can assume interval level.

9 One-tailed (expect positive correlation).

10 a) No **b)** $p < 0.005$

11 As one increased the other decreased. ('Negative correlation' would not be an adequate answer.)

12 a) Correlation between IQ scores at ages nine and 15 is zero.
   b) Rejected.

13 New researcher has a smaller sample.

14 The non-significant result fails to support; the significant result supports.

15 Cultural bias. Only useful with population on whom test was standardised. Tests narrow range of intellectual skill – not creative problem-solving, for instance.

Structured question 3

1 *Advantages*: no participant variables; participant is own control; quicker; cheaper. *Disadvantages*: generalising to larger group is hazardous; participant becomes specialised – not representative behaviour.

2 IV – left- or right-side presentation. DV – reaction time.

3 Words are comparatively similar (in size, length, frequency etc.).

4 Participant may be trying to be fast by guessing.

5 a) So participant cannot predict nature or position of next item.
   b) Tables, computer, selection from jumbled item numbers.

6 Ratio/interval.

7 a) Data do not come from a normal distribution. Also data are unrelated so perhaps variances were very different.
   b) Mann–Whitney or Wilcoxon Rank Sum.

8 See Figure 13.21, page 226.

9 a) Perhaps, contrary to instruction, participant always looks to the left of the screen. Perhaps participant does not have language centres mostly left hemisphere located (perhaps a left-hander).
   b) It should be retained; although difference was significant, researcher made a one-tailed prediction in the opposite direction from that found.

10 p at less than 0.01.

11 a) Independent samples.
   b) *Advantage*: no order effects. *Disadvantage*: participant/'subject' variables; requires larger sample than repeated measures.
   c) Random allocation to conditions, to reduce participant variables effect.

Structured question 4

1 Unstructured, therefore richer, perhaps more genuine information. Quicker than participant observation and less likely to cause bias through researcher's deeper personal involvement.

2 Response set; social desirability.

3 Participants may not offer information under questioning of either form. Researcher has longer to gain trust and assure confidentiality.

4 Lecurers may have a lot more work in their department; head may be harder to work for.

5 Test is consistent within itself. Participants do not score high on some items yet low on other items with similar sense and direction.

6 Items randomly split into two equal sets (or split into odd and even items) and participants' results on the two sets correlated.

7 Give lowest rank to lowest score; give average of shared ranks to tied scores.

8 Spearman's correlation.

9 It is high.

10 Number in sample; significance level set.

11 Strength relates to the actual correlation value. Significance relates to the improbability of obtaining that value, given the number of participants.

12 More specific questionnaire. Look for similar effects in similar departments elsewhere.

13 Questionnaires more impersonal; participants may not have trusted assurances of confientiality.

14 Disclosure, perhaps indirectly, of participants' views and consequences for them. Effect on morale of departments. Checking report with participants first.

STRUCTURED QUESTION 5

1 They are volunteers.

2 **a)** Cues to participant about research aim.
  b) The impossibility of the tasks, if extreme, may alert participants to experimenter's aim.

3 Inter-rater reliability. Ensure consistent meeasurement.

4 Correlation.

5 Control group not given frustrating tasks.

6 See Glossary, Chapter 2.

7 Ordinal.

8 Wilcoxon Signed Ranks.

9 **a)** Post-treatment scores will be significantly higher than pre-treatment scores.
  b) One-tailed.

10 Less than 0.05.

11 Subjective assessment/interpretation of rating scale; generally low reliability.

12 Open questionnaire; reactions to violent film; physiological measures.

13 **a)** Steps taken to measure phenomenon.
  b) Responses scored on Rorschach rating scale.

STRUCTURED QUESTION 6

1 IV: common or uncommon words. DV: median solution time.
2 Repeated measures.
3 **a)** To avoid order effects.
   b) Half the participants do common words first. The other half do uncommon words first.
   c) Randomising the anagrams into one list (or leaving a long time between testing each condition).
4 Presence of participant/'subject' variables.
5 Participants' unfamiliarity with certain words; anxiety; timing errors.
6 Variations in wording and approach cannot be said to be responsible for any changes observed. Sticking to this procedure, experimenters cannot be tempted to give help or clues to the design.
7 **a)** Mean would be distorted in value by the last, very high value.
   b) *H* (because median is 125).
8 Ratio/Interval.
9 **a)** Yes
   b) Values must come from normally distributed population. Variances should not be too dissimilar.
10 More sensitive, power efficient, generalisable.
11 Related *t* test.
12 Level of probability at which null hypothesis rejected. Results too unlikely to be chance fluctuation.
13 Yes. Nine out of 10 uncommon times are longer than common. Differences are mostly quite large.
14 Uncommon words formed by unusual letter combinations (e.g. *'psychology'*).

STRUCTURED QUESTION 7

1 No. Independent variable not controlled.
2 Participants drawn at same time from several target groups, in this case age groups of mothers.
3 *Advantage*: don't lose participants, as happens in longitudinal studies; immediate results. *Disadvantages*: participant variables; one group may have experienced social changes which other group haven't.
4 *Advantage*: more natural behaviour. *Disadvantage*: less control.
5 Can code all behaviour in detail after data collection at appropriate speed.
6 **a)** So results can be generalised, and effects noted aren't linked to particular features of this sample.
   b) Class, area, schooling etc.

7 Variables (such as arrival of post) might otherwise affect any consistency in behaviour observed.

8 So they don't slant their ratings towards or away from it.

9 Use correlation between their two sets of results.

10 Human judgements like these can't be said to have equal intervals between the whole number units.

11 34(1) 45(2) 56(4) 56(4) 56(4) 65(6) 68(7) 78(8.5) 78(8.5) 89(10)

12 Mann–Whitney or Wilcoxon Rank Sum.

13 No. Although we can't reject the null hypothesis, a result with probability less than 0.07 is so close to significance that we may well be making a type II error. It is worth replicating.

14 Ask mothers about discipline and why it is necessary. Look for categories of response, including those stressing need to control.

15 All participants should be given a complete report. Researcher should anyway sit and explain the project in non-specialist language. The mother has the right to remove her material, though researcher might try to assuage her doubts about confidentiality and the security of the raw video data.

STRUCTURED QUESTION 8

1 No. Independent variable not manipulated.

2 No. The participants are volunteers.

3 **a)** Can't bias rating in favour of expected results.
  b) Can't guess research aim.

4 Responding to questionnaire with others around might well have an unwanted effect on a variable like anxiety.

5 To reduce random errors; to be able to check rater reliability.

6 Both tests are standardised.

7 See Question 6, **9 b)**.

8 Pearson's.

9 Inverse relationship; as one variable increases, other decreases.

10 *Higher* anxiety scores are expected to be paired with *lower* health scores and vice versa.

11 Such an extreme correlation would only occur by chance (i.e. if the null hypothesis is true) less than one time in 100.

12 If results likely to be controversial; if only one chance to test.

13 Fairly weak.

14 Depends on sample size; with high sample size a low correlation is significant.

15 To return participants to normal, remove negative impressions, feelings about performance, lowered self esteem etc.; to inform of exact research aims.

16 People with poor health might (understandably) be more anxious about it.

Structured question 9

1 Volunteers; already experienced.

2 IV: two word-processing packages. DVs: time taken and evaluation.

3 Independent samples; no order effects; participants can't guess aims.

4 **a)** Trying out a draft version on an initial sample.
  b) To identify faults and ambiguities so final version is improved; also, in order to check for reliability and to conduct item analysis to create final version.

5 A measure of dispersion (spread of scores around the mean) in a sample of scores.

6 One standard deviation cuts off top 16% of distribution. Standard score of 1 is one standard deviation above mean. This secretary is 1.3 standard deviations above the mean and therefore, in top 16%.

7 Mann–Whitney or Wilcoxon Rank Sum.

8 Any of: (1) Interval level data; (2) and (3) see answer to Question 6, **9 b)**.

9 Standard deviations (and therefore variances) are very different and there are quite different sample numbers. (The design is unrelated.)

10 Two tailed. Researcher didn't predict which programme would be superior.

11 Differences were more likely to occur by chance than 5 in 100 ($p > 0.05$) and, at this level, it is conventional not to reject the view that the differences could be mere chance fluctuations.

12 Since one sample is so much smaller, more chance that it would vary markedly from the other; could be just sample differences; also, perhaps one programme had a bad reputation (but is, in fact, no different from the other).

13 Participant has the right to have results withdrawn. Researcher might attempt to persuade the secretary that confidence is absolute, but must concede if this fails.

Structured question 10

1 **a)** Matched pairs design.
  b) Reduces likelihood of participant variables being responsible for differences observed.

2 Interpersonal factors can influence participants' responses; unstructured and therefore less reliable.

3 Various question weaknesses, see page 143. Making questionnaire reliable.

4 Participants might try to 'look good' on the questionnaire. Therapist can perhaps get closer to the truth.

5 Good agreement between methods since correlation is high.

6 **a)** Because participants in the experimental programme might improve solely because they know they're expected to or are getting special attention.
  b) They would be given an arbitrary treatment, say simple discussion of irrelevant issues. Otherwise, their experience would be identical.

7 Standardised questionnaire.

8 Related t test.

9 Less powerful/power efficient; less sensitive.

10 The difference, though large, might still be the result of chance variation between the two groups, i.e. random/participant variables.

11 Scores on one variable tend to be paired with scores of a similar size and direction on the other variable.

12 If the sample size were smaller.

13 The treatment group volunteered – may have had higher motivation to improve; participants may improve because their expectancy of improvement provides motivation.

14 The controls should also join the programme if they wish to. They would now be disadvantaged if treatment was withheld, since it is now seen as effective.

REFERENCES

Ainsworth, M. D. S. (1967) *Infancy in Uganda.* Baltimore: John Hopkins University Press.

Ainsworth, M. D. S., Bell, S. M. & Stayton, D. J. (1971) Individual differences in strange situation behaviour of one-year-olds. In Schaffer, H. R. (ed.) (1971) *The Origins of Human Social Relations.* London: Academic Press.

Alexander, L. & Guenther, R. K. (1986) The effect of mood and demand on memory, *British Journal of Psychology,* 77(3), 342–51.

Allport, G. W. (1947) *The Use of Personal Documents in Psychological Science.* London: Holt, Rinehart and Winston.

American Psychological Association (1987) *Casebook on Ethical Principles of Psychologists.* Washington: American Psychological Association.

Aronson, E. & Carlsmith, J. M. (1968) Experimentation in social psychology. In Lindzey, G. & Aronson, E. (eds.) (1968) *Handbook of Social Psychology,* 2: Reading, Mass.: Addison–Wesley.

Asch, S. E. (1956) Studies of independence and submission to group pressure. 1. A minority of one against a unanimous majority. In *Psychological Monographs,* 70 (9) (Whole No. 416).

Atkinson, R. L., Atkinson, R. C., Smith, E. E. & Bem, D. J. (1993) *Introduction to Psychology,* Fort Worth: Harcourt Brace Jovanovitch.

Baars, B. J. (1980) Eliciting predictable speech errors in the laboratory. In V. Fromkin (ed.) *Errors in Linguistic Performance: Slips of the Tongue, Ear, Pen and Hand.* New York: Academic Press, 1980.

Baddeley, A. (1992) Is memory all talk? *The Psychologist,* 5, 10 (October).

Bandura, A. (1965) Influence of models' reinforcement contingencies on the acquisition of imitative responses. *Journal of Personality and Social Psychology,* 1, 589–95.

Bandura, A. (1977) *Social Learning Theory.* Englewood Cliffs, NJ: Prentice-Hall.

Barber, T. X. (1976) *Pitfalls in Human Research.* Oxford: Pergamon.

Becker, H. S. (1958) Inference and proof in participant observation. *American Sociological Review,* 23, 652–60.

Beltramini, R. F. (1992) Explaining the effectiveness of business gifts: a controlled field experiment. *Journal of the Academy of Marketing Science,* 20(1), 87–91.

Benedict, R. (1934) *Patterns of Culture.* Boston: Houghton Mifflin.

Berry, J. W., Poortinga, Y. H., Segall, M. H. & Dasen, P. R. (1992) *Cross-cultural Psychology: Research and Applications.* Cambridge: CUP.

Block, N. J. & Dworkin, G. (1974) IQ – heritability and inequality. *Philosophy and Public Affairs,* 3, 331–407.

Bogardus, E. S. (1925) Measuring social distance. *Journal of Applied Sociology,* 9, 299–308.

Born, M. P. (1987) Cross-cultural comparison of sex-related differences on intelligence tests: a meta-analysis. *Journal of Cross Cultural Psychology,* 18(3), 283–314.

Bowlby, J. (1951) *Maternal Care and Mental Health.* Geneva: World Health Organisation.

Bowlby, J. (1953) *Child Care and the Growth of Love.* Harmondsworth: Penguin.

Bracht, G. H. & Glass, G. V. (1968) The external validity of experiments. *American Educational Research Journal,* 5, 437–74.

Bramel, D. A. (1962) A dissonance theory approach to defensive projection. *Journal of Abnormal and Social Psychology,* 64, 121–9.

Brislin, R. (1990) *Applied Cross-cultural Psychology.* Newbury Park, CA: Sage.

British Psychological Society (1985) A code of conduct for psychologists. *Bulletin of the British Psychology Society,* 38, 41–3.

British Psychological Society (1993) *Code of Conduct, Ethical Principles and Guidelines*, Leicester: British Psychological Society.

Broadbent, D. E., Fitzgerald, P. & Broadbent, M. H. P. (1986) Implicit and explicit knowledge in the control of complex systems. *British Journal of Psychology*, 77, 33–50.

Bromley, D. B. (1986) *The Case Study Method in Psychology and Related Disciplines*. Chichester: Wiley.

Brown, R. (1965) *Social Psychology*. New York: Free Press.

Brown, R., Fraser, C. & Bellugi, U. (1964) *The Acquisition of Language*. Monographs of the Society for Research in Child Development 29. 92.

Bruner, E. M. & Kelso, J. P. (1980) Gender differences in graffiti: a semiotic perspective. In *Women's Studies International Quarterly*, 3, 239–52.

Brunswik, E. (1947) *Systematic and Unrepresentative Design of Psychological Experiments with Results in Physical and Social Perception*. Berkeley: University of California Press.

Bryant, B. Harris, M. & Newton, D. (1980) *Children and Minders*. London: Grant McIntyre.

Burgess, R. G. (1984) *In the Field: an Introduction to Field Research*. Allen & Unwin: Hemel Hempstead.

Caldwell, B. M. & Bradley, R. H. (1978) Manual for the home observation of the environment, Unpublished manuscript. Little Rock, Ark.: University of Arkansas.

Campbell, D. T. & Stanley, J. C. (1966) *Experimental and Quasi-experimental Designs for Research*. Chicago: Rand McNally.

Campbell, D. T. (1970) Natural selection as an epistemological model. In R. Naroll & R. Cohen (eds.) *A Handbook of Method in Cultural Anthropology* 51–85). New York: Natural History Press.

Carlsmith, J., Ellsworth, P. & Aronson, E. (1976) *Methods of Research in Social Psychology*. Reading, Mass.: Addison–Wesley.

Charlesworth, R. & Hartup, W. W. (1967) Positive social reinforcement in the nursery school peer group. *Child Development*, 38, 993–1002.

Cochran, W. G. (1954) Some methods for strengthening the common χ^2 tests. *Biometrics*, 10, 417–51.

Cohen, L. & Holliday, M. (1982) *Statistics for Social Scientists*. London: Harper & Row.

Corcoran, S. A. (1986) Task complexity and nursing expertise as factors in decision making. *Nursing Research*, 35(2), 107–12.

Craik, F. & Tulving, E. (1975) Depth of processing and the retention of words in episodic memory. *Journal of Experimental Psychology*, General, Vol 104.

Crano, W. D. & Brewer, M. B. (1973) *Principles of Research in Social Psychology*. New York: McGraw-Hill.

Cronbach, L. J. (1960) *Essentials of Psychological Testing*. New York: Harper & Row.

Cumberbatch, G. (1990) *Television Advertising and Sex Role Stereotyping: A Content Analysis* (working paper IV for the Broadcasting Standards Council), Communications Research Group, Aston University.

Darwin, C. (1877) A biographical sketch of an infant. *Mind*, 2, 285–94.

David, S. S. J., Chapman, A. J., Foot, H. C. & Sheehy, N. P. (1986) Peripheral vision and child pedestrian accidents. *British Journal of Psychology*, vol 77, 4.

Davie, R., Butler, N. & Goldstein, H. (1972) *From Birth to Seven*. London: Longman.

Davis, J. H., Kerr, H. L., Atkin, R. H. & Meek, D. (1975) The decision processes of 6 and 12 person mock juries assigned unanimous and two thirds majority rules. *Journal of Personality and Social Psychology*, 32, 1–14.

De Waele, J.-P. and Harré, R. (1979) Autobiography as a psychological method. In Ginsburg, G. P. (1979) (ed.) *Emerging Strategies in Social Psychological Research*. Chichester: Wiley.

Diesing, P. (1972) *Patterns of Discovery in the Social Sciences*. London: Routledge and Kegan Paul.

Dilthey, W. (1894) *Descriptive Psychology and Historical Understanding*. The Hague: Martinus Nijhoff. (English translation, 1977.)

Doob, A. N. & Gross, A. E. (1968) Status of frustration as an inhibitor of horn-honking responses. *Journal of Social Psychology*, 76, 213–8.

Douglas, J. D. (1972) *Research on Deviance*. New York: Random House.

Duncan, S. L. (1976) Differential social perception and attribution of intergroup violence: Testing the lower limits of stereotyping of blacks. *Journal of Personality and Social Psychology*, 34, 590–8.

Edwards, D. & Potter, J. (1992) *Discursive Psychology*. London: Sage.

Elton, B. (1989) *Stark*. London: Sphere Books.

Enriquez, V. (ed.) (1990) *Indigenous Psychologies*. Quezon City: Psychology Research and Training House.

Ericcson, K. A. & Simon, H. A. (1980) Verbal reports as data. *Psychological Review*, 87, 215–51.

Ericcson, K. A. & Simon, H. A. (1984) *Protocol Analysis: Verbal Reports as Data.* Cambridge, Mass.: MIT Press.

Eron, L. D., Huesmann, L. R., Lefkowitz, M. M. & Walder, L. D. (1972) Does television violence cause aggression? *American Psychologist*, 27, 253–63.

Eysenck, H. J. (1970) *The Structure of Human Personality.* London: Methuen.

Eysenck, H. J. & Eysenck, S. B. G. (1975) *Manual of the Eysenck Personality Questionnaire.* London: Hodder and Stoughton.

Festinger, L., Riecken, H. W. & Schachter, S. (1956) *When Prophecy Fails.* Minneapolis: University of Minnesota Press.

Finch, J. (1984) 'It's great to have someone to talk to': the ethics and politics of interviewing women. In Bell, C. & Roberts, H. (eds.) (1984) *Social Researching: Policies, Problems and Practice.* London: Routledge and Kegan Paul.

Frankenburg, R. (1957) *Village on the Border.* London: Cohen and West.

Friedman, N. (1967) *The Social Nature of Psychological Research.* New York: Basic Books.

Friedrich, L. K. & Stein, A. H. (1973) Aggressive and prosocial television programs and the natural behaviour of pre-school children. *Monographs of the Society for Research in Child Development.* 38(4, serial No. 51).

Ganster, D. C., Mayes, B. T., Sime, W. E. & Tharp, G. D. (1982) Managing organisational stress: a field experiment. *Journal of Applied Psychology*, 67(5), 533–42.

Ginsberg, G. P. (1979) (Ed.) *Emerging Strategies in Social Psychological Research.* Chichester: Wiley.

Glaser, B. G. & Strauss, A. L. (1967) *The Discovery of Grounded Theory: Strategies for Qualitative Research.* Chicago: Aldine.

Godden, D. & Baddeley, A. D. (1975) Context-dependent memory in two natural environments: on land and under water. *British Journal of Psychology*, 66, 325–31.

Gregory, R. L. & Wallace, J. G. (1963) *Recovery from Early Blindness.* Cambridge: Heffer.

Gross, R. D. (1992) *Psychology: the Science of Mind and Behaviour.* (2nd ed.): London: Hodder and Stoughton.

Gross, R. D. (1994) *Key Studies in Psychology* (2nd ed.). London: Hodder and Stoughton.

Gulian, E. & Thomas, J. R. (1986) The efffects of noise, cognitive set and gender on mental arithmetic and performance. *British Journal of Psychology*, Vol 77, 4.

Guttman, L. (1950) The third component of scalable attitudes. *International Journal of Opinion and Attitude Research*, 4, 285–7.

Hall, B. L. (1975) Participatory research: an approach for change. *Convergence, an International Journal of Adult Education*, 8(2), 24–32.

Halliday, S. & Leslie, J. C. (1986) A longitudinal semi-cross-sectional study of the development of mother–child interaction. *British Journal of Developmental Psychology*, 4(3), 221–32.

Hammond, K. R. (1948) Measuring attitudes by error-choice: an indirect method. *Journal of Abnormal Social Psychology*, 43, 38–48.

Hampden-Turner, C. (1971) *Radical Man.* London: Duckworth.

Harré, R. (1981) The positivist–empiricist approach and its alternative. In Reason, R. & Rowan, J. (1981) *Human Inquiry: A Sourcebook of New Paradigm Research.* Chichester: Wiley.

Hatfield, E. & Walster, G. W. (1981) *A New Look at Love.* Reading, Mass.: Addison–Wesley.

Hays, W. L. (1973) *Statistics for the Social Sciences.* London: Holt Rinehart Winston.

Heather, N. (1976) *Radical Perspectives in Psychology.* London: Methuen.

Henwood, K. I. & Pidgeon, N. F. (1992) Qualitative research and psychological theorizing. *British Journal of Psychology*, 83, 97–111.

Hinckley, E. D. (1932) The influence of individual opinion on construction of an attitude scale. *Journal of Social Psychology*, 3, 283–96.

Hitch, G. J. (1992) Why isn't discourse analysis more popular in the study of memory? *The Psychologist*, 5, 10 (October).

Horowitz, I. A. & Rothschild, B. H. (1970) Conformity as a function of deception and role-playing. *Journal of Personality and Social Psychology*, 14, 224–6.

Howell, D. C. (1992) *Statistical Methods for Psychology.* Boston: PWS-Kent.

Humphreys, L. (1970) *Tearoom Trade.* Chicago: Aldine.

Hyman, I. E. Jr (1992) Multiple approaches to remembering. *The Psychologist*, 5, 10 (October).

Jack, S. (1992) Certified to perform. *Retail Week* 6.11.1992.

Jahoda-Lazarsfeld, M. & Zeisl, H. (1932) *Die Arbeitslosen von Marienthal.* Leipzig: Hirzel.

Jefferson, G. (1985) An exercise in the transcription and analysis of laughter. In T. van Dijk (ed.) *Handbook of Discourse Analysis*, Vol 3. London: Academic Press.

Joe, R. C. (1991) *Effecten van taaltonaliteit op het cognitied functioneren: Een cross-cultureel onderzoek* [Effects of tonality in language on cognitive functioning]. PhD thesis, Tilburg: Tilburg University.

Jones, E. E. & Sigall, H. (1971) The bogus pipeline: a new paradigm for measuring affect and attitude. *Psychological Bulletin*, 76, 349–64.

Jones, F. & Fletcher, C. B. (1992) Transmission of occupational stress: a study of daily fluctuations in work stressors and strains and their impact on marital partners. *VIth European Health Psychology Society Conference* (presented as poster) University of Leipzig (August).

Jowell, R. & Topf, R. (1988) *British Social Attitudes.* London: Gower.

Joynson, R. B. (1989) *The Burt Affair.* London: Routledge.

Jung, C. G. (1930) Your Negroid and Indian behaviour. *Forum*, 83, 4, 193–99.

Kagan, J., Kearsley, R. B. & Zelazo, P. R. (1980) *Infancy – Its Place in Human Development.* Cambridge, Mass.: Harvard University Press.

Kamin, L. J. (1977) *The Science and Politics of IQ.* Harmondsworth: Penguin.

Kerlinger, F. N. (1973) *Foundations of Behavioural Research.* London: Holt, Rinehart and Winston.

Kidder, L. H. (1981) *Selltiz Wrightsman and Cook's Research Methods in Social Relations*, 4th ed. New York: Holt, Rinehart and Winston.

Kinsey, A. C., Pomeroy, W. B., Martin, C. E. & Gebhard, P. H. (1953) *Sexual Behavior in the Human Female.* Philadelphia: Saunders.

Kinsey, A. C., Pomeroy, W. B. & Martin, C. E. (1948) *Sexual Behavior in the Human Male.* Philadelphia: Saunders.

Kohlberg, L. (1981) *Essays on Moral Development.* New York: Harper and Row.

Kohler, W. (1925) *The Mentality of Apes.* New York: Harcourt Brace Jovanovich.

Kounin, J. & Gump, P. (1961) The comparative influence of punitive and non-punitive teachers upon children's concepts of school misconduct. *Journal of Educational Psychology*, 52, 44–9.

Kuhn, T. (1962) *The Structure of Scientific Revolutions.* Chicago, Ill.: University of Chicago.

Latané, B. & Darley, J. M. (1976) *Help in a Crisis: Bystander Response to an Emergency.* Morristown, NJ: General Learning Press.

Latour, B. (1987) *Science in Action.* Milton Keynes: Open University Press.

Latour, B. (1988) The politics of explanation: An alternative. In S. Woolgar (ed.) *Knowledge and Reflexivity: New Frontiers in the Sociology of Knowledge*, London: Sage.

Levin, R. B. (1978) An empirical test of the female castration complex. In Fisher, S. & Greenberg, R. P. (1978) *The Scientific Evaluation of Freud's Theories and Therapy.* New York: Basic Books.

Lewis, G., et al. (1990) Are British psychiatrists racist? *British Journal of Psychiatry*, 157, 410–15.

Leyens, J., Camino, L., Parke, R. D. & Berkowitz, L. (1975) Effects of movie violence on aggression in a field setting as a function of group dominance and cohesion. *Journal of Personality and Social Psychology*, 32, 346–60.

Likert, R. A. (1932) A technique for the measurement of attitudes, *Archives of Psychology*, 140, 55.

Luria, A. R. (1969) *The Mind of a Mnemonist.* London: Jonathan Cape.

Littlewood, R. (1989) *Aliens and Alienists.* London: Hyman.

Ma, H. K. (1988) The Chinese perspective on moral judgement development. *International Journal of Psychology*, 23, 201–27.

Madge, J. (1953) *The Tools of Social Science.* London: Longman.

Malim, T., Birch, A. & Wadeley, A. (1992) *Perspectives in Psychology.* Basingstoke: Macmillan.

Manstead, A. S. R. & McCulloch, C. (1981) Sex-role stereotyping in British television advertisements. *British Journal of Social Psychology*, 20, 171–80.

Marsh, P. (1978) *The Rules of Disorder.* London: Routledge.

Martin, S. L. & Klimoski, R. J. (1990) Use of verbal protocols to trace cognitions associated with self- and supervisor evaluations of performance. *Organizational Behaviour and Human Decision Processes*, 46(1), 135–54.

Masling, J. (1966) Role-related behaviour of the subject and psychologist and its effect upon psychological data. In Levine, D. (ed.) (1966) *Nebraska Symposium on Motivation.* Lincoln, Neb.: University of Nebraska Press.

Mead, M. (1928) *Coming of Age in Samoa.* Harmondsworth Middlesex: Penguin.

Mead, M. (1930) *Growing up in New Guinea.* Harmondsworth Middlesex: Penguin.

Medawar, P. B. (1963) Is the scientific paper a fraud? *The Listener*, 10, 377–8.

Menges, R. J. (1973) Openness and honesty versus coercion and deception in psychological research. *American Psychologist*, 28, 1030–34.

Middleton, D. & Edwards, D. (1990) *Collective Remembering.* London: Sage.

Middleton, D., Buchanan, K. & Suurmond, J. (1993) Communities of memory: issues of 'remembering' and belonging in reminiscence work with the elderly. Mimeo, Loughborough University.

Milgram, S. (1961) Nationality and conformity. *Scientific American*, 205, 45–51.

Milgram, S. (1963) Behavioural study of obedience. *Journal of Abnormal and Social Psychology*, 67, 371–8.

Milgram, S. (1974) *Obedience to Authority.* New York: Harper and Row.

Miller, J. G., Bersoff, D. M. & Harwood, R. L. (1990) Perceptions of social responsibilities in India and the United States: Moral imperatives or personal decisions? *Journal of Personality and Social Psychology*, 58, 33–47.

Mitroff, I. I. (1974) Studying the lunar rock scientist. *Saturday Review World*, 2 Nov. 64–5.

Mixon, D. (1974) If you won't deceive what can you do? In Armistead, N. (ed.) (1974) *Reconstructing Social Psychology.* London: Penguin Education.

Mixon, D. (1979) Understanding shocking and puzzling conduct. In Ginsburg, G. P. (ed.) (1979) *Emerging Strategies in Social Psychological Research.* Chichester: Wiley.

Nisbet, R. (1971) Ethnocentrism and the comparative method. In A. Desai (ed.) *Essays on modernisation of underdeveloped societies* (Vol 1, 95–114), Bombay: Thacker.

Ogilvie, D. M., Stone, D. J. & Shniedman, E. S. (1966) Some characteristics of genuine versus simulated suicide notes. In Stone, P. J., Dunphy, C., Smith, M. S. & Ogilvie, D. M. (eds.) (1966) *The General Enquirer: A Computer Approach to Content Analysis in the Behavioral Sciences.* Cambridge: MIT Press.

Ora, J. P. (1965) Characteristics of the volunteer for psychological investigations. Office of Naval Research Contract 2149(03), Technical Report 27.

Orne, M. T. (1962) On the social psychology of the psychological experiment: with particular reference to demand characteristics and their implications. *American Psychologist*, 17, 776–83.

Osgood, C. E., Luria, Z., Jeans, R. F. & Smith, S. W. (1976) The three faces of Evelyn: a case report. *Journal of Abnormal Psychology*, 85, 247–86.

Osgood, C. E., Suci, G. J. & Tannenbaum, P. H. (1957) *The Measurement of Meaning.* Urbana: University of Illinois.

Patton, M. Q. (1980) *Qualitative Evaluation Methods.* London: Sage.

Penny, G. N. & Robinson, J. O. (1986) Psychological resources and cigarette smoking in adolescents. *British Journal of Psychology*, 77(3), 351–8.

Peronne, V., Patton, M. Q. & French, B. (1976) *Does Accountability Count without Teacher Support?* Minneapolis: Centre for Social Research, University of Minnesota.

Petty, R. E. & Cacioppo, J. T. (1984) The effects of involvement on responses to argument quantity and quality: central and peripheral routes to persuasion. *Journal of Personality and Social Psychology*, Vol 46.

Piliavin, I. M., Rodin, J. & Piliavin, J. A. (1969) Good samaritanism: an underground phenomenon? *Journal of Personality and Social Psychology*, 13, 289–99.

Popper, K. R. (1959) *The Logic of Scientific Discovery.* London: Hutchinson.

Potter, J. & Wetherell, M. (1987) *Discourse and Social Psychology: Beyond Attitudes and Behaviour.* London: Sage.

Potter, J. & Wetherell, M. (1993) Analyzing discourse. In A. Bryman & R. G. Burgess (eds.) (1993) *Analysing qualitative data.* London: Routledge.

Presby, S. (1978) Overly broad categories obscure important differences between therapies. *American Psychologist*, 33, 514–15.

Raffetto, A. M. (1967) Experimenter effect on subjects' reported hallucinatory experiences under visual and auditory deprivation. Master's thesis, San Francisco State College.

Reason, P. & Rowan, J. (1981) (eds.) *Human Enquiry: A Sourcebook in New Paradigm Research.* Chichester: Wiley.

Reicher, S. & Emmler, N. (1986) Managing reputations in adolescence: the pursuit of delinquent and non-delinquent identities. In H. Beloff (ed.) *Getting into life.* London: Methuen.

Reinharz, S. (1983) Experiential analysis: a contribution to feminist research: In G. Bowles & R. Duelli Klein (eds.) *Theories of Women's Studies.* London: Routledge and Kegan Paul.

Rice, A. K. (1958) *Productivity and Social Organisations: The Ahmedabad Experiment.* London: Tavistock Publications.

Ring, K., Wallston, K. & Corey, M. (1970) Mode of debriefing as a factor affecting subjective reaction to a Milgram-type obedience experiment: an ethical inquiry. *Representative Research in Social Psychology*, 1, 67–88.

Roethlisberger, F. J. & Dickson, W. J. (1939) *Management and the Worker*. Cambridge, Mass.: Harvard University Press.

Rogers, C. R. (1961) *On Becoming a Person: a Therapist's View of Psychotherapy*. London: Constable.

Rokeach, M. (1960) *The Open and Closed Mind*. New York: Basic Books.

Rosenhan, D. L. (1973) On being sane in insane places. *Science*, 179, 250–8.

Rosenthal, R. (1966) *Experimenter Effects in Behavioral Research*. New York: Appleton-Century-Crofts.

Rutter, M. (1971) Parent–child separation: psychological effects on the children. *Journal of Child Psychology and Psychiatry*, 12, 233–60.

Samuel, J. & Bryant, P. (1984) Asking only one question in the conservation experiment. *Journal of Child Psychology and Psychiatry*, Vol 25, 2.

Sears, R. R., Maccoby, E. & Levin, H. (1957) *Patterns of Child Rearing*. Evanston, Ill.: Row, Petersen & Co.

Seligman, M. (1972) *Biological Boundaries of Learning*. New York: Appleton- Century-Crofts.

Shaffer, D. R. (1985) *Developmental Psychology: Theory, Research and Applications*. Pacific Grove, Ca.: Brooks/Cole.

Shneidman, E. S. (1963) Plan 11. The logic of politics. In Arons, L. & May, M. A. (eds.) (1963) *Television and Human Behavior*. New York: Appleton-Century-Crofts.

Shotland, R. L. & Yankowski, L. D. (1982) The random response method: a valid and ethical indicator of the 'truth' in reactive situations. *Personality and Social Psychology Bulletin*, 8(1), 174–9.

Sinha, D. (1986) *Psychology in a Third World Country: The Indian Experience*. New Delhi: Sage.

Sims, D. (1981) From ethogeny to endogeny: how participants in research projects can end up doing action research on their own awareness. In Reason, P. and Rowan, J. (1981) (eds.) *Human Enquiry: A Sourcebook in New Paradigm Research*. Chichester: Wiley.

Smith, M. L. & Glass, G. V. (1977) Meta-analysis of psychotherapeutic outcome studies. *American Psychologist*, 32, 752–60.

Storms, M. D. (1973) Videotape and the attribution process: reversing actors' and observers' points of view. *Journal of Personality and Social Psychology*, 27, 165–75.

Tandon, R. (1981) Dialogue as inquiry and intervention. In Reason, P. & Rowan, J. (1981) *Human Inquiry: A Sourcebook in New Paradigm Research*. Chichester: Wiley.

Thurstone, L. L. (1931) The measurement of social attitudes. *Journal of Abnormal and Social Psychology*, 26, 249–69

Torbert, W. R. (1981) Why educational research has been so uneducational: the case for a new model of social science based on collaborative enquiry. In Reason, P. & Rowan, J. (1981) *Human Inquiry*. Chichester: Wiley.

Trist, E. L. & Bamforth, K. W. (1951) Some social and psychological consequences of the longwall method of coal-cutting. *Human Relations*, 4(1), 3–38.

Tukey, J. W. (1977) *Exploratory Data Analysis*. Reading, Mass.: Addison–Wesley.

Valentine, E. R. (1982) *Conceptual Issues in Psychology*. London: Routledge.

Valentine, E. R. (1992) *Conceptual Issues in Psychology* (2nd ed.). London: Routledge.

Vidich, A. J. & Bensman, J. (1958) *Small Town in Mass Society*. Princeton, NJ: Princeton University Press.

Watson, J. B. & Rayner, R. (1920) Conditioned emotional reactions. *Journal of Experimental Psychology*, 3, 1–14.

Weber, S. J. & Cook, T. D. (1972) Subject effects in laboratory research: an examination of subject roles, demand characteristics and valid inference. *Psychological Bulletin*, 77, 273–95.

Whorf, B. L. (1957) *Language, Thought and Reality*. Cambridge, Mass.: MIT Press.

Whyte, W. F. (1943) *Street Corner Society: the Social Structure of an Italian Slum*. Chicago: The University of Chicago Press.

Wilkinson, S. (1986) *Feminist Social Psychology*. Milton Keynes: Open University Press.

Williams, J. E., Bennett, S. M. & Best, D. L. (1975) Awareness and expression of sex stereotypes in young children. *Developmental Psychology*, 11, 635–42.

Williams, J. E. & Berry, J. W. (1991) Primary prevention of acculturative stress among refugees: the application of psychological theory and practice. *American Psychologist*, 46, 632–41.

Williams, J. E. & Best, D. L. (1982) *Measuring sex stereotypes: A Thirty Nation Study*. London: Sage.

Word, C. H., Zanna, M. P. & Cooper, J. (1974) The non-verbal mediation of self-fulfilling prophecies in interracial interaction. *Journal of Experimental Social Psychology*, 10, 109–20.

Wright, R. L. D. (1976) *Understanding Statistics*. New York: Harcourt Brace Jovanovich.

Zimbardo, P. G. (1972) Pathology of imprisonment. *Society*, April 1972.

INDEX

NOTE:
Bold *page numbers refer to glossaries at the ends of* chapters.

A

a priori comparisons............. 327, 335, 336–8, **340**
ABBA 84
absolute value 209, **226**
abstracts
    reports 415–16
accountability
    discourse analysis 389
acculturation 165
acquiescence set
    response 135, 144, **157**
action research............................... 169, 175, **184**
active role-play... 101
activity factor 142
aims
    reports 408, 415–16
ambiguity
    attitude scales.. 143
American Psychological Association (APA)
    ethics 393–4
analysis
    early... 387, **390**
    research planning 19
analysis of covariance (ANCOVA) 367, 368–9, **373**
analysis of variance (ANOVA) 327–342, **340**
    mixed design...363–5
    multi-factor...343–54
    repeated measures 355–66
    unequal samples 340
analytical surveys 130–1
ANCOVA *see* analysis of covariance
animal research... 403–5
ANOVA *see* analysis of variance
anthropomorphism 97
appendices
    report writing 420
archival data 106, **111**
arithmetic mean *see* mean
artificial conditions/artificiality...................70, 171
association
    tests of 263, 312, 313

asymmetrical order effects 84, **91**
attitude scales 136, 138–45
audio recording... 129
averages.. 201, **226**
    see also mean

B

bar charts 200, 215–16, **226**
between conditions variation 358, 359, **366**
between groups designs 87, **91**
between groups sum of squares............... 333, **341**
between subjects variation 355, 356–8, 359, **366**
bi-modal data 206
bi-modal distributions 200, 226, **227**
bias
    experimenter... 58
    observer 97, **112**
    removal...76–7
    sampling 35, **45**
    scientists 11–12
binomial sign test 256, **268**
blinds 76–7
Bogardus scale 140–1, **156**
bogus pipeline disguise................................. 116
Bonferroni *t* tests 337, 340, **341**
box plots 219–20, **226**
British Psychological Society (BPS)
    ethics 393–4
    'subjects' or 'participants' 19

C

cardinal numbers 189
carpentered world hypothesis 164
case history... 123, **132**
case-studies 114, 119, 123–6, **132**
categorical variables 196, **197**
categories 188–9

categorisation 385–7
ceiling effects 225
cell frequencies
    low 256, 266–7
census 131, **132**
central tendency...............200, 202–6, 225–6, **226**
chi-squared test 259–68, **268**
    critical value table..................................... 453
    goodness of fit 264–5, **268**
    limitations 266–7
    one variable/two categories.......................265–6
    quick formula 262
    test choice 376
class intervals............................ 205, 213–14, **226**
clinical method/interview...... 102, 114, 122–3, **132**
cluster samples..................................... 34, 40, **45**
co-related values 281
co-variates 367, 369, **373**
coding 95, **111**
coding units 109–10
coefficient of correlation 295, **314**
coefficient of determination 309, **315**
cohort 160, 167
cohort effects 160, 167
collaborative research 169, 176, **184**
comparison studies 156–68
complexity
    attitude scales.. 143
computers
    programs...377, 379
    random sampling... 38
conclusions
    reports 420
concurrent validity 142, 153–4, **157**
condition order
    randomisation 85
conditions
    more than two 316–19
confidentiality...............................127, 393, 395–6
confounding/confounding variables
    ANCOVA... 367
    description 22, 29–31, **32**
    example 7
    loose procedure 58
    order effects 83
connotative meaning 142
consent.. 401
constant error 22, 29, **32**
construct validity 56, 70, 149, 154, **157**
constructionist view 180
constructs
    hypothetical 22, 24
    organisation 24–5
    psychological.. 23
consultation
    participants 388
content analysis 107, 108–11, **111**
content validity 153, **158**
continuous scales 187, 196–7, **198**
contrast coefficients 338
control
    laboratory research 69–70
control groups 34, 43, **44**

controlled observation............................ 97–8, **112**
convenience sample 41
correction factor
    ANOVA... 333, **341**
correlated *t*-test *see* related *t* test
correlated tests... 281
correlation 293–316, **314**
    cause and 309
    coefficient 295, **314**
    common uses 313–14
    dichotomous nominal variable............... 312–13
    measurement..295–6
    significance 305–8
    strength.. 308
correlational studies 78
counterbalancing 83–4, **91**
criterion validity................................153–4, **158**
criterion variables 367, 370, **373**
critical cases....................................... 34, 40, **44**
critical values 245–6, 250, **251**, 307
Cronbach's alpha coefficient................... 151, **157**
cross-cultural studies................... 159, 162–7, **168**
cross-generational problem.................... 161, **167**
cross-sectional studies 159–62, 167, **168**
cultural relativity 164, **167**
cumulative frequency 213–14, 218, **227**
cumulative scaling....................................141–2
curvilinear relationships.......................... 299, **314**

D

DA *see* discourse analysis
data..6, **20**
    access..394–5
    descriptive statistics 200–30
    gathering systems 95–7
    measurement..187–99
    prediction testing................................231–391
    ranking 190–1
    recording 129–30
debriefing 393, 398–9, **406**
deception........................ 104, 393, 397–398, **406**
deciles 213, **226**
decimal conversion 238
deduction..8, **20**
deductive logic...8–9
degrees of freedom.......................... 261, **267**, 333
dehumanisation 18–19, 66, 77–8
demand characteristics 66, 75, **78**, 116, 144
dependent variables............................ 22, 27, **32**
descriptive statistics................. 12–13, **20**, 200–30
descriptive surveys 130
design
    experimental 81–91
    observation.. 94
    practicals.................................... 411–12, 419
    research 18, **20**
    surveys 131
deviation 203
deviation value....................................... 208, **226**
diagnostic item 140, **156**

diary method 102–3, **111**
dimensions 386
directed graphs 147, **156**
directional hypothesis........................ 16, 247, **251**
   see also one-tailed tests
disclosed participant observation 105
disclosure **111**
discomfort
   participants 399, 400
discourse analysis (DA) 169, 178–9, **184**, 389
discrete scales 187, 196–7, **198**
discriminatory power.............................. 138, **156**
discursive action model (DAM) 178
discussion
   reports 419
disguise
   attitude scales... 138
   research 114, 115–16, **132**
dispersion................................... 200, 202, **227**
dispersion measures 206–12
distributions 200, 212–26
   see also normal distributions
   bi-modal 200, 226, **227**
   skewed.. 200, 225–6
   tails..247–8
double blind procedure 76–7, **78**
double-barrelled items
   attitude scales... 143
DV *see* dependent variables

E

ecological validity............................. 55–6, **64**, 70
emotive language
   attitude scales... 144
empirical method.................................... 6–7, **20**
empirical probability 233, 238–9, **251**
endogenous research 169, 176, **184**
enlightenment... 75
equal appearing intervals 138–9
error rate
   family-wise.. 327, **341**
   per comparison.................................... 337, **341**
error sum of squares................................ 333, **341**
errors
   constant 22, 29, **32**
   guessing **315**
   multi-factor ANOVA 343, 349, 355, 359
   one-way ANOVA 331, 332
   random 22, 28–9, **32**
   sampling 211, 228
   standard.. 284, **291**
   type I/II........................... 233, 250–1, **252**
establishment paradigm.............................. 171
ethical issues 391–407
   planning practicals..............................411–12
   undisclosed participant observation 104–5
ethnicity
   interviews... 117
   intra-cultural studies..............................165–6
ethnocentrism................................... 163, **167**

ethogenic perspective 173
evaluation apprehension 75, **78**
evaluative cues.. 118
evaluative factors 142
event sampling.......................................97, **111**
ex *post facto* research........................73, **79**, 313–14
expectancy... 66
expected frequencies 260, **267**
   low 266–7
experimental designs................................81–91
experimental groups................................43, **44**
experimental hypothesis 13, **20**
experimental method 66–92
experimental realism 55, **63**, 75
experimenter
   bias... 58
   effects 74–5
   expectancy 74–5, **78**
   pleasing.................................. 75, **79**, 85, 145
   reliability..74, **78**
experiments 66–78
   criticisms..74–8
   definition **78**
   field 13–14, 71–2, 76, 77, **78**
   laboratory........................ 66, 69–71, 76, 77, **78**
   natural 73, **78**
   quasi-...............................66, 67, 72–3, **78**
   scientific research 11
   true... 66
explicit knowledge.. 111
exploratory data analysis................. 200, 217, **227**
external reliability 151, **157**
external validity 49, 50–1, 53–7, 59, **64**
extraneous variables 28–30, **32**
eyeball test...242–3, **251**

F

F ratio 329–30
   critical value tables 465–6
   test 280, 335, **341**
face validity 138, 153, **158**
face-to-face questioning.................. 115, 132, **133**
   see also interviews
factor analysis 135, 149–50, **156**, 314
factorial designs 344–5, 346–7, **353**
factors
   multi-factor ANOVA 343, 344–5, **353**
falsifiability 9
family-wise error rate 327, **341**
feedback
   interviews..128–9
feelings
   interviews... 128
feminist psychology........................ 169, 177, **184**
field experiments.............. 13–14, 71–2, 76, 77, **78**
Fisher's exact test.................................... 267
fixed action patterns................................. 405
fixed questions 135, 137
floor effects 225
focus groups 131, 132, **133**

formal roles
    interviews 117
formative approach **112**
formative revision 100
formula
    definition 202
frequencies/frequency data 189, **197**
frequency distributions 200, 212, **227**
frequency polygons 216, 217, 218, **227**
Friedman test 323–4, **325**

G

Gaussian curve 221
gender
    interviews 17
goodness of fit test 264–5, **268**
grand mean 330–2, **341**
graphical representation 214–17
grounded theory 387, **390**
groups
    research designs 43–4
guessing error **315**
Guttman scale 141–2, **156**

H

histograms 200, 214–15, **227**
holist studies 99–100
homogeneity of variance 280, **290**, 330
hypotheses
    see also null hypothesis
    description 7, **20**
    directional 247, **251**
    experimental 13, **20**
    features 14
    one tailed 16, 20, **251**
    reports 416–17
    research 13
    testing 13–14
    two tailed 16, 20, **252**
hypothetical constructs 22, 24, **32**, 149
hypothetico-deductive method 7–8, **20**, 170

I

implicit knowledge 111
independent samples (independent groups/
    subjects) design 67, 81,
86–8, 90, **91**
independent variable 22, 27–8, **32**, 343–52
indigenous psychologies 165, **167**
indirect observation 106–7, **112**
induction 6, **20**
inductive analysis 173, **184**
inferential statistics 13, **20**
informal interviews 119–21
ink blot tests 146

interaction effects 343, 344, 346–7, 351, **353**
interaction variation 343
interest
    interviewers 127
internal consistency 151
internal reliability 151, **157**
internal validity 49, 50–4, **64**
interpersonal variables 114, 116–18
interrater reliability 97, **112**
interval level
    correlation 299
    measurement 187, 192–3, **198**, 206
    tests 278–92
intervention 402–3, **407**
interviews 118–22
    data recording 129–30
    influential factors 117–18
    question sequence/progress 128
    question types 128
    techniques 126–30
intra-cultural studies 162, 165
introduction
    reports 415
investigations 66, 67–9, **79**
investigator effects 74
involuntary participation 402, **407**
item analysis 151–2, **157**
item discrimination methods 151
IV see independent variables

J

Jonckheere trend test 321–3, **325**

K

Kalamazoo study 115
knowledge elicitation 110–11, **112**
known groups criterion 153, **158**
Kruskal-Wallis-one-way analysis of variance ....
    320–1, **325**
Kuder-Richardson method 151, **157**

L

L critical value table 468
laboratory research
    experiments 66, 69–71, 76, 77, **78**
    hypothesis testing 13
language
    interviews 126
laws 6
leading questions
    attitude scales 144
levels
    independent variables 27
    multi-factor ANOVA 343, 344–5, **353**
levels of measurement 187–99, 200, 206

Likert method...................................139–40, **156**
line charts.. 217
linear coefficients **341**
linear contrasts 327, 337, 340, **341**
listening skills
    interviewers 127
literature review 59
logic
    deductive 8–9
logical probability 233, 236–8, **252**
longitudinal studies.....................159, 160–2, **168**

M

main effects 343, 344, 347 **353**
Mann-Whitney U test 273–5, **277**
    critical value table....................................454–7
MANOVA *see* multivariate analysis of variance
matched-pairs design 81, 88–9, 90, **91**
mean 202–3, **227**
mean deviation 208–9, **227**
mean sum of squares...........................333–4, **341**
measured variables................................. 196, **197**
measurement 187–99
median 203–5, **227**
median position/location 204, **227**
mental stress
    participants 399–400
meta-analysis 49, 59–60, **63**
meta-reflexivity 181
methods
    reports 417–18
Milgram, S.
    obedience studies 396–7
MINITABSTMs 379
mixed design
    ANOVA....................342, 345, **353**, 354, 363–5
modal value *see* mode
mode..205–6, **227**
mono method bias 56
multi-condition designs.................................... 85
multi-factor ANOVA 343–54
multi-level tests.. 318
multiple predictions 371–2
multiple regression...... 309, **315**, 367, 369–72, **373**
multiple regression coeficient.................... 372, **373**
multivariate analysis of variance (MANOVA)........
    367, 368, **373**
multivariate tests............................... 318, 367–73
mundane realism 55, **63**

N

narrowness
    studies 171
natural experiments.......................................73, **78**
naturalistic observations 98–9, **112**
naturalistic studies 55, 56, 62
negative cases analysis 388, **390**
negative correlations 294, **314**

negative skewed distributions 225, **227**
negatives
    attitude scales...143–4
neutrality
    interviews.. 126
Newman-Keuls test.......................... 338, 340, **342**
nominal level
    measurement................. 187, 188–90, **198**, 206
    tests 256–68
non-active role-play...................................... 101
non-directional hypotheses................ 16, 247, **251**
    see also two-tailed tests
non-directive interviews 119
non-experimental research....................... 66, 67–9
    see also investigations
    confounding... 31
    hypothesis elimination 69
non-parametric tests
    see also individual tests
    more than two conditions 320–6
    parametric comparison 281
non-participant observation............ 93–4, 100, **112**
non-participation 401
non-reactive studies **79**
non-verbal communication
    interviewers 127
normal distribution
    area under curve.......................222–3, 449–51
    description 200, 220–2, **227**
    goodness of fit 265
    parametric tests 280
    significance tests 248–9
    standardisation 155
normal distribution
    area under.................................222–3, 449–51
    characteristics..221–2
notation
    statistical formulae................................229–30
note taking 129
null hypothesis......................... 14–15, **20**, 256, 416

O

observational methods........................93–113, **112**
observational studies **79**
observed frequencies 260, **267**
observer
    bias.. 97, **112**
    reliability.. 97, **112**
ogive 216–17, **227**
one-tailed tests
    chi-squared 261
    hypotheses 16, **20**, **251**
    probability..................................... 233, 246–7
    t-test 283
one-way ANOVA.................................... 327–342
open-ended questions 128, **133**, 135, 137
operational definitions........................ 22, 25–7, **32**
opportunity samples.............................. 34, 41, **45**
order effects...83–5, **92**

ordinal level
    correlation... 299
    measurement.................... 187, 190–2, **198**, 206
    tests 269–77
outriders... 203

P

P critical value table 467
Page trend test.....................................324–5, **325**
pairwise comparisons 336, **342**
panels..131–2, **133**
paradigm shift... 172
paradigms
    definition 170, **184**
    new.. 169–83
parameters................................... 200, 211, 279
parametric tests
    see also individual tests
    assumptions 280, 374
    descriptive statistics 200, 202, 211
    interval/ratio level 195, 278–92, **290**
    non-parametric comparison 281
participant variables 29, 35–6, **44**, 87–8
participant variance.......................................57–8
participants
    see also respondents; subjects
    confidentiality 395–6
    consultation 388
    debriefing..398–9
    deception..397–8
    observation............................ 94–5, 103–6, **112**
    quotations..386–7
    random allocation.....................................67, 87
    reactions 75
    stress discomfort................................. 399–400
    terminology debate 18–19
participative research.............................. 175, **184**
partitioning
    sum of squares 349
Pascal's triangle 240, 241
Pearson's product-moment correlation coefficient .
    293, 299–302, **315**
    critical value table..................................... 464
percentiles 213, **228**
personal qualities
    interviews... 117
Phi coefficient................................... 313, **315**
physical discomfort
    participants 401
piloting/pilot trials.......................................11, **21**
placebo effect...30, **44**
placebo group 34, 43–4, **44**
plagiarism.. 414
planned comparisons 336, 340, **342**
planning
    practicals..408–12
    research 17–19
plastic interval scales 193, **198**
point biserial correlation.......................... 313, **315**
point sampling................................. 97, **112**

population parameters........ 200, 211–12, **227**, 278
population standard deviation 210
population validity 55
population variance... 211
populations...34–5, **44**
positive correlations 294, **314**
positive skewed distribution.................... 225, **227**
positivism 60, **63**, 169–71, **184**, 383
post hoc comparisons 327, 335, 336, 338, **342**
postal surveys 132
potency factor... 142
power
    definition 291
    parametric tests 279–80
    repeated measures 358
power efficiency 279, 290, **291**
practicals
    planning..408–12
pre-test/treatment/post-test design 72–3
pre-tests 88
prediction error... 370
prediction testing 231–390
predictive validity.................................. 154, **158**
predictor variables........................... 367, 370, **373**
preparedness.. 404
prior variable 310
privacy
    attitude scales... 144
    ethics 393, 395–6, **407**
probability 233–42
    empirical...............................233, 238–9, **251**
    logical 233, 236–8, **252**
    subjective 235, **252**
probability distributions 233, 239, **252**
procedure
    loose 58, 63, 66
    planning practicals..................................... 411
projective tests 145–6
psychological constructs 23
psychometric tests..................... 135, 148–50, **156**
psychometrists 192, **197**
psychometry 148
publication 394–5

Q

qualitative approach/research.............................**63**
    new paradigm.....................................169, 174
    non-participant observation 100
    qualitative-quantitative dimension........ 49, 60–3
qualitative data
    analysis 382–90
    description 13, **21**, 63
qualitative differences.............................. 188, **197**
quantification
    definition 60
quantitative data 12, **21**
quantitative differences 188, **197**
quantitative research 49, 60–3, **64**
quartiles 213, **228**
quasi-experiments.....................66, 67, 72–3, **78**

quasi-random sampling 37, **45**
questionnaires 136–8, 143–5
questions
  asking 114–33, 135–58
  questioning mode 132
  sequence/progress 128–9
  types 128
quota sampling 34, 40, **45**
quotations 386–7

R

RxCχ^2 test 264
racism 165–6
random allocation
  participants 38, 67, 87
random error/variables 22, 28–9, **32**
random number tables 38, 450
random numbers **44**
random ordering 38–9
random samples 36–9, **45**
random sequencing 39
random variables 28–9
randomisation
  condition order 85
  stimulus items 85
  stimulus position 29
randomised response 118
range 206–8, **228**
ranks 190–1
rating behaviour 95, **112**
ratio data 191
ratio level
  correlation 299
  measurement 187, 194–6, **198**
  tests 278–92
raw data 201, **228**
reactive design 75–6, **79**
references
  report writing 420
reflexivity 169, 179–81, **184**
regression 309, 367, 369–70, **373**
regression coefficients 371, **373**
reification 24, **32**, 193
related data
  nominal level tests 256–9
  ordinal level tests 269–72
  t-test 281–6
related designs
  ANOVA 345, 360–2
  definition **91**
  non-parametric tests 323–5
  repeated measures 82, 281
  single participant 89
related t-test
  summary 278, 289, **291**
relativist view 180, **184**
reliability
  case-studies 125
  correlation 314
  description 49, 50, **64**
  external 151, **157**

internal 151, **157**
  observational techniques 97
  qualitative analysis 388
  questionnaires 138, 145
  test-retest 152
  tests 135, 150–2
repeated measures
  description **91**
  order effects 83
  strengths/weaknesses 81, 82–6, 90
repeated measures ANOVA 343, 345, 355–66
replication 49, 57, 58–9, **64**
reports
  qualitative data 387
  writing 413–33
representative allocation 88
representative samples 34, 36, 39, **45**
research 3–21, **20**
  aim 18
  appropriate test choice 374–81
  cycle
  description 10
  repetition 388
  ethical isssues 394–408
  hypothesis 13
  myths 6–12
  planning 17–19, 409–13
  repeating 18
  researcher's attitude 18
  subject matter 12
researcher see experimenter
residual 358, **366**, 367, 370, **373**
resources 18
respondent interpretation 144
respondents 115, **133**
response acquiescence set 135, 144, **157**
results
  reports 418–19
reversal
  Bogardus scale 140
rhetorical organisation
  discourse analysis 389
robust tests 280, **291**
role-play 100–2, **112**, 399
roles 117
Rorschach ink blot tests 146

S

sample size 34, 41–3
sample statistics 200, **228**
sample variance 211
samples
  cluster 34, 40, **45**
  more than two 377
  opportunity 34, 41, **45**
  planning practicals 410
  quota 34, 40, **45**
  random 36–9, **45**
  research 18–19, 21, 34–6, **44**
  self-selecting 34, 40–1, **45**
  snowball 34, 40, **45**

samples, *continued*
  stratified.. 34, 39, **45**
  surveys.. 131–2
  unequal numbers, one-way ANOVA 340
sampling..36–43
  bias... 35, 36, **45**
  content analysis 109
  distribution 284, 289, **291**
  error 211, **228**
  event... 97, **111**
  point.. 97, **112**
  time 97
scale value 139, **156**
scales *see* attitude scales
scales of measurement................187–99, 200, 206
scattergrams 293, 296–9, **315**
Scheffé test..**342**
schema 6
science
  definition 4
scientific method................................... 9–10, **21**
'screw you' effect 75
self-report method 114, **133**
self-selecting sample......................... 34, 40–1, **45**
semantic differential............................... 142, **156**
semi-interquartile range.......................207–8, **228**
sign test....................................... 254, 256–9, **268**
significance
  correlation.....................................305–8, **314**
  hypotheses 14
  levels..........................233, 243–4, 249–50, **252**
  testing........................16, 233–53, **252**, 254–5
simple effects 343, 347, **353**
simulation 100–2, 401
single blind procedure 76, **79**
single participant design 81, 89–91, **92**
skewed distributions............................. 200, 225–6
snowball sampling............................... 34, 40, **45**
social desirability
  interviews...117–18
  participants 75, **79**
  questionnaires 145
social distance scale....................................140–1
socio-technical systems.................................. 175
sociograms..................................... 135, 147, **157**
sociometric matrix 147, **157**
sociometry..147–8
Spearman's rho...........................293, 302–5, **315**
  critical value table 463
split half method 151, **157**
SPSS™ 379
stability.. 151
standard deviation
  descriptive statistics 209–11, **228**
  normal distribution curve........................... 223
standard errors................................... 284, **291**
standard scores *see* z-scores
standardisation
  attitude scales 136
  description 135, **157**
  measurement 187
  normal distribution..................................... 155
  questionnaires **138**

z-scores..224–5
standardised procedures 54, 57–60, **64**
statistical significance *see* significance
statistical tables...447–68
STATPAK 379
stem and leaf displays.................................218–19
stimulus items
  randomisation 85
stratified sampling............................... 34, 39, **45**
stress
  participants 399–400
structured interviews....................................121–2
structured observations 95–7, **112**
  objections..99–100
structured questions............................... 114, 115
Student's *t* 285
subject variables *see* participant variables
subjective probability 235, **252**
subjects
  see also participants
  terminology debate 18–19
sum of squares 332–3, **341**
  partitioning 349
summated ratings....................................139–40
suppressor variables 372, **373**
surveys 130–2
  see also questionnaires
  description 114, **133**
  design 131
  sample 131–2
systematic error *see* constant error
systematic observations 95–7
systematic sampling 37, **45**

T

T signed ranks test *see* Wilcoxon signed ranks test
t-test
  critical values table 462
  in ANOVA contrasts.................................... 337
  related data 281–6, 289
  SD automatic calculation........................283–4
  unrelated data 286–90
talk aloud instruction 110–11
target population....................................35, **45**
technical terms
  attitude scales 143
telephone surveys.. 132
test statistic...**268**
test-retest reliability...................................... 152
tests
  choosing...374–81
thematic apperception test (TAT) 146
theories 6, 7–9, 14, **21**
think aloud instruction 110–11
three-way ANOVA....................................... 352
Thurstone method............................138–9, **156**
ties (in values or ranks)................................**277**
  median calculation 204
  Spearman's rho 304
time lag study 161, **168**

time sampling 97
titles
    reports 414
total sum of squares 333
traditional research paradigm 171–2
training
    interviewers 127–8
transcription 385, **390**
treatment groups *see* experimental groups
trends 318–19, **325**
triangulation 388, **390**
Tukey's (honestly significant difference) test ....
    339, 340, **342**
twin studies 89, 314
two sample tests.. 374
two-tailed tests
    chi-squared 261
    hypotheses 16, **20**, 252
    probability 233, 246–7
two-way repeat measure ANOVA 360–2
two-way unrelated ANOVA...................... 347–51
type I/II errors 233, 250–1, **252**
typologies 386

questionnaires 138
tests 135, 152–4
    threats to 49, 51, 52–4, **64**, 66
variables **21**, 22–33
    see also confounding variables
    defining...23–4
    dependent 22, 27, **32**
    extraneous..................................... 28–30, **32**
    independent 22, 27–8, **32**, 343–52
    interpersonal 114, 116–18
    measurement.. 23
    participant........................... 29, 35–6, **44**, 87–8
    random 28–9
    research planning 17
variance................................... **64**, 209–11, **228**
    estimate 308, **315**
    one-way ANOVA 330–2, 333–5
    parametric tests 278
    standardised procedures..........................49, 57
variance ratio test *see* F test
variation
    ANOVA.. 328
    discourse analysis 389
verbal protocols 110–11, 179
video recording 129–30
vignette studies 86, **92**

U

U test *see* Mann-Whitney U test
unbiased standard deviation 210
uncorrelated *t*-test *see* unrelated *t* test
undisclosed participant observation 104–5
unrelated data
    nominal level tests 259–68
    ordinal level tests 273–5
    t-test 278, 286–90, **291**
unrelated designs
    ANOVA.. 345
    independent samples 86
    non-parametric..................................320–3
    single participant 89
unrelated *t*-test
    summary..286–90
unstructured questions.................................. 115

V

validity 50–7
    case-studies 125
    concurrent 142, 153–4, **157**
    construct........................ 56, 70, 149, 154, **157**
    content 153, **158**
    criterion 153–4, **158**
    description 49, **64**
    ecological 55–6, **64**, 70
    external......................... 49, 50–1, 53–7, 59, **64**
    face 138, 153, **158**
    internal 49, 50–4, **64**
    predictive 154, **158**
    qualitative analysis 388

W

Wilcoxon rank sum test 269, 275–6, **277**, 320
    critical value table...................................458–60
Wilcoxon signed ranks test . 269–72, 275, 276, **277**
    critical value table...................................... 461
within subjects variation 343, 355, 359
within subjects/groups design 82, **91**, 343
writing reports 413–32

X

χ^2 test...259–68, **268**
    critical value table..................................... 453
    goodness of fit 264–6, **268**
    limitations 266–7
    one variable/two categories....................265–6
    quick formula 262
    test choice 376

Y

Yates' correction.. 261

Z

z-scores 200, 223–6, **228**, 248–9